READINGS IN STRATEGIC MARKETING

Analysis, Planning, and Implementation

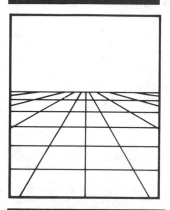

Barton A. Weitz
University of Florida
Robin Wensley
University of Warwick, England

The Dryden Press
Chicago   New York   San Francisco   Philadelphia
Montreal   Toronto   London   Sydney   Tokyo

Acquisitions Editor: Rob Zwettler
Project Editor: Teresa Chartos
Design Director: Alan Wendt
Production Manager: Barb Bahnsen
Permissions Editor: Cindy Lombardo
Director of Editing, Design, and Production: Jane Perkins

Text and Cover Designer: Hunter Graphics
Copy Editor: Siobhan Granner
Compositor: The Clarinda Company
Text Type: 10/12 Times Roman

Library of Congress Cataloging-in-Publication Data

Readings in strategic marketing.

Includes bibliographies and index.
1. Marketing—Decision making.   2. Marketing—
Management.   I. Weitz, Barton A.   II. Wensley,
Robin, 1944-   .
AF5415.135.R42   1988   658.8'02   87-22274
ISBN 0-03-020864-5

Printed in the United States of America
890-066-987654321
Copyright © 1988 by The Dryden Press, a division of
Holt, Rinehart and Winston, Inc.

Address orders:
111 Fifth Avenue
New York, NY 10003

Address editorial correspondence:
One Salt Creek Lane
Hinsdale, IL 60521

The Dryden Press
Holt, Rinehart and Winston
Saunders College Publishing

Preface

Recently, managers, professors, and students have been focusing more attention on strategic issues in marketing. Most undergraduate and MBA programs now offer courses that include marketing strategy and planning concepts. This rapid development of marketing strategy has raised a number of questions: What is marketing strategy? How do strategic marketing decisions differ from tactical decisions? What is the role of strategic marketing in strategic management? The answers to these questions determine what should be taught in strategic marketing courses. Since there is no consensus on the answers to these questions, it is very difficult at this time to develop a traditional textbook that provides a comprehensive synthesis of strategic marketing knowledge and practice. This book represents a first step by grouping key articles that deal with strategic marketing issues and providing introductory material to integrate these articles. The first section of the book addresses the definitions of marketing strategy.

This book is organized around a traditional planning framework: identification of opportunities, evaluation of alternatives, models for allocating resources, planning and development, and finally implementation and control. However, we emphasize in the introductory sections that the development and implementation of ''real world'' marketing strategies are not as orderly as this planning model indicates.

The central theme is the creation and maintenance of a competitive, marketing-based advantage in a dynamic business environment—an environment in which customer needs are changing, new technologies are emerging, and competitors are attempting to replace established firms and develop their own sustainable advantage. Unfortunately, there are no easy formulas for developing marketing strategies to realize sustainable competitive advantages.

There are several differing but important perspectives on some marketing strategy issues. Thus, we have included articles that describe potentially conflicting perspectives so that the underlying issues can be discussed. Our hope is that this book, in conjunction with case studies, will assist students in understanding and assessing the strengths and weaknesses of various approaches. However, the central dilemmas between analysis and implementation, top-down and bottom-up planning, marketing and finance, and generalities and details will not disappear. While consideration of the issues discussed in text will improve strategic marketing decision making, such analysis will never completely replace the need for creativity and good fortune.

In preparing this book, we owe a great deal to colleagues *and* students. Our former students at UCLA, the London Business School, the Wharton School, Warwick University, and the University of Florida have provided a testing ground for the ideas and teaching materials presented here. They have willingly accepted this role and provided valuable insights. Numerous colleagues have contributed to the development of our ideas concerning marketing strategy. We are particularly indebted to George Day of the University of Toronto for his insights and responses to our ideas. Thanks must go to our editor, Rob Zwettler, and, finally, to our families for their patience.

Barton A. Weitz
Robin Wensley
February 1988

About the Authors

Barton A. Weitz (Ph.D., M.B.A., Stanford University; B.S.E.E., Massachusetts Institute of Technology) is professor of marketing and J.C. Penney Eminent Scholar Chair of the University of Florida. Prior to joining the faculty of the University of Florida, he taught marketing strategy at the Wharton School, University of Pennsylvania and at UCLA. Professor Weitz has lectured on marketing strategy in numerous executive education programs including programs for General Electric, Continental Airlines, Harris Corporation, and Stromberg-Carlson. His research has been published in leading marketing and management journals and he was editor for a special issue of the *Journal of Marketing Research* devoted to competition in marketing.

Robin Wensley is professor of strategic management and marketing at the Warwick Business School, England. He previously taught at the London Business School and has been visiting professor at UCLA and the University of Florida. Professor Wensley has acted as a consultant for many major companies including British Telecom, ICI, Philips MV, ICL, IBM, and Glaxo. His research and consulting interests include marketing strategy and planning, investment decision making, and the analysis of qualitative market research. Professor Wensley received the AMA's best publication award prize in 1982 for his *Journal of Marketing* article on strategic marketing and has published a number of other articles in the areas of strategy and marketing.

The Dryden Press Series in Marketing

Balsley and Birsner
Selling: Marketing Personified

Barry
Marketing: An Integrated Approach

Blackwell, Engel, and Talarzyk
Contemporary Cases in Consumer Behavior, Revised Edition

Blackwell, Johnston, and Talarzyk
Cases in Marketing Management and Strategy

Block and Roering
Essentials of Consumer Behavior, Second Edition

Boone and Kurtz
Contemporary Marketing, Fifth Edition

Churchill
Basic Marketing Research

Churchill
Marketing Research: Methodological Foundations, Fourth Edition

Czinkota and Ronkainen
International Marketing

Dunn and Barban
Advertising: Its Role in Modern Marketing, Sixth Edition

Engel, Blackwell, and Miniard
Consumer Behavior, Fifth Edition

Futrell
Sales Management, Second Edition

Hutt and Speh
Industrial Marketing Management: A Strategic View of Business Markets, Second Edition

Kurtz and Boone
Marketing, Third Edition

Park and Zaltman
Marketing Management

Patti and Frazer
Advertising: A Decision-Making Approach

Rachman
Marketing Today, Second Edition

Rogers and Grassi
Retailing: New Perspectives

Rosenbloom
Marketing Channels: A Management View, Third Edition

Schellinck and Maddox
Marketing Research: A Computer-Assisted Approach

Schnaars
MICROSIM
A marketing simulation available for IBM PC® and Apple®

Sellars
Role Playing the Principles of Selling

Shimp and DeLozier
Promotion Management and Marketing Communications

Talarzyk
Cases and Exercises in Marketing

Terpstra
International Marketing, Fourth Edition

Weitz and Wensley
Readings in Strategic Marketing: Analysis, Planning, and Implementation

Zikmund
Exploring Marketing Research, Second Edition

Contents

Section One
Introduction to Strategic Marketing

1

Introduction

Reading 1
"Marketing Theory with a Strategic
Orientation," *George S. Day and Robin Wensley*

17

Reading 2
"Marketing, Strategic Planning and the Theory
of the Firm," *Paul F. Anderson*

37

Section Two
The Identification of Strategic Opportunities

57

Introduction

Customer and Competitive Analysis

Reading 3
"Customer-Oriented Approaches to Identifying
Product-Markets," *George S. Day, Allan D. Shocker,
and Rajendra K. Srivastava*

67

Reading 4
"How Competitive Forces Shape Strategy,"
Michael E. Porter

87

Internal Analysis: Identifying Areas of Competitive Advantage

Reading 5
"Marketing Cost Analysis: A Modularized
Contribution Approach," *Patrick M. Dunne
and Harry I. Wolk*

101

Reading 6
"The Marketing Audit Comes of Age,"
Philip Kotler, William Gregor, and William Rodgers

117

Definition of Strategic Opportunities

Reading 7
"Strategic Segmentation: How to Carve Niches for   135
Growth in Industrial Markets,"   *Robert A. Garda*

Section Three
Concepts for Evaluating Strategic Market   149
Opportunities

Introduction

Experience Curve and Market Share Considerations

Reading 8
"A Fundamental Approach to Strategy   161
Development,"   *Barry Hedley*

Reading 9
"Diagnosing the Experience Curve,"   177
George S. Day and David B. Montgomery

Product Life Cycle Analysis

Reading 10
"Forget the Product Life Cycle Concept!"   201
Nariman K. Dhalla and Sonia Yuspeh

Reading 11
"Don't Forget the Product Life Cycle for Strategic   217
Planning,"   *Lester A. Neidell*

Reading 12
"Strategic Responses to Technological Threats,"   229
Arnold C. Cooper and Dan Schendel

Section Four
Strategic Marketing Models for Allocating   241
Resources

Introduction

Financial Model

Reading 13
"STRATPORT: A Decision Support System   257
for Strategic Planning,"   *Jean-Claude Larreche*
and V. Srinivasan

PIMS Model

Reading 14
"PIMS: A Reexamination," *Carl R. Anderson*   281
and Frank T. Paine

Matrix Portfolio Models

Reading 15
"Strategy and the 'Business Portfolio,'"   295
Barry Hedley

Reading 16
"The Directional Policy Matrix—Tool for Strategic   307
Planning," *S. J. Q. Robinson, R. E. Hichens,*
and D. P. Wade

Reading 17
"Strategic Marketing: Betas, Boxes, or Basics,"   325
Robin Wensley

Section Five
The Planning Process for Marketing Strategy   341

Introduction

Reading 18
"Strategic Market Analysis and Definition: An   351
Integrated Approach," *George S. Day*

Reading 19
"Strategic Goals: Process and Politics,"   373
James Brian Quinn

Reading 20
"Strategic Windows," *Derek F. Abell*   389

Section Six
Implementation of Marketing Strategies   399

Introduction

Market Share Strategies

Reading 21
"Is Market Share All That It's Cracked   409
Up to Be?" *Robert Jacobson and David A. Aaker*

Reading 22
"Product Quality, Cost Position, and Business   433
Performance: A Test of Some Key Hypotheses,"
Lynn W. Phillips, Dae R. Chang, and Robert D. Buzzell

Relationships with Customers

Reading 23
"Positioning Your Product," *David A. Aaker*   467
and J. Gary Shansby

Reading 24
"Brand Franchise Extension: New Product Benefits   479
from Existing Brand Names," *Edward M. Tauber*

Reading 25
"Make Sure Your Customers Keep Coming   489
Back," *F. Stewart DeBruicker and Gregory L. Summe*

Channel Relationships

Reading 26
"Make-or-Buy Decisions," *Erin Anderson*   499
and Barton A. Weitz

Organization

Reading 27
"Manage beyond Portfolio Analysis,"   519
Richard G. Hamermesh and Roderick E. White

Index   530

Section
One

Introduction to Strategic Marketing

THE orientation of marketing management is rapidly changing. Marketing executives have traditionally been concerned with the operating or tactical decisions outlined in their annual marketing plans. During the last five years, this short-term orientation has been supplanted by a growing interest in long-term strategic issues.

The emphasis on strategic marketing issues represents a response to changes in the business environment. Over the last 20 years, the rate of change in political, economic, and technological events has increased dramatically. Marketers must develop strategies for coping with the new developments in communications, bioengineering, electronics, and production methods; changing government policies concerning regulation and antitrust issues; and increased domestic and foreign competition.

In addition to enormous environmental changes, the increased complexity of business organizations has also created the need for a strategic orientation. Between 1949 and 1970, the majority of the Fortune 500 companies shifted from single-product-line firms to multiple industries, and even multinational organizations.[1] Thus, a business can no longer be guided by an enterpreneur's single key idea.

Analytical tools are being developed to assist corporate managers directing complex organizations in rapidly changing environments. A wide variety of consultants, corporate planners, and academicians have made contributions to our understanding of strategic issues. The most well-known of these models— the experience curve and the growth-share product portfolio matrix—were developed by Bruce Henderson, the founder of the Boston Counsulting Group. Such efforts have added a litany of new buzz words to the business vocabulary, including terms such as *cash cow, dog, harvest, milk, SBU, niche, entry barriers, PAR ROI* and *directional policy matrix.* The first article in this section, "Marketing Theory with a Strategic Orientation," emphasizes the need for marketers to reorient themselves, complementing their traditional customer approach with a strategic orientation that considers competitive activity.

What Is Marketing Strategy?

Strategy is one of the most overused terms in the business vocabulary. Corporate planners deal with financial strategies, production strategies, R&D strategies, and marketing strategies. Within the domain of marketing, there are product strategies, advertising strategies, pricing strategies, and copy strategies. This obsession with the word *strategy* has led Pascale to conclude, "our [the U.S. businessperson's] strategy fetish is a cultural peculiarity. We get off on strategy like the French get off on good food and romance."[2]

Does this excessive use of the term *strategy* imply that marketing strategy is just another word for marketing management? Are strategic marketing decisions different from tactical decisions? What is marketing strategy?

Military Analogy

The term *strategy* is derived from a Greek term which is roughly translated as "the art of the general (or commander-in-chief)." Thus, the analogous concept of military strategy provides a logical starting point for developing a definition of marketing strategy.[3] Like all analogies, however, it can be extended too far. As we analyze the readings in this book, we will note the limitations as well as the strengths of the military analogy.

A military strategy provides a framework for action during a confrontation. It indicates where the point of attack will be made, how personnel and equipment will be deployed across a battlefield, and how the anticipated position achieved will be defended against a counterattack. Applying the military analogy to marketing suggests that a statement of marketing strategy should indicate the direction a business plans to take in terms of the products and markets that will be emphasized (the point of attack) and the basis upon which the business will defend itself against competitive response.

To defend its position, a business must develop a sustainable competitive advantage. Merely identifying an exciting opportunity is not enough. The firm must realize that competitors will also recognize these attractive opportunities. Most marketers are aware of the significant profit potential in product ideas such as premium quality, conveniently prepared, frozen foods; computers for small businesses; robotics and factory automation; and genetically engineered products. However, only firms that have or are able to develop sustainable competitive advantages in a given area will realize the potential profits.

Thus, we define a marketing strategy as a statement that indicates *(1) the specific market toward which activities are to be targeted, and (2) the type of competitive advantage(s) that are to be developed and exploited.*

Strategic versus Tactical Decisions

Typically, a number of decisions and events occur as a marketing strategy is articulated and implemented. Some of these decisions are strategic and some are tactical. Our definition of marketing strategy suggests that strategic decisions are identified by the following two characteristics:

1.   They involve a significant resource commitment and thus they are considered to be "important."

2.   They consider competitive activity and focus on establishing a sustainable competitive advantage in a defined market.

As a result of differences in importance and focus, strategic and tactical decisions differ in terms of time horizon and decision-making process. Since strategies consider obtaining a *sustainable* competitive advantage, they are developed with a long-term time horizon and are concerned with achieving long-term competitive advantages. Tactical decisions, on the other hand, typically have a much shorter time horizon. For example, the objective of a new promotion program for Maxwell House coffee or a sales contest for Compaq computers may be to increase sales by 30 percent over a period of several months. However, the degree to which this sales increase can be maintained over the long run is typically beyond the scope of decision making associated with tactical programs. Consideration of long-term implications would make tactical decision making hopelessly complex.

Because strategic decisions are more concerned with long-term implications, the process for making strategic decisions differs from the process for making tactical decisions. Strategic decisions emphasize the relationship between the business and its environment, specifically the actions of potential competitors. While strategic decisions are driven by external considerations, tactical decisions have a more internal focus. Tactical decisions are typically undertaken periodically to coordinate the efforts required to implement a long-term strategy.

Finally, strategic problems are typically unique and less structured than tactical problems. It is difficult to employ simple models to develop marketing strategy statements. Considerable creativity is required to synthesize large amounts of external and internal information and arrive at a concise statement outlining the direction a business should take in the future. On the other hand, tactical decisions concerning advertising budgets and sales territory evaluations are made on a more frequent basis. Because strategic decisions provide structure, tactical decisions become more amendable to the use of models and decision support systems.

The preceding discussion emphasizes a distinction between strategic and tactical decisions based on competitive considerations, time horizons, and decision-making processes. This distinction suggests that strategic decisions can be made at all levels of the corporation—an issue which will be discussed in more detail in the introduction to Section V.

Corporate, Business, and Marketing Strategy

The responsibility for making strategic decisions does not reside solely with top-level management. Strategic decisions are made at all levels of the corporation from the chief executive officer (CEO) to the individual salesperson. The CEO's strategic decisions determine how the corporation allocates capital to various divisions, while the salesperson's strategic decisions determine how the salesperson allocates his or her resource—selling time—to various customers. While reading the articles in this book it is important to recognize that there is a hierarchy of strategic decisions for a corporation and that the focus of these decisions differs across the organizational hierarchy.

Many modern corporations are complex. They are often composed of numerous divisions and even separate legal entities. Corporate-level strategy primarily determines which portfolio of businesses the corporation should hold. Strategic decisions at the corporate level are concerned with acquisition, divestments, and diversification. Thus, a corporate strategist manages a portfolio of businesses just as a mutual fund manager manages a portfolio of stocks. The businesses in a corporate portfolio are frequently referred to as strategic business units (SBUs).

Both business and marketing strategies focus on how to compete in an industry or a product-market. However, they differ in the bases of sustainable competition considered in formulating a strategy. Some methods for building a sustainable competitive advantage are listed in Table I.1. These methods are divided into three groups: (1) advantages relating to the business as a whole; (2) advantages residing in a functional area of the business such as R&D, production, purchasing, or marketing; and (3) advantages based on relationships between the firm and external entities. This categorization is somewhat arbitrary because a sustainable competitive advantage often is based on a combination of the advantages listed in Table I.1. However, the list also illustrates the focus of this book.

Although business strategy is concerned with the entire list of potential advantages in Table I.1, it primarily focuses on advantages residing in the integration of the functional areas. Marketing strategy concentrates on competitive advantages of activities undertaken by the marketing function and advantages derived from relationships typically governed by the marketing function—those between the firm, its customers, and the distribution channels. While these sources of advantages associated with marketing can arise from activities performed by other functional areas within the business, the marketing function is typically responsible for directing the firm's resources toward satisfying customer needs. The marketing function develops long-term relationships with cus-

---

Table I.1   Sources of Competitive Advantage

Organization
Economies of scope
Intraorganizational synergies
Flexibility
Speed of response

Production
Process technology
Production efficiency
Scale economies
Experience
Product quality

Research and Development
Product technology
Patents

Marketing
Skills in developing new products
Communication (advertising, sales force) efficiency
Pricing policy
Knowledge of customer
Services provided—credit, technical assistance location

Relationships with External Entities
Customer loyalty
Channel control
Preferential political/legislative treatment
Access to financial resource

---

tomers, just as the purchasing function creates competitive advantages through supplier relations. Cost and technology advantages developed by the production and R&D functions often interact with market-based advantages. Low production costs can be translated into low prices and high value delivered to customers. Unique technology can be used to provide customer benefits that cannot be offered by competitors. While some of the readings in this book examine competitive advantages developed in functional areas other than marketing, the emphasis is on how cost and technology advantages can be integrated with customer-based marketing advantages.

The second article in this section, "Marketing, Strategic Planning, and the Theory of the Firm," considers various theories of the firm and how these theories imply different objectives for strategic decision making. It also proposes a specific role for the marketing function in influencing both the process by which the firm defines its constituency and the process by which the firm defines its strategy and objectives. Finally, this article suggests a specific role for marketing in aiding the firm to achieve its objectives.

Is an Explicit Marketing Strategy Needed?

After reading this introduction, you might think: "What's all this marketing strategy stuff? Who needs marketing strategy? It makes decision making overly complex, when the key issue is quite simple—buy low and sell high. Make as much profit as you can on each decision. A business should just try to increase sales and sell anything to anyone as long as the price enables the firm to make a profit." This perspective is similar to that of a general indicating that the strategy is to gain as much territory as possible and ordering troops to simply charge ahead in any direction they can. Such global, nondirective approaches are unsuccessful in both marketing and military contexts. They often result in a marketplace or battlefield position that cannot be defended against competitive attack. Spreading resources across a wide range of alternatives hinders the development of a sustainable competitive advantage for any single opportunity.

In general, the marketing strategy must be explicit in terms of specific product-market direction because successfully achieving a sustainable competitive advantage depends on people working together so that their efforts are mutually reinforcing. Without an explicit marketing strategy statement, the marketing efforts of a business can work at cross purposes. Advertising campaigns may be directed toward a product-market while the salesforce fails to call on retailers and wholesalers supporting that product-market. Products may be developed for markets that are not compatible with the firm's channels of distribution. The marketing strategy statement provides a vehicle for communicating the firm's future direction and coordinating efforts throughout the organization.

One must recognize that the amount of detail contained in the marketing strategy statement may vary from a broad statement about direction to a detailed description of target product-markets and business activities. The appropriate amount of detail depends on the business environment. Hayes uses the analogy of a road map for guiding travel through a swamp: while road maps are useful for navigating well-defined terrain, they are almost useless in a swamp.[4] In poorly defined geographic areas (or a highly uncertain business environment), a simple, broad statement about direction such as "Always go north" (or "Always emphasize product quality") may be the only meaningful guide.

Finally, an explicit marketing strategy statement sometimes allows a firm to respond more effectively to changing market conditions. When conditions change, the current marketing strategy statement and the reasons for it can be reexamined. The implications of the changing conditions often can be identified and the firm can then determine what, if any, changes need to be made in its marketing strategy statement.

Developing a Marketing Strategy

A typical prescriptive planning process model for developing a marketing strategy is illustrated in Figure I.1. The portions associated with strategic decisions resulting in a strategic marketing plan are indicated by bold type while the portions associated with tactical implementation issues are indicated by regular type. Such a distinction, however, is potentially misleading on the following points:

1.   "Tactical" and "implementation" are not synonymous. Implementation is an action while, as we discussed previously, tactical refers to the degree of routineness or simplification that is assumed. Actions taken during implementation can be highly strategic, but it is reasonable to assume that, in the process of implementation, the subsequent decisions that emerge are of a "fine-tuning" nature and can be characterized as tactical.

2.   The decisions identified are actually objectives and resource allocations. As we discussed earlier, it is the content of a marketing decision (a targeted product-market and a specified type of competitive advantage) as well as the category of decision that makes it strategic.

3.   The notion of planning process and the plan itself are confused. A plan is a mechanism designed to enable a decision(s) to be translated into action(s) by others, possibly over an extended time period. A planning process, on the other hand, covers the overall activity from developing a definition of strategic direction to actually implementing it.

Thus, the planning process also covers the range of options available for enacting the development of a marketing strategy. For example, in most firms a choice is made either to use the established procedures of corporate and marketing planning as well as capital budgeting or else to conduct a study and make a decision based on examining a particular issue, undertaken by a formal planning group, external consultant, or an "ad hoc" study group within the firm.

The underlying notion of strategy development, therefore, implies a number of important amplifications to Figure I.1. First, we believe that implementation often has important implications for overall strategy development. Second, we need to distinguish between the description of how strategy develops and the attempt to impose some sort of order on development using a planning process. Recent research emphasizes that the process of strategy development is considerably more complex than the simple procedural model illustrated in Figure I.1.[5] Feedback loops arise between stages and the ordering, particularly of forms of analysis, can change to the extent that various stages are completely omitted.

Despite the problems with the descriptive validity of the planning model, it does provide a useful framework for arranging the articles in this book. In broad terms, we can describe the shaded portion as an analytical perspective in the development of a marketing strategy leading to issues of implementation, while the issues of planning process involve attempts to conduct the whole operation of the organization in a systematic manner. In the remaining portion of this section we look at the elements of this framework and relate the stages more directly to the organization of the book.

Figure I.1   The Strategic Marketing Planning Process

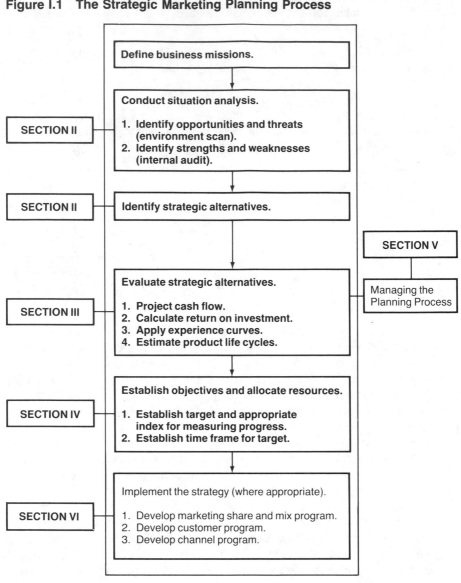

Define business missions.

Conduct situation analysis.

1. **Identify opportunities and threats (environment scan).**
2. **Identify strengths and weaknesses (internal audit).**

SECTION II

Identify strategic alternatives.

SECTION II

SECTION V

Evaluate strategic alternatives.

1. **Project cash flow.**
2. **Calculate return on investment.**
3. **Apply experience curves.**
4. **Estimate product life cycles.**

SECTION III

Managing the Planning Process

Establish objectives and allocate resources.

1. **Establish target and appropriate index for measuring progress.**
2. **Establish time frame for target.**

SECTION IV

Implement the strategy (where appropriate).

1. Develop marketing share and mix program.
2. Develop customer program.
3. Develop channel program.

SECTION VI

Define Business Mission

The first decision in the prescriptive planning process shown in Figure I.1 is the definition and purpose of the business unit. At this stage, managers address the following questions: Who are our customers and what value are we providing them? What business are we in? What should our business be? The answers to these simple-sounding questions can determine the future success of the organization. Levitt suggested that railroad companies would not be in their present deplorable condition if they had defined their mission as transporting people and products rather than simply as "being in the railroad business."[6] By adopting a broader definition, railroad companies could have taken advantage of transportation opportunities involving airplanes, trucks, and pipelines.

Another example of the breadth of definition of the business mission concerns Gillette. During the fluorocarbon propellant controversy, a number of Gillette's customers were switching to competitive roll-on and stick deodorants. In analyzing this situation, one executive commented:

We were like the railroad (that) didn't realize they were in the transportation business. We thought we were in the aerosol business because 80 percent of all users preferred aerosols and we were the leader in that segment. But when the ozone controversy broke, we found we were really in the underam business.[7]

Once Gillette redefined its mission as being in the underarm business, it allocated significant resources to develop alternate deodorant delivery systems.

The two preceding examples are compelling, but, as several writers have recognized, the "correct" answers to the question of business mission are far from clear in most specific situations.[8] The question "What business are we in?" is often really a question about the nature of the firm's capabilities and customer franchise. It could be argued, particularly in the railroad example, that it would be more valuable to ask: "In what businesses are we capable of maintaining a competitive advantage?" and "What business do our customers think we are in?"

We have seen that there can be problems with narrowly defined missions, but problems can also arise when the mission statement is too broad. For example, it would be dangerous for a manufacturer of felt-tip pens to say that its mission was manufacturing communication equipment. Such a broad statement could lead the company to attempt to develop products for which it had no experience or expertise and thus no competitive advantage. A too-broad mission statement can result in a business failing to exploit its differential advantage, while a too-narrow mission definition can result in a failure to capitalize on new opportunities.

Conduct Situation Analysis

Since a marketing strategy indicates the direction that a business takes to realize a sustainable competitive advantage in the marketplace, an analysis of the position of a business relative to its environment is an important input throughout the planning process. Figure I.1 indicates that this analysis is typically composed of two elements: (1) the identification of opportunities and threats that might arise from changes in economic, political, social, legal, technological, and competitive factors and (2) the identification of the strengths and weaknesses of the business relative to competition. These strengths and weaknesses indicate the degree to which the business can exploit the environmental opportunities and blunt the threats. It is important to note that competitive analysis plays a key role in both aspects of the situation analysis.

Identify Strategic Alternatives

The next decision in the planning process is to identify strategic alternatives. Typically, alternatives are defined in terms of products provided to a market. For example, an SBU in the climate control business might consider products such as central, room, and automobile air conditioners for OEM (original equipment manufacturers), industrial, replacement, new construction, and consumer markets. The product-market alternatives facing a pet food business might be dry, canned, and semimoist products to be sold to dog owners and cat owners.

These alternatives may include product-markets that the business is presently serving as well as new opportunities identified by a scan of the environment. Of course, the business mission restricts the nature of the alternatives that are considered: a firm in the climate control business would not consider the growing market for home video tape recorders because this opportunity would be inconsistent with its business mission. Factors related to conducting a situation audit and identifying strategic alternatives are presented in Section II.

Evaluate Strategic Alternatives

After a number of alternatives have been identified, the next decision is to evaluate each of these alternatives. This evaluation is accomplished by an assessment of the degree to which the business can develop a sustainable competitive advantage and realize long-term profits in a product-market. The assessment weighs the characteristics of the product-market opportunity against the characteristics of the business that enable it to exploit this potential. Thus, the business considers the match between its strengths and weaknesses and its opportunities.

On the basis of this evaluation, managers decide that some product markets will receive major investments, in terms of financial resources and human effort; other alternatives will receive little or no investment; and still other alternatives receive negative investments. This final group of alternatives is expected to generate funds rather than receive them. Thus strategic decisions are reflected in the level of investment made in a product-market; the pattern of investments across product-markets reflects the strategy of the business.

The traditional methods for evaluating strategic investment opportunities rely on financial analysis—the projection of cash flows and the calculation of return on investment. But currently there is more emphasis on the use of the concepts of the experience curve and the product life cycle. All these approaches are taken up in Section III.

Establish Objectives and Allocate Resources

The next set of decisions in the planning process establishes objectives for each of the product-markets in which the business will be participating. Each objective should have the following two components: (1) the target sought, with an appropriate index for measuring progress, and (2) a time frame within which the goal is to be achieved. In conjunction with each objective, an appropriate investment level is established so that the business will have sufficient resources to achieve the objectives.

Traditionally, businesses have adopted financial performance targets— such as profits as a percent of sales, earnings per share, dividends, and return on assets employed. Some of the new strategic planning models discussed in Section IV suggest that these financial objectives should be supplanted by market share and cash flow targets.

Implement the Strategy

The next set of decisions in the planning process develops a marketing mix program for each product-market, often based on a specific market share target. This program is designed to achieve the objective with the resources that have been allocated. It requires decisions about product characteristics, price, promotional activities, and distribution functions.

Equally important, managers need to consider the extent to which implementation should also involve the development of specific programs to reinforce customer and distribution channel relationships. Issues related to the implementation of marketing strategies are discussed in Section VI.

Illustrations of Marketing Strategy Development

Since its inception, the mission of Walt Disney Productions has been to provide entertainment for children.[9] The specific product-markets emphasized were theme parks, television programs, and motion pictures directed toward U.S. families with children between 6 and 13 years old. The phenomenal success of Walt Disney Productions is, in part, due to the fact that the 6- to 13-year-old segment grew from 14.7 percent of the U.S. population in 1950 to 18.2 percent of the population in 1960. But this market segment is beginning to decline. In 1980, it accounted for only 15 percent of the U.S. population, and by 1990 it is expected to fall to 12 percent.

This change in the business environment has led Walt Disney Productions to recognize the disadvantages of continuing to aim at a declining product-market, and to place more emphasis instead on the growing segment of 21- to 24-year-old adults. To implement this new strategy, Disney has made changes in its marketing mix. "PG" rated movies are replacing the traditional "G" rated movies, thrill rides are being added to the amusement parks, and new entertainment products (ski resorts) and international markets (Japan) are being pursued.

Decisions made at Texas Instruments in the early 1970s offer another illustration of strategy development and reformation. Prior to 1971, TI's efforts had been directed primarily toward supplying semiconductor products to industrial customers. When surveying the environment, TI recognized that recent technological advances would result in a large, rapidly growing market for consumer electronics. TI felt that it was in a good position to exploit this opportunity because of their experience in manufacturing the critical components in consumer electronic products. Thus, TI decided to

". . . put most of its development money for the next few years into the consumer business rather than into computer memories and microprocessors, as its competitors did. 'We penalized semiconductors—that was the price for allocating our resources,' Bucy [CEO of TI] said."[10]

While this strategic decision resulted in TI playing a major role in the consumer hand-held calculator and digital watch product-market, the limited resources directed toward semiconductors was a major factor in Intel's domination of semiconductor memories.

Most of the examples presented in this book concern profit-oriented corporations. However, nonprofit institutions also develop and reformulate strategies. For example, the University of California has a mission to provide graduate and undergraduate education to the residents of California. The departments (management, law, history, physics, etc.) at the seven campuses can be considered the product-market alternatives toward which resources can be directed. In light of declining enrollments, the total resources allocated to the university system have been reduced. Thus the university is forced to reevaluate its strategy—its pattern of resource allocations. One option would be to reduce the funding to each department by the same percentage as the entire university funding is reduced. Another option would be to direct resources toward strong departments on campuses with high student demand and reduce funding or even eliminate funding to weak departments. Whatever strategy is selected, operational changes will have to be made. The price charged to students (tuition) might be increased and the quality of the service might be altered by increasing class sizes.

Comparisons of Prescriptive and Actual Planning Processes

The prescriptive planning process shown in Figure I.1 implies that strategic decisions are made in a hierarchical process. After the business mission is defined, the situation analysis is performed, the product-market alternatives are identified, objectives are established, and finally resources are allocated. However, one must recognize that there are substantial interactions between the decisions made at each step of the process. For example, when strategic alternatives are identified, they may lead to a reformulation of the business mission; or an analysis of implementation decisions might lead to a reevaluation of the resource allocation decisions previously made, and perhaps ultimately to a reevaluation of the entire strategic decision.[11]

Even though we acknowledge these interactions in the prescriptive planning model, the model still seems to imply that the process is dominated by a top-down rather than a bottom-up direction. In addition, the model may suggest that a clear distinction exists between the strategic marketing decisions made by top management and tactical decisions made at operating levels.

Much of this book is devoted to the hierarchical rational analytic perspective for making strategic marketing decisions. This perspective emphasizes the application of prescriptive principals within a fixed decision-making framework. However, alternative perspectives on strategic decision making suggest that strategies are enacted by simply indicating important criteria that need to be considered when making business decisions or that strategies arise through the definition of the process of decision making and the structure of the organization. These alternative views will be examined in Section V. Specifically, we will examine the contention that, in practice, strategy formulation and evaluation cannot be so readily differentiated from implementation. This problem concerns strategists continually: the tradeoff between the top-down approaches that incorporate the grand view but lack practicality and the bottom-up views which are clearly practical but may be unnecessarily limited in perspective. The top-management perspective is "strategic," but its high-level generalities may mask the richness of options that a different approach could suggest. For example, product positioning and distribution are operating-level decisions which may be critical in creating a strategic advantage over competition.

Organization of the Book

This book primarily addresses the development of analytical skills and thus it is organized around the rational analytical model of strategic formulation in Figure I.1. Section II, following this introduction, contains articles that address the identification of strategic marketing opportunities. The environmental and internal analyses are also considered in this section.

Section III examines concepts used to evaluate the identified alternatives, or opportunities. This section contains articles that illustrate how financial, product life cycle, and experience curve analyses are used to determine the attractiveness of a strategic market opportunity.

Section IV focuses on normative models used to determine objectives and investment levels for strategic opportunities. The three models presented in this section are the market-share/market-growth matrix associated with the Boston Consulting Group; the market-attractiveness/competitive-position matrix associated with GE, McKinsey, and UK Shell; and the PIMS model associated with the Strategic Planning Institute. In addition to articles describing each model, there are also some articles examining the strengths and weaknesses of these models.

While the first four sections are primarily concerned with analytical approaches to strategy development, the remaining two sections introduce issues related to alternative perspectives of strategy development. Section V contains articles that examine how marketing strategies are developed and the planning process.

Section VI is devoted to considerations in implementing marketing strategies. Topics discussed in the articles in this section include examples of the development of sustainable competitive advantages through channel control and customer loyalty, the organization of the strategic effort, and approaches for building market share.

Footnotes

1.   Richard P. Rumelt, *Strategy, Structure and Economic Performance* (Boston: Graduate School of Business Administration, Harvard University, 1974).

2.   R. T. Pascale, "Our Curious Addiction to Corporate Grand Strategy," *Fortune,* January 25, 1982, 115–116.

3.   See Phillip Kotler and Ravi Singh, "Marketing Welfare in the 1980's," *Journal of Business Strategy* (1981):30–41; and Jack Trout and Al Ries, *Marketing Welfare* (New York: McGraw-Hill, 1985).

4.   Robert H. Hayes, "Strategic Planning—Forward in Reverse?" *Harvard Business Review* (November–December 1985):111–119.

5.   Henry Mintzberg and James Walters, "Of Strategies Deliberate and Emergent," *Strategic Management Journal* (July–September 1985):255–272.

6.   Theodore Levitt, "Marketing Myopia," *Harvard Business Review* 38 (July–August 1960):26–34.

7.   "Gillette: After Diversification that Failed," *Business Week,* February 28, 1977, 59.

8.   Ken Simmonds, "Removing the Chains from Product Strategy," *Journal of Marketing Studies* 5 (1968):29–40.

9.   "Can Disney Still Grow on Its Founder's Dream?" *Business Week,* July 31, 1978, 58–63.

10.   "Texas Instruments Shows U.S. Business How to Survive in the 1980's," *Business Week,* September 18, 1978, 66–92.

11.   See Henry Mintzberg and Alexandria Mattush, "Strategy Formulation in Ad hoc racy," *Administrative Science Quarterly* 30 (June 1985):160–197; and James Brian Quinn, *Strategies for Change: Logical Incrementalism* (Homewood, Ill.: Irwin, 1980).

Additional Readings for Section One

Ansoff, Ingor H. "The Changing Shape of the Strategic Problem," In *Strategic Management,* Dan Schendel and Charles W. Hofer, eds. (Boston: Little, Brown and Company, 1979), 30–44.

Biggadike, Ralph E. "The Contributions of Marketing to Strategic Management." *Academy of Management Review* (October 1981):621–632.

Bower, J. L. "Business Policy in the 1980's." *Academy of Management Review* 7 (1982):630–638.

Burgelman, R. "Model of the Interaction of Strategic Behavior, Corporate Context, and the Concept of Strategy." *Academy of Management Review* 8 (1983):61–79.

Caves, R. E. "Industrial Organization, Corporate Strategy, and Structure." *Journal of Economic Literature* 18 (1980):64–92.

Gerstner, L. V. "Can Strategic Planning Pay Off?" *Business Horizons* (December 1972):5–16.

Glueck, F. W., S. P. Kaufman, and A.S. Walleck. "Strategic Management for Competitive Advantage." *Harvard Business Review* 58 (July–August 1980):154–161.

Gray, Daniel E. "Uses and Misuses of Strategic Planning." *Harvard Business Review* (January–February 1986):89–97.

Hayes, Robert H. "Strategic Planning—Forward in Reverse?" *Harvard Business Review* (November–December 1985):111–119.

Mintzberg, H. and J. A. Waters. "Of Strategies Deliberate and Emergent." *Strategic Management Journal* (July–September 1985):257–272.

Porter, M. E. "The Contributions of Industrial Organization to Strategic Management." *Academy of Management Review* 6(1981):609–620.

Schendel, D.E. "Strategic Management and Strategic Marketing: What's Strategic About Either One?" In *Strategic Marketing and Management,* H. Thomas and D. Gardner, eds., (John Wiley and Sons, 1985): 41–63.

Tilles, S. "How to Evaluate Corporate Strategy." *Harvard Business Review* 41 (1963):47–61.

Webster, Frederick E., Jr. "Top Management's Concerns About Marketing Issues for the 1980's." *Journal of Marketing* (Summer 1981):9–16.

Wensley, Robin. "The Effective Strategic Analyst." *Journal of Management Studies* (1979):16, 283–293.

Wind, Y. and T.S. Robertson. "Marketing Strategy: New Directions for Theory and Research." *Journal of Marketing* (Spring 1983):12–25.

Books on Marketing Strategy

Aaker, David A. *Strategic Market Management.* New York: Wiley, 1984. *A paperback book that focuses on the basic concept involved in developing a business strategy. Includes chapters on external and self-analysis, diversification, acquisitions, and multinational strategies.*

Abell, Derek F. *Defining the Business.* Englewood Cliffs, N.J.: Prentice-Hall, 1980. *Focuses on identifying strategic opportunities. Proposes a three-dimensional scheme for defining opportunities, based on customer segments, customer uses, and substitute technology. Particularly relevant to the material in Section II of this book.*

Abell, Derek F., and John S. Hammond. *Strategic Marketing Planning: Problems and Analytical Approaches.* Englewood Cliffs, N.J.: Prentice-Hall, 1979. *A textbook on strategic marketing, containing sections on methods for assessing the strategic position of a company, analytical tools for making strategic decisions, and creative aspects of the planning process. About 50 percent of the book is devoted to cases that illustrate the use of strategic planning tools.*

Ansoff, H. Igor. *Corporate Strategy: An Analytic Approach to Business Policy for Growth and Expansion.* New York: McGraw-Hill, 1965. *A classic book on the steps involved in strategy formulation. Extensive and highly readable discussion of the concept of synergy and the use of this concept to generate and evaluate strategic alternatives.*

Bonoma, Thomas V. *The Marketing Edge: Making Strategy Work.* New York: Free Press, 1985. *This book is unique in that it focuses on strategic implementation issues rather than concepts related to the development of strategies; however, the book lacks a framework for organizing the discussion of implementation issues. Written for a business audience.*

Cravens, David W. *Strategic Marketing.* Homewood, Ill.: Richard D. Irwin, 1982. *A textbook of strategic marketing that discusses the relationship between corporate and marketing strategies, the identification and selection of target markets, the link between marketing strategy and the marketing mix variables, and strategic planning process.*

Day, George S. *Analysis for Strategic Market Decisions.* St. Paul, Minn.: West, 1986. *A paperback that offers comprehensive manager-oriented treatment of methods and concepts used in the development of business strategies such as the product life cycle, experience curves, portfolio models, and PIMS models.*

Day, George S. *Strategic Market Planning: The Pursuit of Competitive Advantage.* St. Paul, Minn.: West, 1984. *A paperback that discusses some key strategic issues such as the concept of sustainable competitive advantage, the definition of strategic opportunities, and the integration of top-down and bottom-up planning perspectives. Contains numerous examples of business strategies.*

Henderson, Bruce D. *Henderson on Corporate Strategy,* Cambridge, Mass.: Abt Books, 1979. *A collection of short essays written by the founder of the Boston Consulting Group. Essays are directed toward senior-level management in large businesses.*

Hofer, Charles W., and Dan E. Schendel. *Strategy Formulation: Analytical Concepts.* St. Paul: West Publishing, 1978. *A paperback book that defines the concept of strategy; ex-*

plains why strategic decisions play a central role in organizational performance; and describes the analytical concepts, models, and techniques that are useful for the formulation of strategy. Distinctions are made between strategy formulation at the corporate, business, and functional level. More oriented toward academics and students than toward a business audience.

Jain, Subhash C., *Marketing Planning and Strategy.* Cincinnati: South-Western Publishing, 1981, Second Edition. *A textbook on marketing strategy that is quite similar to the textbook by Cravens.*

Kerin, Roger A., and Robert A. Peterson, eds. *Perspectives on Strategic Marketing Management.* Boston: Allyn & Bacon, 1980. *A collection of 31 articles on strategic marketing. The articles are divided between the formulation of corporate and marketing strategies and marketing management decisions concerning the implementation of the marketing strategy. There are a mix of theoretical articles and practical articles from trade magazines. Some attempt has been made to develop a framework to link the articles together.*

Larreche, Jean-Claude and Edward C. Straus. *Readings in Marketing Strategy.* Palo Alto, Calif.: Scientific Press, 1982. *Collection of 41 articles on a variety of marketing strategy topics.*

Levitt, Theodore. *Marketing for Business Growth.* New York: McGraw-Hill, 1974. *A very readable book for executives on how to get more out of people, products, and resources. Discusses the importance and role of marketing in the strategic planning process.*

Levitt, Theodore. *The Marketing Imagination.* New York: Free Press, 1983. *Book contains reprints of seven insightful articles rewritten by Levitt on a variety of marketing strategy issues including the gobalization of markets, marketing intangibles, and building long-term relationships.*

Peters, Thomas. *A Passion for Excellence.* New York: Random House, 1985. *A best-selling book written for a practitioner audience that includes numerous examples of how firms achieve excellent performance often through an unrelenting focus on product/service quality and customer satisfaction.*

Peters, Thomas and Robert Waterman. *In Search of Excellence.* New York: Random House, 1982. *A best seller describing a set of principles for achieving excellence. These principles were developed by in-depth case studies of corporations which have been successful over a 50-year period.*

Porter, Michael E. *Competitive Advantage.* New York: Free Press, 1985. *A highly readable book which describes how to achieve competitive advantage by analyzing the value-added cost chain of a firm's offerings compared with that of its competitors.*

Porter, Michael E. *Competitive Strategy: Techniques for Analyzing Business, Industry and Competitors.* New York: Free Press, 1980. *Excellent book describing how to analyze the degree of competition and profit potential in an industry. Also, it includes techniques for examining vertical integration and new business entry decisions.*

Rothschild, William E. *Putting It All Together: A Guide to Strategic Thinking.* New York: ATA-CON, 1976. *An excellent "how-to" book written by a strategic planning specialist of General Electric. Provides an opportunity for business people to think through their own environment, develop strategic alternatives, and evaluate those alternatives.*

Schendel, Dan E., and Charles W. Hofer, eds. *Strategic Management: A New Business Policy and Planning.* Boston: Little, Brown, 1979. *Collection of fourteen commissioned papers plus two commentaries per paper that were presented at a conference in 1977. The papers are written by leading scholars with the objectives of defining the field of strategic management, presenting major research findings, and suggesting the direction for future research in strategic management. This is a comprehensive book covering goal formulation, strategy formulation, evaluation and implementation of strategies, and company organizational forms; it was written primarily for an academic audience.*

1

Marketing Theory with a Strategic Orientation

George S. Day and Robin Wensley

Marketing Theory with a Strategic Orientation

The discipline of marketing is constantly being reshaped by internal and external forces. Seldom have the pressures for change been so compelling as in the present period of ferment. The most obvious forces stem from developments in strategic management and planning, plus substantial restructuring of many traditional markets into networks of long-term cooperation. These developments represent significant challenges to the accepted paradigms within the field of marketing. The effects are being magnified because they frequently have a counterpart in growing dissatisfaction with the restrictive view of marketing that characterizes much of the present theory and research in the field.

From this ferment productive new directions for theory development are emerging. However, because of the multifunctional nature of strategic concepts, much of the initiative behind these new directions is presently coming from the related fields of industrial organization economics and administrative behavior.

This article identifies the pressures for change and their implications for theory development. From this analysis comes a number of specific research priorities to pursue. These priorities are based on judgments about the advantages that research in marketing has relative to other disciplines that also address strategic issues.

This article first appeared in the *Journal of Marketing* 47 (Fall 1983):79–89. Reprinted with permission from *Journal of Marketing,* published by the American Marketing Association.

When this article was published the authors were Professor, Faculty of Management Studies, University of Toronto; and Lecturer in Marketing, London Business School, respectively.

Trends in the Business Environment

During the 1970s the position of marketing within most firms was eroded or displaced by developments in strategic planning. In some cases the role was completely transformed by the emergence of domesticated markets in which competition was replaced by long-term cooperative agreements. Neither of these trends has been adequately captured within our existing body of theory.

Marketing's Influence on Strategy

In retrospect, the 1960s was the era of marketing's greatest influence and promise, when a marketing orientation was accepted as an essential element of profitable progress in growing markets. Because of the inadequacies of corporate long-range planning (Ansoff 1980), the marketing plan became an influential instrument for strategic change by guiding the product-market choices of the firm.

During the 1970s the influence of marketing noticeably waned, while strategic planning was in ascendance. First, the pressure of environmental changes forced many firms toward a financially driven portfolio logic, within the context of an organizational framework where the strategic business unit was the focal point of analysis and planning. Consequently the strategic emphasis shifted to consolidating strong competitive positions and conserving scarce resources. Increasingly the marketing plan was restricted to a tactical support role at the brand level (Hopkins 1981), and thereby lost its earlier strategic focus.

Also during this period, the marketing concept was being viewed with growing skepticism. Strong supporters among senior management were reporting frustration with getting the concept implemented (Webster 1981). Others were questioning the value of satisfied customers in the short run, at the expense of unnecessary product proliferation, inflated costs, unfocused diversification, and a weak commitment to R&D (Hayes and Abernathy 1980). Similar concerns have recently been voiced by marketers (Bennett and Cooper 1982), who argue that the marketing concept has shifted the emphasis from R&D and product innovation toward the supporting elements of the marketing mix, which do not offer a basis for long-run competitive advantage.

Finally, the basic structure of world markets became increasingly distorted during the 1970s. As international trade was increasingly afflicted by protectionism, a growing proportion of market segments were closed to free competition. One recent estimate is that 25–30% of total world trade is subject to *countertrade* requirements (*Business Week* 1982). This refers to transactions in which sellers are forced to take goods they would not otherwise buy. While the arrangements are often incredibly complex, they are all variations on barter. For example:

. counterpurchases—a set of parallel cash sales agreements in which a supplier sells a plant or a product such as aircraft, and orders unrelated products to offset the cost to the buyer.

. buybacks—under a separate agreement to the sale of a plant, the supplier agrees to purchase part of the plant's output for up to 20 years.

Many of these agreements are negotiated with state-owned enterprises or governments to whom profitability may be a secondary objective. The resulting trading patterns continue to rearrange the landscape of marketing.

Toward Strategic Management

The advent of the eighties has required a significant evolution in planning practice (Gluck, Kaufman, and Walleck 1980) that presents an opportunity for marketing to reassert its traditional influence (see Figure 1).

Figure 1   The Changing Role of Marketing

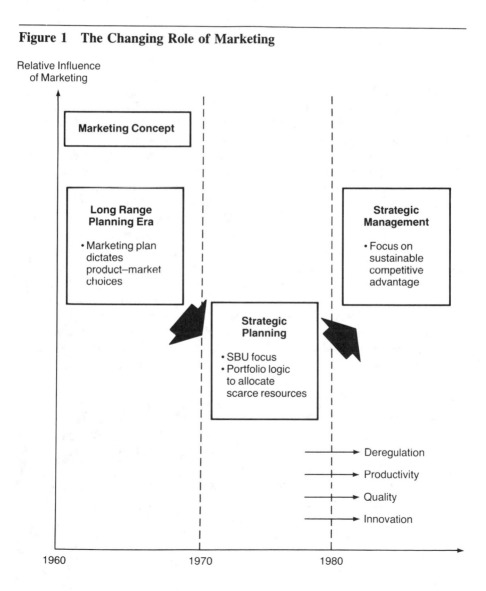

The challenges of the eighties are different from those that earlier spawned corporate strategic planning. Most notably, competitive pressures have become even more acute as companies recognize that in a slower growth economy, they must actively seek new opportunities in order to grow or even hold their position. It is not enough to attempt merely to consolidate present positions. At the same time technological advances, deregulation, pressures for productivity, increased emphasis on quality, an aging population, and innumerable other factors are presenting new challenges and new sources of competition.

The essence of strategic management is an integrated organizational emphasis on securing and sustaining a competitive advantage within the markets served by individual business units. Two patterns of response to this competitive imperative have evolved. The first is to "domesticate" the market by suppressing or controlling competition. The second seeks specific market-based mechanisms for advantage in the face of direct competition.

Domesticated Markets.   Arndt (1979) has observed that many markets that once were competitive have now been restructured as a result of voluntary, long-term binding agreements among participating organizations. As a result of agreements such as joint ventures, franchises, subcontracts, vertical integration, and joint product development and marketing contracts, transactions are planned and administered on the basis of negotiated rules of exchange. Such arrangements offer participants the benefits of reduced uncertainty of operations, reduced transaction costs, and access to economies of scale by bypassing traditional market arrangements. These potential benefits were significant considerations in the recent decision by IBM to invest in Intel Corp., one of their primary microprocessor suppliers. A number of similar linkages have been arranged in the semiconductor industry to strengthen the ability of U.S. chip makers to meet Japanese competition (*Business Week* 1983). The networks of long-term cooperation resulting from such transactions have a degree of stability simply not envisioned in most theories of marketing as a boundary function managing a continuing series of impersonal, discrete exchanges. Indeed, when markets become domesticated, the boundary between the firm and its environment becomes blurred and perhaps meaningless.

Strategic Segments.   Within those markets where overt competition remains, there is growing recognition of the complexity of competitive interplay and the consequent fuzziness of market boundaries. Within this context most businesses make most of their profits from a very limited portion of their served market. These are the segments where their competitive advantages are most distinct (Henderson 1983). Segments are delineated by the boundary line along which two segments come into contact, and no competitor has an advantage. The challenge for marketing is to extend the present theories of segmentation and positioning to encompass this broader perspective.

The Paradigm Shift within Marketing

A paradigm is a loose consensus regarding the fundamental nature of a discipline. The scope of the paradigm dictates the important questions in the field and thereby guides research and theory development. By this definition the marketing concept, with the allied notions of consumer choice and consumer satisfaction and the four Ps are arguably the most accepted general paradigms for the field (Arndt 1979, Hunt 1979). Their acceptance is most evident in the marketing management literature, and especially in their dominant role in the majority of texts.

A strong case could be made for also considering the notion of *exchange,* and the related concepts of exchange rules, transaction costs, information alternatives, and power, as a general paradigm (Carman 1980). Other elements of the field of marketing that have been proposed as candidates for general paradigms include: the *systems* that relate marketing institutions, the *influence* approaches used to bring about desired responses (Kotler 1972), or the pattern and resolution of *conflicts* among buyers and sellers. Overall, these additional elements have not been the catalyst for the development of a sufficient body of theory and research to be considered as dominant features of the discipline. Clearly this is a matter of judgment, which is especially difficult during periods when the essential consensus on the nature of the field is changing.

Disciplines evolve by progressively refining and articulating the accepted paradigms. This process continues until the discrepancies between the most widely accepted paradigms and reality become too large to be ignored (Kuhn 1962). This is the situation we are encountering within marketing. The manifestations are an absence of consensus as to the nature and boundaries of the field, and a relative neglect of significant issues in the field.

The present general paradigms are vulnerable to attack from several directions:

- the implicit one-way model of an exchange transaction is clearly at odds with contemporary exchange theory and research.
- the dominant orientation toward customers has deflected attention from the pursuit of competitive advantage.
- there is little recognition of the role of marketing as an innovating and adaptive force in the organization. The 4 Ps are misleading in the sense that they imply static distinctions.
- the marketing concept relies on inappropriate neoclassical economic premises and should be grounded in a more relevant constituency-based theory of the firm.

In short, the generally accepted paradigms for marketing are simplistic and incomplete in their consideration of major elements of both the practice and the discipline of marketing. However, the growing recognition of these shortcomings provides the goundwork for an integrative paradigm that can effectively guide future theory development. As Figure 2 implies, the eighties should see a broad consensus emerging regarding the role of marketing within the firm. One theme underlying this emerging consensus is the need to incorporate the relationships of the marketing function with constituencies both inside and outside the firm.

Figure 2   The Paradigm Shift within Marketing

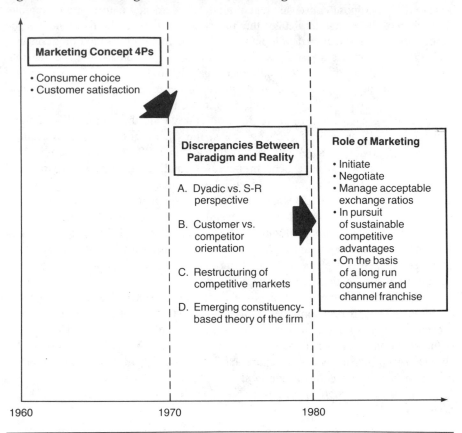

Each of the next four sections elaborates one of the major challenges to the traditional paradigms and contributes a specific element to an emerging integrative paradigm.

The Dyadic Exchange Paradigm

The traditional paradigm incorporates an implicit unidirectional stimulus → response mechanism to explain the reaction of customers and markets to management actions (Arndt 1979). By contrast, the dyadic exchange paradigm focuses on two-way or transactional relations between sellers and buyers. The outcome of this relationship depends on bargaining, negotiation, the balance of power, and the sources of conflict between the parties (Bagozzi 1978). This perspective has much greater potential to be congruent with the realities of domesticated markets. At the same time, it does not imply the abandonment of previous research in marketing, although it does force consideration of the limits to the situations in which this research is relevant.

Customer versus Competitor Orientation

Traditional paradigms in marketing give little explicit attention to competitive forces. Yet the benefits of a marketing exchange depend on the ability of each prospective supplier to create and sustain a competitive advantage over all other competitors. The argument for expanding the paradigm in this direction is persuasive.

> *The reward potential for a successful strategy is only large where the size of the advantage that can be created is also large. The long-term value of any business is determined by the size of its advantage versus the marginal, but viable competitor. When all or most competitors can achieve equal costs without price differentiation, then returns of the whole industry will be depressed to a level sufficient only to fund capacity additions to meet market growth requirements (Lochridge 1981).*

The basic issue for marketers was posed by Oxenfeldt and Moore (1978). In their view, a customer orientation implies a battle for ultimate customers that is won by direct appeal to these customers. However, it is derived from premises they find questionable, including assumptions that (1) customers know what they want, (2) marketing research can ascertain what potential customers want, (3) satisfied customers will reward marketers with repeat purchases, and (4) competitive offering differences are great enough to be important to the customers. By contrast, a competitor orientation views customers as an ultimate "prize" gained at the expense of rivals in many ways other than by simply offering a better match of products to customer needs. Sources of advantage over rivals can also be found in strong distribution arrangements, preferential treatment by suppliers, and lower costs.

Marketing theory has not always been silent about the need to pursue competitive advantage. Alderson (1957, 1965) advanced a number of propositions that could serve as a useful theoretical foundation for a revised paradigm. The pertinent propositions have recently been formalized by Hunt, Muncy, and Ray (1981):

- competition consists of the constant struggle of firms to develop, maintain, or increase their differential advantages over other firms.
- competition for differential advantage is the primary force for innovation in marketing.
- the bases for differential advantage are: market segmentation, selection of appeals, product improvement, process improvement, and product innovation.
- through time competitors will attempt to neutralize the differential advantage of an entrant.
- the existence of a differential advantage gives the firm a position in the marketplace known as an "ecological niche."

Marketing as Innovation

Simmonds has also drawn from Alderson's early work to propose that innovation be recognized as one of the core concepts on which marketing theory rests. Here again, a customer orientation leads to a potentially myopic focus on customer innovation in the adoption of products, while overlooking the functional role of marketing as ". . . organized, rational innovation. It is organized innovation because it is the marketer's function to identify the opportunity for change, initiate it, and monitor it. It is rational, in the sense of reasoned, because marketers must identify from the subset of innovations which are possible and innovations which are wanted" (Simmonds 1982).

A Constituency-Based Theory of the Firm

Implicit in the marketing concept is an acceptance of neoclassical economic theory that views firms solely as profit maximizing units. This acceptance can only be inferred from the normative decision rules incorporated in marketing models and theories, for there has been little or no questioning within the marketing literature as to whether it is an appropriate theory of the firm.

Recently Anderson (1982) has argued that behaviorally-oriented theories of the firm are superior in capturing the reality of marketing's internal and external relationships. The foundation of his constituency-based theory is the notion that the task of the organization is "to maintain itself by negotiating resource exchanges with external interests. Over time the internal coalitions within corporate organizations have adapted themselves to enhance the efficiency and effectiveness with which they perform these negotiating functions."

In general, functional areas that negotiate especially crucial resource exchanges will have greater power within the firm. This power will be manifested in many ways, including the ability to influence and to negotiate objectives. Indeed, from this perspective, the strategic thrust of the firm is also shaped by a bargaining process among functional areas. "Each area attempts to move the corporation toward what it views as the preferred position for long-run survival, subject to the constraints imposed by the positioning strategies of the other functional units" (P. Anderson 1982). Direct support for this view of strategic decision making comes from Quinn's (1981) field research into the political processes by which top management negotiates to obtain the support of the firm's various coalitions and interest groups. While it is possible to argue that such behavior can be consistent with a neoclassical economic theory, it is also true that a behavioral perspective is much more useful for understanding most marketing practice.

Toward an Integrative Paradigm

Several themes are woven through the four preceding challenges to the traditional paradigm. The implications of these themes can be translated into an integrative paradigm for marketing that has growing theoretical support and also speaks directly to the role of marketing in the strategy formulation process. For these reasons we foresee a growing consensus around the notion that the marketing function

- initiates,
- negotiates, and
- manages acceptable exchange relationships with key interest groups, or constituencies,

- in the pursuit of sustainable competitive advantages,
- within specific markets, on the basis of long-run consumer and channel franchises.

Responses to the Emerging Paradigm

The challenge to incorporate an orientation toward competitive advantage in both theory and research has not been widely accepted by marketing scholars. Indeed, many of the developments in strategic marketing analysis that strive to provide generalized diagnoses and prescriptions have deflected marketers' attention from the critical issue of the demand-based sources of competitive advantage (Wensley 1981, 1982). Consequently, the theoretical initiative has passed to economists by default. At the same time, many of the substantive issues of strategic marketing are also being addressed within the emerging field of strategic management. The purpose of this section is to clarify the nature of these related areas of theory and research as a prelude to specifying an appropriate role for marketing in addressing strategic issues.

Strategic Management and the Reinvention of Strategic Marketing

The traditional field of business policy or general management has recently been transformed and expanded into the field of strategic management. To a considerable extent the development of this field has occurred independently of work in related functional areas, notably marketing (see, for example, a study by Jauch 1981). One explanation was provided by Schendel (1983) who recently observed that:

. . . *What goes unrecognized in the literature of most functional areas, especially marketing . . . is that modern day, complex organizations have evolved well past the notion of the president with [functional] vice presidents . . . and have gone on to variations of a corporate/multiple business/functional area type . . . [S]uch parochialism is perhaps more true of academic people than of practitioners or consultants . . . . Increasingly we are seeing distinctions between how the matter of strategy making is approached (strategic management) and how strategy usage is conducted (operations management) . . .*

While the dichotomy between strategy and operations management has some utility, it is ultimately misleading, for it discounts the necessity for strategic thinking at the product-market level of the firm. An alternative perspective that accords a strategic role to marketing within product-markets and business units, holds that the primary concern of strategic management should be the formulation and implementation of corporate level strategy. Within diversified firms this encompasses:

- the *organizational context* of strategic decisions, and the relationship of strategy and organizational structure.

- the strategic *decision processes,* including formal systems for planning, implementing, and controlling.
- the specific *resource allocations* to existing businesses or major growth ventures.

Marketers can contribute to both theory and practice within each of these areas, and especially to decision process and resource allocation questions. The fundamental reason is that the appropriate level of analysis for addressing these two areas is more likely to be the individual product-market or business unit, and not the firm as a whole. Inevitably, a corporate or "top-down" perspective can only be partially informed about the threats and opportunities at this level of competitive interaction and the specific details of the company's franchise with their customers and distribution channels. The strategic decision process requires a dialogue between the corporate and business unit levels to develop individual strategies based on the specifics of market segments and competitive positions. Such a dialog can only be effective if marketing management reasserts its role in providing strategic direction at the product-market level.

There is also an analogous opportunity for marketing theory to make a contribution to the theoretical issues within the field of strategic management, while also expanding the understanding of the integrative paradigm. The clarification of this role will be complicated by the extent of shared interests between strategic marketing and strategic management. A further complication lies in the general difficulty of integrating distinct research streams employing different paradigms, units of analysis, causal presumptions, and researcher biases (Jemison 1981).

Advances in Industrial Organization Economics

The problem of integrating different research streams is especially evident when assessing recent research in economics that addresses the theoretical issues of industry structure and competitive advantage. The traditional industrial organization paradigm of structure → conduct → performance was of little interest to marketers or corporate strategists. Typically, the unit of analysis was the industry, with no recognition of strategic differences among firms. Further irrelevance was introduced by the assumption that because structure determined conduct (strategy), which in turn determined performance, it was possible to ignore strategy and explain performance solely in terms of the industry structure. More recent work has made progress in overcoming these limitations by broadening the research focus to include both the firm and the industry, the factors determining the nature of competition, and feedback effects of strategies on market structure (Porter 1981).

A major premise underlying economic theory is that competitive advantages are essentially temporary, but may be extended if the firm faces few direct competitors. Two developments in industrial organization economics that build on this premise are of particular interest to marketing theorists. The first is the generalization of the market entry barriers concept to embrace all *mobility barriers* that could deter a firm from shifting its strategic position by product or segment diversification, opening up new distribution channels, and so forth.

At first glance mobility barriers appear to be nothing more than fixed costs. Some of these costs are reasonably identifiable, such as capital requirements or access to channels with a new sales force. Other costs, including search and switching costs and reputation and brand image, are less readily determined. In fact, what is crucial is the proportion of any of these fixed costs that is irrevocably and exclusively committed to the particular opportunity—the sunk costs (Baumol and Willig 1981). The existence of substantial sunk costs in specific areas suggests strategic market segments in which certain firms, either by accident or design, find themselves with a pattern of sunk cost commitments very similar to some others and equally very different from others. We can also assume that for many firms, it will be more efficient to concentrate on developing the skills and assets required to compete within a restricted set of such segments, rather than broadly across a wide range.

The second development is the notion that industries can be broken into *strategic groups* of firms that all follow the same strategy, such as full line national brand versus narrow line specialist, and consequently have similar reactions to environmental changes (Caves and Porter 1977). Mobility barriers both define these strategic groups and are reinforced by the patterns of rivalry of group members. The persistence of these barriers determines the stability of competitive positions and the ability of the firm or firms within the group to resist the downward pressure on profits from direct competition.

The appeal of these developments is diminished by the extent to which ad hoc approaches are used to identify mobility barriers. Given that firms within the same product-market are different in many respects, it is inevitably possible to define various discriminating dimensions. The question remains how far such dimensions reflect the underlying economic logic of sunk costs that was developed above. The most consistent and useful distinction would appear to be between manufacturers who brand their own products and those who provide for retailer branding, as in the consumer durables industry (Hunt 1972). In other instances, however, the strategic groups have not proved to be stable over time (a critical requirement if any strategic prescriptions are to be drawn from the analysis). For instance, Hatten and Schendel (1977) claimed to show that the U.S. brewery industry actually consisted of three specific groups: national, large regional, and small regional. In a recent paper, however, Hatten and Hatten (1983) show that both the membership and the classifications of the strategic groups do not appear to be stable over time. Hence, what are needed are sound theoretical and methodological grounds for identifying the few crucial barriers from among many candidates.

Implications for Theory and Research in Marketing

Productive research and theory development in strategic marketing will be characterized by sensitivity, both to significant issues in the environment and opportunities for cross-fertilization with other disciplines. Such research will also enhance theory development in marketing if it expands the traditional paradigm to incorporate negotiated exchanges with internal and external coalitions, in the pursuit of competitive advantage. Productivity will be further assured by building upon existing conceptual and methodological strengths within marketing, and focusing these strengths on the development of mid-range integrative theories. The remainder of this section will elaborate on these last two notions.

Building on Strengths

A recent analysis of the contributions of marketing to strategic management (Biggadike 1981) concluded that although marketers have the tools and concepts to tackle strategic management issues, they are unlikely to do so because their orientation is toward technological solutions to short-term problems at a brand or product level. Indeed, the question was posed whether "marketers are interested in raising their level of aggregation to the business unit or industry unit level, and their time horizon to the long run . . . [Consequently] it will be up to strategic management students to make the transfer of marketing concepts and methods to strategic issues."

In our view, marketing has a broader strategic capability than is suggested by this conclusion. Indeed, while many strategic analysts have attempted to translate marketing theory and practice into the strategic context, in areas such as product and market segmentation they have often failed to recognize the complexity of the underlying theory (Day, Shocker, and Srivastava 1979; Wind 1978). There are three aspects of the strategic context where a marketing perspective should offer a distinctive if not the dominant view. These include the analysis of competitive market behavior, the definition of viable organization boundaries, and the processes by which resources are allocated.

Competitive Market Behavior.   Here we can identify a number of strategic themes: the behavior of existing markets, identifying and estimating new opportunities, and the specific assessment of resource allocation choices. In strategic terms the behavior of existing markets includes both the theory and application of segmentation and positioning approaches. The language of strategy encompasses such terminology as "niches" or "strategic segments." Such terms, as we suggested above, often mask a failure to look in detail at the marketing evidence. Indeed, the literature on marketing management (Kotler 1980) has emphasized that we need to consider four key factors in determining an appropriate basis for segmentation of any particular market:

- *measurability:* the degree to which the size and purchasing power of the resulting segments can be measured,
- *accessibility:* the degree to which the resulting segments can be effectively reached and served,
- *substantiality:* the degree to which the resulting segments are large and/or profitable enough to be worth considering for separate marketing attention, and
- *durability:* whether or not the distinctions between segments will diminish as the product category or industry matures.

Such factors are a valuable starting point for evaluating proposals for strategic segmentation (Garda 1981).

   To understand the behavior of existing markets in strategic terms, we also need to look more closely at the analysis of market responses. We would expect the marketing function to be the area where information should reside about the responsiveness of the market under consideration and also in analogous ones. Since many strategic judgments are inevitably based on similarities and distinctions between the assumed market responses in different product-markets, the lack of an appropriate marketing data base merely means that corporate management will tend to make "blind," and often implicit, assumptions which cannot be challenged against the evidence.

   In strategic terms, the simplest portfolio model of the firm's product-market positions involves the balancing of existing operations against new opportunities. Here also marketing theory has a considerable contribution to make, including the identification of market opportunities, the analysis of new product demand, and the development of a sensible use of product life cycle analysis for forecasting. These are key methodological inputs into any attempt to achieve an effective commercial balance in the portfolio. But here again there have been problems from too rapid transfer of a complex and detailed marketing concept to the strategic arena. For instance, many of the strategic portfolio models rely on a misleading and simplified concept of the product life cycle (Wensley 1981).

Defining Viable Organization Boundaries.   These definitions (Wensley 1983) require specific choices about which activities should be retained within the organizations as opposed to contracted from the external market. Choices cover a wide range of specific options, with the fully integrated organizations at one extreme and the totally independent external market at the other. One of the promising frameworks that can be used to assess the value of internal organizational mechanisms versus the external market is based on transaction cost analysis (Williamson 1979). Such a framework can also be useful in anticipating organizational changes necessitated by shifts in cost structures, due to changes in production technology or distribution channels (Rumelt 1981).

   Marketing practitioners and researchers are well-placed to test and evaluate an approach based on transaction cost analysis because they have experienced such choices within the marketing function and have an understanding of how markets actually operate. For instance, the marketing function has frequently had to consider the "make or buy" choice with respect to both advertising and selling activities. The transaction cost approach provides an opportunity to reinterpret previous work and identify new areas for research (Anderson and Weitz 1982). In such an evaluation, it is important to recognize that actual markets do not operate solely as impersonal mechanisms between individuals with short time horizons. Much of the industrial marketing literature testifies to the existence of longer-term relationships, which may help in the development of a more general model of the practical choices between internal and external markets.

The Process of Allocating Resources.   Many of the models of strategic management, including that developed by Schendel (1983) discussed above, tend to assume too simple a link between the development of strategic direction and its actual implementation via the allocation of resources. In practice, as both Bower (1970) and Mintzberg, Raisinghani, and Theoret (1976) have observed, the actual process of resource allocation often incorporates a number of implicit but critical strategic moves. In the area of resource allocation and particularly the information systems to support such decisions, marketing theory and practice has a key role to play. This role involves not only the extension of previous work on decision support systems (Little 1979) but also more direct attempts to integrate such approaches with current work in finance. It is a major challenge to those designing marketing information systems to ensure that the systems developed also interact with financial and accounting data. This implies a definition of asset values that reflects competitive market economics as well as closer attention to the relationship between specific advantages in the product-markets and the nature of competitive forces. Until the advantages of both consumer and distribution channel franchises are reflected in asset valuations, it will be difficult to recognize the real strategic significance of many marketing actions.

Indeed, this concern for asset valuations can be expressed in a way that represents the real concerns of strategic marketing. Individual firms face choices based on both past and future investment in sunk costs. Such sunk costs not only restrict the areas in which a firm can effectively compete but also act to reduce the extent to which others can imitate and therefore compete effectively. Sunk costs, however, only have strategic value when they facilitate actions that consumers and distributors will value. Strategic marketing is, therefore, concerned with market-based valuations of sunk costs and the incorporation of such valuations into the decision process within the firm.

Priorities for Mid-Range Theory Development

The complexity of strategic environments has led theorists to converge on a middle ground between the view that there are universal principles and the view that each organizational situation is unique (Steiner 1978). This middle ground is similar to the concept of "middle range" theories developed by Merton (1968); the emphasis, in Cohen and Lindblom's (1979) terms, is on usable knowledge that is only applicable within a defined range. These mid-range theories include simple contingency theories in which the validity of the relationship is controlled by the presence or absence of a particular independent variable, as well as more complex models in which independent variables can have an interactive effect on the nature of the relationship. There are a number of potential research topics within this middle ground that would yield considerable dividends.

The proposed research and theory development priorities can be hierarchically ordered. As Figure 3 suggests, our theories about the *outcomes* of competitive market interactions and the *process* of designing strategies for a business must be based on an improved understanding of market and industry evolution.

The Nature of Industry and Market Evolution

Present theories and research tend to focus either on the nature of the suppliers, as in industrial organization economics, or on the nature of the buyers, as in research on customer choice and diffusion processes. In fact, industry evolution is an adaptive process in which customers respond to the options that are avail-

Figure 3   A Hierarchy of Research and Theory Development Issues

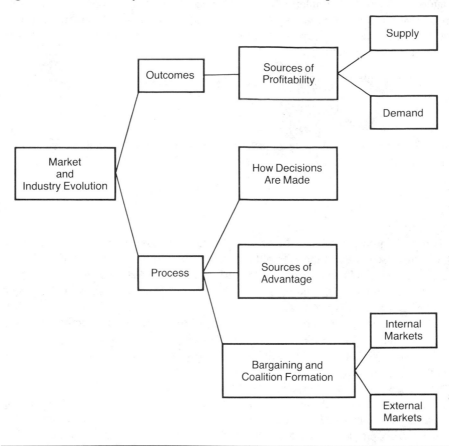

able, and in so doing, generate signals that suppliers respond to by changing the options that they offer. A better understanding of this evolutionary process can be obtained from historical and longitudinal analyses of various industries. Such studies would provide a basis for the identification of common stages, and also help to address such issues as the extent to which a firm's choice of strategy can influence the evolution of the relevant market. This research approach would avoid the confusion that exists in some models of the product life cycle between competitive supplier effects and changing consumer tastes. However, such research would involve considerable effort. One has only to look at Chander's original work on the impact of organizational structure in strategy, or the work of others, such as Rumelt (1974) to appreciate the depth of analysis that is required.

Research on Outcomes

A more focused search for relationships between forms of sunk costs and their strategic value in terms of consumer and channel franchises, would be productive. The most obvious departure point for this search is the impact of various independent variables on the relationship between a specific strategy and a performance outcome. Even the formulation of testable theories is a challenge. A prerequisite is a robust taxonomy of strategies and an adequate measure of performance outcomes. A further complication is the variety of candidates for important independent variables, including:

- product life cycle parameters
- experience effects
- perceived relative product quality and customer satisfaction
- market position

Composite models of profitability determinants also need to be developed and tested. Three classes of determinants have been identified:

- industry forces and strategic group membership
- competitive advantage
- operating productivity

There is a need for a much better understanding of the relative contributions of these three sources and the extent to which their contributions are modified by the independent variables discussed above. Merely to formulate the problem in these terms raises substantial methodological problems: We need to define and measure the three classes of profitability determinants so they are conceptually distinct. Currently, competitive advantage seems to be assumed to be directly correlated with the other "independent" variables. As Day (1983) has suggested, we can more usefully group the independent variables into two sources of competitive advantage and distinguish demand factors, such as market position, from supply factors, such as scale economies and experience curve effects.

A further research priority derived from this perspective is the identification of strategic group structures and mobility barriers. The utility of these concepts is considerably diminished by problems in designing an appropriate and independent form of measurement. To the extent that strategic groups are manifested in differences in consumer perceptions and behavior, existing methodologies can contribute to the resolution of this problem.

Research on the Firm's Strategic Market Planning Process

One of the major concerns for research in marketing strategy is the way in which consumer valuations are reflected in the strategic choice process within the firm. This also suggests a number of specific areas for research.

First, there is the relationship between the strategic decision-making process—in terms of the balance between top-down and bottom-up perspectives (Day 1981)—and the nature of the resultant strategic decisions. This is a particularly important question in regard to assumptions about market segmentation, positioning, and sales response to marketing decision variables. Work in this area should look closely at the role of middle managers, who were seen to be critical in Bower's work (1970), and also consider the relationship between tactical market planning and strategic decision making. We must be wary of two potential errors. First, we must not confuse more extensive and systematic procedures as evidence of better process. Although Wind and Robertson (1983) present a more comprehensive procedure to guide the process of marketing strategy development, there is little evidence that such procedures are sufficient in themselves to improve either the decision process or the quality of decisions. The second problem stems from the nature of process research. Within the broad field of organizational behavior, many research design, measurement, and interpretive problems have been recognized (see Van Mannen 1979). On the other hand, many marketing researchers have had experiences of analogous problems and solutions in the analysis of qualitative market research data.

Such research would necessarily focus on the factors that prove to be sources of competitive advantage at the time decisions are made. Such factors are more likely to include the availability of and ability to utilize market-based data and the particular skills of key managers, rather than measures such as market share and strategic group membership. As a related development, there are key areas for improvement in the models currently available for product and strategy evaluation. In particular, appropriate ways need to be found to incorporate assessments of market risk and competitive expectations.

Finally, the development of models of internal markets and bargaining and coalition formation within external markets would provide a means of assessing the viability of internal market mechanisms in vertically integrated firms, as well as the strategic significance of interorganizational marketing systems.

Summary

Marketing theory has tended to focus on operational problems relating to customer decision making within the confines of the marketing concept. In marketing practice another set of priorities has emerged, with the emphasis on the development of sustainable competitive positions in product-markets. Marketing theory has only tackled those issues indirectly, but can be redirected to explore a number of crucial consequences. On the basis of such an effort, it will be possible for marketing to reassert its role in the strategic dialog within the firm. Such a role would be based on clear functional responsibility for the maintenance and development of key commercial assets in terms of customer and distribution channel franchises.

References

Alderson, Wroe (1957), *Marketing Behavior and Executive Action,* Homewood, IL: Irwin.

———— (1965), *Dynamic Marketing Behavior,* Homewood, IL: Irwin.

Anderson, Erin and Barton Weitz (1982), "Make or Buy Decisions: A Framework for Analyzing Vertical Integration Issues in Marketing," unpublished working paper, Philadelphia: Wharton School, University of Pennsylvania.

Anderson, Paul F. (1982), "Marketing, Strategic Planning, and the Theory of the Firm," *Journal of Marketing,* 46 (Spring), 15–26.

Ansoff, H. Igor (1980), "Strategic Issue Management," *Strategic Management Journal,* 1 (April/June), 131–148.

Arndt, Johan (1979), "Toward a Concept of Domesticated Markets," *Journal of Marketing,* 43 (Fall), 69–75.

Bagozzi, Richard P. (1978), "Marketing as Exchange: A Theory of Transactions in the Marketplace," *American Behavioral Scientist,* 21 (March/April), 535–555.

Baumol, William J. and Robert D. Willig (1981), "Fixed Costs, Sunk Costs, Entry Barrier, and Sustainability of Monopoly," *Quarterly Journal of Economics,* 96 (August), 405–431.

Bennett, Roger C, and Robert G. Cooper (1982), "The Misuse of Marketing: An American Tragedy," *Business Horizons* (no. 2), 51–61.

Biggadike, E. Ralph (1981), "The Contributions of Marketing to Strategic Management," *Academy of Management Review,* 6 (no. 4), 621–632.

Bower, Joseph L. (1970), *Managing the Resource Allocation Process,* Boston: Division of Research, Graduate School of Business Administration, Harvard University.

Business Week (1982), "New Restrictions on World Trade" (July 19), 118–122.

—— (1983), "IBM and Intel Link Up to Fend Off Japan" (January 10), 96–98.

Carman, James M. (1980), "Paradigms for Marketing Theory," in *Research in Marketing,* 3, Jagdish M. Sheth, ed., Greenwich, CT: JAI Press, 1–36.

Caves, R. E. and M. E. Porter (1977), "From Entry Barriers to Mobility Barriers: Conjectural Decisions and Contrived Deterrence to New Competition," *Quarterly Journal of Economics,* 91 (May), 241–262.

Cohen, D. K. and D. E. Lindblom (1979), *Usable Knowledge: Social Science and Social Problem Solving,* New Haven, CT: Yale University Press.

Day, George S. (1981), "Strategic Market Analysis and Definition: An Integrated Approach," *Strategic Management Journal,* 2 (July–September), 281–301.

—— (1983), "Gaining Insights Through Strategy Analysis," *Journal of Business Strategy,* 4 (Summer), 51–58.

——, Allan D. Shocker, and Rajendra K. Srivastava (1979), "Customer-Oriented Approaches to Identifying Product-Markets." *Journal of Marketing,* 43 (Fall), 8–19.

Garda, Robert A. (1981), "Strategic Segmentation: How to Carve Niches for Growth in Industrial Markets," *Management Review* (August), 15–22.

Gluck, Frederick W., Stephen P. Kaufmann, and A. Steven Walleck (1980), "Strategic Management for Competitive Advantage," *Harvard Business Review,* 58 (July–August), 154–161.

Hatten, Kenneth J. and Mary Louise Hatten (1983), "Some Empirical Insights for Strategic Marketers: The Case of Beer," in *Strategic Marketing and Strategic Management,* D. Gardner and H. Thomas, eds., New York: Wiley.

—— and Dan E. Schendel (1977), "Heterogeneity within an Industry: Firm Conduct in the U.S. Brewing Industry 1952–71," *Journal of Industrial Economics,* 26 (December), 97–113.

Hayes, Robert H. and William J. Abernathy (1980), "Managing Our Way to Economic Decline," *Harvard Business Review,* 58 (July–August), 67–77.

Henderson, Bruce D. (1983), "The Concept of Strategy," in *Handbook of Business Strategy,* Kenneth J. Albert, ed., New York: McGraw-Hill.

Hopkins, David S. (1981), *The Marketing Plan,* New York: Conference Board.

Hunt, Michael S. (1972), *Competition in the Major Home Appliance Industry,* Ph.D. dissertation, Boston: Harvard University.

Hunt, Shelby D. (1979), "Positive vs. Normative Theory in Marketing: The Three

Dichotomies Model as a General Paradigm for Marketing,'' paper presented at the AMA Marketing Theory Conference.

_____, James A. Muncy, and Nina M. Ray (1981), ''Alderson's General Theory of Marketing: A Formalization,'' in *Review of Marketing 1981,* Ben Enis and Kenneth Roering, eds., Chicago: American Marketing.

Jauch, Lawrence R. (1981), ''A Descriptive Inventory of Some Cutting Edge Research on Strategic Management,'' working paper, Carbondale, IL: Southern Illinois University (April).

Jemison, David B. (1981), ''The Importance of an Integrative Approach to Strategic Management Research,'' *Academy of Management Review,* 6 (no. 4), 601–608.

Kotler, Philip (1972), ''A Generic Concept of Marketing,'' *Journal of Marketing,* 36 (April), 46–54.

_____ (1980), *Marketing Management: Analysis, Planning and Control,* 4th ed., Englewood Cliffs, NJ: Prentice-Hall.

Kuhn, Thomas S. (1962), *The Structure of Scientific Revolutions,* Chicago: University of Chicago Press.

Little, John D. C. (1979), ''Decision Support Systems for Marketing Managers,'' *Journal of Marketing,* 43 (Summer), 9–26.

Lochridge, Richard K. (1981), ''Strategy in the Eighties, *Annual Perspective,* Boston: Boston Consulting Group.

Merton, Robert K. (1968), ''On Sociological Theories of the Middle Range,'' in *Social Theory and Social Structure,* New York: The Free Press.

Mintzberg, H. D., D. Raisinghani, and A. Theoret (1976), ''The Structure of Unstructured Decision Processes,'' *Administrative Science Quarterly,* 23 (June), 246–275.

Oxenfeldt, Alfred R. and William L. Moore (1978), ''Customer or Competitor: Which Guideline for Marketing?,'' *Management Review* (August), 43–48.

Porter, Michael E. (1981), ''The Contributions of Industrial Organization to Strategic Management,'' *Academy of Management Review,* 6 (no. 4), 609–620.

Quinn, James Brian (1981), ''Formulating Strategy One Step at a Time,'' *Journal of Business Strategy,* 1 (Winter), 42–63.

Rumelt, Richard P. (1974), *Strategy, Structure, and Economic Performance,* Boston: Division of Research, Graduate School of Business Administration, Harvard University.

_____ (1981), ''The Electronic Re-Organization of Industry,'' unpublished paper presented at the First Strategic Management Conference, London.

Schendel, Dan (1983), ''Strategic Management and Strategic Marketing: What is Strategic About Either One?,'' in *Strategic Marketing and Strategic Management,* D. Gardner and H. Thomas, eds., New York: Wiley.

Simmonds, Ken (1982), ''Marketing as Innovation,'' *Research in Marketing Series,* London: London Business School, July.

Steiner, George A. (1978), ''Contingency Theories of Strategy and Strategic Management,'' in *Strategic Management: A New View of Business Policy and Planning,* Dan E. Schendel and Charles W. Hofer, eds., Boston: Little, Brown.

Van Mannen, John (1979), ''Reclaiming Qualitative Methods for Organizational Research,'' *Administrative Science Quarterly,* 26 (no. 6), 520–526.

Webster, Frederick, E., Jr. (1981), ''Top Management's Concerns about Marketing Issues for the 1980s'' *Journal of Marketing,* 45 (Summer), 9–16.

Wensley, Robin (1981), ''Strategic Marketing: Betas, Boxes or Basics,'' *Journal of Marketing,* 45 (Summer), 173–182.

_____ (1982), "PIMS and BCG: New Horizons or False Dawn?," *Strategic Management Journal,* 3 (April–June), 147–158.

_____ (1983), "Strategy as Maintaining a Viable Organizational Entity in a Competitive Market," in *Strategic Marketing and Strategic Management,* D. Gardner and H. Thomas, eds., New York: Wiley.

Williamson, Oliver E. (1979), "Transaction-Cost Economics: The Governance of Contractual Relations," *Journal of Law and Economics,* 22 (October), 233–262.

Wind, Yoram (1978), "Issues and Advances in Segmentation Research," *Journal of Marketing Research,* 15 (August), 317–337.

_____ and Thomas S. Robertson (1983), "Marketing Strategy: New Directions for Theory and Research," *Journal of Marketing,* 47 (Spring), 12–25.

Marketing, Strategic Planning and the Theory of the Firm

Paul F. Anderson

Would you tell me, please, which way I ought to go from here? asked Alice.
That depends a good deal on where you want to get to, said the Cat.
I don't much care where, said Alice.
Then it doesn't matter which way you go, said the Cat.
Lewis Carroll—*Alice's Adventures in Wonderland*

The obvious wisdom of the Cheshire's statement reveals an important fact concerning strategic planning: without a clear set of objectives, the planning process is meaningless. Two authorities on the subject refer to strategy as "the major link between the goals and objectives the organization wants to achieve and the various functional area policies and operating plans it uses to guide its day-to-day activities" (Hofer and Schendel 1978, p. 13). Other strategy experts generally agree that the process of goal formulation must operate prior to, but also be interactive with, the process of strategy formulation (Ackoff 1970, Ansoff 1965, Glueck 1976, Newman and Logan 1971). Given the growing interest of marketers in the concept of strategic planning, it would appear fruitful to assess the current state of knowledge concerning goals and the goal formulation process.

Over the years, this general area of inquiry has fallen under the rubric of the "theory of the firm." One objective of this paper is to review some of the major theories of the firm to be found in the literature. The extant theories have emerged in the disciplines of economics, finance and management. To date, mar-

This article first appeared in the *Journal of Marketing* (Spring 1982): 15–26. Reprinted with permission from *Journal of Marketing*, published by the American Marketing Association.

When the article was published the author was Associate Professor of Marketing, Virginia Polytechnic Institute and State University.

keting has not developed its own comprehensive theory of the firm. Generally, marketers have been content to borrow their concepts of goals and goal formulation from these other disciplines. Indeed, marketing has shown a strange ambivalence toward the concept of corporate goals. The recent marketing literature pays scant attention to the actual content of corporate goal hierarchies. Even less attention is focused on the normative issue of what firm goals and objectives ought to be. Moreover, contemporary marketing texts devote little space to the subject. Typically, an author's perspective on corporate goals is revealed in his/her definition of the marketing concept, but one is hard pressed to find further development of the topic. There is rarely any discussion of how these goals come about or how marketing may participate in the goal formulation process.

This is not to say that received doctrine in marketing has been developed without regard for corporate objectives. The normative decision rules and procedures that have emerged always seek to attain one or more objectives. Thus it could be said that these marketing models implicitly assume a theory of the firm. However, the particular theory that serves as the underpinning of the model is rarely made explicit. More importantly, marketing theorists have devoted little attention to an exploration of the nature and implications of these theories. For example, the product portfolio (Boston Consulting Group 1970, Cardozo and Wind 1980), and PIMS (Buzzell, Gale and Sultan 1975) approaches that are so much in vogue today implicitly assume that the primary objective of the firm is the maximization of return on investment (ROI). This objective seems to have been accepted uncritically by many marketers despite its well-documented deficiencies (e.g., its inability to deal with timing, duration and risk differences among returns and its tendency to create behavioral problems when used as a control device; Hopwood 1976, Van Horne 1980). However, the concern expressed in this paper is not so much that marketers have adopted the wrong objectives, but that the discipline has failed to appreciate fully the nature and implications of the objectives that it has adopted.

As a result, in the last sections of the paper the outline of a new theory of the firm will be presented. It will be argued that the theories of the firm developed within economics, finance and management are inadequate in varying degrees as conceptual underpinnings for marketing. It is asserted that the primary role of a theory of the firm is to act as a kind of conceptual backdrop that functions heuristically to guide further theory development within a particular discipline. As such, the proposed model is less of a theory and more a Kuhnian-style paradigm (Kuhn 1970). Moreover, for a theory of the firm to be fruitful in this respect it must be congruent with the established research tradition of the field (Laudan 1977). It will be demonstrated, for example, that the theories emerging from economics and finance are inconsistent with the philosophical methodology and ontological framework of marketing. However, the proposed model is not only fully consonant with marketing's research tradition, but, unlike existing theories, it explicitly considers marketing's role in corporate goal formulation and strategic planning. Thus it is hoped that the theory will be able to provide a structure to guide future research efforts in these areas.

Economic Theories of the Firm

In this section three theories of the firm are reviewed. The first, the neoclassical model, provides the basic foundation of contemporary microeconomic theory. The second, the market value model, performs a similar function within financial economics. Finally, the agency costs model represents a modification of the market value model to allow a divergence of interests between the owners and managers of the firm. In this sense, it operates as a transitional model between the economically oriented theories of this section and the behavioral theories of the section to follow. However, all three may be classified as economic models since they share the methodological orientation and conceptual framework of economic theory. Note that each postulates an economic objective for the firm and then derives the consequences for firm behavior under different assumption sets.

The Neoclassical Model

The neoclassical theory of the firm can be found in any standard textbook in economics. In its most basic form the theory posits a single product firm operating in a purely competitive environment. Decision making is vested in an owner-entrepreneur whose sole objective is to maximize the dollar amount of the firm's single period profits. Given the standard assumptions of diminishing returns in the short run and diseconomies of scale in the long run, the firm's average cost function will have its characteristic U-shape. The owner's unambiguous decision rule will be to set output at the point where marginal costs equal marginal revenues. The introduction of imperfections in the product market (such as those posited by the monopolistically competitive model) represent mere elaborations on the basic approach. The objective of the firm remains single period profit maximization.

The neoclassical model is well known to marketers. Indeed, it will be argued below that the profit maximization assumption of neoclassical economics underlies much of the normative literature in marketing management. It will be shown that this is true despite the fact that neoclassical theory is inconsistent with the basic research tradition of marketing. Moreover, the neoclassical model suffers from a number of limitations.

For example, the field of finance has challenged the profit maximization assumption because it fails to provide the business decision maker with an operationally feasible criterion for making investment decisions (Solomon 1963). In this regard, it suffers from an inability to consider risk differences among investment alternatives. When risk levels vary across projects, decision criteria that focus only on profitability will lead to suboptimal decisions (Copeland and Weston 1979, Fama and Miller 1972, Van Horne 1980). As a result of these and other problems, financial economists have generally abandoned the neoclassical model in favor of a more comprehensive theory of the firm known as the market value model.

The Market Value Model

Given the assumptions that human wants are insatiable and that capital markets are perfectly competitive, Fama and Miller (1972) show that the objective of the firm should be to maximize its present market value. For a corporation this is equivalent to maximizing the price of the firm's stock. In contrast to the profit maximization objective, the market value rule allows for the consideration of risk differences among alternative investment opportunities. Moreover, the model is applicable to owner-operated firms as well as corporations in which there is likely to be a separation of ownership and control.

The existence of a perfectly competitive capital market allows the firm's management to pursue a single unambiguous objective despite the fact that shareholders are likely to have heterogeneous preferences for current versus future income. If, for example, some stockholders wish more income than the firm is currently paying in dividends, they can sell some of their shares to make up the difference. However, if other shareholders prefer less current income in favor of more future income, they can lend their dividends in capital markets at interest. In either case shareholder utility will be maximized by a policy that maximizes the value of the firm's stock.

The value maximization objective is implemented within the firm by assessing all multiperiod decision alternatives on the basis of their risk-adjusted net present values (Copeland and Weston 1979, Fama and Miller 1972, Van Horne 1980):

$$NPV_j = \sum_{i=1}^{n} \frac{A_i}{(1 + k_j)^i} \qquad (1)$$

where NPV_j equals the net present value of alternative j, A_i equals the net after-tax cash flows in year i, n is the expected life of the project in years, and k_j is the risk-adjusted, after-tax required rate of return on j. In the absence of capital rationing, the firm should undertake all projects whose net present values are greater than or equal to zero. Assuming an accurate determination of k_j, this will ensure maximization of the firm's stock price. The discount rate k_j should represent the return required by the market to compensate for the risk of the project. This is usually estimated using a parameter preference model such as the capital asset pricing model or (potentially) the arbitrage model (Anderson 1981). However, it should be noted that there are serious theoretical and practical difficulties associated with the use of these approaches (Anderson 1981; Meyers and Turnbull 1977; Roll 1977; Ross 1976; 1978).

From a marketing perspective this approach requires that all major decisions be treated as investments. Thus the decision to introduce a new product, to expand into new territories, or to adopt a new channel of distribution should be evaluated on the basis of its risk-adjusted net present value. While similar approaches have been suggested in marketing (Cravens, Hills and Woodruff 1980; Dean 1966; Howard 1965; Kotler 1971; Pessemier 1966), it has generally not been recognized that this implies the adoption of shareholder wealth maximization as the goal of the firm. Moreover, these approaches are often offered in piecemeal fashion for the evaluation of selected decisions (e.g., new products), and are not integrated into a consistent and coherent theory of the firm.

Despite the deductive logic of the market value model, there are those who question whether corporate managers are motivated to pursue value maximization. An essential assumption of the market value theory is that stockholders can employ control, motivation and monitoring devices to ensure that managers maximize firm value. However, in the development of their agency theory of the firm, Jensen and Meckling (1976) note that such activities by shareholders are not without cost. As a result, it may not be possible to compel managers to maximize shareholder wealth.

The Agency Costs Model

The separation of ownership and control in modern corporations gives rise to an agency relationship between the stockholders and managers of the firm. An agency relationship may be defined as "a contract under which one or more persons (the principal(s)) engage another person (the agent) to perform some service on their behalf which involves delegating some decision making authority to the agent" (Jensen and Meckling 1976, p. 308). In any relationship of this sort, there is a potential for the agent to expend some of the principal's resources on private pursuits. As such, it will pay the principal to provide the agent with incentives and to incur monitoring costs to encourage a convergence of interests between the objectives of the principal and those of the agent. Despite expenditures of this type, it will generally be impossible to ensure that all of the agent's decisions will be designed to maximize the principal's welfare. The dollar value of the reduction in welfare experienced by the principal along with the expenditures on monitoring activities are costs of the agency relationship. For corporate stockholders these agency costs include the reduction in firm value resulting from management's consumption of nonpecuniary benefits (perquisites) and the costs of hiring outside auditing agents.

The tendency of managers of widely held corporations to behave in this fashion will require the stockholders to incur monitoring costs in an effort to enforce the value maximization objective. Unfortunately, perfect monitoring systems are very expensive. Thus the stockholders face a cost-benefit trade-off in deciding how much to spend on monitoring activities. Since it is unlikely that it will pay the shareholders to implement a "perfect" monitoring system, we will observe corporations suboptimizing on value maximization even in the presence of auditing activities. This leads to implications for managerial behavior that are quite different from those predicted by the market value model. For example, the Fama-Miller model predicts that managers will invest in all projects that will maximize the present value of the firm. However, the agency costs model suggests that management may actually invest in suboptimal projects and may even forego new profitable investments (Barnea, Haugen and Senbet 1981).

The recognition that a firm might not pursue maximization strategies is a relatively new concept to the literature of financial economics. However, in the middle 1950s and early 1960s, various economists and management specialists began to question the neoclassical assumption of single objective maximization on the basis of their observations of managerial behavior. This led directly to the development of the behavioral theory of the firm.

Behavioral Theories of the Firm

In this section two behaviorally oriented theories of the firm will be reviewed. While other approaches could also be included (Bower 1968, Mintzberg 1979), these models will lay the foundation for the development of a constituency-based theory in the last sections of the paper. The first approach is the behavioral model of the firm that emerged at the Carnegie Institute of Technology. The behavioral model can best be understood as a reaction against the neoclassical model of economic theory. The second approach is the resource dependence model of Pfeffer and Salancik (1978). The resource dependence perspective builds on a number of ideas contained in the behavioral model. For example, both approaches stress the coalitional nature of organizations. Moreover, both models emphasize the role of behavioral rather than economic factors in explaining the activities of firms.

The Behavioral Model

The behavioral theory of the firm can be found in the writings of Simon (1955, 1959, 1964), March and Simon (1958), and especially in Cyert and March (1963). The behavioral theory views the business firm as a coalition of individuals who are, in turn, members of subcoalitions. The coalition members include "managers, workers, stockholders, suppliers, customers, lawyers, tax collectors, regulatory agencies, etc." (Cyert and March 1963, p. 27).

The goals of the organization are determined by this coalition through a process of quasi-resolution of conflict. Different coalition members wish the organization to pursue different goals. The resultant goal conflict is not resolved by reducing all goals to a common dimension or by making them internally consistent. Rather, goals are viewed as "a series of independent aspiration-level constraints imposed on the organization by the members of the organizational coalition" (Cyert and March 1963, p. 117).

As Simon (1964) points out, in real world decision making situations acceptable alternatives must satisfy a whole range of requirements or constraints. In his view, singling out one constraint and referring to it as the goal of the activity is essentially arbitrary. This is because in many cases, the set of requirements selected as constraints will have much more to do with the decision outcome than the requirement selected as the goal. Thus he believes that it is more meaningful to refer to the entire set of constraints as the (complex) goal of the organization.

Moreover, these constraints are set at aspiration levels rather than maximization levels. Maximization is not possible in complex organizations because of the existence of imperfect information and because of the computational limitations faced by organizations in coordinating the various decisions made by decentralized departments and divisions. As a result, firm behavior concerning goals may be described as satisficing rather than maximizing (Simon 1959, 1964).

Cyert and March (1963) see decentralization of decision making leading to a kind of local rationality within subunits of the organization. Since these subunits deal only with a small set of problems and a limited number of goals, local optimization may be possible, but it is unlikely that this will lead to overall optimization. In this regard, the firm not only faces information processing and coordination problems but is also hampered by the fact that it must deal with problems in a sequential fashion. Thus organizational subunits typically attend to different problems at different times, and there is no guarantee that consistent objectives will be pursued in solving these problems. Indeed, Cyert and March argue that the time buffer between decision situations provides the firm with a convenient mechanism for avoiding the explicit resolution of goal conflict.

Thus in the behavioral theory of the firm, goals emerge as "independent constraints imposed on the organization through a process of bargaining among potential coalition members" (Cyert and March 1963, p. 43). These objectives are unlikely to be internally consistent and are subject to change over time as changes take place in the coalition structure. This coalitional perspective has had a significant impact on the development of management thought. Both Mintzberg (1979) and Pfeffer and Salancik (1978) have developed theories of the firm that take its coalitional nature as given. In the following section the resource dependence approach of Pfeffer and Salancik is outlined.

The Resource Dependence Model

Pfeffer and Salancik (1978) view organizations as coalitions of interests which alter their purposes and direction as changes take place in the coalitional structure. Like Mintzberg (1979) they draw a distinction between internal and external coalitions, although they do not use these terms. Internal coalitions may be viewed as groups functioning within the organization (e.g., departments and functional areas). External coalitions include such stakeholder groups as labor, stockholders, creditors, suppliers, government and various interested publics. Pfeffer and Salancik place their primary emphasis on the role of environmental (i.e., external) coalitions in affecting the behavior of organizations. They believe that "to describe adequately the behavior of organizations requires attending to the coalitional nature of organizations and the manner in which organizations respond to pressures from the environment" (Pfeffer and Salancik 1978, p. 24).

The reason for the environmental focus of the model is that the survival of the organization ultimately depends on its ability to obtain resources and support from its external coalitions. Pfeffer and Salancik implicitly assume that survival is the ultimate goal of the organization and that to achieve this objective, the organization must maintain a coalition of parties willing to "legitimize" its existence (Dowling and Pfeffer 1975, Parsons 1960). To do this, the organization offers various inducements in exchange for contributions of resources and support (Barnard 1938, March and Simon 1958, Simon 1964).

However, the contributions of the various interests are not equally valued by the organization. As such, coalitions that provide "behaviors, resources and capabilities that are most needed or desired by other organizational participants come to have more influence and control over the organization" (Pfeffer and Salancik 1978, p. 27). Similarly, organizational subunits (departments, functional areas, etc.) which are best able to deal with critical contingencies related to coalitional contributions are able to enhance their influence in the organization.

A common problem in this regard is that the various coalitions make conflicting demands on the organization. Since the satisfaction of some demands limits the satisfaction of others, this leads to the possibility that the necessary coalition of support cannot be maintained. Thus organizational activities can be seen as a response to the constraints imposed by the competing demands of various coalitions.

In attempting to maintain the support of its external coalitions, the organization must negotiate exchanges that ensure the continued supply of critical resources. At the same time, however, it must remain flexible enough to respond to environmental contingencies. Often these objectives are in conflict, since the desire to ensure the stability and certainty of resource flows frequently leads to activities limiting flexibility and autonomy. For example, backward integration via merger or acquisition is one way of coping with the uncertainty of resource dependence. At the same time, however, this method of stabilizing resource exchanges limits the ability of the firm to adapt as readily to environmental contingencies. Pfeffer and Salancik suggest that many other activities of organizations can be explained by the desire for stable resource exchanges, on the one hand, and the need for flexibility and autonomy on the other. They present data to support their position that joint ventures, interlocking directorates, organizational growth, political involvement and executive succession can all be interpreted in this light. Other activities such as secrecy, multiple sourcing and diversification can also be interpreted from a resource dependence perspective.

This the resource dependence model views organizations as "structures of coordinated behaviors" whose ultimate aim is to garner the necessary environmental support for survival (Pfeffer and Salancik 1978, p. 32). As in the behavioral model, it is recognized that goals and objectives will emerge as constraints imposed by the various coalitions of interests. However, the resource dependence model interprets these constraints as demands by the coalitions that must be met in order to maintain the existence of the organization.

Research Traditions and the Theory of the Firm

In reflecting on the various theories of the firm presented herein, it is important to recognize that one of their primary roles is to function as a part of what Laudan calls a "research tradition" (Laudan 1977). A research tradition consists of a set of assumptions shared by researchers in a particular domain. Its main purpose is to provide a set of guidelines for theory development. In so doing it provides the researcher with both an ontological framework and a philosophical methodology.

The ontology of the research tradition defines the kinds of entities that exist within the domain of inquiry. For example, in the neoclassical model such concepts as middle management, coalitions, bureaucracy and reward systems do not exist. They fall outside the ontology of neoclassical economics. Similarly, the concepts of the entrepreneur, diminishing returns and average cost curves do not exist (or at least are not used) in the resource dependence model. The ontology of the research tradition defines the basic conceptual building blocks of its constituent theories.

The philosophical methodolgy, on the other hand, specifies the procedure by which concepts will be used to construct a theory. Moreover, it determines the way in which the concepts will be viewed by theorists working within the research tradition. For example, the neoclassical, market value and agency costs models have been developed in accordance with a methodology that could be character-ized as deductive instrumentalism. The models are deductive in that each posits a set of assumptions or axioms (including assumptions about firm goals) from which implications for firm behavior are deduced as logical consequences (Hempel 1965, p. 336). The models are also instrumentalist in that their component concepts are not necessarily assumed to have real world referents. Instrumentalism views the-ories merely as calculating devices that generate useful predictions (Feyerabend 1964, Morgenbesser 1969, Popper 1963). The reality of a theory's assumptions or its concepts is irrelevant from an instrumentalist point of view.

It is essentially this aspect of economic instrumentalism that has drawn the most criticism from both economists and noneconomists. Over 30 years ago con-cerns for the validity of the theory among economists emerged as the famous "marginalism controversy" which raged in the pages of the *American Economic Review* (Lester 1946, 1947; Machlup 1946, 1947; Stigler 1946, 1947). More re-cently, much of the criticism has come from proponents of the behavioral theory of the firm (Cyert and March 1963, Cyert and Pottinger 1979). Perhaps the most commonly heard criticism of the neoclassical model is that the assumption of a rational, profit-maximizing decision maker who has access to perfect information is at considerable variance with the real world of business management (Cyert and March 1963, Simon 1955). Moreover, these critics fault the "marginalists" for concocting a firm with "no complex organization, no problems of control, no standard operating procedures, no budget, no controller, [and] no aspiring middle management" (Cyert and March 1963, p. 8). In short, the business firm assumed into existence by neoclassical theory bears little resemblance to the modern cor-porate structure.

Concerns with the realism of assumptions in neoclassical theory have been challenged by Friedman (1953) and Machlup (1967). In Friedman's classic state-ment of the "positivist" viewpoint, he takes the position that the ultimate test of a theory is the correspondence of its predictions with reality. From Friedman's perspective the lack of realism in a theory's assumptions is unrelated to the ques-tion of its validity.

Machlup, in a closely related argument, notes that much of the criticism of neoclassical theory arises because of a confusion concerning the purposes of the theory (1967). He points out that the "firm" in neoclassical analysis is nothing more than a theoretical construct that is useful in predicting the impact of changes in economic variables on the behavior of firms in the aggregate. For example, the neoclassical model performs well in predicting the *direction* of price changes in an industry that experiences an increase in wage rates or the imposition of a tax. It does less well, however, in explaining the complex process by which a partic-ular firm decides to implement a price change. Of course, this is to be expected since the theory of the firm was never intended to predict the real world behavior of individual firms.

Thus the question of whether corporations really seek to maximize profits is of no concern to the economic instrumentalist. Following Friedman, the only consideration is whether such assumptions lead to "sufficiently accurate predictions" of real world phenomena (1953, p. 15). Similarly, the financial economist is unmoved by criticism related to the lack of reality in the market value and agency cost models. The ultimate justification of a theory from an instrumental viewpoint comes from the accuracy of its predictions.

In contrast to the instrumentalism of the first three theories of the firm, the behavioral and resource dependence models have been developed from the perspective of realism. The realist believes that theoretical constructs should have real world analogs and that theories should describe "what the world is really like" (Chalmers 1978, p. 114). Thus, it is not unexpected that these models are essentially inductive in nature. Indeed, in describing their methodological approach Cyert and March state that they "propose to make detailed observations of the procedures by which firms make decisions and to use these observations as a basis for a theory of decision making within business organizations" (1963, p. 1).

Thus it can be seen that the theories of the firm that have been developed in economics and financial economics emerged from a very different research tradition than the behaviorally oriented theories developed in management. This fact becomes particularly significant in considering their adequacy as a framework for marketing theory development. For example, the discipline of marketing appears to be committed to a research tradition dominated by the methodology of inductive realism, yet it frequently employs the profit maximization paradigm of neoclassical economic theory. Despite the recent trend toward the incorporation of social objectives in the firm's goal hierarchy, and the recognition by many authors that firms pursue multiple objectives, profit or profit maximization figures prominently as the major corporate objective in leading marketing texts (Boone and Kurtz 1980, p. 12; Markin 1979, p. 34; McCarthy 1978, p. 29; Stanton 1978, p. 13). More significantly perhaps, profit maximization is the implicit or explicit objective of much of the normative literature in marketing management. While the terms may vary from return on investment to contribution margin, cash flow or cumulative compounded profits, they are all essentially profit maximization criteria. Thus such widely known and accepted approaches as product portfolio analysis (Boston Consulting Group 1970), segmental analysis (Mossman, Fischer and Crissy 1974), competitive bidding models (Simon and Freimer 1970), Bayesian pricing procedures (Green 1963), and many others all adhere to the profit maximization paradigm. It may seem curious that a discipline that drifted away from the research tradition of economics largely because of a concern for greater "realism" (Hutchinson 1952, Vaile 1950) should continue to employ one of its most "unrealistic" assumptions. In effect, marketing has rejected much of the philosophical methodology of economics while retaining a significant portion of its ontology.

It would seem that what is required is the development of a theory of the firm that is consistent with the existing research tradition of marketing. Such a theory should deal explicit with the role of marketing in the firm and should attempt to explicate its relationship with the other functional areas (Wind 1981) and specify its contribution to the formation of corporate "goal structures" (Richards 1978). In this way it would provide a framework within which marketing theory development can proceed. This is particularly important for the development of theory within the area of strategic planning. It is likely that greater progress could be made in this area if research is conducted within the context of a theory of the firm whose methodological and ontological framework is consistent with that of marketing.

Toward a Constituency-Based Theory of the Firm

The theory of the firm to be outlined in this section focuses explicitly on the roles performed by the various functional areas found in the modern corporation. There are basically two reasons for this. First, theory development in business administration typically proceeds within the various academic disciplines corresponding (roughly) to the functional areas of the firm. It is felt that a theory explicating the role of the functional areas will be of greater heuristic value in providing a framework for research within these disciplines (and within marketing in particular).

Second, a theory of the firm that does not give explicit recognition to the activities of these functional subunits fails to appreciate their obvious importance in explaining firm behavior. As highly formalized internal coalitions operating at both the corporate and divisional levels, they often share a common frame of reference and a relatively consistent set of goals and objectives. These facts make the functional areas an obvious unit of analysis in attempting to explain the emergence of goals in corporations.

The proposed theory adopts the coalitional perspectives of the various behaviorally oriented theories of the firm and relies especially on the resource dependence model. As a matter of analytical convenience, the theory divides an organization into both internal and external coalitions. From a resource dependence perspective, the task of the organization is to maintain itself by negotiating resource exchanges with external interests. Over time the internal coalitions within corporate organizations have adapted themselves to enhance the efficiency and effectiveness with which they perform these negotiating functions. One approach that has been taken to accomplish this is specialization. Thus certain coalitions within the firm may be viewed as specialists in negotiating exchanges with certain external coalitions. By and large these internal coalitions correspond to the major functional areas of the modern corporate structure.

For example, industrial relations and personnel specialize in negotiating resource exchanges with labor coalitions; finance, and to a lesser extent, accounting specialize in negotiating with stockholder and creditor groups; materials management and purchasing specialize in supplier group exchanges; and, of course, marketing specializes in negotiating customer exchanges. In addition, public relations, legal, tax and accounting specialize to a greater or lesser extent in negotiating the continued support and sanction of both government and public coalitions. In most large corporations the production area no longer interacts directly with the environment. With the waning of the production orientation earlier in this century, production gradually lost its negotiating functions to specialists such as purchasing and industrial relations on the input side and sales or marketing on the output side.

The major resources that the firm requires for survival include cash, labor and matériel. The major sources of cash are customers, stockholders and lenders. It is, therefore, the responsibility of marketing and finance to ensure the required level of cash flow in the firm. Similarly, it is the primary responsibility of industrial relations to supply the labor, and materials management and purchasing to supply the matériel necessary for the maintenance, growth and survival of the organization.

As Pfeffer and Salancik point out, external coalitions that control vital resources have greater control and influence over organizational activities (1978, p. 27). By extension, functional areas that negotiate vital resource exchanges will come to have greater power within the corporation as well. Thus the dominance of production and finance in the early decades of this century may be attributed to the fact that nearly all vital resource exchanges were negotiated by these areas. The ascendance, in turn, of such subunits as industrial relations and personnel (Meyer 1980), marketing (Keith 1960), purchasing and materials management (*Business Week* 1975) and public relations (Kotler and Mindak 1978) can be explained in part by environmental changes which increased the importance of effective and efficient resource exchanges with the relevant external coalitions. For example, the growth of unionism during the 1930s did much to enhance the role and influence of industrial relations departments in large corporations. Similarly, the improved status of sales and marketing departments during this same period may be linked to environmental changes including the depressed state of the economy, the rebirth of consumerism, and a shift in demand away from standardized "Model-T type products" (Ansoff 1979, p. 32). More recently, the OPEC oil embargo, the institutionalization of consumerism, and the expansion of government regulation into new areas (OSHA, Foreign Corrupt Practices Act, Affirmative Action, etc.) has had a similar impact on such areas as purchasing, public relations and legal.

Thus the constituency-based model views the major functional areas as specialists in providing particular resources for the firm. The primary objective of each area is to ensure an uninterrupted flow of resources from the appropriate external coalition. As functional areas tend to become specialized in dealing with particular coalitions, they tend to view these groups as constituencies both to be served and managed. From this perspective, the chief responsibility of the marketing area is to satisfy the long-term needs of its customer coalition. In short, it must strive to implement the marketing concept (Keith 1960, Levitt 1960, McKitterick 1957).

Of course, in seeking to achieve its own objectives, each functional area is constrained by the objectives of the other departments. In attempting to assure maximal consumer satisfaction as a means of maintaining the support of its customer coalition, marketing will be constrained by financial, technical and legal considerations imposed by the other functional areas. For example, expenditures on new product development, market research and advertising cut into the financial resources necessary to maintain the support of labor, supplier, creditor and investor coalitions. When these constraints are embodied in the formal performance measurement system, they exert a significant influence on the behavior of the functional areas.

In this model, firm objectives emerge as a series of Simonian constraints that are negotiated among the various functions. Those areas that specialize in the provision of crucial resources are likely to have greater power in the negotiation process. In this regard, the marketing area's desire to promote the marketing concept as a philosophy of the entire firm may be interpreted by the other functional areas as a means of gaining bargaining leverage by attempting to impress them with the survival value of customer support. The general failure of the other areas to embrace this philosophy may well reflect their belief in the importance of their own constituencies.

Recently, the marketing concept has also been called into question for contributing to the alleged malaise of American business. Hayes and Abernathy (1980) charge that excessive emphasis on marketing research and short-term financial control measures has led to the decline of U.S. firms in world markets. They argue that American businesses are losing more and more of their markets to European and Japanese firms because of a failure to remain technologically competitive. They believe that the reliance of American firms on consumer surveys and ROI control encourages a low-risk, short run investment philosophy, and point out that market research typically identifies consumers' current desires but is often incapable of determining their future wants and needs. Moreoever, the short run focus of ROI measures and the analytical detachment inherent in product portfolio procedures tends to encourage investment in fast payback alternatives. Thus Hayes and Abernathy believe that American firms are reluctant to make the higher risk, longer-term investments in new technologies necessary for effective competition in world markets. They feel that the willingness of foreign firms to make such investments can be attributed to their need to look beyond their relatively small domestic markets for success. This has encouraged a reliance on technically superior products and a longer-term payoff perspective.

From a resource dependence viewpoint the Hayes and Abernathy argument seems to suggest that the external coalitions of U.S. firms are rather myopic. If the survival of the firm is truly dependent on the adoption of a longer-term perspective, one would expect this to be forced on the firm by its external coalitions. Indeed, there is ample evidence from stock market studies that investor coalitions react sharply to events affecting the longer run fortunes of firms (Lev 1974, Lorie and Hamilton 1973). Moreover, recent concessions by government, labor and supplier coalitions to Chrysler Corporation suggest a similar perspective among these groups.

However, the real problem is not a failure by internal and external coalitions in recognizing the importance of a long run investment perspective. The real difficulty lies in designing an internal performance measurement and reward system that balances the need for short run profitability against long-term survival. A number of factors combine to bias these reward and measurement systems in favor of the short run. These include:

- Requirements for quarterly and annual reports of financial performance.
- The need to appraise and reward managers on an annual basis.

- The practical difficulties of measuring and rewarding the long-term performance of highly mobile management personnel.
- Uncertainty as to the relative survival value of emphasis on short run versus long run payoffs.

As a result of these difficulties, we find that in many U.S. firms the reward system focuses on short run criteria (Ouchi 1981). This naturally leads to the use of short-term financial control measures and an emphasis on market surveys designed to measure consumer reaction to immediate (and often minor) product improvements. In some cases the marketing area has adopted this approach in the name of the marketing concept.

However, as Levitt (1960) noted more than two decades ago, the real lesson of the marketing concept is that successful firms are able to recognize the fundamental and enduring nature of the customer needs they are attempting to satisfy. As numerous case studies point out, it is the *technology* of want satisfaction that is transitory. The long run investment perspective demanded by Hayes and Abernathy is essential for a firm that focuses its attention on transportation rather than trains, entertainment rather than motion pictures, or energy rather than oil. The real marketing concept divorces strategic thinking from an emphasis on contemporary technology and encourages investments in research and development with long-term payoffs. Thus, the "market-driven" firms that are criticized by Hayes and Abernathy have not really embraced the marketing concept. These firms have simply deluded themselves into believing that consumer survey techniques and product portfolio procedures automatically confer a marketing orientation on their adopters. However, the fundamental insight of the marketing concept has little to do with the use of particular analytical techniques. The marketing concept is essentially a state of mind or world view that recognizes that firms survive to the extent that they meet the real needs of their customer coalitions. As argued below, one of the marketing area's chief functions in the strategic planning process is to communicate this perspective to top management and the other functional areas.

Implications for Strategic Planning

From a strategic planning perspective, the ultimate objective of the firm may be seen as an attempt to position itself for long run survival (Wind 1979). This, in turn, is accomplished as each functional area attempts to determine the position that will ensure a continuing supply of vital resources. Thus the domestic auto industry's belated downsizing of its product may be viewed as an attempt to ensure the support of its customer coalition in the 1980s and 1990s (just as its grudging acceptance of the UAW in the late 1930s and early 1940s reflected a need to ensure a continuing supply of labor).

Of course, a firm's functional areas may not be able to occupy all of the favored long run positions simultaneously. Strategic conflicts will arise as functional areas (acting as units at the corporate level or as subunits at the divisional level) vie for the financial resources necessary to occupy their optimal long-term positions. Corporate management as the final arbiter of these disputes may occasionally favor one area over another, with deleterious results. Thus, John De Lorean, former group executive at General Motors, believes that the firm's desire for the short run profits available from larger cars was a major factor in its reluctance to downsize in the 1970s (Wright 1979). He suggests that an overwhelming financial orientation among GM's top executives consistently led them to favor short run financial gain over longer-term marketing considerations. Similarly, Hayes and Abernathy (1980) believe that the growing dominance of financial and legal specialists within the top managements of large U.S. corporations has contributed to the slighting of technological considerations in product development.

Against this backdrop marketing must realize that its role in strategic planning is not preordained. Indeed, it is possible that marketing considerations may not have a significant impact on strategic plans unless marketers adopt a strong advocacy position within the firm (Mason and Mitroff 1981). On this view, strategic plans are seen as the outcome of a bargaining process among functional areas. Each area attempts to move the corporation toward what it views as the preferred position for long run survival, subject to the constraints imposed by the positioning strategies of the other functional units.

This is not to suggest, however, that formal-analytical procedures have no role to play in strategic planning. Indeed, as Quinn's (1981) research demonstrates, the actual process of strategy formulation in large firms is best described as a combination of the formal-analytical and power-behavioral approaches. He found that the formal planning system often provides a kind of infrastructure that assists in the strategy development and implementation process, although the formal system itself rarely generates new or innovative strategies. Moreover, the study shows that strategies tend to emerge incrementally over relatively long periods of time. One reason for this is the need for top management to obtain the support and commitment of the firm's various coalitions through constant negotiation and implied bargaining (Quinn 1981, p. 61).

Thus, from a constituency-based perspective, marketing's role in strategic planning reduces to three major activities. First, at both the corporate and divisional levels it must identify the optimal long-term position or positions that will assure customer satisfaction and support. An optimal position would reflect marketing's perception of what its customers' wants and needs are likely to be over the firm's strategic time horizon. Since this will necessarily involve long run considerations, positioning options must be couched in somewhat abstract terms. Thus the trend toward smaller cars by the domestic auto industry represents a very broad response to changing environmental, social and political forces and will likely affect the industry well into the 1990s. Other examples include the diversification into alternative energy sources by the petroleum industry, the movement toward "narrowcasting" by the major networks, and the down-sizing of the single family home by the construction industry. The length of the time horizons involved suggests that optimal positions will be determined largely by fundamental changes in demographic, economic, social and political factors. Thus strategic positioning is more likely to be guided by long-term demographic and socioeconomic research (Lazer 1977) than by surveys of consumer attitudes.

Marketing's second major strategic planning activity involves the development of strategies designed to capture its preferred positions. This will necessarily involve attempts to gain a competitive advantage over firms pursuing similar positioning strategies. Moreover, the entire process is likely to operate incrementally. Specific strategies will focus on somewhat shorter time horizons and will be designed to move the firm toward a particular position without creating major dislocations within the firm or the marketplace (Quinn 1981). Research on consumers' current preferences must be combined with demographic and socioeconomic research to produce viable intermediate strategies. For example, Detroit's strategy of redesigning all of its subcompact lines has been combined with improved fuel efficiency in its larger cars (*Business Week* 1980).

Finally, marketing must negotiate with top management and the other functional areas to implement its strategies. The coalitional perspective suggests that marketing must take an active role in promoting its strategic options by demonstrating the survival value of a consumer orientation to the other internal coalitions.

Marketing's objective, therefore, remains long run customer support through consumer satisfaction. Paradoxically, perhaps, this approach requires marketers to have an even greater grasp of the technologies, perspectives and limitations of the other functional areas. Only in this way can marketing effectively negotiate the implementation of its strategies. As noted previously, the other functional areas are likely to view appeals to the marketing concept merely as a bargaining ploy. It is the responsibility of the marketing area to communicate the true long run focus and survival orientation of this concept to the other interests in the firm. However, this cannot be accomplished if the marketing function itself does not understand the unique orientations and decision methodologies employed by other departments.

For example, the long run investment perspective implicit in the marketing concept can be made more comprehensible to the financial coalition if it is couched in the familiar terms of capital budgeting analysis. Moreover, the marketing area becomes a more credible advocate for this position if it eschews the use of short-term ROI measures as its sole criterion for internal decision analysis. At the same time, an appreciation for the inherent limitations of contemporary capital investment procedures will give the marketing area substantial leverage in the negotiation process (Anderson 1981).

In the final analysis, the constituency model of the firm suggests that marketing's role in strategic planning must be that of a strong advocate for the marketing concept. Moreover, its advocacy will be enhanced to the extent that it effectively communicates the true meaning of the marketing concept in terms that are comprehensible to other coalitions in the firm. This requires an intimate knowledge of the interests, viewpoints and decision processes of these groups. At the same time, a better understanding of the true nature of the constraints imposed by these interests will allow the marketing organization to make the informed strategic compromises necessary for firm survival.

References

Ackoff, Russell (1970), A *Concept of Corporate Planning,* New York: John Wiley & Sons.

Anderson, Paul F. (1981), "Marketing Investment Analysis," in *Research in Marketing,* 4, Jagdish N. Sheth, ed., Greenwich, CT: JAI Press 1–37.

Ansoff, Igor H. (1965), *Corporate Strategy,* New York: McGraw-Hill.

_____ (1979), "The Changing Shape of the Strategic Problem," in *Strategic Management: A View of Business Policy and Planning,* Dan E. Schendel and Charles W. Hofer, eds., Boston: Little, Brown and Company, 30–40.

Barnard, Chester I. (1938), *The Functions of the Executive,* London: Oxford University Press.

Barnea, Amir, Robert A. Haugen and Lemma W. Senbet (1981), "Market Inperfections, Agency Problems and Capital Structure: A Review," *Financial Management,* 10 (Summer), 7–22.

Boone, Louis E. and David L. Kurtz (1980), *Foundations of Marketing,* 3rd ed., Hinsdale, IL: Dryden Press.

Boston Consulting Group (1970), *The Product Portfolio,* Boston: The Boston Consulting Group.

Bower, Joseph L. (1968), "Descriptive Decision Theory from the 'Administrative' Viewpoint," in *The Study of Policy Formation,* Raymond A. Bauer and Kenneth J. Gergen, eds., New York: Collier-Macmillan, 103–148.

Business Week (1975), "The Purchasing Agent Gains More Clout," (January 13), 62–63.

_____ (1980), "Detroit's New Sales Pitch," (September 22), 78–83.

Buzzell, Robert D., Bradley T. Gale and Ralph G. M. Sultan (1975), "Market Share: A Key to Profitability," *Harvard Business Review,* 53 (January–February), 97–106.

Cardozo, Richard and Yoram Wind (1980), "Portfolio Analysis for Strategic Product—Market Planning," working paper, The Wharton School, Unviersity of Pennsylvania.

Chalmers, A. F. (1978), *What is This Thing Called Science?* St. Lucia, Australia: University of Queensland Press.

Copeland, Thomas E. and J. Fred Weston (1979), *Financial Theory and Corporate Policy,* Reading, MA: Addison-Wesley Publishing Company.

Cravens, David W., Gerald E. Hills and Robert B. Woodruff (1980), *Marketing Decision Making,* rev. ed., Homewood, IL: Richard D. Irwin.

Cyert, Richard M. and James G. March (1963), *A Behavioral Theory of the Firm,* Englewood Cliffs, NJ: Prentice-Hall.

_____ and Garrel Pottinger (1979), "Towards a Better Microeconomic Theory," *Philosophy of Science,* 46 (June), 204–222.

Dean, Joel (1966), "Does Advertising Belong in the Capital Budget?" *Journal of Marketing,* 30 (October), 15–21.

Dowling, John and Jeffrey Pfeffer (1975), "Organizational Legitimacy," *Pacific Sociological Review,* 18 (January), 122–36.

Fama, Eugene and Merton H. Miller (1972), *The Theory of Finance,* Hinsdale, IL: Dryden Press.

Feyerabend, Paul K. (1964), "Realism and Instrumentalism: Comments on the Logic of Factual Support," in *The Critical Approach to Science and Philosophy,* Mario Bunge, ed., London: The Free Press of Glencoe, 280–308.

Friedman, Milton (1953), "The Methodology of Positive Economics," in *Essays in Positive Economics,* Chicago: University of Chicago Press.

Glueck, William (1976), *Policy, Strategy Formation and Management Action,* New York: McGraw-Hill.

Green, Paul E. (1963), "Bayesian Decision Theory in Pricing Strategy," *Journal of Marketing,* 27 (January), 5–14.

Hayes, Robert H. and William J. Abernathy (1980), "Managing Our Way to Economic Decline," *Harvard Business Review,* 58 (July–August), 67–77.

Hempel, Carl G. (1965), *Aspects of Scientific Explanation,* New York: Macmillan Publishing Co.

Hofer, Charles W. and Dan Schendel (1978), *Strategy Formulation: Analytical Concepts,* St. Paul, MN: West Publishing Company.

Hopwood, Anthony (1976), *Accounting and Human Behavior,* Englewood Cliffs, NJ: Prentice-Hall.

Howard, John A. (1965), *Marketing Theory,* Boston: Allyn and Bacon.

Hutchinson, Kenneth D. (1952), "Marketing as a Science: An Appraisal," *Journal of Marketing,* 16 (January), 286–93.

Jensen, Michael C. and William H. Meckling (1976), "Theory of the Firm: Managerial Behavior, Agency Costs and Ownership Structure," *Journal of Financial Economics,* 3 (October), 305–60.

Keith, Robert J. (1960), "The Marketing Revolution," *Journal of Marketing,* 24 (January), 35–38.

Kotler, Philip (1971), *Marketing Decision Making,* New York: Holt, Rinehart and Winston.

_____ and William Mindak (1978), "Marketing and Public Relations," *Journal of Marketing,* 42 (October), 13–20.

Kuhn, Thomas S. (1970), *The Structure of Scientific Revolutions,* 2nd ed., Chicago: University of Chicago Press.

Laudan, Larry (1977), *Progress and Its Problems,* Berkeley, CA: University of California Press.

Lazer, William (1977), "The 1980's and Beyond: A Perspective," *MSU Business Topics,* 25 (Spring), 21–35.

Lester, R. A. (1946), "Shortcomings of Marginal Analysis for Wage-Employment Problems," *American Economic Review,* 36 (March), 63–82.

_____ (1947), "Marginalism, Minimum Wages, and Labor Markets," *American Economic Review,* 37 (March), 135–48.

Lev, Baruch (1974), *Financial Statement Analysis: A New Approach,* Englewood Cliffs, NJ: Prentice-Hall.

Levitt, Theodore (1960), "Marketing Myopia," *Harvard Business Review,* 38 (July–August), 24–47.

Lorie, James H. and Mary T. Hamilton (1973), *The Stock Market: Theories and Evidence,* Homewood, IL: Richard D. Irwin.

Machlup, Fritz (1946), "Marginal Analysis and Empirical Research," *American Economic Review,* 36 (September), 519–54.

_____ (1947), "Rejoinder to an Antimarginalist," *American Economic Review,* 37 (March), 148–54.

_____ (1967), "Theories of the Firm: Marginalist, Behavioral, Managerial," *American Economic Review*, 57 (March), 1–33.

March, James G. and Herbert A. Simon (1958), *Organizations*, New York: John Wiley & Sons.

Markin, Rom (1979), *Marketing*, New York: John Wiley & Sons.

Mason, Richard O. and Ian I. Mitroff (1981), "Policy Analysis as Argument," working paper, University of Southern California.

McCarthy, E. Jerome (1978), *Basic Marketing*, 6th ed., Homewood, IL: Richard D. Irwin.

McKitterick, J. B. (1957), "What is the Marketing Management Concept?" in *Readings in Marketing 75/76*, Guilford, CT: Dushkin Publishing Group, 23–26.

Meyer, Herbert E. (1980), "Personnel Directors Are the New Corporate Heros," in *Current Issues in Personnel Management*, Kendrith M. Rowland et al., eds., Boston: Allyn & Bacon, 2–8.

Meyers, Stewart C. and Stuart M. Turnbull (1977), "Capital Budgeting and the Capital Asset Pricing Model: Good News and Bad News," *Journal of Finance*, 32 (May), 321–336.

Mintzberg, Henry (1979), "Organizational Power and Goals: A Skeletal Theory," in *Strategic Management*, Dan E. Schendel and Charles W. Hofer, eds., Boston: Little, Brown and Company.

Morgenbesser, Sidney (1969), "The Realist-Instrumentalist Controversy," in *Philosophy, Science and Method*, New York: St. Martin's Press, 200–18.

Mossman, Frank H., Paul M. Fischer and W. J. E. Crissy (1974), "New Approaches to Analyzing Marketing Profitability," *Journal of Marketing*, 38 (April), 43–48.

Newman, William H. and James P. Logan (1971), *Strategy, Policy and Central Management*, Cincinnati: South-Western Publishing Company.

Ouchi, William G. (1981), *Theory Z*, Reading, MA: Addison-Wesley.

Parsons, Talcott (1960), *Structure and Process in Modern Societies*, New York: Free Press.

Pessemier, Edgar A. (1966), *New-Product Decisions: An Analytical Approach*, New York: McGraw Hill.

Pfeffer, Jeffrey and Gerald R. Salancik (1978), *The External Control of Organizations*, New York: Harper and Row.

Popper, Karl R. (1963), *Conjectures and Refutations*, New York: Harper & Row.

Quinn, James Brian (1981), "Formulating Strategy One Step at a Time," *Journal of Business Strategy*, 1 (Winter), 42–63.

Richards, Max D. (1978), *Organizational Goal Structures*, St. Paul: West Publishing Company.

Roll, Richard (1977), "A Critique of the Asset Pricing Theory's Tests: Part I," *Journal of Financial Economics*, 4 (March), 129–76.

Ross, Stephen A. (1976), "The Arbitrage Theory of Capital Asset Pricing," *Journal of Economic Theory*, 13 (December), 341–360.

_____ (1978), "The Current Status of the Capital Asset Pricing Model (CAPM)," *Journal of Finance*, 33 (June), 885–901.

Simon, Herbert A. (1955), "A Behavioral Model of Rational Choice," *Quarterly Journal of Economics*, 69 (February), 99–118.

_____(1959), ''Theories of Decision Making in Economics and Behavioral Science,''
American Economic Review, 49 (June), 253–83.

_____ (1964), ''On the Concept of Organizational Goal,'' *Administrative Science Quarterly,* 9 (June), 1–22.

Simon, Leonard S. and Marshall Freimer (1970), *Analytical Marketing,* New York: Harcourt, Brace & World.

Solomon, Ezra (1963), *The Theory of Financial Management,* New York: Columbia University Press.

Stanton, William J. (1978), *Fundamentals of Marketing,* 5th ed., New York: McGraw-Hill.

Stigler, G. J. (1946), ''The Economics of Minimum Wage Legislation,'' *American Economic Review,* 36 (June), 358–65.

_____ (1947), ''Professor Lester and the Marginalists,'' *American Economic Review,* 37 (March), 154–57.

Vaile, Roland S. (1950), ''Economic Theory and Marketing,'' in *Theory in Marketing,* Reavis Cox and Wroe Alderson, eds., Chicago: Richard D. Irwin.

Van Horne, James C. (1980), *Financial Management and Policy,* 5th ed., Englewood Cliffs, NJ: Prentice-Hall.

Wind, Yoram (1979), ''Product Positioning and Market Segmentation: Marketing and Corporate Perspectives,'' working paper, The Wharton School, University of Pennsylvania.

_____ (1981), ''Marketing and the Other Business Functions,'' in *Research in Marketing,* 5, Jagdish N. Sheth, ed., Greenwich, CT: JAI Press, 237–64.

Wright, Patrick J. (1979), *On A Clear Day You Can See General Motors,* Grosse Pointe, MI: Wright Enterprises.

Section
Two

The Identification of
Strategic Opportunities

Product-Markets

From a marketing perspective, a strategic opportunity arises within a product-market. A product-market consists of a group of potential customers with similar needs and sellers who employ similar methods (technologies and marketing programs) to provide products or services to satisfy customers' needs. A product-market space is a set of product-markets in specific industry or business domain. Thus, the product-market space is the commercial arena in which sellers compete against each other for customers.

Figure II.1 illustrates a product-market space in which manufacturers involved in the microcomputer industry might compete. Product offerings are listed in the left-hand column, ranging from retailing microcomputers to manufacturing systems emphasizing a specific benefit such as communications between microcomputers and mainframe computers. Market segments are described on the top row of Figure II.1.

Each square in the matrix describes a potential product-market in which a set of firms compete to provide microcomputer-related products to a group of customers. For example, Atari and Commodore produce low-priced microcomputers for consumers who are interested in using them for educational purposes; Radio Shack and Computerland compete in retailing computers; and

Figure II.1 Product–Market Space for Microcomputer Industry

		Educational Home Applications	Financial Home Applications	Educational Institutions	Small Businesses	Large Businesses
Manufacturers of Computers Offering Specific Capabilities	Communications					
	Portability					
	Graphics					
	Ease of Use					
Developers of Software Products	Operating Systems					
	Spread sheets					
	Data Base Management					
	Games					
Retailing	Computers					

Compaq and IBM produce microcomputers that provide portability capabilities.[1] Note that many firms compete in more than one square of the matrix.

The product-market space shown in Figure II.1 is only one of many possible representations of the microcomputer industry. The space could be expanded using more offering categories. Manufacturing printers could be included in the set of offerings. Some offerings could be subdivided. For example, manufacturers of computers offering graphics capabilities could be subdivided into microcomputers versus full systems including the monitor and printer. The markets also can be segmented differently and expanded to include original equipment manufacturers (OEMs) and value-added resellers. However, for this illustration, we will limit our attention to the 45 product-market alternatives in Figure II.1.

Consider the strategic marketing decisions facing AT&T—a firm that competes in the microcomputer industry. Should AT&T engage competition in each of the 45 product-market alternatives shown in Figure II.1 or focus on a limited number of alternatives? If AT&T focuses on a few alternatives, which product-markets should it pursue? Should it aggressively attack all alternatives selected or pursue holding actions in some alternatives?

Notice that all of these questions can be translated into resource allocation decisions. AT&T's marketing strategy statement will indicate which product-markets will receive no resources, which will receive limited resources to maintain a holding position, and which will receive substantial resources.

In the introduction to Section I, we indicate parallels between military strategy and marketing strategy; however, there are also some important differences. Classic military strategy is implemented in physical terrain which does not change over time—valleys remain valleys and high ground remains high ground. However, the product-market "battlefield" is constantly changing. In addition to external forces of change such as technology and customer values, businesses are continually changing the product-market space as they attempt to erode advantages established by competitors. Consider changes that have occurred in the microcomputer industry product-market space over the last 10 years: the growth and decline of home video games, the entry of IBM and withdrawal of Texas Instruments, the emergence of IBM-clones, and the changing nature of computer retail outlets. Thus, marketing strategy operates in a less stable environment than that of classic military strategy.[2]

The evolving nature of product-markets is demonstrated by the recent interest in the globalization of markets. Some large businesses are beginning to recognize that local markets cannot be effectively defended against international competitors. In some markets, a long-term, sustainable advantage can be achieved only by taking a global perspective, while continuing to respond to the needs of local markets.

Analyzing the Product-Market Space

An important step in developing a marketing strategy is analyzing the battlefield—the product-market space. Where are the customers located and what is the nature of demand? Where are competitors located? Are there positions that can be defended effectively because of either naturally occurring barriers or barriers that can be erected by explicit unique capabilities of the firm? How is the product-market space likely to change in the future? Will there be shifts in demand? What are competitors likely to do?

We can answer some of these questions by thinking carefully about this simple principle. Overall success in a competitive marketplace depends on marketing one's products to customers in a more cost-effective manner than do competitors. Using this principle, we can consider the following three dimensions of strategic opportunities: (1) customers, (2) competitors, and (3) company capabilities. Traditional economic analysis focuses on the first and third dimensions which represent demand and supply. The dimension of competitive analysis is added because actual business practice indicates that, contrary to the classic economic assumption, competitors are not homogeneous. Most competitor companies exhibit as many differences as similarities. Hence, we need to recognize explicitly that competition in the marketplace is critical.

The degree to which businesses compete is determined, to a considerable extent, by customers. Customers define the nature of competition by the alternatives they consider when making purchase decisions. Some definitions of competitive products are obvious, for example, Coca-Cola and Pepsi-Cola in the cola-drink market. However, Coca-Cola also competes against Seven-Up in the broader soft-drink market, and against Maxwell House coffee in the still broader beverage market. Some competitive products, however, are less obvious. For example, convenience foods prepared at home compete with fast-food outlets. Microcomputers with word-processing capabilities compete with secretarial services.

It is often easier to identify competition in terms of products that look alike and perform similar functions. In some markets, this may be an appropriate way to characterize customer perceptions as well. After all, customers are also likely to think that one brand of detergent competes against another brand if they look alike and are both used to launder clothes. When this product-based approach is justified by consumer behavior and perceptions, it is certainly a convenient approach to take. It is easier to relate market-based product dimensions to internal measures of production and distribution.

However, there is a growing number of markets where product-related distinctions are less and less justified. There is ample evidence, both at the broad level of industry sectors and in many specific markets, that physical characteristics of a product are becoming less important relative to services associated with the overall offering. In this situation, we have to consider two crucial issues in our analysis of customers. First, we cannot identify competitive offerings purely in terms of the characteristics of physical products. Second, we must therefore be careful to base our analysis on customers perceptions of crucial competitor offerings.

Customer perceptions of service are increasingly important. "Service" has traditionally been considered the product of businesses such as hotels and banking. But with the advent of store and generic brands, firms are compelled to recognize that service plays a wider role. Service implies not only the convenience and choice of products the retailer provides but also the quality certification proffered by the retailer rather than merely the traditional certification manufacturers offer with their brand names.

With increased emphasis on service, we can expect to encounter many situations in which the nature of the market as perceived by customers is significantly different from the nature of the market defined in terms of companies' physical products.

A number of businesses successfully compete against manufacturers of brand-name products by adopting new approaches. Rather than competing for customers by offering similar brand-name products, they specialize in low-cost manufacturing and supply store-brand products instead. For example, Design and Manufacturers, one of the largest worldwide manufacturers of appliances during the 1960s and early 1970s, had no brand-name products.[3] Thus, powerful competition can exist between businesses that have chosen very different strategic directions.

Finally, a business, in an effort to exploit its strengths, may embrace opportunities that are not related to its existing customer franchise and not related to activities of existing competitors. Texas Instruments and IBM both entered into retailing activity to have direct access to new customers; in so doing, they found themselves competing with retail outlets, somewhat unsuccessfully, as well as with electronics manufacturers.

The preceding discussion illustrates that we must not expect our analyses of customer, competitor, and capabilities dimensions of competition to yield the same sets of opportunities. In addition, there is another problem. So far we have considered analysis of the past and the present, but what we really want to know is what might happen in the future, at least we want to ensure that we are reasonably aware of any large changes around the corner. We must consider how far the overall process of information gathering and analysis can be taken. It is the essence of strategy that, since decisions have to be made in an ambiguous and confusing world, we cannot expect to arrive at neat, unambiguous answers. Indeed, those who arrive at unambiguous solutions are either deceiving themselves or doctoring the data.

In the process of strategic analysis, companies should be looking for something different from a single, neat answer. Analysts need to seek various partial facts derived form empirical data, information that will either cast doubt on or support one or more of the critical assumptions in the proposed strategy.[4] The fact that such a process is incomplete does not mean it is of limited value. It is critical that as much information as possible be gathered and analyzed so that reasoned judgments can be made about appropriate opportunities.

Customers

While customers are not forgotten in strategy, there is a danger that strategic analysts can talk rather glibly about market niches in which the premium price can be sustained when, in fact, there is little real evidence that such niches exist. Understanding customers is one way of avoiding such pitfalls and of identifying more meaningful ways in which to split up the market. The only critical proviso is that analysts must remember that customers are not a very reliable source of information on the nature of market evolution. A business cannot expect its customers to forecast how the market will develop, since customers typically have not been exposed to the developing products and choices.

On the other hand, market research can provide a lot of information on current behaviors and attitudes toward existing offerings. There are essentially two different ways of obtaining information about customer behavior and attitudes—from an analysis of purchase and usage behavior and from customer judgments. A balance between these two sources is critical: ever since Mason Hair's classic article demonstrating the usefulness of projective market research techniques, we have recognized the need to relate empirical evidence to attitude data.[5] The first article in this section, "Customer-Oriented Approaches to Identifying Product-Markets," evaluates the approaches for defining product-markets based on customer inputs.

Competitors

One of the more recent and obvious developments in marketing strategy has been a renewed focus on the impact of competitors on strategies. This focus was first developed within the context of cost competition (the experience curve described in Section III), in which emphasis was placed in descending the experience curve faster than the competition. More recently, however, firms have recognized both the more complex nature of the experience curve, with its many shared components, and the heterogeneity of most competition. Heterogeneous competition indicates that firms have to expect to find themselves competing not only with businesses that are very similar but also with some that are very different.[6]

Competition can be considered from a number of different points of view. There are companies that:

- provide the same product or service to the market,
- provide a substitute product or service, or
- use a similar production technology

In addition, each competitor must be considered from a number of different perspectives:

- their relative performance in terms of costs,
- the relationship between the specific products and related products that they produce or sell, and
- the relationship of this product group to competitors' overall portfolio.

Any analysis of competition must therefore consider two distinct elements: first, the overall nature of competition in terms of the institutional structure of the market (including both alternative intermediate suppliers and alternative distribution channels); second, a more detailed analysis of how individual competitors are changing in response to their objectives, priorities, and overall portfolios.

The second article in this section, "How Competitive Forces Shape Strategy," details the issues raised by the competitive structure of the market.

The Company Itself

The final input into the process of identifying opportunities is the detailed analysis of the company itself. One traditional component in such a corporate appraisal has been a strengths-and-weaknesses analysis. This analysis is often combined with the competitive and market analyses previously discussed; the combination is described by the acronym SWOT—Strengths, Weaknesses, Opportunities, and Threats. A number of critics have claimed that the output from a strengths-and-weaknesses analysis is often either trivial or so broad as to be relatively meaningless in making actual strategic decisions. For example, Stevenson describes evaluations made by managers of their firm's strengths and weaknesses and the reasons underlying their evaluations.[7] The results of his study illustrate the difficulty in developing a consistent and meaningful assessment. The descriptions by managers may tell us more about the person performing the analysis than about the firm. Such research clearly suggests that one should be wary of the results of a traditional SWOT analysis. However, such an analysis is often useful as feedback to the relevant managers who formulate and recommend strategy.

An understanding of both current and future performance also requires a clear idea of the firm's actual costs associated with serving a particular market segment. Unfortunately, many accounting systems tend to reflect a rather restricted set of distinct elements in the costing system. To make more effective marketing strategy decisions, we need a refined costing structure capable of analyzing contribution margins at various levels of aggregation—including products, distribution channels, and customers. Such information can be generated at a cost in response to each particular inquiry. The development of a cost accounting system having such built-in flexibility would have a significant impact on strategy development even though the set-up costs are likely to be quite high. Article 5 in this section, "Marketing Cost Analyses: A Modularized Contribution Approach," describes such a system in detail.

Finally, marketing analysis has a traditional method to identify the current corporate position: the marketing audit. A well-executed marketing audit results in the recognition of important questions and new options to consider. On the other hand, it often works most effectively as feedback into the relevant organization, to be assessed and acted upon. In Article 6 in this section, "The Marketing Audit Comes of Age," the process and types of questions are described in some detail; the final emphasis is on the fact that the audit report will help place priorities on ideas and directions already within the company rather than propose startling new opportunities.

The last article in this section, "Strategic Segmentation: How to Carve Niches for Growth in Industrial Markets," provides a framework in which information about customers, competitors, and firms can be integrated to identify product-market opportunities—"real" niches that can be defended against competitive activity.

Footnotes

1. See "The PC Wars: IBM vs. the Clones," *Business Week,* July 28, 1986, 62–68; "The Next Boom in Computers: Service," *Business Week,* July 7, 1986, 72–73; "The Computers that Refuse to Die," *Business Week,* July 21, 1986, 123–126; "Software: The Growing Gets Rough," *Business Week,* March 24, 1986, 128–139; "The Schoolyard Brawl Breaking Out in Classroom Computers," *Business Week,* April 7, 1986, 90–91; "Changing Channels in the Microcomputer Market," *Business Marketing,* September 1986, 89–94.

2. Modern perspectives on military strategy (Lidell-Hart) adopt a broader perspective which emphasizes a more dynamic environment for the conduct of military strategy.

3. The original research work in this area was in domestic appliances; see M. S. Hunt, "Competition in the Major Home Appliance Industry" (Ph.D. diss., Harvard University, 1972).

4. Such a process is discussed in more detail in Robin Wensley, "The Effective Strategic Analyst," *Journal of Management Studies* 16 (1979) and also relates to the concept of strategic assumptions analysis developed by James R. Emshoff and Ian I. Mitroff, "Improving the Effectiveness of Corporate Planning," *Business Horizons,* October 1976, 49–60.

5. Mason Haire, "Projective Techniques in Marketing Research," *Journal of Marketing* (April 1950):646–656.

6. See Michael Porter, *Competitive Advantage* (New York: Free Press, 1985) for detailed discussion of competitive advantage gained through concentration on specific elements of the value-added chain.

7. Howard W. Stevenson, "Defining Corporate Strengths and Weaknesses," *Sloan Management Review* 17, 3 (Spring 1976):51–68.

Additional Readings for Section Two

Customer Analysis

Srivastava, Rajendra K., Mark I. Alpert, and Allan D. Shocker. "A Customer-oriented Approach for Determining Market Structures." *Journal of Marketing* (Spring 1984):32–45.

Srivastava, Rajendra K., Robert P. Leone, and Allan D. Shocker. "Market Structure Analysis: Hierarchical Clustering of Products Based on Substitution in Use." *Journal of Marketing* (Summer 1981):38–48.

Competitor Analysis

Brock, John J. "Competitor Analysis: Some Practical Approaches." *Industrial Marketing Management* (October 1984):225–231.

Rothschild, William E. "Competitor Analysis: The Missing Link in Strategy." *Management Review* (July 1979):22–28, 37, 38.

Company Analysis

Beik, Leland L. and Stephen L. Buzby. "Profitability Analysis by Market Segments." *Journal of Marketing* (July 1973):48–53.

Cook, Victor J. Jr. "Marketing Strategy and Differential Advantage." *Journal of Marketing* (Spring 1983):68–75.

Kirpalani, V. H. and S. S. Shapiro. "Financial Dimensions of Marketing Management." *Journal of Marketing* (Fall 1973):40–47.

Lenz, R. T. "Strategic Capability: A Concept and Framework for Analysis." *Academy of Management Review* 2 (1980):225–234.

Mossman, Frank H., Paul Fisher, and W. J. E. Crissy. "New Approaches to Analyzing Marketing Profitability." *Journal of Marketing* (April 1974):43–48.

Snow, C. and L. Hrebiniak. "Strategy and Distinctive Competence." *Administrative Science Quarterly* 25 (1980):317–335.

Venkatraman, N. and J. Camillus. "Explaining the Concept of 'Fit' in Strategic Management." *Academy of Management Review* 9 (1984):513–525.

Auditing the Environment

Hambrick, D. "Environmental Scanning and Organizational Strategy." *Strategic Management Journal* 3 (1982):159–174.

Montgomery, David B. and Charles B. Weinberg. "Toward Strategic Intelligence Systems." *Journal of Marketing* (Fall 1979):41–52.

Definition of Product-Market Alternatives

Buzzell, Robert D. "Are There 'Natural' Market Structures?" *Journal of Marketing* (Winter 1981):42–51.

Caves, R. and M. Porter. "From Entry Barriers to Mobility Barriers." *Quarterly Journal of Economics* 91 (1977):241–262.

Frazier, Gary and Roy Howell. "Business Definition and Performance." *Journal of Marketing* (Spring 1983):68–75.

Hammell, G. and C. K. Prahlad. "Do You Really Have a Global Strategy?" *Harvard Business Review* (July-August 1985):139–148.

Hout, Thomas, Michael E. Porter, and Eileen Rudden. "How Global Companies Win Out." *Harvard Business Review* (September-October 1982):98–108.

Levitt, T. "The Globalization of Markets." *Harvard Business Review* (May-June 1983):92–102.

Watson, C. M. "Counter Competition Abroad to Protect Home Markets." *Harvard Business Review* (January-February 1982):40–42.

3

Customer-Oriented Approaches to Identifying Product-Markets

George S. Day, Allan D. Shocker, and Rajendra K. Srivastava

The problems of identifying competitive product-markets pervade all levels of marketing decisions. Such strategic issues as the basic definition of the business, the assessment of opportunities presented by gaps in the market or threats posed by competitive actions, and major resource allocation decisions are strongly influenced by the breadth or narrowness of the competitive arena. Share of market is a crucial tactical tool for evaluating performance and guiding territorial advertising, sales force, and other budget allocations. The quickening pace of antitrust prosecution is a further source of demands for better definitions of relevant market boundaries that will yield a clearer understanding of the competitive consequences of acquisitions.

This paper is primarily concerned with the needs of marketing planners for strategic analyses of competitive product-markets.[1] Their needs presently are

---

[1]Many of the same issues are encountered during efforts to define the relevant product-market for antitrust purposes. Here the question is whether a company so dominates a market that effective competition is precluded, or that a past or prospective merger has lessened competition. The conceptual approach to this question is very similar to the one developed in this paper (Day, Massy, and Shocker 1978). However, because of the adversarial nature of the proceedings and the existence of prior hypotheses of separation to be tested, the treatment of "relevant market" issues is otherwise quite different.

This article first appeared in the *Journal of Marketing* 43 (Fall 1979):8–19. Reprinted with permission from *Journal of Marketing*, published by the American Marketing Association.

When this article was published the authors were Professor of Marketing at the University of Toronto, Toronto, Ontario, Canada; Associate Professor of Business Administration at the University of Pittsburgh, Pa.; and Associate Professor of Business Administration at the University of Texas, Austin, Tex., respectively.

served by approaches to defining product-markets which emphasize similarity of production processes, function, or raw materials used. Seldom do these approaches give a satisfactory picture of either the threats or the opportunities facing a business. In response, there has been considerable activity directed toward defining product-markets from the customers' perspective. Our objectives are first, to examine the merits of a customer perspective in the context of a defensible definition of a product-market, and second, to evaluate progress toward providing this perspective. The paper's structure corresponds to these objectives. The first two sections are concerned with the nature of the strategic problem, and the development of a customer-oriented definition of a product-market. This definition is used in the third section to help evaluate a variety of methods for identifying product-market boundaries. In this discussion, a sharp distinction is drawn between methods which rely on purchase or usage behavior and those which use customer judgments.

Sources of Demand for Better Insights

Ultimately all product-market boundaries are arbitrary. They exist because of recurring needs to comprehend market structures and impose some order on complex market environments. But this situation could not be otherwise. One reason is the wide variety of decision contexts which dictate different definitions of boundaries.

Market and product class definitions appropriate for tactical decisions tend to be narrow, reflecting the short-run concerns of sales and product managers who regard a market as "a chunk of demand to be filled with the resources at my command." These resources are usually constrained by products in the present product line. A longer-run view, reflecting strategic planning concerns, invariably will reveal a larger product-market to account for (1) presently unserved but potential markets; (2) changes in technology, price relationships, and supply which broaden the array of potential substitute products; and (3) the time required by present and prospective buyers to react to these changes.

Of necessity, a single market definition is a compromise between the long-run and the short-run views. All too often, the resulting compromise is not consistent with customer's views of the competitive alternatives to be considered for a particular usage situation or application. One consequence of these problems is the development of different definitions for different purposes. Thus, for some strategic planning purposes, General Electric treats hair dryers, hair setters, and electric brushes as parts of distinct markets while for other purposes they are part of a "personal appliance" business since they tend to compete with one another in a "gift market." General Foods has taken an even broader approach in a reorganization of its process-oriented divisional structure into strategic business units. Each SBU now concentrates on marketing families of products made by different processing technologies but consumed by the same market segments (Hanon 1974). Thus, all desserts are in the same division whether they are frozen, powdered, or ready-to-eat.

A further reason for the inevitable arbitrariness of product-market boundaries is the frequent absence of natural discontinuities which can be readily identified—and accepted—without argument. Moran (1973) states the problem bluntly:

In our complex service society, there are no more product classes—not in any meaningful sense, only as a figment of file clerk imagination . . . To some degree, in some circumstances, almost anything can be a partial substitute for almost anything else. A (fifteen-cent) stamp substitutes to some extent for an airline ticket.

When a high degree of ambiguity or compromise is present in the identification of the product-market, a number of problems are created. Some will stem from inadequate and delayed understanding of emerging threats in the competitive environment. These threats may come from foreign competition, product substitution trends, shifts in price sensitivity, or changed technological possibility. Thus fiberglass and aluminum parts have displaced steel in many automotive applications due in some measure to increasing willingness to pay higher prices to obtain lower weight and consequent gas economy. Conversely, opportunities may be overlooked when the definition is drawn too narrowly for tactical purposes and the nature and size of the potential market are understated. Finally, whenever market share is used to evaluate the performance of managers or to determine resource allocations (Day 1977), there is a tendency for managers to manipulate the market boundaries to show an increasing or at least static share.

A Customer-Oriented Concept of a Competitive Product-Market

Market definitions have, in the past, focused on either the *product* (as with the following definition, ". . . products may be closely related in the sense that they are regarded as substitutes by consumers" [Needham 1969], which assumes homogeneity of consumer behavior), or on the *buyers* (". . . individuals who in the past have purchased a given class of products" [Sissors 1966]). Neither approach is very helpful for clarifying the concept, or evaluating alternative approaches for identifying product-market boundaries.

A more productive approach can be derived from the following premises:

- People seek the benefits that products provide rather than the products per se. Specific products or brands represent the available combinations of benefits and costs.
- Consumers consider the available alternatives from the vantage point of the usage contexts with which they have experience or the specific applications they are considering (Belk 1975; Lutz and Kakkar 1976; Stout et al. 1977). It is the usage requirement which dictates the benefits being sought.[2]

---

[2]This premise was directly tested, and supported, in a study of the variation of judged importance of various fast-food restaurant attributes across eating occasions (Miller and Ginter 1979). This study and others also have found that some needs, and benefits sought, are reasonably stable across situations. Thus it is usually productive to segment a market on the basis of both people and occasions (Goldman and McDonald 1979).

From these two premises, we can define a product-market as the *set of products* judged to be substitutes, within those usage situations in which similar patterns of benefits are sought, and the *customers* for whom such usages are relevant.

This definition is *demand* or customer-oriented in that customer needs and requirements have primacy. The alternative is to take a *supply* perspective and define products by such operational criteria as similarity of manufacturing processes, raw materials, physical appearance, or function. These criteria are the basis of the Standard Industrial Classification (SIC) system—and have generally wide acceptance because they appear easy to implement. They lead to seemingly stable and clear-cut definitions, and importantly, involve factors largely controllable by the firm, implying that the definition is somehow controllable as well. They are also helpful in identifying potential competitors, because of similarities in manufacturing and distribution systems. Demand-oriented criteria, on the other hand, are less familiar and consequently appear more difficult to implement (as a consequence of the variety of methods available and the inevitable problems of empirical measurement, sampling errors, and aggregation over individual customer differences). Moreover, such definitions may be less stable over time because of changing needs and tastes. Finally, the organization must initiate a research program to collect and analyze relevant data and monitor change rather than relying on government or other external sources to make the information available. The consequence is most often a decision to use supply-oriented measures despite their questionable applicability in many circumstances (Needham 1969).

Hierarchies of Products.   The notion of a unique product category is an oversimplification in the face of the arbitrary nature of the boundaries. Substitutability is a measure of degree. Thus it is better to think in terms of the levels in a hierarchy of products within a generic product class representing all possible ways of satisfying a fundamental consumer need or want. Lunn (1972) makes the following useful distinctions between:

- Totally different *product types* or subclasses which exist to satisfy significantly different patterns of needs beyond the fundamental or generic. For example, both hot and cold cereals serve the same need for breakfast nutrition, but otherwise are different. Over the long run, product types may behave like substitutes.
- Different *product variants* are available within the same overall type, e.g., natural, nutritional, presweetened, and regular cereals. There is a high probability that some short-run substitution takes place among subsets of these variants (between natural and nutritional, for example). If there is too much substitution, then alternatives within the subset do not deserve to be distinguished.
- Different *brands* are produced within the same specific product variant. Although these brands may be subtly differentiated on many bases (color, package type, shape, texture, etc.), they are nonetheless usually direct and immediate substitutes.

There may be many or few levels in such a hierarchy, depending on the breadth and complexity of the genuine need and the variety of alternatives available to satisfy it. Thus, this typology is simply a starting point for thinking about the analytical issues.

Submarkets and Strategic Segments.   The product-market definition proposed above implies submarkets composed of customers with common uses or applications of the product. These are segments according to the traditional definition of groups that have similar purchase or usage behavior or reactions to marketing efforts (Frank, Massy, and Wind 1973). For our purposes, it is more useful to consider these as submarkets within *strategic market segments*. While each of these submarkets may serve as the focus of a positioning decision, the differences between them may not present significant strategic barriers for competitors to overcome. Such barriers may be based on factors such as differences in geography, order quantities, requirements for technical assistance and service support, price sensitivity, or perceived importance of quality and reliability. The test of strategic relevance is whether the segments defined by these or other characteristics must be served by substantially different marketing mixes. The boundaries could then be manifested by discontinuities in price structures, growth rates, share patterns, and distribution channels when going from one segment to another.

Analytical Methods for Customer-Oriented Product-Market Definitions

Customer-oriented methods for identifying product-markets can be classified by whether they rely upon behavioral or judgmental data. Purchase behavior provides the best indication of what people actually do, or have done, but not necessarily what they might do under changed circumstances. As such, its value is greater as a guide to tactical planning. Judgmental data, in the form of perceptions or preferences, may give better insights into future patterns of competition and the reasons for present patterns. Consequently, it may better serve as the basis for strategic planning. In this section we will evaluate seven different analytical approaches within the two basic classes as follows:

Purchase or Usage Behavior	Customer Judgments
A1. Cross-elasticity of demand	B1. Decision sequence analysis
A2. Similarities in behavior	B2. Perceptual mapping
A3. Brand switching	B3. Technology substitution analysis
	B4. Customer judgments of substitutability

Within the broad category of customer judgments of substitutability (B4), five related approaches, using free associations, the "dollar metric," direct grouping of products, products-by-uses analysis and substitution-in-use analysis will be examined.

Analysis of Purchase or Usage Behavior

A1. *Cross-elasticity of demand* is considered by most economists to be the standard against which other approaches should be compared (Scherer 1970). Despite the impressive logic of the cross-elasticity measure, it is widely criticized and infrequently used:

- The conceptual definition of this measure presumes that there is no response by one firm to the price change of another (Needham 1969). This condition is seldom satisfied in practice.
- It is a static measure, and "breaks down in the face of a market characterized by changing product composition" (Cocks and Virts 1975). This is so because a priori it is not known what all the potential substitutes or complements may be. Over time new entrants or departures from a market may affect the cross-elasticity between any two alternatives.
- Finally, "in markets where price changes have been infrequent, or all prices change together, or where factors other than prices have also changed, there is simply not enough information contained in the data to permit valid statistical estimation of the elasticities," (Vernon 1972).

These problems may be overcome with either an experimental study, which can introduce problems of measure validity, or extensive monitoring of the factors affecting demand and use of econometric methods to control, where possible, for the effects of such factors. Not surprisingly, such studies are expensive and rather infrequently undertaken. Generally, empirical cross-elasticity studies have focused on only two goods (typically product-types as opposed to variants or brands). It is also worth noting that if simultaneous estimation of all cross-elasticities were to be attempted, some a priori determination of the limits to a product-market would be needed in order to include price change and other market data for all potential competitive brands. The estimation of any specific cross-elasticity should be sensitive to such product-market definition.

A2. *Similarities in customer usage behavior.* This approach was successfully used in a study of the ethical pharmaceutical market (Cocks and Virts 1975). The basic question was the extent to which products made up of different chemicals, but with similar therapeutic effects, could be significant substitutes. The key to answering this question was the availability of a unique set of data on physician behavior. Each of the 3,000 physicians in a panel recorded: (1) patient characteristics, (2) the diagnosis, (3) the therapeutic measures—drugs—used to treat the patient, (4) the desired action of the drugs being used, and (5) characteristics of the reporting physician.

The first step in the analysis was to estimate the percentage usage of each drug in the treatment of patients diagnosed as having the same ailment. When a drug was found to be the only one used for a certain disease, and seldom or never used in the treatment of any other diagnosis, it was assumed to represent a distinct class. Generally, it was found that several drugs were used in several diagnosis categories. The next step was to see if drugs which were used together had similar desired actions. Some drugs, such as analgesics, are frequently used along with other drugs, without being substitutes (strictly speaking, they also are not complements). Finally, drugs were classed as substitutes—and hence in the same product class—if 10% or more of the total usage of each drug was in the treatment of a specific diagnosis.

While it was not claimed that every drug in the resulting product-market competed for all uses of every other drug in that market, the data revealed a substantial amount of substitutability. The key to understanding the patterns of competition in this market was knowledge of the usage situation. As yet, few consumer panels have incorporated similar data with the usual measures of purchase behavior. The potential to conduct similar analyses suggests that usage data could be valuable when available for categories which are purchased for multiple uses.

A3. *Brand-switching* measures are usually interpreted as conditional probabilities, i.e., the probability of purchasing brand Λ, given that brand B was purchased on the last occasion. Such measures are typically estimated from panel data where the purchases of any given respondent are represented by a sequence of indefinite length. The probabilities are computed from counts of the frequency with which each condition arises in the data (e.g., purchases of brand A are preceded by different brands in the sequence). The premise is that respondents are more likely to switch between close substitutes than distant ones and that brand-switching proportions provide a measure of the probability of substitution.

As with cross-elasticity, the brand-switching measure is usable only after a set of competitive products has first been established. Since estimation of brand-switching rates is based upon a sequence of purchases, there must be some logical basis to determine which brands to include in such a sequence. Similarity of usage patterns, as discussed above, is one promising basis.

Brand-switching rates as measures of degree of substitutability are flawed in several respects. (1) Applicability is typically limited to product categories having high repeat purchase rates to ensure that a sufficiently long sequence of purchases is available over a short time period for reliable estimates of switching probabilities. (2) The customer choice process, which determines switching, must be presumed stable throughout the sequence of purchases. If a long time series is used to provide reliable estimates, this assumption may be questionable. (3) Panel data, upon which switching probabilities are based, often obscure individual switching behavior since data are typically reported by only one member of a family who completes a diary of purchases. Apparent switching can result from different members of the family making consistent but different brand choices at differing points in time. A similar distortion is created by an individual who regularly purchases different brands for different usage occasions. (4) Analyses of panel data are further complicated by multiple brand purchases at the same time (does purchase of A precede B or vice versa in determining the sequence?), by lack of uniformity in package sizes across brands (since package size affects frequency of purchase), and by different sized packages of the same brand (is purchase of a large size equivalent to some sequence of purchases of smaller sizes?).

The Hendry model (Butler and Butler 1970, 1971) uses brand-switching data directly to determine the market structure. Although details have been slow to appear in the literature (Kalwani and Morrison 1977; Rubison and Bass 1978) there has been a good deal of utilization of the empirical regularities uncovered by the model for marketing planning purposes.

This model does not rely solely on behavioral data, as it can also incorporate retrospective reports of switching or purchase intentions data from surveys. In essence, the model seeks an underlying structure of brand-switching maximally "consistent" with the input data. It posits a hierarchical ordering in consumer decision making: consumers are presumed to form categories within the product class (e.g., cold or hot, presweetened or regular, Kellogs, General Mills, or Post cereals), select those classes in which they are interested, and then consider for purchase only the alternatives within the chosen class (e.g., brands within a particular type of product *or* product types within a brand name). Analysis is carried out at each submarket level. Customers may purchase brands within more than one submarket, but within any submarket all customers are considered potential purchasers of all brands. Each customer is assumed, at equilibrium, to have stable purchase probabilities.

To determine which ordering or structuring of the market best characterizes customer views, a heuristic procedure is employed. Initially, judgment is used to hypothesize a limited number of plausible partitionings of a market, i.e., *alternative* submarket definitions. For each hypothesized definition, the Hendry framework is used to predict various switching probabilities among the products/brands within each submarket and between submarkets (switching *between* submarkets should be much less than *within* any one submarket). The predictions can then be compared with the actual data. That hypothesized partitioning (market structure) yielding switching patterns in closest correspondence with actual data is selected as the appropriate definition for the structure of the market.

A procedure elaborating hierarchical partitioning concepts similar to those of Hendry, but with the ability to incorporate usage occasion has recently been discussed by Urban and Hauser (1979). As in the Hendry model, a hierarchical tree structure is specified. More switching should occur within than between branches. Individual probability estimates are derived by measuring preferences among products with a consumer interview and statistically matching these preferences to observed or reported purchase behavior using the conditional logit model (McFadden 1970). The derived trees are tested by comparing predicted with actual choices in a simulated buying situation which occurs at the end of the consumer interview.

The Hendry procedure has a substantial subjective component, depending upon the criterion used to generate the hypothetical market structure definitions to be evaluated. (The alternative to a good criterion is the testing of potentially large numbers of definitions.) It is also quite arbitrary, possessing elements of the chicken-egg controversy: the prior specification of "the market" is quite critical to the empirical determination of "market shares" for each brand but these in turn are necessary to calibrate the Hendry model (i.e., estimate its parameters). Thus the "correct" definition of the market will depend upon how well predictions of the model correspond to the actual data. The model ought to always do reasonably well in predicting switching patterns in the same market environment from which share data were taken. In other words, to use the model for purposes of selecting the superior market definition, one must presume the model valid. But to test its validity, one must already possess a valid definition of the market. Thus the Hendry model may provide a reasonable approach to market definition only if either the model itself can be independently validated or if independent criteria exist for validating the market definition it suggests.

The Hendry model presumes all customers have stable probabilities of purchasing every brand within a partition (submarket). This assumes preferences, market shares, attitudes, and all other factors of significance are stable and that learning is negligible. Such assumptions may suggest applicability of the Hendry framework only in mature product categories, where such conditions may reasonably hold. Moreover, confirmation of any a priori partitioning of a market rests solely upon analysis of the aggregate switching probabilities as these become the measures of substitutability. Since analysis is carried out on an aggregate level, individual or segment differences are largely ignored. The premise that any given brand may have a varying set of competitors depending upon intended usage and brand familiarity is assumed away by such aggregation.

Summary. Behavioral measures suffer from an endemic weakness because they are influenced by what "is" or "was" rather than what "might be." Actual switching is affected by current market factors such as the set of existing brands, their availability, current pricing structures, promotional message and expenditures, existing legislation and social mores, etc. An imported beer could be substitutable for a local brand insofar as usage is concerned, but price differences may discourage actual substitution. Similarly, a private label brand may be substitutable for a nationally distributed one, but unless the customer shops the stores in which the private label is sold, they cannot make the substitution. If data are developed over long periods of time or from a diverse set of people in differing circumstances, sufficient variability may have taken place in the determinants of demand to reveal such potential substitutability. Otherwise, if some kind of behavioral measure is desired, laboratory manipulation may be necessary.

Analyses Based upon Customer Judgments

Customers often have considerable knowledge of existing brands through personal or friends' experiences and exposure to promotion. Their perceptions may not always correspond to what manufacturers may believe about their own or competitive products. They may have purchase and consumption objectives which influence their consideration of alternatives and choices among them. They may create new uses for existing products. If such perceptual and decision making processes prove relatively stable, they may be useful for predicting which products and brands will be regarded as potential or actual substitutes and why.

B.1. *Decision Sequence Analysis* utilizes protocols of consumer decision making, which indicate the sequence in which various criteria are employed to reach a final choice (Bettman 1971; Haines 1974). The usual procedure asks individuals to verbalize what is going through their mind as they make purchase decisions in the course of a shopping trip. This verbal record is called a protocol as distinguished from retrospective questioning of subjects about their decisions. With such data, a model of the way the subject makes decisions can be developed. These models specify the *attributes* of the choice objects or situations that are considered and the *sequence* and *method* of combination of these attributes or cues. Generally, the attributes or cues are arrayed in a hierarchical structure called a decision tree. The order in which they are examined is modeled by the path structure of the tree. The branches are based merely on whether or not the level of the attribute is satisfactory or a certain condition is present ("is the price too high?" "is the store out of my favorite brand?").

Analysis of protocols is at the individual level. This has the advantage of enabling individual differences in knowledge and beliefs about alternative products and choice criteria to be recognized. Individuals may, in principle, be grouped into segments on the basis of similar decision procedures. Measures of the extent of competition between brands can be obtained from protocols of different segments by noting which alternatives are even considered and when they are eliminated from further consideration by criteria used at each stage of the decision process (alternatives eliminated at later stages should be more competitive than those eliminated earlier).

Applications of decision sequence analysis have focused on choices at the brand level. Yet the real benefits of this approach would seem to be better insights into the hierarchy of product types and variants within a generic product class. Thus in understanding patterns of competition in the vegetable market, it is important to know whether buyers first decide on the type of vegetable (corn, beans, peas, etc.) or the form (fresh, frozen, or canned). Proposals for a similar kind of study have been made by economists in connection with the concept of a "utility tree" (Strotz 1957) and are similar in intent to the Hendry procedure.

There are numerous empirical problems to be considered in any effort to collect protocols of choice hierarchies. The typical representations of decision sequences appear quite complex and pose serious difficulties for aggregation of the individual models into any small number of segments. Aggregation requires some definition of "similarity" in order to group different decision structures. Further, since it is generally expensive to develop protocols, a representative sample of customers may be unrealizable. Customers are not used to reporting their decision processes so explicitly. A trained interviewer is needed to coax information which is specific enough to be meaningful (e.g., what is too high a price or a satisfactory level of preference?) and yet not unduly bias the process. Since customer decision making for some product categories may take place over prolonged periods of time it may be necessary for the length of the interviewing to be similarly extended or to rely on respondent's recall of certain events. Finally, since protocol data are collected in the context of the purchase situation, factors associated with that situation may assume greater importance than factors of intended usage. This could place misleading emphasis on in-store factors as determinants of competition.

B.2. *Perceptual mapping* includes a large family of techniques used to create a geometric representation of customer's perceptions of the qualities possessed by products/brands comprising a previously defined product-market (Green 1975). Brands are represented by locations (points or, possibly, regions) in the space. The dimensions of this space distinguish the competitive alternatives and represent benefits or costs perceived important to the purchase. Thus any product/brand might be located in such a space according to a set of coordinates which represent the extent to which the product is believed to possess each benefit or cost attribute. Relative "distances" between product alternatives may be loosely interpreted as measures of perceived substitutability of each alternative for any other.

There are several different techniques which can be used to create perceptual configurations of product-markets (e.g., direct scaling, factor analysis, multiple discriminant analysis, multidimensional scaling). Analysis may be based upon measures of perceived overall similarity/dissimilarity, perceived appropriateness to common usage situations, and correlations between attribute levels for pairs of products. Unfortunately such diversity of criteria and method can lead to somewhat different perceptual maps and possibly different product-market definitions. Much empirical research is still needed to compare the alternatives and assess which produce definitions are more valid for particular purposes (Shocker and Srinivasan 1979).

When perceptual maps can be represented in two or three dimensions without destroying the data, there is a great improvement in the understanding of the competitive structure. Further, to the extent that substitutability in such a representation corresponds in some straightforward way to interproduct distance, analytic techniques such as cluster analysis (or simply looking for "open spaces" in the map) could prove useful in identifying product-market boundaries. The eventual decision must necessarily be judgmental, with the geometric representation simply facilitating that judgment. Customers or segments may also be represented in such a space by the location of their "most preferred" combination of attribute levels—termed their ideal point.

The major advantage offered by perceptual mapping methods is versatility. Maps can be created for each major usage situation. When care is taken to control for customer knowledge of available product/brand alternatives, perceptual homogeneity may be sufficient to permit the modeling of preference and choice for different user segments within a common perceptual representation (Pessemier 1977). Moreover, perceptual maps can be created for different levels of product competition to explore competitive relations at the level of product types, variants, or brands. For example, Jain and Etgar (1975) have used multidimensional scaling to provide a geometric representation of the beverage market which incorporates all these different levels in the same configuration. These analyses become cumbersome when it is not possible to assume perceptual homogeneity (Day, Deutscher, and Ryans 1976). Then it is necessary to cluster the respondents into homogeneous "points-of-view" groups, based on the commonality in their perceptions, and conduct a separate analysis for each group. Alternatively, one can assume that respondents use the same perceptual dimensions, but differ with respect to the weights they attach to the various dimensions.

In principle, new product concepts can be positioned in the space, or existing brands repositioned or deleted, and the effects on the individual or segment choice behavior predicted. Unfortunately, the relation between interproduct distances in the perceptual space and substitutability is not rigorously established. Stefflre (1972) has argued that a perceptual space contains only labeled regions and hence that gaps may simply represent discontinuities. The question is not whether such discontinuities in fact exist, but rather whether a preference model based upon distances from ideal-points to products remains a reasonable predictor of individual or segment behavior. If so, the decision framework of a common perceptual space coupled with models of individual/segment decision making can be used to assess the relative substitutability of different brands for each segment. These measures can then be aggregated over segments to estimate patterns of competition for the broader market.

B.3. *Technology substitution analysis* adapts the idea of preference related to distance in a multiattribute space to the problem of forecasting the substitution of one material, process, or product for another—aluminum for copper in electrical applications and polyvinyl for glass in liquor bottles, for example. Each successful substitution tends to follow an S-shaped or "logistic" curve representing a slow start as initial problems and resistance to change have to be overcome, followed by more rapid progress as acceptance is gained and applications can be publicized, and finally a slowing in the pace of substitution as saturation is reached.

A simple approach to forecasting the course and speed of the substitution process is to project a function having the appropriate logistics curve, using historical data to determine its parameters (Lenz and Lanford 1972). This curve-fitting method overlooks many potential influences on the process, such as: the age, condition, and rate of obsolescence of the capital equipment used in the old technology; the price elasticity of demand; and the "utility-in-use" or relative performance advantage. Recent efforts to model substitution rates have focused on relative "utility" as the basis for improvements in forecasting ability (Stern, Ayres, and Shapanko 1975). The procedure for assessing "utility-in-use" involves: first, identifying the relevant attributes and performance characteristics of each of the competing products or technologies, followed by ratings by experts of the extent to which each alternative possesses each attribute and the perceived importance of each attribute in each end-use market. Finally, an overall utility for each product in each usage situation is obtained by multiplying the attribute possession score by the importance ratings, summing the resulting products, and adjusting for differences in unit price. While criticism can be made of the model structure and the seeming reliance on measurable physical properties to specify the attributes, the value of the basic approach should not be discounted. The outcome is a highly useful quantitative measure of utility which can be used to estimate substitutability among competing products or technologies in specific usage situations.

B.4. *Customer judgments of substitutability* may be obtained in a variety of ways. The simplest is to ask a sample of customers to indicate the degree of substitutability between possible pairs of brands on a rating scale such as: none, low, some, or substantial substitutability. Beyond this familiar approach, several methods of utilizing customer judgments have recently been developed which provide far greater diagnostic insights into patterns of competition.

1. *The free response approach* (Green, Wind, and Jain 1973). Respondents are presented with various brands and asked to free-associate the names of similar or substitute brands. Two kinds of data are obtained. One is the *frequency* of mention of one brand as a substitute for another, which could be used as a measure of similarity of the two brands in order to establish a perceptual space. Secondly, the *order of mention* of substitute brands can be treated as rank-order data (Wind 1977). These data represent an aggregate judgment across situations, and leave it to the respondent to decide how similar two brands must be before they become substitutes.

    A useful variant of the free-response question asks respondents what they would do if they were unable to buy their preferred brand. One advantage of this question is that it can realistically be tailored to specific situations. For example, one study asked scotch drinkers what they would do if scotch were not available in a variety of situations, such as a large cocktail party in the early evening. Evidently, there were some situations where white wine was the preferred alternative.

2.   *The dollar metric approach* (Pessemier et al. 1970/71). Respondents first are presented with all possible pairs of brands, each of the brands being marked with their regular prices. In each case, the respondent selects the brand he/she would buy in a forced choice purchase. They are then asked the price to which the preferred brand must rise before they would switch their original preference. Strength of preference is measured in terms of this price increment. Such data must be further "processed" to compute aggregated preference measures.

   This procedure is somewhat analogous to a laboratory measurement of cross-elasticity of demand. The set of potentially competitive brands must be again identified in advance. The procedure is reasonably easy to administer and analyze; although the simplicity may be eroded if considerations of intended usage, brand familiarity, and market segmentation are incorporated. It appears that respondents are able to reveal their preferences for different alternatives in the forced-choice situation. Whether they can relate validly how they arrived at the preference—by estimating the minimum price change that would cause a switch—remains an open question (Huber and James 1977).

3.   *Direct grouping into product categories*. Bourgeois, Haines, and Sommers (1979) have taken broadly related sets of brands and asked samples of customers to: (1) divide the set into as many groups as they consider meaningful, (2) explain the criteria used for each grouping, and (3) judge the similarity of the brands within each group. A measure of the similarity of brands is created by summing across customers to find the frequency with which pairs of brands are assigned to the same group. These data are analyzed by nonmetric, multidimensional scaling programs to obtain interval-scaled measures of brand similarity (according to their proximity in a reduced space). These are input to a cluster analysis routine to obtain groupings of brands regarded as "customer product types." Products are assigned to one type only. An application of this procedure to the generic "personal care" market yielded intuitively appealing groups of brands. However the data were reported to be quite "noisy," which is not surprising in view of the wide latitude given the respondents. Potentially, respondents could differ both in the frame of reference for the task (the intended application or usage) and the criterion for grouping. Some, for example, might emphasize physical similarity while others might elect appropriateness-in-use or similarity of price as the criterion.

4.   *Products-by-uses analysis*. In the procedure developed by Steffire (1979; Myers and Tauber 1977), a sample of customers is given a list of target products or brands and asked to conjecture as many uses for them as possi-

ble. They are then asked to suggest additional products or brands appropriate to these same uses and additional uses appropriate to these new products. This sequence of free response questions generates large lists of products/ brands and potential uses. An independent sample is then asked to judge the appropriateness of each product for each use. In one study of proprietary medicines, for example, respondents were asked to judge the acceptability of each of 52 medicines for 52 conditions of use ranging from "when you have a stuffy nose" to "when the children have a fever."

Two assumptions underlie analyses of the products-by-uses matrix: (1) the set of products constitutes a representative sample of the benefits sought by customers and (2) two usage situations are similar if similar benefits are desired in both situations. If these assumptions are valid, then grouping usage situations according to similarity of products judged appropriate should be equivalent to grouping them explicitly by the benefits desired. The net result is a somewhat circular procedure:

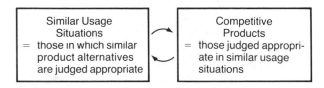

The merits of the Stefflre (1972, 1979) procedure are first, that the introduction of specific situations gives respondents frames of reference for their judgments of substitutability or appropriateness and second, that the criteria can be modified to reflect greater concern with *potential* competition (respondents are asked which existing products or descriptions of concepts would be appropriate to specified uses) or with *actual* competition (which products they would consider for purchase in the situation). This ability to use descriptions of concepts greatly extends the flexibility of the approach to provide data relevant to actual or proposed changes in the product-market. A further advantage, shared with the direct grouping approach, is an ability to cope with large numbers of alternatives if necessary, without a require- ment for large numbers of respondents because of a high degree of homo- geneity in perceptual judgments.

These advantages are seemingly offset by the evident impracticability of the demands on respondents to complete a matrix with as many as 2,500 cells. For many purposes, however, it is not necessary that each respondent complete the entire matrix. A related problem is the lack of a sound basis for deciding how many situations and at what level of specificity, to include in the matrix.

5.   *Substitution-in-use analysis.* This extends the Stefflre procedure in two di- rections (Srivastava, Shocker, and Day 1977). First, a separate analysis step is introduced to ensure that the set of usage situations is parsimonious and representative. If the latter condition is not met, it is likely there will be too many of one "type" of situation, with consequent distortion in the grouping

of products. Secondly, the measure of appropriateness-in-use is modified to measure the degree of suitability. This is feasible as the number of situations the respondents are given is significantly smaller than in the Stefflre procedure. The result is a three-stage procedure:

1.   The *exploratory* stage uses free response plus repertory grid and focused group methods to elicit usage situations associated with a generic need.

2.   A *typology* of usage situations is then developed from principal components analysis of the products-by-uses matrix (after a check for perceptual homogeneity). Both uses and products can be plotted in the reduced space described by the first two or three principal components. A typology of uses may be derived from factorial combinations of different levels of the independent dimensions of this space.

3.   A new sample is employed to obtain a measure of the suitability or appropriateness of each brand or product for each of the usage situations in the typology. Each alternative can be rated separately, or all alternatives can be ranked, within each situation.

There are several ways to analyze the resulting matrix. Insights into a firm's competitive position within distinct situational submarkets can be obtained from a principal components analysis similar to stage 2 of the procedure described above. Experience with breath fresheners and banking services (Srivastava and Shocker 1979) indicates that ideas for new products or product positions can come from the identification of inadequately served usage situations. A useful test of the effectiveness of a company's positioning efforts is the extent of variability of customer perceptions of the appropriateness of a specific brand for a distinct usage submarket. The analysis can also help assess the possibility of cannibalization. If two or more products or brands of a single manufacturer are seen as appropriate for the same usage submarket, then efforts to promote one may be at the expense of a loss in sales of the other.

The data can also be analyzed with categorical conjoint or similar procedures, as long as the factorial combinations of usage situations are properly balanced. Here the focus would be on both the patterns of competition within a usage situation and the elements of the situation which have the greatest influence on these patterns. Wind (1977) used this approach to study the relative positions of finance companies. Automobile dealers were given 16 different financing situations and asked to assign each to one of five possible financing alternatives. The situations represented combinations of six different factors including customer's credit rating, familiarity with customer, amount to finance, and length of term. The estimated utility functions suggested the degree of appropriateness of each source of financing for each level of the six factors. It was found, for example, that the client (a finance company associated with an automobile dealer) faced quite different competition depending on the amount to be financed.

Many of the advantages of the substitution-in-use approach derive from the consistency of the approach with the conceptual definition of a product-market. Despite these potential advantages, the procedure produces only a relative measure of substitutability. Managerial judgment must still decide the level of judged appropriateness that permits each product/brand to be considered as part of a situational submarket.

Summary and Conclusions

The questions of how to identify product-market boundaries cannot be separated from the ways results are to be used. Strategic or long-run definitions of market structure inevitably hold more significance even though they are mainly obtainable from customer judgments rather than behavior. Very narrowly defined boundaries appear adequate for short-run, tactical decisions in most product categories. The value of a valid and strategically relevant product-market definition lies in "stretching" the company's perceptions appropriately far enough so that significant threats and opportunities are not missed, but not so far as to dissipate information gathering and analysis efforts on "long shots." This is a difficult balance to achieve given the myriad of present and potential competitors faced by most companies.

The principal conclusions from the analysis of the nature of boundaries and the various empirical methods for identifying competitive product-markets are:

- boundaries are seldom clear-cut—ultimately, all boundaries are arbitrary,
- the suitability of different empirical methods is strongly influenced by the character of the market environment,
- on balance, those empirical methods which explicitly recognize the variety of usage situations have widest applicability and yield maximum insights. The concept of usage situation appears to be the most prevalent common denominator of market environments which can be used as the basis for empirical methods,
- most methods, particularly those based upon behavioral measures are static and have difficulty coping with changes in preferences or additions and deletions of choice alternatives in the market,
- regardless of method, the most persistent problem is the lack of defensible criteria for recognizing boundaries.

These conclusions add up to a situation where the state of knowledge has not kept abreast of either the present need to understand, or the changing technological, social, and economic factors which are constantly reshaping market environments. To redress this situation, there is a clear need for a strategically oriented program of research in a variety of market situations. Research in each market should be characterized by the use of multiple techniques to seek confirmation through cross validation and longitudinal approaches in which judgmental methods are followed by behavioral methods which can validate inferences. As we have noted, different methods have different strengths and weaknesses, and more needs to be learned about the sensitivity of results to the shortcomings of each method. Also there will inevitably be points of contradiction and consistency in the insights gained from boundaries established by different methods. The process of resolution should be most revealing, both in terms of understanding a firm's competitive position and suggesting strategy alternatives.

References

Belk, Russell (1975), "Situational Variables and Consumer Behavior," *Journal of Consumer Research,* 2 (December), 157–164.

Bettman, James R. (1971), "The Structure of Consumer Choice Processes," *Journal of Marketing Research,* 8 (November), 465–471.

Bourgeois, Jacques D., George H. Haines, and Montrose S. Sommers (1979), "Defining an Industry," paper presented to the TIMS/ORSA Special Interest Conference on Market Measurement and Analysis, Stanford, CA, March 26.

Butler, Ben Jr. and David H. Butler (1970 and 1971), "Hendrodynamics: Fundamental Laws of Consumer Dynamics," Hendry Corp., Croton-on-Hudson, NY, Chapter 1 (1970) and Chapter 2 (1971).

Cocks, Douglas L. and John R. Virts (1975), "Market Definition and Concentration in the Ethical Pharmaceutical Industry," Internal publication of Eli Lilly and Co., Indianapolis.

Day, George S. (1977), "Diagnosing The Product Portfolio," *Journal of Marketing,* 41 (April), 29–38.

———, Terry Deutscher, and Adrian Ryans (1976), "Data Quality, Level of Aggregation and Nonmetric Multidimensional Scaling Solutions," *Journal of Marketing Research,* 13 (February), 92–97.

———, William F. Massy, and Allan D. Shocker (1978), "The Public Policy Context of The Relevant Market Question," in *Public Policy Issues in Marketing,* John F. Cady, ed., Cambridge, MA: Marketing Science Institute, 51–67.

Frank, Ronald, William F. Massy, and Yoram Wind (1973), *Market Segmentation,* Englewood Cliffs, NJ: Prentice-Hall, Inc.

Goldman, Alfred and Susan S. McDonald (1979), "Occasion Segmentation," paper presented to American Marketing Association Attitude Research Conference, Hilton Head, S.C., Feb. 25–28.

Green, Paul E. (1975), "Marketing Applications of MDS: Assessment and Outlook," *Journal of Marketing,* 39 (January), 24–31.

———, Yoram Wind, and Arun K. Jain (1973), "Analyzing Free Response Data in Marketing Research," *Journal of Marketing Research,* 10 (February), 45–52.

Haines, George H. (1974), "Process Models of Consumer Decision-Making," in *Buyer/ Consumer Information Processing,* G. D. Hughes and M. L. Ray, eds., Chapel Hill, NC: University of North Carolina Press.

Hanon, Mack (1974), "Reorganize Your Company Around Its Markets," *Harvard Business Review,* 79 (November-December), 63–74.

Huber, Joel and Bill James (1977), "The Monetary Worth of Physical Attributes: A Dollarmetric Approach," in *Moving A Head with Attitude Research,* Yoram Wind and Marshall Greenberg, eds., Chicago: American Marketing Association.

Jain, Arun K. and Michael Etgar (1975), "How to Improve Antitrust Policies with Marketing Research Tools," in *1975 Combined Proceedings of the American Marketing Association,* Edward M. Mazze, ed., Chicago: American Marketing Association, 72–75.

Kalwani, Manohar U. and Donald G. Morrison (1977), "A Parsimonious Description of the Hendry System," *Management Science,* 23 (January), 476–477.

Lenz, Ralph C. Jr. and H. W. Lanford (1972), "The Substitution Phenomena," *Business Horizons,* 15 (February), 63–68.

Lunn, Tony (1972), "Segmenting and Constructing Markets," in *Consumer Market Research Handbook,* R. M. Worcester, ed., Maidenhead, Berkshire: McGraw-Hill.

Lutz, Richard J. and Pradeep Kakkar (1976), "Situational Influence in Interpersonal Persuasion," in *Advances in Consumer Research,* Vol. III, Beverlee B. Anderson, ed., Atlanta: Association for Consumer Research, 370–378.

McFadden, Daniel (1970), "Conditional Logit Analysis of Qualitative Choice Behavior" in *Frontiers in Econometrics,* P. Zarembka, ed., New York: Academic Press, 105–142.

Miller, Kenneth E. and James L. Ginter (1979), "An Investigation of Situational Variation in Brand Choice Behavior and Attitude," *Journal of Marketing Research,* 16 (February), 111–123.

Moran, William R. (1973), "Why New Products Fail," *Journal of Advertising Research,* 13 (April), 5–13.

Myers, James H. and Edward Tauber (1977), *Market Structure Analysis,* Chicago: American Marketing Association.

Needham, Douglas (1969), *Economic Analysis and Industrial Structure,* New York: Holt, Rinehart, and Winston, Chapter 2.

Pessemier, Edgar A. (1977), *Product Management: Strategy and Organization,* Santa Barbara, CA: Wiley/Hamilton, 203–254.

————, Philip Burger, Richard Teach, and Douglas Tigert (1970/71), "Using Laboratory Brand Preference Scales to Predict Consumer Brand Purchases," *Management Science,* 17 (February), 371–385.

Rubison, Joel R. and Frank M. Bass (1978), "A Note on 'A Parsimonious Description of the Hendry System,' " paper 658, West Lafayette, IN: Krannert School, Purdue, March.

Scherer, Frederic (1970), *Industrial Market Structure and Economic Performance,* Chicago: Rand McNally.

Shocker, Allan D. and V. Srinivasan (1979), "Multi-Attribute Applications for Product Concept Evaluation and Generation: A Critical Review," *Journal of Marketing Research,* 16 (May), 159–180.

Sissors, Jack Z. (1966), "What is a Market?" *Journal of Marketing,* 30 (July), 17–21.

Srivastava, Rajendra and Allan D. Shocker (1979), "The Validity/Reliability of a Method for Developing Product-Specific Usage Situational Taxonomies," working paper, Pittsburgh: University of Pittsburgh, Graduate School of Business (September).

————, ————, and George S. Day (1978), "An Exploratory Study of Situational Effects on Product Market Definition," in *Advances in Consumer Research,* Vol. V, H. Keith Hunt, ed., Ann Arbor: Association for Consumer Research, 32–38.

Stefflre, Volney (1972), "Some Applications of Multidimensional Scaling to Social Science Problems," in *Multidimensional Scaling: Theory and Applications in the Behavioral Sciences,* Vol. III, A. K. Romney, R. N. Shepard, and S. B. Nerlove, eds., New York: Seminar Press.

————(1979), "New Products: Organizational and Technical Problems and Opportunities," in *Analytic Approaches to Product and Marketing Planning,* A. D. Shocker, ed., Cambridge, MA: Marketing Science Institute, April Report 79–104, 415–480.

Stern, M. O., R. V. Ayres, and A. Shapanko (1975), "A Model for Forecasting the

Substitution of One Technology for Another,'' *Technological Forecasting and Social Change,* 7 (February), 57–59.

Stout, Roy G., Raymond H. S. Suh, Marshall G. Greenberg, and Joel S. Dubow (1977), ''Usage Incidents as a Basis for Segmentation,'' in *Moving A Head with Attitude Research,* Yoram Wind and Marshall Greenberg, eds., Chicago: American Marketing Association.

Strotz, Robert H. (1957), ''The Empirical Implications of a Utility Tree,'' *Econometrica,* 25 (April), 269–280.

————, and John R. Hauser (1979), ''Market Definition'' in *Design and Marketing of New Products and Services,* Cambridge, MA: MIT, Sloan School of Management, Ch. 5.

Vernon, John (1972), *Market Structure and Industrial Performance,* Boston: Allyn and Bacon.

Wind, Yoram (1977), ''The Perception of a Firm's Competitive Position,'' in *Behavioral Models for Market Analysis,* F. M. Nicosia and Y. Wind, eds., New York: The Dryden Press, 163–181.

How Competitive Forces Shape Strategy

Michael E. Porter

The essence of strategy formulation is coping with competition. Yet it is easy to view competition too narrowly and too pessimistically. While one sometimes hears executives complaining to the contrary, intense competition in an industry is neither coincidence nor bad luck.

Moreover, in the fight for market share, competition is not manifested only in the other players. Rather, competition in an industry is rooted in its underlying economics, and competitive forces exist that go well beyond the established combatants in a particular industry. Customers, suppliers, potential entrants, and substitute products are all competitors that may be more or less prominent or active depending on the industry.

The state of competition in an industry depends on five basic forces, which are diagrammed in the *exhibit* on page 88. The collective strength of these forces determines the ultimate profit potential of an industry. It ranges from *intense* in industries like tires, metal cans, and steel, where no company earns spectacular returns on investment, to *mild* in industries like oil field services and equipment, soft drinks, and toiletries, where there is room for quite high returns.

In the economists' "perfectly competitive" industry, jockeying for position is unbridled and entry to the industry very easy. This kind of industry structure, of course, offers the worst prospect for long-run profitability. The weaker the forces collectively, however, the greater the opportunity for superior performance.

Whatever their collective strength, the corporate strategist's goal is to find a position in the industry where his or her company can best defend itself against these forces or can influence them in its favor. The collective strength of the

This article first appeared in the *Harvard Business Review*. Reprinted by permission of the *Harvard Business Review,* March-April 1979, pp. 137–145. Copyright © 1979 by the President and Fellows of Harvard College, all rights reserved.

When the article was published the author was Associate Professor of Business Administration at the Harvard Business School.

Forces Governing Competition in an Industry

forces may be painfully apparent to all the antagonists; but to cope with them, the strategist must delve below the surface and analyze the sources of each. For example, what makes the industry vulnerable to entry? What determines the bargaining power of suppliers?

Knowledge of these underlying sources of competitive pressure provides the groundwork for a strategic agenda of action. They highlight the critical strengths and weaknesses of the company, animate the positioning of the company in its industry, clarify the areas where strategic changes may yield the greatest payoff, and highlight the places where industry trends promise to hold the greatest significance as either opportunities or threats. Understanding these sources also proves to be of help in considering areas for diversification.

Contending Forces

The strongest competitive force or forces determine the profitability of an industry and so are of greatest importance in strategy formulation. For example, even a company with a strong position in an industry unthreatened by potential entrants will earn low returns if it faces a superior or a lower-cost substitute product—as the leading manufacturers of vacuum tubes and coffee percolators have learned to their sorrow. In such a situation, coping with the substitute product becomes the number one strategic priority.

Different forces take on prominence, of course, in shaping competition in each industry. In the ocean-going tanker industry the key force is probably the buyers (the major oil companies), while in tires it is powerful OEM buyers coupled with tough competitors. In the steel industry the key forces are foreign competitors and substitute materials.

Every industry has an underlying structure, or a set of fundamental economic and technical characteristics, that gives rise to these competitive forces. The strategist, wanting to position his company to cope best with its industry environment or to influence that environment in the company's favor, must learn what makes the environment tick.

This view of competition pertains equally to industries dealing in services and to those selling products. To avoid monotony in this article, I refer to both products and services as "products." The same general principles apply to all types of business.

A few characteristics are critical to the strength of each competitive force. I shall discuss them in this section.

Threat of Entry

New entrants to an industry bring new capacity, the desire to gain market share, and often substantial resources. Companies diversifying through acquisition into the industry from other markets often leverage their resources to cause a shake-up, as Philip Morris did with Miller beer.

The seriousness of the threat of entry depends on the barriers present and on the reaction from existing competitors that the entrant can expect. If barriers to entry are high and a newcomer can expect sharp retaliation from the entrenched competitors, obviously he will not pose a serious threat of entering.

There are six major sources of barriers to entry:

1. *Economies of scale*—These economies deter entry by forcing the aspirant either to come in on a large scale or to accept a cost disadvantage. Scale economies in production, research, marketing, and service are probably the key barriers to entry in the mainframe computer industry, as Xerox and GE sadly discovered. Economies of scale can also act as hurdles in distribution, utilization of the sales force, financing, and nearly any other part of a business.

2. *Product differentiation*—Brand identification creates a barrier by forcing entrants to spend heavily to overcome customer loyalty. Advertising, customer service, being first in the industry, and product differences are among the factors fostering brand identification. It is perhaps the most important entry barrier in soft drinks, over-the-counter drugs, cosmetics, investment banking, and public accounting. To create high fences around their businesses, brewers couple brand identification with economies of scale in production, distribution, and marketing.

3. *Capital requirements*—The need to invest large financial resources in order to compete creates a barrier to entry, particularly if the capital is required for unrecoverable expenditures in up-front advertising or R&D. Capital is necessary not only for fixed facilities but also for customer credit, invento-

The Experience Curve as an Entry Barrier

In recent years, the experience curve has become widely discussed as a key element of industry structure. According to this concept, unit costs in many manufacturing industries (some dogmatic adherents say in *all* manufacturing industries) as well as in some service industries decline with "experience" or a particular company's cumulative volume of production. (The experience curve, which encompasses many factors, is a broader concept than the better-known learning curve, which refers to the efficiency achieved over a period of time by workers through much repetition.)

The causes of the decline in unit costs are a combination of elements, including economies of scale, the learning curve for labor, and capital-labor substitution. The cost decline creates a barrier to entry because new competitors with no "experience" face higher costs than established ones, particularly the producer with the largest market share, and have difficulty catching up with the entrenched competitors.

Adherents of the experience curve concept stress the importance of achieving market leadership to maximize this barrier to entry, and they recommend aggressive action to achieve it, such as price cutting in anticipation of falling costs in order to build volume. For the combatant that cannot achieve a healthy market share, the prescription is usually, "Get out."

Is the experience curve an entry barrier on which strategies should be built? The answer is: not in every industry. In fact, in some industries, building a strategy on the experience curve can be potentially disastrous. That costs decline with experience in some industries is not news to corporate executives. The significance of the experience curve for strategy depends on what factors are causing the decline.

If costs are falling because a growing company can reap economies of scale through more efficient, automated facilities and vertical integration, then the cumulative volume of production is unimportant to its relative cost position. Here the lowest-cost producer is the one with the largest, most efficient facilities.

A new entrant may well be more efficient than the more experienced competitors; if it has built the newest plant, it will face no disadvantage in having to catch up. The strategic prescription, "You must have the largest, most efficient plant," is a lot different from, "You must produce the greatest cumulative output of the item to get your costs down."

Whether a drop in costs with cumulative (not absolute) volume erects an entry barrier also depends on the sources of the decline. If costs go down because of technical advances known generally in the industry or because of the development of improved equipment that can be copied or purchased from equipment suppliers, the experience curve is no entry barrier at all—in fact, new or less experienced competitors may actually enjoy a cost *advantage* over the leaders. Free of the legacy of heavy past investments, the newcomer or less experienced competitor can purchase or copy the newest and lowest-cost equipment and technology.

If, however, experience can be kept proprietary, the leaders will maintain a cost advantage. But new entrants may require less experience to reduce their costs than the leaders needed. All this suggests that the experience curve can be a shaky entry barrier on which to build a strategy.

While space does not permit a complete treatment here, I want to mention a few other crucial elements in determining the appropriateness of a strategy built on the entry barrier provided by the experience curve:

- The height of the barrier depends on how important costs are to competition compared with other areas like marketing, selling, and innovation.
- The barrier can be nullified by product or process innovations leading to substantially new technology and thereby creating an entirely new experience curve.* New entrants can leapfrog the industry leaders and alight on the new experience curve, to which those leaders may be poorly positioned to jump.
- If more than one strong company is building its strategy on the experience curve, the consequences can be nearly fatal. By the time only one rival is left pursuing such a strategy, industry growth may have stopped and the prospects of reaping the spoils of victory long since evaporated.

---

*For an example drawn from the history of the automobile industry, see William J. Abernathy and Kenneth Wayns, "The Limits of the Learning Curve," *HBR*, September–October 1974, p. 109.

ries, and absorbing start-up losses. While major corporations have the financial resources to invade almost any industry, the huge capital requirements in certain fields, such as computer manufacturing and mineral extraction, limit the pool of likely entrants.

4. *Cost disadvantages independent of size*—Entrenched companies may have cost advantages not available to potential rivals, no matter what their size and attainable economies of scale. These advantages can stem from the effects of the learning curve (and of its first cousin, the experience curve), proprietary technology, access to the best raw materials sources, assets purchased at preinflation prices, government subsidies, or favorable locations. Sometimes cost advantages are legally enforceable, as they are through patents. (For an analysis of the much-discussed experience curve as a barrier to entry see the ruled insert above.)

5.   *Access to distribution channels*—The new boy on the block must, of course, secure distribution of his product or service. A new food product, for example, must displace others from the supermarket shelf via price breaks, promotions, intense selling efforts, or some other means. The more limited the wholesale or retail channels are and the more that existing competitors have these tied up, obviously the tougher that entry into the industry will be. Sometimes this barrier is so high that, to surmount it, a new contestant must create its own distribution channels, as Timex did in the watch industry in the 1950s.

6.   *Government policy*—The government can limit or even foreclose entry to industries with such controls as license requirements and limits on access to raw materials. Regulated industries like trucking, liquor retailing, and freight forwarding are noticeable examples; more subtle government restrictions operate in fields like ski-area development and coal mining. The government also can play a major indirect role by affecting entry barriers through controls such as air and water pollution standards and safety regulations.

The potential rival's expectations about the reaction of existing competitors also will influence its decision on whether to enter. The company is likely to have second thoughts if incumbents have previously lashed out at new entrants or if:

- The incumbents possess substantial resources to fight back, including excess cash and unused borrowing power, productive capacity, or clout with distribution channels and customers.
- The incumbents seem likely to cut prices because of a desire to keep market shares or because of industrywide excess capacity.
- Industry growth is slow, affecting its ability to absorb the new arrival and probably causing the financial performance of all the parties involved to decline.

Changing Conditions.   From a strategic standpoint there are two important additional points to note about the threat of entry.

First, it changes, of course, as these conditions change. The expiration of Polaroid's basic patents on instant photography, for instance, greatly reduced its absolute cost entry barrier built by proprietary technology. It is not surprising that Kodak plunged into the market. Product differentiation in printing has all but disappeared. Conversely, in the auto industry economies of scale increased enormously with post–World War II automation and vertical integration—virtually stopping successful new entry.

Second, strategic decisions involving a large segment of an industry can have a major impact on the conditions determining the threat of entry. For example, the actions of many U.S. wine producers in the 1960s to step up product introductions, raise advertising levels, and expand distribution nationally surely strengthened the entry roadblocks by raising economies of scale and making access to distribution channels more difficult. Similarly, decisions by members of the recreational vehicle industry to vertically integrate in order to lower costs have greatly increased the economies of scale and raised the capital cost barriers.

Powerful Suppliers and Buyers

Suppliers can exert bargaining power on participants in an industry by raising prices or reducing the quality of purchased goods and services. Powerful suppliers can thereby squeeze profitability out of an industry unable to recover cost increases in its own prices. By raising their prices, soft drink concentrate producers have contributed to the erosion of profitability of bottling companies because the bottlers, facing intense competition from powdered mixes, fruit drinks, and other beverages, have limited freedom to raise *their* prices accordingly. Customers likewise can force down prices, demand higher quality or more service, and play competitors off against each other—all at the expense of industry profits.

The power of each important supplier or buyer group depends on a number of characteristics of its market situation and on the relative importance of its sales or purchases to the industry compared with its overall business.

A *supplier* group is powerful if:

- It is dominated by a few companies and is more concentrated than the industry it sells to.

   Its product is unique or at least differentiated, or if it has built up switching costs. Switching costs are fixed costs buyers face in changing suppliers. These arise because, among other things, a buyer's product specifications tie it to particular suppliers, it has invested heavily in specialized ancillary equipment or in learning how to operate a supplier's equipment (as in computer software), or its production lines are connected to the supplier's manufacturing facilities (as in some manufacture of beverage containers).

- It is not obliged to contend with other products for sale to the industry. For instance, the competition between the steel companies and the aluminum companies to sell to the can industry checks the power of each supplier.

- It poses a credible threat of integrating forward into the industry's business. This provides a check against the industry's ability to improve the terms on which it purchases.

- The industry is not an important customer of the supplier group. If the industry *is* an important customer, suppliers' fortunes will be closely tied to the industry, and they will want to protect the industry through reasonable pricing and assistance in activities like R&D and lobbying.

A *buyer* group is powerful if:

- It is concentrated or purchases in large volumes. Large-volume buyers are particularly potent forces if heavy fixed costs characterize the industry—as they do in metal containers, corn refining, and bulk chemicals, for example—which raise the stakes to keep capacity filled.

- The products it purchases from the industry are standard or undifferentiated. The buyers, sure that they can always find alternative suppliers, may play one company against another, as they do in aluminum extrusion.

- The products it purchases from the industry form a component of its product and represent a significant fraction of its cost. The buyers are likely to shop for a favorable price and purchase selectively. Where the product sold by the industry in question is a small fraction of buyers' costs, buyers are usually much less price sensitive.

- It earns low profits, which create great incentive to lower its purchasing costs. Highly profitable buyers, however, are generally less price sensitive (that is, of course, if the item does not represent a large fraction of their costs).

- The industry's product is unimportant to the quality of the buyers' products or services. Where the quality of the buyers' products is very much affected by the industry's product, buyers are generally less price sensitive. Industries in which this situation obtains include oil field equipment, where a malfunction can lead to large losses, and enclosures for electronic medical and test instruments, where the quality of the enclosure can influence the user's impression about the quality of the equipment inside.

- The industry's product does not save the buyer money. Where the industry's product or service can pay for itself many times over, the buyer is rarely price sensitive; rather, he is interested in quality. This is true in services like investment banking and public accounting, where errors in judgment can be costly and embarrassing, and in businesses like the logging of oil wells, where an accurate survey can save thousands of dollars in drilling costs.

- The buyers pose a credible threat of integrating backward to make the industry's product. The Big Three auto producers and major buyers of cars have often used the threat of self-manufacture as a bargaining lever. But sometimes an industry engenders a threat to buyers that its members may integrate forward.

Most of these sources of buyer power can be attributed to consumers as a group as well as to industrial and commercial buyers; only a modification of the frame of reference is necessary. Consumers tend to be more price sensitive if they are purchasing products that are undifferentiated, expensive relative to their incomes, and of a sort where quality is not particularly important.

The buying power of retailers is determined by the same rules, with one important addition. Retailers can gain significant bargaining power over manufacturers when they can influence consumers' purchasing decisions, as they do in audio components, jewelry, appliances, sporting goods, and other goods.

Strategic Action. A company's choice of suppliers to buy from or buyer groups to sell to should be viewed as a crucial strategic decision. A company can improve its strategic posture by finding suppliers or buyers who possess the least power to influence it adversely.

Most common is the situation of a company being able to choose whom it will sell to—in other words, buyer selection. Rarely do all the buyer groups a company sells to enjoy equal power. Even if a company sells to a single industry, segments usually exist within that industry that exercise less power (and that are therefore less price sensitive) than others. For example, the replacement market for most products is less price sensitive than the overall market.

As a rule, a company can sell to powerful buyers and still come away with above-average profitability only if it is a low-cost producer in its industry or if its product enjoys some unusual, if not unique, features. In supplying large customers with electric motors, Emerson Electric earns high returns because its low cost position permits the company to meet or undercut competitors' prices.

If the company lacks a low cost position or a unique product, selling to everyone is self-defeating because the more sales it achieves, the more vulnerable it becomes. The company may have to muster the courage to turn away business and sell only to less potent customers.

Buyer selection has been a key to the success of National Can and Crown Cork & Seal. They focus on the segments of the can industry where they can create product differentiation, minimize the threat of backward integration, and otherwise mitigate the awesome power of their customers. Of course, some industries do not enjoy the luxury of selecting "good" buyers.

As the factors creating supplier and buyer power change with time or as a result of a company's strategic decisions, naturally the power of these groups rises or declines. In the ready-to-wear clothing industry, as the buyers (department stores and clothing stores) have become more concentrated and control has passed to large chains, the industry has come under increasing pressure and suffered falling margins. The industry has been unable to differentiate its product or engender switching costs that lock in its buyers enough to neutralize these trends.

Substitute Products

By placing a ceiling on prices it can charge, substitute products or services limit the potential of an industry. Unless it can upgrade the quality of the product or differentiate it somehow (as via marketing), the industry will suffer in earnings and possibly in growth.

Manifestly, the more attractive the price-performance trade-off offered by substitute products, the firmer the lid placed on the industry's profit potential. Sugar producers confronted with the large-scale commercialization of high-fructose corn syrup, a sugar substitute, are learning this lesson today.

Substitutes not only limit profits in normal times; they also reduce the bonanza an industry can reap in boom times. In 1978 the producers of fiberglass insulation enjoyed unprecedented demand as a result of high energy costs and severe winter weather. But the industry's ability to raise prices was tempered by the plethora of insulation substitutes, including cellulose, rock wool, and styrofoam. These substitutes are bound to become an even stronger force once the current round of plant additions by fiberglass insulation producers has boosted capacity enough to meet demand (and then some).

Substitute products that deserve the most attention strategically are those that (a) are subject to trends improving their price-performance trade-off with the industry's product, or (b) are produced by industries earning high profits. Substitutes often came rapidly into play if some development increases competition in their industries and causes price reduction or performance improvement.

Jockeying for Position

Rivalry among existing competitors takes the familiar form of jockeying for position—using tactics like price competition, product introduction, and advertising slugfests. Intense rivalry is related to the presence of a number of factors:

- Competitors are numerous or are roughly equal in size and power. In many U.S. industries in recent years foreign contenders, of course, have become part of the competitive picture.
- Industry growth is slow, precipitating fights for market share that involve expansion-minded members.
- The product or service lacks differentiation or switching costs, which lock in buyers and protect one combatant from raids on its customers by another.
- Fixed costs are high or the product is perishable, creating strong temptation to cut prices. Many basic materials businesses, like paper and aluminum, suffer from this problem when demand slackens.
- Capacity is normally augmented in large increments. Such additions, as in the chlorine and vinyl chloride businesses, disrupt the industry's supply-demand balance and often lead to periods of overcapacity and price cutting.
- Exit barriers are high. Exit barriers, like very specialized assets or management's loyalty to a particular business, keep companies competing even though they may be earning low or even negative returns on investment. Excess capacity remains functioning, and the profitability of the healthy competitors suffers as the sick ones hang on.[1] If the entire industry suffers from overcapacity, it may seek government help—particularly if foreign competition is present.
- The rivals are diverse in strategies, origins, and "personalities." They have different ideas about how to compete and continually run head-on into each other in the process.

As an industry matures, its growth rate changes, resulting in declining profits and (often) a shakeout. In the booming recreational vehicle industry of the early 1970s, nearly every producer did well; but slow growth since then has eliminated the high returns, except for the strongest members, not to mention many of the weaker companies. The same profit story has been played out in industry after industry—snowmobiles, aerosol packaging, and sports equipment are just a few examples.

An acquisition can introduce a very different personality to an industry, as has been the case with Black & Decker's takeover of McCullough, the producer of chain saws. Technological innovation can boost the level of fixed costs in the production process, as it did in the shift from batch to continuous-line photo finishing in the 1960s.

While a company must live with many of these factors—because they are built into industry economics—it may have some latitude for improving matters through strategic shifts. For example, it may try to raise buyers' switching costs or increase product differentiation. A focus on selling efforts in the fastest-growing segments of the industry or on market areas with the lowest fixed costs can reduce the impact of industry rivalry. If it is feasible, a company can try to avoid confrontation with competitors having high exit barriers and can thus sidestep involvement in bitter price cutting.

---

[1]For a more complete discussion of exit barriers and their implications for strategy, see Michael L. Porter, "Please Note Location of Nearest Exit," *California Management Review,* Winter 1976, p. 21.

Formulation of Strategy

Once the corporate strategist has assessed the forces affecting competition in his industry and their underlying causes, he can identify his company's strengths and weaknesses. The crucial strengths and weaknesses from a strategic standpoint are the company's posture vis-à-vis the underlying causes of each force. Where does it stand against substitutes? Against the sources of entry barriers?

Then the strategist can devise a plan of action that may include (1) positioning the company so that its capabilities provide the best defense against the competitive force; and/or (2) influencing the balance of the forces through strategic moves, thereby improving the company's position; and/or (3) anticipating shifts in the factors underlying the forces and responding to them, with the hope of exploiting change by choosing a strategy appropriate for the new competitive balance before opponents recognize it. I shall consider each strategic approach in turn.

Positioning the Company

The first approach takes the structure of the industry as given and matches the company's strengths and weaknesses to it. Strategy can be viewed as building defenses against the competitive forces or as finding positions in the industry where the forces are weakest.

Knowledge of the company's capabilities and of the causes of the competitive forces will highlight the areas where the company should confront competition and where to avoid it. If the company is a low-cost producer, it may choose to confront powerful buyers while it takes care to sell them only products not vulnerable to competition from substitutes.

The success of Dr Pepper in the soft drink industry illustrates the coupling of realistic knowledge of corporate strengths with sound industry analysis to yield a superior strategy. Coca-Cola and Pepsi-Cola dominate Dr Pepper's industry, where many small concentrate producers compete for a piece of the action. Dr Pepper chose a strategy of avoiding the largest-selling drink segment, maintaining a narrow flavor line, forgoing the development of a captive bottler network, and marketing heavily. The company positioned itself so as to be least vulnerable to its competitive forces while it exploited its small size.

In the $11.5 billion soft drink industry, barriers to entry in the form of brand identification, large-scale marketing, and access to a bottler network are enormous. Rather than accept the formidable costs and scale economies in having its own bottler network—that is, following the lead of the Big Two and of Seven-Up—Dr Pepper took advantage of the different flavor of its drink to "piggyback" on Coke and Pepsi bottlers who wanted a full line to sell to customers. Dr Pepper coped with the power of these buyers through extraordinary service and other efforts to distinguish its treatment of them from that of Coke and Pepsi.

Many small companies in the soft drink business offer cola drinks that thrust them into head-to-head competition against the majors. Dr Pepper, however, maximized product differentiation by maintaining a narrow line of beverages built around an unusual flavor.

Finally, Dr Pepper met Coke and Pepsi with an advertising onslaught emphasizing the alleged uniqueness of its single flavor. This campaign built strong brand identification and great customer loyalty. Helping its efforts was the fact that Dr Pepper's formula involved lower raw materials cost, which gave the company an absolute cost advantage over its major competitors.

There are no economies of scale in soft drink concentrate production, so Dr Pepper could prosper despite its small share of the business (6%). Thus Dr Pepper confronted competition in marketing but avoided it in product line and in distribution. This artful positioning combined with good implementation has led to an enviable record in earnings and in the stock market.

Influencing the Balance

When dealing with the forces that drive industry competition, a company can devise a strategy that takes the offensive. This posture is designed to do more than merely cope with the forces themselves; it is meant to alter their causes.

Innovations in marketing can raise brand identification or otherwise differentiate the product. Capital investments in large-scale facilities or vertical integration affect entry barriers. The balance of forces is partly a result of external factors and partly in the company's control.

Exploiting Industry Change

Industry evolution is important strategically because evolution, of course, brings with it changes in the sources of competition I have identified. In the familiar product life-cycle pattern, for example, growth rates change, product differentiation is said to decline as the business becomes more mature, and the companies tend to integrate vertically.

These trends are not so important in themselves; what is critical is whether they affect the sources of competition. Consider vertical integration. In the maturing minicomputer industry, extensive vertical integration, both in manufacturing and in software development, is taking place. This very significant trend is greatly raising economies of scale as well as the amount of capital necessary to compete in the industry. This in turn is raising barriers to entry and may drive some smaller competitors out of the industry once growth levels off.

Obviously, the trends carrying the highest priority from a strategic standpoint are those that affect the most important sources of competition in the industry and those that elevate new causes to the forefront. In contract aerosol packaging, for example, the trend toward less product differentiation is now dominant. It has increased buyers' power, lowered the barriers to entry, and intensified competition.

The framework for analyzing competition that I have described can also be used to predict the eventual profitability of an industry. In long-range planning the task is to examine each competitive force, forecast the magnitude of each underlying cause, and then construct a composite picture of the likely profit potential of the industry.

The outcome of such an exercise may differ a great deal from the existing industry structure. Today, for example, the solar heating business is populated by dozens and perhaps hundreds of companies, none with a major market position. Entry is easy, and competitors are battling to establish solar heating as a superior substitute for conventional methods.

The potential of this industry will depend largely on the shape of the future barriers to entry, the improvement of the industry's position relative to substitutes, the ultimate intensity of competition, and the power captured by buyers and suppliers. These characteristics will in turn be influenced by such factors as the establishment of brand identities, significant economies of scale or experience curves in equipment manufacture wrought by technological change, the ultimate capital costs to compete, and the extent of overhead in production facilities.

The framework for analyzing industry competition has direct benefits in setting diversification strategy. It provides a road map for answering the extremely difficult question inherent in diversification decisions. "What is the potential of this business?" Combining the framework with judgment in its application, a company may be able to spot an industry with a good future before this good future is reflected in the prices of acquisition candidates.

Multifaceted Rivalry

Corporate managers have directed a great deal of attention to defining their businesses as a crucial step in strategy formulation. Theodore Levitt, in his classic 1960 article in *HBR*, argued strongly for avoiding the myopia of narrow, product-oriented industry definition.[2] Numerous other authorities have also stressed the need to look beyond product to function in defining a business, beyond national boundaries to potential international competition, and beyond the ranks of one's competitors today to those that may become competitors tomorrow. As a result of these urgings, the proper definition of a company's industry or industries has become an endlessly debated subject.

One motive behind this debate is the desire to exploit new markets. Another, perhaps more important motive is the fear of overlooking latent sources of competition that someday may threaten the industry. Many managers concentrate so single-mindedly on their direct antagonists in the fight for market share that they fail to realize that they are also competing with their customers and their suppliers for bargaining power. Meanwhile, they also neglect to keep a wary eye out for new entrants to the contest or fail to recognize the subtle threat of substitute products.

The key to growth—even survival—is to stake out a position that is less vulnerable to attack from head-to-head opponents, whether established or new,

---

[2]Theodore Levitt, "Marketing Myopia," reprinted as an *HBR* Classic, September-October 1975, p. 26.

and less vulnerable to erosion from the direction of buyers, suppliers, and substitute goods. Establishing such a position can take many forms—solidifying relationships with favorable customers, differentiating the product either substantively or psychologically through marketing, integrating forward or backward, establishing a technological leadership.

5

Marketing Cost Analysis: A Modularized Contribution Approach

For managers concerned with the profitability of their various products, territories, and types of customers.

Patrick M. Dunne and Harry I. Wolk

In recent years, an increasing use of accounting information for planning, controlling, and evaluating the firm's marketing performance has been advocated in the literature.[1] Some of this published material is very sophisticated, and indeed there is almost no limit to how far one can go in analyzing the effectiveness of marketing operations by accounting techniques. At the same time, it is truly astounding that many marketing managers do not use even some of the more elementary accounting tools that are available.

The authors know of one company where Product X was generating an annual profit of $800,000 and Product Y was losing money at $600,000 per year—and management was totally unaware of the situation, just pleasantly happy to be making $200,000! They were simply astounded when a little accounting by product line revealed Product Y to be such a drain.

Not quite that elementary, but still well within the group of non-accounting trained managers, is the *modular contribution-margin income statement*. This technique spotlights the behavior of controllable costs and indicates each seg-

This article first appeared in the *Journal of Marketing* (July 1977):83–94. Reprinted with permission from *Journal of Marketing*, published by the American Marketing Association.

When this article was published the authors were Associate Professor of Marketing, Texas Tech University, Lubbock; and Professor of Accounting, Drake University, Des Moines, respectively.

ment's contribution to profit and indirect fixed costs. It is a very useful tool for marketing managers who are concerned not only with the efficiency of the operation for which they are responsible, but also with the profitability of the product, various territories, channels, types and sizes of customer, etc.

In order to generate accounting information for specific market segments, a detailed data base is a necessity. All transactions entering the system must be classified and coded so that costs can be matched with revenues at desired aggregation levels for different combinations of relevant factors. But the payoff is usually worth the effort. The modular contribution margin approach to marketing analysis enables management (a) to judge the profitability of a specific marketing mix in a specific area and (b) to decide whether or not to take action to change it.

Case Example

Consider the D-W Appliance Company, a small appliance manufacturer that produces blenders and mixers on separate production lines. The firm's marketing division is organized along territorial lines (East and West), and the products are sold by sales representatives through two marketing channels: (1) to wholesalers, who, in turn, distribute to small retailers, and (2) directly to large retailers. Order size is also important: channel costs are lower for orders of 100 units or more of either product.

If the Marketing Division Manager wanted to assess the profitability of his functional area, he might request an income statement. Under the full-cost approach to financial statements, costs would be separated according to function: cost of goods sold and operating expenses. A portion of the general expense of the company cost centers (accounting, corporate headquarters, etc.) would arbitrarily be allocated to the operating expense of the Marketing Division. (See Exhibit 1.)

This type of statement is, however, better suited to external reporting than to internal managerial planning and control, since it contains costs which do not directly affect decisions in the marketing area and which are not controllable by the Marketing Division Manager. Furthermore, in order to apply variance analysis to this kind of statement, comparing budgeted results with actual results for control purposes, the costs would first have to be separated by activity before the analysis could distinguish between cost changes in the level of an activity and those due to other causes.

The main advantage of the modular contribution margin approach as a managerial tool for planning and control is that it separates costs, by behavior, into variable and fixed costs.[2]

Variable costs are those costs which vary predictably with some measure of activity during a given time-period. For example, commissions on sales for D-W are set at 10% of sales revenue. Total commission expense varies as sales vary.

Fixed costs, on the other hand, are costs which do not change in the short-run, e.g., the Marketing Division Manager's salary.

Exhibit 1   Income Statement Models

Full-Cost Approach

Revenue
Less: Cost of Goods Sold

Gross Margin
Less: Operating Expenses
        (including the division's allocated share of company administrative and general expenses)

Net Income

Contribution Margin Approach

Revenue
Less: Variable Manufacturing Costs
        Other Variable Costs directly traceable to the segment

Contribution Margin
Less: Fixed Costs directly traceable to products
        Fixed Costs directly traceable to the market segment

Segment Net Income

Cost Behavior and Controllability

The modular contribution margin model, which allows separation of costs by behavior, can be expanded to include separation of costs by controllability. (See Cost Analysis Model table.)

Cost Analysis Model

Controllable Variable Costs	Controllable Fixed Costs
Uncontrollable Variable Costs	Uncontrollable Fixed Costs

Controllable costs are those costs which originate in the particular organizational unit under consideration. Whether a cost is classified as controllable or uncontrollable obviously depends on the organizational segment under consideration. Territorial expenses in the statement for East Territory would be controllable costs for that territory and for the Marketing Division, but not for the West Territory.

As just suggested, controllability relates to the degree of influence over a cost by the relevant division manager. Labor costs that exceed standard costs for actual production in a particular department are a classic example of a cost for which the appropriate manager would be held accountable. However, even for this classification, a great deal of care must be exercised. Actual controllable labor costs may exceed standard because of many reasons beyond the manager's scope or control. For example, delivery time for shipments may be delayed by severe weather. Furthermore, controllability may be constrained by economic externalities. Selling costs would be a controllable variable cost of the Marketing Division, while the manager probably has little, if any, influence over a price decline precipitated by a competitor's action.

Controllable fixed costs are rarely controllable in the very short run. Once a fixed asset is acquired, there is virtually no control over the annual depreciation charges. One may select the depreciation method, but no differences will arise between actual and budgeted costs except in those situations where depreciation can be calculated on usage. There are, however, some intermediate-term fixed costs (often called discretionary or programmed costs because they are determined annually on a budgetary basis) which may be highly controllable; i.e., actual costs may exceed budgeted costs. Advertising and R&D costs fall into this category.

Uncontrollable variable costs are variable costs which are not incurred in the segment under consideration. Therefore, the costs should be expressed as standard costs so that a manager will not be held responsible for the inefficiencies of another department. Variable manufacturing costs of blenders and mixers would be indirect variable costs for the Marketing Division, and should be expressed in the budget at standard costs.

Uncontrollable fixed costs are not included in segmental income statements since any basis of allocation to the segment would necessarily be arbitrary. Uncontrollable costs are often called common costs and for the Marketing Division would include a portion of those costs of the corporate headquarters and those manufacturing costs which couldn't be directly allocated to blenders and mixers, such as the plant manager's salary.

Segmental Analysis

Contribution margin income statements by department are useful for budgeting, performance analysis, short-run decision-making, pricing, and decisions between alternatives—e.g., whether to close down a warehouse or relocate it; whether to lease a fleet of trucks or own them. Market segment income statements are also useful for such marketing decisions as whether to drop a product line and whether to alter the physical distribution system; and they aid in the redirection of effort to the company's more profitable markets. The usual market segmentation is by product line, territory, channel, order size, and customer, but any of the segmentation bases of the marketing matrix of the firm's target markets could be used.

A modular data base also facilitates statements focusing on functional areas, depending on management's judgment about what information is relevant for decision-making and control. For example, if transportation is judged to be a crucial function in the case of blenders, then the expense for shipping blenders would be coded by that function and by the relevant variables (territory, channel, product, order size, customer, date). Revenue, in turn, would be coded at the time of each transaction.

Unless the company's information system is somewhat sophisticated, there is usually some initial difficulty in constructing accounting statements of functional/departmental areas.[3] Costs for a specific department must be broken out of the natural accounts via estimation techniques. (Since costs are usually accumulated in natural accounts, such as salary expense, the salary expense for the Marketing Division would have to be calculated.)

Under the modular contribution margin approach not all costs are allocated to segments. Rather, only those costs are considered which would disappear if the company were to drop that department or segment. Note that this is acceptable only for purposes of internal decision-making, and *not* for differential cost justification under the Robinson-Patman Act (as demonstrated in the Borden case) or for general financial reporting purposes (audited reports to stockholders, IRS returns, and SEC reports).

Allocation of Costs

Other refinements can be added to the modular contribution margin model. The charge for the specific assets used by the department (depreciation) could be based on the decline in the market value of the resources during the period. Or an interest charge on the working capital used by the department (based on the firm's actual cost of capital) could be included to give a clear picture of the department's operations and actual contribution.

Allocation, however, cannot be made arbitrarily on the basis of sales volume since that focus might overlook other relevant information. For example, how do you attach distribution expense to blenders and mixers for a mixed shipment of both products, when blenders are bulkier, heavier, and require more handling? Or if mixers are easy to sell to large retailers, while blenders require extensive sales effort, the entry of salesmen's expenses to blenders and mixers should reflect this difference.

If costs are based on a factor such as weight or space occupied, this may allow an equitable basis of cost assignment. This does not always happen, though, and so assigning costs to departments on the basis of weight can be highly misleading for analytical purposes. Suffice it to say that wherever variable costs are predictable and vary with a given base, standard costs should be used in budgeting for the Marketing Division.

The value of a modular contribution margin statement is the ability to match costs with revenues for the smallest market segments desired and then to aggregate these modules into statements for larger segments. Essentially, the modular data base provides management with the capability of transforming accounting information into two systems: one based on departments within the firm, the other based on market segments.

Useful Information

The flexibility and responsiveness of the modular contribution margin approach for market segments can be shown by applying it to the D-W Appliance Company. The first step is for management to decide on the relevant factors for ex-

**Exhibit 2   Segmental Contribution Income Statements:
D-W Appliance Company**

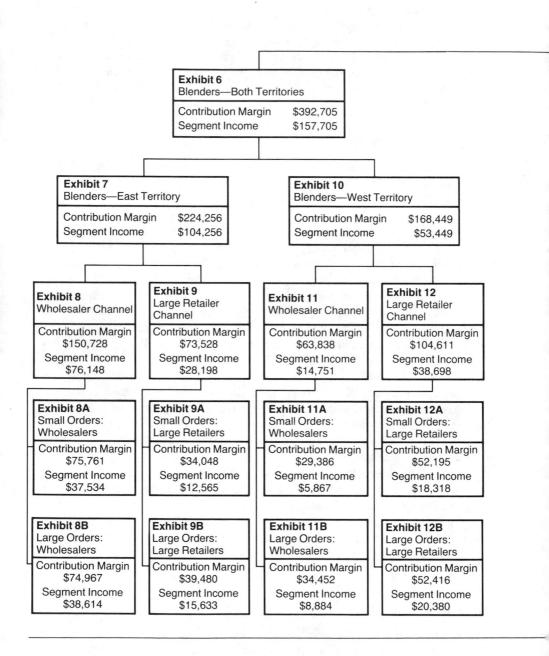

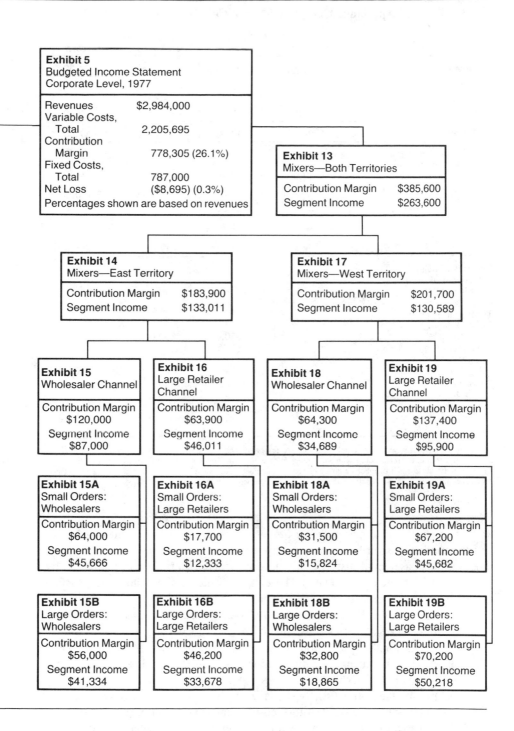

Exhibit 5
Budgeted Income Statement
Corporate Level, 1977

Revenues	$2,984,000
Variable Costs,	
Total	2,205,695
Contribution	
Margin	778,305 (26.1%)
Fixed Costs,	
Total	787,000
Net Loss	($8,695) (0.3%)

Percentages shown are based on revenues

Exhibit 13
Mixers—Both Territories

Contribution Margin	$385,600
Segment Income	$263,600

Exhibit 14
Mixers—East Territory

Contribution Margin	$183,900
Segment Income	$133,011

Exhibit 17
Mixers—West Territory

Contribution Margin	$201,700
Segment Income	$130,589

Exhibit 15
Wholesaler Channel

Contribution Margin
$120,000
Segment Income
$87,000

Exhibit 16
Large Retailer
Channel

Contribution Margin
$63,900
Segment Income
$46,011

Exhibit 18
Wholesaler Channel

Contribution Margin
$64,300
Segment Income
$34,689

Exhibit 19
Large Retailer
Channel

Contribution Margin
$137,400
Segment Income
$95,900

Exhibit 15A
Small Orders:
Wholesalers

Contribution Margin
$64,000
Segment Income
$45,666

Exhibit 16A
Small Orders:
Large Retailers

Contribution Margin
$17,700
Segment Income
$12,333

Exhibit 18A
Small Orders:
Wholesalers

Contribution Margin
$31,500
Segment Income
$15,824

Exhibit 19A
Small Orders:
Large Retailers

Contribution Margin
$67,200
Segment Income
$45,682

Exhibit 15B
Large Orders:
Wholesalers

Contribution Margin
$56,000
Segment Income
$41,334

Exhibit 16B
Large Orders:
Large Retailers

Contribution Margin
$46,200
Segment Income
$33,678

Exhibit 18B
Large Orders:
Wholesalers

Contribution Margin
$32,800
Segment Income
$18,865

Exhibit 19B
Large Orders:
Large Retailers

Contribution Margin
$70,200
Segment Income
$50,218

Exhibit 3   D-W Appliance Company Master Cost Data Sheet for 1977

	East		West	
	Blenders	Mixers	Blenders	Mixers
Revenue (per unit)	$ 42.00	$ 26.00	$ 38.00	$ 24.00
Variable Manufacturing Costs	$ 20.00	$ 15.00	$ 20.00	$ 15.00
Variable Selling Costs (10% of revenue)	4.20	2.60	3.80	2.40
Total	**$ 24.20**	**$ 17.60**	**$ 23.80**	**$ 17.40**
Contribution Margin Per Unit Before Channel Costs	$ 17.80	$ 8.40	$ 14.20	$ 6.60
Programmed Advertising Costs[a]	$20,000	$12,000	$15,000	$10,000
Budgeted Sales (units)	15,000	28,000	15,000	44,000

	Blenders	Mixers	East	West	Unallocated
Controllable Direct Manufacturing Costs	$200,000	$100,000			
Territorial Fixed Costs (joint to products)			$50,000	$30,000	
Joint Fixed Manufacturing Costs					$100,000
Corporate Headquarters Costs					$250,000

[a]Programmed advertising costs are fixed costs that are reviewed each year through the budget process. (Therefore, they are not in a direct relationship with sales revenue or units sold. This could result from having a particular ad aimed at only one channel member or group of channel members. An example would be a trade magazine ad in a conference program for a Wholesalers Convention. Such an ad would not reach the retailer.)

amination. In this example, *product line* was chosen as the basic unit of interest, and the market was further segmented by territory, channel, and order size. (The modular data base could just as easily have provided for primary segmentation by territory or channel, or whatever.) The exhibits which follow show the possible modular income statements that can be constructed.

Exhibit 2 shows the hierarchy and linkages among the segmental contribution margin income statements illustrated here.

Basic data for the illustration is shown in Exhibit 3, the Master Cost Data Sheet. Unit sales and channel of distribution costs are broken down by territory, product, and channel in Exhibit 4.

Income for the entire firm is shown in Exhibit 5. It is the only statement containing $430,000 of costs (territory costs, joint manufacturing costs, and corporate headquarters costs) which are joint to the product oriented segmental income statements shown in Exhibits 6–19.

Exhibit 4   Budgeted Channel of Distribution Costs

	Wholesaler Small Order	Channel Large Order	Large Retailer Small Order	Channel Large Order
East:				
Blenders:				
Budgeted Sales (units)	5,119	4,868	2,381	2,632
Cost Per Unit	$ 3.00	$ 2.40	$ 3.50	$ 2.80
Total	$15,357	$11,683	$ 8,334	$ 7,370
Mixers:				
Budgeted Sales (units)	10,000	8,000	3,000	7,000
Cost Per Unit	$ 2.00	$ 1.40	$ 2.50	$ 1.80
Total	$20,000	$11,200	$7,500	$12,600
West:				
Blenders:				
Budgeted Sales (units)	2,881	3,132	4,619	4,368
Cost Per Unit	$ 4.00	$ 3.20	$ 2.90	$ 2.20
Total	$11,524	$10,022	$13,395	$ 9,610
Mixers:				
Budgeted Sales (units)	9,000	8,000	14,000	13,000
Cost Per Unit	$ 3.10	$ 2.50	$ 1.80	$ 1.20
Total	$27,900	$20,000	$25,200	$15,600

Clues for Action

The loss at the corporate level (as shown in Exhibit 5), indicates that the firm should either strengthen, if possible, those segments which are weakest and/or reallocate more of its resources to those segments which are strongest.

In Exhibits 6 and 13, Total Income Statements for blenders and mixers, blenders are stronger than mixers in terms of Contribution Margin (32.7% versus 21.6%) although slightly less profitable after taking into account direct fixed costs (13.1% versus 14.8%). This may indicate that not enough programmed advertising costs are being budgeted to blenders. More advertising effort may be needed to effectively exploit higher Contribution Margin of blenders.

At the same time, the further breakdowns indicate that the Segment Income of the West Territory is lagging behind the East Territory for both blenders and mixers (see Exhibits 7, 10, 14, and 17). The biggest reason for this poor performance is the very low Segment Income of the Wholesaler Channels in the West Territory (Exhibits 11 and 18).

Action to improve the situation is especially called for in the Wholesaler Channel for blenders in the West Territory. Not only is the Segment Income per-

Exhibits 5 and 6–12   Total Income Statements

Exhibit 7
Blenders—East Territory

Revenues (15,000 units)	**$630,000**
Variable Costs:	
Manufacturing Marketing:	$300,000
Selling	63,000 10.0%
Channel Costs	42,744 6.8%
Total	**$405,744**
Contribution Margin	**$224,256 35.6%**
Fixed Costs:	
Programmed Advertising	$ 20,000 3.2%
Direct (to product) Manufacturing Costs	100,000
Total	**$120,000**
Segment Income	**$104,256 16.5%**

Exhibit 8
Wholesaler Channel

	Small Order (5119 units)	Large Order (4868 units)	Total
Revenues	$214,998	$204,456	$419,454
Variable Costs:			
Manufacturing			
Marketing:	$102,380	$ 97,360	$199,740
Selling	21,500 10.0%	20,446 10.0%	41,946 10.0%
Channel Costs	15,357 7.1%	11,683 5.7%	27,040 6.4%
Total	**$139,237**	**$129,489**	**$268,726**
Contribution Margin	**$ 75,761 35.2%**	**$ 74,967 36.7%**	**$150,728 35.9%**
Fixed Costs:			
Programmed Advertising[1]	$ 4,100 1.9%	$ 3,900 1.9%	$ 8,000 1.9%
Direct (to product) Manufacturing Costs[2]	34,127	32,453	66,580
Total	**$ 38,227**	**$ 36,353**	**$ 74,580**
Segment Income	**$ 37,534 17.5%**	**$ 38,614 18.9%**	**$ 76,148 18.2%**

Exhibit 9
Large Retailer Channel

	Small Order (2381 units)	Large Order (2632 units)	Total
Revenues	$100,002	$110,544	$210,546
Variable Costs:			
Manufacturing			
Marketing:	$ 47,620	$ 52,640	$100,260
Selling	10,000 10.0%	11,054 10.0%	21,054 10.0%
Channel Costs	8,334 8.3%	7,370 6.7%	15,704 7.5%
Total	**$ 65,954**	**$ 71,064**	**$137,018**
Contribution Margin	**$ 34,048 34.0%**	**$ 39,480 35.7%**	**$ 73,528 34.9%**
Fixed Costs:			
Programmed Advertising[1]	$ 5,700 5.7%	$ 6,300 5.7%	$ 12,000 5.7%
Direct (to product) Manufacturing Costs[2]	15,783	17,547	33,330
Total	**$ 21,483**	**$ 23,847**	**$ 45,330**
Segment Income	**$ 12,565 12.6%**	**$ 15,633 14.1%**	**$ 28,198 13.4%**

[1] Direct to the Large Retailer Channel and allocated in accordance with revenues. The same procedure is used for channel analysis in later exhibits.

[2] Allocated in proportion of number of units sold in each order size for this channel to total sales. The same procedure is used in later exhibits.

Exhibit 5
Corporate Level, 1977

Revenues	$2,984,000
Variable Costs:	
Manufacturing Marketing:	$1,680,000
Selling	298,400 10.0%[1]
Channel Costs	227,295 7.6%
Total	**$2,205,695**
Contribution Margin	**$ 778,305 26.1%**
Fixed Costs:	
Programmed Advertising	$ 57,000 1.9%
Direct (to product) Manu-	
facturing Costs	300,000
Territory Costs	80,000
Joint Manufacturing Costs	100,000
Corporate Headquarters Costs	250,000
Total	**$ 787,000**
Net Loss	**($8,695) (.3%)**

[1]Percentages shown are
based upon revenues.

Exhibit 6
Blenders—Both Territories

Revenues (30,000 units)	$1,200,000
Variable Costs:	
Manufacturing Marketing:	$ 600,000
Selling	120,000 10.0%
Channel Costs	87,295 7.3%
Total	**$ 807,295**
Contribution Margin	**$ 392,705 32.7%**
Fixed Costs:	
Programmed Advertising	$ 35,000 2.9%
Direct (to product) Manu-	
facturing Costs	200,000
Total	**$ 235,000**
Segment Income	**$ 157,705 13.1%**

Exhibit 10
Blenders—West Territory

Revenues (15,000 units)	$570,000
Variable Costs:	
Manufacturing Marketing:	$300,000
Selling	57,000 10.0%
Channel Costs	44,551 7.8%
Total	**$401,551**
Contribution Margin	**$168,449 29.6%**
Fixed Costs:	
Programmed Advertising	$ 15,000 2.6%
Direct (to product) Manu-	
facturing Costs	100,000
Total	**$115,000**
Segment Income	**$ 53,449 9.4%**

Exhibit 11
Wholesaler Channel

	Small Order (2881 units)	Large Order (3132 units)	Total
Revenues	$109,478	$119,016	$228,494
Variable Costs:			
Manufacturing			
Marketing:	$ 57,620	$ 62,640	$120,260
Selling	10,948 10.0%	11,902 10.0%	22,850 10.0%
Channel Costs	11,524 10.5%	10,022 8.4%	21,546 9.4%
Total	**$ 80,092**	**$ 84,564**	**$164,656**
Contribution Margin	**$ 29,386 26.8%**	**$ 34,452 28.9%**	**$ 63,838 27.9%**
Fixed Costs:			
Programmed Advertising	$ 4,312 3.9%	$ 4,688 3.9%	$ 9,000 3.9%
Direct (to product) Manufacturing Costs	19,207	20,880	40,087
Total	**$ 23,519**	**$ 25,568**	**$ 49,087**
Segment Income	**$ 5,867 5.4%**	**$ 8,884 7.5%**	**$ 14,751 6.5%**

Exhibit 12
Large Retailer Channel

	Small Order (4619 units)	Large Order (4368 units)	Total
Revenues	$175,522	$165,984	$341,506
Variable Costs:			
Manufacturing			
Marketing:	$ 92,380	$ 87,360	$179,740
Selling	17,552 10.0%	16,598 10.0%	34,150 10.0%
Channel Costs	13,395 7.6%	9,610 5.8%	23,005 6.7%
Total	**$123,327**	**$113,568**	**$236,895**
Contribution Margin	**$ 52,195 29.7%**	**$ 52,416 31.6%**	**$104,611 30.6%**
Fixed Costs:			
Programmed Advertising	$ 3,084 1.8%	$ 2,916 1.8%	$ 6,000 1.8%
Direct (to product) Manufacturing Costs	30,793	29,120	59,913
Total	**$ 33,877**	**$ 32,036**	**$ 65,913**
Segment Income	**$ 18,318 10.4%**	**$ 20,380 12.3%**	**$ 38,698 11.3%**

Exhibits 5 and 13–19   Total Income Statements

Exhibit 5
Corporate Level, 1977

Revenues	**$2,984,000**
Variable Costs:	
Manufacturing Marketing:	$1,680,000
Selling	298,400 10.0%[1]
Channel Costs	227,295 7.6%
Total	**$2,205,695**
Contribution Margin	**$ 778,305 26.1%**
Fixed Costs:	
Programmed Advertising	$ 57,000 1.9%
Direct (to product) Manu-	
facturing Costs	300,000
Territory Costs	80,000
Joint Manufacturing Costs	100,000
Corporate Headquarters Costs	250,000
Total	**$ 787,000**
Net Loss	**($8,695) (.3%)**

Exhibit 14
Mixers—East Territory

Revenues (28,000 units)	**$728,000**
Variable Costs:	
Manufacturing Marketing:	$420,000
Selling	72,800 10.0%
Channel Costs	51,300 7.0%
Total	**$544,100**
Contribution Margin	**$183,900 25.3%**
Fixed Costs:	
Programmed Advertising	$ 12,000 1.6%
Direct (to product) Manu-	
facturing Costs	38,889
Total	**$ 50,889**
Segment Income	**$133,011 18.3%**

Exhibit 13
Mixers—Both Territories

Revenues (72,000 units)	**$1,784,000**
Variable Costs:	
Manufacturing Marketing:	$1,080,000
Selling	178,400 10.0%
Channel Costs	140,000 7.8%
Total	**$1,398,400**
Contribution Margin	**$ 385,600 21.6%**
Fixed Costs:	
Programmed Advertising	$ 22,000 1.2%
Direct (to product) Manu-	
facturing Costs	100,000
Total	**$ 122,000**
Segment Income	**$ 263,600 14.8%**

Exhibit 15
Wholesaler Channel

	Small Order (10,000 units)	Large Order (8,000 units)	Total
Revenues	$260,000	$208,000	$468,000
Variable Costs:			
Manufacturing Marketing:	$150,000	$120,000	$270,000
Selling	26,000 10.0%	20,800 10.0%	46,800 10.0%
Channel Costs	20,000 7.7%	11,200 5.4%	31,200 6.7%
Total	**$196,000**	**$152,000**	**$348,000**
Contribution Margin	**$ 64,000 24.6%**	**$ 56,000 26.9%**	**$120,000 25.6%**
Fixed Costs:			
Programmed Advertising	$ 4,445 1.7%	$ 3,555 1.7%	$ 8,000 1.7%
Direct (to product) Manufacturing Costs	13,889	11,111	25,000
Total	**$ 18,334**	**$ 14,666**	**$ 33,000**
Segment Income	**$ 45,666 17.6%**	**$ 41,334 19.8%**	**$ 87,000 18.6%**

Exhibit 16
Large Retailer Channel

	Small Order (3,000 units)	Large Order (7,000 units)	Total
Revenues	$78,000	$182,000	$260,000
Variable Costs:			
Manufacturing Marketing:	$45,000	$105,000	$150,000
Selling	7,800 10.0%	18,200 10.0%	26,100 10.0%
Channel Costs	7,500 9.6%	12,600 6.9%	20,100 7.7%
Total	**$60,300**	**$135,800**	**$196,100**
Contribution Margin	**$17,700 22.7%**	**$ 46,200 25.4%**	**$ 63,900 24.6%**
Fixed Costs:			
Programmed Advertising	$ 1,200 1.5%	$ 2,800 1.5%	$ 4,000 1.5%
Direct (to product) Manufacturing Costs	4,167	9,722	13,889
Total	**$ 5,367**	**$ 12,522**	**$ 17,889**
Segment Income	**$12,333 15.8%**	**$ 33,678 18.5%**	**$ 46,011 17.7%**

Exhibit 17
Mixers—West Territory

Revenues	$1,056,000
Variable Costs: Manufacturing Marketing: Selling Channel Costs	$ 660,000 105,600 10.0% 88,700 8.4%
Total	$ 854,300
Contribution Margin	$ 201,700 19.1%
Fixed Costs: Programmed Advertising Direct (to product) Manu- facturing Costs	$ 10,000 .9% 61,111
Total	$ 71,111
Segment Income	$ 130,589 12.4%

Exhibit 18
Wholesaler Channel

	Small Order (9000 units)	Large Order (8000 units)	Total
Revenues	$216,000	$192,000	$408,000
Variable Costs: Manufacturing Marketing: Selling Channel Costs	$135,000 21,600 10.0% 27,900 12.9%	$120,000 29,200 10.0% 20,000 10.4%	$255,000 40,800 10.0% 47,900 11.7%
Total	$184,500	$159,200	$343,700
Contribution Margin	$ 31,500 14.6%	$ 32,800 17.1%	$ 64,300 15.8%
Fixed Costs: Programmed Advertising Direct (to prod- uct) Manufac- turing Costs	$ 3,176 1.5% 12,500	$ 2,824 1.5% 11,111	$ 6,000 1.5% 23,611
Total	$ 15,676	$ 13,935	$ 29,611
Segment Income	$ 15,824 7.3%	$ 18,865 9.8%	$ 34,689 8.5%

Exhibit 19
Large Retailer Channel

	Small Order (14,000 units)	Large Order (13,000 units)	Total
Revenues	$336,000	$312,000	$648,000
Variable Costs: Manufacturing Marketing: Selling Channel Costs	$210,000 33,600 10.0% 25,200 7.5%	$195,000 31,200 10.0% 15,600 5.0%	$405,000 64,800 10.0% 40,800 6.3%
Total	$268,800	$241,800	$510,600
Contribution Margin	$ 67,200 20.0%	$ 70,200 22.5%	$137,400 21.2%
Fixed Costs: Programmed Advertising Direct (to prod- uct) Manufac- turing Costs	$ 2,074 .6% 19,444	$ 1,926 .6% 18,056	$ 4,000 .6% 37,500
Total	$ 21,518	$ 19,982	$ 41,500
Segment Income	$ 45,682 13.6%	$ 50,218 16.1%	$ 95,900 14.8%

centage (6.5%) the lowest for any segment in the whole analysis, but the corresponding Contribution Margin is relatively strong (27.9%). The problem is one of spreading heavy fixed costs of manufacturing over more sales. The solution, again, would be to take advantage of the good contribution margin percentage through increased advertising effort or, perhaps in this case, by expanding the sales force.

As another indication of the revealing capability of this kind of analysis, consider the profitability of the two channels. If they had simply been compared in total (as a form of primary segmentation), the figures would have been:

Channel	Contribution Margin %	Segment %	Income $
Wholesaler	26.3%	12.9%	$212.588
Large Retailer	27.8%	14.3%	$208,807

The two channels would have appeared to be very even in profitability. Yet recombining in various ways brings out still more information. Exhibit 20 shows that if the Wholesaler Channel in the West could be improved to match the

Exhibit 20   Aggregate Comparison of Wholesaler Channel and Large Retailer Channel

Channel	Contribution Margin (%)	Segment %	Income $	Total
WHOLESALERS[a]	[26.3%][c]	[12.9%][c]		[$212,588][c]
West				
blenders	27.9%	6.5%	$14,751	
mixers	15.8%	8.5%	$34,689	
Subtotal				$ 49,440
East				
blenders	35.9%	18.2%	$76,148	
mixers	25.6%	18.6%	$87,000	
Subtotal				$163,148
LARGE RETAILERS[b]	[27.8%][c]	[14.3%][c]		[$208,807][c]
West blenders	30.6%	11.3%	$38,698	
mixers	21.2%	14.8%	$95,900	
Subtotal				$134,598
East				
blenders	34.9%	13.4%	$28,198	
mixers	24.6%	17.7%	$46,011	
Subtotal				$74,209

[a]Exhibits 8, 11, 15, and 18.
[b]Exhibits 9, 12, 16, and 19.
[c]Aggregate totals.

Wholesaler Channel in the East, the total Wholesaler Channel would have outper-formed the Large Retailer Channel.

Within the Large Retailer Channel, blenders and mixers in the East are rel-atively more profitable in terms of both Contribution Margin and Segment Income percentages than their counterparts in the West. However, Segment Income in total dollars for blenders and mixers in the East ($74,209) is barely half of that for the corresponding products in the West for the Large Retailer Channel ($134,598). Maybe the East Territory for Large Retailers needs a greater dosage of advertising dollars to exploit its relative advantage. Perhaps the whole Large Retailer Channel needs some kind of revamping—a need that otherwise would never have been revealed except through segmental analysis.

Another aspect of the problem lies in order size. Exhibit 21 reveals that this is most evident within the Large Retailer Channel in the West. Within that terri-tory and channel, distribution costs for small order sizes of mixers are 50% greater per dollar of revenue than for large orders. Similarly, small orders of blenders in the West in the Large Retailer Channel are out of line relative to large orders (31% excess). Small order costs are also out of line relative to large orders for mixers in the East in both channels (39.1% and 42.6% for Large Retailers and Wholesalers). Efforts must be made to increase the size of Large Retailers' small orders, or the retailers responsible for these orders must be converted to buying from wholesalers.

Exhibit 21   Relative Distribution Costs by Order Size

Territory	Product	Large Order[1]	Small Order[1]	Relative Cost Excess[2]
Large Retailers				
West	Blenders	5.8%	7.6%	31.0%
West	Mixers	5.0%	7.5%	50.0%
East	Blenders	6.7%	8.3%	23.9%
East	Mixers	6.9%	9.6%	39.1%

Territory	Product	Large Order[3]	Small Order[3]	Relative Cost Excess[2]
Wholesalers				
West	Blenders	8.4%	10.5%	25%
West	Mixers	10.4%	12.9%	24%
East	Blenders	5.7%	7.1%	24.6%
East	Mixers	5.4%	7.7%	42.6%

[1]Channel costs as a percentage of revenues from Exhibits 9, 12, 16, 19.

[2]Percentage is based on large order size; for example, $7.6\% - 5.8\% = 1.8\%$ and $\dfrac{1.8\%}{5.8\%} = 31\%$.

[3]Channel costs as a percentage of revenues from Exhibits 8, 11, 15, 18.

Benefits of Segmentation

These are just a few of the possible areas where the use of the modular contribution margin income statement could improve management control and planning, for the sake of greater profitability. In addition, actual results can be compared against the projected budget for each segment to analyze management's performance or the effect of uncontrollable factors on that performance.

If segmental analysis had not been done at all, or if the segmentation had been conducted just by product (or just by territory, just by channel, or just by order size) many ideas for corrective action or expanded effort might not have been generated.

While the benefits of segmental statements must exceed costs of preparation, the power of the computer should lessen costs enough to make segmental analysis beneficial to an increasing number of companies.

Endnotes

1. For example, "Report of the Committee on Cost and Profitability Analyses for Marketing," *The Accounting Review Supplement* (1972), pp. 575–615; W. J. E. Crissy, Paul Fischer, and Frank H. Mossman, "Segmental Analysis: Key to Marketing Profitability," *Business Topics* (Spring 1973), pp. 42–49; V. H. Kirpalani and Stanley J. Shapiro, "Financial Dimensions of Marketing Management," **Journal of Marketing,** Vol. 37 No. 3 (July 1973), pp. 40–47; Leland L. Beik and Stephen L. Buzby, "Profitability Analysis by Market Segments," **Journal of Marketing,** Vol. 37 No. 3 (July 1973), pp 48–53; Frank H. Mossman, Paul Fischer and W. J. E. Crissy, "New Approaches to Analyzing Marketing Profitability," **Journal of Marketing,** Vol. 38 No. 2 (April 1974), pp. 43–48; Merritt J. Davoust, "Analyzing a Client's Customer Profitability Picture," *Management Adviser,* May-June 1974, pp. 15–19; Harry I. Wolk and Patrick M. Dunne, "Modularized Contribution Margin Income Statements for Marketing and Physical Distribution Analysis," *Research Issues in Logistics,* James F. Robeson and John Grabner, eds., (Columbus: The Ohio State University, 1975), pp. 199–210; Stephen L. Buzby and Lester E. Heitger, "Profit Oriented Reporting for Marketing Decision Makers," *Business Topics,* Summer 1976, pp. 60–68; Richard L. Lewis and Leo G. Erickson, "Distribution System Costing: An Overview," *Distribution System Costing: Concepts and Procedures,* John R. Grabner and William S. Sargent, eds. (Columbus: The Ohio State University, 1972), pp. 1–30.

2. Sophisticated methods for separating fixed and variable costs are shown in William J. Baumol and Charles H. Sevin, "Marketing Costs and Mathematical Programming," *New Decision-Making Tools for Managers,* Edward C. Bursk and John F. Chapman, eds. (New York: New American Library, Inc., 1963), pp. 247–65; and R. S. Gynther, "Improving Separation of Fixed and Variable Expenses," *Management Accounting,* June 1963, pp. 29–38.

3. Mossman, same as reference 1, pg 44.

6

The Marketing Audit Comes of Age

Philip Kotler, William Gregor, and William Rodgers

Comparing the marketing strategies and tactics of business units today versus ten years ago, the most striking impression is one of marketing strategy obsolescence. Ten years ago U.S. automobile companies were gearing up for their second post-war race to produce the largest car with the highest horsepower. Today companies are selling increasing numbers of small and medium-sized cars and fuel economy is a major selling point. Ten years ago computer companies were introducing ever-more powerful hardware for more sophisticated uses. Today they emphasize mini- and microcomputers and software.

It is not even necessary to take a ten-year period to show the rapid obsolescence of marketing strategies. The growth economy of 1950–1970 has been superseded by a volatile economy which produces new strategic surprises almost monthly. Competitors launch new products, customers switch their business, distributors lose their effectiveness, advertising costs skyrocket, government regulations are announced, and consumer groups attack. These changes represent both opportunities and problems and may demand periodic reorientations of the company's marketing operations.

Many companies feel that their marketing operations need regular reviews and overhauls but do not know how to proceed. Some companies simply make many small changes that are economically and politically feasible, but fail to get to the heart of the matter. True, the company develops an annual marketing plan but management normally does not take a deep and objective look at the market-

This article first appeared in the *Sloan Management Review*. Reprinted from *Sloan Management Review,* Winter 1977, pp. 25–43, by permission of the publisher. Copyright © 1977 by the Sloan Management Review Association. All rights reserved.

When the article was published the first author was Professor at Northwestern University and the following two were employed at the Management Analysis Center.

ing strategies, policies, organizations, and operations on a recurrent basis. At the other extreme, companies install aggressive new top marketing management hoping to shake down the marketing cobwebs. In between there must be more orderly ways to reorient marketing operations to changed environments and opportunities.

Enter the Marketing Audit

One hears more talk today about the *marketing audit* as being the answer to evaluating marketing practice just as the public accounting audit is the tool for evaluating company accounting practice. This might lead one to conclude that the marketing audit is a new idea and also a very distinct methodology. Neither of these conclusions is true.

The marketing audit as an idea dates back to the early fifties. Rudolph Dallmeyer, a former executive in Booz-Allen-Hamilton, remembers conducting marketing audits as early as 1952. Robert J. Lavidge, President of Elrick and Lavidge, dates his firm's performance of marketing audits to over two decades ago. In 1959, the American Management Associations published an excellent set of papers on the marketing audit under the title *Analyzing and Improving Marketing Performance,* Report No. 32, 1959. During the 1960s, the marketing audit received increasing mention in the lists of marketing services of management consulting firms. It was not until the turbulent seventies, however, that it began to penetrate management awareness as a possible answer to its needs.

As for whether the marketing audit has reached a high degree of methodological sophistication, the answer is generally no. Whereas two certified public accountants will handle an audit assignment using approximately the same methodology, two marketing auditors are likely to bring different conceptions of the auditing process to their task. However, a growing consensus on the major characteristics of a marketing audit is emerging and we can expect considerable progress to occur in the next few years.

In its fullest form and concept, a marketing audit has four basic characteristics. The first and most important is that it is *broad* rather than narrow in focus. The term "marketing audit" should be reserved for a *horizontal (or comprehensive) audit* covering the company's marketing environment, objectives, strategies, organization, and systems. In contrast, a *vertical (or in-depth) audit* occurs when management decides to take a deep look into some key marketing function, such as sales force management. A vertical audit should properly be called by the function that is being audited, such as a sales force audit, an advertising audit, or a pricing audit.

A second characteristic feature of a marketing audit is that it is conducted by someone who is *independent* of the operation that is being evaluated. There is some loose talk about self-audits, where a manager follows a checklist of questions concerning his own operation to make sure that he is touching all the bases.[1]

---

[1]Many useful checklist questions for marketers are found in C. Eldridge, *The Management of the Marketing Function* (New York: Association of National Advertisers, 1967).

Most experts would agree, however, that the self-audit, while it is always a useful step that a manager should take, does not constitute a *bona fide* audit because it lacks objectivity and independence. Independence can be achieved in two ways. The audit could be an *inside audit* conducted by a person or group inside the company but outside of the operation being evaluated. Or it could be an *outside audit* conducted by a management consulting firm or practitioner.

The third characteristic of a marketing audit is that it is *systematic*. The marketing auditor who decides to interview people inside and outside the firm at random, asking questions as they occur to him, is a "visceral" auditor without a method. This does not mean that he will not come up with very useful findings and recommendations; he may be very insightful. However, the effectiveness of the marketing audit will normally increase to the extent that it incorporates an orderly sequence of diagnostic steps, such as there are in the conduct of a public accounting audit.

A final characteristic that is less intrinsic to a marketing audit but nevertheless desirable is that it be conducted *periodically*. Typically, evaluations of company marketing effort are commissioned when sales have turned down sharply, sales force morale has fallen, or other problems have occurred at the company. The fact is, however, that companies are thrown into a crisis partly because they have failed to review their assumptions and to change them during good times. A marketing audit conducted when things are going well can often help make a good situation even better and also indicate changes needed to prevent things from turning sour.

The above ideas of a marketing audit can be brought together into a single definition:

A marketing audit is a *comprehensive, systematic, independent,* and *periodic* examination of a company's—or business unit's—marketing environment, objectives, strategies, and activities with a view of determining problem areas and opportunities and recommending a plan of action to improve the company's marketing performance.

What Is the Marketing Audit Process?

How is a marketing audit performed? Marketing auditing follows the simple three-step procedure shown in Figure 1.

Setting the Objectives and Scope

The first step calls for a meeting between the company officer(s) and a potential auditor to explore the nature of the marketing operations and the potential value of a marketing audit. If the company officer is convinced of the potential benefits of a marketing audit, he and the auditor have to work out an agreement on the objectives, coverage, depth, data sources, report format, and the time period for the audit.

Consider the following actual case. A plumbing and heating supplies wholesaler with three branches invited a marketing consultant to prepare an audit of its

Figure 1   Steps in a Marketing Audit

overall marketing policies and operations. Four major objectives were set for the audit:

- Determine how the market views the company and its competitors.
- Recommend a pricing policy.
- Develop a product evaluation system.
- Determine how to improve the sales activity in terms of the deployment of the sales force, the level and type of compensation, the measurement of performance, and the addition of new salesmen.

Furthermore, the audit would cover the marketing operations of the company as a whole and the operations of each of the three branches, with particular attention to one of the branches. The audit would focus on the marketing operations but also include a review of the purchasing and inventory systems since they intimately affect marketing performance.

The company would furnish the auditor with published and private data on the industry. In addition, the auditor would contact suppliers of manufactured plumbing supplies for additional market data and contact wholesalers outside the company's market area to gain further information on wholesale plumbing and heating operations. The auditor would interview all the key corporate and branch management, sales and purchasing personnel, and would ride with several of those salesmen on their calls. Finally, the auditor would interview a sample of the major plumbing and heating contractor customers in the market areas of the two largest branches.

It was decided that the report format would consist of a draft report of conclusions and recommendations to be reviewed by the president and vice-president of marketing, and then delivered to the executive committee which included the three branch managers. Finally, it was decided that the audit findings would be ready to present within six to eight weeks.

Gathering the Data

The bulk of an auditor's time is spent in gathering data. Although we talk of a single auditor, an auditing team is usually involved when the project is large. A detailed plan as to who is to be interviewed by whom, the questions to be asked, the time and place of contact, and so on, has to be carefully prepared so that auditing time and cost are kept to a minimum. Daily reports of the interviews are to be written up and reviewed so that the individual or team can spot new areas requiring exploration while data are still being gathered.

The cardinal rule in data collection is not to rely solely for data and opinion on those being audited. Customers often turn out to be the key group to interview. Many companies do not really understand how their customers see them and their competitors, nor do they fully understand customer needs. This is vividly demonstrated in Figure 2 which shows the results of asking end users, company salesmen, and company marketing personnel for their views of the importance of different factors affecting the user's selection of a manufacturer. According to the figure, customers look first and foremost at the quality of technical support services, followed by prompt delivery, followed by quick response to customer needs. Company salesmen think that company reputation, however, is the most important factor in customer choice, followed by quick response to customer needs and technical support services. Those who plan marketing strategy have a different opinion. They see company price and product quality as the two major factors in buyer choice, followed by quick response to customer needs. Clearly, there is lack of consonance between what buyers say they want, what company salesmen are responding to, and what company marketing planners are emphasizing. One of the major contributions of marketing auditors is to expose these discrepancies and suggest ways to improve marketing consensus.

Preparing and Presenting the Report

The marketing auditor will be developing tentative conclusions as the data comes in. It is a sound procedure for him to meet once or twice with the company officer before the data collection ends to outline some initial findings to see what reactions and suggestions they produce.

When the data gathering phase is over, the marketing auditor prepares notes for a visual and verbal presentation to the company officer or small group who

Figure 2   Factors in the Selection of a Manufacturer*

Factor	All Users Rank	Company Salesmen Rank	Company Non-Sales Personnel Rank
Reputation	5	①	4
Extension of Credit	9	11	9
Sales Representatives	8	5	7
Technical Support Services	①	△3	6
Literature and Manuals	11	10	11
Prompt Delivery	☐2	4	5
Quick Response to Customer Needs	△3	☐2	△3
Product Price	6	6	①
Personal Relationships	10	7	8
Complete Product Line	7	9	10
Product Quality	4	8	☐2

*Marketing and Distribution Audit, A Service of Decision Sciences Corporation, p. 32.

hired him. The presentation consists of restating the objectives, showing the main findings, and presenting the major recommendations. Then, the auditor is ready to write the final report, which is largely a matter of putting the visual and verbal material into a good written communication. The company officer(s) will usually ask the auditor to present the report to other groups in the company. If the report calls for deep debate and action, the various groups hearing the report should organize into subcommittees to do follow-up work with another meeting to take place some weeks later. The most valuable part of the marketing audit often lies not so much in the auditor's specific recommendations but in the process that the managers of the company begin to go through to assimilate, debate, and develop their own concept of the needed marketing action.

Marketing Audit Procedures for an Inside Audit

Companies that conduct internal marketing audits show interesting variations from the procedures just outlined. International Telephone and Telegraph, for example, has a history of forming corporate teams and sending them into weak divisions to do a complete business audit, with a heavy emphasis on the marketing component. Some teams stay on the job, often taking over the management.

General Electric's corporate consulting division offers help to various divisions on their marketing problems. One of its services is a marketing audit in the sense of a broad, independent, systematic look at the marketing picture in a division. However, the corporate consulting division gets few requests for a marketing audit as such. Most of the requests are for specific marketing studies or problem-solving assistance.

The 3M Company uses a very interesting and unusual internal marketing plan audit procedure. A marketing plan audit office with a small staff is located at corporate headquarters. The main purpose of the 3M marketing plan audit is to help the divisional marketing manager improve the marketing planning function, as well as come up with better strategies and tactics. A divisional marketing manager phones the marketing plan audit office and invites an audit. There is an agreement that only he will see the results and it is up to him whether he wants wider distribution.

The audit centers around a marketing plan for a product or product line that the marketing manager is preparing for the coming year. This plan is reviewed at a personal presentation by a special team of six company marketing executives invited by the marketing plan audit office. A new team is formed for each new audit. An effort is made to seek out those persons within 3M (but not in the audited division) who can bring the best experience to bear on the particular plan's problems and opportunities. A team typically consists of a marketing manager from another division, a national sales manager, a marketing executive with a technical background, a few others close to the type of problems found in the audited plan, and another person who is totally unfamiliar with the market, the product, or the major marketing techniques being used in the plan. This person usually raises some important points others forget to raise, or do not ask because "everyone probably knows about that anyway."

The six auditors are supplied with a summary of the marketing manager's plan about ten days before an official meeting is held to review the plan. On the audit day, the six auditors, the head of the audit office, and the divisional marketing manager gather at 8:30 A.M. The marketing manager makes a presentation for about an hour describing the division's competitive situation, the long-run strategy, and the planned tactics. The auditors proceed to ask hard questions and debate certain points with the marketing manager and each other. Before the meeting ends that day, the auditors are each asked to fill out a marketing plan evaluation form consisting of questions that are accompanied by numerical rating scales and room for comments.

These evaluations are analyzed and summarized after the meeting. Then the head of the audit office arranges a meeting with the divisional marketing manager and presents the highlights of the auditor's findings and recommendations. It is then up to the marketing manager to take the next steps.

Components of the Marketing Audit

A major principle in marketing audits is to start with the marketplace first and explore the changes that are taking place and what they imply in the way of problems and opportunities. Then the auditor moves to examine the company's marketing objectives and strategies, organization, and systems. Finally he may move to examine one or two key functions in more detail that are central to the marketing performance of that company. However, some companies ask for less than the full range of auditing steps in order to obtain initial results before commissioning further work. The company may ask for a marketing environment audit, and if satisfied, then ask for a marketing strategy audit. Or it might ask for a marketing organization audit first, and later ask for a marketing environment audit.

We view a full marketing audit as having six major components, each having a semiautonomous status if a company wants less than a full marketing audit. The six components and their logical diagnostic sequence are discussed below. The major auditing questions connected with these components are gathered together in Appendix A at the end of this article.

Marketing Environment Audit

By marketing environment, we mean both the *macro-environment* surrounding the industry and the *task environment* in which the organization intimately operates. The macro-environment consists of the large scale forces and factors influencing the company's future over which the company has very little control. These forces are normally divided into economic-demographic factors, technological factors, political-legal factors, and social-cultural factors. The marketing auditor's task is to assess the key trends and their implications for company marketing action. However, if the company has a good long-range forecasting department, then there is less of a need for a macro-environment audit.

The marketing auditor may play a more critical role in auditing the company's task environment. The task environment consists of markets, customers, competitors, distributors and dealers, suppliers, and marketing facilitators. The marketing auditor can make a contribution by going out into the field and interviewing various parties to assess their current thinking and attitudes and bringing them to the attention of management.

Marketing Strategy Audit

The marketing auditor then proceeds to consider whether the company's marketing strategy is well-postured in the light of the opportunities and problems facing the company. The starting point for the marketing strategy audit is the corporate goals and objectives followed by the marketing objectives. The auditor may find the objectives to be poorly stated, or he may find them to be well-stated but inappropriate given the company's resources and opportunities. For example, a chemical company had set a sales growth objective for a particular product line at 15 percent. However, the total market showed no growth and competition was fierce. Here the auditor questioned the basic sales growth objective for that product line. He proposed that the product line be reconsidered for a maintenance or harvest objective at best and that the company should look for growth elsewhere.

Even when a growth objective is warranted, the auditor will want to consider whether management has chosen the best strategy to achieve that growth.

Marketing Organization Audit

A complete marketing audit would have to cover the question of the effectiveness of the marketing and sales organization, as well as the quality of interaction between marketing and other key management functions such as manufacturing, finance, purchasing, and research and development.

At critical times, a company's marketing organization must be revised to achieve greater effectiveness within the company and in the marketplace. Companies without product management systems will want to consider introducing them; companies with these systems may want to consider dropping them, or trying product teams instead. Companies may want to redefine the role concept of a product manager from being a promotional manager (concerned primarily with volume) to a business manager (concerned primarily with profit). There is the issue of whether decision-making responsibility should be moved up from the brand level to the product level. There is the perennial question of how to make the organization more market-responsive including the possibility of replacing product divisions with market-centered divisions. Finally, sales organizations often do not fully understand marketing. In the words of one vice-president of marketing: "It takes about five years for us to train sales managers to think marketing."

Marketing Systems Audit

A full marketing audit then turns to examine the various systems being used by marketing management to gather information, plan, and control the marketing operation. The issue is not the company's marketing strategy or organization per se but rather the procedures used in some or all of the following systems: sales forecasting, sales goal and quota setting, marketing planning, marketing control, inventory control, order processing, physical distribution, new products development, and product pruning.

The marketing audit may reveal that marketing is being carried on without adequate systems of planning, implementation, and control. An audit of a consumer products division of a large company revealed that decisions about which products to carry and which to eliminate were made by the head of the division on the basis of his intuitive feeling with little information or analysis to guide the decisions. The auditor recommended the introduction of a new product screening system for new products and an improved sales control system for existing products. He also observed that the division prepared budgets but did not carry out formal marketing planning and hardly any research into the market. He recommended that the division establish a formal marketing planning system as soon as possible.

Marketing Productivity Audit

A full marketing audit also includes an effort to examine key accounting data to determine where the company is making its real profits and what, if any, marketing costs could be trimmed. Decision Sciences Corporation, for example, starts its marketing audit by looking at the accounting figures on sales and associated costs of sales. Using marketing cost accounting principles,[2] it seeks to measure the marginal profit contribution of different products, end user segments, marketing channels, and sales territories.

We might argue that the firm's own controller or accountant should do the job of providing management with the results of marketing cost analysis. A handful of firms have created the job position of marketing controllers who report to financial controllers and spend their time looking at the productivity and validity of various marketing costs. Where an organization is doing a good job of marketing cost analysis, it does not need a marketing auditor to study the same. But most companies do not do careful marketing cost analysis. Here a marketing auditor can pay his way by simply exposing certain economic and cost relations which indicate waste or conceal unexploited marketing opportunities.

Zero-based budgeting[3] is another tool for investigating and improving marketing productivity. In normal budgeting, top management allots to each business unit a percentage increase (or decrease) of what it got last time. The question is not raised whether that basic budget level still makes sense. The manager of an operation should be asked what he would basically need if he started his operation from scratch and what it would cost. What would he need next and what would it cost? In this way, a budget is built from the ground up reflecting the true needs of the operation. When this was applied to a technical sales group within a large

---

[2]See P. Kotler, *Marketing Management Analysis, Planning and Control* (Englewood Cliffs, N.J.: Prentice-Hall, Inc., 1976), pp. 457–462.

[3]See P. J. Stonich, "Zero-Base Planning—A Management Tool," *Managerial Planning*, July-August 1976, pp. 1–4.

industrial goods company, it became clear that the company had three or four extra technical salesmen on its payroll. The manager admitted to the redundancy but argued that if a business upturn came, these men would be needed to tap the potential. In the meantime, they were carried on the payroll for two years in the expectation of a business upturn.

Marketing Function Audit

The work done to this point might begin to point to certain key marketing functions which are performing poorly. The auditor might spot, for example, sales force problems that go very deep. Or he might observe that advertising budgets are prepared in an arbitrary fashion and such things as advertising themes, media, and timing are not evaluated for their effectiveness. In these and other cases, the issue becomes one of notifying management of the desirability of one or more marketing function audits if management agrees.

Which Companies Can Benefit Most from a Marketing Audit?

All companies can benefit from a competent audit of their marketing operations. However, a marketing audit is likely to yield the highest payoff in the following companies and situations:

- *Production-Oriented and Technical-Oriented Companies.* Many manufacturing companies have their start in a love affair with a certain product. Further products are added that appeal to the technical interests of management, usually with insufficient attention paid to their market potential. The feeling in these companies is that marketing is paid to sell what the company decides to make. After some failures with its "better mousetraps," management starts getting interested in shifting to a market orientation. But this calls for more than a simple declaration by top management to study and serve the customer's needs. It calls for a great number of organizational and attitudinal changes that must be introduced carefully and convincingly. An auditor can perform an important service in recognizing that a company's problem lies in its production orientation, and in guiding management toward a market orientation.
- *Troubled Divisions.* Multidivision companies usually have some troubled divisions. Top management may decide to use an auditor to assess the situation in a troubled division rather than rely solely on the division management's interpretation of the problem.
- *High Performing Divisions.* Multidivision companies might want an audit of their top dollar divisions to make sure that they are reaching their highest potential, and are not on the verge of a sudden reversal. Such an audit may also yield insights into how to improve marketing in other divisions.
- *Young Companies.* Marketing audits of emerging small companies or young divisions of large companies can help to lay down a solid marketing ap-

proach at a time when management faces a great degree of market inexperience.

- *Nonprofit Organizations.* Administrators of colleges, museums, hospitals, social agencies, and churches are beginning to think in marketing terms, and the marketing audit can serve a useful educational as well as diagnostic purpose.

What Are the Problems and Pitfalls of Marketing Audits?

While the foregoing has stressed the positive aspects of marketing audits and their utility in a variety of situations, it is important to note some of the problems and pitfalls of the marketing audit process. Problems can occur in the objective-setting step, the data collection step, or the report presentation step.

Setting Objectives

When the marketing audit effort is being designed by the auditor and the company officer who commissioned the audit, several problems will be encountered. For one thing, the objectives set for the audit are based upon the company officer's and auditor's best *a priori* notions of what the key problem areas are for the audit to highlight. However, new problem areas may emerge once the auditor begins to learn more about the company. The original set of objectives should not constrain the auditor from shifting his priorities of investigation.

Similarly, it may be necessary for the auditor to use different sources of information than envisioned at the start of the audit. In some cases this may be because some information sources he had counted on became unavailable. In one marketing audit, the auditor had planned to speak to a sample of customers for the company's electro-mechanical devices, but the company officer who hired him would not permit him to do so. In other cases, a valuable new source of information may arise that was not recognized at the start of the audit. For example, the auditor for an air brake system manufacturer found as a valuable source of market intelligence a long-established manufacturers' representatives firm that approached the company after the audit had begun.

Another consideration at the objective-setting stage of the audit is that the management most affected by the audit must have full knowledge of the purposes and scope of the audit. Audits go much more smoothly when the executive who calls in the auditor either brings the affected management into the design stage, or at least has a general introductory meeting where the auditor explains his procedures and answers questions from the people in the affected business.

Data Collection

Despite reassurances by the auditor and the executive who brought him in, there will still be some managers in the affected business who will feel threatened by the auditor. The auditor must expect this, and realize that an individual's fears and biases may color his statements in an interview.

From the onset of the audit, the auditor must guarantee and maintain confidentiality of each individual's comments. In many audits, personnel in the company will see the audit as a vehicle for unloading their negative feelings about the company or other individuals. The auditor can learn a lot from these comments, but he must protect the individuals who make them. The auditor must question interviewees in a highly professional manner to build their confidence in him, or else they will not be entirely honest in their statements.

Another area of concern during the information collection step is the degree to which the company executive who brought in the auditor will try to guide the audit. It will be necessary for this officer and the auditor to strike a balance in which the executive provides some direction, but not too much. While overcontrol is the more likely excess of the executive, it is possible to undercontrol. When the auditor and the company executive do not have open and frequent lines of communication during the audit, it is possible that the auditor may place more emphasis on some areas and less on others than the executive might have desired. Therefore, it is the responsibility of both the auditor and the executive who brought him in to communicate frequently during the audit.

Report Presentation

One of the biggest problems in marketing auditing is that the executive who brings in the auditor, or the people in the business being audited, may have higher expectations about what the audit will do for the company than the actual report seems to offer. In only the most extreme circumstances will the auditor develop surprising panaceas or propose startling new opportunities for the company. More likely, the main value of his report will be that it places priorities on ideas and directions for the company, many of which have already been considered by some people within the audited organization. In most successful audits, the auditor, in his recommendations, makes a skillful combination of his general and technical marketing background (e.g., designs of salesman's compensation systems, his ability to measure the size and potential of markets) with some opportunistic ideas that people in the audited organization have already considered, but do not know how much importance to place upon them. However, it is only in the company's implementation of the recommendations that the payoff to the company will come.

Another problem at the conclusion of the audit stems from the fact that most audits seem to result in organizational changes. Organizational changes are a common outcome because the audit usually identifies new tasks to be accomplished and new tasks demand people to do them. One thing the auditor and the executive who brought him in must recognize, however, is that organizational promotions and demotions are exclusively the executive's decision. It is the executive who has to live with the changes once the auditor has gone, not the auditor. Therefore, the executive should not be lulled into thinking that organizational moves are any easier because the auditor may have recommended them.

The final problem, and this is one facing the auditor, is that important parts of an audit may be implemented incorrectly or not implemented at all, by the executive who commissioned the audit. Non-implementation of key parts of the audit undermines the whole effectiveness of the audit.

Summary

The marketing audit is one important answer to the problem of evaluating the marketing performance of a company or one of its business units. Marketing audits are distinguished from other marketing exercises in being *comprehensive, independent, systematic,* and *periodic*. A full marketing audit would cover the company's (or division's) external environment, objectives, strategies, organization, systems, and functions. If the audit covers only one function, such as sales management or advertising, it is best described as a marketing function audit rather than a marketing audit. If the exercise is to solve a current problem, such as entering a market, setting a price, or developing a package, then it is not an audit at all.

The marketing audit is carried out in three steps: developing an agreement as to objectives and scope; collecting the data; and presenting the report. The audit can be performed by a competent outside consultant or by a company auditing office at headquarters.

The possible findings of an audit include detecting unclear or inappropriate marketing objectives, inappropriate strategies, inappropriate levels of marketing expenditures, needed improvements in organization, and needed improvements in systems for marketing information, planning, and control. Companies that are most likely to benefit from a marketing audit include production-oriented companies, companies with troubled or highly vulnerable divisions, young companies, and nonprofit organizations.

Many companies today are finding that their premises for marketing strategy are growing obsolete in the face of a rapidly changing environment. This is happening to company giants such as General Motors and Sears as well as smaller firms that have not provided a mechanism for recycling their marketing strategy. The marketing audit is not the full answer to marketing strategy recycling but does offer one major mechanism for pursuing this desirable and necessary task.

Appendix A—Components of a Marketing Audit
The Marketing Environment Audit

I. Macro-Environment

Economic-Demographic

1. What does the company expect in the way of inflation, material shortages, unemployment, and credit availability in the short run, intermediate run, and long run?

2. What effect will forecasted trends in the size, age distribution, and regional distribution of population have on the business?

Technology

1. What major changes are occurring in product technology? In process technology?

2. What are the major generic substitutes that might replace this product?

Political-Legal

1. What laws are being proposed that may affect marketing strategy and tactics?

2. What federal, state, and local agency actions should be watched? What is happening in the areas of pollution control, equal employment opportunity, product safety, advertising, price control, etc., that is relevant to marketing planning?

Social-Cultural

1. What attitudes is the public taking toward business and toward products such as those produced by the company?

2. What changes are occurring in consumer life styles and values that have a bearing on the company's target markets and marketing methods?

II. Task Environment

Markets

1. What is happening to market size, growth, geographical distribution, and profits?

2. What are the major market segments? What are their expected rates of growth? Which are high opportunity and low opportunity segments?

Customers

1. How do current customers and prospects rate the company and its competitors, particularly with respect to reputation, product quality, service, sales force, and price.

2. How do different classes of customers make their buying decisions?

3. What are the evolving needs and satisfactions being sought by the buyers in this market?

Competitors

1. Who are the major competitors? What are the objectives and strategy of each major competitor? What are their strengths and weaknesses? What are the sizes and trends in market shares?

2. What trends can be foreseen in future competition and substitutes for this product?

Distribution and Dealers

1. What are the main trade channels bringing products to customers?

2. What are the efficiency levels and growth potentials of the different trade channels?

Suppliers

1. What is the outlook for the availability of different key resources used in production?

2. What trends are occurring among suppliers in their pattern of selling?

Facilitators

1. What is the outlook for the cost and availability of transportation services?

2. What is the outlook for the cost and availability of warehousing facilities?

3. What is the outlook for the cost and availability of financial resources?

4. How effectively is the advertising agency performing? What trends are occurring in advertising agency services?

Marketing Strategy Audit

Marketing Objectives

1. Are the corporate objectives clearly stated and do they lead logically to the marketing objectives?

2. Are the marketing objectives stated in a clear form to guide marketing planning and subsequent performance measurement?

3. Are the marketing objectives appropriate, given the company's competitive position, resources, and opportunities? Is the appropriate strategic objective to build, hold, harvest, or terminate this business?

Strategy

1. What is the core marketing strategy for achieving the objectives? Is it a sound marketing strategy?

2. Are enough resources (or too much resources) budgeted to accomplish the marketing objectives?

3. Are the marketing resources allocated optimally to prime market segments, territories, and products of the organization?

4. Are the marketing resources allocated optimally to the major elements of the marketing mix, i.e., product quality, service, sales force, advertising, promotion, and distribution?

Marketing Organization Audit

Formal Structure

1. Is there a high level marketing officer with adequate authority and responsibility over those company activities that affect the customer's satisfaction?

2. Are the marketing responsibilities optimally structured along functional, product, end user, and territorial lines?

Functional Efficiency

1. Are there good communication and working relations between marketing and sales?

2. Is the product management system working effectively? Are the product managers able to plan profits or only sales volume?

3. Are there any groups in marketing that need more training, motivation, supervision, or evaluation?

Interface Efficiency

1. Are there any problems between marketing and manufacturing that need attention?

2. What about marketing and R&D?

3. What about marketing and financial management?

4. What about marketing and purchasing?

Marketing Systems Audit

Marketing Information System

1. Is the marketing intelligence system producing accurate, sufficient, and timely information about developments in the marketplace?

2.   Is marketing research being adequately used by company decision makers?

Marketing Planning System

1.   Is the marketing planning system well-conceived and effective?

2.   Is sales forecasting and market potential measurement soundly carried out?

3.   Are sales quotas set on a proper basis?

Marketing Control System

1.   Are the control procedures (monthly, quarterly, etc.) adequate to insure that the annual plan objectives are being achieved?

2.   Is provision made to analyze periodically the profitability of different products, markets, territories, and channels of distribution?

3.   Is provision made to examine and validate periodically various marketing costs?

New Product Development System

1.   Is the company well-organized to gather, generate, and screen new product ideas?

2.   Does the company do adequate concept research and business analysis before investing heavily in a new idea?

3.   Does the company carry out adequate product and market testing before launching a new product?

Marketing Productivity Audit

Profitability Analysis

1.   What is the profitability of the company's different products, served markets, territories, and channels of distribution?

2.   Should the company enter, expand, contract, or withdraw from any business segments and what would be the short- and long-run profit consequences?

Cost-Effectiveness Analysis

1.   Do any marketing activities seem to have excessive costs? Are these costs valid? Can cost-reducing steps be taken?

Marketing Function Audits

Products

1.   What are the product line objectives? Are these objectives sound? Is the current product line meeting these objectives?

2.   Are there particular products that should be phased out?

3.   Are there new products that are worth adding?

4.   Are any products able to benefit from quality, feature, or style improvements?

Price

1.   What are the pricing objectives, policies, strategies, and procedures? To what extent are prices set on sound cost, demand, and competitive criteria?

2.   Do the customers see the company's prices as being in line or out of line with the perceived value of its offer?

3.   Does the company use price promotions effectively?

Distribution

1.   What are the distribution objectives and strategies?

2.   Is there adequate market coverage and service?

3.   Should the company consider changing its degree of reliance on distributors, sales reps, and direct selling?

Sales Force

1.   What are the organization's sales force objectives?

2.   Is the sales force large enough to accomplish the company's objectives?

3.   Is the sales force organized along the proper principle(s) of specialization (territory, market, product)?

4.   Does the sales force show high morale, ability, and effort? Are they sufficiently trained and incentivized?

5.   Are the procedures adequate for setting quotas and evaluating performances?

6.   How is the company's sales force perceived in relation to competitors' sales forces?

Advertising, Promotion, and Publicity

1.   What are the organization's advertising objectives? Are they sound?

2.   Is the right amount being spent on advertising? How is the budget determined?

3.   Are the ad themes and copy effective? What do customers and the public think about the advertising?

4.   Are the advertising media well chosen?

5.   Is sales promotion used effectively?

6.   Is there a well-conceived publicity program?

7

Strategic Segmentation: How to Carve Niches for Growth in Industrial Markets

Robert A. Garda

Over the past two decades, some industrial companies have rediscovered Demosthenes' idea: "Small opportunities are often the beginning of great enterprises." Unable to compete broadly against entrenched competitors, they have adopted a successful niche, or divide-and-conquer, strategy of identifying a market need and then focusing their resources and energies on meeting that need better than anyone clsc.

Since the oil embargo of 1973 and the subsequent impact of high energy costs on global economics, many managers have realized that in most industries corporate growth can come only from market-share gains, not general expansion of the market as in the past. Niche strategies thus have become more interesting than ever to growth-minded managers.

Although the niche approach is well known and frequently attempted, niche strategies are seldom as successful as they should be. Many industrial companies have toyed with the approach without ever really giving it a fair try. Because they still regard volume as the swing factor for profitable growth, they can't bring themselves to concentrate on the few markets where they have, or could have, a real competitive advantage. Instead, they continue to favor a shotgun approach to marketing strategy, although both their volume and their profit picture would improve if they abandoned the shotgun for a rifle.

Another reason why successful niche strategies are few and far between lies in the reluctance of most top managements to change a business unit's strategic approach, especially if it has enjoyed reasonable profit success. Developing a niche strategy requires rethinking one's market on a long-term basis—anything but an easy task for managers beset by pressure to achieve short-term results and attend to today's urgent problems.

Still another reason is that most industrial companies don't understand how to segment the market to their advantage. They divide it into either too many (and therefore too narrow) or into too few (and therefore too broad) segments. In the first instance, the result is confusion; in the second, failure to achieve a real competitive advantage.

Finally, a good many industrial companies find that segmentation, though it often works well for consumer goods manufacturers, has a way of losing its magic in an industrial marketing environment. Segmentation itself becomes the name of the game, and the development of winning strategies gets lost in the shuffle. Consider these complaints:

Our division people have lost sight of what we are trying to accomplish with the niche approach. They produce mountains of data—market size and growth, shares, profits, channels—but the strategies they come up with are just the same old stuff in twice the detail. No creative breakthroughs, nothing that could give us a competitive advantage.

They've segmented our market into 62 segments. I've got a sneaking suspicion that's about four dozen too many. Even if it isn't, there's no way we can develop useful competitive strategies for each one in less than five years, and we haven't got five years.

Now that they've identified the 90 core product/market and geographic segments, my marketing people tell me they can't develop the necessary facts to develop winning niche strategies because the data just aren't available. Maybe we were taking too broad an approach to the market in the old days, but we're certainly no better off now. If this is market segmentation, you can have it.

A New View of Segmentation

Recently a number of companies have begun to experiment with a segmentation concept that focuses analysis on the strategic implications of market segments, thus leading to a level of aggregation for which implementable niche strategies can be developed. To reinforce the objective of the effort, they call it "strategic market segmentation," and they have changed the rules of the game in a way that is both subtle and radical. Simply stated, SMS is a method of aggregating customer groups so as to maximize (1) homogeneity of demand within segments and (2) differentiation of demand between segments (Figure 1).

In dividing a market into strategic market segments, analysts are instructed to forget about traditional product or product groupings and to search out, instead,

Figure 1 Strategic Market Segmentation by a Heavy Machinery Manufacturer

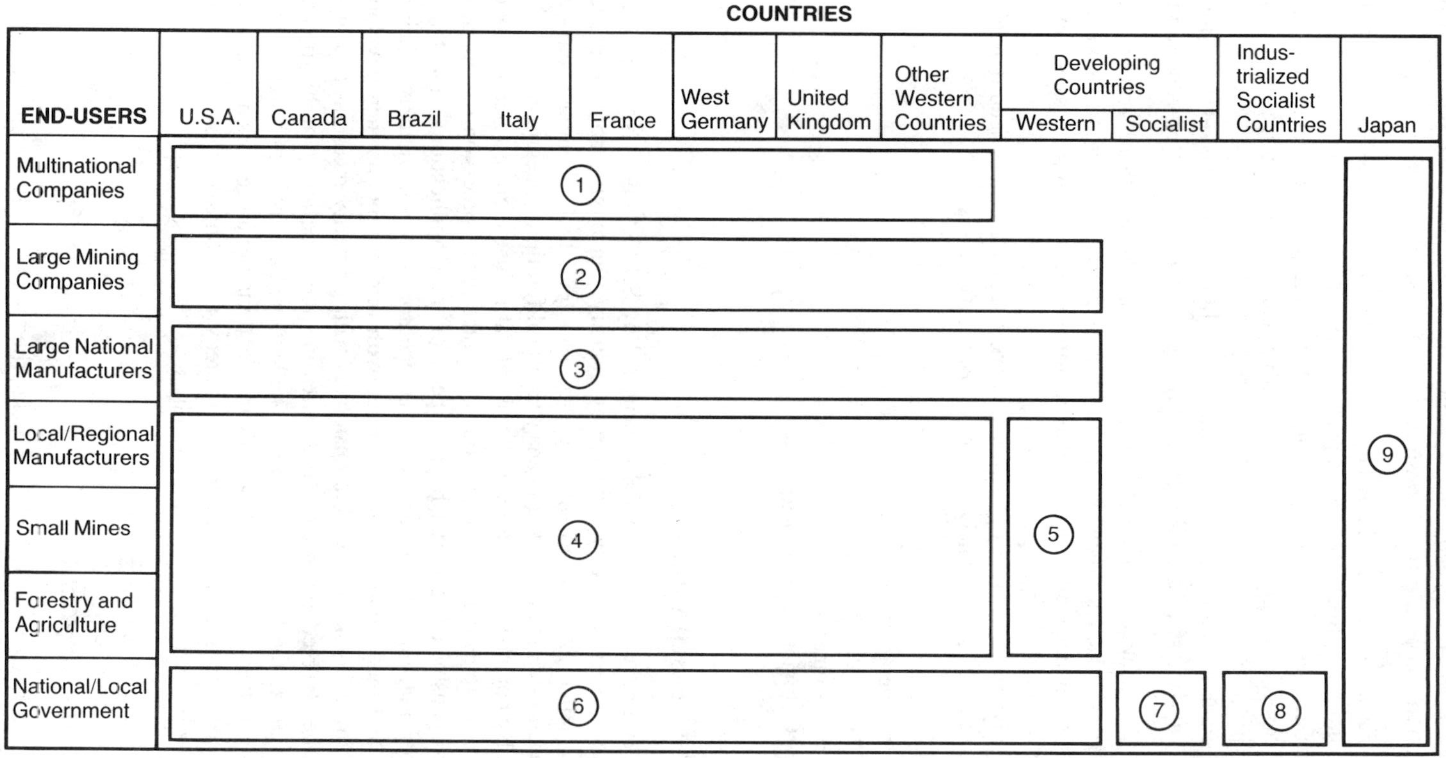

COUNTRIES

END-USERS	U.S.A.	Canada	Brazil	Italy	France	West Germany	United Kingdom	Other Western Countries	Developing Countries — Western	Developing Countries — Socialist	Industrialized Socialist Countries	Japan
Multinational Companies	①											
Large Mining Companies	②											
Large National Manufacturers	③											
Local/Regional Manufacturers	④								⑤			⑨
Small Mines												
Forestry and Agriculture										⑦	⑧	
National/Local Government	⑥											

any areas of homogeneity and disparity that might make the basis of a new segmentation, subject to three constraints:

- Each segment should be large enough so that a successful niche strategy will have a significant profit impact.
- Each segment should be identifiable by measurable characteristics (e.g., customer size, growth rate, competitive market shares, price levels, profitability).
- Each segment should be characterized by a distinctive set of customer buying factors (e.g., sales effort, pricing, product line, after-sales service).

To check further on a tentative SMS that meets these criteria, determine whether (1) each segment is served by a single channel of distribution and (2) whether segment by segment, competitors' strengths, weaknesses, and market share fall logically into place.

Five different types of strategic market segments have been defined and put into use (and creative analysts may well identify others):

- *End-use
- *Geographic
- *Product
- *Customer-size
- *Common buying factor

End-Use Segments

End-use markets are traditionally identified by S.I.C. codes. Not only are market data usually more readily available by industry, but buying criteria, product uses and benefits, and decision-making processes tend to be homogeneous. But this approach often leads to an unmanageable proliferation of segments.

By contrast, SMS users look not only at industry groups but at how customers use a product. For example, one manufacturer of precision motors discovered that his customers differed by the speed of their applications, and that a new, cheaper machine introduced by his competitor wore out quickly when used in high- and medium-speed work. Armed with this insight, he then developed segment strategies (Figure 2). For customers with primarily medium- and high-speed uses, he doubled his sales effort, stressing the superiority of his product. For customers in the low-speed segment, he launched a long-term program to develop a competitively priced product with an added maintenance advantage; at the same time, he altered his short-term sales strategy to emphasize the life-cycle-cost advantage offered by his existing machines.

Product Segments

Products are customarily grouped by families—essentially a technological cut. Alternatively, they can sometimes be usefully grouped by production economics. Consider the experience of a components manufacturer who was barely breaking

Figure 2 Resegmentation by Redefining End-Use Markets

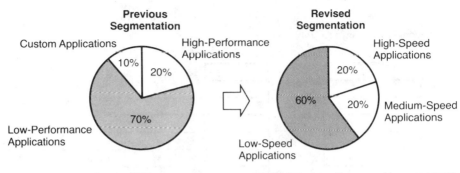

Previous strategy: Serve all segments with a
single product

Competitor's strategy: Concentrate on low-
performance segment; provide higher-priced
options for other segments

Revised strategy: Serve each new segment
with separate products

even at full capacity. Studying the profitability of all his products, he discovered:
(1) that contribution per machine hour varied widely (Figure 3); (2) that contribution per machine hour–contrary to conventional wisdom in the industry—was
more a function of pounds produced per hour than of price realized per pound; (3)
that pounds produced per hour were directly related to size and simplicity of parts.
Testing the new concept, management found that its policy of pricing bids to
provide a set 30 percent gross profit was losing the company bid orders that would
actually have been more profitable than many of those it won (Figure 4). Accordingly, this manufacturer resegmented his market, basing the new strategic segments on size and complexity of parts. This entailed drastic shifts in pricing and
customer focus: The company raised its prices on orders for small, complex parts
and went aggressively after customers who used simple, large parts. The change
was risky, but within two years it had paid off handsomely with a 20 percent
after-tax return on investment.

Geographic Segments

Geography offers a third basis for defining strategic market segments. Geographic
segments may be defined by boundaries between countries, or by regional differences within them.

An example of ingenious geographic SMS is the case of a midwestern commodity construction materials firm that found itself faced with overcapacity and
unable to take share away from its competition in its 200-mile trading area without
starting a price war.

Industry folklore maintained that because of high transport costs, no producer could ship more than 300 miles from plant to customer and make money.

Figure 3   Two Ways of Looking at Product Profitability

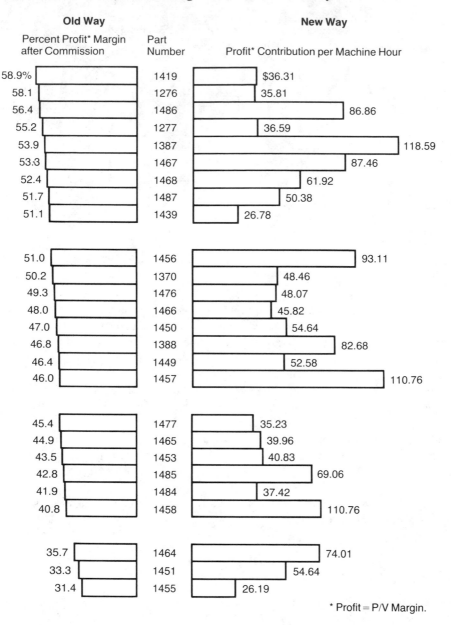

Old Way   **New Way**

Percent Profit* Margin   Part
after Commission   Number   Profit* Contribution per Machine Hour

Old Way	Part Number	New Way
58.9%	1419	$36.31
58.1	1276	35.81
56.4	1486	86.86
55.2	1277	36.59
53.9	1387	118.59
53.3	1467	87.46
52.4	1468	61.92
51.7	1487	50.38
51.1	1439	26.78
51.0	1456	93.11
50.2	1370	48.46
49.3	1476	48.07
48.0	1466	45.82
47.0	1450	54.64
46.8	1388	82.68
46.4	1449	52.58
46.0	1457	110.76
45.4	1477	35.23
44.9	1465	39.96
43.5	1453	40.83
42.8	1485	69.06
41.9	1484	37.42
40.8	1458	110.76
35.7	1464	74.01
33.3	1451	54.64
31.4	1455	26.19

* Profit = P/V Margin.

Figure 4   Alternative Uses for Same Press Capacity

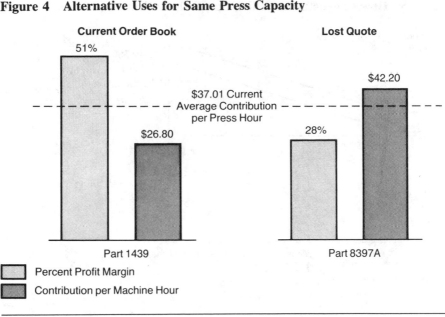

Current Order Book

Lost Quote

51%

$42.20

$37.01 Current
Average Contribution
per Press Hour

$26.80

28%

Part 1439

Part 8397A

Percent Profit Margin

Contribution per Machine Hour

This was true on an all-in cost basis; yet—as this company discovered—the fixed costs included in its all-in costs were so high that sales to customers as much as 700 miles away would still contribute to overhead (Figure 5). The result of its analysis was three strategic market segments: core markets (up to 200 miles distant); secondary markets (200 to 400 miles); and fringe markets (400 to 700 miles).

Each of these segments had its own pricing strategy. In the core market, the strategy was business as usual; in the secondary markets, prices were cut to take a few selected bids away from competitors, but not enough to provoke retaliation; in the fringe market, prices were reduced in order to fill the plants—but again, not frequently enough or severely enough to provoke retaliation.

With this strategy, the company tripled its volume in the first year. Although much of the added volume was from marginal business, its profits doubled. And the industry price structure remained intact.

Common Buying-Factor Segments

Because common buying characteristics of customers often cut across logical product, market, and geographic segments, this approach may be the most difficult mode of market segmentation. But the insights it yields are often both simple and creative.

For example, a heavy capital goods manufacturer, after months of analyzing its 50 end-use markets, came to the conclusion that for strategic purposes they

Figure 5   How Restructuring Selling Economics Enlarged a Market

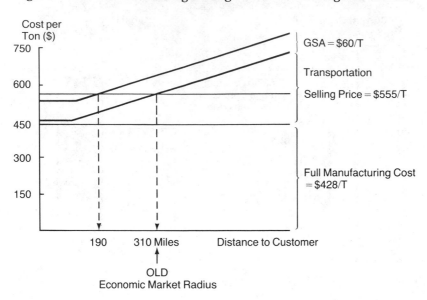

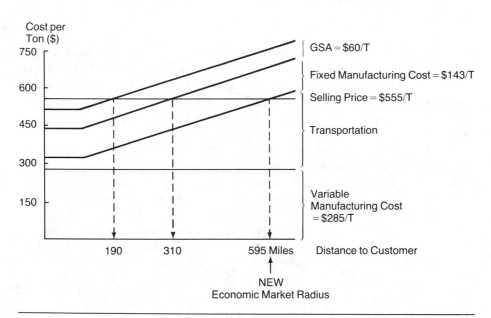

could be grouped into only two segments: "entrenched" customers (60 percent of the market) and "open" customers (the remainder).

Entrenched customers, once they had standardized on maintenance and parts inventories, rarely changed suppliers. To hold an entrenched customer of one's own, good technical service and fast delivery of machines and parts were required; to crack another supplier's entrenched customer meant waiting until the competitor gouged the customer on price or made a major error in serving the account.

Open customers, in contrast, tended to buy on price and machine availability. Accordingly, management developed three different strategies based on common buying characteristics—one for its own entrenched customers, another for those of its competitors, and a third for open customers.

Another company had a more complicated problem. To combat increasing price competition, a leading electrical components manufacturer spent two years trying to develop detailed niche strategies for its 47 S.I.C. markets. The breakthrough came when it discovered that its customers could be aggregated into four strategic market segments based on common buying characteristics (Figure 6). Segment A consisted of large-lot buyers who were extremely price sensitive (because the component was a significant portion of their product cost), did their own applications engineering, required dedicated capacity to meet their demand for a standard product, demanded only a very basic quality standard, and cared little for features.

At the other end of the spectrum, Segment D comprised a host of small-lot buyers, mostly makers of specialty products, who insisted on high quality and special features, relied on the supplier for applications engineering, and (because they lacked buying clout) were not noticeably price sensitive. The buying characteristics of Segments B and C fell between these two extremes.

Having defined these simplified strategic market segments, the manufacturer was able to address the key issues in each segment and develop marketing strategies for attacking them. For example, its marketing analysts were surprised to find that in the price-sensitive Segment A, the company had only an 11 percent market share, as against a 24 percent share overall; more importantly, in a market where its competitors were averaging $20,000 per order, its own average order size was only $2,260. Further digging revealed that the company was receiving only special orders, and that although its prices were 10 percent higher than those of the competition, they were still too low to offset marketing and setup costs. As often happens when share is low, the sales department had held prices down relative to other specialty segments in the hope of maintaining market presence and eventually of winning volume orders. Consequently, true profits in Segment A were (as they always had been) the lowest among the four segments.

Sensing that the company with its antiquated facilities could not compete for large orders on price, and unwilling to dedicate any of its existing capacity for customers as competitors had been doing, top management chose to price itself "up or out" of Segment A by raising prices 25 percent. As anticipated, the price increase stuck; none of the competitors wanted the specialty business. Next, top management launched a facilities study to determine whether it could meet the low price and dedicated capacity requirements for the high-volume business in Segment A. Equally creative strategies were developed for other segments. Altogether, top management was convinced that the SMS approach based on common buying characteristics had given the company what in the long run would prove to be a decisive competitive advantage.

Figure 6   Segmentation by Key Buying Factors

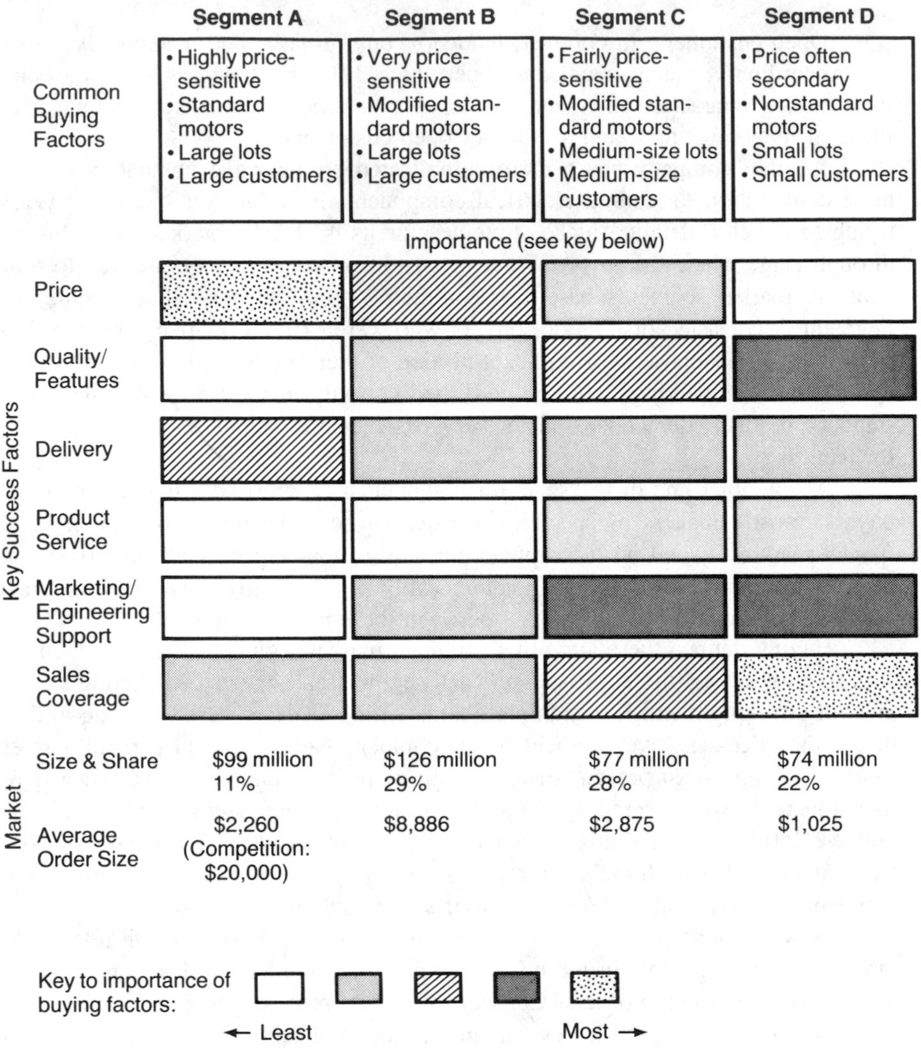

	Segment A	Segment B	Segment C	Segment D
Common Buying Factors	• Highly price-sensitive • Standard motors • Large lots • Large customers	• Very price-sensitive • Modified standard motors • Large lots • Large customers	• Fairly price-sensitive • Modified standard motors • Medium-size lots • Medium-size customers	• Price often secondary • Nonstandard motors • Small lots • Small customers

Importance (see key below)

Key Success Factors:
- Price
- Quality/Features
- Delivery
- Product Service
- Marketing/Engineering Support
- Sales Coverage

Market:

	Segment A	Segment B	Segment C	Segment D
Size & Share	$99 million 11%	$126 million 29%	$77 million 28%	$74 million 22%
Average Order Size	$2,260 (Competition: $20,000)	$8,886	$2,875	$1,025

Key to importance of buying factors: ← Least   Most →

Customer-Size Segments

In some industries, where buying criteria differ with predictable consistency by customer size, it becomes possible to develop niche strategies for different customer-size groups. (Logically, this could be called a subset of SMS by common buying factors, but its practical importance entitles it to separate treatment.)

Sales managers are accustomed to grouping customers by size for planning purposes, but until recently few top managers had thought to try developing niche strategies on this basis. Yet the the opportunity often exists.

For example, an electrical equipment manufacturer isolated 187 key accounts, accounting for 60 percent of the market, each of whom bought direct and selected suppliers on the basis of price and sales coverage. These large accounts made up one strategic market segment. A second segment consisted of medium-sized OEM accounts who bought through distributors; a third comprised maintenance, repair, and operating supply accounts who required distributor servicing. Having identified these three strategic market segments, the company was able to develop programs (product pricing, distribution channels, and service policies) tailored to each.

As all these examples suggest, defining the strategic market segments is the first step in developing a creative niche strategy. Strategic market segmentation alerts the marketer to the critically important trends and opportunities in his market. And it gives him a precise view of his competition, making it easy to determine what weaknesses he needs to correct and what strengths he has to exploit. In short, it gives management a uniquely effective basis for determining where the company should concentrate its resources.

The Story of Segmentation

Approaches to market segmentation have been gaining in sophistication ever since the late 1950s and early 1960s, when industrial companies selling several products to the same general market—following the lead of consumer good manufacurers—discovered the significance of product segmentation. That discovery led to the installation of product managers to make certain that each product received its fair share of support from the various functional groups influencing its success in the marketplace.

The next stage in the evolution of segmentation was characterized by a focus on end-use markets. In the mid- to late 1960s, many industrial companies began to recognize that they were selling basically the same products to a variety of customer groups, whose requirements were typically quite different. Taking the lead once again from consumer companies, they set up market or industry managers to plan for these end-use markets, each served by a particular group of products.

The shift from a product focus to a market focus added a new dimension to niche strategies. Some companies, recognizing the competitive advantage that could be gained by meeting all the needs of a selected market segment, even went so far as to acquire other companies with compatible offering. In the power transmission market, for example, Litton, North American Rockwell, and Reliance Electric acquired companies in the drive chain, gear, speed reducer, V-belt, and/or hydrostatic drive businesses. Thus was born the systems approach to markets: offering a broad range of products to selected segments, or leveraging a common distributor network.

From this it was a short step to the concept of product/markets. In the early 1970s, strategists began to concentrate on defining the product/market combinations in which their companies were involved and designing specific strategies for each segment. The results were impressive. A manufacturer of electric and elec-

Figure 7   How Market Segmentation Evolved

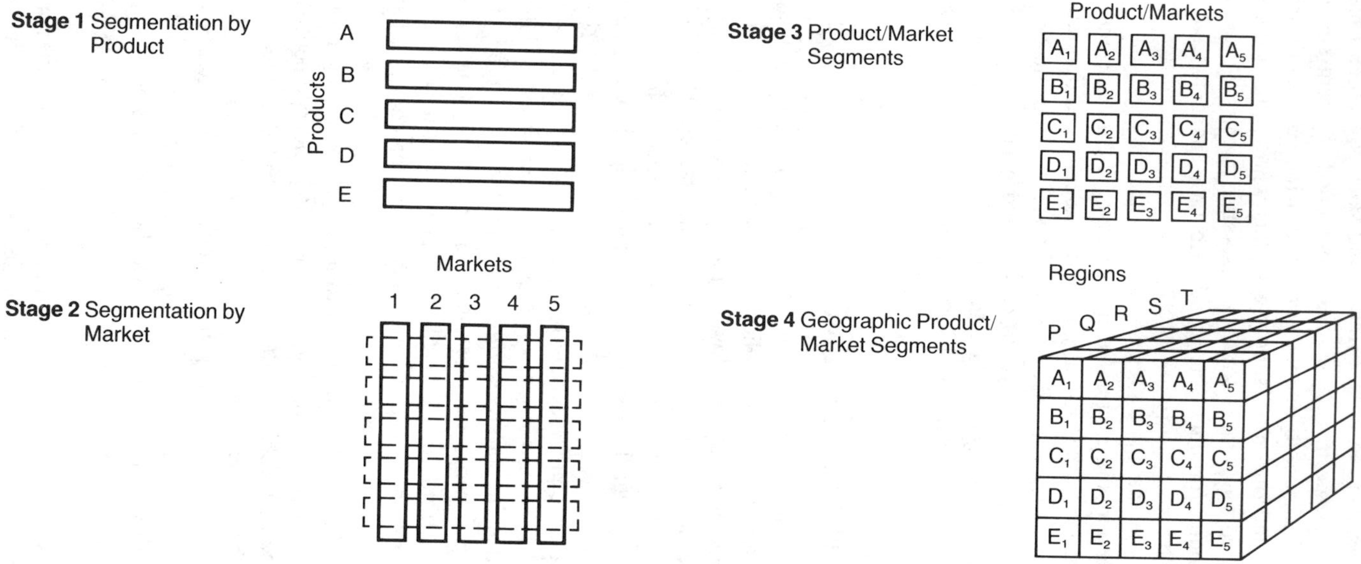

Stage 1 Segmentation by
Product

Products

A
B
C
D
E

Stage 2 Segmentation by
Market

Markets

1 2 3 4 5

Stage 3 Product/Market
Segments

Product/Markets

A_1	A_2	A_3	A_4	A_5
B_1	B_2	B_3	B_4	B_5
C_1	C_2	C_3	C_4	C_5
D_1	D_2	D_3	D_4	D_5
E_1	E_2	E_3	E_4	E_5

Stage 4 Geographic Product/
Market Segments

Regions

P Q R S T

A_1	A_2	A_3	A_4	A_5
B_1	B_2	B_3	B_4	B_5
C_1	C_2	C_3	C_4	C_5
D_1	D_2	D_3	D_4	D_5
E_1	E_2	E_3	E_4	E_5

tromechanical products captured the No. 1 position in its market by developing different strategies for each of eight product/market segments, while its prime competitors continued to treat all eight segments the same. A material supplier turned a losing division into a highly profitable one by cutting back eight product lines to two and 12 market segments to two, thus focusing all its efforts on only four product/market segments instead of the previous 96.

Although the concept of product/markets was a natural outgrowth of the systems approach, finding a way to manage it turned out to be a struggle. Some companies resorted to matrix organizations with both product and market managers.

For the multinational corporation of today, the geographic dimension has been added. Many companies are now trying to develop niche strategies for each product/region that they serve. In short, the art of market segmentation has been growing more and more sophisticated. But with sophistication has come complexity, and many managers are now concerned that in contending with complexity, their marketing analysts have lost sight of the real objective of market segmentation, gaining competitive advantage.

Section
Three

Concepts for Evaluating Strategic Market Opportunities

IN the introductory section, strategic marketing decisions were characterized as investment decisions—decisions concerning the allocation of resources across product-market alternatives to achieve a sustainable competitive advantage. Financial theory provides some classic capital budgeting methods for evaluating such investment opportunities. While these methods typically are applied to decisions concerning the purchase of revenue-producing assets, they can also be used for strategic marketing decisions.

The capital budgeting approach is conceptually appealing: if this approach is used to make investment decisions, the firm will realize its objective of maximizing stockholder wealth. However, the capital budgeting approach has some practical limitations that lead us to consider additional factors in evaluating strategic opportunities. The articles in this section discuss two of these factors: the experience curve and the importance of market share, and the product life cycle. First, we will review the traditional capital budgeting approach for evaluating investment opportunities. After discussing the limitations of this approach, we will look at the concepts of the experience curve and the product life cycle.

Traditional Capital Budgeting

Strategic marketing decisions parallel the investment decisions encountered in capital budgeting.[1] A company faces a number of product-markets to which it can allocate resources and must decide the amount of resources to allocate to each product-market opportunity. The basis for making these decisions is the expected yield from the resources allocated.

In the conventional method for allocating resources, individuals, typically at an operating level, make investment proposals to a person or group responsible for capital budgeting. Each proposal is accompanied by an estimate of the investment required, the expected revenues to be generated by the investment, and the cost associated with generating these revenues. For example, an investment program involving the purchase and installation of an industrial robot would include the cost of programming and installing the robot and the cost of training operators in the investment required. The proposal might assume that revenues will not increase—potential improvements in quality of products produced by the robot may not result in increased sales. However, the robot may result in an annual cost savings over the operating life of the robot. Such proposals are then evaluated and funds are allocated to those that seem promising.

Evaluating Proposals

A variety of methods are used to evaluate the financial viability of capital budgeting proposals. Some firms simply determine the net profit each proposal generates by adding up the additional revenues generated over a ten-year time horizon and subtracting the investment costs and additional costs. Another common method is to calculate a pay-back period. The pay-back period is the number of years of anticipated profit increases needed to recover the initial cost of the investment. Conceptually, these methods for evaluating capital budgeting proposals are not very appealing because they do not consider the time value of money—they do not recognize that a dollar spent on an investment today is worth more than future income generated from the investment. This concern raises the issue of discounting future income and defining a net present value (NPV) criterion for evaluating investments.

The theoretically correct method for evaluating investment opportunities is to determine the anticipated cash flow for each future time period and then convert the stream of cash flows into a net present value (NPV) using an appropriate discount rate. Note that the cash flows typically will be negative during the initial time periods because of investment expenditures; however, they will become positive during later periods as the benefits of the investment are realized. Having determined the NPV for all investment opportunities, financial theory suggests that the firm should fund all investment proposals with a positive NPV.

From a normative economic perspective, evaluating investment proposals based on their NPV will maximize stockholder wealth.[2] Most financial theorists believe that maximizing stockholder wealth is the appropriate objective for the firm because it is viewed as consistent with maximizing social welfare. As James Van Horne described it: the use of any other objective by the firm "is likely to result in the sub-optimal capital formation and growth in the economy as well as less than optimal level of economic want satisfaction."[3]

The objective of maximizing stockholder wealth is superior to the traditional profit maximization objective because profit maximization fails to consider the timing of investments and returns. In addition, it is not characterized by a unique measure of profits because different accounting procedures can produce a wide range of profit levels.

The second reading, "Marketing, Strategic Planning, and the Theory of the Firm," discussed a variety of objectives. While the article supports the normative value of maximizing stockholder wealth, it also discussed how conflicting interests within the firm can result in the pursuit of other objectives.

Discount Rate and NPV

In determining the NPV for an investment, a critical aspect is selecting the appropriate discount rate to apply to future cash flows. The discount rate should reflect the firm's cost of capital which, according to the Capital Pricing Model (CAPM), is a function of the riskiness of the firm's future cash flow.

The cost of capital (R_c) is calculated using the following CAPM formula:

$$R_c = R_f + \beta [R_m - R_f]$$

where R_f is the risk-free rate, R_m is the expected return on the stock market portfolio, and β is the beta coefficient for the stock.

Beta is the relationship between the stock price of the firm and the stock market portfolio, often measured by S&P 500-stock index. Thus, beta is the unavoidable or systematic risk of the firm's stock. A beta of 1.00 indicates that the stock has the same systematic risk as the stock market as a whole, while a beta less than 1.00 indictates that the stock has less systematic risk than the market.

Assume that the risk-free rate, based on the yield of one-year treasury bills, is 5.5 percent and expected return for the stock market, as a whole, is 14 percent. The beta for the firm, determined by comparing the stock market index with firm's stock price over the last 60 months, is 1.50. Thus, the cost of capital is:

$$R_c = .055 + (.14 - .055) \times 1.5 = 18.25\%.$$

While the cost of capital for the firm is important, investment opportunities may have different systematic risks and thus should be evaluated using different discount rates. Determining the systematic risk for an investment opportunity is not as straightforward as indicated above because there is no stock price for the investment that can be compared against the market index. Thus, the appropriate beta for an investment typically is determined by using the beta of firms engaged in an industry similar to the investment opportunity. For example, the beta for an investment in microcomputer software development might be determined using the average beta of publicly traded firms that develop and market microcomputer software such as Ashton-Tate, Microsoft, and Lotus Development.[4]

Implications of the CAPM for Evaluating Opportunities

The preceding example illustrates how risk can be incorporated into the net present value (NPV) calculation used to evaluate investment opportunities. The technique can be easily applied to the evaluation of new-product proposals, major salesforce expansion decisions, changes in distribution channels, and other marketing strategies and tactics.

The CAPM approach outlined in this section has interesting implications for the diversification of a company's portfolio of product-market investments. The CAPM suggests that managers acting in the shareholders' interest should evaluate opportunities individually, adjusting the discount rate for each opportunity's level of systematic risk. Despite a popular notion that companies should invest in a diversified portfolio of product-market opportunities to reduce risk or uncertainty, the CAPM approach suggests that such diversification by the firm will not maximize stockholder wealth. Individual investors can diversify their portfolios more efficiently than can the firm. Thus, the manager should be concerned simply with achieving an appropriate return for a given risk level, and not with minimizing the risks of different projects.

The marketing strategy undertaken by the Kellogg Company is consistent with the CAPM approach. In 1978, 75 percent of Kellogg's revenues and 80 percent of its profits came from the cereal market. The market faced significant risks: consumer groups were denouncing the company's presweetened cereals; the FTC was mounting antitrust legislation against the company; and the proportion of children, the large cereal consumers, was declining. Competitors General Mills and General Foods also faced this high-risk environment and diversified into other food and nonfood products. Kellogg's, however, made the strategic decision to continue major investments in cereal products and has outperformed the competition. Kellogg's was able to achieve a high return on their cereal investment strategy commensurate with the associated risks.[5]

Drawbacks of the Capital Budgeting Approach

While the capital budgeting approach has strong theoretical support, practical problems arise when it is used as the sole guide for strategic investment decisions.[6] First, the procedure may limit the range of opportunities considered. Second, the approach may result in focusing attention on a calculation rather than on the calculation's underlying assumptions. Finally, the capital budgeting approach tends to assume that the status quo will be maintained if a proposal is rejected, but this assumption may be unwarranted. The rejection of a new strategic direction may result in a gradual deterioration of the present position.

Limited Focus.   When a capital budgeting approach is used, the strategic proposals are usually generated by line managers, such as brand managers or sales managers. Proposals generated by operating managers tend to be narrowly focused on modifications to existing strategic directions. For example, a brand manager may propose a significant increase in support for his or her brand, without considering the positive or negative effects on other brands. It is unlikely that a brand manager would propose a major divestment of a group of brands due to a shift in the environment.

Lack of Attention to Assumptions.   To develop a capital budgeting proposal, all the benefits and costs associated with the proposal need to be quantified. The process of calculating a net present value for each opportunity focuses attention on selecting the alternative with the highest net present value rather than on questioning the assumptions on which the calculations are based. These assumptions are critical since there are significant uncertainties in forecasting investment levels, revenues, and costs over a long-term strategic time horizon. In addition, there are likely to be biases in these forecasts when the proposals are generated by managers with a vested interest in the strategic decision.

Status Quo.   The basic principle underlying an NPV evaluation is incremental analysis: the cost-benefit cash flow to be discounted is the difference between the cash flow that would have occurred with and without the specific proposal. Hayes and Abernathy have criticized NPV analysis because the analyst often implicitly assumes that the base case—the cash flow without the specific proposal—is the status quo.[7] Defining a realistic base cost is often difficult and uncomfortable since it requires an explicit recognition of weaknesses in a previously formulated strategy.

Any manager can develop a proposal showing a positive net present value. The crucial question is not whether the NPV is positive but What justifies the positive NPV? What is the nature of the strategic investment opportunity that will result in a positive NPV? This question has led to the search for critical factors that should be used to evaluate strategic opportunities. The articles in this section examine two important factors—the experience that a company acquires in a product-market and the life cycle stage of the product-market.

Experience Curves and Market Share

One of the major concepts used to evaluate strategic market opportunities is the experience curve. This concept suggests that the cost per unit of manufacturing and marketing a product declines as a function of the number of units produced—the cumulative production volume. This phenomenon was observed over 40 years ago with respect to labor costs,[8] but the Boston Consulting Group has more recently extended the concept to all costs—direct labor, overheard, distribution, and selling. Article 8, "A Fundamental Approach to Strategy Development," provides evidence of the experience curve and discusses its implications.

The principal implication of the experience curve phenomenon concerns the setting of marketing objectives. As discussed in the article, because costs decline with accumulated experience, the company with the most accumulated experience will have the lowest costs, the highest margins, and the highest profits. The level of the market share is usually proportional to the level of accumulated experience. Thus, the profitability of a company relative to its competitors will be related to its relative market share. The company that dominates a product-market will make more money than its competitors. Hence, market share becomes a key strategic objective.

The relationship between market share and profitability has been demonstrated empirically. Analyses of more than 1,000 business units have shown a significant relationship among these elements: return on investment (ROI), relative market share, and absolute market share.[9] These findings, summarized in Figure III.1, clearly indicate that high-share businesses are more profitable than low-share businesses. Additional analyses suggest that high-share businesses have lower costs. These findings support the experience curve explanation of the profitability–market share relationship, supplanting any explanation claiming that the effect can be explained solely by a process in which market power had permitted monopolistic pricing.

Reevaluating the Implications of the Experience Curve

The experience curve concept and market share play an important role in the strategic marketing planning models examined in Section IV of this book. These

Figure III.1   Market Share Helps Profitability

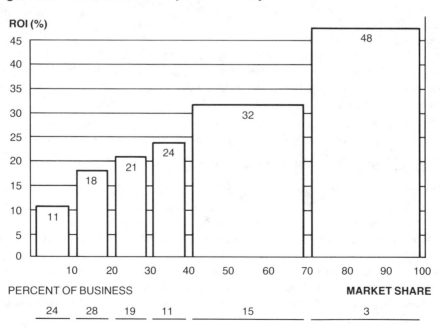

models were the cornerstone of strategic marketing in the 1970s; however, the role of market share is now being questioned:

> *The sweeping downward arc of the experience curve hung like a guiding constellation over the business landscape of the 1970s. What's happening now, though, is that the curve is being consigned to a much reduced place in the firmament of strategic concepts. With it is going a good bit of the importance originally attached to market share.*[10]

The second article in this section, "Diagnosing the Experience Curve," suggests that strategic insights gained from the experience curve concept may be misleading. The article outlines some issues related to the measurement of experience curves and emphasizes that the unit of analysis and shared costs must be considered before developing strategic implications. Finally, the dangers of overemphasis on developing a cost advantage to the exclusion of satisfying customer needs are discussed.

Cost Dynamics

The experience curve concept emphasizes that managers should examine the cost advantage of their business in a product-market relative to their competition. It is important to realize that product-markets evolve over time. Changes in the nature of a product-market may be caused by a variety of factors, such as new customer needs and product technologies. When these changes arise, the relative importance of the various cost elements in a product may also change. Since the nature of shared costs among competitors differs, the relative cost advantage of competitors will differ as major cost elements become more or less important. The electronic calculator market, described in Table 8.1 of Article 8, illustrates how different cost elements and competitors prevail during the evaluation of the product-market.

From Table 8.1 we can learn that the evolutionary phase of a product-market is an important consideration in evaluating strategic market opportunity. For example, a key ingredient for success in the electronic calculator market during Phase 2 was the capability to assemble discrete semiconductors at low cost. However, a technological change, the availability of integrated circuits, shifted the product-market to Phase 3. A competitive advantage in low-cost assembly was no longer important in evaluating this product-market opportunity. The key consideration became capability in integrated circuit design, fabrication, and production. Product life cycle analysis is one method for anticipating the evolution of product-markets.

Product Life Cycle

The product life cycle (PLC) is a concept used to describe and predict product-market evolution, such as that of the electronic calculator market mentioned previously.[11] Charles Hofer suggests: "The most fundamental variable in determining an appropriate strategy is the stage of the product life cycle."[12]

From a strategic perspective, the PLC concept proposes that product-markets undergo an inevitable evolution from introduction (birth) through growth and maturity to decline (death). The effectiveness of marketing variables changes from stage to stage due to differences in consumer knowledge, market structure, and competitive behavior. The PLC concept suggests that if strategic investments are made during the introductory and early-growth phases, returns will accrue during the late-growth and maturity phases. Investments are discouraged during the maturity phase because intense competition during this phase will not permit the firm to achieve appropriate returns.

Article 10, "Forget the Product Life Cycle Concept!" describes the traditional view of the product life cycle as a strategic marketing tool and discusses how life cycle analysis can result in inappropriate business decisions. This article questions the very existence of life cycles. On the other hand, Article 11, "Don't Forget the Product Life Cycle for Strategic Planning," reemphasizes the usefulness of life cycle analysis. The contrasting views presented in these two articles reflect the diversity of opinion among marketers concerning the PLC. As you read these articles, note the different perspectives that the authors take concerning both the key forces driving demand and the unit of analysis.

Determinants of Product Demand[13]

The PLC concept purports to represent the demand for a product over time, but there is no well-defined theory of product demand to support the PLC. While the classic PLC curve has been observed in a number of product-markets, the factors shaping the curve have not been clearly articulated. The application of a biological model to the PLC's would suggest that the demand for a product, like the activity of a living organism, goes through inevitable, preordained changes over time and, thus, that product demand is predictable over time and is beyond the control of marketers. Accordingly, while marketers need to alter the nature of their tactical marketing programs during the various stages, they cannot affect the basic demand for the product by marketing efforts. Clearly, this biological analogy begins to look inappropriate. We know that a wide range of PLC shapes have been observed. Thus, we can see that product demand is not highly predictable or beyond the control of marketers.

Research on the diffusion of innovation has also been used to explain the evolutionary nature of product demand and PLC.[14] This research suggests that the S-shaped curve of the introductory, growth, and maturity phases represents the rate at which consumers adopt new products or concepts: demand remains at a low level in the introductory stage while innovators and early adopters become familiar with the new concept; growth in demand accelerates when the early adopters spread the information about the new concept; finally, demand levels off in the maturity stages when all potential adopters of the new concept have been exposed to it.

In addition, theories on the diffusion of innovations suggest that the specific shape of the S-shaped curve is determined by the nature of the product, the consumer's adoption decision, and the communication efforts concerning the products. The diffusion process will occur sooner (the introductory and growth stages will be shorter) when the product benefits can be communicated easily, when the product is simple, when consumers can try the product with low risk, and so on.

Thus, the research on diffusion of innovation indicates that product demand and the PLC is determined by the nature of the product and the marketing efforts concerning the product. However, the diffusion of innovation explains only the factors causing the first three stages in the PLC. The decline phase cannot be explained by the diffusion of innovation process.

A fully developed PLC theory requires a mechansim that accounts for the decline in demand. The decline in product demand usually results from a shift in demand to a different product. Such shifts arise when new technology provides products that will better satisfy customer needs or when new customer needs develop in response to changes in societal values. At this time we do not have adequate theories to account for the role of new technologies or new social values. The last article in this section, "Strategic Responses to Technological Threats," discusses how technological changes affect the nature of competitive activities.

The Level of Aggregation for PLC Analysis[15]

A problem confronted by all strategy analysis is determining the appropriate level of aggregation. Traditionally, the product in product life cycles is defined at one of three hierarchical levels of aggregation: (1) product class, such as passenger automobiles; (2) product form, such as sports cars; and (3) brand, such as Datsun 280ZX. Should the unit of analysis be the brand, the product form, the product class, the market segment, or the industry? The previous discussion of the PLC demonstrates that when analyses are made at different levels—the brand versus the product form—the conclusions can be dramatically different. Based on their analyses at the brand level, Dhalla and Yuspeh reject the PLC concept, while Neidel accepts the PLC concept on the basis of his analysis at the product form level.

The key question is: Which level of aggregation best captures the changing nature of the environment to which marketing strategies must respond? George Day, building on the work of Derek Abell, suggests that a useful level of aggregation is

the application of a distinct technology to the provision of a particular function for a specific customer group. Only when there is a change along one or more of these dimensions that involves a sharp departure from the present strategies of the participating competitors is a separate life cycle needed.[16]

An analysis of the PLC for nylon illustrates how this heuristic approach is applied. In a classic article, Ted Levitt discusses how Du Pont extended the PLC for nylon by sequentially marketing the product for different applications.[17] After an initial effort directed toward parachute cords, the marketers undertook applications to women's hosiery, tire cords, and carpeting. Should the marketing strategist consider one extended PLC for nylon or separate PLCs for each application? The previously stated heuristic suggests that separate PLCs are appropriate because each application is characterized by a different function and customer group; each application represents a separate strategic market opportunity and should be considered individually in the development of a marketing strategy.

In conclusion, we can say that the following elements are determinants of the nature of product demand and the PLC.

1.   The nature of the customer adoption decision.

2.   Characteristics of the product.

3.   Marketing efforts.

4.   The availability of substitutes arising from new technologies.

5.   The degree to which those customer needs satisfied by the product are changing.

The relative importance of these factors is determined, in part, by how the product is defined.

Footnotes

1.   An excellent and more detailed presentation of the concepts in this section can be found in Paul F. Anderson, "Marketing Investment Analysis," in *Research in Marketing*, vol. 4, ed. J. N. Sheth (Greenwich, Conn.: JAI Press, 1980). A more advanced and complete treatment of capital budgeting can be found in Thomas E. Copeland and J. Fred Weston, *Financial Theory and Corporate Policy* (Reading, Mass.: Addison-Wesley, 1979), chaps. 2 and 3.

2.   Eugene Fama and Merton H. Miller, *The Theory of Finance* (Hinsdale, Ill.: Dryden Press, 1972).

3.   James C. Van Horne, *Financial Management and Policy*, 4th ed. (Englewood Cliffs, N.J.: Prentice-Hall, 1977), 98. Alternatives to this perspective concerning the theory of the firm can be found in Paul F. Anderson, "Marketing, Strategic Planning, and the Theory of the Firm," *Journal of Marketing* (Reading #1 in this book).

4.   The estimation of beta using appropriate firms whose stock is traded ignores bankruptcy risk affects and tax implications of alternative capital structures. However, these effects typically have minimal consequences in the context of practical investment decisions. (See Patrick Barwise, Paul March, and Robin Wensley, "Strategic Investment Decisions," in *Research in Marketing*, ed. J. Sheth, vol. 9, 1987.)

5.   "Kellogg Still the Cereal People," *Business Week*, November 26, 1979, 80–93.

6.   Seymour Tilles, "Strategies for Allocating Funds," *Harvard Business Review* (January-February 1966):72–80.

7.   Robert Hayes and William Abernathy, "Managing Our Way to Economic Decline," *Harvard Business Review* (July-August 1980):67–77.

8.   See Louis E. Yelle, "The Learning Curve: Historical Review and Comprehensive Survey," *Decision Sciences* 10 (1979):302–328.

9.   R. D. Buzzell, B. T. Gale, and R. G. M. Sullen, "Market Share—A Key to Profitability," *Harvard Business Review* (January-February 1975):97–106; and R. D. Buzzell and F. D. Wiersema, "Successful Share Building Strategies," *Harvard Business Review* (January-February 1981):133–144.

10.   Walter Kiechel III, "The Decline of the Experience Curve," *Fortune*, October 5, 1981, 139.

11.   For a review of research concerning the product life cycle, see D. R. Rink and J. Swan, "Product Life Cycle Research: A Literature Review," *Journal of Business Research* (September 1979):219–242.

12.   C. W. Hofer, "Toward a Contingency Theory of Business Strategy," *Academy of Management Journal* (December 1975):785.

13.   The Fall 1981 issue of the *Journal of Marketing* contains a special section on the product life cycle. Articles in this section review the recent conceptual thinking and empirical results concerning the PLC.

14.   See E. V. Roger and F. F. Shoemaker, *Communication of Innovations* (New York: Collier McMillian, 1971) and T. S. Robertson, *Innovative Behavior and Communication* (New York: Holt, Rinehart, & Winston, 1971).

15.   This discussion draws heavily on George S. Day, "The Product Life Cycle: Analysis and Applications Issues," *Journal of Marketing* 45 (Fall 1980):60–67.

16.   Ibid., 61.

17.   Theodore Levitt, "Exploiting the Product Life Cycle," *Harvard Business Review* 43 (November-December 1965):81–94.

Additional Readings For Section Three

Financial Analysis

Mossman, Frank, W. J. E. Crissey, and Paul Fischer, *Financial Dimensions of Marketing Management*. New York: Wiley, 1978.

Shapiro, Stanley J. and V. H. Kirpalani. *Marketing Effectiveness*. Boston: Allyn and Bacon, 1984.

Experience Curves

Abernathy, William J. and Kenneth Wayne. "Limits of the Learning Curve." *Harvard Business Review* (September-October 1974):109–119.

Beckenstein, A. R. and H. L. Gabel. "Experience Curve Pricing Strategy: The Next Target of Antitrust?" *Business Horizons* (September-October 1982):71–77.

Ghemawat, Pankaj. "Building Strategy on the Experience Curve." *Harvard Business Review* (March-April 1984):143–149.

Product Life Cycle

Anderson, C. and C. Reithaml. "Stages of the Product Life Cycle." *Academy of Management Journal* 27 (1984):5–24.

Bennett, R. and R. B. Cooper. "The Product Life Cycle Trap." *Business Horizons* (September-October 1984):1–16.

Cox, William E. "Product Life Cycles as Marketing Models." *Journal of Business* (October 1967):375–384.

Day, George S. "The Product Life Cycle: Analysis and Applications Issues." *Journal of Marketing* (Fall 1981):60–67.

Enis, B., R. LaGarca, and A. E. Prell. "Extending the Product Life Cycle." *Business Horizons* (June 1977):46–56.

Levitt, Theodore. "Exploit the Product Life Cycle." *Harvard Business Review* (November-December 1965):81–94.

Polli, Rolando and Victor Cook. "Validity of the Product Life Cycle." *Journal of Business* (October 1969):385–400.

Rink, David R. and John E. Swan. "Product Life Cycle Research: A Literature Review." *Journal of Business Research* (September 1979):219–242.

Rink, David R. and Robert H. Dodge. "Industrial Sales Emphasis Across the Life Cycle." *Industrial Market Management* (1980):305–310.

Smallwood, John E. "The Product Life Cycle: A Key to Strategic Marketing Planning." *MSU Business Topics* (Winter 1973):29–35.

Tellis, A. J. and C. M. Crawford. "An Evolutionary Approach to Product Growth Theory." *Journal of Marketing* (Fall 1983):125–132.

Thorelli, H. and S. Burnett. "The Nature of Product Life Cycles for Industrial Goods Businesses." *Journal of Marketing* (Fall 1981):97–108.

Wasson, Chester R. "The Importance of the Product Life Cycle to the Industrial Marketer." *Industrial Marketing Management* 5 (1975):299–308.

Wasson, Chester R. *Dynamic Competitive Strategy and Product Life Cycles*. St. Charles, Ill.: Challenge, 1974.

Yelle, Louis E. "Industrial Life Cycles and Learning Curves: Interaction of Marketing and Production." *Industrial Marketing Management* (1980):311–318.

8

A Fundamental Approach to Strategy Development

Barry Hedley

In the face of continuing economic and environmental uncertainty, an increasing number of companies are rejecting traditional approaches to long-range planning. These approaches were frequently "extrapolative" in nature, and in the absence of smooth economic trends it seems right that they should be discarded. Yet there is considerable confusion concerning what should take their place.

It is, however, possible to specify the requirements which must be satisfied by any approach to strategy development which can hope to be successful in today's changeable world. First, the approach must provide a means for identifying the underlying factors which are critical for long-term success at the individual business level, and which are sufficiently fundamental that their effects can be expected to persist indefinitely in the face of continual general environmental change. Second, the framework must offer a way of establishing the implications of these factors for the allocation of limited resources—and especially of cash—within a company which is comprised of a number of businesses. This allocation must take place in such a way that the performance of the multibusiness company *overall* can be optimized.

These are in fact the same problems companies have always faced in trying to develop sound corporate strategy. What has happened is simply that changes in the environment have brought the requirements into sharper focus, made the constraints more severe. Indeed it could be argued that the recent crises of inflation and recession may yet have at least one beneficial effect: under sheer fear for survival they could force companies to focus carefully on the *fundamentals* for the first time. It is not an exaggeration to say that, properly directed, this focus could convert the crisis into a real opportunity for more effective corporate strategy development in the future.

This article first appeared in *Long Range Planning*. Reprinted with permission from *Long Range Planning*, December 1976, pp 2–11. Copyright 1976, Pergamon Press, Ltd.

When this article was published, the author was director of The Boston Consulting Group Ltd.

The remainder of this article is devoted to a description of a suitable approach for identifying the fundamental strategic factors at the level of the individual business. [In the February edition of *Long Range Planning* the approach is extended to the process of overall strategy development for the multibusiness company.]

Strategy for Individual Businesses

At its most basic, long-term strategic success in an individual business depends on a company's ability to achieve a position such that its costs incurred in making the product concerned and delivering it to the relevant market are as low or lower than its competitors'. Since all competitors in a given business will tend to enjoy similar price levels for their products, having lower costs than competition will naturally result in superior profitability. This will be true regardless of general fluctuations in economic conditions and indeed the lower cost competitor should enjoy both superior and more stable profitability, as illustrated schematically in Figure 8.1. Developing sound strategy for an individual business thus requires a good understanding of the factors influencing long-run costs.

The Experience Curve Effect

It has long been recognized that the labor input required to manufacture a product tends to decline systematically with increases in accumulated production.[1] The Boston Consulting Group has found that the type of relationship involved—originally called the "learning curve"—frequently applies also to the *total cost* in-

---

Figure 8.1   The Benefits of Lower Costs (Schematic)

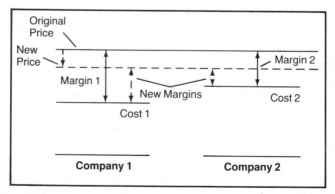

Company 1 has lower costs than Company 2 in the same business. It thus enjoys superior profitability. Should economic conditions change adversely, as represented by the price fall indicated by the broken line, Company 1's margins will drop proportionately less than Company 2's (by roughly one-third versus one-half in the diagram as indicated).

---

volved in manufacturing, distributing, and selling a product. The relationship can be expressed simply as follows: each time the accumulated experience of manufacturing a particular product doubles, the total unit cost in real terms (i.e., in "constant money", net of GDP inflation) can be made to decline by a characteristic percentage. The decline is normally in the region of 20–30 percent.

The fundamental nature of this relationship—note especially that it deliberately factors out the influence of inflation—makes it a particularly useful tool for product management and strategy development. The relationship has now been explored in a broad range of industries in many different countries, and it has been found to apply extremely widely. It is best illustrated by plotting real unit cost against cumulative production volume (a quantitative measure of "accumulated experience"). If logarithmic scales are used, a straight line normally results, as shown in the actual examples in Figure 8.2. This line typically has a slope such that the real unit cost drops to around 70–80 percent of its former value for each

Figure 8.2   Some Examples of Cost Experience Curves

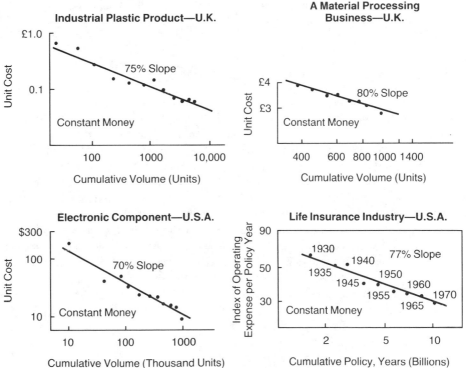

With the exception of the Life Insurance example which is derived from published data, the other curves were derived for products of clients in the course of consulting assignments performed by The Boston Consulting Group. The curves are therefore presented anonymously.

doubling of cumulative volume, and is usually referred to as an "experience curve."[2]

There are a variety of factors which contribute to the cost reduction performance implicit in the experience curve effect. These include:

- productivity improvement due to technological change and/or "learning" effects leading to adoption of new production methods,
- economies of scale and of specialization,
- displacement of less efficient factors of production, especially investment for cost reduction and capital-for-labor substitution,
- modifications and redesign of product for lower costs.

For present purposes, however, it is less important to catalogue all the means by which real costs can be reduced than it is to note the key strategic implications of the experience curve:

- failure to reduce costs along an appropriate experience curve slope (i.e., equivalent to that achieved by competitors) will lead to an uncompetitive cost position,
- failure to grow as rapidly as competitors will lead to an uncompetitive cost position: the competitor with the largest market share and hence, over time, the largest accumulated experience, should have the lowest costs and thus the highest profitability.

Achieving Real Cost Reduction in Practice

With respect to the first of these, it is by no means unusual to find managers who are skeptical about the possibility of achieving continuous real cost reductions over long periods of time. Indeed in our consulting practice we do occasionally find companies whose real cost performance has been on an upward, rather than a downward trend. This raises an important point: cost reductions are not *automatic*. Real costs have to be aggressively managed downwards. Poor control of operations; lack of investment in new methods enabling cost reduction; allowing an excessive build-up of nonproductive overhead: these can all lead to adverse real cost performance. The overwhelming evidence is, however, that given good management real costs *can* be made to decline *forever*. After all, this simply means that over time, and as a function of experience, we should get better (in real terms) in making and selling things—that we do not "un-learn" as experience builds. This is hardly counterintuitive!

It is often easiest to find means for real cost reduction in high growth businesses. Production scale is expanding, and there is plenty of scope for the introduction of new technology and labor-saving production methods without redundancy programs (the latter is often a problem in low growth U.K. industries). Under these conditions alert management will find many opportunities for reducing the level of "laggards" in the overall cost mix. In experience curve terms, the growth is simply resulting in rapidly expanding accumulated experience, and rapid progress is made along the cost curve. The rates of real cost decline which result can easily outstrip inflation, so that costs even decline when expressed in current money terms.

An Example: Electronic Calculators

Electronic calculators, which in the space of a few years have been transformed from expensive luxuries into everyday items, provide a very good example of this. Events in the calculator market also illustrate the strategic need for management to understand the dynamics of experience curve cost reduction if they are to remain effective competitors. A simplified history of the development of solid state electronic calculators is outlined in Table 8.1. Electronic calculators first appeared on the scene around the beginning of the 1960s, various rival firms claiming their invention. In the very early days it seems that the major element of cost was that of the discrete semiconductor devices (transistors, diodes) from which the calculators were made. The leading competitors were probably those based in the U.S.A. close to the best source of solid state components and technology.

At this time the calculators were extremely expensive. As a result the market was limited to those few applications for which they were cost effective. Meanwhile, however, tremendous expansion was taking place in solid state electronics in general: the market for solid state diodes, for example, regularly expanded in unit volume at a rate in excess of 50 percent per annum during the early and mid 1960s. This rapid growth engendered correspondingly rapid experience curve based cost and price declines in discrete devices: for example, between 1960 and 1965 the price of the average germanium diode in the U.S.A. fell by a factor of seven in real terms as illustrated in the price curves in Figure 8.3. Before long, the main concern in calculator costs became the labor costs, largely related to assembly.

As a result of this, during the mid 1960s the advantage passed to the low labor cost countries, including—at that time—Japan. Japanese companies had assumed virtual control of the market by the end of the decade. Costs continued to come down on an experience curve basis and the market expanded as prices dropped lower and lower, bringing electronic calculators within the range of more pockets. The overall size of the market was now beginning to look very attractive and in the early 1970s the American semiconductor manufacturers themselves entered the market. They realized that with the use of integrated circuits—the so-called LSI ("large scale integration") chips—many assembly operations could be

Table 8.1   Electronic Calculators (Solid State)

	Major Cost Elements	Dominant Competitors
Phase 1	Semiconductors (Discrete Devices)	Americans (e.g., Wang)
Phase 2	Assembly	Japanese (e.g., Sharp, Casio) S.E.Asia
Phase 3	Integrated Circuits	Americans (e.g., Texas Instruments)
Phase 4	Assembly Plus **Distribution**	? (Unresolved) (Tesco, Woolworth, Boots)

Figure 8.3   Price Experience Curves for Semiconductors

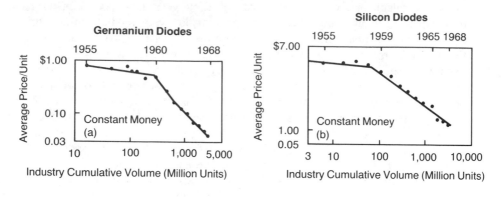

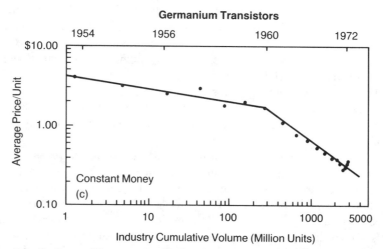

Notes on price patterns: The very steep price declines at certain times in some of these curves resulted from a competitive "shakeout" in which intense competitive activity was following a previous price "umbrella" period in which price reductions were not matching underlying experience curve cost decreases. This rapid decline normally only abates when one or more competitors relinquish their fierce attack on the market (or defenders relinquish their hold on market share) and stability returns. The alternative is stable pricing (parallel to costs) throughout. This appears to have been the pattern with integrated circuits. These price patterns are repeated in many different businesses.

Source: Perspective on Experience, The Boston Consulting Group Inc., Boston 1968, 1970, 1972.

made unnecessary. The overall cost advantage thus lay with the integrated circuit manufacturers themselves, and these companies entered the market in a big way, most notably Texas Instruments, who clearly set out to dominate the business.

Calculators were now at price levels such that they were becoming a consumer item. Growth was large: the annual market for consumer (as opposed to desk-top) calculators expanded from only 2 million units in 1972 to almost 20 million units by the end of 1974. Prices dropped dramatically, both as a result of experience curve cost reductions and also under the influence of aggressive com-

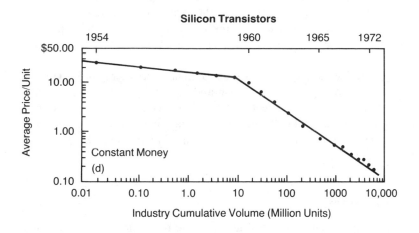

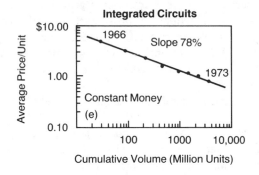

petition for market shares: a "shakeout" was occurring, rather as had happened in discrete semiconductor devices themselves early in the 1960s. This shakeout is not yet complete, and in cost experience curve terms there are some interesting considerations for the protagonists to bear in mind.

First, under the influence of the experience curve, the cost structure of making calculators must unquestionably be changing again: the integrated circuits and displays will be becoming a smaller part of the total cost. Labor costs and assembly in particular will be resuming their relative importance. This could well return the advantage to the low labor cost countries unless overall volume and experience have now reached a level at which highly automated assembly methods can be used enabling cost-effective manufacture in the U.S.A. and other advanced countries. The other consideration is the relative importance of distribution costs now that calculators themselves are so cheap. This encourages the distribution of calculators through mass merchandizing outlets such as those indicated in Table 8.1 rather than through specialty business machine stores. The manufacturers who win in the end may well be those with the best distribution links. Meanwhile, costs and prices continue to decline. Prices are probably declining even more rapidly than costs, for some competitors at least: Bowmar, the second largest U.S.A. manufacturer, quit the business in mid-1975 and filed for reorganization under U.S.A. bankruptcy laws. Texas Instruments, the largest manufacturer—not even in the business at the start of the decade—appears to be prepared to tolerate heavy losses in order to make the market its own. The competitive struggle continues.

The story of calculators is, of course, a dramatic tale of rapid growth and spectacular cost and price declines. A clear understanding of experience curve effects is obviously necessary for effective strategic management in that business. Electronic watches will undoubtedly be the next significant market to undergo similar dynamic changes as a result of high growth compounding the effects of the experience curve.

Low Growth Businesses

It should not be thought that, based on this extensive discussion of the calculator business, the experience curve is only relevant in high growth businesses. In low growth businesses too real cost reductions are possible, but at a lower rate given the slower rate of accumulation of experience. This is indicated by the examples in Figure 8.4. Thus even in a mature business, any competitor who is not achieving the appropriate experience curve cost reductions can expect to be in profit trouble over the long term.

This is the first simple and fundamental strategic message of the experience curve: never relax on cost control. In many growth businesses, U.S. companies actually control cost monthly on an experience curve basis. All companies, in all businesses, should at least ensure that their real costs are not rising on trend. Analysis often reveals that companies who pride themselves on good cost control are not in fact as tough as this in practice. They should be: the experience curve shows it can be done in the majority of cases.

Profitability and Market Share

The second of the two strategic implications listed earlier has an even more far-reaching significance, which certainly applies in both high and low growth businesses. This implication suggests that—even given good experience curve cost control—profitability, over the long term, will be directly related to market share. It is interesting that extensive independent business research—of which perhaps the best-known example is the recent 'PIMS' study—is also confirming the ubiquitous nature of this relationship.[3] Market share of the acquired firm has also been identified as the critical success requirement in a recent study of European acquisitions.[4] Only rarely is it possible to find explicit cost data for a number of competitors in a single business in order to verify directly the fact that the experience curve effect is at the root of this profit/market share relationship. One example is, however, given by the cost data made public in the U.S.A. in antitrust hearings concerning the business of manufacturing steam turbine electricity generators.

Figure 8.4   Some Experience Curves in Mature Businesses

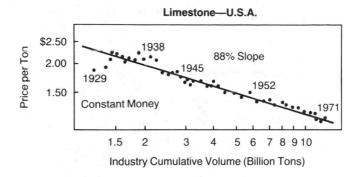

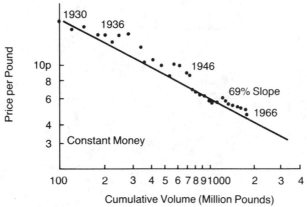

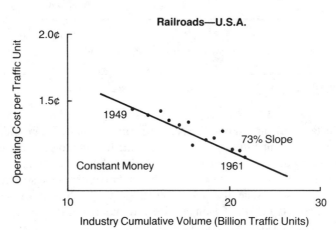

The curves for limestone and viscose rayon are for price; the curve for U.S. railroads is for cost.

Figure 8.5   U.S. Steam Turbine Generators: Competitive Cost Comparison

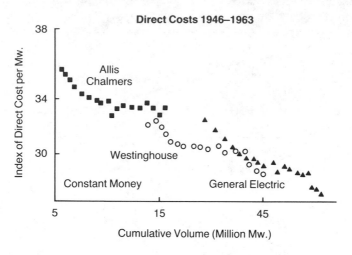

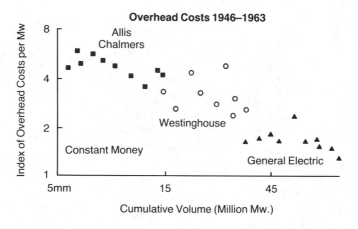

Source: Antitrust Hearings.

These data are displayed on an experience curve basis in Figure 8.5. General Electric, the largest competitor, at any point in time had the lowest unit costs. All three competitors tended to move in step over time down a common experience curve. While the market shares remained stable, relative cost levels stayed stable. General Electric was consistently more profitable than Westinghouse who in turn was more profitable than Allis Chalmers. Despite making real cost reductions on trend over time, Allis Chalmers could never catch up with the leaders unless the relative market share positions were changed. And indeed it looks as though Allis Chalmers even failed to secure real cost reductions on trend over the last 5 to 6 years of the period. It is perhaps not surprising that this has been a perennial problem business for Allis Chalmers.

Incidentally, it is worth noting that the slope of the experience curve relating the three companies' direct costs to each other is closer to 90 percent than to 70–80 percent. This is not uncommon for such "cross-sectional" experience curves and can arise from a variety of factors such as: equal raw material costs for all competitors; commonly available elements of production technology; tendency for the larger share competitor to spend more per unit on marketing to stabilize his higher share; and so forth. The slope is nevertheless sufficiently steep to lead to very marked profitability differences: at a price level yielding Allis Chalmers no margin above direct costs, General Electric's margin on these costs would be in excess of 20 percent.

This type of profitability/market share relationship is exhibited in a large range of effectively "single business" industries. An example from the U.K. is illustrated in Table 8.2.

This example—a low physical growth industry—is particularly interesting since it clearly shows the effects of market share on both absolute levels of profitability and stability of profitability: Transparent Paper, the marginal competitor, swung from loss to profit between 1970—a depressed year for the business—and 1973. British Cellophane, the largest competitor, was consistently the most profitable and experienced a less wild swing in performance between the two years. It is interesting that despite the fact that at a detailed level it is obviously an oversimplification to regard these as "single business" companies, and indeed there is obviously a degree of noncomparability between the three—differing degrees of participation in converting, for example—the overall results of the experience curve effect are quite clearly to be seen.

An Example: The Motor Industry

Perhaps the best known example of the profit/market share relationship is in another low growth business: the motor industry. GM, Ford, Chrysler and American Motors form a very clear pecking order in terms of size and profits. What may be less well known is the closely similar pattern displayed by the higher growth Japanese motor industry, as shown in Figure 8.6.

Table 8.2   The U.K. Cellophane Industry

	1970/1971		1972/1973	
	Sales (£m.)	PBIT/Sales (percent)	Sales (£m.)	PBIT/Sales (percent)
British Cellophane	41	10.0	68	14.9
British Sidac	15	3.1	19	7.8
Transparent Paper	8	(2.1)	11	5.6

Figure 8.6   The U.S. and Japanese Motor Companies

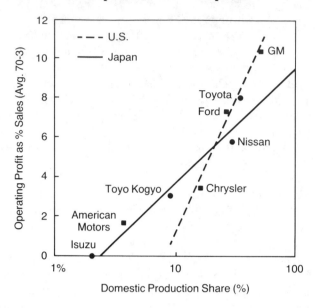

Despite very active competition at an "operational" level between these companies, the experience curve effect indicates that they cannot achieve long-term changes in profitability without changes in market share and hence, over time, relative experience and costs. The strategy implications for a low share competitor, such as American Motors or Chrysler, must include resignation to low profitability as long as market share remains low. This may well seem like a hopeless situation, given that gaining share in a major way against GM would probably be a long and extremely costly task, virtually impossible to fund given the lower present profitability of the companies.

The Need for "Segmentation"

There is, however, an alternative. Curiously, a guide to the solution can be found in the British motor industry, a cursory analysis of which would appear initially to refute the experience curve effect. As shown in Table 8.3 the profit relationship between Ford, Vauxhall and Chrysler is much as one would predict from the experience curve. British Leyland, however, which is almost twice the size of Ford in turnover, has been significantly less profitable on trend. The likely reason for this apparent anomaly is revealed on more detailed examination.

In Table 8.4, the basic product offerings of the U.K. motor companies are listed. The tremendous breadth of Leyland's product line relative to the other manufacturers is startling. This is, of course, partly a legacy of the way Leyland was put together by merger. Yet undoubtedly a detailed experience curve analysis would show that the main determinant of cost in an individual car model is pro-

Table 8.3   The British Motor Industry

	Average 1970–1973	
	Sales (£m.)	Op. Profit Margin (percent)
British Leyland	1261	4.1
Ford (U.K.)	716	4.8
Vauxhall	262	0.3
Chrysler (U.K.)	249	0.6

duction scale of that basic model, although the potential cost level is also likely to be influenced by the overall accumulated experience of the firm as a whole. Clearly Leyland's average volume *per model* is in fact lower than Ford's, and this will put a strategic limitation on the cost level which Leyland can attain even given the good labor relations, smooth production operations, and competitive manning which the CPRS study of the industry showed to be so necessary.[5]

Any future for Leyland in popular cars must surely lie at least in part in the direction of a strategy developing greater volume per model, either through increased market share, increased rationalization or specialization, or some combination of the two. The same could be said of Chrysler in either the U.K. or,

Table 8.4   U.K. Car Manufacturers Base Product Offerings (mid-1975)

Leyland	Ford	Vauxhall	Chrysler
Allegro	Escort	Viva	Imp
Maxi	Cortina	Chevette	Avenger
1800/2200	Capri	Victor	Hunter
MG Midget	Consul/Granada		
MGB			
Mini			
Marina			
Rover Saloon			
Range Rover			
Triumph Spitfire			
Toledo/Dolomite			
2000/2500 Saloon			
TR6			
TR7			
Stag			
Jaguar XJ6 12			
V12 Open E-Type			
(Daimler Limousine)			
(Taxi)			

indeed, the U.S.A., though here the degree of focus would need to be even greater. Again, this conclusion would tend to be supported by the findings of the CPRS study. It is certainly true, however, that huge overall size is not essential for profitability in the car industry: Rolls Royce Motors, with a turnover of the order of £50–60m., shows a before tax return on capital of almost 20 percent; Group Lotus, with a turnover of around £10m., has even higher profitability. Of course, seeking profitability by specialized *segment* based dominance can be risky, as other specialty car manufacturers have discovered from time to time (e.g., Jensen, Aston Martin). But this is the only approach for a small manufacturer if he is to have any chance of profitable survival.

At the other end of the scale, the most secure approach to profitability is to dominate the industry both overall *and* on a segment basis: in the U.S.A., GM is not only the largest manufacturer overall, it also offers the broadest product range. Unlike Leyland, however, its overall volume is such that it is still the largest manufacturer in terms of unit volume per basic model type, whether one is talking about body types or engines (Table 8.5). As a result it should enjoy superior costs (though even GM has suffered from specialist volume-based European and Japanese competition in small cars), and *hence* the higher profitability noted previously in Figure 8.6, which is now seen to be an oversimplification of the way the experience curve effect applies in this particular industry.

The motor industry example is particularly useful, since it demonstrates the need for explicit examination of business segmentation before applying the experience curve concept for purposes of strategy development. Most broad business areas do in fact break down into a number of business segments which have fairly distinct economics. However, the process of developing an understanding of the basis on which a strategic segmentation should be made is often very complex. It normally involves making a detailed examination of each major element of cost and value addition in the business, and exploring the possible basis on which an experience based advantage relative to competition could exist within each element.

It is not possible within the scope of this article to go into the process of segmentation in great depth. It is in any case a process which is difficult to describe in general terms. The motor industry example does, however, give a feel

---

Table 8.5   U.S. Car Manufacturers: Volume by Model (1974)

Company	Total Volume	Base Body Types		Engine Types	
		No. Offered	Vol. per Type	No. Offered	Vol. per Type
GM	4440	6	740	4	1110
Ford	2300	5	460	4	580
Chrysler	1270	4	320	3	420
American Motors	260	4	65	2	130

The manufacturing approach adopted by the U.S. manufacturers is such that quite a broad range of superficially different vehicles can be produced on a few identical chassis.

for some of the issues which can be raised concerning production costs. Frequently there are also important segmentation issues in the marketing area as well. For example, this is undoubtedly a further dimension which would actually need to be considered in practice in the motor industry before strategy could be finally determined. The reason American Motors lies so much above the profit trend of the other three U.S.A. manufacturers undoubtedly results to a significant degree from a market segmentation approach on their part (e.g., focus on smaller cars).

The overall aim of segmentation can be summarized, then, as the identification of product-market segments which are sufficiently distinct, economically and competitively, that it is meaningful to develop strategy for them separately as "individual businesses." The segmentation process must also identify clearly the experience curve basis on which a superior cost position can be developed in the business segment, to enable competitive strategy to be properly developed. In some cases simple relative market share in the segment may not be the sole determinant: all elements of cost do not always have the same experience base, also, some cost elements may share in experience with other business segments. In these cases, it may be necessary to focus directly on likely relative costs by synthesizing a view of the effects of the company's varying position in the different experience bases into its implications for overall costs.

Summary
The Experience Curve and Individual Business Strategy

It is in practice at the more detailed business segment level that the concept of the value of relative scale and market share is applicable. The basic strategic message of the experience curve can thus be summarized as follows:

The largest competitor in a particular business area should have the potential for the lowest unit costs and hence greatest profits. If it is unprofitable it is probably either being 'out-segmented' by more focused competition, or it is defective in experience curve cost control.

Smaller competitors in a business area are likely to be unprofitable, and they will remain so unless a strategy can be devised for gaining dominant market share at reasonable cost. If achieving overall dominance is not feasible, then the smaller competitor should seek to identify an economically distinct segment of the business in which he can dominate the relevant experience bases sufficiently to attain a viable cost position overall. If this is not feasible, then the smaller competitor must resign himself to inadequate profitability forever. Under these circumstances the business should really be phased out.

These are the fundamental rules of individual business strategy. They focus on position *relative to competitors*. Relative competitive position thus provides the required simple and unchanging objective towards which strategy development efforts should be single-mindedly focused. This objective will remain valid in spite of unpredictable changes in the economic environment. Come inflation or deflation, boom or bust, the superior business performers will be those in strong market positions relative to competition in the relevant business segment. Strategic planning must concentrate on achieving dominance as its primary object. Any efforts directed towards environmental forecasting or extrapolative long range planning are really only useful in so far as they contribute to this goal.

These conclusions at the individual business level imply that in any multi-business company, the best performers over the long term will tend to be those businesses in which the company has a superior market share; "problem" businesses or divisions will tend to be those where market shares are marginal. This simple observation, coupled with an appreciation of the effect and value of long-term growth, leads to an extremely useful integrated approach to overall strategy development for the multibusiness company.

References

1. One of the earliest references to this phenomenon was Wright, T. P., "Factors Affecting the Cost of Airplanes," *J. Aeron. Sci.* 3, 122–128, February (1936).
2. For a full description of the experience curve effect and further examples of its application in practice see The Boston Consulting Group, *Perspectives on Experience*, 1968, 1970, 1972.
3. A concise report of the main findings of the PIMS study is given in Robert D. Buzzell, Bradley T. Gale, and Ralph G. M. Sultan, "Market Share: Key to Profitability," *Harvard Business Review*, January–February 1975.
4. John Kitching, "Winning and Losing with European Acquisitions," *Harvard Business Review*, March–April 1974.
5. The Central Policy Review Staff, *The Future of the British Car Industry*, Her Majesty's Stationery Office, London (1975).

9

Diagnosing the Experience Curve

George S. Day
and David B. Montgomery

Few strategy concepts have gained wider acceptance than the notion underlying the experience curve, that value-added costs net of inflation decline systematically with increases in cumulative volume. The logic is appealing, the empirical support seems persuasive and the strategic implications are often profound. Yet despite these advantages, acceptance is waning. The application problems were always formidable, but now there is a growing suspicion that some of the key strategic implications may be delusions (Kiechel 1981).

Fortunately, strategic concepts also continue to improve with cumulative research and applications activity. As a result, there is now much better appreciation of the various types of experience curves that are available and the conditions under which they yield meaningful strategic insights. Concurrent progress has been made in identifying the source of observed experience effects and clarifying the measurement and estimation problems. This paper evaluates this progress as a guide for both analysts and managers to the state of the art and suggests productive directions for further work. Before turning to specific applications issues, we will first review the basic concept and the supporting empirical evidence.

The Concept of the Experience Curve

The antecedent of the experience curve is the production learning curve, first observed in the 1930s as a systematic decline in the number of labor hours required to produce an airplane (Yelle 1979). It was only in the mid-1960s that the notion

This article first appeared in the *Journal of Marketing*, 47 (Spring 1983): 44–58. Reprinted with permission from *Journal of Marketing*, published by the American Marketing Association.

When this article was published the authors were Professor of Marketing, University of Toronto, and Professor of Marketing, Stanford University, respectively.

of the learning curve was generalized by the Boston Consulting Group (1972) to encompass the behavior of all value-added costs and prices as cumulative volume or experience increase.

The usual form of the experience curve[1] is:

$$C_n = C_1 \, n^{-\lambda} \tag{1}$$

where

C_n = cost of the nth unit,
C_1 = cost of the first unit,
n = cumulative number of units,
λ = elasticity of unit costs with respect to cumulative volume.

The form of the function reflects a constant elasticity λ and the cost (price) will fall by

$$1 - k = 1 - 2^{-\lambda} \tag{2}$$

percent each time experience doubles. If k = 80, then cost will fall by $1 - 80 = 20\%$ as experience doubles and the experience curve is said to be an 80% curve or have an 80% slope. This slope will only be observed if the effects of inflation have been removed and all costs and prices are stated in real terms. Also, it should be emphasized that the curves apply to cumulative experience and not to calendar time. Experience will tend to cumulate faster in calendar time during periods of rapid growth and relatively early in the product life cycle.

Supporting Evidence

Thousands of experience curves have been plotted during the past 15 years by staff of the Boston Consulting Group (Henderson 1980b). These analyses have ranged from the direct costs of U.S. long distance calls, integrated circuits and life insurance policies, to the prices of bottle caps in Germany, refrigerators in Britain and polystyrene molding resin in the U.S. A typical example is the set of price experience curves for different sizes of Japanese motorcycles, prepared by BCG (1975) as part of a study of the British motorcycle industry, shown in Figure 1.

Unfortunately, the bulk of the evidence in support of the experience curve phenomenon has been graphical in nature and has not focused on the measurement and econometric issues, which would be required for a more scientific assessment. However, several studies that are more carefully prepared also lend credence to the experience phenomenon. Wooley (1972) obtained cost data for 18 products from 10 companies using BCG case files. His sample was carefully selected to avoid most of the difficult application issues discussed in the next section and encompassed products in the chemical, paper, steel, electronic, knit product and mechanical goods industries. His results strongly support the experience phenom-

---

[1]Equation (1) is of the Cobb-Douglas production function and is linear in the logarithm. A form similar to equation (1) is postulated for price, but the elasticity λ may differ from the elasticity corresponding to cost experience.

Figure 1   Japanese Motorcycle Industry: Price Experience Curves (1959–1974)

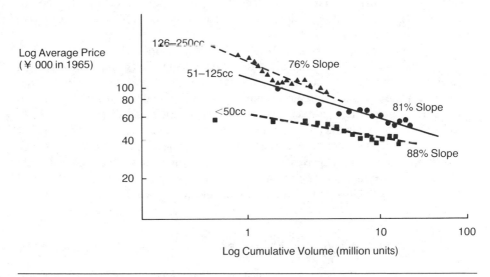

Source: MITI (BCG 1975)

enon with over 80% of the R^2 values exceeding .8 and over 80% of the λs significant at the .01 level. The median experience slope in his sample was 77.5%, with over 75% of the slopes between 70 and 90%, which is the usual range suggested by BCG based upon their client studies.

Rutenberg (1976) cites three rigorous econometric studies that support the experience curve and illustrate its robustness with respect to variations in factor input conditions. The first was a study by Rapping (1965) analyzing the output of WW II liberty ships being manufactured at different sites, each with different rates of cumulative production. His results indicated that with each doubling of accumulated output a ship required 17% less input. At the other extreme were two studies in which the factor inputs were held constant, and yet the rate of output per unit of input improved due to experience. In Arrow's (1961) classic paper on learning by doing, he cites the Horndal iron works in Sweden which experienced productivity increases in output per man hour of 2% per annum even though there had been no new capital investment in 15 years. Similarly, Barkai and Levhari (1973) found that experience steadily increased productivity by 0.4 to 0.6% per annum on an Israeli kibbutz even though capital and labor inputs were held constant. Here the gains came from changes in the output, as experience revealed which crops were best suited to the growing conditions.

Evidence to support the existence of price experience curves comes from studies by Stobaugh and Townsend (1975) and Lieberman (1981). In the former study price changes over intervals of one, three, five and seven years were estimated as a function of number of producers (competition), degree of product standardization, cumulative industry experience and static scale economies. The data were for 82 petrochemicals. Of the four explanatory variables, cumulative experience was the most important in predicting price changes. Further, when the products were divided into 13 homogeneous subsets, adding the other three variables to the experience variable was significant at the .05 level in only three of the 13 instances. For these products at least, the experience effect appears to have a dominant effect on price.

The Lieberman (1981) study analyzed three-year price changes for 37 products in the chemical processing industries. Price changes were postulated to be a function of market concentration, short-run imbalances between supply and demand, experience effects, scale economies, capital embodied technological improvements and changes in factor costs. The results indicated that cumulative experience was very significant, with a coefficient corresponding to a 72% slope.

Although there are several fairly rigorous studies supporting the existence and importance of the experience effect, econometric issues have received scant attention. For example, what should be the specification in terms of variables and functional form?[2] How should the errors be specified? What about errors in the variable measures? What is the potential for simultaneous equations bias?

Sources of the Experience Curve Effect

Given evidence to support the existence of an experience curve effect, the question arises as to why this effect appears. There are three major sources: learning by doing, technological advances and scale effects.

Learning encompasses the increasing efficiency of *all* aspects of labor input as a result of practice and the exercise of ingenuity, skill and increased dexterity in repetitive activities. Learning includes the discovery of better ways to organize work via improved methods and work specialization (for example, doing half as much twice as often). Similarly, the performance of production equipment will improve as personnel become better acquainted with their operation. For example, the capacity of a fluid catalytic cracking unit typically "grows" about 50% over a ten-year period as operators, engineers and managers gain experience in operating the unit (Hirchmann 1964). Similarly, Joskow and Rozanski (1979) found that learning by doing increases the effective capacity or output of a particular piece of nuclear equipment by approximately 5% per year. The reason is that with experience workers were more effective in using and maintaining the equipment and various technical "bugs" were identified and corrected.

Marketing activities also benefit from learning by doing. A recent survey of 13,000 new products in 700 companies (Booz, Allen and Hamilton 1981) found that cost of introduction of new products declined along a 71% slope.

Technological improvements also contribute to the experience curve effect. New production processes, especially in capital intensive industries, often contribute substantial economies. For example, Golden Wonder's introduction of continuous flow potato chip manufacture versus the traditional batch frying mode enabled them to achieve substantial economies in heating and quality control and

---

[2]More attention has been given to these issues in the learning curve literature. Yelle (1979) describes four models other than the log linear, that provide better fits to the data in certain circumstances. See Montgomery and Day (1983) for a further discussion of these issues.

played an important part in Golden Wonder's achievement of market share parity with the formerly dominant firm (Beevan 1974). Changes in the resource mix, such as automation replacing labor, also provide a technology driven basis for the experience effect. Process and product changes that produce yield improvements are yet another source of experience effects. Product standardization and redesign are also sources of the effect, as with the economies achieved in the automobile industry by modularization of the engine, chassis and transmission production.

Economies of scale, from the increased efficiency due to size, are another source of the experience curve effect. These scale effects apply to the majority of investment and operating costs. Seldom does an increase in throughput require an equivalent increase in capital investment, size of sales force or overhead functions. Scale is also an enabling condition for other cost reduction activities. Thus, scale creates the potential for volume discounts, vertical integration and the division of labor, which in turn facilitate learning.

Decomposing the Experience Curve

Most experience curves reflect the joint effects of learning, technological advances and scale.[3] For example, Sultan (1974) found that the costs per megawatt of output of steam turbine generators followed a 70% slope because of (a) practice in making units of each size, which followed an 87% slope, (b) scale economies by building larger units, 600 MW rather than 200 MW units, and (c) technological improvements in turbine bucket design, bearings and high strength steels for rotor shafts, which made possible the designs for larger units. (See Figure 2.)

Normally it is difficult to distinguish the separate contributions of scale, learning and technology, in part because the process of learning usually coincides with the expansion of scale. Only a few efforts have been made to measure the relative importance of the three basic effects, and they only apply to the chemical industry. Hollander (1965) in a study of the sources of efficiency increases at DuPont rayon plants concluded that only 10–15% of the efficiency gains were due to scale effects, whereas the remainder was accounted for by technology and learning. Of this remainder between 32 and 75% (depending on the plant) was ascribed to learning. Hence scale seems relatively less important, while technology and learning have major impact. Interestingly, Hollander found that the largest proportion of the technology-driven cost reductions were due to a series of minor technical changes based on a broad consensus that continuous cost reduction action was a high priority.

Similar results for price experience were found by Stobaugh and Townsend (1975) and Lieberman (1981). Stobaugh and Townsend report that static scale economies did not account for price changes to the same extent that the confounded experience variables of learning, technology and dynamic scale did. Lieberman found a 71% experience curve when scale, new plant introductions and new competitive entry were confounded with cumulative volume, while the slope

---

[3]Some authors, such as Abell and Hammond (1979), prefer to keep scale effects separate from experience effects. Others, such as Pessemier (1980) prefer to distinguish static scale effects from dynamic scale effects that are achieved over time.

Figure 2   Cost Experience for Steam Turbine Generators

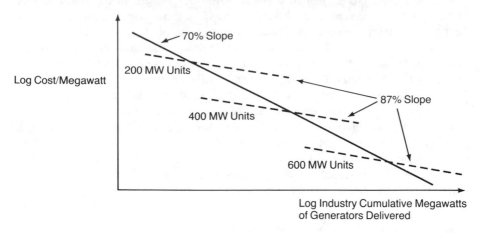

rose to 77% when these variables were separately analyzed. Thus, while scale plays an obvious role, in these instances it does not appear to be a dominant component of the experience effect.

Despite the difficulty of decomposing the experience curve to understand the underlying sources, the effort is critical to informed strategic application because:

- Cost reductions due to learning and technology are the result of continuous, planned efforts by management. Cumulative experience does not guarantee that costs will decline but simply presents management with an opportunity to exploit.
- Where the cost reductions are being achieved primarily from economies of scale through more efficient, automated facilities and vertical integration (Porter 1979), then cumulative experience may be unimportant to the relative cost position. In these situations a new entrant may be more efficient than more experienced producers.

Types of Experience Curves

Within a specific market environment a variety of experience curves can be found, depending on whether one is concerned with:

- costs or prices,
- total costs or elements of cost,
- the effect of industry or company accumulated experience,
- dynamic (time-dependent) or static (cross-sectional) comparisons.

Three combinations of these variables are of particular interest, for they lead to experience curves that are interdependent but offer very different strategic insights. The first is the company cost compression curve that relates changes in the company's costs to accumulated company experience. The second is the competitive cost comparison curve that shows the current costs of all direct competitors as a function of their respective levels of cumulative experience at that point in time. The third curve describes the behavior of industry prices and average costs as total industry experience cumulates. This last curve has a close relationship to the product life, which we will discuss at the end of this section.

Company Cost Compression Curves

This is the easiest curve to establish, for it is derived from internal cost and production records. To be sure there are many hurdles to overcome in establishing the cost corresponding to each level of company production experience with a specific product, service or cost element. Short-term discontinuities will be found due to revisions in accounting procedures, changes in the product and cost variances from fluctuations in the level of capacity utilization. Nonetheless it is usually possible to develop a meaningful company cost curve, which has immediate application as a cost control tool. Standard costs can be set, based on continuing or improving past patterns of reductions with experience, and management can be held to these targets. Abell and Hammond (1979) argue that the discontinuities that occur render the experience curve less useful for short-run cost control. In light of the ambiguities of other kinds of experience curves, some would argue that this is the most useful of all the experience curves.

Competitive Cost Comparison Curves

These are cross-sectional experience curves that relate the relative cost positions of the competitors in an industry (Henderson 1978). With this curve it is possible to estimate the profitability of each of the competitors at the prevailing price. While potentially the most useful experience curve, it is also the most difficult to obtain.

We usually know the slope of our own cost curve and can reasonably estimate the cumulative experience of the relevant competitors from their market shares. Unfortunately we cannot immediately jump to the next step, which is to locate each of these competitors on our cost curve according to their relative experience. This will invariably overstate the cost differences. For example, the real price per unit of a split system central air conditioner (CAC) has been declining about 20% with each doubling of industry experience. Yet a cross-sectional experience curve relating the costs of the major competitors has a 92% slope (Biggadike 1977). There are many reasons why the slope of the cross-section curve is likely to be shallower than other experience curves:

1.   Followers into a market usually have lower initial costs than the pioneer:

   ■   The follower has an opportunity to learn from the pioneer's mistakes by hiring key personnel, "tear-down" analysis of the competitor's product and conducting marketing research to learn the problems and unfulfilled expectations of customers and distributors;

- A follower may leap-frog the pioneer by using more current technology or building a plant with a larger current scale of operations;
- There may be opportunities for followers to achieve advantages on certain cost elements by sharing operations or functions with other parts of the company.

2.   All competitors should benefit from cost reductions achieved by outside suppliers of components or production equipment. For example, in the spinning and weaving industry most of the advances in technology come from textile machinery manufacturers who share these improvements with their customers.

3.   One competitor may have lower factor costs than another for reasons that are independent of experience, such as location advantages, the benefits of government subsidies, and reduced susceptibility to cost element inflation because of differences in cost structure (McLagan 1981).

4.   Another problem that clouds cross-sectional analyses is differences between overhead rates of competitors. A large multidivision company with heavy corporate overhead allocations to each strategic business unit may be at a disadvantage against a specialist producer with very lean and efficient management. Whether there is a disadvantage depends on the ability of the diversified firm to exploit opportunities for shared experience gains through corporate coordination.

5.   Finally, if there have been significant changes in market position, current market shares may not be good measures of relative cumulative output.

The net effect of these factors is a cross-sectional experience curve with shallow slope, masking steeper company cost curves that are often approximately parallel to one another, as in Figure 3. Of course, it is not necessary that the various company cost curves be parallel, since this implies equivalence in both ability to exploit cost reduction opportunities and access to the necessary technology.

Narrowing of Competitive Cost Differentials

As markets mature and the forces acting on the cross-sectional experience curve continue to operate, competitive cost differences tend to narrow. The extent of this narrowing has been documented in the PIMS data base (Buzzell 1981).

Further narrowing of competitive cost differentials may be triggered by changes in industry structure. In some industries the full line manufacturer is also a full service manufacturer, with concomitant high overheads and short production runs with many items in the product line. But as markets mature, an increasing proportion of customers have less need for technical service, engineering and lab support, and applications assistance. Thus the full line, full service manufacturers may be vulnerable to competitors with less experience but who incur fewer cost elements and are attacking specific segments. Indeed, the increasing fragmentation of markets during the maturity stage is a serious challenge to the full line manu-

Figure 3   Competitive Cost Comparison Curves

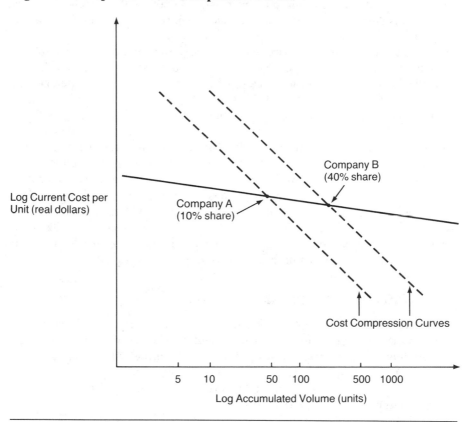

Log Current Cost per Unit (real dollars)

Company B (40% share)

Company A (10% share)

Cost Compression Curves

Log Accumulated Volume (units)

5   10   50   100   500   1000

facturer, for it creates a pressure for a proliferation of products to satisfy the needs of different segments. The ensuing costs may dissipate the advantages of experience.

Industry Price Experience Curves

This curve relates the industry average price to industry cumulative experience. It may be difficult to establish for two reasons. The first question is, what is or was the price prevailing at the time corresponding to an industry cumulative volume? List prices are notoriously unrealistic, given the fluctuating discount structures (hidden and otherwise) that exist to cope with changes in the industry supply picture (Burck 1972). A single price may be misleading if it requires averaging across disparate models, features and accessories, or if different competitors use different marketing mixes. When some competitors are full service high-quality suppliers, and others provide minimal technical support or applications engineering while selling components, there will be a high variance in observed prices. It must always be remembered that the customer is paying for value in use. This value can be enhanced not only by a real price cut but also by adding benefits and services without corresponding price increases. The offer of a warehousing plan that permits customers to lower their component inventories is surely a price reduction.[4]

A meaningful industry price curve also requires we know the industry cumulative volume. This may be a problem simply because good industry data are unavailable or cannot be trusted. The problem is aggravated when different competitors use different strategies. This is one aspect of the question of defining industry boundaries to which we will return shortly.

The Captive Manufacturing Issue.   In some component markets the process of vertical integration is so far advanced that more than 50% of total output is "in-fed" (Wilson and Atkin 1976). If this output is purely captive it may be possible to ignore it. This would be dangerous, however, if the practice is to sell excess output on the open market to ensure optimum capacity utilization. If a beer company periodically sells 20–30% of their output of cans to other companies (especially during nonpeak periods), the long-run price patterns in the industry will eventually reflect the impact of these high-volume, low-cost producers.

Costs, Prices and the Product Life Cycle

The average industry price curve frequently does not decline as fast as the cost curve in the early stages of the life cycle (Hedley 1976). Since the widening gap is inherently unstable, there is a sharp readjustment during a shake-out period and prices eventually establish a stable margin relationship with costs.[5] This pattern is juxtaposed on an idealized product life cycle in Figure 4, as there is often a correspondence of the stages (Day 1981a).

Introductory Period.   During this period prices are held below current costs in expectation of lower costs in the future and to expand the market for the product by increasing the cross-elasticity of demand with existing substitutes. A steep cost compression curve suggests a penetration price, substantially below current costs (Dean 1976). Such a pricing strategy is even more attractive when (1) there is little prospect of creating and maintaining product superiority over competitors, (2) when there are few barriers to entry and expansion by competitors, or (3) when the lower price will significantly expand the current market. When and if the product takes off, the period of negative margins will eventually come to an end. Robinson and Lakhani (1975) have shown that for a new product without direct competition and in the presence of imitative consumer demand, an optimal price

---

[4]Hedonic price studies may prove helpful in disentangling the impact of different product features (Griliches 1961).

[5]Seldom is an average industry cost curve available for this purpose, as it requires knowledge of individual company costs, weighted by the unit production for each competitor, that correspond to each level of industry cumulative volume (Conley 1970).

Figure 4   Product Life Cycle Stages and the Industry Price Experience Curve

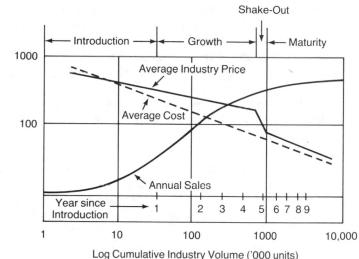

policy would be a penetration price substantially below initial costs.[6] The demand stimulus provided by this very low price coupled with experience based cost declines were found to lead to profits several times greater than those generated by a myopic price policy that sets price to equate marginal revenue and marginal cost each period.

In an economic analysis of the impact of the experience effect on competitive entry into new products, Spence (1981) found that the experience curve could create substantial entry barriers by conveying substantial cost advantages on the early entrants. Surprisingly, his analysis demonstrated that moderate experience slopes create a greater entry barrier than do very small or very large slopes. With small slopes experience gives little advantage to the pioneers, while steep slopes make it relatively easy for late entrants to catch up with the early entrants. Entry was found to cease after three or four firms had entered under conditions of a moderately sloped experience curve. Interestingly, Spence found that market performance improved sharply from monopoly to two or three entrants but rather slowly thereafter. Hence experience-generated concentration may not prove substantially harmful.

[6]Dolan and Jeuland (1981) also have developed a model that derives an optimal pricing policy, which depends on the nature of the demand and experience curves and the type of product, whether a durable or a repeat purchase item.

Growth Period: Building an Umbrella.   The germanium transistor market is a good illustration of what can happen during the growth period. As demand surged, the overriding problem was obtaining product supply. Certainly there was no incentive to cut prices. However, the combination of rising average margins and rapid growth soon attracted a number of new entrants. These new entrants were able to survive profitably because the price umbrella was still high enough to cover their high initial costs. Because of their narrow margins these new entrants were motivated to gain share at the expense of the market leader and thereby reduce costs more rapidly than the leader.

During the growth period of the market leader who condones a high umbrella is trading long-run market share for current profits. There are many reasons for electing this choice. The current profits are often needed to fund the still rapid growth in capacity, working capital, R&D and market development activity. The reward system often puts a premium on immediate profits. This also reduces the incentive to build capacity beyond short-run needs, since poor capacity utilization will penalize profit performance. If market growth is underestimated the market leader may be forced to give up further share because of capacity constraints.

The Shake-Out Period.   The number of competitors attracted by the growth opportunities and high umbrella margins can be quite amazing. In industries such as housewares with modest barriers to entry, it is not uncommon to find 20 to 40 hopefuls entering during the growth period. Sooner or later the umbrella folds, for one or all of the following reasons:

- Growth slows or declines because the market is close to saturation or a recession has intervened;
- Aggressive late entrants buy into the market by cutting prices (a variant is the acquisition of an also-ran by a cash-rich outsider that creates a competitor who can afford to invest in market share gains);
- The market leader attempts to stem the previous erosion of market share or regain previous share levels by cutting price;
- Retailers or wholesalers have limited space or capacity and decide to limit their offerings to the top three or four competitors that have a strong customer franchise.

The observable result is a sharp break in the price trend. The severity of the break will depend on the number of competitors, the size of the umbrella and the abruptness of the slowdown. In the meantime, there are still expansion plans in the pipeline that come into production during this period. The ensuing excess capacity puts further downward pressure on prices. The shake-out period becomes aptly named as marginal producers are eventually squeezed out of the market.

All these factors are currently operating in the personal computer market, where at least 150 companies build computers and another 300 have been formed to cater to the aftermarket for peripherals, software, service and support. Most of these aspirants entered the market within a two-year period. It is now clear that the market cannot support most of these companies, and so it is predicted that by 1986 there could be only a dozen companies offering microcomputer lines (*Business Week* 1982).

Toward Maturity and Beyond.   We have already seen that competitive cost differentials steadily narrow as the market matures. At the same time the effect of experience on real unit costs and prices becomes less evident. Doubling times are longer, so year-to-year cost reductions tend to be swamped by cost fluctuations induced by the economic situation, availability of materials and so on.

Eventually the product progresses into late maturity and decline, with unpredictable consequences for the experience curve. For example, one manufacturer of industrial gases observed that the cost compression curve for their bottled oxygen had not only flattened but was turning up somewhat. This was not happening with either liquified or pipelined oxygen supplied by the same manufacturer. The two latter forms of oxygen supply were newer and their success had pushed bottled oxygen into the decline stage of the life cycle. Despite the drop in industry sales, no competitors had dropped out, which meant everyone was suffering reduced levels of capacity utilization and higher production costs.

Measurement and Interpretation Questions

The insights gained from the three types of experience curves depend on numerous judgments as to the treatment of costs, inflation, shared experience and the definition of the units of analysis. These put significant limitations on the strategic relevance of experience curve analysis.

Which Costs?

Although it is claimed that the experience effect applies to all costs, it is misleading to consider only total costs. Total costs decline from the effect of experience on the cost elements that combine to make up the product, including components, assembly, packaging, distribution and so on. Only some of these costs can be influenced by management. Also the amounts of experience accumulated in each cost element may be very different, as a result of shared experience, and the slopes of the experience curves may also vary between elements. For these reasons, special attention must be given to the controllable elements of value-added costs that have been adjusted for inflation.

Cost Component Analysis.   When the slopes of the experience curves of major elements are different, the relative importance of each component changes as experience with the total product accumulates. As Table 1 shows, this may also lead to a change in the slope of the overall experience curve. In this hypothetical example, cost component B with the shallowest cost curve rapidly becomes the most important cost component. While this is an extreme circumstance, the same general effect is logically at work whenever the experience curves for major cost components have very different slopes. A similar evolution in cost structure would be revealed if component B had a more steeply sloped experience curve, but the total company experience with that component was extensive. This would be another reason for the costs of component B to decline at a much slower rate than the costs of A.

Table 1   Changes in Cost Structure as Experience Cumulates

	Cost per Component at Each Level of Cumulated Experience		
	2000 Units	8000 Units	32,000 Units
Cost Component A (70% slope)	$1.00	$0.49	$0.24
Cost Component B (90% slope)	1.00	0.81	0.66
	$2.00	$1.30	$0.90
Average slope of total cost curve	80%		85%

Another implication of the example of Table 1 is that products are likely to exhibit shallower total cost experience curves as they mature. In effect the slope of the total cost curve is increasingly influenced by the cost element which is declining the slowest with each doubling of total experience. But when the cost components each follow equation (1) with separate elasticities, the total cost function does not have the form of equation (1) and is no longer linear in the logarithms. Thus, what often appears as a straight line on log paper may actually be a poor fit that obscures a gradual flattening of the experience curve. For further elaboration see Montgomery and Day (1983).

Value-Added Costs. The experience effect is largely felt on those costs that contribute to the value added during manufacturing or when providing the service. Inclusion of all costs and especially raw materials costs may mask the desired effect. This was the problem in an analysis of the evolution of costs of insulated wire and cable. The total cost was dominated by raw materials elements, notably aluminum and copper, which are commodities subject to wide price swings. Only when the raw material costs were excluded was any pattern evident. Whether cost elements outside of the value-added portion are included in the analysis depends on the ability of the company to influence the purchase price through scale and experience. For example, significant influence would be implied if a supplier dedicated most of the output of a component to a particular customer. When in doubt, it is always desirable to break total costs into elements.

If value-added costs decline faster than other costs with increasing experience, the industry price experience curve is likely to have a smaller slope than the industry value-added experience curve. In the U.S. brewing industry between 1950 and 1976, value-added costs (payroll, advertising, capital) declined on a 76% curve while prices declined on an 87% curve. Since value-added costs were only about 32% of per barrel costs in the early 1970s, it appears likely that other costs such as taxes, raw materials, freight and containers were not declining as rapidly.

Controllable Costs. Process industries such as chemicals and metal refining, which are subject to rigorous safety and environmental regulations, find that the costs of these regulations behave like an unproductive "add-on." The consequence is most noticeable with the company cost compression curve, which has a dismaying habit of turning up, perhaps with a jump discontinuity, as in Figure 5.

Figure 5   Discontinuities in the Cost Compression Curve

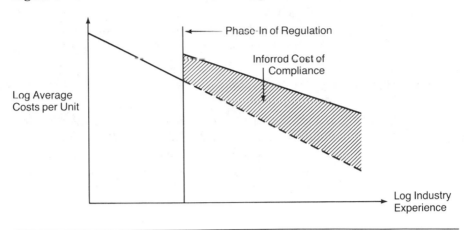

It is less clear what impact a regulation has on relative cost positions within an industry, for regulatory burdens often fall most heavily on smaller producers. This has become very noticeable in the auto industry, as GM spreads the costs of mandated downsizing across many units. Similarly the cost of label changes in the food industry is proportionately greater for small-volume packers.

Identifying Relevant Costs.   Most cost accounting systems are designed to serve many purposes and the resulting costs are often wildly inappropriate for experience curve analysis. The major problems are with the allocation of costs, the treatment of joint costs, and the deferred recognition of actual costs until revenue is realized. Cost allocations may be made of departments or profit centers rather than to specific products. Shared resources, such as pooled sales force, researcher and support staff may be allocated as a percentage of total sales accounted for by the product rather than reflecting the actual use of the resources. There is always the possibility that unit costs are not comparable over time because the allocation of joint costs has been arbitrarily changed or different accounting conventions have been used. Consequently, the analysis should be based on cash inputs rather than costs as recorded by cost accountants (Henderson 1980a).

Choosing the Unit of Analysis.   When costs are averaged across a broad product line, a change in the total cost may be observed simply as a result of a change in the sales mix. For example, refrigerator manufacturers have been producing larger units on average. Here the solution is to define the product as a cubic foot of usable refrigeration space and observe the evolution of costs on this basis. This will only partially control for a shift in the mix of sizes, as the cost of a cubic foot is cheaper in a larger refrigerator. A related problem is the treatment of product variations and modifications, especially where the aim is to enhance the value of the product to the customer. At the extreme the product may have changed so much that it no longer resembles the original.

Which Deflator?

There is no single rate of inflation (Wilson 1982). For example, during 1980 when the GNP deflator was 9.0% and the implicit price deflator for producers' durable equipment was 6.5%, the following industry inflation rates were observed:

Textile machinery	10.2% per year
Underground mining machinery	2.5% per year
Accounting machines and calculators	0.6% per year

On balance the GNP deflator is a poor representation of inflation in any particular industry, although it may be adequate to evaluate long-term shifts in strategy. For shorter-term cost analysis it is better to choose a deflator that reflects the inflation of factor costs within the industry. However, care must be taken that the deflator is not so closely allied with the specific industry that the slope is defined away.

What About Shared Experience?

Cost differences between competitors are often less than we would expect from our knowledge of relative market shares and the slope of the company cost compression curve. A major reason is the effect of shared experience between two or more products using a common resource. The experience gained with one of the products can be applied to a reduction of the costs of related products.

For example, suppose company A and company B both produce product X using the same three steps. However, whereas company A only produces product X using these three steps, company B makes two other products, both of which use the same first two steps as product X. Company B then should have the advantage of the volume generated by these other products, all contributing to its cumulative experience in the first two steps. In this circumstance, if companies A and B have similar cumulative volumes for product X, company B would have lower costs on the first two steps and thereby should have lower costs and higher profits on product X than company A. Company B might well still have a cost advantage even if company A has more experience with product X because of company B's shared experience with the other two products.

Shared experience comes in many guises:

- manufacturer of semi-conductor components for calculators utilize many of the same capabilities to produce random access memories;
- textile fiber manufacturers use similar polymerization and spinning processes for polyesters and nylon;
- the same assembly operation may produce high-torque motors for oil exploration and low-torque motors for conveyors;
- major appliance manufacturers use the same sales and service organization for a variety of products;
- Procter and Gamble was able to overcome a lack of experience in manufacturing paper products by being far along the experience curve in selling packaged consumer products when it entered the disposable diaper market.

Although a common effect of shared experience is to reduce cost differentials between competitors, a useful way to treat shared experience operationally is as an increment to the accumulated output of the specific product or processes of which the product is comprised. The hypothetical example in Table 2 helps to illustrate this point. The cost position of company B is weakened by the lack of transferable experience with related products. Rutenberg (1976) suggests adding factors to equation (1) which reflect the impact of shared experience.

As illustrated in Table 2, the assessment of competitor's shared experience as well as the company's own shared experience is important to understanding the relative economies of the various competitors. One fiber producer has noted that since most competitors in the textile industry produce several fibers, it is necessary to estimate the unique, shared experience base of each competitor in order to understand relative cost positions. This company claims this approach has been used successfully on several occasions and has produced insights into competitive positions that otherwise would have eluded them.

How can the amount of the carryover from shared experience be estimated? As with the basic experience effect, shared experience merely presents an opportunity to reduce costs but does not guarantee it will happen. If a company has two plants making identical products that were constructed independently, and the plants do not exchange cost reduction information, then the shared experience effect will be negligible. To assess whether experience has been shared it is usually necessary to apply expert judgment to each cost element. For example, manufacturing personnel can be asked to estimate where cost reduction projects for individual products have originated in the past. Similar approaches can be used to determine the effect on sales and distribution costs of a pooled sales force and warehousing facility. Needless to say, this kind of analysis represents a formidable amount of work, which possibly accounts for the paucity of published research on this topic.

Which Product-Market?

Few issues create more uncertainty than the choice of product-market boundary for the experience curve analysis. Published evidence suggests that industry-wide cost compression effects are most evident when broad, product-market definition is used:

- kilowatt hours of electricity generated,
- silicon transistors,

Table 2 Effect of Shared Experience

	Accumulated Experience with Product X	Shared Experience from Production of Related Products	Total Accumulated Experience
Company A	1,000,000 units	600,000 units	1,600,000 units
Company B	600,000	—	600,000
Company C	200,000	350,000	550,000

■   gallons of beer, or
■   pounds of viscose rayon.

Such broad definitions work because they are able to encompass most sources of shared experience.

Yet, as Abell and Hammond (1979) observe, a definition that is too broad may mean that an opportunity for cost leadership in a specialized market may be overlooked:

> . . . the grinding wheel industry produces hundreds of thousands of different kinds of wheels, each particularly suited for certain industrial applications. Production of a given type of wheel requires development and control of a "recipe" consisting of quantity, type and size of abrasives, bonding agents, filters, wetting agents, etc.; the timing of adding these to the "mix," baking times and temperatures; finishing techniques and so on. Likewise a firm can gain important experience advantages in the selling and servicing of wheels to a particular application.
>
> Experience advantages on a given type of wheel can yield important cost advantages. Here the unit of analysis should be the type of wheel on the application; if it were simply "grinding wheels" significant cost advantages due to specialization would be missed . . . .

The dilemma of the breadth of product and market boundaries may be resolved if segments can be found such that cost sharing *between* segments is less important than competitive cost differentials that are dependent on the relative position within the segment (Day 1981b). This will yield a useful definition if most competitors approach the market in the same way. However, there are many situations where different competitors define their business very differently. Laboratory ovens, for example, can be manufactured and sold by oven specialists or by laboratory equipment specialists. Whether laboratory ovens constitute a distinct segment depends on whether manufacturing or selling and servicing have the greater influence on total costs. When in doubt it may be necessary to repeat the experience curve analysis using several different definitions of both products and markets.

A recurring problem is the treatment of new technologies. For example, should there be a single experience curve for the tire cord, or separate curves for rayon and nylon tire cord? In general, if the consequence of the new technology is primarily to reduce production costs without a change in the functions provided to customers, then a new curve is not necessary. However, if the new technology offers significant new functions, as happened when cash registers became electronic, then a separate curve is necessary.

What Strategic Relevance?

The experience curve seemingly speaks directly to the long-run strategic concerns of management. According to the Boston Consulting Group (Hedley 1976), the basic strategic message of the experience curve is:

1.   The largest competitor in a particular business area should have the potential for the lowest unit costs and hence greatest profits.

If he is unprofitable he is probably either being "out-segmented" by more focused competitors or he is defective in experience curve cost control.

2. Smaller competitors in a business area are likely to be unprofitable, and they will remain so unless a strategy can be devised for gaining dominant market share at reasonable cost.

    If achieving overall dominance is not feasible, then the smaller competitor should seek to identify an economically distinct segment of the business in which he can dominate the relevant experience bases sufficiently to attain a viable cost position overall.

These implications focus on market position relative to competitors and lead inexorably to the pursuit of dominance as a strategic imperative. However, the broad conclusions must be carefully hedged for there are many reasons why the experience curve may be inaccurate and many situations where the effects are unimportant relative to other variables. We have already seen that competitive cost differentials are dependent on the rate of value added. Thus, most of the successful applications have been within high value-added, continuous processing, capital intensive industries that are usually highly concentrated.

By contrast there is little point in looking for experience effects in custom industries such as tool and die making, which have traditionally been very fragmented (although numerical control machine tools are slowly changing that situation). Service industries have been especially resistant to experience analysis. According to Carman and Langeard (1980), the effect of learning on total costs has never been demonstrated in a service situation. There is also uncertainty as to whether economies of scale exist. Larréché (1980) found a negative association of return on assets and market share among French private commercial banks. However, this may not be true in the U.S. with the advent of new banking services, such as automated teller systems or daily interest checking accounts, which utilize capital-intensive computer systems. Indeed, preliminary PIMS findings from a sample of 85 financial service businesses reveal relationships of share and rate of return that are even stronger than those reported for consumer and industrial product business. Clearly, a great deal of work is needed before the applicability of the experience curve is established.

Risks of a Cost Reduction Strategy

All-out dedication to cost reduction efforts requires maximizing the scale of operations and pursuit of opportunities for specialization of work force, production processes and organizational arrangements. This approach confers a number of advantages, as smaller companies will attest. Unfortunately these cost reduction efforts introduce rigidities that may make the organization slower and less flexible in response to shifts in customers' requirements or competitive innovations (Abernathy and Wayne 1974). Ford recently had this problem when it closed its large, supposedly efficient Flat Rock plant because it was inflexible for conversion to the new types and sizes of engines being demanded by today's energy conscious consumer. Further, a large-scale plant is vulnerable to significant changes in process technology.

A more subtle risk of an experience based strategy is a "definition of the business" that is distorted by an excessive commitment to a particular technology, rather than to satisfying customer needs. This, in turn, may lead to a preoccupation with competitors who make products with similar functions, materials and so on, and a lack of sensitivity of threats from other technologies with capacity to serve the same customer needs. The paper industry, for example, was slow to recognize the threat to paper grocery bags from plastics. Now that a plastic grocery bag is cost competitive, with the bonus of greater strength and reusability, the paper grocery bag is experiencing a competitive setback.

Summary and Conclusions

The simplistic market share dominance prescriptions that marked the early experience curve applications have been replaced with a growing sensitivity to the complexities of this concept. While its appeal as an organizing framework remains high, there is a realization that the experience curve effect is itself a product of underlying scale, technology and learning effects. Whether the experience curve is strategically relevant depends initially on whether these three effects are influential features of the strategic environment. Beyond this there is a growing recognition that there is a family of experience curves, each addressing different strategic issues, from cost component analyses to price forecasting to competitive cost comparisons. One consequence is that the earlier broad generalizations have been replaced with focused applications, where experience curve analysis plays a supportive role as one of a number of analytical methods.

An Agenda for Research

There are significant risks in analyses based on the experience curve concept because the potential for misleading signals is high. Yet when the insights are valid, they are highly valuable. These are conditions where the payoff to research is high. The following topics are judged especially rewarding.

Theory Development.   Few well-supported generalizations can be made about the conditions in which experience effects are significant. Specifically, what are the variables that dictate the slope of both the price curve and the competitive cost compression curve? Numerous hypotheses as to the effects of type of industry, rate of value added, competitive structure and mechanisms for technology diffusion need to be explored. A key unanswered question is the relationship of the experience curve with the product life cycle.

Both theory and practice would benefit from further research on the sources of the experience effect. Many strategic implications are derived from assumptions as to the relative contribution of learning, technology and scale. Yet published work is presently limited to three studies within the chemical industry.

Measurement Sensitivity.   Virtually no work has been reported on the impact of the measures on the results. What are the consequences of different assumptions about inflation, errors in the data or significant discontinuities in data series? When there is shared experience available to new products, how should the base of experience be estimated? How should "augmented" products, including technical service support, inventory financing and other services be treated?

Model Specification and Evaluation. In general, model specification issues have been ignored in the literature. Indeed, most of the reported analyses are straight lines fitted on a graphical plot. Other models than the log linear need to be tested for their econometric characteristics and forecasting accuracy. Forecasting tests are especially important for the industry price curve because of the hypothesized pattern of departure from the underlying cost curve. Finally, the consequences of aggregating a number of cost curves for individual components to obtain a total cost curve are not well understood.

A major area for further development is the integration of product life cycle and experience curve models that incorporate competitive behavior patterns. A recent paper by Harrell and Taylor (1981) illustrates the strategic relevance of such a model in the housewares industry. As with the other research suggested above, the payoff in improved strategic decision making and better understanding of dynamic market processes is substantial.

References

Abell, Derek F. and John S. Hammond (1979), *Strategic Market Planning: Problems and Analytical Approaches,* Englewood Cliffs, NJ: Prentice-Hall.

Abernathy, William J. and K. Wayne (1974), "Limits of the Learning Curve," *Harvard Business Review,* 52 (September-October), 109–119.

Arrow, Kenneth J. (1961), "The Economic Implications of Learning by Doing," in *Review of Economic Studies,* 155–173.

Barkai, Haim and David Levhari (1973), "The Impact of Experience in Kibbutz Farming," *Review of Economics and Statistics,* 55 (February), 56–63.

Beevan, Alan (1974), "The U.K. Potato Crisp Industry, 1960–1972: A Study of New Entry Competition," *Journal of Industrial Economics,* 22 (June), 281–297.

Biggadike, Ralph (1977), *Scott-Air Corporation (B),* working paper, Colgate Darden School, University of Virginia.

Booz, Allen and Hamilton (1982), *New Products: Best Practices—Today and Tomorrow,* New York: Booz, Allen.

Boston Consulting Group (1972), *Perspectives on Experience,* Boston: BCG.

———— (1975), *Strategy Alternatives for the British Motorcycle Industry,* London: Her Majesty's Stationery Office.

Burck, Gilbert (1972), "The Myths and Realities of Corporate Pricing," *Fortune,* 96 (April).

Business Week (1982), "The Coming Shakeout in Personal Computers," (November 22), 72–83.

Buzzell, Robert D. (1981), "Are There Natural Market Structures?," *Journal of Marketing,* 45 (Winter), 42–51.

Carman, James M. and Eric Langeard (1980), "Growth Strategies for Service Firms," *Strategic Management Journal,* 1 (January–March), 7–22.

Conley, Patrick (1970), "Experience Curves as a Planning Tool," *IEEE Spectrum*, 7 (Spring), 63–68.

Day, George S. (1981a), "The Product Life Cycle: Analysis and Application Issues," *Journal of Marketing*, 45 (Fall), 60–67.

——— (1981b), "Strategic Market Analysis and Definition: An Integrated Approach," *Strategic Management Journal*, 2 (July–September), 281–299.

Dean, Joel (1976), "Pricing Policies for New Products," *Harvard Business Review*, 54 (November–December), 141–53.

Dolan, Robert J. and Abel P. Jeuland (1981), "Experience Curves and Dynamic Demand Models: Implications for Optimal Pricing Strategies," *Journal of Marketing*, 45 (Winter), 52–73.

Griliches, Zvi (1961), "Hedonic Price Indices for Automobiles: An Econometric Analysis of Quality Change," *Government Price Statistics*, U.S. Congress Joint Economic Committee, U.S. Government Printing Office (January), 173–96; reprinted in *Readings in Economic Statistics and Econometrics*, A. Zellner, ed., Boston, MA: Little, Brown and Co., 1968, 103–130.

Harrell, Stephen G. and Elmer D. Taylor (1981), "Modeling the Product Life Cycle for Consumer Durables," *Journal of Marketing*, 45 (Fall), 68–75.

Hedley, Barry (1976), "A Fundamental Approach to Strategy Development," *Long Range Planning*, 9 (December), 2–11.

Henderson, Bruce D. (1978), *Cross-Sectional Experience*, Boston, MA: Boston Consulting Group.

——— (1980a), "Caution Based on Experience," in *Shifting Boundaries Between Regulation and Competition*, Betty Bock, ed., New York: Conference Board.

——— (1980b), *The Experience Curve Revisited*, Boston, MA: Boston Consulting Group.

Hirschman, Winfred B. (1964), "Profit from the Learning Curve," *Harvard Business Review*, 42 (January–February).

Hollander, S. (1965), *The Sources of Increased Efficiency: A Study of DuPont Rayon Manufacturing Plants*, Cambridge, MA: MIT Press.

Joskow, Paul L. and George A Rozanski (1979), "The Effect of Learning by Doing on Nuclear Plant Operating Reliability," *Review of Economics and Statistics*, 61 (May), 161–168.

Kiechel, Walter (1981), "The Decline of the Experience Curve," *Fortune*, 105 (October), 139–146.

Larréché, Jean-Claude (1980), "On Limitations of Positive Market Share-Profitability Relationships: The Case of the French Banking Industry," unpublished working paper, Fontainebleau, France: INSEAD.

Lieberman, Marvin B. (1981), "The Experience Curve, Pricing and Market Structure in the Chemical Processing Industries," unpublished working paper, Harvard University.

McLagan, Donald L. (1981), "Market Share: Key to Profitability," *Planning Review*, 9 (March), 26–29.

Montgomery, David B. and George S. Day (1983), "Experience Curves: Evidence, Empirical Issues and Applications," in *Strategic Marketing and Strategic Management*, D. Gardner and H. Thomas, eds., New York: John Wiley.

Pessemier, Edgar A. (1977), *Product Management: Strategy and Organization*, New York: John Wiley.

Porter, Michael E. (1979), "How Competitive Forces Shape Strategy," *Harvard Business Review,* 57 (March–April), 137–145.

Rapping, Leonard (1965), "Learning and World War II Production Functions," *Review of Economics and Statistics,* 47 (February), 81–86.

Robinson, Bruce and Chet Lakhani (1975), "Dynamic Price Models for New Product Planning," *Management Science,* 21 (June), 1113–1122.

Rutenberg, David (1976), "What Strategic Planning Expects from Management Science," working paper 89-75-76, Carnegie-Mellon University (December).

Spence, A. Michael (1981), "The Learning Curve and Competition," *The Bell Journal of Economics,* 12 (Spring), 49–69.

Stobaugh, Robert B. and Philip L. Townsend (1975), "Price Forecasting and Strategic Planning: The Case of Petro Chemicals," *Journal of Marketing Research,* 12 (February), 19–29.

Sultan, Ralph (1974), *Pricing in the Electrical Oligopoly,* Vols. I and II, Cambridge, MA: Harvard Graduate School of Business Administration.

Wilson, Aubrey and Bryan Atkin (1976), "Exorcising the Ghosts in Marketing," *Harvard Business Review,* 54 (September–October), 117–127.

Wilson, Robert G. (1982), "Strategies to Fight Inflation," *Journal of Business Strategy,* 2 (Winter), 22–31.

Wooley, Robert (1972), "Econometric Analysis of the Experience Effect," unpublished Ph.D. dissertation, Stanford University.

Yelle, Louis E. (1979), "The Learning Curve: Historical Review and Comprehensive Survey," *Decision Sciences,* 10 (March), 302–328.

10

Forget the Product Life Cycle Concept!

Nariman K. Dhalla and Sonia Yuspeh

Not long ago, a leading manufacturer was promoting a brand of floor wax. After a steady period of growth, the sales of the product had reached a plateau. Marketing research suggested that an increase in spot television advertising, backed by a change in copy, would help the brand to regain its momentum. Feeling that the funds could be better spent in launching a new product, management vetoed the proposal.

But the new product failed to move off the shelf despite heavy marketing support. At the same time, the old brand, with its props pulled out from under it, went into a sales decline from which it never recovered. The company had two losers on its hands.

This experience is not atypical among the nation's corporations. Many strongly believe that brands follow a life cycle and are subject to inevitable death after a few years of promotion. Like so many fascinating but untested theories in economics, the product life cycle concept (PLC) has proved to be remarkably durable, and has been expounded eloquently in numerous publications. In fact, its use in professional discussions seems to add luster and believability to the insistent claim that marketing is close to becoming a science.

The PLC concept, as developed by its proponents, is fairly simple. Like human beings or animals, everything in the marketplace is presumed to be mortal. A brand is born, grows lustily, attains maturity, and then enters declining years, after which it is quietly buried. *Exhibit I* shows profit-volume relationships that are supposed to prevail in a typical PLC.

This article first appeared in the *Harvard Business Review*. Reprinted by permission of the *Harvard Business Review*, January-February 1976, pp. 102–112. Copyright © 1976 by the President and Fellows of Harvard College; all rights reserved.

When this article was published the authors were with the J. Walter Thompson Company in New York; associate research director in charge of Economic and Econometric Research, and senior vice-president and director of Research and Planning, respectively.

Exhibit I   Generalized PLC Pattern for Sales and Profits

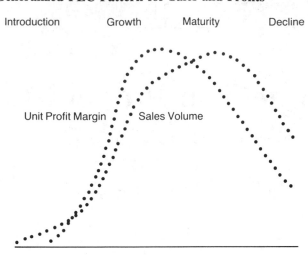

Even a cursory analysis shows flaws in this picture. In the biological world the length of each stage in the cycle is fixed in fairly precise terms; moreover, one stage follows another in an immutable and irreversible sequence. But neither of these conditions is characteristic of the marketing world. The length of different stages tends to vary from product to product. Some items move almost directly from introduction to maturity and have hardly any growth stage. Other products surge to sudden heights of fashion, hesitate momentarily at an uneasy peak, and then quickly drop off into total oblivion. Their introductory and maturity stages are barely perceptible.

What is more, it is not unusual for products to gain "second lives" or even "reincarnation." Thanks to brilliant promotion, many brands have gone from the maturity stage not to decline and death but to a fresh period of rapid growth. Later in this article we shall examine a few examples of the unlifelike and noncyclical behavior of products.

Despite the lack of correspondence between the marketing and the biological worlds, PLC advocates continue to remain dogmatic and proclaim that their concept has wide applications in different areas of planning and policy formulation. *Exhibit II* gives a bird's-eye view of the four stages of the PLC and the type of marketing action that, according to proponents, is suitable for each stage. While there is no unanimity among PLC advocates on details of this pattern, the basic relationships have been described repeatedly by authorities.[1]

---

[1]See, for example, David J. Luck, *Product Policy and Strategy* (Englewood Cliffs, N.J.: Prentice-Hall, 1972); Arch Patton, *Top Management's Stake in a Product's Life Cycle* (New York: McKinsey & Co., Inc., June 1959), Thomas A. Staudt and Donald A. Taylor, *A Managerial Introduction to Marketing,* 2d ed. (Englewood Cliffs, N.J.; Prentice-Hall, 1970); and Chester R. Wasson, *Product Management* (St. Charles, Ill.: Challenge Books, 1971).

Exhibit II How PLC Advocates View the Implications of the Cycle for Marketing Action

Effects and Responses	Stages of the PLC			
	Introduction	Growth	Maturity	Decline
Competition	None of importance	Some emulators	Many rivals competing for a small piece of the pie	Few in number with a rapid shakeout of weak members
Overall strategy	Market establishment; persuade early adopters to try the product	Market penetration; persuade mass market to prefer the brand	Defense of brand position; check the inroads of competition	Preparations for removal; milk the brand dry of all possible benefits
Profits	Negligible because of high production and marketing costs	Reach peak levels as a result of high prices and growing demand	Increasing competition cuts into profit margins and ultimately into total profits	Declining volume pushes costs up to levels that eliminate profits entirely
Retail prices	High, to recover some of the excessive costs of launching	High, to take advantage of heavy consumer demand	What the traffic will bear; need to avoid price wars	Low enough to permit quick liquidation of inventory
Distribution	Selective, as distribution is slowly built up	Intensive; employ small trade discounts since dealers are eager to store	Intensive; heavy trade allowances to retain shelf space	Selective; unprofitable outlets slowly phased out
Advertising strategy	Aim at the needs of early adopters	Make the mass market aware of brand benefits	Use advertising as a vehicle for differentiation among otherwise similar brands	Emphasize low price to reduce stock
Advertising emphasis	High, to generate awareness and interest among early adopters and persuade dealers to stock the brand	Moderate, to let sales rise on the sheer momentum of word-of-mouth recommendations	Moderate, since most buyers are aware of brand characteristics	Minimum expenditures required to phase out the product
Consumer sales and promotion expenditures	Heavy, to entice target groups with samples, coupons, and other inducements to try the brand	Moderate, to create brand preference (advertising is better suited to do this job)	Heavy, to encourage brand switching, hoping to convert some buyers into loyal users.	Minimal, to let the brand coast by itself

Most writers present the PLC concept in qualitative terms, in the form of idealization without any empirical backing. Also, they fail to draw a clear distinction between product class (e.g., cigarettes), product form (e.g., filter cigarettes), and brand (e.g., Winston). But, for our purposes, this does not matter. We shall see that it is not possible to validate the model at any of these levels of aggregation.

Myths of Class and Form

Many product classes have enjoyed and will probably continue to enjoy a long and prosperous maturity stage—far more than the human life expectancy of three score years and ten. Good examples are Scotch whisky, Italian vermouth, and French perfumes. Their life span can be measured, not in decades, but in centuries. Almost as durable are such other product classes as automobiles, radios, mouthwashes, soft drinks, cough remedies, and face creams. In fact, in the absence of technological breakthroughs, many product classes appear to be almost impervious to normal life cycle pressures, provided they satisfy some basic need, be it transportation, entertainment, health, nourishment, or the desire to be attractive.

As for product form, it tends to exhibit less stability than does product class. Form is what most PLC advocates have in mind when they speak of a generalized life cycle pattern for a "product." Even here the model is not subject to precise formulation. Theoretically, it presumes the existence of some rules indicating the movement of the product from one stage to another. However, when one studies actual case histories, it becomes clear that no such rules can be objectively developed.

For evidence of this conclusion, consider *Exhibit III*, which gives examples of life cycles of product forms in four diverse product classes: cigarettes, make-up bases, toilet tissues, and cereals. In order to present a realistic picture, the sales (whether in dollars or units) have been adjusted to a common base in the light of varying annual consumer expenditures on nondurable goods. In this way, it becomes possible to remove changes that do not reflect life cycle patterns, e.g., population growth, inflationary pressures, and cyclical economic fluctuation.

Unpredictable Variations

Although in most cases it is not feasible to go back far enough to get a complete birth-do-death portrayal, certain facts are obvious from *Exhibit III:*

- With the exception of nonfilter cigarettes, year-to-year variations make it difficult to predict when the next stage will appear, how long it will last, and to what levels the sales will reach.
- One cannot often judge with accuracy in which phase of the cycle the product form is.

Exhibit III   Life Cycle Patterns of Product Forms in Four Product Classes

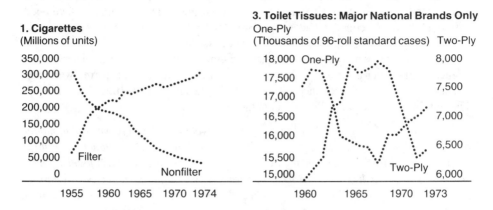

1. Cigarettes
(Millions of units)

3. Toilet Tissues: Major National Brands Only
One-Ply
(Thousands of 96-roll standard cases)   Two-Ply

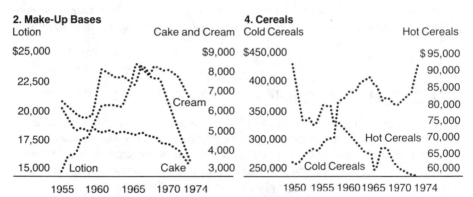

2. Make-Up Bases
Lotion   Cake and Cream

4. Cereals
Cold Cereals   Hot Cereals

Note: Dollar sales figures are in thousands of dollars. Both unit and dollar sales are adjusted to a common base of consumer nondurable goods expenditures.

Sources: For 1, *Advertising Age;* for 2 and 4, *Supermarketing and Food Topics;* for 3, J. Walter Thompson research.

■ The four major phases do not divide themselves into clean-cut compartments. At certain points, a product may appear to have attained maturity when actually it has only reached a temporary plateau in the growth stage prior to its next big upsurge.

One of the most thorough attempts to validate the PLC concept for product classes and product forms was carried out a few years ago by the Marketing Science Institute.[2] The authors examined over 100 product categories in the food, health, and personal-care fields, and measured the number of observations that did

---

[2]See Rolando Polli and Victor J. Cook's "A Test of the Product Life Cycle as a Model of Sales Behavior," *Market Science Institute Working Paper,* November 1967, p. 43, and also their "Validity of the Product Life Cycle," *The Journal of Business,* October 1969, p. 385.

not follow the expected sequence of introduction, growth, maturity, and decline. They compared these actual inconsistent observations with simulated sequences of equal length generated with the aid of random numbers. The hypothesis developed was that the PLC concept had some "raison d'être" only if it was capable of explaining sales behavior better than a chance model could.

The outcome of this test was discouraging. Only 17% of the observed sequences in product classes and 20% of the sequences in product forms were significantly different from chance (at the confidence level of 99 times out of 100). The authors reached the following conclusion:

> After completing the initial test of the life cycle expressed as verifiable model of sales behavior, we must register strong reservations about its general validity, even stated in its weakest, most flexible form. In our tests of the model against real sales data, it has not performed uniformly well against objective standards over a wide range of frequently purchased consumer products, nor has it performed equally well at different levels of product sales aggregation. . . . Our results suggest strongly the life cycle concept, when used without careful formulation and testing as an explicit model, is more likely to be misleading than useful.[3]

No Life Cycles for Brands

When it comes to brands, the PLC model has even less validity. Many potentially useful offerings die in the introductory stage because of inadequate product development or unwise market planning, or both. The much-expected ebullient growth phase never arrives. Even when a brand survives the introductory stage, the model in most cases cannot be used as a planning or a predictive tool.

Exhibit IV shows the life cycle trends of certain brands in the product forms earlier discussed. The evidence for the PLC concept is discouraging. With the exception of nonfilter cigarettes, the brands tend to have different sales patterns, and the product-form curves throw no light on what the sales would be in the future. All that can be said is that if a product form (e.g., nonfilter cigarettes) is truly in a final declining stage, it is very difficult for a brand (e.g., Chesterfield) to reverse the trend. However, with respect to the first three stages of the PLC, no firm conclusions can be drawn about brand behavior from the product-form curve.

Some PLC advocates have tried to salvage their theory by introducing different types of curves to fit different situations. For instance, one authority, in a study of 258 ethical drug brands, suggests six different PLC curves;[4] another develops no less than nine variants: marketing specialties, fashion cycle, high-learning products, low-learning products, pyramided cycles, instant busts, abortive introductions, straight fads, and fads with significant residual markets.[5]

[3]See Polli and Cook, "A Text of the Product Life Cycle," p. 61.

[4]See William E. Cox, "Product Life Cycles as Marketing Models," *The Journal of Business,* October 1967, p. 375.

[5]See Wasson's *Product Management.*

Exhibit IV   Life Cycle Patterns of Brands Compared with Product Forms

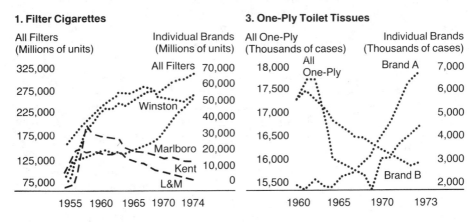

1. Filter Cigarettes

All Filters (Millions of units) — Individual Brands (Millions of units): All Filters, Winston, Marlboro, Kent, L&M

1955 1960 1965 1970 1974

3. One-Ply Toilet Tissues

All One-Ply (Thousands of cases) — Individual Brands (Thousands of cases): All One-Ply, Brand A, Brand B

1960   1965   1970   1973

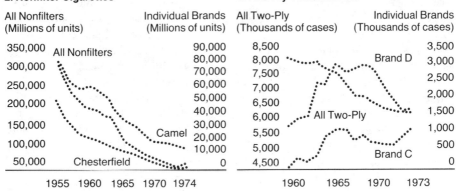

2. Nonfilter Cigarettes

All Nonfilters (Millions of units) — Individual Brands (Millions of units): All Nonfilters, Camel, Chesterfield

1955 1960 1965 1970 1974

4. Two-Ply Toilet Tissues

All Two-Ply (Thousands of cases) — Individual Brands (Thousands of cases): Brand D, All Two-Ply, Brand C

1960   1965   1970   1973

Note: All sales figures are adjusted to a common base of consumer nondurable goods expenditures.

Source: For cigarettes, *Advertising Age;* for toilet tissues, J. Walter Thompson research.

Such efforts at curve fitting leave much to be desired. From the standpoint of practical marketing, they are sterile exercises in taxonomy. It would be better to admit that the whole PLC concept has little value in the world of brands. Clearly, the PLC is a *dependent* variable which is determined by marketing actions; it is not an *independent* variable to which companies should adapt their marketing programs. Marketing management itself can alter the shape and duration of a brand's life cycle.

Of course, a company may not be able to extend the maturity phase indefinitely. When a brand passes "over the hill" in sales, no marketing strategies are effective anymore. Such a drop may be due to changes in consumer tastes and values, or to the fact that users have shifted their preference to a new and improved competitive product. In these instances, euthanasia has to be quietly performed so that the company's capital resources can be used profitably in other ventures.

Blunders Due to PLC Blinders

Unfortunately, in numerous cases a brand is discontinued, not because of irreversible changes in consumer values or tastes, but because management, on the basis of the PLC theory, believes the brand has entered a dying stage. In effect, a self-fulfilling prophecy results.

Suppose a brand is acceptable to consumers but has a few bad years because of other factors—for instance, poor advertising, delisting by a major chain, or entry of a "me-too" competitive product backed by massive sampling. Instead of thinking in terms of corrective measures, management begins to feel that its brand has entered a declining stage. It therefore withdraws funds from the promotion budget to finance R&D on new items. The next year the brand does even worse, panic increases, and new products are hastily launched without proper testing. Not surprisingly, most of the new products fail. Thus management has talked itself into a decline by relying solely on the PLC concept.

The annals of business are full of cases of once strong and prosperous brands that have died—if not with a bang, at least with a whimper—because top management wore PLC blinders. A good example is the case of Ipana. This toothpaste was marketed by a leading packaged-goods company until 1968, when it was abandoned in favor of new brands. In early 1969, two Minnesota businessmen picked up the Ipana name, concocted a new formula, but left the package unchanged. With hardly any promotion, the supposedly petrified demand for Ipana turned into $250,000 of sales in the first seven months of operation. In 1973, a survey conducted by the Target Group Index showed that, despite poor distribution, the toothpaste was still being used by 1,520,000 adults. Considering the limited resources of the owners, the brand would have been in an even stronger position had it been retained by its original parent company and been given appropriate marketing support.

Planning without PLC

In a slightly different vein, there are several cases of companies that have ignored the PLC concept and achieved great success through imaginative marketing strategies. The classic example of the 1940s and 1950s is DuPont's nylon. This product, whose original uses were primarily military (parachutes, rope, and so on), would have gradually faded into oblivion had the company believed that the declining sales curve signaled death. Instead, management boldly decided to enter the volatile consumer textile market. Women were first induced to switch from silk to nylon stockings. The market was later expanded by convincing teenagers and subteens to start wearing hosiery. Sales grew even further when the company introduced tinted and patterned hosiery, thereby converting hosiery from a neutral accessory to a central element of fashion.

Here are other brands whose productive lives have been stretched many decades by sound planning:

- Listerine Antiseptic has succeeded in retaining its lion's share of the mouthwash market despite heavy competitive pressures and the introduction of strongly supported new brands.

- Marlboro is fast edging up to top place in the highly segmented filter-cigarette market by focusing on the same basic theme—only developing different variations of it.
- Seven-up, whose growth had been impeded because of its image strictly as a mixer, now has more room to expand as a result of taking the "Uncola" position against Coke and Pepsi.

This list could be expanded considerably. The following are ten other leading brands that have been around for a long time but are still full of vitality because of intelligent marketing: Anacin analgesic, Budweiser beer, Colgate toothpaste, Dristan cold remedy, Geritol vitamin-mineral supplement, Jell-o gelatin, Kleenex facial tissue, Maxwell House coffee, Planter's peanuts, and Tide detergent.

The importance of a proper marketing effort is further illustrated in *Exhibit V*. Here are comparisons of rival brands in various product forms. In 1961, the

Exhibit V   Growth and Decline of Brand Usage Share within Product Forms, 1961 and 1973

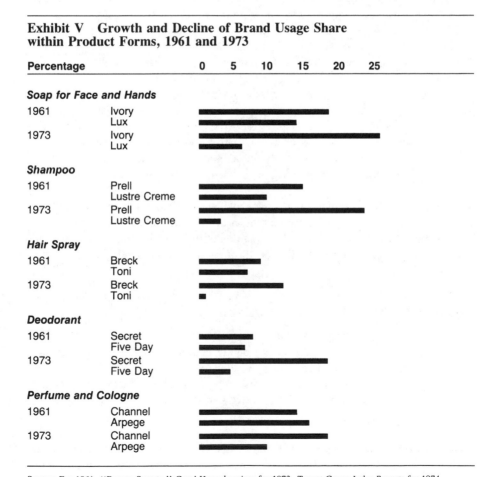

Percentage		0 5 10 15 20 25
Soap for Face and Hands		
1961	Ivory	
	Lux	
1973	Ivory	
	Lux	
Shampoo		
1961	Prell	
	Lustre Creme	
1973	Prell	
	Lustre Creme	
Hair Spray		
1961	Breck	
	Toni	
1973	Breck	
	Toni	
Deodorant		
1961	Secret	
	Five Day	
1973	Secret	
	Five Day	
Perfume and Cologne		
1961	Channel	
	Arpege	
1973	Channel	
	Arpege	

Source: For 1961, "Beauty Secrets," *Good Housekeeping;* for 1973, *Target Group Index Reports* for 1974.

brands in each pairing had approximatley the same share of usage. However, by 1973 one of each two was able to move up substantially, while the other took a reverse turn. Had the PLC forces played an all-important role during this 12-year span, both brands in each pair would have gone downhill. This exhibit demonstrates that the judicious use of advertising and other marketing tools can check the erosion of a consumer franchise. If a brand is widely available at a competitive price, and has certain benefits which are meaningful to a large segment of the population, then well-conceived and properly directed marketing communications will produce the right response at the checkout counter. This is true regardless of whether the brand has been in existence for two years or twenty.

Capitalizing on Today's Products

A major disservice of the PLC concept to marketing is that it has led top executives to overemphasize new product introduction. This route is perilous. Experience shows that nothing seems to take more time, cost more money, involve more pitfalls, or cause more anguish than new product programs.

   Actual statistics are hard to come by, but it is generally believed in business circles that the odds are four to one against a new product becoming a winner. Yet, like a new baby in the house, the new product too often gets all the attention while the older brands are pretty much neglected.

   The point is not that work on new products should be halted. Obviously work should continue, for new products are vital to the future. Yet it is today's products that are closest to the cash register; the company's chances of generating greater profits normally depend on them. It is foolish for a corporation to invest millions of dollars to build goodwill for a brand, then walk away from it and spend additional millions all over again for a new brand with no consumer franchise.

   In these days of inflation, shortages, and slow economic growth, industry can ill afford a system that pushes brand proliferation too far. The challenge to management lies in avoiding market fragmentation and in building up large national franchise for a few key brands through heavy and intelligent marketing support.

An Effective System

How can such support be given? Management needs an approach that will help it to position the brand to a large segment of the population, evaluate different options, and foresee opportunities or dangers that lie ahead. Such an approach can be put together by combining strategic research and tracking studies with marketing and communications models. Let us now consider one example from the snack food industry.

Getting Started.   A branded drink had a small, select group of loyal users who liked its strong, bitter taste. But sales for some time had been gradually declining. Despite the advice of some PLC-oriented marketing consultants, management was

Exhibit VI   Model Showing Relationships of Different Variables to Brand Share

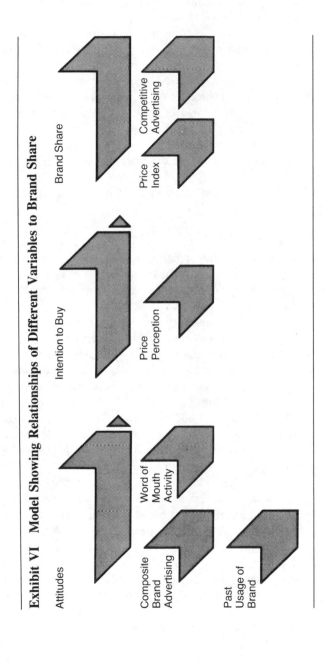

Attitudes

Intention to Buy

Brand Share

Word of Mouth Activity

Price Perception

Price Index

Competitive Advertising

Composite Brand Advertising

Past Usage of Brand

opposed to discontinuing the line and to bringing out a new item. Instead, it initiated a segmentation study in order to find out ways of increasing that franchise among the large body of nonusers. The results indicated that the brand could be best positioned against one segment of the market-nutrition conscious housewives who took their role as custodians of family health and well-being very seriously.

Although never mentioned before in advertising, it so happened that the tangy bitterness of the brand was mainly due to the addition of certain "natural" ingredients. Also this benefit was distinctive and not generic to the whole product category. Hence the company had a clear edge over competition.

New advertising was prepared around nutrition, wholesomeness, and the added ingredients. At the same time, in order to retain loyal users, management continued the old 30-second TV spots emphasizing strong taste. On the research side, arrangements were made to obtain from consumer panels and tracking studies quarterly information on the brand's "share of mind" and share of market. The emphasis in the tracking research was on the target groups, namely, housewives who were (1) fond of the taste, and (2) neutral toward taste but health conscious.

Building an Effective Model.   After three years, it was felt that sufficient data had been collected to start building a marketing-communications model that would bring relevant variables, both controllable and uncontrollable, into a coherent, unified picture. Using this picture, management could examine the effects of its marketing policies on two key consumer targets.

The basic format of the model can be seen at a glance in *Exhibit VI*. The mathematical details are discussed at length in the Appendix.

Once the system was in operation, it was frequently used to predict likely changes in sales as a result of certain actions planned by the company. For example, when preparing his budget for the next quarter, the marketing manager wanted to know what would happen if he kept the price unchanged but augmented advertising from $3.30 million to $3.55 million. As described in the Appendix, the model indicated that an increase of this magnitude would theoretically raise the brand share by 0.3 percentage point. Similar projections could be made for other types of changes contemplated in the marketing mix.

The model was of great value in another way. At one point, discrepancies began to appear between actual and estimated attitude changes. The higher advertising levels were not able to generate better attitudinal ratings, as predicted by the equation. Some part of the system apparently had broken down. Further investigation revealed that the advertising campaign was wearing thin. This problem was solved by developing a fresh program built around the same basic strategy.

Thus, because management had a "radar set" beamed on the marketplace, it was in a position to initiate remedial measures before there was a sharp drop in sales.

A model of this type can also aid management in distinguishing between irreversible sales declines and those which are controllable through a marketing effort. Suppose a brand has taken an irreversible turn for the worse, with the scores on attitudes and intentions continuing to decline and consumer research indicating a fundamental change in consumer tastes and values. Then it is advisable to discontinue the brand and embark upon other profitable ventures. Such drastic action can be justified if based on a careful study of the marketplace rather than on blind faith in the PLC concept.

Conclusion

The PLC concept has little validity. The sequence of marketing strategies typically recommended for succeeding stages of the cycle is likely to cause trouble. In some respects, the concept has done more harm than good by persuading top executives to neglect existing brands and place undue emphasis on new products.

The 1960s were a period of growing affluence, cheap energy, limitless supplies, and rising public expectations. This decade saw brand proliferation, product parity, and market segmentation carried to an extreme. The scenario now has changed. Inflation, shortages, and slow economic growth characterize the 1970s. As a result, aggressive brand proliferation no longer makes sense. The emphasis should shift from spouting out new "me-too" products to prolonging the productive life of existing brands through sound and solid marketing support.

Marketing-communications models can be of great help. They measure quantitatively the influence of different elements on sales, permit the evaluation of different options, and provide advance warning signals so that remedial action can be taken before a crisis occurs. The management that uses them will not be misled by minor sales aberrations into believing erroneously that a brand has entered a declining stage.

Appendix

Model building in the field of marketing and consumer behavior is complex. At the early stages, it is desirable to run a sufficient number of cross-lagged and partial correlations in order to determine the true causal path among the variables under study. The equations, when formulated, should be checked for biases such as multicollinearity and autocorrelation. If a simultaneous-equation model is developed, the parameters should be estimated through two-stage least squares, or through limited or full-information maximum likelihood techniques.

The purpose of this section is not to go into mathematical details but to show how management can make use of the model, assuming that all statistical requirements have been satisfied.

To simplify exposition, the equations for the snack drink brand discussed in the text are presented in the linear form, though actually nonlinear and interactive relationships are more realistic. Here are three equations in a specific marketing-communications model:

$$ATT_t = -3.49 + 1.05\ ADV\text{-}BR_t + 1.50\ WOM_t + 0.88\ BS_{t-1}$$

$$INT_t = 5.13 + 0.74\ ATT_t - 0.44\ PR\text{-}PER_t$$

$$BS_t = 129.57 + 1.03\ INT_{t-1} - 0.94\ PR\text{-}IND_t - 0.90\ ADV\text{-}COM_t$$

The symbols in this equation are defined below. The data source for each symbol is shown in parentheses, with TS standing for tracking studies, CP for consumer panels, and AA for advertising agency:

- ATT (TS)
  Attitudes (sum of ratings on nutrition, natural ingredients, and liking for taste)
- ADV-BR (AA)
  Advertising expenditures on the brand, in millions of dollars (composite figure)
- WOM (TS)
  Word of mouth (percent of respondents who talk about the brand with friends, neighbors, or relatives)
- BS (CP)
  Brand share
- INT (TS)
  Intention to buy the brand at the time of next purchase
- PR-PER (TS)
  Price perception (percent of respondents who regard the brand as high priced)
- PR-IND (CP)
  Ratio of brand's price to the average price of all competitors (100 means the brand price is the same as the average for competition)
- ADV-COM (AA)
  Advertising expenditures of major competitors in millions of dollars
  t, $t-1$
  Time period, t for current quarter and $t-1$ for preceding quarter.

The variables are self-explanatory, except for ADV-BR (Equation 1), which takes into account the lagged effects of advertising. At the preliminary stages of model building, it was found that 80% of the impact was felt almost immediately and 20% was felt in the subsequent quarter. These weights were employed in computing the composite figure.

The following illustration shows how the model could be used to predict likely changes in brand share. Suppose the marketing manager is faced with the following problem: What would be the increase in brand share from the current level of 12.2%, if he keeps the price unchanged but augments advertising from $3.3 million to $3.55 million between the first and the second quarter? (The input in the model for the second quarter would be: $3.55 \times 0.8 + 3.3 \times 0.2$, i.e., $3.5 million.) Much would depend on the accuracy with which he could forecast the four variables that are beyond the company's control—word of mouth (WOM), price perception (PR-PER), the price index (PR-IND), and competitive advertising (ADV-COM).

Assume that the marketing manager is able to prepare the following estimates based on past trends and opinions of some experts in the field:

WOM (2d quarter)	6.5%
PR-PER (2d quarter)	11.6%
PR-IND (3d quarter)	105.5
ADV-COM (3d quarter)	$37.4 million

The three equations in the model can now be used to predict the brand share two quarters ahead. The computations are as follows:

$$ATT_{t+1} = -3.49 + 1.05 \ ADV\text{-}BR_{t+1} + 1.50 \ WOM_{t+1} + 0.88 \ BS_t$$
$$= -3.49 + (1.05)(3.5) + (1.50)(6.5) + (0.88)(12.2)$$
$$= 20.67$$

$$INT_{t-1} = 5.13 + 0.74 \ ATT_{t+1} + 0.44 \ PR\text{-}PER_{t+1}$$
$$= 5.13 + (0.74)(20.67) - (0.44)(11.6) = 15.32$$

$$BS_{t+2} = 129.57 + 1.03 \ INT_{t+1} - 0.94 \ PR\text{-}IND_{t+2} - 0.90 \ ADV\text{-}COM_{t+2}$$
$$= 129.57 + (1.03)(15.32) - (.94)(105.5) - (.90)(37.4) = 12.52$$

Thus a planned increase of $250,000 in advertising in the next quarter would lead to a theoretical brand share of 12.52% in the subsequent quarter, compared to the current share of 12.2%.

The model described has been tailor-made for a particular company. Naturally, the effect of outside influences on corporate efforts would differ from product category to product category and from brand to brand.

11

Don't Forget the Product Life Cycle for Strategic Planning

Lester A. Neidell

Buoyed by a 15% average annual increase in revenue passenger miles from 1963 to 1968, the airline industry ordered dozens of first-generation, wide-bodied jets. But by 1973 (prior to the energy crisis), many airlines had parked these new planes indefinitely because passenger miles increased by only half the expected amount. What went wrong?

During planning, airline officials failed to consider the concept of the *product life cycle* (PLC). They simply extrapolated the increase in air travel that had occurred, without understanding the structural reasons for it. The increase was due principally to the business segment, not to pleasure travelers. In order for these business travelers, who were the "heavy users" of commercial aircraft seats, to fill the seats available in 1973, it would have been necessary for many of them to spend three days each week in airplanes! The American airline industry has paid dearly for its ignorance of potential customer saturation and the resultant overcapacity.

To deal with this sort of problem, a variety of strategic planning models have been developed during the past decade. Among the most prominent are the portfolio models of the Boston Consulting Group and of General Electric (GE)/McKinsey, which utilize two axes or dimensions to portray current and expected positions of strategic business units.[1] One dimension that portfolio models generally include is a growth factor based on the PLC concept. This article will exam-

This article first appeared in *BUSINESS* April-June 1983, pp. 30–35. Reprinted with permission from *BUSINESS* and Lester A. Neidell. Copyright 1983 by the College of Business Administration, Georgia State University, Atlanta.

When the article was published the author was Associate Professor of Marketing at the University of Tulsa, Tulsa, Oklahoma.

ine the usefulness of the PLC as a strategic planning aid independent of portfolio analysis.

Because growth by itself is a vague concept, strategic planning requires that the growth factor be defined in terms of why, when, and how much. The PLC is useful because it portrays changes in sales and market conditions over time. Since opportunities and problems parallel these changes, dynamic strategies (ones that can also change) are required to take advantage of the opportunities and avoid the problems.

The PLC can provide insight into: (1) the types and depth of investment required to develop new products, (2) the number of competitors likely to be encountered, and (3) the likelihood of being profitable. The PLC is a summary concept, one in which the interaction of the environment, customers, and competition is key.

The General PLC Model

An S-shaped curve as shown in Exhibit 1 is accepted as the basic sales pattern under the PLC concept. Typically the sales pattern is divided into the four phases of *introduction, growth, maturity,* and *decline.* Initially, sales are slow as the product is introduced. Depending on the "newness" of the product, potential users and buyers must be informed during the *introduction* phase of its features, uses, and advantages. During the *growth* stage, rapid market acceptance takes

Exhibit 1   Basic PLC Sales Pattern

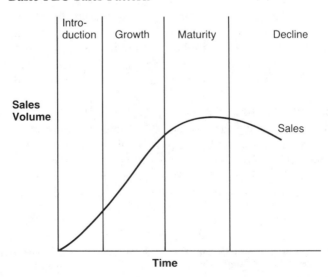

Source: Lester A. Neidell, *Strategic Marketing Management: An Integrated Approach* (Tulsa, Oklahoma: Penn Well Press, 1983).

place; in the *maturity* stage a slowdown in sales growth occurs; while in the *decline* stage the product's unit sales actually decrease.

The unit sales curve in Exhibit 1 is often viewed as the most dominant feature of the PLC. For strategic planning purposes, two other PLC relationships are at least as important as unit sales. These are (1) the investment recovery curve, indicating the scope of preintroduction and postintroduction expenses, and (2) the profit curve, showing how profits accrue in the different PLC stages. The relationship of these factors to the sales curve is shown in Exhibit 2. Notice that each of the investment areas—engineering and development, market planning, manufacturing, and marketing—has a preintroduction and a postintroduction phase.

During the introductory sales phase, it is unlikely that sales levels will become great enough to recoup preintroductory expenses. For many products, introduction costs actually increase the investment. Investment recovery usually begins during the rapid growth stage, and profits ordinarily peak at the end of the rapid growth stage or early in the maturity stage. Typically, the innovator and early entrants reach investment recovery break-even points late in the growth stage or early in the maturity stage. The slowdown in sales growth that characterizes maturity also signals a decrease in industry profitability. Organizations that were late entrants, particularly those with small shares and undifferentiated products, will

---

Exhibit 2 Product Life Cycle: Sales, Investment, and Profits

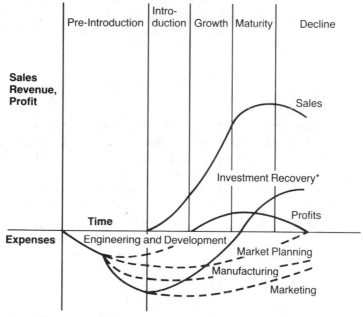

*Investment recovery = Sales revenue – Expenses

Source: Lester A. Neidell, *Strategic Marketing Management: An Integrated Approach* (Tulsa, Oklahoma: Penn Well Press, 1983).

seldom be profitable at maturity; their investment base may never be recovered. But in those organizations with solid market shares, investment recovery will often continue, and substantial profits can be achieved. In the sales decline stage, profits are eroded, and if the decision is made to remain in the market, new investments may be required in production technology and/or product improvement.

The PLC is conceptually appealing because it helps shape corporate strategy and marketing tactics. For example, corporate strategy may focus on the development of a balanced life-cycle mix by creating a stream of new products to replace those in maturity and decline. In marketing, the development of different "mixes" of advertising, selling effort, pricing, and distribution over the PLC dominates managerial thinking.

Other PLC Patterns

The S-shaped, life-cycle pattern shown in Exhibit 1 is an idealized pattern. For example, fashion items often skip the slow introductory period and initially exhibit rapid growth. Other products never exhibit growth rapidly but simply pass directly to the maturity stage. As many as 12 different PLC patterns have been documented; 3 of the more prominent variations of the idealized S-shaped curve are shown in Exhibit 3. They include (1) a *cycle-recycle* pattern, attributed to a traditional promotional push as products enter the decline stage; (2) a *stable maturity* pattern, in which the maturity phase extends for a long period of time; and (3) an *innovative maturity* (or "scalloped") pattern in which new sales are derived from the development of new-product uses, product improvement, and/or the penetration of new markets.

What Is a Product?

One of the enduring enigmas of PLC theory is the definition of "product." Empirical evidence of the PLC has sometimes foundered when rigid definitions of "product" were applied.[2] In general, three levels of product can be defined: (1) product class, (2) product form, and (3) product brand.

Product class has the broadest definition. Items that broadly substitute for the same customer use, such as cigarettes, pipes, and cigars, are each a product class. Product classes tend to exhibit extended or stable maturity patterns (see Exhibit 3), since in maturity product use is often correlated with total population or population within a market segment. In the U.S. automobile market the product class is broadly defined by "number of passenger vehicle registrations" and is an example of one that has reached stable maturity.

Product forms are finer breakdowns within the product class, and can be conceived of as distinct subtypes of a product class. Different definitions of product form often correspond to different ways of achieving customer segmentation. For example, within the product class of cigarettes, product forms would be king-

Exhibit 3   Variations in PLC Patterns

A: Cycle-Recycle Pattern

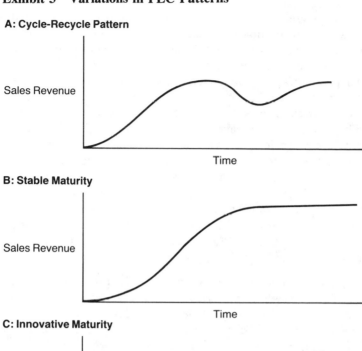

B: Stable Maturity

C: Innovative Maturity

Source: Lester A. Neidell, *Strategic Marketing Management: An Integrated Approach* (Tulsa, Oklahoma: Penn Well Books, 1983). Adapted from David R. Rink and John E. Swan, "Product Life Cycle Research: A Literature Review," *Journal of Business Research* (September 1979).

size, mentholated, low tar, and combinations of these. For passenger vehicles, product forms could include subdivision by size of car (standard, compact, sub-compact), or by type (convertible, station wagon, four-door sedan). Product forms tend to exhibit the standard S-shaped PLC of Exhibit 1 more than product classes or product brands do.

Product forms can be broken down still further into *product brands*. Individual product brands often display erratic sales patterns. This occurs because brands respond more quickly to short-run competitive marketing tactics than do either product forms or product classes. For this reason, brands frequently do not exhibit the S-shaped PLC pattern of Exhibit 1, or the PLC variations shown in Exhibit 2.

Application of the PLC Concept

Product life cycles are closely related to the social-psychological theory of the diffusion of innovations.[3] Innovation theory identifies 5 categories of adopters. Initial sales of a new product are generally low because only "innovators" know about the product or service. Marketing efforts focus on stimulating awareness, interest, trial, and purchase. As customer recognition and acceptance increase, larger numbers of buyers—the "early adopters"—form the vanguard of the growth stage. Product success attracts new competitors and speeds up the adoption process by providing increased information and by pressuring prices downward. The "early majority" provides the nucleus of the growth stage, and as the number of potential new buyers decreases, the rate of growth slows appreciably. In maturity, sales are derived from the "late majority" and "laggards," as well as from replacement or from multiunit sales to earlier purchasers. Sales may also decline when competitive product classes or forms divert the interest of buyers.

When analyzing the American leisure sports industry, G. David Hughes noted the effects of diffusion and the PLC on competitors within this industry. According to Hughes:

> *In the early 1970s, Wilson could sell as many steel-framed tennis rackets as it could make. By 1975, 35 percent of the rackets were steel-framed, but competition was so intense that prices had dropped to one-third of the previous levels. Everyone was caught with expanded distribution, and commitments to import from Taiwan. The shakeout included Chemold, an early metal-racket manufacturer, which filed for a Chapter 11 bankruptcy.*
>
> *Many nonsports conglomerates moved into the manufacturing of sporting goods, e.g., Victor Comptometer (business machines), Colgate-Palmolive (personal care products), S. C. Johnson & Sons (waxes), and American Brands (foods). This diversity of entries made the identification of competitors and the measurement of industry capacity difficult, if not impossible.*
>
> *Golf grew at the rate of 10 percent per year, until its popularity resulted in overcrowded courses. But the high cost of new courses prevented expansion. Ski equipment and apparel businesses too had their shakeout. AMF's Head Ski, the inventor of metal skis, went from a 70 percent to a 12 percent market share. Manufacturers seemed to have overlooked the fact that their growth is limited by the fact that people have only so many leisure hours to spend on sports.[4]*

Another example in which planners ignored PLC implications occurred with the aforementioned original adoption of wide-bodied jets by airlines in the United States.

Market Entry Strategies

At the corporate level, recognition of different stages of the PLC provides insight into the degree of competition, both in terms of number of competitors and the scope of competitive activities. These factors, together with the assessment of an organization's unique capabilities, provide various market entry strategies. Thus,

a firm leading in technology would normally enter the market early; strong promotional tools also justify early entry. Strengths in distribution would warrant
entry in the growth stage. And if production engineering and cost cutting are a
firm's strengths, it may even consider entering late in the PLC.

During the 1950s and 1960s the GE portable appliance division in the
United States adroitly matched its capabilities with PLC concepts and obtained
large market shares for many of its products. Strategy seemed to center not on
product introduction but on significant product improvement (such as rechargeable
batteries in place of a direct electrical connection) as soon as a product passed the
introductory stage. The company's strengths lay in its promotional capabilities and
in its ability to obtain intensive distribution, which made GE products widely
available once promotion had stimulated demand. Retailers were encouraged to
carry GE appliances by: (1) GE's support for resale price maintenance, which
removed price competition as a retail weapon; and (2) GE's assumption of the
service function. (Factory-owned service centers were opened in major cities to
remove the service burden from retailers.) Thus, GE's extensive resources were
used to develop a marketing program that relied on rapid sales growth to recover
substantial investments in product improvement and distribution.

The PLC and Process Life Cycles

Recent empirical investigation has demonstrated that production processes normally move through a *process life cycle* that parallels the PLC.[5] For example, in
the production stage that corresponds to the introductory PLC stage, the production process is usually of the job-shop type: flexible, but not cost-efficient. As the
product matures, production evolves toward standardization and mechanization,
and becomes more capital intensive and less flexible. This concept is shown in
Exhibit 4, which depicts the interaction between the PLC and the process life
cycle. The columns in this figure represent four stages of the PLC, while the rows
of this matrix represent four process-life-cycle stages: job shop, batch assembly,
assembly line, and continuous process. A natural fit exists between these two life
cycles, as shown by the circled examples on the main diagonal. For example,
products in maturity and decline rely on standardized production processes. But,
depending on its competences, an organization may opt to compete in an off-
diagonal position. Thus, Rolls-Royce Limited competes successfully by producing
a limited line of cars using a job-shop process. The more a company moves away
from the diagonal, the more it is likely to become different from its competitors.
This provides greater opportunity to obtain uniqueness. However, off-diagonal
positions increase coordination difficulties between manufacturing and marketing.
This was illustrated by the first entry of Texas Instruments (TI) into the digital
watch market. The company was already established as a major producer of integrated circuits. Its manufacturing process was highly automated, certainly in the
stage III (assembly line) area. Yet TI's first product line in the digital watch field
was a jewelry line that emphasized styling and high prices. This positioned the
product's life cycle in the upper-left-hand quadrant of Exhibit 4, as shown. The
jewelry line was quickly dropped and was replaced with a simplified electronic

Exhibit 4   Product Life Cycles and Process Life Cycles

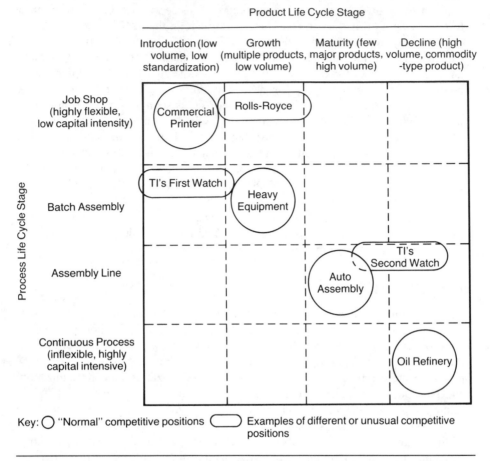

Product Life Cycle Stage

| | Introduction (low volume, low standardization) | Growth (multiple products, low volume) | Maturity (few major products, high volume) | Decline (high volume, commodity -type product) |

Key: ◯ "Normal" competitive positions   ⬭ Examples of different or unusual competitive positions

Source: Lester A. Neidell, *Strategic Marketing Management: An Integrated Approach* (Tulsa, Oklahoma: Penn Well Press, 1983). Adapted from Robert H. Hayes and Steven C. Wheelwright, "Link Manufacturing Process and Product Life Cycles," *Harvard Business Review* (January–February 1979).

watch in a plastic case which could be manufactured by a more standardized process closer to TI's traditional strengths. The position of the simplified watch is also indicated in Exhibit 4 and demonstrates that the simplified product is much closer to TI's distinctive manufacturing competence.

Linking PLC and manufacturing processes is another way of illustrating the need for a dynamic strategic plan, one that changes over the PLC. As product markets mature, companies may find a conflict between manufacturing processes and market needs. Mature products often are commodity-like and require a highly automated, capital-intensive production process to be price competitive. When products approach maturity, the flexibility that yielded higher-than-average returns during introduction and growth often becomes a liability.

Product Class and Product Form/Brand Matching

Earlier it was suggested that the PLC needs to be defined in terms of level of product—either class, form, or brand.[6] Clearly, these levels or different definitions of product may be in different life-cycle stages at the same time. For example, while the American passenger vehicle market (product class) is in the maturity stage or perhaps even in the decline stage, a new product form (economy cars) and a new brand (the Escort) are being introduced. As a result, the marketing program developed by Ford to promote the front-wheel drive Escort (introduction stage) is quite different from that used to promote the LTD Ford (maturity stage). The fact that product classes and product forms or brands can be in different life-cycle stages during a given time period is illustrated in Exhibit 5. The four standard life-cycle stages, which refer to the product form or brand, make up the horizontal axis, while the four analogous terms that define the life cycle for the product class make up the vertical axis.

The often unstated assumption is that product classes and product forms/brands exhibit *simultaneous development,* as illustrated by the main diagonal of Exhibit 5. In simultaneous development, the principal strategic action is to generate product-class awareness during introduction. Heavy promotional expenditures often mark this stage. As product-class sales take off and then mature, the strategic key becomes the development of product-form and product-brand loyalty. Differentiation and segmentation are often used to achieve this. Other marketing mix elements can also be used to establish and maintain customer loyalty. For example, coffee producers often use retail price promotion as a feature of their marketing programs. This tactic has as its principal aim the "rewarding" of brand loyal customers. If customers of some other brand switch because of the price cut, that is simply a bonus. As a rule, simultaneous product-class and product-form/brand development is a competitive situation that requires the ultimate skill in developing dynamic strategies.

The two other situations shown in Exhibit 5 are *market extension* and *market following.* Aggressive marketing can often push a mature product form or brand into a new market without going through a distinct period of product class introduction. This is called *market extension.* The concept involves the discovery of new markets for mature products. Obvious examples exist in international trade, where specific brands of automobiles, jet aircraft, and computers are sold to the Third World or to less-developed countries without an extensive program to promote the need for the product class. Sometimes these efforts fail. Polaroid was unsuccessful in meeting the European objectives for its cameras during the early years of the company's international expansion. This was partly due to erroneous assumptions that European consumers were aware of and appreciated instant photography. Market extension can also be found in the United States. Prime examples are Johnson and Johnson, which promotes its baby shampoo to adults, and Arm and Hammer, which has introduced baking soda as a refrigerator deodorant.

The third condition, *market following,* requires that a product be introduced as a *follower* that lags behind the product-class stage. This replication strategy can involve creative product development and innovative marketing efforts, such as those of GE, or might involve an exploitive strategy, that is, simply copying another's successful strategy.

Exhibit 5   Product Class/Product Form Matching Matrix

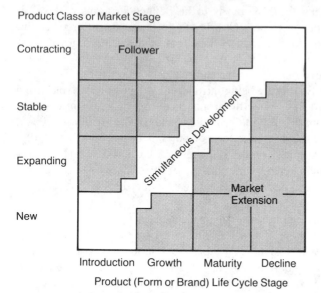

Source: Lester A. Neidell, *Strategic Marketing Management: An Integrated Approach* (Tulsa, Oklahoma: Penn Well Press, 1983). Adapted from Ben M. Enis, "GE, PIMS, BCG, and the PLC," *Business* (May–June 1980).

An Inappropriate Biological Analogy

The truth is that product classes, forms, and brands are born and eventually die. One common analogy suggests that PLCs are similar to ordinary aging associated with biological processes. This is inappropriate, since *the strategic implications of PLC analysis are that PLCs are to a large extent controllable,* while biological aging is largely uncontrollable. Product life cycles result from the interaction of environmental, competitive, and customer forces; strategic planning requires the assessment of these forces. The focus of strategic planning is to assess the strengths of the organization in light of environmental influences and then to select those strategies that seem to assure achievement of organizational goals. Analysis of the PLC provides a model on which environments and strategies can be assessed.

Summary

The PLC has been a durable marketing concept. Its utility and form have been debated, but the current stress on strategic planning reemphasizes the need to evaluate growth paths of products. The PLC concept can, by itself and in concert with other empirical findings and theoretical constructs, be a valuable tool for the analysis and development of competitive strategies. Analysis of the PLC should be the *first* step in strategic analysis; the use of more complex models can follow.

Notes

1. Yoram Wind and Vijay Mahajan, "Designing Product and Business Portfolios," *Harvard Business Review* (January–February 1981): 155—165, and Lester A. Neidell, *Strategic Marketing Management: An Integrated Approach* (Tulsa, Oklahoma PennWell Press, 1983), Chapters 7 and 8.

2. Nariman K. Dhalla and Sonia Yuspeh, "Forget The Product Life Cycle Concept!" *Harvard Business Review* (January–February 1976): 102–112.

3. Everett Rogers, *The Diffusion of Innovations* (New York: The Free Press, 1962).

4. G. David Hughes, *Marketing Management: A Planning Approach* (Reading, Massachusetts: Addison-Wesley), 279.

5. Robert H. Hayes and Steven C. Wheelwright, "Link Manufacturing Process and Product Life Cycles," *Harvard Business Review* (January–February 1979): 133–140.

6. Ben M. Enis, "GE, PIMS, BCG and the PLC," *Business* (May–June 1980): 10–18.

12

Strategic Responses to Technological Threats

Arnold C. Cooper and Dan Schendel

Technological innovation can create new industries and transform or destroy existing ones. At any time, many businesses are confronted with a host of external technological threats. Managements of threatened firms realize that many threats may not materialize, at least in the short run. However, one or more of those potential threats may develop in ways that will have devastating impact. Providers of kerosene lamps, buggy whips, railroad passenger service, steam radiators, hardwood flooring, passenger liner service and motion pictures all have had to contend with such threats. Few environmental changes can have such important strategic implications.

A typical sequence of events involving the traditional firm's responses to a technological threat begins with the origination of a technological innovation outside the industry, often pioneered by a new firm. Initially crude and expensive, it expands through successive submarkets, with overall growth following an S-shaped curve. Sales of the old technology may continue to expand for a few years, but then usually decline, the new technology passing the old in sales within five to fourteen years of its introduction.

The traditional firms fight back in two ways. The old technology is improved and major commitments are made to develop products utilizing the new technology. Although competitive positions are usually maintained in the old technology, the new field proves to be difficult. In addition to the major traditional competitors (who are also fighting for market share in the new field), a host of new competitors must be confronted. Despite substantial commitments, the traditional firm is usually not successful in building a long-run competitive position in the new tech-

This article first appeared in *Business Horizons*, February 1976, pp. 61–69. Copyright, 1976, by the Foundation for the School of Business at Indiana University. Reprinted by permission.

When this article was published the authors were both faculty members in the Krannert Graduate School of Business Administration at Purdue University.

nology. Unless other divisions or successful diversifications take up the slack, the firm may never again enjoy its former success.

Most previous research on technological innovation has been concerned with the practices and problems of innovators. This research is concerned with major technological innovations from the viewpoint of firms in established industries threatened by innovation.

Threatened Industries

The industries and technologies selected for study were the following:

- steam locomotives vs. diesel-electric
- vacuum tubes vs. the transistor
- fountain pens vs. ball-point pens
- boilers for fossil fuel power plants vs. nuclear power plants
- safety razors vs. electric razors
- aircraft propellers vs. jet engines
- leather vs. polyvinyl chloride and poromeric plastics.

Within these traditional industries, twenty-two separate firms were studied, using data available in the secondary literature where over 200 separate sources were examined. The accompanying table lists these firms. Two broad questions are of concern to the study:

- What was the nature of the substitution of the new technology for the old?
- What response strategies were used to counter the technological threats?

Firms Studied

Locomotives

American Locomotive Co.
Baldwin Locomotive Works

Vacuum (Receiving) Tubes

Columbia Broadcasting System (CBS)
Radio Corp. of America (RCA)
Ratheon Mfg. Co.
Sylvania Electric Products, Inc.

Fountain Pens

Esterbrook Pen Co.
Eversharp, Inc.
Parker Pen Co.
Sheaffer Pen Co.
Waterman Pen Co.

Safety Razors

American Safety Razor Corp.
Gillette Safety Razor Co.

Fossil Fuel Boilers

Babcock & Wilcox Co.
Combustion Engineering Inc.

Propellers

Koppers Corp.
Curtiss-Wright Corp.
United Aircraft Corp.

Leather Industry

A. C. Lawrence Leather Co.
Armour Leather Co.
Allied Kid Co. (Cudahy)
Seton Leather Co.

The findings must be regarded as tentative. The data are incomplete in some areas, as should be expected from secondary data. For example, data on the performance and strategies of smaller firms in the threatened industries are not readily available. The relatively small number of industries studied and the complexity of the processes prevent definitive conclusions. However, the experiences of these industries and firms suggest a number of conclusions with implications for managers of threatened firms.

The first section which follows deals with substitution patterns of new technology for the old. The second deals with response strategies by the threatened firms, a subject which has received very little previous attention in the literature. Finally, a section is devoted to implications and conclusions.

Patterns of Substitution

The nature of the substitution of one technology for another is not well known. The product life cycle concept suggests that products move through a classical S-shaped curve: this implies that the sales of a new product grow, slowly at first and then rapidly, and finally mature to a plateau from which they decline. Presumably, this would apply to the sales of a new technology, with the sales of the old technology declining accordingly.

Empirical studies of ethical drug products and of nondurable goods found that new products did not always follow the S-shaped sales curve.[1] J. C. Fisher and R. H. Pry postulated that the substitution of one technology for another follows a hyperbolic tangent or S-shaped curve.[2] On a semilog scale, the market share of the new technology divided by the market share of the old technology plots as a straight line. They reported on some seventeen substitutions, most of which closely followed this pattern. Kenneth Hatten and Mary Louise Piccoli tested the Fisher-Pry model on over forty substitutions and reported that the model was useful, so long as care was exercised in the selection of units and in the application of the results.[3] Generally, then, an S-shaped curve of growth for the

[1]William E. Cox, "Product Life Cycles in Marketing Models," *Journal of Business* (October 1967), pp. 375–384.

Rolando Polli and Victor Cook, "Validity of the Product Life Cycle," *Journal of Business* (October 1969), pp. 385–400.

[2]J. C. Fisher and R. H. Pry, "A Simple Substitution Model of Technological Change," *Technological Forecasting and Social Change* (1971), pp. 75–88.

[3]Kenneth Hatten and Mary Louise Piccoli, "An Evaluation of a Technological Forecasting Method by Computer Based Simulation" (Proceedings of the Division of Business Policy and Planning, Academy of Management, August 1973).

new technology and a similar S-shaped curve of decline for the old technology would be expected.

The data required to plot the product life cycles for the new and old technologies are not always available in the form desired. For instance, the unit sales of piston engines and of jet engines over time do not accurately reflect the much greater horsepower of jet engines. Comparison of leather and vinyl is made difficult by the wide range of uses of both materials, often in applications where they do not compete with each other. Nevertheless, a number of questions of managerial interest can be considered with the data available.

An examination of the sales over time for both the new and old technologies showed variable patterns which do not always duplicate the classical S-shaped pattern. Analysis of this sales data, coupled with extensive examination of other information, leads to a number of conclusions concerning the substitution pattern of new for old technologies.

1.   After the introduction of the new technology, the sales of the old technology did not always decline immediately; in four out of seven cases, sales of the old technology continued to expand.

2.   In two cases, sales of the old technology continued to expand for the entire period studied, despite growth in sales of the new technology.

3.   When sales of the old technology did decline, the time period from first commercial introduction to the time when dollar sales of the new technology exceeded dollar sales of the old ranged from about five to fourteen years.

4.   The first commercial introduction of the new technology was, in four out of seven cases, made by a firm outside the traditional industry. It might have been expected that the traditional competitors would have been the logical sources of industry innovation because of their strong customer relationships, well-developed channels of distribution and organizations oriented toward serving those industries.

5.   In three of the four industries in which capital requirements were not excessive, new firms were the first to introduce the new technology.

6.   The new technology often created new markets which were not available to the old technology. Although the initial ball-point pens were expensive, low-priced pens were later developed which opened up a new market—the "throw-away" pen. It was also estimated that 50% of the applications for the transistor were in equipment made possible by the invention of the transistor. Vinyls were used in floor coverings and building materials, applications not open to leather.

7.   The new technology was expensive and relatively crude at first. Often, its initial shortcomings led observers to believe it would find only limited applications. Although the first ball-point pens wrote under water, they blotted, skipped and stopped writing on paper and even leaked into pockets; after an initial fad phase, public disenchantment set in and sales dropped

dramatically. The first transistors were expensive and had sharply limited frequencies, power capabilities and temperature tolerance; some observers thought they would never find more than limited application. The jet-powered airplane was initially thought to be suitable only for the military market.

8. The new technology often invaded the traditional industry by capturing sequentially a series of submarkets. Although the new technology was crude it often had performance advantages for certain applications. Some submarkets were insulated from competition for extended periods. General Motors' diesel-electric locomotive first invaded the submarket for passenger locomotives, subsequently the submarket for switcher locomotives, and then freight locomotives—the major submarket—accounting for about 75% of industry sales. The transistor found early application in hearing aids and pocket radios, but not in radar systems and television.

9. The new technology did not necessarily follow the standard S-shaped growth curve. Erratic patterns were caused by abnormal economic and social conditions (World War II in the case of the electric razor, propellers and steam locomotives), by faddish phases of sales (ball-point pens), and by a newer technology replacing the original new technology (transistors and integrated circuits).

Some Pitfalls of Appraisals

Many factors affect the rate of penetration of a new technology: it does not capture markets overnight. Substantial sales opportunities may exist in the old technology for extended periods. It may be difficult for management in the traditional firms to judge the eventual impact of a developing threat, but at least there is usually time to develop a new strategy.

However, response presumes the ability to recognize and assess the threatening innovation. Intelligence activities focusing only upon traditional competitors are not enough, inasmuch as nontraditional competitors and new firms may be the originators of the threatening technology. It may be necessary to monitor a variety of innovations, many of which may never have significant impact.

Surviving past technological threats does not confer future immunity. In 1934, when General Motors introduced the first mainline diesel-electric locomotive, the producers of steam locomotives could look back upon two earlier threats which they had survived: the electric locomotive, and, in the 1920s, passenger cars with individual gasoline-powered engines. Both of these prior threats captured only small segments of the American locomotive market. There was no indication that the next threat, the diesel-electric, would destroy the traditional industry within fifteen years.

It would be a mistake to wait until decline in sales of the old technology triggered the need for appraisal of the threat. By then, much of the lead time would have passed. However, this means that the new technology must be appraised when it is still relatively crude. In an earlier article, James C. Utterback and James W. Brown emphasized that hypotheses about directions for change aid in selection of parameters which can be observed and evaluated.[4] For instance, early diesel engines had such a high weight-to-horsepower ratio that a diesel-electric locomotive would have been impossibly large. Managements of steam locomotive firms might have hypothesized that any changes leading to improvements in this weight-to-power ratio were of critical importance and deserved continuous monitoring.

It is not enough to judge that someday a new technology will replace an old one. Rates of penetration must be determined. When the Baldwin Locomotive Works was founded in 1831, it would have been of little value to tell founders that someday their principal product would be obsolete. However, when Sylvania introduced a new line of vacuum tubes for computers in 1957, the rate of improvement of transistors then taking place was extremely relevant.

The forecaster needs to understand differences in needs of market segments and relate these to probable improvements in the new technology. Some market segments in a traditional industry are threatened earlier and to a greater extent than others. Firms should consider strategies involving emphasis on the less threatened segments.

Response Strategies

Once the threat has been recognized, what kind of response is made by the traditional firm? If it decides not to participate in the new technology, management might elect one or a combination of the following specific actions:

- Do nothing.
- Monitor new developments in the competing technology through vigorous environmental scanning and forecasting activity.
- Seek to hold back the new threat by fighting it through public relations and legal action.
- Increase flexibility so as to be able to respond to subsequent developments in the new technology.
- Avoid the threat through decreasing dependence on the most threatened submarkets.
- Expand work on the improvement of the existing technology.
- Attempt to maintain sales through actions not related to technology, such as promotion or price-cutting.

A firm might, however, choose to participate in the new technology. The degree of commitment could vary widely, ranging from a token involvement, such as defensive research and development, to seeking leadership in the new technology through major and immediate commitments. Important dimensions of a strategy for participation in the technology include decisions about the level of acceptable risk, the magnitude of commitments to the new technology, the timing

[4]James C. Utterback and James W. Brown, "Monitoring for Technological Opportunities," *Business Horizons* (October 1972), pp. 5–15.

of those commitments and the extent of reliance on internal development versus acquisition. Against this background of possible responses, the seven industries were studied to determine the response strategies actually used by the threatened firms. Their strategies are shown in the accompanying table.

Participation in the New Technology

Of the twenty-two firms studied, all but five made at least some effort to participate in the new technology. Fifteen of the firms made major efforts to establish positions in the new technology. Firms with small market shares in the old technology were not the focus of this study. However, it does appear that they either did not attempt to establish positions in the new technology, or they achieved no visible success. For instance, the hundreds of small razor blade firms never had successful electric razors, and the five smallest locomotive producers never made the transition to diesel-electrics.

Nature of Participation

The timing of traditional firms' entries in the new technology varied widely. Raytheon and RCA vacuum tube producers were among the first to enter the transistor market. By contrast, Parker Pen brought out its first ball-point pen nine years after its first commercial introduction. Of the nine firms which had traditionally emphasized research and development in their various divisions, six were early entrants in the new technology. By contrast, only two of the firms with a low research and development emphasis were early entrants.

Acquisition was not a widely used means of entry into the new technology. Only four of twenty-two traditional firms used acquisition, and two of these used acquisitions to supplement their internal development. Parker acquired the Writing Division of Eversharp as a means of successfully entering the low-priced ball-point pen market after having first developed a high-priced ball-point pen. Raytheon, having previously made major commitments to germanium transistors, acquired Rheem Semiconductor as a means of entering the silicon transistor field.

Emphasis on Old Technology

In every industry studied, the old technology continued to be improved and reached its highest stage of technical development *after* the new technology was introduced. For instance, the smallest and most reliable vacuum tubes ever produced were developed after the introduction of the transistor. No threatened firm adopted a strategy of early withdrawal from the old technology in order to concentrate on the new. Moreover, all but one of the twenty-two companies continued to make heavy commitments to the improvement of the old technology.

Most of the firms followed a strategy of dividing their resources, so as to participate in a major way in both the old and new technologies. Baldwin Locomotive developed both advanced turbine-powered electric locomotives and diesel-electric locomotives. CBS and Raytheon developed new lines of vacuum tubes and also made major investments in research and development and production

Traditional Industries Studied

	Locomotives	Vacuum (Receiving) Tubes	Fountain Pens	Safety Razors	Fossil Fuel Boilers	Propellers	Leather Industry
Sales decline immediately after new technology introduced?	No	No	*	No	No	No	Yes[1]
Sales eventually begin long-term decline?	Yes	Yes	Yes	No	No	Yes	Yes
Time from introduction of new technology until sales of new technology exceeded old.	Fourteen years[2]	Eleven years	Nine years	Twenty-five years[3]	Not during the twenty years since first sale	Five years[4]	†
New markets created by new technology?	No	Yes	Yes	No	No	No	Yes
New technology limited in application or crude at first?	Yes	Yes	Yes	Yes	Yes	Yes	Yes
New technology applied sequentially to submarkets?	Yes	Yes	Yes[5]	No	No	Yes	Yes
First commercial introduction by a firm in traditional industry?	‡	Yes	No	No	§	Yes[6]	No
First commercial introduction by a new firm?	No	No	Yes	Yes	No	No[6]	Yes
Old firms participate in new technology?	Yes	Yes	Yes (4 of 5)	Yes (briefly)	Yes	Yes (2 of 3)	No (1 of 4)[7]

Acquisitions a means of participating in new technology?	No	Yes Raytheon	Yes Parker	Yes Gillette[8]	No	No	Yes Allied Kid
Old technology improved after new technology was introduced?	Yes	Yes	Yes	Yes	Yes	Yes	Yes
Traditional firms involved in improving old technology and in entering new technology?	Yes	Yes	Yes (4 of 5)	Yes (participation in electric razors short-lived)	Yes	Yes	Yes
Attempt to establish barriers to new technology?	No	No	No	No	No	No	No

---

[1] Production of three of the four types of leather declined in the year after vinyl was first used as a leather substitute.

[2] Available sales data relate to units sold rather than sales dollars, but it appears that diesel-electric sales exceeded steam locomotive sales by 1938, fourteen years after the first diesel-electric switcher was introduced. Subsequently, steam locomotive unit sales exceeded diesel-electric unit sales during World War II, but steam locomotive sales then dropped sharply after the War.

[3] During 1956–1958, electric razor sales exceeded sales of razor blades. Subsequently, however, razor blades regained a sales lead and have maintained it to the time of the study.

[4] Unit production of jet engines exceeded unit production of piston engines during a three-year period in the early 1950s. It appears that the dollar value of jet engines produced exceeded the value of the smaller, less powerful piston engines within about five years of their introduction in the United States.

[5] The pen market is segmented by price. Initially, the ball-point pen was relatively expensive.

[6] Power Jets, a new British firm, developed the first jet engine. General Electric developed and introduced the first American jet engine, relying upon Power Jets' designs.

[7] Allied Kid bought Corfam from DuPont in 1965. Also, all the firms began coating hides with synthetic materials to improve their qualities.

[8] Gillette acquired Braun, A. G., and thereby entered the overseas market for electric razors. Gillette has not reentered the U.S. market since 1938, when its internally developed electric razor was introduced and subsequently withdrawn.

[*] Data were not found to indicate whether sales of fountain pens declined the year the ball-point pen was introduced.

[†] Results are mixed by type of application. By 1950, synthetics had captured 50% of the shoe sole market.

[‡] The first mainline diesel-electric was introduced by General Motors, a firm which never made steam locomotives. However, American Locomotive had earlier introduced an experimental diesel-electric switcher.

[§] The first nuclear power plant was developed by Westinghouse, a firm with a strong position in turbines. However, for the producers of boilers, it was not a traditional competitor which introduced the new technology.

facilities for transistors. This dual strategy was not usually successful, particularly in relation to building a strong competitive position in the new technology. There were no apparent actions taken by the traditional firms to create or strengthen the barriers to adoption and diffusion of the innovations.

Firms that pioneered the new technology generally did not enter the old technology. The only exception was BIC, a successful French producer of low-priced ball-point pens, which acquired Waterman, an American fountain pen manufacturer. The acquisition was apparently for Waterman's U.S. distribution system rather than its product line, inasmuch as the fountain pen line was discontinued four years later.

Overall Performance

The new technical innovations did not always lead to immediate financial returns and, in fact, sometimes presented all participants with severe competitive challenges. The nuclear power field involved very heavy investments for many years by all participants before the first profits were earned. The precipitous sales decline, which occurred after the first cycle of ball-point pen sales, drove more than 200 new firms, as well as several established firms, from the market. DuPont's poromeric leather substitute, Corfam, reportedly resulted in losses of $100 million; Goodrich and Armstrong were also entrants who later withdrew from the leather substitute field.

The new technology often evolved rapidly. Transistors, nuclear power plants and jet engines all confronted participants with a succession of decisions about commitments to evolving technologies. Early leaders, such as Raytheon in transistors and Curtiss-Wright in jet engines, lost their competitive positions as the technology changed.

Where the old technology continued to grow, traditional firms were able to maintain their competitive positions and enjoy financial success. But many of the most successful firms in the new technology had never participated in the old technology. In industries in which capital barriers were not great, new firms were among the most successful. Examples of successful new firms were Papermate in ball-point pens, Fairchild Semiconductor in transistors and Schick in electric razors.

Over the long run most of the traditional firms that tried to participate in the new technology were not successful. Of the fifteen firms making major commitments, only two, Parker in ball-point pens and United Aircraft in jet engines, enjoyed long-term success as independent firms participating in the new technology.

Patterns of Commitment

Managers of threatened firms must decide how to allocate resources in choosing between improving the old technology and attempting to establish a competitive position in the new. If sales of the old continue to grow, as in safety razors or fossil fuel power plants, then the strengthening of the firm's position in the business it knows so well can be rewarding. However, if sales of the old technology are declining, heavy, across-the-board commitments seem questionable. Management should carefully segment its markets and identify those which appear protected from the threat. Strategies based upon maintaining strong competitive positions in these segments seem justified.

It is interesting that the traditional firms studied here continued to make substantial commitments to the old technologies, even when their sales had already begun to decline because of the competitive pressures of the new technologies. Perhaps this demonstrates the difficulty of changing the patterns of resource allocation in an established organization. Decisions about allocating resources to old and new technologies within the organization are loaded with implications for the decision makers; not only are old product lines threatened, but also old skills and positions of influence.

It was common for spokesmen for the traditional firms to emphasize the shortcomings of the new technology with comments such as "It is no wonder if the public feels that the steam locomotive is about to lay down and play dead," and "It is certain that substantially all airplanes which operate at speeds of 550 mph or less will use propeller propulsion." The executives who made these statements, conditioned by life-long involvements with the old technology, may have been slower than others to recognize the declining opportunities for their traditional products.

Commitment to the new technology, with its expanding opportunities and lack of entrenched competitors, may seem attractive. Certainly most of the firms studied here made such strategic investments. Yet such decisions are fraught with risk, as evidenced by the traditional firms being relatively unsuccessful in the new fields.

For these companies, the patterns of commitment seem to be related to the firm's characteristics. One group of firms was relatively undiversified and did not have strong research and development orientations. The producers of locomotives, fountain pens, safety razors and two of the leather producers might be so classified. Except for several of the pen companies, these firms usually were *not* early entrants, and furthermore, never captured substantial market shares in the new technologies. It is tempting to conclude that an innovative technical and managerial organization is required to make a successful transition from the old to the new technology.

Another group of firms had relatively strong research and development traditions and were accustomed to managing multibusiness organizations. Most of this group, which included the producers of vacuum tubes, boilers and propellers, made major commitments to the new technologies and in several instances achieved substantial early success. However, these technologies continued to evolve rapidly, so that it was necessary to generate successive generations of successful new products. Here, companies such as Curtiss-Wright in jet engines and RCA and Raytheon in transistors were unable to continue their early successes.

The reasons for these firms' inability to build and maintain strong competitive positions are not obvious. Resource limitations apparently were not a major factor in the transistor industry, inasmuch as a number of new companies were relatively successful. The traditional firms not only had to develop new products based upon different technologies, but also had to adapt to changing methods of marketing, servicing and manufacturing. Their lack of long-term success may be an indication of the relative difficulty of changing organizational strategy success-fully. The skills, attitudes and assumptions which undergird successful strategy in a traditional technology may require modification in ways both major and subtle to bring about equivalent success in the new technology. Apparently, many orga-nizations found this difficult to do.

Managers of threatened firms should consider carefully commitments to the new technology. Where such commitments are made, it is desirable to recognize ex-plicitly the different strategic requirements for success in the new field. Acquisi-tion, although not widely used by the firms studied here, merits particular consid-eration. This may be a way to acquire not only technical capabilities, but also organizations attuned to competition in the new field. There are no easy paths to success when faced with major technological threats. However, the experiences of these firms illustrate some of the approaches and pitfalls which management should consider.

Section
Four

Strategic Marketing
Models for Allocating
Resources

THE articles in this section discuss normative models that are used by managers to develop marketing strategies.[1] These models—STRATPORT, the
PIMS PAR ROI model, the BCG market growth/market share matrix, and the
market attractiveness/competitive capabilities matrix—are used both to evaluate product-market alternatives and to determine the level of investment that
should be directed toward the product-markets. The financial analysis, product
life cycle, and experience curve concepts discussed in the previous section provide a foundation for these strategic planning models.

STRATPORT—A Decision Calculus Model
for Strategic Decision Making

In the previous section, we discussed how financial models can be used to
evaluate strategic investment opportunities. These financial models are typically
used to examine capital investments such as purchasing new equipment, building a new plant, or funding an R&D project. Such investment decisions are

formulated in a discrete manner: they involve "go—no-go" decisions concerning a specified level of investment and subsequent returns. Strategic decisions, however, often are more continuous in nature. Rather than deciding to fund or not to fund a project, managers may need to determine the level of support that should be provided for various strategic alternatives.

Article 13, "STRATPORT: A Decision Support System for Strategic Planning," describes a decision calculus model developed to assist managers in making strategic resource allocation decisions. While financial evaluation models characterize investments as discrete choices (whether or not to make an investment), the STRATPORT model employs a response function which relates the range of potential investment levels to market position achieved (market share). In addition, the model incorporates some dynamic elements such as the changes in sales and costs over time. Consider whether the model, while providing a useful decision aid for managers, overcomes the limitations of financial planning models discussed in the introduction to Section III.

The PIMS Project

Although the use of traditional financial analysis to evaluate product-market opportunities is theoretically appealing, it does not provide insight into the factors that make an opportunity attractive. Why do some strategic alternatives have a high ROI while other alternatives have a low ROI? The PIMS project, described in Article 14, was established to address this shortcoming of traditional financial analysis.

The principal objective of the PIMS (Profit Impact of Market Strategy) project is to determine empirically the factors that lead to business unit profitability. As a first step toward the realization of this objective, the 200 member corporations of the Strategic Planning Institute (SPI) provided data on the performance, operation, financial structure, and environment of individual business units. This data base was then used (1) to discover empirical generalities concerning factors related to business unit performance and (2) to assist managers in evaluating the performance of their specific business units and in developing strategies for them.

Factors Related to Profitability

Early results of analyzing the PIMS data base indicated that profitability and cash flow are related to nine strategic factors. These nine factors account for almost 80 percent of the determination of business success or failure.[2] In approximate order of importance, they are as follows:

1.   *Investment intensity.* Technology and the business method chosen govern how much fixed capital and working capital are required to produce a dollar of sales or a dollar of value added in the business. Investment intensity generally produces a negative impact on percentage measures of

profitability or net cash flow; that is, businesses that are mechanized or automated or inventory-intensive generally show lower returns on investment and sales than businesses that are not.

2. *Productivity.* Businesses producing high value added per employee are more profitable than those with low value added per employee. ("Value added" is the amount by which the business increases the market value of the raw materials and components it buys.)

3. *Market position.* A business's share of its served market (both absolute and relative to its three largest competitors) has a positive impact on its profit and net cash flow. (The "served market" is the specific segment of the total potential market—defined in terms of products, customers, or areas—in which the business actually competes.)

4. *Growth of the served market.* Growth is generally favorable to dollar measures of profit, indifferent to percentage measures of profit, and negative to all measures of net cash flow.

4. *Quality of the products or services offered.* Quality, defined as the customers' evaluation of the business's product/service package as compared to that of competitors, has a generally favorable impact on all measures of financial performance.

6. *Innovation/differentiation.* Extensive actions taken by a business in the areas of new product introduction, R&D, marketing effort, and so on, generally produce a positive effect on its performance if the company has strong market position to begin with. If a company's market position is weak, such actions usually do not produce a positive effect.

7. *Vertical integration.* For businesses located in mature and stable markets, vertical integration (that is, make rather than buy) generally has a favorable effect on performance. In markets that are rapidly growing, declining, or otherwise changing, the opposite is true.

8. *Cost push.* The rates of increase of wages, salaries, and raw material prices and the presence of a labor union have complex impacts on profit and cash flow—depending on how the business is positioned to pass along the increase to its customers or to absorb the higher costs internally.

9. *Current strategic effort.* The current direction of change of any of the above factors has effects on profit and cash flow that are frequently opposite to that of the factor itself. For example, having strong market share tends to increase net cash flow, but acquiring share drains cash while the business is making that effort.[3]

In addition to these nine general factors, early PIMS researchers also recognized the importance of management capability (although it is difficult to measure its reliability independently in the data itself). There is such a thing as being a good or a poor "operator." A good operator can improve the profitability of a strong strategic position or minimize the damage of a weak one; a poor operator does the opposite. The presence of a management team that functions as a good operator is therefore a favorable element of a business; it produces a financial result better than one would expect from the strategic position of the business alone.[4]

Recent research using the PIMS data base is directed toward elaborating on these relationships. Attention is being directed toward uncovering contingencies and qualifications that must be considered when using the basic PIMS findings. Articles 21 and 22 in Section VI illustrate research utilizing the PIMS data base.[5]

PIMS Models for Strategic Analysis—PAR ROI

The general strategic principles developed through research on the PIMS data base are of interest to managers and scholars, but the SPI has also developed a PAR ROI model and a PAR cash flow model to help individual business unit managers evaluate the performance of their units and make strategic decisions. These models are linear equations derived through regression analysis. With these models, managers can determine what ROI and cash flow would normally be expected from a business unit in a similar strategic situation with average management (and luck). These norms for PAR ROI and cash flow are determined by simply substituting the values describing the specific unit into the regression equation derived by analyzing all business units in the data base. An example of a PAR ROI report is shown in Table IV.1.

Based on the PAR ROI report, managers can assess the performance of their business unit. Are their units above or below expected profits? What strategic factors are responsible for abnormal performance? What would the PAR ROI be if specific changes were made in strategic factors such as market share, marketing expenditures, or product quality? By using the PAR cash flow model, managers also can determine the typical cash flow that would result from making specific strategic changes. Thus the PAR reports are used to evaluate strategic alternatives in terms of the expected ROI and investment level (cash flows) associated with achieving the ROI.

Limitations of the PIMS Model

Article 14, "PIMS: A Reexamination," deals with some problems and limitations with the PIMS project. Criticism of the PIMS model center around the specification of the PAR models and the interpretation of the results.[6]

Model Specification. Specification problems focus on whether important variables have been omitted from the model and whether the structure of the model is appropriate. A critical issue that has not been resolved is whether one complex model can be used to describe the performance of widely diverse businesses. Some managers insist that their business is different, is so unique that the experiences of other businesses are irrelevant to their strategic market ef-

Table IV.1 PAR ROI Report (Impact of ROI-Influencing Factors: A Diagnosis of Strategic Strengths and Weaknesses)

	PIMS Mean	This Business	Impact	Sensitivity A Change Of:	Changes Impact By:
Attractiveness of Environment			0.6		
1 Purchase Amount—Immediate Costs	5.2	4.0	1.8	0.20	−0.31
2 Real Market Growth, Short Run	8.2	−4.1	−0.6	2.00	0.20
3 Industry (SIC) Growth, Long Run	9.1	6.8	−0.5	1.00	0.02
4 Selling Price Growth Rate	6.8	0.5	−0.1	1.00	0.00
Competitive Position			0.2		
5 Market Position			−2.9		
Market Share	23.7	15.0		5.00	3.05
Relative Market Share	61.7	34.8			
6 Industry Concentration Ratio	56.5	51.0	−0.2	5.00	0.19
7 Employees Unionized (%)	48.3	0.0	2.6	5.00	−0.25
8 Immediate Customer Fragmentation	12.2	25.0	0.2	2.00	0.04
9 Market Share Growth Rate	3.3	8.1	0.7	2.00	0.31
10 Market Share Instability	4.0	1.2	−0.3	0.50	0.06

Continued.

Table IV.1 *Continued*

	PIMS Mean	This Business	Impact	Sensitivity A Change Of:	Sensitivity Changes Impact By:
Differentiation from Competitors			2.8		
11 Relative Product Quality	25.9	34.3	0.8	5.00	0.75
12 Price Relative to Competition	103.5	100.3	0.1	1.00	−0.08
13 Standard Products/Services?		Yes	0.5		
14 Relative Compensation	100.9	102.0	0.0	1.00	−0.10
15 New Product Sales/Total Sales	11.9	0.0	1.3	5.00	−0.49
Effectiveness of Investment Use			5.0		
16 Investment Intensity Index			7.3		
Investment/Sales	56.1	33.0		5.00	−2.71
Investment/Value Added	96.7	65.6			
17 Value Added per Employee ($)	30.0	23.8	−1.7	5.00	1.67
18 Vertical Integration	58.8	51.9	−0.8	2.00	0.37
19 Relative Integration Backward		Less	−0.9		

No.	Factor		Same			
20	Relative Integration Forward			-0.3		
21	Fixed Capital Intensity	52.3	42.4	0.5	5.00	-0.36
22	Capacity Utilization	79.6	76.3	-0.4	5.00	0.30
23	Investment per Employee ($)	30.4	15.6	0.4	5.00	-0.12
24	Inventory/Sales	18.8	10.7	1.0	2.00	-0.34
25	FIFO Valuation?		No	0.0		
26	Newness of P&E (NBV/GBV)	55.0	52.0	0.0	2.00	0.27
	Discretionary Budget Expenditures			1.4		
27	Marketing Expense/Sales	10.8	7.7	1.5	2.00	-1.27
28	R&D Expense/Sales	2.4	2.5	-0.1	0.50	-0.23

1. PAR ROI is the sum of the five category impacts added to the all-PIMS average ROI:

Attractiveness of Environment	0.6%
Competitive Position	0.2
Differentiation from Competitors	2.8
Effectiveness of Investment Use	5.0
Discretionary Budget Expenditures	1.4
Sum of Impacts	9.9%
+ Average Return on Investment	22.1
"PAR" Return on Investment	32.0%

2. While useful insights may be gained by looking at individual factor impacts, attention should be focused on the aggregate (categorical) impacts when individual factors are interrelated.

3. Interpretation of Purchase Amount Immediate Customers:
   4 = from $100 up to $999

Source: Reprinted from Bradley T. Gale, Donald F. Heany, and Donald J. Swire, "The PAR ROI Report: Explanation and Commentary," *The Strategic Planning Institute* (1977):8–9.

forts. While each business may be unique, the factors driving performance may be similar. Analogously, medical practitioners appreciate that each patient is unique, but they focus on a set of common characteristics (pulse rate, blood pressure, body temperature, body weight to height, etc.) to evaluate the patient's health.

Another issue concerning the PIMS models is the choice of dependent and independent variables. Is ROI the best measure of business unit performance? Should managerial intentions and environmental characteristics be incorporated into the model?

A final issue concerns the estimation bias resulting from a confounding of the dependent and independent variables. In the PAR ROI model, the investment, revenue, and cost terms appear on both sides of the model equation. Investment is the denominator of ROI (the dependent variable) and also the numerator of investment intensity (an independent variable). Sales and costs are also components of both the dependent and independent variables. Profit (sales minus costs) is the numerator of ROI (the dependent variable) and part of investment intensity and marketing expenditure (the independent variables). The result is that the high explanatory power of the PAR models (80 percent of the variance explained) may be due in part to the tautological nature of the model.

Interpretation of Results.   Perhaps the most serious problem with the PIMS models is the implication that the relationships in the model are causal. The PAR models describe static relationships between variables at a specific time. Due to the cross-sectional nature of the analysis, one cannot infer that changes in the independent variables will cause changes in the dependent variable—the ROI or cash flow. For example, even though relative market share is significantly related to ROI, an increase in market share may not lead to a higher ROI because the cost of increasing market share may be greater than the benefit realized.

Summary—The PIMS Models

While there are many problems with the PIMS models, the PIMS project is one of the few strategy research efforts based on empirical research; most observations on strategy are based on management experience, simple rules of thumb, and case studies. Thus, the PIMS models provide a unique source of information for making strategic decisions.

Portfolio Models

The remaining articles in this section deal with two portfolio classification models: the BCG market growth/market share model and the market attractiveness/ competitive capabilities model. These models represent the two types of portfolio classification models that have been virtually synonymous with strategic market planning since the early 1970s.[7] On the basis of an extensive survey,

Phillippe Haspeslagh estimates that as of 1979, 36 percent of the *Fortune* 1000 and 45 percent of the *Fortune* 500 industrial companies use, to some extent, the portfolio planning approach associated with these models.[8]

When using these portfolio classification models, one must first undertake the following three steps:

1.   Define the strategic product-market opportunities. (The considerations associated with defining these strategic opportunities are discussed in Section II of this book.)

2.   Plot each product-market opportunity on a two-dimensional grid. Classify the opportunity on the basis of its position in this grid.

3.   Assign a classification to the product-market opportunity, thereby determining the strategic objective for the opportunity and the level of resources to be allocated so that the objective can be realized.

The market growth/market share and market attractiveness/competitive position models differ in terms of variables used to classify opportunity. However, there are strong similarities between these models in terms of objectives and resource allocation patterns associated with positions on the grid.

Market Growth/Market Share Model

The market growth/market share model, developed by the Boston Consulting Group, is described in Article 15, "Strategy and the Business Portfolio." The two dimensions used to classify strategic opportunities in this model are related to the product life cycle and experience curve concepts (discussed in Section III of this book). The vertical axis—long-term market growth—divides the opportunities into those in the introductory/growth stage of the product life cycle and those in the mature/decline stage of the product life cycle. The horizontal dimension uses relative market share as a surrogate for relative position on the experience curve: opportunities are classified by whether or not they have dominant market share opportunities. Opportunities with a dominant share typically have the most cumulative experience and hence the lowest cost.

Classification in Terms of the Model. Using these two dimensions, each strategic opportunity is classified as star, cash cow, dog, or problem. The strategy for the product-market is determined by the classification. Note that the potential strategies can be ordered in terms of the resources to be allocated to the product-market.

Investment Level	Strategy	Objective	Classification
+ +	invest	gain share	problem
+	maintain	hold share	star
−	harvest	lose share	problem, dog
− −	milk	maintain share	cash cow

It is important to realize that product-market opportunities are classified according to their long-term growth rate and relative market share—not profitability or cash generation. Thus, a product-market with high growth and low relative share is classified as a problem, even if it is generating a high positive cash flow. The actual cash situation of the relevant business unit becomes a diagnostic measure. For example, a unit in the problem category actually generating cash is seen as the result of a harvesting strategy, an improper definition of the market, or improper long-term management of the unit.

Criticism of the Market Growth/Market Share Matrix.   The market growth/market share matrix has certainly received substantial acceptance and has spawned a new vocabulary for marketing strategy; but it is not universally accepted. Concerns about the validity of the model center around the following premises basic to the model:

1.   Relative market share and long-term market growth are the most important considerations for making strategic marketing decisions. By focusing on these two factors, the BCG product portfolio approach ignores a number of factors empirically related to profitability that were found in the PIMS studies and also other factors theoretically related to performance in financial models, such as risk.

2.   Cash flow is a function of relative market share. Relative market share is token to represent relative competitive position on the relevant experience curve. Article 8 provides some empirical support for the notion that a business with the most cumulative experience in a product-market will have the lowest cost. However, there are a number of product-markets in which experience effects are quite weak. In addition, there are situations in which market share is a poor indicator of relative cost. For example, Apple had the largest market share in personal computers, but when IBM entered the market it may have had the lowest cost due to share experience gained through manufacturing larger computers.

3.   It is "easier" to gain share in high-growth markets. This premise is based on the idea that competitive reaction is greater in a mature market. On this assumption, the prescriptions of the market growth/market share matrix indicate that strategic investments should be restricted to high-growth product-markets (stars or problems). But there is little evidence to support this premise. Many managers are wary of restricting investments to high-growth markets. Roy Ash followed a course of investing in high-growth, high-technology businesses when he was CEO of AM International. This strategy resulted in the near collapse of AM. Richard Black, who replaced Ash,

> . . . favors a slower, more methodical growth strategy. He sees great appeal in businesses that operate in markets growing at a 3 percent to 5 percent annual rate. "If you've got a 30 percent to 40 percent growth business, you've got everybody looking at the business and jumping in," he explains. "I have nothing against high technology, but why do I want to get into a pot-limit poker game [such as word processing] with giant companies that have money coming out of their ears? . . ."[9]

4. A company should be in cash balance. While the market growth/market share model does not preclude raising cash externally, there is an implied assumption that cash must be generated from some product-markets (cash cows) to fund growth and share-gaining activities in other product-markets (problems and stars). Thus the portfolio of product-market opportunities needs to be balanced between problems, stars, and cash cows. However, many companies have made strategic investments with funds raised externally rather than generated internally.

5. Interdependencies between product-markets is limited to the generation and use of cash. Basically, the product portfolio approach treats each strategic alternative as an independent unit. The business unit manager manages a portfolio of product-markets just as a mutual fund manager manages a portfolio of stocks. This perspective ignores potential synergies between product-markets, such as shared experience. Such synergies often form the basis of unique competitive advantages that determine why one company is successful in a product-market and another is not.

In Article 17, "Strategic Marketing: Betas, Boxes, or Basics," these concerns are described in more detail.

In addition to these conceptual concerns, there are a number of implementation problems when using portfolio models to classify products. It is often difficult to define the unit of analysis and measure its position. There are also administrative problems in aligning the objective for the product managers with their rewards. Clearly, the manager of a "cash cow" should not be rewarded on the basis of growth and the manager of a "problem child" should not be rewarded on the basis of profitability. Such reward structures would result in managerial decisions counter to the generation of cash or the achievement of a dominant market position. Finally, assigning labels to product-markets may lead to a self-fulfilling prophecy, precluding the investigation of new directions that might alter the long-term prospects in the product-market.

Market Attractiveness/Competitive Capabilities Model

Article 16 in this section, "The Directional Policy Matrix—Tool for Strategic Planning," describes procedures for considering a broader array of variables for positioning strategic opportunities on a grid. The principal difference between this portfolio approach and the BCG approach discussed previously is the use of multiple factors rather than a single factor to assess each dimension. When using the market attractiveness/competitive capabilities model, market size, market profitability, and environmental factors are considered in addition to long-term market growth to assess the position of a product-market on the market attractiveness dimension. Similarly, the assessment of position on the competitive capabilities dimension considers technological, financial, and managerial capabilities in addition to relative market share and the associated curve cost advantages.

When comparing these two types of product portfolio models, one should consider issues such as: (1) for which model is the classification of product-markets more objective? (2) which one provides clearer objectives for marketing strategies? (3) which model provides greater insights into specific business unit performance?

Identifying and Exploiting Competitive Advantage—Back to Basics

The final article in this section, Article 17, "Strategic Marketing: Betas, Boxes, or Basics," reviews the two portfolio approaches and concludes that these models offer limited insight and may even provide misleading guidance in some situations. The author suggests that a return to basics—the search for sustainable competitive advantage—would provide more meaningful guidance for strategic decision modeling. This basic principle was incorporated in our definition of marketing strategy presented in the introduction to Section I.

Focusing on building sustainable competitive advantage means that managers should evaluate strategic alternatives primarily in terms of the strengths and weaknesses of business. Opportunities are attractive when they build on unique competitive capabilities possessed by the business. Obviously, these unique capabilities give the business an advantage over competition in the product-market. Such capabilities reflect synergies between the core activities of the business unit and the strategic alternatives that are being considered.

H. Igor Ansoff's growth vector matrix, shown in Figure IV.1 is a useful, analytical tool for assessing broadly the competitive advantage and synergy that a business can bring to a product-market opportunity.[10] The dimensions of this matrix are the similarity or synergy between the core marketing and production/technological capabilities of a business and the capabilities it needs to be successful in each product opportunity being considered. Clearly, a business has its greatest competitive advantage in product-markets very similar to its core business activities, and will not have an advantage in product-markets requiring new and different marketing and technological capabilities.

The usefulness of the Ansoff matrix can be illustrated by examining strategic opportunities considered by Gillette.[11] Gillette's core business was razors and razor blades for men. As Gillette explored growth opportunities, some of the strategic investments made were in razors for women (Daisy), shaving cream for men, disposable lighters (Cricket), digital watches, and pocket calculators. The manufacture of razors for women requires that a similar product be delivered to a new market, but there is a high degree of synergy between the core business and this new opportunity. The marketing and production of razors for men and women are quite similar. Making shaving cream for men is another example of a highly synergistic strategic opportunity. The Gillette brand name is useful in developing a consumer franchise. Shaving cream is purchased in the same location as razors, and thus Gillette's distribution network for razors can be used for shaving cream. On the other hand, new production capabilities, technologies, and marketing skills are needed to be successful in digital watches and pocket calculators. These opportunities do not exploit Gillette's unique manufacturing or marketing capabilities. Digital watches and pocket calculators, while they are positioned toward high-volume consumer markets, they

Figure IV.1   Assessing Relative Competitive Advantage

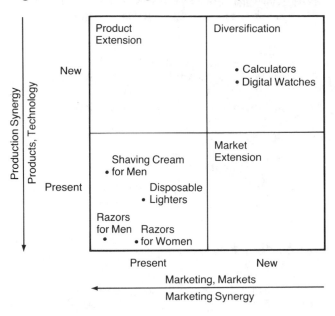

have a low degree of overall synergy with Gillette's core capabilities; and, predictably, Gillette was unsuccessful in these ventures.

We can see that shaving cream and women's razors are obviously synergistic to Gillette's core business; however, we find that an assessment of Gillette's capabilities in disposable lighters is not as straightforward at first glance. Disposable lighters and razors and razor blades do not appear to be very similar. However, an examination of Gillette's unique capabilities reveals substantial synergy: namely, the mass production of low-cost products utilizing precision plastic molded parts and the marketing of low-cost, disposable, brand-name, consumer products through mass distribution. Even though the Gillette brand name may not be useful in marketing disposable lighters, Gillette's manufacturing and marketing skills give Gillette a competitive advantage in this product-market.

Notes

1. For a complete review of analytical methods for strategic decision making, see George S. Day, "Analytical Approaches to Strategic Market Planning," in *Review of Marketing 1981,* eds. Ben Enis and Kenneth Roering (Chicago: American Marketing Association, 1981), 89–105.

2. Note that the percentage of variance explained by the PIMS PAR ROI model is probably inflated due to the exclusion of outliers and data compression.

3. Sidney Schoeffler, "Nine Basic Findings on Business Strategy," PIMS Letter, No. 1, The Strategic Planning Institute, 1977.

4.   Ibid.

5.   See also V. Ramanujan and N. Venkataraman, "An Inventory and Critique of Strategy Research Using the PIMS Database," *Academy of Management Review* (January 1984):138–151.

6.   Ibid.

7.   For a description of additional portfolio models, see Yoram Wind and Vijay Mahajan, "Designing Product and Business Portfolios," *Harvard Business Review* (January–February 1981):155–165.

8.   Phillippe Haspeslagh, "Portfolio Planning: Uses and Limits," *Harvard Business Review* (January–February 1982):58–81.

9.   *Business Week,* January 25, 1982, 63.

10.   H. Igor Ansoff, *Corporate Strategy: An Analytic Approach to Business Policy for Growth and Expansion* (New York: McGraw-Hill, 1965).

11.   "Gillette: After the Diversification That Failed," *Business Week,* February 28, 1977, 58–62.

Additional Readings for Section Four

Financial Models

Hayes, R. H. and J. W. Abernathy. "Managing Our Way to Economic Decline." *Harvard Business Review* (July–August 1980):67–77.

PIMS

Labatkin and Pitts. "PIMS: Fact or Folklore." *Journal of Business Strategy* (Winter 1983):38–43.

Schoeffler, Sidney, Robert D. Buzzell, and Donald F. Heany. "Impact of Strategic Planning on Profit Performance." *Harvard Business Review* (March–April 1974):137–145.

Portfolio Models

Ansoff, H. Igor, Werner Kirsch, and Peter Roventa. "Dispersed Positioning in Portfolio Analyses." *Industrial Marketing Management* (Fall 1982):237–252.

Cardozo, Richard N. and David K. Smith, Jr. "Applying Financial Portfolio Theory to Product Portfolio Decisions: An Empirical Study." *Journal of Marketing* (Spring 1983):110–119.

Day, George S. "Diagnosing the Product Portfolio." *Journal of Marketing* (April 1977):29–38.

Hambrick, D., I. MacMillan, and D. Day. "Strategic Attributes and Performance in the BCG Matrix—A PIMS-Based Analysis of Industrial Product Businesses." *Academy of Management Journal* 25 (1982):510–31.

Harrell, Gilbert D. and Richard O. Kiefer. "Multinational Strategic Market Portfolios." *MSU Business Topics* (Winter 1981):5–15.

Haspeslagh, Philippe. "Portfolio Planning Uses and Limits." *Harvard Business Review* (January–February 1982):58–73.

Hurst. "Of Boxes, Bubbles and Effective Management." *Harvard Business Review* (May–June 1984):78–88.

Hussey, D. E. "Portfolio Analysis: Practical Experience with the Directional Policy Matrix." *Long Range Planning* (August 1979):2–8.

MacMillan, I., D. Hambrick, and D. Day. "The Product Portfolio and Profitability—A PIMS-based Analysis of Industrial Product Businesses." *Academy of Management Journal* 25 (1982):733–755.

Sheth, Jagdish N. and Gary L. Frazier. "A Margin-Return Model for Strategic Market Planning." *Journal of Marketing* (Spring 1983):100–109.

Wind, Yoram and Henry J. Claycamp. "Planning Product Line Strategy: A Matrix Approach." *Journal of Marketing* (January 1976):2–9.

Wind, Yoram, Vijay Mahajan, and Donald J. Swire. "An Empirical Comparison of Standardized Portfolio Models." *Journal of Marketing* (Spring 1983):89–99.

Wernerfelt, Birger and Cynthia A. Montgomery. "What Is An Attractive Industry?" *Management Science* (October 1986):1223–1230.

13

STRATPORT: A Decision Support System for Strategic Planning

Jean-Claude Larreche and V. Srinivasan

In the seventies, increasing environmental and competitive pressures have induced corporations to redefine to some extent the role of marketing in the firm. Instead of implementing the marketing philosophy mainly towards the achievement of growth objectives for individual products in a typical brand management organization, firms have given increasing importance to other factors such as profitability, market share, competition, product line management, and allocation of resources among products (see, for instance, Hopkins 1976).

The more strategic orientation of marketing has already been integrated, to some extent, in marketing education (Abell and Hammond 1979, Kotler 1980, Larréché and Gatignon 1977). This evolution is also reflected in the development of new marketing approaches and models to assist managers in the formulation of segmentation and positioning strategies in the context of a product line (Jackson and Shapiro 1979, Pessemier 1977, Shocker and Srinivasan 1979, Wind and Clay-camp 1976). But marketing modeling has failed, so far, to assist top managers or corporate planners in the allocation of marketing resources across product lines or business units. This is reflected, in particular, by the poor quality of the marketing component in most corporate models (Larréché and Montgomery 1981). Naylor and Schauland (1976) identified close to 2,000 firms in North America and Europe that made use of some type of corporate model. Marketing modelers seem to have overlooked such wide use of corporate models.

This article first appeared in the *Journal of Marketing* 45 (Fall 1981): 39–52. Reprinted with permission from *Journal of Marketing*, published by the American Marketing Association.

When this article was published the authors were Associate Professor of Marketing, INSEAD, Fontainbleau, France; and Professor of Marketing and Management Science, Graduate School of Business, Stanford University, respectively.

Marketing modelers now face the challenge of adapting their efforts to the increasing strategic orientation of marketing. The purpose of this paper is to present the result of such an effort, and STRATPORT (for STRATegic PORTfolio planning) decision support system, an on-line computerized mathematical model utilizing empirical and (managerial) judgment-based data. This system was designed to assist top managers and corporate planners in the evaluation and formulation of business portfolio strategies, and it represents both an operationalization and extension of the business portfolio analysis approaches developed in the seventies by a number of firms. This article will review and critique the main aspects of these approaches, present the basic structure of the STRATPORT model, describe a hypothetical example of its utilization, and discuss the contributions and limitations of the model in the allocation of resources among business units.

A Brief Review of Business Portfolio Analysis Approaches

Following the pioneering work of General Electric in the late sixties, a number of business portfolio analysis approaches have been proposed and applied by various firms, including the Boston Consulting Group, McKinsey, Arthur D. Little, and Royal Dutch Shell (see, for instance, Hedley 1977; Robinson, Hickens, and Wade 1978). These different approaches have been compared by Boyd and Larréché (1978) and Wind and Mahajan (1981). Only their main characteristics will be reviewed here.

These approaches conceptualize the firm as a portfolio of business units and identify the major corporate strategic decision as being the allocation of resources among these business units. To aid top managers in this decision, they provide different procedures to cluster the business units into more homogeneous groups in terms of their expected contribution to the dynamic evolution of the portfolio.[1] In the Boston Consulting Group approach, relative market share and the market growth are used to classify business units as Question Marks, Stars, Cash Cows, or Dogs. In the General Electric/McKinsey approach, the business units are classified into nine groups according to company strength and industry attractiveness. The position of a given business unit on each of these dimensions is determined qualitatively from a number of market, competitive, environmental, and internal factors. The Royal Dutch Shell approach is somewhat similar although the two dimensions are called company's competitive capabilities and prospects for sector profitability, and the set of factors and their integration into these composite dimensions are also different.

The philosophy underlying these approaches is, however, similar. At a given point in time, each business unit has a specific role in the portfolio accord-

---

[1]These approaches are usually presented as classification procedures so that a finite number of typical strategies may be conveniently identified. In a more detailed analysis the posture of business units is more accurately defined in terms of continuous dimensions. The distinction between these two levels of analysis is particularly clear in the Boston Consulting Group approach.

ing to its short-term and long-term economic potential. This role determines the allocation of financial resources among elements of the portfolio. Minimum or maintenance investments will be made in a group of business units so that they generate a maximum cash flow in the short term. These may be business units that have a strong market position and are not vulnerable to competitive pressures, or do not represent satisfactory long-term potential. This generated cash flow allows investments in other business units, which will provide growth in the short and medium term. In the long term, these business units will, in turn, become net cash generators and will contribute to financing the growth of other units of the portfolio. The development and renewal of a balanced portfolio of business units through careful resource allocation is considered essential to the long-term survival and growth of the firm.

Business portfolio analysis approaches are being increasingly used in corporations (see, for instance, *Business Week* 1975, Kiechel 1979) for a number of reasons. They have effectively formulated the key strategic corporate decision as being the allocation of resources among business units. They provide a simple framework and language to classify business units into more homogeneous groups to facilitate this decision. From the position of a business unit on some dimensions, such as market growth and relative market share, they readily provide inferences on the cash requirements or cash generation of the business unit. These inferences are supported by past experience as well as empirical studies on cost and price dynamics (Boston Consulting Group 1972, Stobaugh and Townsend 1975) and on the relationship between market share and profitability (Buzzell, Gale, and Sultan 1975). Finally, they aid strategic thinking by graphically representing business units on two critical dimensions.

Different authors (Channon 1977, Day 1977, Wensley 1981, Wind and Mahajan 1981) have already discussed the limitations of these business portfolio approaches that stem from three main sources: the representation of the portfolio situation, the implicit relationships assumed in drawing inferences on desirable strategies, and the scope of the analysis. The representation of the current business portfolio situation involves a definition of the business units and the measurement of their position on the two dimensions considered. The analysis requires that business units should not share any cost or marketing interdependency. Implementation of the portfolio strategy, on the other hand, requires that delineation of business units should be coherent with the organizational structure of the firm. In practice, it is unlikely that all these conditions will be met simultaneously. The only safeguard available is to define business units in such a way as to minimize potential problems in analysis, and implementation, and explicitly to consider the implications of the assumptions when interpreting a given portfolio strategy.

The definition of business units will also have a critical impact on the measurement of their position on the dimensions of analysis. The Boston Consulting Group approach considers two quantitative dimensions, relative market share and market growth, which can be determined based on the (difficult) definition of the relevant market and competitors for each business unit. The other approaches raise the additional issues of eliciting managerial judgments on the position of business units on qualitative factors, and of integrating these factors into composite dimensions.

Another commonly cited limitation of the business portfolio analysis approaches is the implicit relationship that they assume between the position of a business unit on the dimensions of analysis and its cash requirements or cash generation capabilities. In the Boston Consulting Group approach, cash flows are inferred from relative market share and market growth. For instance, a higher market growth is implicitly associated with a more unstable market structure and with higher marketing and production investments. A higher relative market share is implicitly associated with a competitive cost advantage and higher profit margins. Combining the effects of these two factors, a business unit having a dominant posture in a high growth market will be expected to have a relatively small positive or negative cash flow, the high marketing and production investments being approximately financed by the high profit margin. These implicit relationships are generally valid and provide a basis to evaluate the overall balance of a business portfolio in a preliminary screening stage. They may, however, not hold under specific competitive and environmental conditions, and it is indeed possible to find business units that are highly profitable without enjoying a high relative market share (Hall 1980, Hamermesh, Anderson, and Harris 1978). Moreover, these implicit relationships can at best provide only an indication, but not a quantitative appraisal of the financial implications of a given portfolio strategy.

The use of these portfolio analysis approaches is also limited in practice by other aspects not given due emphasis in the literature. The limitations are due to the fact that a number of important elements have been left out of the scope of the analysis. The previous approaches do not explicitly distinguish between cash flows and profits. In fact, cash flows represent constraints on the strategic options that may be adopted while profits are required to provide a satisfactory return to shareholders and to have further access to external financial sources. The previous approaches concentrate on total cash flow levels and do not explicitly distinguish between capacity, working capital, R&D, or marketing investments. As a result, they are valuable in diagnosing an existing situation but offer only an indication of the financial implications of changes in the market postures of business units. Furthermore, they center on existing business units while a long-term profitability of the firm may require investing in new business units (Wind and Saaty 1980, p. 648.) Finally, these business portfolio analysis approaches do not explicitly consider the different financial risks involved in each business unit (Wind and Mahajan 1981).

The development of the STRATPORT decision support system was guided by two main considerations. The first one was to overcome some of the limitations of current business portfolio analysis approaches, especially by extending the scope of the analysis and by making explicit some of the relationships on which these approaches are built. In particular, STRATPORT explicitly considers marketing, capacity and working capital investments, potential new business units, cash flows, profits, external financial resources, and financial risks. In addition, it provides an explicit specification of the relationship between changes in the market posture of a business unit and its cash flow requirements, as well as its long-term profit potential.

The second consideration in the development of STRATPORT was to provide an operationalization of the business portfolio analysis concept so that a number of alternative portfolio strategies and their underlying assumptions could be effectively investigated. In particular, STRATPORT allows:

- An integration of empirically based data with managerial judgments. The system may be used to study the sensitivity of outcomes to specific inputs and to guide accordingly the gathering of additional empirical data in areas where it is most valuable.
- A determination of business portfolio strategies appropriate for different financial requirements, on the basis of key quantifiable factors.
- A rapid investigation of the robustness of a given business portfolio strategy to changes in the underlying assumptions.

The STRATPORT system does not resolve all of the limitations of the business portfolio analysis approaches. In particular, it assumes that the firm has appropriately defined its business units. Although progress is currently being made in this difficult area (Day, Shocker, and Srivastava 1979), no ideal solution will usually exist. The STRATPORT system provides, however, a convenient support to test the robustness of a given portfolio strategy to alternative definitions of business units.

In addition, because of the complex and long-term nature of corporate strategy, top executives will continuously have to cope with incomplete and approximate data, imperfect knowledge of the outcome of alternative actions, uncertainties on market, competitive, and environmental dynamics, and factors that do not lend themselves to quantitative analysis. In this context, STRATPORT does not claim to determine *the* optimum business portfolio strategy. STRATPORT is a decision support system. It tries to extract relevant information from existing empirical data and managerial judgments and to integrate this information to assist decision making, while relieving corporate planners from fastidious computations. It provides a framework to investigate strategic factors and key assumptions. It identifies optimum portfolio strategies on the basis of critical quantifiable factors. Taking other qualitative considerations into account, top management may then concentrate on a more complete analysis of the proposed strategies, which may lead to the selection of a strategy or to further investigation of other alternative strategies.

An Overview of the Model

STRATPORT is composed of a mathematical model and extensive input and output capabilities. Only the model will be described here, in the context of the portfolio planning framework represented in Figure 1.

At any point in time, the firm has internal cash resources from its equity and earnings retained from past operations. It also has access to external financial sources. For a given dividend policy, the maximum sustainable growth that the firm may afford can be investigated from the current capital structure and an anticipation of profits and cost structure (see, for instance, Babcock 1970, Higgins

Figure 1   Overview of the Model

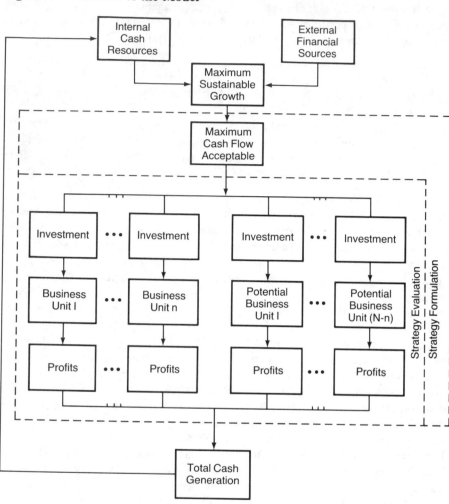

1977). The choice of a maximum sustainable growth for the firm determines the maximum amount of external financial funds that it can attract. The sum of these external financial funds and of internal cash resources provide the maximum cash resources available.

For a given amount of total cash resources available, the strategic portfolio problem is to determine how they should be allocated among the N business units considered in the firm's portfolio. These include ongoing operations of the firm as well as potential new business units that do not currently exist but may be either developed internally or acquired externally. The main investments considered will usually be in the areas of production capacity, working capital, marketing, and R&D. Over a certain period of time and for a given investment, a business unit will generate a level of profits and the resulting cash flow. This cash flow will affect the internal cash resources of the firm, which will in turn influence the maximum cash resources available. Thus the problem is highly dynamic.

In STRATPORT, the time horizon for the analysis is divided into two parts. The *planning period* is the one over which investments and cash constraints are explicitly considered. Marketing investments are expected to result in changes in market share and sales, which may require additional investments in the expansion of capacity and for working capital. The purpose of the *post-planning period* is to provide an evaluation of the long-term profit implication of actions taken during the planning period. For this reason, market shares are treated as if they remain constant during the post-planning period. Marketing investments are set at maintenance levels, while capacity expenditures and changes in working capital follow the evolution of sales.

The distinction between the planning and post-planning periods is illustrated in Figure 2 in terms of the evolution of the market share for different business units. The lengths of these two periods are chosen according to the characteristics

Figure 2 Planning and Post-Planning Periods

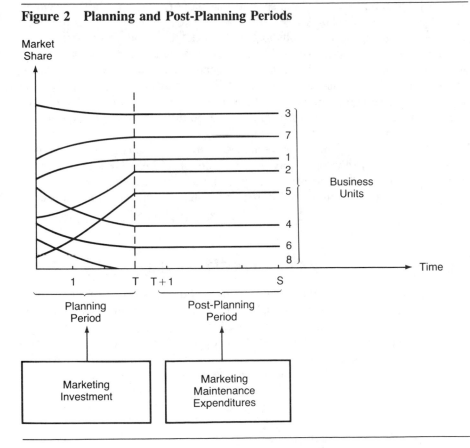

of the industries considered and the confidence of management in the reliability of data for different time horizons. Typically, the planning period will cover from two to five years and the post-planning period from five to 15 years. The time horizon is further divided into time units typically representing quarters, semesters, or years and are the basis for representing different elements of the model.

The STRATPORT model may be used at two different levels represented by the dotted lines in Figure 1.

Strategy Evaluation.   The user of the model may evaluate a given portfolio strategy by indicating specific marketing investment levels (or, alternatively, market share objectives) for each business unit. The model will project for each business unit the expected market share (or marketing investment), capacity expenditures, working capital, profit, and cash flow resulting from such a strategy. Aggregation of these results over the business units provides an evaluation of the total cash flow requirements in the planning period and of the total profits over the planning and post-planning periods. The model may in particular be used in this fashion to project the long-term implications of a status quo strategy, or of incremental changes to the current strategy.

Strategy Formulation.   Given a specific cash flow requirement in the planning period, the model may be used to formulate a strategy in terms of the allocation of resources among business units that maximizes total profits over the planning and post-planning periods. The user may specify a range of values for the cash flow limit based on the maximum external financial funds available, or the maximum cash inflow that should be generated by the portfolio during the planning period. The optimum resource allocations recommended by the model may be used by the manager as a basis to formulate a portfolio strategy, taking into account factors not incorporated in the model.

Recognizing the inherent uncertainties in strategic planning, it is extremely important to analyze the sensitivity of the results of STRATPORT to changes in the data inputs. In fact, such sensitivity analyses may distinguish inputs where more accurate information is needed from inputs having relatively little impact on the results.

The Structure of the STRATPORT Model

The core of the STRATPORT model is composed of a business unit module representing the cash flow and profit implications of a given marketing investment in a specific business unit. This module is used for both the evaluation of a specific portfolio strategy and the formulation of appropriate portfolio strategies. We will successively describe the overall structure of the business unit module, the key functional relationships in this module, and the principles of the optimization routine.[2]

---

[2]For a detailed mathematical formulation, see Larréché and Srinivasan (1981).

Overall Structure of the Business Unit Module

The structure of the model is common to all business units and is represented in Figure 3. The values of parameters and inputs are obviously specific to each business unit.

The marketing investment made in the business unit considered during the planning period results in an expected market share m_T for that business unit at the end of the planning period. This also determines the values for market share over the planning period and the marketing expenditures required to maintain market share in the post-planning period. The sales are obtained for each time unit by

---

Figure 3   Structure of STRATPORT for a Single Business Unit

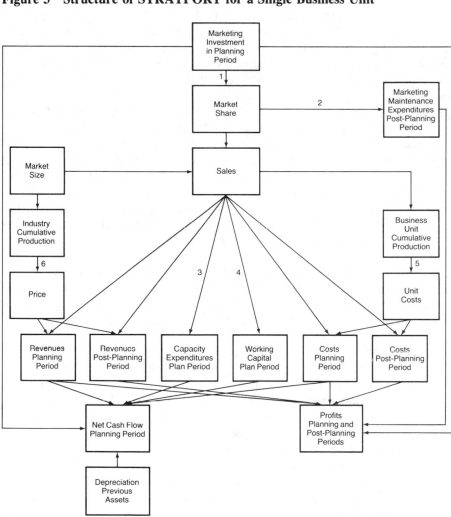

multiplying the market share by the market size. Different market growth rates for the planning and post-planning periods may be specified by the user.

At a given point in time, the market size determines the cumulative production of the industry, which influences the competitive price level for the firm. The revenues of the business unit are obtained from the sales volume and price level during each time unit. Similarly, the sales volume determines the cumulative production of the business unit at a given point in time, which influences the unit costs. The total costs of the business unit are computed directly from the sales volume and unit costs during each time unit. Finally, the sales level determines the capacity expenditures and working capital required during the planning period.

The cash flow during the planning period is computed as the after tax profits from the business unit (revenues minus costs minus marketing investments, adjusted by the appropriate tax rate), minus the portion of the increase in working capital not expensed during the planning period, minus the portion of the additional capacity investment not depreciated during the planning period, plus the depreciation during the planning period of assets acquired before the beginning of the planning period. The total after tax profits over the time horizon considered are obtained form total revenues minus total costs, marketing investments during the planning period, and marketing expenditures during the post-planning period, adjusted by the appropriate tax rate.

All the financial entities in the STRATPORT model are expressed in constant dollars. Consequently, the model may be used to determine portfolio strategies that would maximize the total after-tax profits in constant dollars cumulative over the planning and post-planning periods, subject to a cash flow constraint in the planning period. Although this approach may be desirable as a first step of the analysis, it does not take into account the time value of money, and thus discounted cash flows will usually be more appropriate. Consequently, the STRATPORT model allows a maximization of net present value over the planning and post-planning periods subject to a constraint on discounted cash flow during the planning period.

There is, for any given business unit, a level of risk associated with its projected profits and cash flows. To reflect this risk, the financial entities for that business unit should be discounted at a rate higher than the exptected rate of return for risk-free assets. Following the capital asset pricing model (see Van Horne 1980, Chapters 7 and 8), a different discounting rate can be specified in STRATPORT for each business unit to correspond to its level of systematic risk, which is the risk that cannot be avoided by diversification (Sharpe 1964). The discounting rate for a specific business unit can be estimated from the Beta coefficients published by various financial services for corporations operating in closely related industries (see Larréché and Srinivasan 1981 for details). The STRATPORT model consequently combines the strategic perspective of business portfolio analysis with the risk considerations of finanical portfolio theory. (For other approaches to the incorporation of risk, see Corstjens and Weinstein 1981 and Mahajan, Wind, and Bradford 1981.) In addition to considering systematic financial risk, management may want to limit the activity of a business unit to reduce the total risks stemming from a variety of sources such as antitrust or competitive and labor reactions. These limits on total risk are incorporated in the model through upper and lower bound constraints on the market share of each business unit.

Main Functional Relationships

The six main functional relationships of the business unit module are (1) the market response function; (2) the maintenance marketing function; (3) the capacity expenditures function; (4) the working capital function; (5) the cost function; and (6) the price function. They are identified by the corresponding numbers in Figure 3 and illustrated graphically in Figure 4.

Figure 4   Main Functional Relationships

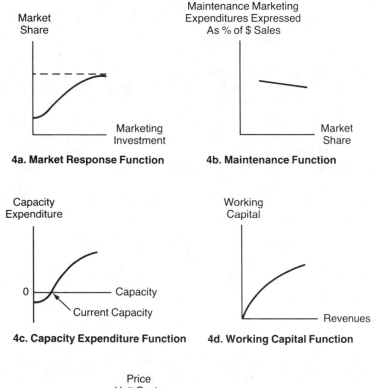

4a. Market Response Function

4b. Maintenance Function

4c. Capacity Expenditure Function

4d. Working Capital Function

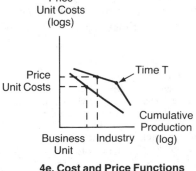

4e. Cost and Price Functions

1. The Market Response Function.   The market response function specifies the market share m_T, on a quantity basis, which may be expected at the end of the planning period for a given marketing investment. It will generally be S-shaped, reflecting an increasing marginal response for small investments and a decreasing marginal response for large investments, but it may also assume a concave form. Since the market response function is strictly monotone increasing, it is feasible and managerially more attractive to interpret this curve as a specification of the marketing investments required to obtain different market share levels. These marketing investments will typically include personal selling and advertising expenditures, but also developmental costs to improve product quality or to modify the product line within a business unit.[3]

Following a procedure proposed by Little (1970), the market response function is estimated from four managerial inputs: the market share expected at the end of the planning period if no marketing investment is made, the marketing investment required to achieve a reference market share level, the expected market share for a higher marketing investment, and the maximum market share expected for an unlimited marketing investment. For an existing business unit, the reference market share is taken as the current market share, while for a potential business unit, the minimum expected market share is set to zero.

To provide the market response judgments, the manager should be encouraged to think in terms of the best tactics (such as segmentation strategy, consumer and trade promotions, product line changes including new products, improvements in product quality, acquisitions of small competitors, advertising and personal selling) that can be used in the product-market(s) corresponding to the business unit under consideration. Substantial attention needs to be paid to likely competitive reactions, the strengths and weaknesses of the firm, and the best ways to market to different segments constituting the product-market(s). The market response function is likely to be a critical component of the proposed approach, and the quality of the results from the model will reflect the intensity of analysis done before providing the subjective judgments. The S-shaped market response function has been successfully used in several decision calculus models (e.g., Little 1970, Lodish 1971).

2. The Maintenance Marketing Function.   This function specifies the marketing expenditures required during the post-planning period, expressed as a percentage of sales, to maintain market share at the level reached at the end of the planning period. It will generally decrease as market share increases, reflecting economies of scale in marketing, although it may increase in some situations. This

---

[3]A distinction is made between R&D investments concerning product development, which is an integral part of a business unit strategy, and more fundamental research, which, because of the unpredictability and distant nature of its outcome, is unlikely to affect the market posture of the business unit during the planning horizon. The former is included as part of the marketing investment required to obtain a specific market share level. The latter reflects a policy decision made to protect the firm beyond the current planning horizon and is not directly incorporated in the model. The minimum cash flow acceptable for the firm should, however, be determined after allowing for the investments resulting from such policy decisions.

may, for instance, be the case if a higher market share is anticipated to generate more than a proportionate increase in competitive reactions. A linear functional form was assumed in modeling the variation of relative marketing maintenance expenditure as a function of market share. It is estimated from managerial inputs corresponding to two market share levels.

3. The Capacity Expenditure Function. This function represents the additional investment required to expand the current capacity to be consistent with the market share to be achieved. It also specifies the additional resources available if the activity level of the business unit is decreased. These additional resources represent the resale value of the freed capacity or the cash equivalent when transferred to other business units. The capacity expenditures are the proportion of the investment not accounted as depreciation in the computation of costs during the planning period.

    The capacity expenditure function for an existing business unit is evaluated from five estimates provided by the user: the cash flow generated by a complete sale or transfer of the current capacity, the additional investment required for two expansion levels, and the investment required for a marginal expansion beyond a high capacity level. If the firm is not able to sell off a business unit or to use freed capacity for other activities, the cash flow corresponding to a complete sale may be set to a small value. The capacity expenditure function may be S-shaped or concave depending on the estimates provided by the user.

    In the case of business unit with no existing capacity, the capacity expenditure function has a concave form and is evaluated from estimates of the investment required for two capacity levels.

4. The Working Capital Function. The working capital requirements (cash + inventory + equipment on lease + accounts receivable − accounts payable) are usually expected to differ for various levels of market share. Working capital is specified as a function of revenues. The parameters of this function are evaluated on the basis of estimates expressing the appropriate working capital as a proportion of revenues for two revenue levels. The working capital function may be expected to be generally concave, but it may also be convex when, for instance, an increase in market share will result in penetrating market segments requiring more favorable credit or delivery terms. Since the financing of working capital is already included under costs, additional working capital is defined as only that portion that is not expensed during the planning period.

5. The Cost Function. Following the works of the Boston Consulting Group on experience effects (1972), the STRATPORT model assumes that unit costs, expressed in constant dollars, decline as a function of the business unit's cumulative production. In STRATPORT, however, unit costs incorporate all costs (including depreciation) with the exception of marketing investments, which are accounted for separately. The evaluation of the cost function is based on a loglinear regression of past data or, alternatively, on current unit costs and a managerial estimate of the cost reduction anticipated for an increase in cumulative production. If, however, the evolution of unit costs is estimated to be more a function of time than of cumulative production, the model can be extended to handle such cases. This extension may be particularly appropriate when raw materials costs are anticipated to evolve significantly and when they represent a substantial amount compared to value added.

6. The Price Function.   The price function also assumes a decline in average industry unit price as a function of industry cumulative production, similar to the behavior of unit costs. The evolution of price may, however, be different in the planning and post-planning periods to reflect different patterns of price competition over time, which have been empirically identified by the Boston Consulting Group (1972). For instance, the average industry price may decline at a lower rate than unit costs for a new industry and decrease at a faster rate later as the market matures and competition intensifies.

This formulation does not assume that there is a market price followed by the firm. The price set by the firm may actually be above or below average industry prices according to the price positioning strategy adopted. Moreover, just as in the case of costs, the model can be extended to consider price as a function of time as opposed to a function of industry cumulative sales.

The Optimization Module

The business unit module described above is sufficient for the evaluation of a specific portfolio strategy. In addition, STRATPORT may be used to determine the allocation of resources among business units that provides the maximum net present value over the time horizon considered, subject to a constraint on the discounted cash flow during the planning period. This cash constraint may be evaluated over a range of levels as indicated earlier.

The optimization procedure follows the Generalized Lagrange Multiplier technique (Everett 1963) and transforms the simultaneous optimization of N variables to N univariate maximizations.[4] The univariate maximization algorithm is based on the decomposition of the Lagrangean derivative into a difference between two monotone increasing functions. It automatically provides the expected net present value for alternative cash flow constraints as well as an estimate of the marginal increase in net present value for an increase in the level of the cash flow constraint.

This optimization procedure is highly efficient, and the computer time required to find an optimum allocation goes up only linearly with the number of business units. It determines the optimum allocations to 10 business units for 11 different levels of the cash flow constraint in less than 20 seconds of CPU time on a DEC 2050 system. This high efficiency makes feasible the on-line interaction to conduct sensitivity analysis.

---

[4]For a mathematical description of the optimization routine, see Larréché and Srinivasan (1981).

An Illustrative Use of the Model

Figure 5 contains selected parts of a computer terminal printout corresponding to a hypothetical utilization of the STRATPORT. The inputs provided by the user have been underlined to distinguish them from the text printed by the computer. In a previous utilization of STRATPORT, a data file had been created, containing the appropriate inputs for six business units over a planning period of three years and a post-planning period of five years. Without going into the detailed characteristics of the business units, we may summarize that, in terms of the Boston Consulting Group terminology, business units 1, 2, 3, and 4 are a Cash Cow, a Star, a Dog, and a Problem Child, with current market shares of 20%, 30%, 5%, and 5% respectively. Business units 5 and 6 are new opportunities that the firm is considering entering into.

The strategy evaluation and strategy formulation modes of STRATPORT are illustrated in Figure 5. For simplification, the financial entities in these examples are presented only before tax and without discounting. In the first part, the model is used to project the current situation over the time horizon. Over the planning period, the marketing investments required to maintain the current market share of each business unit are $45, $150, $40, and $30 million for business units 1, 2, 3, and 4, respectively. This status quo strategy implies that the firm will not make new entries into business units 5 and 6.

The results of this evaluation indicate that this strategy would generate a net cash flow of $297 million over the three-year planning period and profits of $1366 million over the total eight-year time horizon considered. The detailed results show that all business units would, under this strategy, be net cash generators, although business unit 1 would account for close to 70% of the cash flow in the planning period. Over the long term, business units 1 and 2 would generate close to 90% of the total profits of the firm.

There are some indications that this status quo strategy may be far from optimum. There are obvious disparities between the marketing investments made in the business units and their long-term profit potential. It is possible, in particular, that more cash could be generated by business units 1 and 3 and invested more profitably into business units 2, 4, 5, and 6. Moreover, it is difficult to evaluate whether the total cash flow generated in the planning period corresponds to the appropriate level for the firm without knowing the long-term profit implications of alternative cash flow levels.

For these different reasons, in the second part of Figure 5 the strategy formulation mode of STRATPORT is used to investigate a range of portfolio strategies from a net cash generation of $600 million to a net cash need of $200 million. The detailed results of the optimization routine are saved in an output file for off-line printing. They can also be selectively displayed on-line, but only the key results of the optimization are presented here. They represent the profit, marginal percent yield, and market share for 11 portfolio strategies (options) corresponding to different cash flow levels. These cash flow levels correspond to constant steps in the marginal yield. At one extreme, option 1 would require $206 million of additional cash in the planning period and would provide a total profit of $2911

Figure 5 An Illustrative Run of the STRATPORT Model

INDICATE MARKETING INVESTMENT FOR

    BUSINESS UNIT 1 : 45
    BUSINESS UNIT 2 : 150
    BUSINESS UNIT 3 : 40
    BUSINESS UNIT 4 : 30
    BUSINESS UNIT 5 : 0
    BUSINESS UNIT 6 : 0

OUTPUT SAVED IN FILE FOR OFF-LINE PRINTING.
DO YOU WANT TO PROCEED (0), OR TO DISPLAY RESULTS (1)? 1

EVALUATION OF PORTFOLIO STRATEGY
······························

CASH NEEDS	−297.
PROFIT LEVEL	1366.
MARKET SHARE	
B. U. 1	.202
B. U. 2	.300
B. U. 3	.050
B. U. 4	.050
B. U. 5	.000
B. U. 6	.000

SOURCES AND USES OF FUNDS
·······························

B. U. NUMBER	1	2	3	4	5	6
CASH NEEDS	824.	1372.	345.	190.	0.	0.
REVENUE PL.	551.	1082.	295.	127.	0.	0.
COSTS PL.	45.	150.	40.	30.	0.	0.
MKTG. IN. PL.	25.	79.	−11.	23.	0.	0.
CAPA. IN. PL.	−204.	−61.	−21.	−10.	0.	0.
TOTAL						

PROFITS

REVENUE PL.	824.	1372.	345.	190.	0.
COSTS PL.	551.	1082.	295.	127.	0.
MKTG. IN. PL.	45.	150.	40.	30.	0.
REVENUE PP.	1623.	3838.	623.	468.	0.
COSTS PP.	1089.	2969.	530.	302.	0.
MKTG. IN. PP.	98.	460.	67.	84.	0.
TOTAL	665.	550.	37.	115.	0.

INPUT MINIMUM AND MAXIMUM LEVELS OF EXTERNAL CASH AVAILABILITY: -600,200

OUTPUT SAVED IN FILE FOR OFF-LINE PRINTING.

DO YOU WANT TO PROCEED (0), OR TO DISPLAY KEY RESULTS (1),
PROFIT CONTRIBUTIONS (2), OR CASH FLOWS (3) 1

KEY OPTIMIZATION RESULTS

OPTIONS	1	2	3	4	5	6
CASH NEEDS	206.	195.	185.	175.	165.	106.
PROFIT LEVEL	2911.	2894.	2877.	2860.	2842.	2735.
MARG. % YIELD	19.53	20.26	21.00	21.73	22.46	23.19
MARKET SHARE						
B. U. 1	.203	.201	.198	.195	.193	.150
B. U. 2	.394	.393	.391	.390	.389	.387
B. U. 3	.010	.010	.010	.010	.010	.010
B. U. 4	.171	.170	.170	.169	.169	.168
B. U. 5	.360	.358	.355	.353	.351	.349
B. U. 6	.000	.000	.000	.000	.000	.000

OPTIONS	7	8	9	10	11
CASH NEEDS	-383.	-386.	-389.	-393.	-609.
PROFIT LEVEL	1813.	1807.	1801.	1793.	1330.
MARG. % YIELD	23.92	24.66	25.39	26.12	26.85
MARKET SHARE					
B. U. 1	.150	.150	.150	.150	.150
B. U. 2	.050	.050	.050	.050	.050
B. U. 3	.010	.010	.010	.010	.010
B. U. 4	.168	.167	.167	.166	.166
B. U. 5	.346	.344	.342	.339	.000
B. U. 6	.000	.000	.000	.000	.000

PL. = Planning Period   B. U. = Business Unit
PP. = Post-Planning Period   IN. = Investment

million. At the other extreme, option 11 would generate a net cash flow of $609 million and a total profit of $1330 million.

Business unit 6 does not appear to be an attractive opportunity over the whole range of cash flows considered. Similarly, the most appropriate strategy for business unit 3 in all options is a minimum marketing investment resulting in a minimum market share. At the other extreme, business unit 4 appears to warrant a sustained marketing investment that would result in a substantial market share increase under all options.

The optimum strategies for the remaining three business units appears to differ widely for different cash flow levels. These strategies vary from a sustained marketing investment for a given cash flow level to a minimum marketing investment when the cash flow requirement becomes very stringent. For instance, if a net cash generation of at least $383 million is required, a sustained marketing investment cannot be made in business unit 2; its market share will drop to a minimum level of 5% at the end of the planning period (see option 7). The user could also look at the detailed cash flow and profit projections made available by the model for each option, although this capability is not presented here because of space limitations.

An analysis could be performed to compare the long-term profitability of different strategies with their cash requirements. Such an analysis is represented graphically in Figure 6 from the information obtained from the interaction with STRATPORT. The curve obtained by linking the points corresponding to different optimum strategies determines the profit/cash flow envelope of optimum strategies, and it increases at a declining rate. The slope of this envelope represents the marginal profit from the additional amount of investment involved in one option compared to the next. Comparing the marginal profit with the marginal cost of external financing can aid in the determination of a desirable cash flow level.

A more complete analysis would obviously require the incorporation of the effects of tax, discounting, and risk as well as a number of additional runs of the model to investigate the sensitivity of the results to changes in the input parameters. Final recommendations would also have to consider a number of factors not explicitly included in the STRATPORT model, such as implications for the labor force and financing possibilities. But this example clearly shows that the choice of an investment strategy may depend mainly on the characteristics of a business unit, as in the case of business units 3, 4, and 6, or be significantly affected by the net cash flow requirements of the firm, as in the case of business units 1, 2, and 5.

Finally, this analysis also provides a perspective on the adequacy of the status quo strategy. As represented in Figure 6, this strategy would be far from optimum. For the same cash flow level in the planning period, the profits of the firm could be increased by $500 million over the next eight years by a better allocation of resources among business units. Alternatively, the same level of long-term profits could be achieved while providing an additional $300 million surplus to the net cash flow during the planning period.

Figure 6   Optimum Profit/Cash Flow Envelope

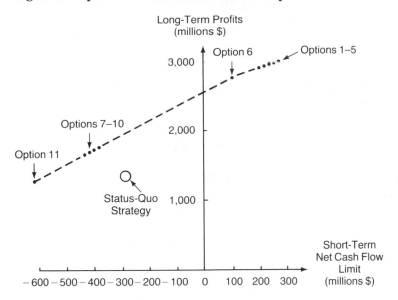

Conclusion

STRATPORT is a decision support system designed to assist top managers and corporate planners in the formulation of business portfolio strategies. The development of this system has been based on two specific research areas that have had a substantial impact on marketing in recent years: the decision calculus approach to marketing models (Little 1970) and strategic planning techniques.

The overall structure of the STRATPORT system is easy to understand and use. Yet it is reasonably complete in integrating the key aspects of the business portfolio problem. The complexities inherent in the mathematical formulation of the model, in the estimation of function parameters, or in the optimization procedure have been transferred to the computer so as to facilitate the use of the model by corporate planners and managers. The model attempts to make the best use of existing empirical data as well as managerial judgment. Judgmental inputs are elicited from managers on issues with which they are familiar and in a way that is coherent with managerial thinking. The model provides information readily interpreted by managers. These features are the result of an implementation-oriented decision-calculus approach to model design as advocated by Little (1970). Despite our best efforts, however, there remains the question of whether the present approach provides a valid representation of managers' beliefs and whether the approach would, in fact, improve management decisions. Research along the lines of Chakravarti, Mitchell, and Staelin (1979) and McIntyre (1980) may shed more light on these issues.

STRATPORT represents simultaneously an extension and operationalization of current business portfolio analysis approaches. The main extensions included in the model are the distinction made between specific types of investments, the inclusion of potential new business units in the analysis, the explicit specification of the relationship between changes in the market posture of a business unit, its short-term cash flow requirements and its long-term profit potential, and the incorporation of risk considerations. The operationalization of the business portfolio concept allows a more extensive and easier investigation of this complex problem, in particular by providing: a better exploitation of existing information, either empirical or judgmental, and guiding the gathering of additional data; a rapid evaluation and formulation of a large number of alternative business portfolio strategies; and an investigation of the robustness of a given portfolio strategy to changes in the underlying assumptions. A further benefit from the operationalization of the business portfolio concept into an interactive model is the potential linkage that one may anticipate, at least partially, between the STRATPORT decision support system and data bases as well as explanatory models developed by some firms in the context of the PIMS (Schoeffler, Buzzell, and Heany 1974) and ADVISOR (Lilien 1979) projects.

The appropriate use of the STRATPORT decision support system also requires an understanding of its key limitations, which stem from three main sources:

Restricted Scope.   The model centers uniquely on critical quantifiable factors in the formulation of business portfolio strategies. The main types of investments that it considers explicitly are capacity, working capital, and marketing investments (including product development). Other types of investments such as basic R&D are not directly incorporated in the model. Personnel, manufacturing, and financial policies (e.g., debt/equity, dividend) are not explicitly addressed. Nor are qualitative elements such as quality of management and political risks. The conclusions obtained from using the model have to be interpreted in the light of these missing factors.

Structural Assumptions.   The main assumptions in the structure of the model concern the specific forms selected for each function, the absence of market or cost interactions between business units, and the treatment of price behavior and market size as exogeneous. The functional forms specified in the model are relatively general and will not usually represent a serious limitation. The other assumptions were made mainly because of the difficulty in obtaining reliable data, either empirically or through managerial judgments, to represent these more complex phenomena. The assumptions of cost and market independence of business units are usually quite reasonable when the model is used at the corporate or divisional level. In the context of a hierarchical approach (Wind and Mahajan 1981), they become less tenable at lower levels in the organization. Interactions between business units as well as the potential impact of marketing investments on price and market-size evolutions can, however, be taken into account by updating the values of the parameters in an iterative fashion in successive runs of STRATPORT.

External Aggregation.   Some aspects of the business portfolio problem that are kept outside the scope of the model have to be integrated in the formulation of the managerial judgments provided as inputs. In particular, the use of an aggregate response function of market share to marketing investment assumes that the manager providing the inputs for estimation will integrate such factors as the presence of multiple products and market segments, potential opportunities and threats, strengths and weaknesses of the firm, development of adequate marketing programs, and possible competitive reactions.

The adequate utilization of a model requires an understanding of its basic structure, capabilities, and limitations. We have attempted to provide such an understanding of the STRATPORT model. It is hoped that by providing a simple approach to comprehend better the quantitative aspects of corporate resource allocation, the model will enable top managers to give greater attention to the more qualitative issues involved in strategic decisions on business portfolios.

References

Abell, Derek F. and John S. Hammond (1979), *Strategic Market Planning*, Englewood Cliffs, NJ: Prentice-Hall.

Babcock, Guilford C. (1970), "The Concept of Sustainable Growth," *Financial Analyst Journal*, 26 (May-June), 108–114.

Boston Consulting Group (1972), *Perspectives on Experience*, Boston: The Boston Consulting Group Inc.

Boyd, Harper W., Jr. and Jean-Claude Larréché (1978), "The Foundations of Marketing Strategy," in *Review of Marketing* 1978, Gerald Zaltman and Thomas V. Bonoma, eds., Chicago: American Marketing Association, 41–72.

Business Week (1975), "Piercing Future Fog in the Executive Suite," April 28, 46–54.

Buzzell, Robert D., Bradley T. Gale, and Ralph S. M. Sultan (1975), "Market Share: A Key to Profitability," *Harvard Business Review*, 53 (January-February), 97–106.

Chakravarti, Dipankar, Andrew Mitchell, and Richard Staelin (1979), "Judgment Based Marketing Decision Models: An Experimental Investigation of the Decision Calculus Approach," *Management Science*, 25 (March), 251–263.

Channon, Derek F. (1977), "Use and Abuse of Analytical Techniques for Strategic Decisions," paper presented at the 23rd International Meeting of the Institute of Management Sciences, Athens, Greece (July).

Corstjens, Marcel and David Weinstein (1981), "Optimal Strategic Business Unit Portfolio Analysis," in *Marketing Planning Models*, A. A. Zoltners, ed., TIMS Studies in the Management Sciences, New York: North Holland, forthcoming.

Day, George S. (1977), "Diagnosing the Product Portfolio," *Journal of Marketing*, 41 (April), 29–38.

———, Allan D. Shocker, and Rajendra K. Srivastava (1979), "Customer-Oriented Approaches to Identifying Product Markets," *Journal of Marketing*, 43 (Fall), 8–19.

Everett, Hugh, III (1963), "Generalized Lagrange Multiplier Method for Solving Problems of Optimum Allocation of Resources," *Operations Research*, 11 (May-June), 399–417.

Hall, William K. (1980), "Survival Strategies in a Hostile Environment," *Harvard Business Review*, 58 (September-October), 75–85.

Hamermesh, R. G., M. J. Anderson, and J. E. Harris (1978), "Strategies for Low Market Share Businesses," *Harvard Business Review*, 56 (May-June), 95–102.

Hedley, Barry (1977), "Strategy and the Business Portfolio," *Long Range Planning*, 10 (February), 9–15.

Higgins, Robert C. (1977), "How Much Growth Can a Firm Afford?," *Financial Management*, 6 (Fall), 7–16.

Hopkins, David S. (1976), "New Emphasis in Marketing Strategies," *The Conference Board Record*, 13 (August), 35–39.

Jackson, Barbara B. and Benson P. Shapiro (1979), "New Way to Make Product Line Decisions," *Harvard Business Review*, 57 (May-June), 139–149.

Kiechel, Walter, III (1979), "Playing by the Rules of the Corporate Strategy Game," *Fortune*, 100 (September 24), 110–115.

Kotler, Philip (1980), *Marketing Management: Analysis, Planning and Control*, 4th edition, Englewood Cliffs, NJ: Prentice-Hall.

Larréché, Jean Claude and Hubert Gatignon (1977), *MARK-STRAT: A Marketing Strategy Game*, Palo Alto, CA: The Scientific Press.

———, and David B. Montgomery (1981), "Strategic Marketing and Corporate Modeling," unpublished paper.

———, and V. Srinivasan (1981), "STRATPORT: A Model for the Evaluation and Formulation of Business Portfolio Strategies," Research Paper No. 572, Stanford, CA: Stanford University, Graduate School of Business.

Lilien, Gary L. (1979), "ADVISOR 2: Modeling the Marketing Mix Decision for Industrial Products," *Management Science*, 25 (February), 191–204.

Little, John D. C. (1970), "Models and Managers: The Concept of a Decision Calculus," *Management Science*, 16 (April), B466–B485.

Lodish, Leonard M. (1971), "CALLPLAN: An Interactive Salesman's Call Planning System," *Management Science*, 18 (December, Part II), P25–P40.

Mahajan, Vijay, Yoram Wind, and John W. Bradford (1981), "Stochastic Dominance Rules for Product Portfolio Analysis," in *Marketing Planning Models*, A. A. Zoltners, ed., TIMS Studies in the Management Sciences, New York: North Holland, forthcoming.

McIntyre, Shelby H. (1980), "The Leverage Impact of Judgment-Based Marketing Models," in *Market Measurement and Analysis*, David B. Montgomery and Dick R. Wittink, eds., Cambridge, MA: Marketing Science Institute, 551–573.

Naylor, Thomas N. and Horst Schauland (1976), "A Survey of Users of Corporate Planning Models," *Management Science*, 22 (May), 927–937.

Pessemier, Edgar A. (1977), *Product Management*, New York: John Wiley.

Robinson, S. J. Q., R. E. Hickens, and D. P. Wade (1978), "The Directional Policy Matrix—Tool for Strategic Planning," *Long Range Planning*, 11 (June), 8–15.

Schoeffler, Sidney, Robert D. Buzzell, and Donald F. Heany (1974), "Impact of Strategic Planning on Profit Performance," *Harvard Business Review*, 52 (March-April), 137–145.

Sharpe, William F. (1964), "Capital Asset Prices: A Theory of Market Equilibrium Under Conditions of Risk," *Journal of Finance*, 19 (September), 425–442.

Shocker, Allan D. and V. Srinivasan (1979), "Multi-Attribute Approaches for Product Concept Evaluation and Generation: A Critical Review," *Journal of Marketing Research*, 16 (May), 159–180.

Stobaugh, Robert B. and Phillip L. Townsend (1975), "Price Forecasting and Strategic

Planning: The Case of Petrochemicals,'' *Journal of Marketing Research*, 12 (February), 19–29.

Van Horne, James C. (1980), *Financial Management and Policy*, 5th edition, Englewood Cliffs, NJ: Prentice-Hall.

Wensley, Robin (1981), ''Strategic Marketing: Betas, Boxes or Basics?'', *Journal of Marketing*, 45 (Summer), 173–182.

Wind, Yoram and Henry J. Claycamp (1976), ''Planning Product Line Strategy: A Matrix Approach,'' *Journal of Marketing*, 40 (January), 2–9.

———, and Vijay Mahajan (1981), ''Designing Product and Business Portfolios,'' *Harvard Business Review*, 59 (January-February), 155–165.

———, and Thomas L. Saaty (1980), ''Marketing Applications of the Analytic Hierarchy Process,'' *Management Science*, 26 (July), 641–658.

14

PIMS: A Reexamination[1]

Carl R. Anderson and Frank T. Paine

A major thrust in current policy research has been development of predictive models which enhance analysis of various strategic alternatives. In the forefront of this model development are studies undertaken in conjunction with the PIMS (Profit Impact of Market Strategies) project. Since its initial development at General Electric and eventual transfer to the Strategic Planning Institute (SPI), the PIMS program has generated considerable interest in the business and academic community. Because it was designed as a program for analyzing strategic moves based on extensive use of confidential data from many businesses (including direct competitors), a minimum of actual data has been made available to the academic community concerning its operation and results. Within the last few years, sufficient information has become available to allow at least a general critique of the PIMS approach.

Background

Begun in 1960 by Schoeffler and associates at General Electric, the project has since moved to SPI, enabling considerable expansion of the original data base. In 1977, over 1,000 "businesses" are contained in the PIMS data base. A "busi-

[1]Portions of this article were presented at the 37th Annual Meeting of the National Academy of Management, Orlando, Florida, August, 1977.

This article first appeared in the *Academy of Management Review* (July 1978):602–612. Reprinted with permission from the *Academy of Management Review*, published by the Academy of Management.

When this article was published the authors were Associate Professor of Management and Organizational Behavior, College of Business and Management, University of Maryland, College Park, Maryland; and Professor of Organizational Behavior and Business Policy, College of Business and Management, University of Maryland, College Park, Maryland, respectively.

The PIMS research program is examined in eight key areas. In general, the PIMS approach was found to be the best current attempt to gather and analyze data on strategic actions of businesses. Suggested improvments will enhance its usefulness to the practitioner. These improvements will further the state of theoretical model building and validation in the strategy field.

ness'' is congruent with the term ''strategic business unit (SBU)'' and is defined as an operating unit which sells a distinct set of products to an identifiable group of customers in competition with a well defined set of competitors. The most publicized use of the PIMS data is a regression model which contains 37 independent variables and predicts 80 percent of the criterion variable, return on investment (ROI) (2, 28, 29). This model is used to diagnose strategic variables at the level of the SBU. In conjunction with this diagnosis, several reports are routinely generated during PIMS analysis.

The *PAR Report* is concerned with ROI and cash flow which is normal for the combination of circumstances which a particular business faces, (market share, competition, market position, production process, capital/cost structure). The generated ROI figure is based on past performance of real businesses under ''comparable'' conditions and assumes that managerial skills and decision abilities are at ''average'' levels.

The *Strategy Report* analyzes short- and long-term effects of strategic changes on ROI. Usual strategic changes analyzed include changes in market share, changes in degree of vertical integration, and changes in capital intensity. The report summarizes the effect of these changes in several financial areas, including ROI.

The *Optimum Strategy Report* is concerned with isolating a particular combination of strategic moves which optimize a particular criterion (including profit, cash, or growth), again judging by the past experiences of others in similar situations.

SPI argues for this approach on the grounds of learning about strategy from experience for which diversity is required. From this diverse experience they derive ''principles'' which are usually expressed in the form of a 3 × 3 matrix (3 levels of each of 2 variables) with ROI as the criterion (see Tables 2 and 3).

The following sections express general observations based on our evaluation of publicly available data concerning the PIMS approach. Hopefully, these observations will lead to further improvement and refinement of the technique.

Basic Assumptions and Philosophy

Observation 1: *PIMS achieves its primary usefulness in the analysis and diagnostic appraisal phase of the policy formation process. Problem finding and solution generating phases are deemphasized.*

A number of broad issues describe the basic approach taken by SPI in constructing the PIMS program. First, the PIMS program is not a total strategy concept but is useful primarily as an analysis and diagnostic appraisal device. In this sense, it does not deal with the problem finding and solution generating phase which still requires a great deal of managerial creativity nor with the set of objectives likely to arise from individual and interpersonal decision making within the organization. It assumes a single objective (maximization of ROI) in much of its analysis. It is useful through its various reports as a method for evaluating a particular strategy based on comparisons with other firms and for suggesting factors that should be examined in selecting one particular strategy.

Observation 2: *The complexity of the PIMS model may lead to problems of inter-pretation and understanding and to a tendency for the user to rely on the "exact-ness" of the technique.*

The PIMS model is described as a complex rather than a simplistic model of strategy. On one hand, the rationale for this approach is based on the assumption that complex models are more likely to be right than simplistic models. On the other hand, they introduce problems of understanding and interpretation which may hinder their usefulness. Although SPI cautions against this, there may be a tendency for the user to rely on the generated figures as exact measures or fore-casts of future performance, an especially important problem with regard to the generated Strategy Reports.

Observation 3: *Current analysis of the PIMS data is largely a retrospective ap-proach to strategy formulation.*

By this we mean that, generally, future possibilities or opportunities which result from changed environmental conditions are largely ignored in analysis of effects of planned strategies. Rather, what other organizations have done in the *past* serves as the basis for analysis. "Organizational retrospection," as we have termed this framework, may be a suitable approach for firms operating in rela-tively stable situations, but it cannot be applied with validity to all environmental conditions, especially those where significant discontinuities occur or change is rampant. These require a more sophisticated analysis/forecasting technique and/or flexibility strategies for preparedness and readiness (2).

Observation 4: *Positive (or negative) effects of synergy are deemphasized in the PIMS approach.*

The PIMS approach concentrates on the isolation of relatively independent SBUs as the basic unit of analysis. While this has become accepted practice in recent years for analysis of business-level strategy, it has an inherent weakness in that effects of synergy are ignored for the organization as a whole—interaction among SBUs may create substantial benefits or negative contributions for the en-tire organization. For example, goodwill on one product line may have substantial carryover to other lines. This "partialling out" of strategies requires a more so-phisticated analysis with the total system in mind. The PIMS program might be modified to conduct such an analysis in the future (13).

Suitability of ROI as a Criterion

Observation 5: *The ROI criterion employed in the PIMS program may not be a suitable global criterion for the measurement of strategic performance.*

A number of sources (15, 16, 32) have criticized use of ROI as a measure of organizational performance. In general, these criticisms have centered around ROI which may inhibit long-term goal attainment, especially investment in plant and equipment and similar capital spending; there is an unwillingness to take growth related risks, since ROI is usually measured in the short-term. Strategic decisions which may result from the use of ROI include analysis of and possible elimination of marginal products or product groups, price adjustments for low return items, and decreasing inventories to improve returns. New investment is particularly neglected since these investments may not produce a significant return for several years, thereby leading to poor performance ratings for the manager. Problems resulting from these decisions may include long-term unemployment, capacity shortages, and diminished sales growth. In summary, one original purpose of PIMS was to provide a yardstick to counteract enthusiasm (unwarranted) which often enters at the conclusion of the planning cycle. We feel that the criterion may be overly conservative and short-sighted.

Cross-Sectional Data Base

Observation 6: *The cross-sectional data base employed by PIMS has certain identifiable, inherent weaknesses which can lead to erroneous conclusions.*

For a number of years, critics of policy research pointed to a lack of empirical data as a major weakness in development of policy as a field of study. To date, PIMS has been the only attempt to overcome this major weakness through collection of accurate data on a large scale. The method and rationale for this collection has been criticized (12, 30). The PIMS approach is based on data from many firms which are pooled and then treated as being from the same population. Researchers have pointed to a better methodology which would involve time series (trends) on every firm as well as cross-sectional comparisons. The lack of time-series analysis to date is probably due to the newness of the PIMS data base rather than to the oversight of this obviously rich analytical field.

There are some important considerations for the time series approach which may discount validity of current conclusions derived from the cross-sectional analysis. First, the goals—strategies employed by an organization—change over time, and these changes must be documented and compared to results. To date this has not been done. Further, the environmental variables analyzed vary over time for each firm in an industry (and across industries). For example, changes in competitive postures over time must be considered. Finally, in the current data, the number of observations of any particular environment is limited; thus, the variation due to that environment may not be picked up in the model. PIMS reports similar factors influencing performance across obviously different environmental sectors (see Observation 16). A longitudinal analysis of any particular sector should pick up these changes.

Incorporation of Goal Structures

Observation 7: *PIMS analysis has not identified intended goals—strategies for which performance was measured. In the future, goal structures should be added to the data base.*

Both Kirchoff (15) and Hatten and Schendel (12) point to the need for identifying goals of organizations under study in the PIMS project (what were they trying to do when performance was measured?). Paine (20) goes one step further in suggesting the use of goal structures or hierarchies as a means of identifying the particular strategy (and level of implementation) for the organization.

In a broader sense, the PIMS data base consists of mostly interval data; nominal and ordinal data are neglected for either statistical (the regression model and associated assumptions) or definitional reasons. Several researchers have pointed to this factor as a deficiency in the data which may lead to erroneous or simplistic conclusions through omission of important nominal or ordinal variables including goals. Apparently use of noninterval data is not completely rejected because of statistical reasons since certain noninterval data are currently incorporated in the model.

Methodology

Observation 8: *Analysis of independent variables in the absence of remaining model variables may lead to erroneous conclusions primarily due to problems of multicollinearity.*

A number of criticisms of PIMS research methodology especially concern the regression model. As noted in the introduction, the major use of PIMS data is the association between ROI and 37 independent variables incorporated in a linear regression model. As part of the explanation of their strategic findings, SPI presents a series of 3×3 matrices which relate variables two at a time to ROI. Many difficulties have been noted with this approach. Rumelt (27) criticizes the analysis of these associations in the absence of the remaining variables (or if they were held constant). Fruhan (8) concurs with this conclusion especially concerning the relationship between market share and ROI (see Contingency Factors). In general, when there is a great deal of multicollinearity in the independent variable set (28), this becomes a valid criticism. One can expect changes in the magnitude of the relationships or, more seriously, sign changes in the direction of the relationship.

Observation 9: *Omission of key strategic variables from the model may lead to erroneous conclusions.*

In the case of high multicollinearity, the researcher must be extremely careful to specify as exactly as possible the independent variable set. Omission of a variable which has an important impact on the dependent variable or specified independent variables can result in changes in both sign and magnitude of coefficients. This problem may occur in PIMS analysis due to omission of goals and strategies and related decision-making variables. One analysis undertaken to date (18) appears to provide substantial evidence for both Observations 8 and 9.

Observation 10: *The standard error of the estimate for the regression model should be specified.*

Kirchoff (15) points out that the accuracy claims of SPI (80 percent predictability of ROI) may be magnified since they do not report the standard error of the estimate for their model. Kirchoff suggests that the error may be in excess of $\pm$ 12 percent. When predicting an average ROI of 17 percent, this magnitude of error certainly questions the accuracy of the prediction. A partial test of the model by the Carnegie group seems to support this contention (18).

Observation 11: *The PIMS data base represents the most reliable and accurate data relevant to strategy formulation currently available.*

It would be easy to criticize the accuracy (quality) of the PIMS data collection process. For example, some accounting judgments must be made in reporting certain variables; but given the overwhelming superiority of PIMS data to other sources in quantity, number of measured variables, timeliness, conscientious attempt to minimize potential sources of input error through the collection of valid data, and the qualitative nature of our science, we feel that criticism here is unwarranted at present.

"Similar Businesses Under Similar Conditions"

Observation 12: *Criteria for selection of "similar" businesses appear arbitrary. In addition, relevant ranges which determine the degree of "similarity" are not specified.*

Since the basis of the PAR report is comparison of the particular business being analyzed with "similar businesses under similar circumstances," it is important to specify the conditions necessary for a business to be classified as similar. PIMS claims that similarities are not necessarily confined to industry categories. It would appear that the basis of comparison is market share, competition, market position, production process, and capital/cost structure. We could find no specific definitions for some of these variables, and no relevant ranges were specified within which a business could fall and be considered similar.

Given these unspecified factors, it is difficult for the researcher (or the user) to arrive at generalizable conclusions for selection of "similar" businesses. It is a particular problem for practitioners since they are responsible for selection of comparison businesses. As indicated in future directions for research, recent advances in organizational and strategic theory can make a significant contribution in this area.

Causality Assumptions

The most critical fault with PIMS approach is its supposition of causal relationships with little theoretical or statistical basis. The problem occurs most frequently with the construction of and relationships among the 37 independent variables used to predict ROI. The following discussion centers on a number of causal inconsistencies which may influence PIMS results, including directly and indirectly controllable factors, theoretical relationships among variables, and variable construction inconsistencies.

Observation 13: *Differences in management controllability exist among the 37 independent variables. These differences suggest a causal sequence.*

Significant differences exist among PIMS independent variables regarding the degree of controllability which management may exercise over them. Table 1 presents a categorization of the variables according to whether they are directly controllable by management, partially controllable, or largely uncontrollable (environmental). As the table indicates, about 50 percent of the variables are at least partially beyond the direct control of management, thus impacting generally on

Table 1.   Categorization of PIMS Independent Variables According to the Degree to Which They May Be Controlled by Management

Directly Controllable by Management (Goals-Strategies)	Partially Controllable by Management	Largely Uncontrollable by Management (Environmental)
Market position	Instability of market share	Industry long-run growth
Price relative to competition	Relative pay scale[a]	Short-run market growth
Product quality	Capacity utilization[b]	Industry exports
New product sales	Corporate size	Sales direct to end user
MFG costs/sales	Change in market share	Share of 4 largest firms
Receivables/sales	Change in selling price index	Buyer fragmentation index
Vertical integration	Change in vertical integration	Investment intensity[c]
Inventory/purchases	Market position impact	Fixed capital intensity[c]
Sales/employee		Competitive market activity
Marketing less sales force expenses/sales		Change in capital activity
R&D expenses/sales		Investment intensity impact
Corporate payout		
Degree of diversification		
Growth of sales		
Change in product quality		
Change in advertising and promotion/sales		
Change in sales force expenses/sales		
Change in return on sales		

[a]Only controllable by increasing.
[b]Only controllable in the short run.
[c]Only controllable at the entry level.

business strategy as situational factors (constraints, threats, or opportunities). Several authors (14, 19) suggest that these variables may impact on one another (the apparently high degree of correlation among the variables discussed in the methodology section provides a statistical indication that this may be the case). For example, a decision to increase product quality through investment in research and development, upgrading of manufacturing costs, and higher inventory turnover (controllable factors) has an impact on short-run market growth as well as on long-run growth of the industry (uncontrollable factors). A number of authors (21, 23, 31) have suggested causal sequences which may be useful in further defining the nature of the relationships among these factors. For example, the current state of environmental uncertainty (Where are we now?) could first be defined in terms of the uncontrollable factors. This serves to define the current and past position of the organization with respect to key environmental variables. As a second step, we suggest a closer examination of the controllable and partially controllable factors to determine the consistency between environment, strategy, and capabilities. Such an analysis should be undertaken in the future as part of the PIMS research program.

Observation 14: *Theoretical frameworks from strategic management and organization theory suggest causal relationships among the independent variable set.*

Other advances in strategic management and organization theory (1, 2, 10, 11, 12, 13, 21, 23, 26) suggest that causal relationships may exist among many variables included in the PIMS model. Examples include the effect of environmental uncertainty on the organization's structure and decision making. For example, high growth, highly fragmented buyers, low degree of capital intensity, and highly active competitors (see Table 1) should lead to a different mix of controllable factors than the opposite set of conditions. In addition, several variables measured in the PIMS data base are not included in the analysis; they have significant impact on the firm according to organization theory (see Future Directions). Examples include frequency of product and technological change.

Observation 15: *Some variables included in the PIMS regression model may have an impact due to their construction rather than to a "true" causal impact.*

There must be a sharp distinction drawn between variables used as predictors and those used to extend causal theory. Some variables included in the PIMS model to predict ROI apparently do so through the method of construction. Examples include investment intensity and various expense items. Since ROI is defined as:

$$\frac{\text{Sales} - \text{(certain) Expenses}}{\text{Investment}}$$

Investment intensity naturally would be expected to show an inverse relationship to ROI and in fact does so (see Table 2). Similarly, market expense tends to depress ROI as its level increases (see Table 3). In other words, rationale for the relationship may be unjustified as presented by the SPI group (29).

Finally, some causal relationships assumed in the PIMS analysis are unjustified for several previously cited reasons. Foremost is the conclusion that firm

---

Table 2.   Impact of Strategic Planning on Profit Performance: Investment Intensity and Market Share

Investment Intensity	Market Share		
	Under 12%	12%–26%	Over 26%
Under 45%	21.2%	26.9%	34.6%
45%–71%	8.6	13.1	26.2
Over 71%	2.0	6.7	15.7

PIMS Conclusion: Low market share plus high investment intensity equals disaster.

Source: Schoeffler, S., R. D. Buzzell, and D. F. Heany, "Impact of Strategic Planning on Profit Performance," *Harvard Business Review* (March-April 1974), 137–145.

Table 3.   Impact of Strategic Planning on Profit Performance: Product Quality and Ratio of Marketing Expenditures to Sales

Product Quality	Ratio of Marketing Expenditures to Sales		
	Low Under 6%	Average 6%–11%	High Over 11%
Inferior	15.4%	14.8%	2.7%
Average	17.8	16.9	14.2
Superior	25.2	25.5	19.8

PIMS Conclusion: A high marketing expenditure damages profitability when quality is low.

Source: Schoeffler, S., R. D. Buzzell, and D. F. Heany, "Impact of Strategic Planning on Profit Performance," *Harvard Business Review* (March-April 1974), 137–145.

performance above the level of PAR ROI is due to management effectiveness. Model error and environmental (contingency) factors may contribute equally to this result.

Contingency Factors

Although certain aspects of the PIMS analysis define factors upon which selected strategies are contingent, many aspects of the analysis do not utilize currently accepted contingency factors or prescribe strategy influencing actions on a "principle" basis (4, 5, 21, 29). (The Strategy Report, for example, makes "most likely environment" assumptions based on industry sales growth, change in selling price, change in wage rates, and change in various cost factors.)

Observation 16: *Conclusions derived from the PIMS analysis may be misleading due to omission of certain contingency factors including inconsistencies across industries and neglect of relevant ranges for variables.*

The PIMS conclusions with regard to market share have been criticized most heavily because of their neglect of contingencies (3, 4, 7, 8). PIMS concludes that increasing market share is a key factor which influences profitability and supports this contention with several explanatory tables (see Table 2). Fruhan (8) questions such a conclusion on the basis that the analysis ignores factors such as adequacy of financial resources, viability of position if the effort to increase market share fails, and influence of environmental factors in allowing the company to pursue the chosen strategy.

Bloom and Kotler (4) attack PIMS's results with regard to market share on the basis of specification of relevant range for their results:

. . . *the PIMS study does not reveal whether profitability eventually turns down at very high market-share levels. The study lumps together all market shares above 40%; therefore the behavior of ROI in response to still higher market shares is undisclosed. Consequently, a high market-share company must itself analyze whether profitability will fall with further gains in market share (4, p. 65).*

The relevant range problem can be further extended to other variables in the analysis. Table 2, for example, suggests that decreasing investment intensity leads to higher profit levels. Extension of this concept would require liquidation of all plant and equipment, an obvious case for specifying the turnaround point. A similar argument can be advanced for marketing in Table 3.

Contingencies which exist across various industries present further problems in the PIMS analysis. Much work in the area of organization theory, beginning with the pioneering efforts of Lawrence and Lorsch (17), has identified those factors which differentiate one industry from another. Among the more important variables which have been documented are size (24), degree of technological intensity (25, 33), uncertainty of the environment (6, 7), and degree of centralization (9). It is not our purpose to review this large body of literature here other than to suggest that future research with the PIMS data base should concentrate on developing and testing this important theoretical area. The next section examines some variables available in the PIMS data which can prove useful in testing several suggested hypotheses.

Future Dimensions

The previous 16 observations suggest a number of improvements which can be made in the PIMS system, both to enhance its applicability to the practitioner and to aid in the testing and construction of policy-related theories. First, and most importantly, it seems necessary to classify the PIMS variables into categories which reflect the causal relationships among them. This will enable the practitioner to better evaluate the strategies under consideration, since the current situation can be more exactly compared to that defined in the PIMS model. Improved variable specification also will enhance development of consistent theories of strategy and policy analysis; without additional specification, the model cannot be adequately compared to those model developments undertaken in the past and those which will be developed in the future.

Second, it appears necessary to examine additional data which are available in the PIMS data base but which are not now included in the model. Many of these data are related to suggested relationships from organization theory and are discussed in the following paragraphs. Further, although many of these data may not have a strong *direct* relationship (which appears to be the criterion for selection of those variables included in the model), the indirect relationships in a further specified model may be quite strong. Examples of variables which are available and should be tested include the following. In particular, these serve to define further the turbulence or uncertainty of the environment, a factor given increased importance in recent policy and strategy models (1, 7, 14):

1. Frequency of product changes.

2. Technological change.

3. Development time for new products.

4. Change in market in terms of end users.

5.   Capacity and supply problems.
    a.   Scarcity of materials, personnel, energy, plant capacity.
    b.   Alternate sources of supply available.

These variables and the associated performance measures provide an obviously rich source of information concerning recent hypotheses generated in the strategy field. As an example, the following hypothesis taken from Khandwalla (14) could easily be tested using the PIMS data base:

The more turbulent the external environment, the more strategically important to management are uncertainty absorption and avoidance mechanisms like market research, forecasting, advertising, and vertical integration (14, p. 335).

Further, hypotheses proposed by Anderson and Paine (1) are subject to PIMS data evaluation. In particular the following type of hypothesis is relevant:

The more uncertain the external environment, the more management is likely to undertake search for advance information, especially through market research and technological R&D.

An outgrowth of these hypothesis tests would be corroboration of the various models recently proposed for evaluation of strategic decisions. Looking further ahead, several writers have pointed to the difficulty of defining what is meant by the term ''strategy'' (or ''policy''). The PIMS program is in a position to provide such a definition since it is currently the only source for verification of conclusions with varied, accurate empirical data.

Conclusions

The PIMS program probably is the most substantial empirical attempt yet in the policy field. Generally the program has succeeded to a large degree in accomplishing its lofty goals; it is the most comprehensive analysis system currently in use. However, if a number of its weaknesses were removed, its usefulness to both the practitioner and to those interested in advancing the theoretical base of policy and strategy formulation would be enhanced.

One major outgrowth of the PIMS program is its initiation of thought about the true nature of the relationships among those variables incorporated in strategy. Obviously, the practitioner must deal with these relationships on a daily basis, but attempts at conceptualizing these relationships by the theorist have been lacking. Perhaps the major function of the PIMS program in the future will be to serve as a catalyst to further sophistication of these models and as a measure of their true applicability in the real world.

References

1. Anderson, C. R., and F. T. Paine. ''Managerial Perceptions and Strategic Behavior,'' *Academy of Management Journal,* Volume 18, Number 4 (December 1975), pp. 811–823.

2. Ansoff, H. I. *Corporate Strategy: An Analytic Approach to Business Policy for Growth and Expansion.* (New York: McGraw-Hill, 1965).
3. Ansoff, H. I. *Business Strategy* (New York: Penguin, 1970).
4. Bloom, P. N., and P. Kotler. "Strategies for High Market-Share Companies," *Harvard Business Review* (November-December 1975), 63–72.
5. Buzzell, R. D., T. G. Bradley, and R. G. M. Sultan. "Market Share—A Key to Profitability," *Harvard Business Review* (January-February 1975), 97–106.
6. Downey, H. K., and J. W. Slocum, Jr. "Uncertainty Measures, Research, and Sources of Variation," *Academy of Management Journal,* Vol. 18 (1975), 562–578.
7. Duncan, R. "Characteristics of Organizational Environments and Perceived Environmental Uncertainty," *Administrative Science Quarterly,* Vol. 17 (1972), 313–327.
8. Fruhan, W. E., Jr. "Pyrrhic Victories in Fights for Market Share," *Harvard Business Review* (September-October 1972), 100–107.
9. Galbraith, J. *Designing Complex Organizations.* (Reading, Mass.: Addison, Wesley, 1973).
10. Glueck, W. F. *Business Policy: Strategy Formation and Management Action* (New York: McGraw-Hill, 1976).
11. Hatten, K. J. "Strategic Models in the Brewing Industry" (Ph.D. dissertation, Purdue University, 1974).
12. Hatten, K. J., and D. E. Schendel. "Strategy's Role in Policy Research," *Journal of Economics and Business,* Vol. 28 (1975–1976), 196–202.
13. Hofer, C. W. "Toward a Contingency Theory of Business Strategy," *Academy of Management Journal,* Vol. 18, No. 4 (December 1975), 184–810.
14. Khandwalla, P. N. *The Design of Organizations* (New York: Harcourt, Brace, Jovanovich, 1977).
15. Kirchoff, B. A. "Discussant's Response to Strategy Evaluation: The State of the Art and Future Directions," Business Policy and Planning Research State of the Art Workshop, Pittsburgh, May 1977.
16. Kirchoff, B. A. "Organization Effectiveness Measurement and Policy Research," *Academy of Management Review,* Vol. 2, No. 3 (July 1977), 347–355.
17. Lawrence, P. R., and J. W. Lorsch. *Organization and Environment* (Boston: Harvard Business Review, Division of Research, 1967).
18. Magid, W., J. Roman, and R. Santoski. "Critical Analysis of PIMS." Working paper prepared for C. Kriebel (Pittsburgh: Carnegie-Mellon University, 1977).
19. Montanari, J. "An Expanded Theory of Structural Determination: An Empirical Investigation of the Impact of Managerial Discretion on Organizational Structure," (Ph.D. dissertation, University of Colorado, 1976).
20. Paine, F. T. "Towards an Integrated Contingency Theory of Strategy." Business Policy and Planning State of the Art Workshop, Pittsburgh, May 1977.
21. Paine, F. T., and C. R. Anderson. "Contingencies Affecting Strategy Formulation and Effectiveness: An Empirical Study," *Journal of Management Studies,* Vol. 14, No. 2 (May 1977), 147–158.
22. Paine, F. T., and C. R. Anderson. "Strategic Management: An Intervention Approach," *Proceedings of the National Academy of Management* (Orlando, Florida: August 1977).
23. Patton, R. A. "A Simultaneous Equation Model of Corporate Strategy: The Case of the U.S. Brewing Industry," (Ph.D. dissertation, Purdue University, 1976).
24. Porter, L. W. *Organizational Patterns of Managerial Job Attitudes* (New York: American Foundation for Management Research, 1964).
25. Pugh, D. S., D. J. Hickson, and C. R. Hinings. "An Empirical Taxonomy of Structures of Work Organizations," *Administrative Science Quarterly,* Vol. 14 (1969), 115–126.

26. Rumelt, R. P. *Strategy, Structure, and Economic Performance* (Boston: Division of Research, Harvard University, Graduate School of Business Administration, 1974).

27. Rumelt, R. P. "Strategy Evaluation: The State of the Art and Future Directions," Business Policy and Planning State of the Art Workshop, Pittsburgh, May, 1977.

28. Schoeffler, S. "Cross-Sectional Study of Strategy, Structure, and Performance: Aspects of the PIMS Program," in H. B. Thorelli (Ed.), *Strategy + Structure = Performance: The Strategic Planning Imperative* (Bloomington, Ind.: Indiana University Press, 1977).

29. Schoeffler, S., R. D. Buzzell, and D. F. Heany. "Impact of Strategic Planning on Profit Performance," *Harvard Business Review* (March-April 1974), pp. 137–145.

30. Utterback, J. M. "Environment Analysis and Forecasting," Business Policy and Planning State of the Art Workshop, Pittsburgh, May, 1977.

31. Winn, D. N. *Industrial Market Structure and Performance 1960–1968* (Ann Arbor, Michigan: Division of Research, Graduate School of Business Administration, University of Michigan, 1975).

32. Winter, Ralph E. "Stress and Fast Profits Called A Key Deterrent to Capital Spending," *The Wall Street Journal* (June 10, 1977), p. 1.

33. Woodward, J. *Industrial Organization: Theory and Practice* (London: Oxford University Press, 1965).

15

Strategy and the "Business Portfolio"

Barry Hedley

All except the smallest and simplest companies comprise more than one business. Even when a company operates within a single broad business area, analysis normally reveals that it is, in practice, involved in a number of product-market segments which are distinct economically. These must be considered separately for purposes of strategy development.

[It has been] shown [in Article 8] that the fundamental determinant of strategy success for each individual business segment was relative cost position. As a result of the experience curve effect the competitor with high market share in the segment relative to competition should be able to develop the lowest cost position and hence the highest and most stable profits. This will be true regardless of changes in the economic environment. Hence relative competitive position in the appropriately defined business segment forms a simple but sound strategic goal. Focusing on this goal provides a basis for effective long-range planning even in the face of considerable environmental uncertainty.

Almost invariably, any company which reviews its various businesses carefully in this light will discover that they occupy widely differing relative competitive positions. Some businesses will be competitively strong already, and may appear to present no strategic problem; others will be weak, and the company must face the question of whether it would be worthwhile to attempt to improve their position, making whatever investments might be required to achieve this; if this is not done, the company can only expect poor performance from the business and the best option economically will be divestment.

Even in quite small companies, the total number of possible combinations of individual business strategies can be extremely large. The difficulty of making a firm final choice on strategy for each business is normally compounded by the

This article first appeared in *Long Range Planning*. Reprinted with permission from *Long Range Planning* 10 (February 1977):9–15. Copyright 1977, Pergamon Press, Ltd.

When this article was published, Mr. Hedley was a director of The Boston Consulting Group Ltd.

fact that most companies must operate within constraints established by limited resources, particularly cash resources. This is an especially vital concern in times of high inflation or recession such as have been experienced in recent years.

An effective solution to this problem requires the development of a framework enabling the selection of the optimum combination of individual business strategies from the spectrum of possible alternatives and opportunities open to the company, while at the same time remaining within the boundaries set by the company's overall constraints. The purpose of this article is to discuss an approach to doing this, which has evolved considerably in the course of its regular application in consulting assignments. The approach hinges on the integration of the implications of the experience curve effect for profit performance at the individual business level with an understanding of the nature of the strategy alternatives open to each business as a function of its overall growth rate. Final decisions on strategy for each business are then taken within the context of the company viewed explicitly as a portfolio of individual businesses. Hence the approach has come to be termed the product or *business portfolio* today. However, there seems to be some confusion in practice as to exactly what it is and how it is meant to be applied. It is hoped that this article will help clarify the nature of the approach and its power as an aid to effective strategy development.

The Business Portfolio Concept[1]

The Effect and Value of Growth

At its most basic level, the importance of growth in shaping strategy choice is twofold. First, the growth of a business is a major factor influencing the likely ease—and hence cost—of gaining market share. In low growth businesses, any market share gained will tend to require an actual volume reduction in competitors' sales. This will be very obvious to the competitors and they are likely to fight to prevent the throughput in their plants dropping. In high growth businesses, on the other hand, market share can be gained steadily merely by securing the largest share of the *growth* in the business: expanding capacity earlier than the competitors, ensuring product availability and effective selling support despite the strains imposed by the growth, and so forth. Meanwhile competitors may even be unaware of their share loss because their actual volume of throughput has been well maintained. Even if aware of their loss of share, the competitors may be unconcerned by it given that their plants are still well loaded. This is particularly true of competitors who do not understand the strategic importance of market share for long-term profitability resulting from the experience curve effect.

An unfortunate example of this is given by the history of the British motorcycle industry. British market share was allowed to erode in motorcycles worldwide for more than a decade, throughout which the British factories were still fairly full: British motorcycle production volumes held up at around 80,000 units per year throughout the sixties; in sharp contrast, Japanese export volumes leapt from only about 60,000 in 1960 to 2.5 million in 1973; their total production volumes roughly tripled in the same period. The long term effect was that while

Japanese real costs were falling rapidly British costs were not: somewhat oversimplified, this is why the British motorcycle industry faced bankruptcy in the early seventies.[2]

The second important factor concerning growth is the opportunity it provides for investment. Growth businesses provide the ideal vehicles for investment, for ploughing cash into a business in order to see it compound and return even larger amounts of cash at a later point in time. Of course this opportunity is also a need: the faster a business grows, the more investment it will require just to maintain market share. Yet the experience curve effect means that this is essential if its profitability is not to decline over time.

Importance of Relative Competitive Position for Cash Generation

While these growth considerations affect the rate at which a business will *use* cash, the relative competitive position of the business will determine the rate at which the business will *generate* cash: the stronger the company's position relative to its competitors the higher its margins should be, as a result of the experience curve effect. The simplest measure of relative competitive position is, of course, relative market share. A company's relative market share in a business can be defined as its market share in the business divided by that of the largest other competitor. Thus only the biggest competitor has a relative market share greater than one. All the other competitors should enjoy lower profitability and cash generation than the leader.

The Growth-Share Matrix

Individual businesses can have very different financial characteristics and face different strategic options depending on how they are placed in terms of growth and relative competitive position. Businesses can basically fall into any one of four broad strategic categories, as depicted schematically in the growth-share matrix in Figure 15.1.

Stars—high growth, high share—are in the upper left quadrant. Growing rapidly, they use large amounts of cash to maintain position. They are also leaders in the business, however, and should generate large amounts of cash. As a result, *star* businesses are frequently roughly in balance on net cash flow, and can be self-sustaining in growth terms. They represent probably the best profit growth and investment opportunities available to the company, and every effort should therefore be made to maintain and consolidate their competitive position. This will sometimes require heavy investment beyond their own generation capabilities and low margins may be essential at times to deter competition, but this is almost invariably worthwhile for the longer term: when the growth slows, as it ultimately does in all businesses, very large cash returns will be obtained if share has been maintained so that the business drops into the lower left quadrant of the matrix, becoming a *cash cow*. If *star* businesses fail to hold share, which frequently happens if the attempt is made to net large amounts of cash from them in the short

Figure 15.1   The Business Portfolio or Growth-Share Matrix

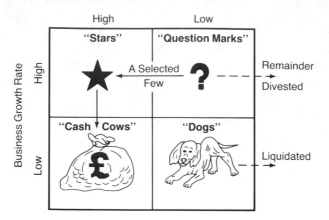

and medium term (e.g., by cutting back on investment and raising prices, creating an "umbrella" for competitors), they will ultimately become *dogs* (lower right quadrant). These are certain losers.

Cash cows—low growth, high share—should have an entrenched superior market position and low costs. Hence profits and cash generation should be high, and because of the low growth reinvestment needs should be light. Thus large cash surpluses should be generated by these businesses. *Cash cows* pay the dividends and interest, provide the debt capacity, pay for the company overhead *and* provide the cash for investment elsewhere in the company's portfolio of businesses. They are the foundation on which the company rests.

Dogs—low growth, low share—represent a tremendous contrast. Their poor competitive position condemns them to poor profits. Because the growth is low, there is little potential for gaining sufficient share to achieve a viable cost position at anything approaching a reasonable cost. Unfortunately, the cash required for investment in the business just to maintain competitive position, though low, frequently exceeds that generated, especially under conditions of high inflation. The business therefore becomes a "cash trap" likely to absorb cash *perpetually* unless further investment in the business is rigorously avoided. The colloquial term *dog* describing these businesses, though undoubtedly pejorative, is thus rather apt. A company should take every precaution to minimize the proportion of its assets that remain in this category.

Question marks—high growth, low share—have the worst cash characteristics of all. In the upper right quadrant, their cash needs are high because of their growth, but their cash generation is small because of their low share. If nothing is done to change its market share, the *question mark* will simply absorb large amounts of cash in the short term and later, as the growth slows, become a *dog*. Following this sort of strategy, the *question mark* is a cash loser throughout its existence. Managed this way, a *question mark* becomes the ultimate "cash trap."

In fact there is a clear choice between only two strategy alternatives for a *question mark,* hence the name. Because growth is high, it should be easier and less costly to gain share here than it would be in a lower growth business. One strategy is therefore to make whatever investments are necessary to gain share, to try to fund the business to dominance so that it can become a *star* and ultimately a *cash cow* when the business matures. This strategy will be very costly in the short term—growth rates will be even higher than if share were merely being maintained, and additional marketing and other investments will be required to make the share actually change hands—but it offers the only way of developing a sound business from the *question mark* over the long term. The only logical alternative is divestment. Outright sale is preferable; but if this is not possible, then a firm decision must be taken not to invest further in the business and it must be allowed simply to generate whatever cash it can while none is reinvested. The business will then decline, possibly quite rapidly if market growth is high, and will have to be shut down at some point. But it will produce cash in the short term and this is greatly preferable to the error of sinking cash into it perpetually without improving its competitive position.

Some Examples

These then, are the four basic categories to which businesses can belong. Some companies tend to fit almost entirely into a single quadrant. General Motors and English China Clays are examples of predominantly *cash cow* companies. Chrysler, by comparison, is a *dog* which compounded its fundamental problem of low share in its domestic U.S. market by acquiring further mature low share competitors in other countries (e.g., Rootes which became Chrysler U.K.). IBM in computers, Xerox in photocopiers, and BSR in low-cost record autochangers are all examples of predominantly *star* businesses. Xerox's computer operation XDS was clearly a *question mark* and it is not surprising that Xerox effectively gave it away free to Honeywell, and considered itself lucky to escape at that price! When RCA closed down its computer operation, it had to sustain a write-off of about $490 million. *Question marks* are costly.

Portfolio Strategy

Most companies have their portfolio of businesses scattered through all four quadrants of the matrix. It is possible to outline quite briefly and simply what the appropriate overall portfolio strategy for such a company should be. The first goal should be to maintain position in the *cash cows,* but to guard against the frequent temptation to reinvest in them excessively. The cash generated by the *cash cows* should be used as a first priority to maintain or consolidate position in those *stars* which are not self sustaining. Any surplus remaining can be used to fund a *se-*

lected number of *question marks* to dominance. Most companies will find they have inadequate cash generation to finance market share–gaining strategies in all their *question marks*. Those which are not funded should be divested either by sale or liquidation over time.

Finally, virtually all companies have at least some *dog* businesses. There is nothing reprehensible about this, indeed on the contrary, an absence of *dogs* probably indicates that the company has not been sufficiently adventurous in the past. It is essential, however, that the fundamentally weak strategic position of the *dog* be recognized for what it is. Occasionally it is possible to restore a *dog* to viability by a creative business segmentation strategy, rationalizing and specializing the business into a small niche which it can dominate. If this is impossible, however, the only thing which could rescue the *dog* would be an increase in share taking it to a position comparable to the leading competitors in the segment. This is likely to be unreasonably costly in a mature business, and therefore the only prospect for obtaining a return from a *dog* is to manage it for cash, cutting off all investment in the business. Management should be particularly wary of expensive "turn around" plans developed for a *dog* if these do not involve a significant change in fundamental competitive position. Without this, the *dog* is a sure loser. An indictment of many corporate managements is not the fact that their companies have *dogs* in the portfolio, but rather that these *dogs* are not managed according to logical strategies. The decision to liquidate a business is usually even harder to take than that of entering a new business. It is essential, however, for the long-term vitality and performance of the company overall that it be prepared to do *both* as the need arises.

Thus the appropriate strategy for a multibusiness company involves striking a balance in the portfolio such that the cash generated by the *cash cows,* and by those *question marks* and *dogs* which are being liquidated, is sufficient to support the company's *stars* and to fund the selected *question marks* through to dominance. This pattern of strategies is indicated by the arrows in Figure 15.1. Understanding this pattern conceptually is, however, a far cry from being able to implement it in practice. What any company should do with its own specific businesses is of course a function of the precise shape of the company's portfolio, and the particular opportunities and problems it presents. But how can a clear picture of the company's portfolio be developed?

The Matrix Quantified

Based on careful analysis and research it is normally possible to divide a company into its various business segments appropriately defined for purposes of strategy development. Following this critical first step, it is usually relatively straightforward to determine the overall growth rate of each individual business (i.e., the growth of the *market,* not the growth of the company within the market), and the company's size (in terms of turnover or assets) and relative competitive position (market share) within the business.[3]

Armed with these data it is possible to develop a precise overall picture of the company's portfolio of businesses graphically. This can greatly facilitate the identification and resolution of the key strategic issues facing the company. It is a particularly useful approach where companies are large, comprising many separate businesses. Such complex portfolios often defy description in more conventional ways.

The nature of the graphical portfolio display is illustrated by the example in Figure 15.2. In this chart, growth rate and relative competitive position are plotted on continuous scales. Each circle in the display represents a single business or business segment, appropriately defined. To convey an impression of the relative significance of each business, size is indicated by the area of the circle, which can be made proportional to either turnover or assets employed. Relative competitive position is plotted on a logarithmic scale, in order to be consistent with the experience curve effect, which implies that profit margin or rate of cash generation differences between competitors will tend to be related to the *ratio* of their relative competitive positions (market shares). A linear axis is used for growth, for which the most generally useful measure is *volume* growth of the business concerned. In general, rates of cash use should be directly proportional to growth.

The lines dividing the portfolio into four quadrants are inevitably somewhat arbitrary. "High growth," for example, is taken to include all businesses growing in excess of 10 percent per annum in volume terms. Certainly, above this growth rate market share tends to become fairly fluid and can be made to change hands quite readily. In addition many companies have traditionally employed a figure of 10 percent for their discount rate in times of low inflation, and so this also tends to be the growth rate above which investment in market share becomes particularly attractive financially.[4]

Figure 15.2   Graphical Representation of the Portfolio

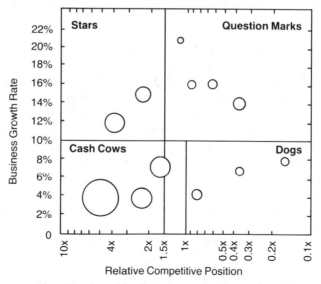

Circle area is proportional to size of business concerned, e.g., turnover or assets.

The line separating areas of high and low relative competitive position is set at 1.5 times. Experience in using this display has been that in high-growth businesses relative strengths of this magnitude or greater are necessary in order to ensure a sufficiently dominant position that the business will have the characteristic of a *star* in practice. On the other hand, in low-growth businesses acceptable cash generation characteristics are occasionally, but not always, observed at relative strengths as low as 1 times; hence the addition of a second separating line at 1 times in the low-growth area to reflect this. These lines should, of course, be taken only as approximate guides in characterizing businesses in the portfolio as *dogs* and *question marks, cash cows* and *stars*. In actuality, businesses cover a smooth spectrum across both axes of the matrix. There is obviously no "magic" which transforms a *star* into a *cash cow* as its growth declines from 10.5 to 9.5 percent. It is undeniably useful, however, to have some device for broadly indicating where the transition points occur within the matrix, and the lines suggested here have worked well in practical applications of the matrix in a large number of companies.

Portfolio Approaches in Practice

The company shown in Figure 15.2 would be a good example of a potentially well balanced portfolio. With a firm foundation in the form of two or three substantial *cash cows,* this company has some well placed *stars* to provide growth and to yield high cash returns in the future when they mature. The company also has some *question marks* at least two of which are probably sufficiently well placed that they offer a good chance of being funded into *star* positions at a reasonable cost, not out of proportion to the company's resources. The company is not without *dogs,* but properly managed there is no reason why these should be a drain on cash.

The Sound Portfolio, Unsoundly Managed

Companies with an attractive portfolio of this kind are not rare in practice. In fact Figure 15.2 is a disguised version of a representation of an actual U.K. company analyzed in the course of a Boston Consulting Group assignment. What is much rarer, however, is to find that the company has made a clear assessment of the matrix positioning and appropriate strategy for each business in the portfolio.

Ideally, one would hope that the company in Figure 15.2 would develop strategy along the following lines. For the *stars,* the key objectives should be the maintenance of market share; current profitability should be accorded a lower priority. For the *cash cows,* however, current profitability may well be the primary goal. *Dogs* would not be expected to be as profitable as the *cash cows,* but would be expected to yield cash. Some *question marks* would be set objectives in terms of increased market share; others, where gaining dominance appeared too costly, would be managed instead for cash.

The essence of the portfolio approach is therefore that strategy objectives must vary between businesses. The strategy developed for each business must fit its own matrix position *and* the needs and capabilities of the company's overall portfolio of businesses. In practice, however, it is much more common to find all businesses within a company being operated with a common overall goal in mind. "Our target in this company is to grow at 10 percent per annum and achieve a return of 10 percent on capital." This type of overall target is then taken to apply to every business in the company. *Cash cows* beat the profit target easily, though they frequently miss on growth. Nevertheless, their managements are praised and they are normally rewarded by being allowed to plough back what only too frequently amounts to an *excess* of cash into their "obviously attractive" businesses—attractive businesses, yes, but *not* for growth investment. *Dogs* on the other hand rarely meet the profit target. But how often is it accepted that it is in fact unreasonable for them *ever* to hit the target? On the contrary, the most common strategic mistake is that major investments are made in *dogs* from time to time in hopeless attempts to turn the business around without actually shifting market share. Unfortunately, only too often *question marks* are regarded very much as *dogs,* and get insufficient investment funds ever to bring them to dominance. The *question marks* usually do receive some investment, however, possibly even enough to maintain share. *This is throwing money away into a cash trap.* These businesses should either receive enough support to enable them to achieve segment dominance, *or none at all*.

These are some of the strategic errors which are regularly committed even by companies which have basically sound portfolios. The result is a serious suboptimization of potential performance in which some businesses (e.g., *cash cows*) are not being called on to produce the full results of which they are actually capable, and resources are being mistakenly squandered on other businesses *(dogs, question marks)* in an attempt to make them achieve performance of which they are intrinsically incapable without a fundamental improvement in market share. Where mismanagement of this kind becomes positively dangerous is when it is applied within the context of a basically unbalanced portfolio.

The Unbalanced Portfolio

The disguised example in Figure 15.3 is another actual company. This portfolio is seriously out of balance. As shown in Figure 15.3(a), the company has a very high proportion of *question marks* in its portfolio, and an inadequate base of *cash cows.* Yet at the time of investigation this company was in fact taking such cash as was being generated by its mature businesses and spreading it out amongst all the high growth businesses, only one of which was actually receiving sufficient investment to enable it even to maintain share! Thus the overall relative competitive position of the portfolio was on average declining. At the same time, the balance in the portfolio was shifting: as shown in the projected portfolio in Figure 15.3(b), because of the higher relative growth of the *question marks* their overall weight in the portfolio was increasing, making them even harder to fund from the limited resources of the mature businesses. If the company continued to follow the same strategy of spreading available funds between all the businesses, then the rate of decline could only increase over time leading ultimately to disaster.

Figure 15.3   An Unbalanced Portfolio

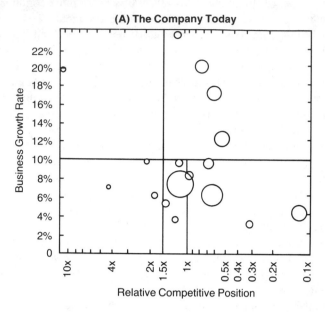

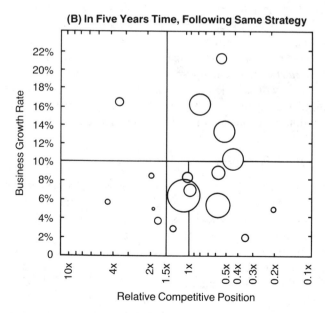

This company was caught in a vicious circle of decline. To break out of the circle would require firm discipline and the strength of will to select only one or two of the *question marks* and finance those, while cutting off investment in the remainder. Obviously the choice of which should receive investment involves rather more than selection at random from the portfolio chart. It requires careful analysis of the actual nature of the businesses concerned and particularly the characteristics and behavior of the competitors faced in those businesses. However, the nature of the strategic choice facing the company is quite clear, when viewed in portfolio terms. Without the clarity of view provided by the matrix display, which focuses on the real fundamentals of the businesses and their relationships to each other within the portfolio, it is impossible to develop strategy effectively in any multibusiness company.

Implications for Strategy Development Today

The need for an approach of this kind is more acute than ever today. In recent times business managers and planners have had to adapt to a new norm of continual change and unpredictability in economic affairs. The difficulty of adapting has been compounded over the last few years by persistent pressures of inflation and recession. Inflation, of course, results in pressure on profits—certainly on "real" profits—and even more importantly on cash. More cash is required for the same physical stocks, net debtors inflate and, of course, investment in plant and equipment becomes much more costly in cash terms. Apparent profits can normally be increased in inflationary times, though taxes and dividends take their share. The net result, however, especially in a climate of price and marginal control, is that cash available for reinvestment is insufficient to finance real growth at anything like historic rates. Introduction of accounting changes, spearheaded by the provision of tax relief on "stock profits," helps the situation but is by no means a complete solution in itself. The influence of recession, superimposed on the inflation, has been to increase further the pressure on profits. In a few instances, recession may have reduced cash needs as working capital needs declined and short-term capacity expansion requirements were revised downwards. But that has been cold comfort, at best.

The Predictable Reactions

How are companies reacting to these pressures? It is, of course, difficult and dangerous to generalize. It appears, however, that the most common corporate response has been simply a general "tightening of the belt." The call has gone out to all businesses both to generate more profits in the short-term, and to control cash tightly. The results have been predictable. Prices have been increased as much as is legally possible. Expenditures which look "postponable" have been eliminated. This has covered everything from company cars and office paintings to more important expenditures—such as plant overhaul, market research, product research and development—which may produce only "intangible" short-term benefits. Cash has been conserved both by tight stock control, and by energetically trying to take increased supplier credit at the same time as reducing the level of one's own debtors. Significantly, investments in plant and equipment have frequently been refused, unless they offered a very high return and rapid payback. And perhaps most importantly of all, these measures tend to have been applied virtually across the board, affecting all the businesses within large multibusiness companies more or less equally.

Actions such as these are understandable reflex managerial responses. They have alleviated the pressures to which companies have been exposed. Unfortunately, however, they are only acceptable in the short term. They must not be continued now even if the pressures which originally stimulated them persist into the longer term. It is particularly important that they be discontinued if the maximum benefit is to be taken of any near term improvement in trading conditions. If these "across the board" measures *are* continued, then severe and lasting damage will be done in some businesses for which they are wholly inappropriate long term.

Many companies have been living from day to day for too long. Clear and explicit consideration of long range strategy must be restored to our business consciousness and decision making, or we shall find that we have mortgaged the future irretrievably. Relative competitive position within the context of the portfolio concept can provide the simple and sound individual business objectives which are needed for any company to optimize its strategic opportunities.

Notes

1. A number of discussions of the business portfolio concept have appeared previously at various times in publications by The Boston Consulting Group. These include: *Perspectives,* The Product Portfolio (1970); *Commentary,* Growth and Financial Strategies (1971); and *Perspectives,* The Growth Share Matrix (1973).

2. The Boston Consulting Group Ltd., *Strategy Alternatives for the British Motorcycle Industry,* a Report prepared for the Secretary of State for Industry, HMSO (1975).

3. Frequently the ratio of the market share of the company in the business relative to that of the largest competitor can be used for the latter measure. In some business segments with more complex economics, different cost elements may have differing experience curve bases for cost reduction. In such cases a simple measure of overall relative competitive position is given by the weighted average of the company's relative position in each of these separate experience curve bases. The weights to be used in computing the average are the proportion of the total cost or value added accounted for by the cost element related to each experience base. The average relative share thus still represents an experience curve based proxy for relative cost position in this complex situation, just as it does in the simpler case where all costs in the business segment are simply a reflection of accumulated experience in that segment alone.

4. It is an interesting mathematical fact that if the market were expected to grow in excess of the discount rate *forever,* the discounted present value of increased market share would actually be infinite!

16

The Directional Policy Matrix—Tool for Strategic Planning

S. J. Q. Robinson, R. E. Hichens, and D. P. Wade

In diversified business organizations one of the main functions of the management is to decide how money, materials, and skilled manpower should be provided and allocated between different business sectors in order to ensure the survival and healthy growth of the whole. Good management allocates resources to sectors where business prospects appear favorable and where the organization has a position of advantage.

In a reasonably stable economic environment the normal method of comparing the prospects of one business sector with another, and for measuring a company's strengths and weaknesses in different sectors, is to use historical and forecast rates of return on capital employed in each sector to provide a measure of the sector's prospects or the company's strength. This is because a sector where business prospects are favorable and the company's position is strong tends to show higher profitability than one in which business prospects are less attractive and the company's position is weak. But records and forecasts of profitability are not sufficient yardsticks for guidance of management in corporate planning and allocation of resources.

The main reasons are:

(a) They do not provide a systematic explanation

    (1) Why one business sector has more favorable prospects than another.

    (2) Why the company's position in a particular sector is strong or weak.

This article first appeared in *Long Range Planning*. Reprinted with permission from *Long Range Planning* 11 No. 3 (June 1978):8–15. Copyright 1978, Pergamon Press, Ltd.

When this article was published, the authors were, respectively, in the Corporate Planning Division of Shell Chemical UK, Ltd.; with Shell International Chemical Co., Ltd.; and in the Planning and Economics Division of Shell International Chemical UK.

(b)   They do not provide enough insight into the underlying dynamics and balance of the company's individual business sectors and the balance between them.

(c)   When new areas of business are being considered, actual experience, by definition, cannot be consulted. Even when entry to a new area is to be achieved by acquiring an existing business the current performance of the existing business may not be reliable as a guide to its future.

(d)   World-wide inflation has severely weakened the validity and credibility of financial forecasts, particularly in the case of businesses which are in any way affected by oil prices.

Corporate managements which recognize these shortcomings bring a variety of other qualitative and quantitative considerations to bear on the decision-making process in addition to the financial yardsticks. These are described in the following sections.

Outline of Technique

In building up a corporate plan, a company will normally have available a number of plans and investment proposals for individual business sectors. These will include historical data on the company's past financial performance in the sector, and financial projections embodying the future investment plans. Such projections will reflect the expectations of those responsible for the company's business in that particular sector in relation to:

(a)   Market growth;

(b)   Industry supply/demand balance;

(c)   Prices;

(d)   Costs;

(e)   The company's future market shares;

(f)   Manufacturing competitiveness;

(g)   Research and development strength;

(h)   The activities of competitors; and

(i)   The future business environment.

The basic technique of the Directional Policy Matrix is to identify:

(a)   the main criteria by which the prospects for a business sector may be judged to be favorable or unfavorable; and

(b)   those by which a company's position in a sector may be judged to be strong or weak.

Favorable in this context means with high profit and growth potential for the industry generally.

These criteria are then used to construct separate ratings of "sector prospects" and of "company's competitive capabilities" and the ratings are plotted on a matrix. It is convenient to divide the matrix into three columns and three rows, but other layouts are equally feasible. The ratings can be plotted in various ways. Figure 16.1 displays the position of a number of different sectors in a hypothetical company's portfolio. Alternatively, the matrix can be used to display all the competitors in one particular business sector, since the method lends itself to evaluating competitors' ratings as well as those of one's own company.

Details of Technique

Scope of the Analysis

The detailed techniques have been developed by reference to the petroleum-based sector of the chemical industry, but the general technique is applicable to almost any diversified business with separately identifiable sectors. It could be applied to a diversified shipping company where the separate business sectors might be dif-

Figure 16.1   Positions of Business Sectors in a Hypothetical Company's Portfolio

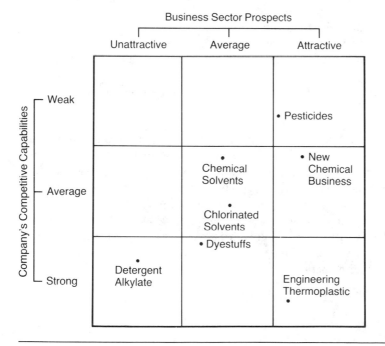

ferent types of cargo, or to an engineering company offering a range of products and services. In most cases there is no difficulty in identifying a logical business sector to analyze. In the chemical industry business sectors can generally be identified with product sectors, since these form distinct businesses with well defined boundaries and substantial competition within the boundaries.

Any particular geographical area may be defined for study. For the majority of petroleum-based chemicals it has been found most convenient to consider economic blocs (e.g., Western Europe) since there is generally greater movement of chemicals within these blocs than between them.

The time scale of assessment is the effective forecasting horizon. This will vary according to the business growth rate and the lead time needed to install new capacity or develop new uses. For most petroleum-based chemicals a time scale of 10 years has been found appropriate.

Analysis of Business Sector Prospects

There are four main criteria by which the profitability prospects for different sectors of the petroleum-based chemical business may be judged. These are:

(a)   Market growth rate;

(b)   Market quality;

(c)   Industry feedstock situation; and

(d)   Environmental aspects.

Some of these criteria are not applicable to other industries and other criteria have to be introduced. Industry feedstock situation, for example, would not be of significance in evaluating sectors of the engineering industry. Market growth and market quality, however, are fundamental to any analysis of business sector prospects.

The significance of these four criteria and the way in which they are rated is as follows.

Market Growth.   Sectors with high market growth are not always those with the greatest profit growth. Nevertheless market growth is a necessary condition for growth of sector profits even if it is not a sufficient condition. It has therefore been included in the rating of sector prospects on the basis of an appropriate scale. For sector analysis in the chemical industry the scale given below is the one used in Shell chemical companies. The center point, or average rating, corresponds roughly with the five-year average growth rate predicted for the heavy organic chemical industry in Western Europe. A star rating system gives more visual impact than a display of numerals.

Sector Growth Rate Per Year	Market Growth Rating
0–3 percent	* (minimum)
3–5 percent	**
5–7 percent	*** (average)
7–10 percent	****
10 percent and over	***** (maximum)

When applying this rating system to another industry it would be necessary to construct a different scale with a center point appropriate to the average growth rate for that industry.

The other criteria are used to qualify the basic forecast of growth of demand so far as their effect on growth of profits is concerned.

Market Quality.   Certain sectors of the chemical industry show a consistent record of higher and/or more stable profitability than others. These differences can be ascribed in part to differences in the quality of the markets which the various sectors serve. For example, in some sectors, notably those of a commodity type, profitability can be highly variable as profit margins contract and expand over a wide range as market conditions swing between under- and over-supply. This problem is often most severe in the case of commodity type products with a large number of producers. Again some sectors may have a chronically poor profitability record because the market is dominated by a small group of powerful customers who are able to keep prices down.

Other sectors remain profitable even in depressed periods of the economic cycle. This may be due to a variety of causes. For example, the market may be supplied by a few well entrenched producers who are content to let sales fall when demand goes down, rather than reduce prices. Or it may be that the consuming industry, able to add a high value, and having a prospect of further substantial growth accepts the need for suppliers to earn a reasonable living. Or, again, the determining factor may be the high technical content of the product, the performance of which has been carefully tailored to the needs of the consumer.

Market quality is difficult to quantify; in order to arrive at a sector rating it is necessary to consider a number of criteria in relation to the sector and try to assess their impact. The following are some of the more important questions:

(a)   Has the sector a record of high, stable profitability?

(b)   Can margins be maintained when manufacturing capacity exceeds demand?

(c)   Is the product resistant to commodity pricing behavior?

(d)   Is the technology of production freely available or is it restricted to those who developed it?

(e)   Is the market supplied by relatively few producers?

(f)   Is the market free from domination by a small group of powerful customers?

(g)   Has the product high added value when converted by the customer?

(h)   In the case of a new product, is the market destined to remain small enough not to attract too many producers?

(i)   Is the product one where the customer has to change his formulation or even his machinery if he changes supplier?

(j)   Is the product free from the risk of substitution by an alternative synthetic or natural product?

A sector for which the answers to all or most of these questions are yes would attract a four- or five-star market quality rating.

Industry Feedstock Situation.   Normally in the chemical industry, expansion of productive capacity is often constrained by uncertainty of feedstock supply. If this is the case, or if the feedstocks for the sector in question have a strong pull towards an alternative use, or are difficult to assemble in large quantities, this is treated as a plus for sector prospects and attracts a better than average rating.

Conversely if the feedstock is a by-product of another process, and consumption of the main product is growing faster than the by-product, pressure may arise, either from low prices or direct investment by the by-product producer, to increase its consumption. This would attract a lower than average rating.

Environmental (Regulatory) Aspects.   Sector prospects can be influenced by the extent of restrictions on the manufacture, transportation or marketing of the product. In some cases the impact of such restrictions is already quantifiable and has been built into the forecasts of market growth. If it has not, it must be assessed if there is a strongly positive or negative environmental or regulatory influence to be taken into account for the product.

Analysis of a Company's Competitive Capabilities

Three main criteria have been identified by which a company's position in a particular sector of the chemical business may be judged strong, average or weak. With suitable adaption they can probably be applied to the analysis of companies' positions in almost any business sector. The three criteria are:

(a)   Market position;

(b)   Production capability; and

(c)   Product research and development.

The significance of these criteria and the ways in which they are rated are shown below. In general it is convenient to review the position of one's own company in relation to that of all the significant competitors in the sector concerned as this helps to establish the correct relativities.

Normally the position being established is that of the companies *today*. Other points can be plotted for one's own company to indicate possible future positions which might result from implementing alternative investment proposals and product strategies.

Market Position.   The primary factor to consider here is percentage share of the total market. Supplementary to this is the degree to which this share is secured. Star ratings are awarded against the following guidelines:

***** Leader. A company which, from the mere fact of its preeminent market position, is likely to be followed normally accompanied by acknowledged technical leadership. The market share associated with this position varies from case to case. A company with 25 percent of West European consumption in a field of ten competitors may be so placed. A company with 50 percent in a field of two competitors will not be.

**** Major Producer. The position where, as in many businesses, no one company is a leader, but two to four competitors may be so placed.

*** A company with a strong viable stake in the market but below the top league. Usually when one producer is a leader the next level of competition will be three-star producers.

** Minor market share. Less than adequate to support R&D and other services in the long run.

* Current position negligible.

Production Capability.   This criterion is a combination of process economics, capacity of hardware, location and number of plants, and access to feedstock. The answers to all the following questions need to be considered before awarding a one- to five-star production capability rating:

Process economics. Does the producer employ a modern economic production process? Is it his own process or licensed? Has he the research and development capability or licensing relationships that will allow him to keep up with advances in process technology in the future?

Hardware. Is current capacity, plus any new capacity announced or building, commensurate with maintaining present market share? Does the producer have several plant locations to provide security to his customers against breakdown or strike action? Are his delivery arrangements to principal markets competitive?

Feedstock. Has the producer secure access to enough feedstocks to sustain his present market share? Does he have a favorable cost position on feedstock?

Product Research and Development.   In the case of performance products this criterion is intended to be a compound of product range, product quality, a record of successful development in application, and competence in technical service. In other words, the complete technical package upon which the customer will pass judgment. In awarding a one- to five-star rating, judgment should be passed on whether a company's product R&D is better than, commensurate with, or worse than its position in the market.

In the case of commodity products, this criterion is not relevant and is not rated.

Assignment of Ratings—Plotting the Matrix

The most straightforward method of assigning ratings for each of the criteria is discussion by functional specialists. They should be drawn from the particular sector of the company's business which is being studied and assisted by one or two nonspecialists to provide the necessary detached viewpoint and comparability with other sector assessments.

Although members of the group may differ in the initial ratings which they assign, it is usually possible to arrive at a set of consensus ratings. Where there are still unresolved differences, a representative rating can generally be obtained by averaging. More sophisticated methods of sampling opinion have been designed, using computer techniques, but experience shows that the group discussion method was to be preferred as the end result is reached by a more transparent series of steps which make it more credible both to those participating and to management.

Simplified System

In the simplified form of the technique each of the main criteria is given an equal weighting in arriving at an overall rating for business sector prospects and for company's competitive capabilities. This system of equal weighting may be open to question in comparing certain business sectors but has been found to give good results when applied to a typical chemical product portfolio.

In converting star ratings into matrix positions it is necessary (in order to avoid distortion) to count one, two, three, four and five stars as zero, one, two, three, four points respectively. One star is thus equivalent to a nil rating and a three star rating scores two points out of four and occupies a midway position where three points out of five would not.

It is also convenient in practice to quantify the criteria in half-star increments so that there are effectively eight half-star graduations between one star and five star. Half stars are shown as: (*).

The working of the system is illustrated by the hypothetical example in Table 16.1. In this, the technique is being used to assess the competitors in a particular business sector. In general it is desirable to record the arguments and supporting data in considerable detail but in this case the results of the matrix analysis are summarized in highly abbreviated form.

Weighting System

In certain businesses it is unrealistic to suppose that each factor is equally important, in which case an alternative method of analyzing company's competitive capabilities can be used, introducing objectively determined weightings.

An example of such weightings is given in Table 16.2. This is taken from a particular study on specialty chemicals, in which the four functions were considered to be the most important.

(a)   Selling and distribution;

(b)   Problem solving;

(c)   Innovative research and development; and

(d)   Manufacturing.

In addition to giving a more refined approach to the company competitive axis, the set of weighting factors is useful in its own right, indicating what sort of organizational culture is most apt in this particular business.

Interpretation of Matrix Positions

The results of the hypothetical example in Table 16.1 can be plotted on the matrix as shown in Figure 16.2.

Since the various zones of the matrix are associated with different combinations of sector prospects and company strength or weakness, different product strategies are appropriate to them. These are indicated by the various key words which suggest the type of strategy or resource allocation to be followed for products falling in these zones.

The zones covered by the various policy key words are not precisely defined by the rectangular subdivision arbitrarily adopted for the matrix. Experience suggests that:

(a)   The zones are of irregular shape;

(b)   They do not have hard and fast boundaries but shade into one another; and

(c)   In some cases they are overlapping.

The most appropriate boundaries can only be determined after further practical experience of comparing business characteristics with positions plotted in the matrix.

Matrix Positions in the Right Hand Column

Leader.   Competitor A, the largest producer with the lowest unit costs and a commanding technical situation, is in the highly desirable position of leader in a business sector with attractive prospects. His indicated strategy is to give absolute priority to the product with all the resources necessary to hold his market position. This being a fast growing sector he will, before long, need to install extra capacity. Although in all probability he is already earning satisfactory profits from Product X his current cash flow from this source may not be sufficient to finance a high rate of new investment. In that case the cash must be found from another sector of his business. Later, as the growth rate slows down Product X should be able to finance its own growth and eventually to become a net generator of cash.

However, in this hypothetical example, competitor A's position on process and feedstock economics is threatened by second generation processes. This suggests that he may need to strengthen his process R&D. A production capability of one star below market position reflects A's slight weakness in this area.

Try Harder.   Competitor B is in this position. It implies that products located in this zone can be moved down towards at least an equality position by the right allocation of resources. However competitor B does not appear to have any very special advantages in this sector and unless he can strengthen his position by, for example, licensing one of the new processes, he may be condemned to remain No. 2. This is not necessarily an unacceptable position in the short term but is likely to become increasingly vulnerable with the passage of time.

Double or Quit.   This is the zone of the matrix from which products that are destined to become the future high fliers should be selected. A company should

Table 16.1 Examples of Simplified Weighting System

Sector Prospects Analysis (Western Europe, 1975–1980)

		Stars	Points
Market growth	15–20% per year forecast	*****	4
Market quality			
Sector profitability record?	Above average.		
Margins maintained in over-capacity?	Some price-cutting has taken place but product has not reached commodity status.		
Customer to producer ratio?	Favorable. Numerous customers; only two producers so far.		
High added value to customer?	Yes. The product is used in small scale, high value, engineering applications.		
Ultimate market limited in size?	Yes. Unlikely to be large enough to support more than three or four producers.		
Substitutability by other products?	Very limited. Product has unique properties.		
Technology of production restricted?	Moderately. Process is available under license from Eastern Europe.		
Overall market quality rating:	Above average.	****	3
Industry feedstock	Product is manufactured from an intermediate which it-self requires sophisticated technology and has no other outlets.	****	3
Environmental aspects	Not rated separately.	—	—
Overall sector prospects rating			10

Product sector: Product X is a semi-mature thermoplastic suitable for engineering industry applications. There are two existing producers in Western Europe and a third producer is currently building plant.

Companies Competitive Capabilities Analysis (Competitors A, B and C)

	A	B	C	A	B	C
Market position						
Market share	65%	25%	10%	*****	***	***
Production capability						
Feedstock	Manufactures feedstock by slightly out-dated process from bought-in precursors	Has own precursors. Feedstock manufactured by third party under process deal	Basic position in precursors. Has own second process for feedstock			
Process economics	Both A and B have own "first generation" process supported by moderate process R&D capacity		C is licensing "second generation" process from Eastern Europe			
Hardware	A and B have one plant sufficient to sustain their respective market shares		None as yet. Market product imported from Eastern Europe			
Overall production capability ratings				****	***	**(*)
Product R&D (in relation to market position)	Marginally weaker	Comparable	Stronger	****	***	**(*)
Overall competitors' ratings				10/12	6/12	4/12

Table 16.2   Example of Weightings on Company's Competitive Capabilities Axis

	Businesses			
	W	X	Y	Z
Selling and distribution	2	3	6	3
Problem solving	2	4	3	1
Innovative R&D	4	1	0	1
Manufacturing	2	2	1	5
	10	10	10	10

not normally seek to diversify into any new sector unless the prospects for it are judged to be attractive. Only a small number of the most promising should be picked for doubling and the rest should be abandoned. Competitor C, on the strength of his successful feedstock process development and his licensing relationships with Eastern Europe for the X process, has already decided to double, i.e., invest in a commercial plant. He is therefore on the borderline of the Double or Quit and Try Harder zones: his production capability and product R&D ratings

Figure 16.2   Comparison of Competitive Capabilities—Product X

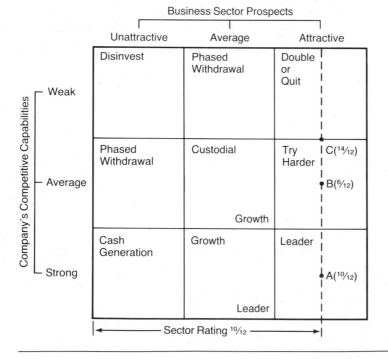

are both higher than his present market rating. Competitor C faces a more uncertain prospect of reaching a viable position in this sector than if he had been first in the field like competitor A.

Matrix Positions in the Left Hand Column

Business sectors falling in the middle column of the matrix are in general those in which market growth has fallen to around the average for the industry. In many cases they are the high growth sectors of a decade or two previously which have now reached maturity. Sector prospects can range, however, from 0.33 (below average) to 0.66 (above average) according to market quality, industry feedstock situation and environmental considerations. The significance of the key words in this column is as follows:

Growth.   Products will tend to fall in this zone for a company which is one of two to four major competitors (four-star market position) backed up by commensurate production capability and product R&D. In this situation no one company is in a position to be a leader and the indicated strategy for the companies concerned is to allocate sufficient resources to grow with the market in anticipation of a reasonable rate of return.

Products in this zone will in general be earning sufficient cash to finance their own (medium) rate of expansion.

Custodial.   A product will fall in the custodial zone of the matrix when the company concerned has a position of distinct weakness either in respect of market position (below three star), process economics, hardware, feedstock or two or more of these in combination. Typically, custodial situations apply to the weaker brethren in sectors where there are too many competitors. The indicated strategy in these situations is to maximize cash generation without further commitment of resources.

Experience shows that for any individual company's portfolio there tend to be more products in the center box of the matrix than in any other, and that these products do not just fall into the custodial and growth zones but also occupy intermediate positions between the two. In such cases the matrix gives less clear-cut policy guidance but the relative positions of the sectors still enable a ranking to be drawn up for resource allocation.

Matrix Positions in the Left Hand Column

Business sectors falling in this column are those in which a growth rate below the average for the industry as a whole is combined with poor market quality and/or weaknesses in the industry feedstock situation and environmental outlook. A typical case would be a sector in which the product itself is obsolescent and is being replaced by a quite different product of improved performance and environmental acceptability or one in which the product is serving a customer-dominated industry which has fallen into a low rate of growth.

Cash Generation.   A company with a strong position in such a sector can still earn satisfactory profits and for that company the sector can be regarded as a cash generator. Needing little further finance for expansion it can be a source of cash for other faster growing sectors.

Phased Withdrawal.   A company with an average-to-weak position in a low-growth sector is unlikely to be earning any significant amount of cash and the key word in this sector is phased withdrawal. This implies that efforts should be made to realize the value of the assets and put the money to more profitable use. The same policy would apply to a company with a very weak position in a sector of average prospects.

Disinvest.   Products falling within this zone are likely to be losing money already. Even if they generate some positive cash when business is good, they will lose money when business is bad. It is best to dispose of the assets as rapidly as possible and redeploy more profitably the resources of cash, feedstock, and skilled manpower so released.

In general, unless the prospects for the sector have been completely transformed as the result of some rapid technological or environmental change, it will be rare for a well managed company to find that any of its business sectors lie within the disinvest area; it will be more usual for a company to be able to foresee the decline in sector prospects in the phased withdrawal stage.

The Second Order Matrix

The second order matrix enables one to combine two parameters of an *investment* decision. This is distinct from examining the parameters of product strategy, the object of the first order matrix. In this instance we are relating the product strategy parameters with our priorities in nonproduct strategy notably location and feedstock security aspects.

Table 16.3 shows a classification of the business sectors in Figure 16.1, in order of priority for resources. It will be noted that new ventures and double or quit businesses only receive attention after those with proven profitability or cash generation have been allocated sufficient resources to get the best advantage from existing commitments.

Table 16.4 shows a list of nonproduct strategic options. These will usually have been developed at the corporate level and the company management will have a clear idea of relative preferences.

These two desiderata can then be combined in the second order matrix shown as Figure 16.3. It will be noted that three of the businesses appear twice, as their future development can be used to satisfy alternative non-product priorities, whereas three of them do not appear at all.

This matrix gives a very convenient method of presentation of priorities and feasible alternatives, from which the most appropriate decisions can be more easily resolved.

Table 16.3   Classification of Business Sectors in Order of Priority

Criteria	—Matrix position —Profit record —Other product related criteria —Judgment
Category I	Hard core of good quality business consistently generating good profits. Example: Engineering Thermoplastic
Category II	Strong company position. Reasonable to good sector prospects. Variable profit record. Examples: Dyestuffs. Chlorinated Solvents
Category III	Promising product sectors new to company. Example: New Chemical Business
Category IV	Reasonable to modest sector prospects in which the company is a minor factor. Variable profit record. Example: Chemical Solvents
Category V	Businesses with unfavorable prospects in which the company has a significant stake. Example: Detergent Alkylate

Other Uses of the DPM

In addition to the applications described, the Directional Policy Matrix can be used in several other ways.

Analyzing the Dynamics and Financial Balance of the Portfolio

The general shape of the product matrix plot for a diversified business will give an insight into its financial position. Thus a company in which the majority of products plotted fall in the mature phase (cash generator or custodial) may be expected to generate more cash than it needs to pursue its total strategy. If so it must either seek new areas of business in the double or quit or try harder areas, or else act in effect as a banker to other businesses.

Table 16.4   Nonproduct Strategic Options

Category	
1	—Joint venture to make olefins with petroleum company having secure oil feed-stocks.
2	—Make maximum use of land and infrastructure at existing sites.
3	—Develop new major coastal manufacturing site in the EEC.
4	—Develop a foothold in the US market.
5	—Reduce dependence upon investment in Europe in order to spread risk. Develop manufacturing presence in, *inter alia,* Ruritania.

Figure 16.3   Second Order Matrix

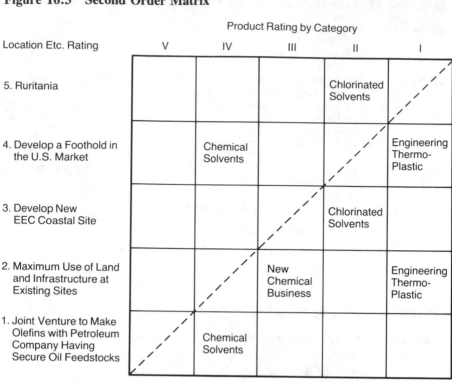

Conversely a company that has the majority of its individual product sectors in the double or quit, try harder or leadership areas will need more cash if it is to pursue the opportunities open to it.

Ideally the overall strategy should aim at keeping cash surplus and cash deficit sectors in balance, with a regular input or promising new business coming forward from research or to take up the surplus cash generated by the businesses already in or moving into the mature phase.

Building up a Picture of Competitors

The DPM can also be used to build up a qualitative picture of the product portfolios of other companies. Some insight into competitors' market positions, production capability and product R&D is in any case a prerequisite to arriving at one's own company's ranking in a particular sector. The matrix analysis will perform a useful function in codifying this information and highlighting areas where more needs to be obtained.

Once competitors' matrices have been plotted, and assuming that competitors will base their investment decisions on broadly the same logic, one can gain an insight into their likely future moves. For example, the matrix analysis will identify the points at which a competitor's production capability is weaker than his market position and hence will indicate that he is likely to lose market share unless he strengthens his position by further investment in manufacturing plant. Conversely it will also identify where production capability is stronger and a competitor is likely to seek to gain market share.

17

Strategic Marketing: Betas, Boxes, or Basics

Robin Wensley

The problem of resource allocation within the multiproduct, multimarket firm has received considerable attention in both the finance and marketing literature. Although much of the work in finance and marketing has been independent, a number of authors have recognized the potential interrelationships. Wind (1974), for instance, suggested the application of financial portfolio theory to product mix decisions, while Grant and King (1979) proposed that at a corporate level of analysis, the financial approach based on portfolio theory should be considered alongside such marketing classification schemes as the business planning matrix and the directional policy matrix. More recently, Mahajan, Wind, and Bradford (1981) have commented on the failure of many marketing schemes to reflect the distinction between risk and return that is so fundamental to the financial approaches.

This paper will develop further the comparison between the financial and marketing approaches. The current financial approach has developed from traditional capital budgeting based on discounting methods to the Capital Asset Pricing Model (CAPM) and the use of discount rates related to the systematic risk of the project, its beta, while the marketing approach has relied on the classification of either products or business units into various boxes. The marketing strategy literature contains numerous individual approaches for such box classifications, but as Wind and Mahajan (1980) imply, it is possible to consider such standardized models in two broad categories: those based on univariate dimensions, best exemplified by the market share/growth matrix; and those based on composite dimensions involving the subjective weighting of a number of factors, exemplified by the directional policy matrix but including others such as the A. D. Little and GE/McKinsey schemes.

This article first appeared in the *Journal of Marketing* 45 (Summer 1981):173–182. Reprinted with permission from the *Journal of Marketing*, published by the American Marketing Association.

When the article was published the author was Visiting Associate Professor in Marketing at the Graduate School of Management, University of California at Los Angeles.

In comparing resource allocation models consideration is given first to theoretical assumptions and the supporting empirical evidence and then to the relevance of each approach to crucial strategic issues at the corporate level. It is not possible to include in such a comparison the customized marketing strategy models (Wind and Saaty 1980), since as Mahajan, Wind, and Bradford (1981) recognize, such models tend to rely primarily on management's subjective judgment and, therefore, cannot be tested against either their theoretical assumptions or any general empirical evidence.

A Framework for Evaluation of Corporate Level Models

In economic terms the underlying principle of corporate level models can be simply stated: They are decision rules or heuristics for detecting areas of sustainable competitive advantage whereby the firm can realize economic profits or rents. Firms have been searching for profit long before the advent of the new strategy models, but at least in principle, such techniques offer an opportunity for a more focused search. To achieve such an objective, however, any particular model must satisfy three requirements:

- an internal consistency in the implied economic processes
- must be based on established empirical regularities
- must focus the search along critical dimensions rather than trivial ones, if it is claimed (Hopkins 1977) that a particular approach is to help managers think rather than give them answers.

The issue of simplicity is in itself not particularly relevant. A simple model that focuses on a particular critical dimension is likely to be more cost effective than a more complex one that concentrates on the same dimension. Indeed it has been argued that effective strategic analysis is more likely from simple add-on models that contradict the results of established analysis under certain conditions and, hence, generate a level of surprise. Provided such models are based on established empirical regularities, the simplicity of the model increases the likelihood that the surprises will be acted upon rather than the model ignored (Wensley 1979a).

Financial Models for Resource Allocation

Although the concept of discounting future cash flows has existed in economics for a long time, it was during the fifties and sixties that the Discounted Cash Flow (DCF) approach towards project selection became widely adopted in both U.S. and U.K. corporations. Considerable efforts were extended, both academically

---

[1]Customized strategy models do, of course, make implicit assumptions about the economic value of a more systematic and consistent apprasial of project characteristics. As such there are close relationships with the arguments for procedural rationality (Burton and Naylor 1980). These assumptions could also be tested against the evidence, but this is outside the scope of this paper.

and practically, to establish the relevant Weighted Average Cost of Capital (WACC), which could then be used as the criterion for project selection or rejection (Merrett and Sykes 1963). In a number of instances it became clear that such a DCF approach was being used not only as a method of identifying attractive opportunities but also as a means of generating an exclusive ranking on the basis of each opportunity's internal rate of return.

Such developments led some strategic analysts to voice strident criticisms of such a rigidly quantified and unidimensional perspective:

In evaluating the deployment of assets, the rigidity of quantification (DCF, for example) can distort the true picture of the various alternatives open to the firm seeking growth; those factors which do not lend themselves under conventional methods to numerical analysis tend to be left to intuition (e.g., risk analysis).

The reinforcement of "minimum rates" or uniform return criteria can often result in foreclosing growth through implicitly limiting a company's strategic choices.

Failure to come to grips explicitly with risk/return tradeoffs often displaces logical strategic analysis with traditional policies or "conventional wisdom" (Zakon 1971, p. 1).

The general criticism that overreliance on the now traditional means of project selection based exclusively on ranking by internal rate of return could lead to undesirable effects, became widely recognized. New developments occurred in both the areas of finance and marketing partially at least in response to such problems. Such developments were, however, independent and have remained virtually unrelated; as Anderson recently commented (1979, p. 325): "A virtual revolution has occurred in financial thinking in the last two decades, but few of the new technologies and approaches from finance have filtered into marketing."

Portfolio Theory and the Capital Asset Pricing Model

The finance approach starts from the appropriate rules to construct an efficient portfolio of financial investments. The most widely developed approach is that based on the mean-variance rule suggested by Markowitz (1952). At a technical level, however, it has been recognized that the mean-variance rule is only optimally efficient under certain assumptions, in particular that the investor's utility function is quadratic and the probability distribution of returns is normal. Such issues have led to the development of rather different rules under stochastic dominance principles (Mahajan, Wind, and Bradford 1981). Whether such concerns will in the end prove significant in the area of strategic marketing is a moot point. At the moment it seems likely that the basic principles underlying the CAPM approach, which is the means to apply Markowitz' portfolio theory to resource allocation decisions both at the level of the individual investor (Linter 1965, Mossin 1966, Sharpe 1964, and Weston 1973) and of the firm (Rubinstein 1973), will prove to be fairly robust to most of these issues.

The CAPM approach is concerned with the selection of the appropriate discount rate to apply to the cost and benefit stream for any particular project. The approach rejects the use of the same discount rate for all projects the WACC approach discussed earlier, and recommends a project specific rate related to the systematic risk of the project. The systematic risk is not the total risk but only that portion of total risk that is nondiversifiable from the point of view of the portfolio investor.

In the usual finance terminology, the level of systematic risk is characterized by its "beta," which is strictly the covariance between the asset returns and returns from a fully diversified market portfolio. The higher the beta of any particular project, the higher the required return for that project. A number of financial analysts have argued that there is a general relationship between increased market uncertainties and systematic risk. This would imply, for instance, that new project ventures may involve higher systematic risks than line extension projects for established products. On this basis, projects should first be sorted into different general classes:

Various types of projects are separated into risk classes according to their perceived risk, and each risk class is assigned a discount rate . . . for example, cost reduction projects are put into Class A (low risk), scale expansion projects into Class B (average risk), new projects into Class C (high risk) (Franks and Broyles 1979, p. 118).

Then higher return targets should be set for the higher risk categories so that, for instance, the required ROI is higher for new products than for line extensions to mature products.

Limitations in the CAPM

Because the CAPM has been derived from finance theory, it has a high degree of internal consistency. There are, however, a number of problems in extending the CAPM to resource allocation decisions on projects within the firm. An analysis of the project cash flows on the basis of a discount rate related to the project's beta gives reasonable answers. The problem is that the determinants of the correct beta in this case are complicated and related to such factors as the link between cash flow forecast errors and the forecast errors of market return as well as asset life, the growth trend in case flows, and the pattern of expected cash flows over time (Myers and Turnbull 1977).

On the issue of empirical evidence, despite extensive testing of the CAPM, Roll (1977) has shown that the many empirical tests purporting to show that the CAPM is descriptively valid, i.e., that the actual pricing of capital assets in the market follows the predicted behavior of the model, are, in reality, joint tests of both the CAPM and market efficiency, and that the CAPM cannot be tested directly on its own.

Finally, it has been recognized that the existence of a positive Net Present Value (NPV) against the appropriate risk adjusted discount rate cannot be taken as the automatic indicator of acceptance. A large NPV must reflect anticipated scarcity or competitive advantage. Management must, therefore, decide how much effort should be expended on the basic application of the CAPM compared with a strategic analysis of competitive advantage in any resource allocation decision.

Box Models for Resource Allocation

The Market Share/Growth Matrix

The development of the approach derived from the CAPM can be seen as one means of responding to many of the criticisms of the traditional capital budgeting methodology. Another approach to such problems has been the market share/ growth box classification system, probably best described by Hedley (1977) and principally attributed to the Boston Consulting Group (BCG).

The BCG approach focuses the analysis on the two axes of market share and market growth. Market share or relative market share is seen to be important as an indicator of relative competitive position, particularly in cost terms. Such an assumption is supported by the empirical evidence of the relationship between market share and profitability (Buzzell, Gale, and Sultan 1975) as well as the somewhat more indirect evidence of the experience curve effect (Hedley 1976). Market growth is, on the other hand, seen to be important partly because of the substantial cash costs of funding activity in high-growth markets; the need for substantial annual additions to both fixed and working capital often dominates any cash generated by the operation. Market growth is also seen as significant because of a hypothesized interaction effect with market share itself: It is suggested that it is easier to gain market share in high-growth markets.

The BCG matrix, therefore, appears to be an appropriate means of comparing the market position, in terms of share and growth, with the cash performance of any particular product. It also has the advantage that in many cases it is simple and easy to use, although problems of market definition and measurement have been recognized by other commentators (Channon 1979, Day 1977).

Limitations in the BCG Matrix

The BCG matrix has, however, been commonly extended from a simple diagnostic tool to a framework within which future strategic actions can be proposed. In such a situation we are not considering an approach derived from financial economic theory, as in the case of the CAPM, but one that is essentially ad hoc, and we need to look much more closely at two critical assumptions:

- the need for the corporation to maintain a degree of cash balance by the recycling of cash between products within the corporate portfolio;
- preferential investment in high market growth businesses.

The Need for Cash Balance

The capital market as a source of funds seems to be almost ignored in some approaches. Hedley (1977), for instance, states that most companies will have to divest themselves of certain activities solely because they will not be able to generate enough cash from other areas. The extent to which such an approach can only be effective with strict cash budgeting is left somewhat unclear, but the strong implication in this direction has been developed much further by other authors (Gray and Green 1976, Hall 1978).

This whole approach brings us back to the strategic mistake in seeing the corporation as an independent cash recycling entity. There are times in any corporation's history when it is difficult to raise either debt or equity, but this is very different from the assumption that in the long run the corporation cannot raise funds even if it can offer a portfolio of attractive projects to the market. This is back to defining the attractiveness of any particular investment from the market point of view. If we argue that we need an internal cash control policy to avoid investing in reasonable return projects in mature markets, then logically this must be because we are claiming that the opportunity cost of cash within the firm is above such a rate for relatively low risk projects. In this case, the corporation should probably be out in the market raising further funds.[2]

Preferential Investment in High Market Growth Businesses

In a similar approach to that of Hedley, Zakon (1971) implies that cash should be preferentially directed towards high-growth markets and away from established businesses in slower growth markets. The logic behind the need for such redirection seems to rest on two further assumptions: there are more opportunities for investing in high-growth areas, and the payoff for such investment is better, or at least it is easier to gain market share in high-growth markets.

In a simple sense, the question of more opportunities is clearly irrelevant because there is no need to direct cash towards a particular area when it already generates a large number of demands. The more subtle argument for such a bias rests on the assumption that it is in high-growth markets that technology is changing fastest, and so the competitive advantage of investing in the latest technology is the greatest. This was an argument used very effectively by the BCG (1975) to explain the rapid demise of the U.K. motorcycle industry at the hands of the Japanese. However, while there may be some correlation between market growth and the rate of technological change, it would seem more appropriate to focus the analysis on the critical variable of technological change rather than a partial proxy such as market growth, particularly in the context of a market such as the worldwide motorcycle market.

The issue of better payoffs is potentially very relevant, but the model is not well formulated. It is, therefore, not clear to what extent the ease of gaining share in high-growth markets refers to the short-run cost of gaining market share or to the long-run incremental benefit of increasing market share. There is very little empirical evidence, but Kijewski (1978) did undertake an analysis of the PIMS data in an attempt to estimate the cash costs of gaining market share points in different market environments. By looking at the difference between the cash flow/investment ratios for businesses that gained share as opposed to those that held share steady over one year as a means of estimating the short-term cash flow costs of gaining share, she concluded:

---

[2]This principle also works in the reverse situation. If the corporation is unable to find sufficient projects with adequate returns to use up all the funds available from its retained earnings, it should be returning such additional funds to its shareholders rather than investing in projects with inadequate returns.

Contrary to conventional wisdom, we do not find that the cash costs of gaining share vary substantially between moderate and rapid growth markets. When the cash costs are appropriately adjusted for average point change in market share in each environment, the cost of a point in share is only slightly lower in the more rapidly growing markets (and, indeed, lowest in low-growth markets) (Kijewski 1978, p. 8).

On such evidence it would be difficult to make a good general case for investing in market share gains in rapid growth markets because the short-term costs were substantially lower. Indeed on such criteria there might even be a bias towards investments in low-growth markets. To jusitify a general bias towards high-growth markets there must be significant evidence that the long-run incremental benefits of market share gains in such markets are greater.

If we were willing to postulate a model in which all product/markets followed the same Product Life Cycle (PLC) pattern of the same duration, then gains in market share would have greater longevity in terms of benefits if they were achieved at earlier stages in the cycle. Such a model would in fact appear to be fairly close to that implicity assumed by those who attempt to tie budgeting procedures to the PLC (Savich and Thompson 1978). The PLC, however, has been a notable empirical failure if the analysis focuses too directly on the issue of stages (Dhalla and Yuspeh 1976, Polli and Cook 1969). Such failure led a recent reviewer to comment that "The concept of PLC stages may be hindering PLC research by diverting attention from other issues concerning product life cycles" (Rink and Swan 1979, p. 232).

It would seem that the current limited state of empirical knowledge about the costs and benefits of investing in market share shifts does not support the contention that, on average, the payoff is better from investing cash in gaining market share in rapid growth markets. The market share/growth matrix approach also fails to reflect the considerably greater degree of risk attached to major and substantial diversification moves, which has been widely recognized in more traditional work on corporate strategy since Ansoff's (1965) famous four boxes.

In conclusion, any attempt to use the market share/growth matrix for resource allocation decisions implies a preference for high market growth businesses and the need to maintain a cash balance within the firm. There is little current empirical or theoretical work to justify such a preference.

The Directional Policy Matrix

A number of other criticisms have been levelled against the market growth/share matrix. Day (1977) in the most comprehensive critique focused on the problems of assumptions, measurement, and strategic feasibility. In particularly he indicated that feasibility was often dominated by other factors beyond share and market growth, which was suggestive of the nine-box classification. Some other critics have chosen to concentrate solely on the oversimplistic nature of the market growth/share approach (*Marketing News* 1978). Such critics have often been much more emphatic than Day in advocating the Directional Policy Matrix or its cousins (Hussey 1978, Robinson, Hitchens, and Wade 1978). In principle the Directional

Policy Matrix involves expanding the dimensions of the BCG matrix so that market growth attractiveness, and market share equally becomes a part of a composite measure of business position.

Limitations in the DPM

Applications of the DPM approach is complicated by the problem of weighting and combining different factors to generate the two dimensions, and it is in grave danger of leading the analyst to the tautological position of recommending preferential investment in those areas of highest market attractiveness and strongest business position. Hussey (1978) implicitly recognizes this with his tentative conclusion that the DPM analysis results in no surprises and, even to a limited extent, that there was a direct correlation between the discount rates shown by the projects via the normal appraisal system and those predicted by the position of the projects on the DPM. This would come as no surprise to those who see a positive net present value as a reflection of competitive advantage anyway, but Hussey does not address the question of whether he is claiming that a DPM approach would prove to be a less costly means of achieving the same result as the traditional method.

The DPM approach brings us back to the basic search for areas of sustainable competitive advantage, but there is limited evidence that it provides a useful additional form of analysis in such circumstances beyond a fairly comprehensive checklist and an idiosyncratic weighting of factors by corporate management.

Betas or Boxes: Projects or Business Units

The evaluation of the CAPM, BCG, and DPM schemes as corporate level models is given in Table 1.

We should have severe doubts about the theoretical and empirical support for the BCG market share/growth boxes when used to identify areas of sustainable competitive advantage. Both the CAPM and the DPM do remain focused on such an economic principle, but there remain considerable doubts as to the extent to which either can be seen as the critical determinant.

In practice the difference between financial approaches such as the CAPM and box classification systems is greater. A CAPM approach is related to individual projects, whereas box classification systems are most often applied at higher levels of aggregation, in particular Strategic Business Units. Indeed, it would be difficult to justify the cost effectiveness of box classification at the level of individual projects, since in most cases this would involve adding a more superficial approach onto the existing appraisal process within the firm.

In the context of project appraisal most evidence suggests that the sustainable competitive advantage resides in the specifics of the particular project. Hence, much of the current work on the issues of Strategic Business Units (SBUs) is likely to be based on an inappropriate grouping of product-market opportunities into a single unit. For instance, the current literature on the problems of managing units in mature markets contains the implicit assumption that few, if any, worth-

Table 1 An Evaluation of Corporate Level Models

Approach	Exemplar	Internal Consistency	Empirical Evidence	Critical Issue
Risk/Return	CAPM	OK	OK	Unlikely because numbers less important than competitive market assumptions
Unidimensional Classification	BCG	Dubious assumption about the importance of market growth	No supporting evidence for costs of gaining market share	Very unlikely because of doubts about the validity of the whole approach
Composite Dimensions	DPM	No clear theoretical or empirical statements to be assessed—seems broadly in line with competitive advantage approach but no additional empirical tests		Unlikely because it depends on management to make their own idiosyncratic assessments and adds little to current procedures

while projects will be generated by such SBUs (Hall 1978). Such an assumption challenges not only economic logic but market evidence. Goodyear, for instance, has decided quite consciously to commit its resources to increasing market share in the low growth auto tire business (*Business Week* 1978), while most of its major competitors such as Goodrich are clearly planning to reduce capacity and future capital commitments in the market. Many firms will have also experienced the fact that it is often economic for the major supplier to expand production in apparently low-growth markets as have Philips N.V. in the worldwide electric light bulb market; even more will have encountered the considerable number of highly profitable cost saving investments in such areas.

It is not, of course, difficult to see why such opportunities are geniunely attractive. As the more marginal firms drop out of the business, there are real opportunities for the dominant firm(s) to pick up additional sales. Such opportunities are reinforced when technical change requires all firms to reinvest in new facilities as the switch to radial tires has done in the U.S. market. Similar situations often occur when extra market effects such as tighter pollution regulations require significant incremental investment and, therefore, often encourage marginal firms to leave the market. The dominant firm that invests in such situations is really doing no more than building on its existing market strengths.

This all suggests that corporate management cannot avoid ensuring that each particular strategic investment proposal is assessed individually. A critical component of such an appraisal is the interrelatedness of the particular project with other current or potential activities of the firm, but such interrelatedness is not adequately represented by the generalized dimensions of box classification systems such as the DPM. Conceptually this implies that the distinction between the corporate level approach and the product/market level as proposed by Grant and King (1979) cannot yet be sustained. In principle, if we could identify classificatory systems at the corporate level that meet the classical criterion that the intraclass variability of projects was substantially less than the interclass variability, then we could maintain the distinction. We have argued that against such a criterion we really have nothing better than the traditional budgetary limits method in which projects are essentially classified purely by size or the broad categories of cost saving, line or volume extension, and new products proposed by financial analysts.

The Basic Issue: Aids to Assessing Competitive Advantage

We have argued that any analytical approach in marketing strategy must not be followed to monopolize the search for areas of sustainable competitive advantage. Wensley (1981) has argued that no economic theory can be expected to give us all the right answers, but can provide useful diagnostic questions that will indicate things to be done. Such approaches suggest, as already discussed, that any competitive advantage is much more likely to reside in the specific nature of a particular project rather than the broad characteristics of the particular business division that is sponsoring it. Economic analysis starts from the assumption that any such competitive advantage is essentially temporary but that it can be extended if the firm faces few direct competitors.

The economic analysis of barriers to direct competition starts from Bain's (1956) initial study. Bain's conception of such barriers was that new entrants into a particular market were likely to face substantial costs before being able to compete on equal terms with the established firms. The rather simplified conception of distinct but homogeneous markets inherent in this approach was, however, at variance with the market realities of customer segmentation, alternative distribution channels, and product differentiation. Caves and Porter (1977) have recently extended the barriers concept to mobility barriers reflecting the initial costs faced by any firm that wishes to change its overall position in the marketplace by opening up a new distribution channel, extending the product line, etc. The whole approach implies that because of such barriers, the level of competitive activity in any market will be less than it would otherwise be since existing firms are in some senses protected from further competition. Porter has also extended the concept to the implication that in certain declining markets the competition may also be more intense than it would otherwise be because of analogous barriers to exit (Porter 1976).

Mobility barriers distinguish between the performance of established firms in a particular market and that of new entrants. In developing markets the overall entry costs will be different for different firms; some will be better placed to develop production opportunities, while others will have better access to distribution channels and face lower entry costs in terms of this dimension. However, since there is by definition no such thing as established competition, the analysis of actual outcomes has to consider game theoretic assumptions (Shubik 1975), which creates further complications (Salop 1979).

Porter (1979) has argued that the principal empirical base of the BCG approach—the experience curve effect—can be seen as a particular form of a barrier to entry. However, the learning curve phenomena (Andress 1954, Hirschmann 1964) has been extended from direct production costs first to production overhead costs and then to all other value added items in the product. This development means that experience economies can be categorized in two ways:

- Some value added elements such as advertising should be assessed much more on the demand effect rather than actual cost;
- Experience in the various value added components in the final product market can be shared with developments in other, sometimes apparently unrelated areas.

As Day (1977) has indicated, the oversimple extension of the experience curve concept to all value added elements has created the danger that analysis is conducted in terms of building experience curve economies in the production and marketing of Product X.

More Comprehensive Analysis of Experience

In practice, in any experience analysis we should distinguish between both cost and demand effects and also specific and shared benefits. In particular, we should recognize the problems of cost-based, specific analysis and the benefits of other approaches.

For instance, an obsession with reaping the benefits of experience curve cost economies can result in a strategic posture in the marketplace that is severely disadvantaged in the case of significant shifts in market response. Such a problem is clearly documented for Ford and the Model T by Abernathy and Wayne (1974), and should be uppermost in the minds of any executives if they feel they are being persuaded to take major investment decisions based on relatively naive and unchanging models of market behavior.

However, some cost-based approaches require a broader sense of the related markets. For instance, the burgeoning market for solid-state devices in autos will substantially affect the scale economies for the production of such items in apparently unrelated markets (Boyd and Headen 1978) but the problem goes much further than this. The value added structure of particular products is likely to change over time, hence, the questions of relevant experience become more complex: Will the calculator market become an area where much of the value added is in distribution and marketing? If this is the case, the critical experience curve economies may well switch from production to such areas and thus change the set of corporations that are most competitively placed.

Demand based approaches may offer a way of avoiding some of these problems. For specific products the process of branding offers a way in which, if successful, a premium in the market can be maintained often over a long period. Shared opportunities come from activities in the market that provide future options for further development, such as the opening up of a new distribution channel.

We can, therefore, summarize the four broad options for experience-based strategies, and the examples in Table 2.

To avoid an overemphasis in our strategic analysis on specific, cost-based benefits, we should recognize some of the additional advantages of the other approaches.

Additional Considerations

Demand-based approaches have the advantage that, if successful, they are often difficult to imitate:

> In general there may be a high level of uncertainty as to the outcome of an advertising campaign. If advertising is successful or a new styling takes, an opponent may not be able to make a strategically successful countermove. If a price cut is successful, an opponent can counter by also cutting prices (Shubik 1959, p. 349).

Table 2   Examples of Experience-based Strategies

	Specific	Shared
Cost-based	Model T	Solid-state components
Demand-based	Branding	Distribution channel

In mobility barriers terms certain demand-based investments can carry the additional benefit that the relevant barrier grows for those following, either because of a direct increase in costs or the need to use less effective measures because direct imitation is not feasible.

Shared experience approaches offer two potential benefits: a greater degree of flexibility in the face of market uncertainties, and the development of positions that can be exploited at a later date. Within the study of the economics of internal organizations (Alchian and Demsetz 1972, Williamson 1975), it has been recognized that firms already in a particular market have the opportunity to adapt their behavior more efficiently than potential new entrants by selective managerial intervention.

There has also been a growing body of literature on strategic analysis that has focused on this issue either directly or indirectly (Ackoff 1970, Ball and Lorrange 1979, Per Strangert 1977). However, the limited empirical evidence is rather pessimistic about the ability of particular activities to adapt to major environmental change (Cooper and Schendel 1976), and indeed suggests that such activities as more effective environmental scanning (Montgomery and Weinberg 1979) often only delay rather than avoid the threatened demise. This would suggest that corporate management should assess the flexibility in any particular project in terms of monitoring as well as future potential changes, rather than rely on statements about general management skills.

The benefit of building a position, particularly in distribution and customer terms, resides in the options that are made possible before, and often long before, these options are actually realized (Wensley 1979b). Logically, such benefits are a result of the original investment decisions, and the additional value of these optional benefits should have been considered at the time when the investments were being made to develop a positional strength.

The basic conception of positional advantages is very close to the multidimensional definition of corporate strengths proposed by Simmonds (1968), but includes the explicit recognition that today's strategy is tomorrow's history and, therefore, the strategic decisions of today are shaping the strengths and weaknesses of tomorrow. In this direction, certain strategic actions will have much greater payoffs in terms of potential benefits to future actions than others. It is important in the strategic analysis of any particular action that the nature, scale, and value of such benefits is evaluated.

Conclusion

In undertaking strategic marketing analysis of any particular investment option it is important to avoid the use of classificatory systems that deflect the analysis from the critical issue of why there is a potential sustainable competitive advantage for the corporation. The market growth/share portfolio approach advocated by BCG encourages the use of general rather than specific criteria as well as implying assumptions about mechanisms of corporate financing and market behavior that are either unnecessary or false. The DPM approach, on the other hand, appears to add little to a more specific project-based form of analysis.

Both classificatory schemes would be positively harmful if used to justify some form of cash budgeting, since it is essential that any major project is assessed independent of its box classification. The financial basis of such an assessment should be an evaluation of the project's benefits against the appropriate discount rate related to the project's systematic risk or beta. It is critical, however, that the financial analysis should not dominate a thorough evaluation of the competitive market assumptions upon which the project is based. Such a project-based evaluation must focus not only on direct cost experience effects but also on the degree to which the project can be effectively imitated by others if it proves to be successful, the extent to which the project's progress will be adequately monitored and suitable changes implemented at a later date, and the particular ways in which the project will beyond its direct substantive benefits, also enhance the firm's ability to exploit further opportunities at a later stage.

References

Abernathy, William J. and Kenneth Wayne (1974), "Limits of the Learning Curve," *Harvard Business Review,* 52 (Sept-Oct.), 109–119.

Ackoff, R. L. (1970), *A Concept of Corporate Planning,* New York: John Wiley.

Alchian, A. A. and H. Demsetz (1972), "Production, Information Costs and Economic Organizations," *American Economic Review,* 62 (December), 777–795.

Anderson, Paul F. (1979), "The Marketing Management/Finance Interface," in *1979 AMA Educators Proceedings,* N. Beckwith et al., eds., Chicago: American Marketing Association, 325–329.

Andress, Frank J. (1954), "The Learning Curve as a Production Tool," *Harvard Business Review,* 32 (January-February) 87–97.

Ansoff, I. (1965), *Corporate Strategy,* New York: McGraw Hill.

Bain, J. S. (1956), *Barriers to New Competition,* Cambridge, MA: Harvard University Press.

Ball, Ben C., Jr., and Peter Lorange (1979), "Managing Your Strategic Responsiveness to the Environment," *Managerial Planning,* 28(3) (November/December), 3–9.

Boston Consulting Group (1975), *Strategic Alternatives for the British Motorcycle Industry,* London: Her Majesty's Stationers Office.

Boyd, Harper W., and Robert S. Headen (1978), "Definition and Management of the Product-Market Portfolio," *Industrial Marketing Management,* 7 (no. 5), 337–346.

Burton, Richard M. and Thomas N. Naylor (1980), "Economic Theory in Corporate Planning," *Strategic Management Journal,* 1 (no. 3), 249–263.

Business Week (1978), "Goodyear's Solo Strategy: Grow Where Nobody Else Sees It," (August 1), 67–104.

Buzzell, R. D., B. T. Gale, and R. G. M. Sultan (1975), "Market Share—A Key to Profitability," *Harvard Business Review,* 53 (Jan.-Feb.), 97–106.

Caves, R. E., and M. E. Porter (1977), "From Entry Barriers to Mobility Barriers, Conjectural Decisions and Contrived Deterrence to New Competition," *Quarterly Journal of Economics,* XCI (May), 241–261.

Channon, Derek F. (1979) "Commentary on Strategy Formulation," in *Strategic Management: A New View of Business Policy and Planning,* D. E. Schendel and C. W. Hofer, eds., Boston: Little, Brown and Co.

Cooper, A. C. and D. Schendel (1976), "Strategic Responses to Technological Threats," *Business Horizons,* 19 (February), 61–69.

Day, George (1977), "Diagnosing the Product Portfolio," *Journal of Marketing,* 41 (April), 29–38.

Dhalla, Nariman K. and Sonia Yuspeh (1976), "Forget the Product Life Cycle Concept," *Harvard Business Review,* 54 (Jan.-Feb.), 102–109.

Franks, J. R., and J. Broyles (1979), *Modern Managerial Finance,* Chichester: Wiley.

Grant, John H. and William R. King (1979), "Strategy Formulation: Analytical and Normative Models," in *Strategic Management: A New View of Business Policy and Planning,* D. E. Schendel and C. W. Hofer, eds., Boston: Little, Brown and Co.

Gray, E. G. and H. B. Green (1976), "Cash Throw-Off: A Resource Allocation Strategy," *Business Horizons,* 19 (June), 29–33.

Hall, W. K. (1978), "SBUs: Hot, New Topic in the Management of Diversification," *Business Horizons,* 21 (February), 17–25.

Hedley, Barry (1976), "A Fundamental Approach to Strategy Development," *Long Range Planning,* 9 (December), 2–11.

_____ (1977), "Strategy and the Business Portfolio," *Long Range Planning,* 10 (Feb.), 9–15.

Hirschmann, W. D. (1964), "Profit from the Learning Curve," *Harvard Business Review,* (Jan.-Feb.), 125–139.

Hopkins, D. S. (1977), "New Emphasis in Product Planning and Strategy Development," *Industrial Marketing Management,* 6 (no. 6), 410–419.

Hussey, D. E. (1978), "Portfolio Analysis: Practical Experience with the Directional Policy Matrix," *Long Range Planning,* 11 (August), 2–8.

Kijewski, V. (1978), "Marketing Share Strategy: Beliefs vs. Actions," PIMS letter 9/2, Strategic Planning Institute, Cambridge, MA.

Linter, John (1965), "Security Prices, Risk, and Maximal Gains from Diversification," *Journal of Finance,* 20 (December), 587–615.

Mahajan, Vijay, Yoram Wind, and John W. Bradford (1981), "Stochastic Dominance Rules for Product Portfolio Analysis," *Management Science, in press, special issue on Marketing Policy Models, Andy Zoltners, ed.*

Marketing News (1978), "Market-Share ROI Corporate Strategy Approach Can be an 'Oversimplistic' Snare," 12 (December 15), 12.

Markowitz, H. (1952), "Portfolio Selection," *Journal of Finance,* 7 (March), 77–91.

Merritt, A. and A. Sykes (1963), *The Finance and Analysis of Capital Projects,* London: Longmans.

Montgomery, David B. and Charles B. Weinberg (1979), "Towards Strategic Intelligence Systems," *Journal of Marketing,* 43 (Fall), 41–52.

Mossin, Jan (1966), "Equilibrium in a Capital Asset Market," *Econometics,* 34 (October), 768–783.

Myers, S. and S. M. Turnbull (1977), "Capital Budgeting and the Capital Asset Pricing Model: Good News and Bad News," *Journal of Finance,* 32 (May), 321–333.

Per Strangert (1977), "Adaptive Planning and Uncertainty Resolution," *Futures,* 9 (February), 32–42.

Polli, R. and V. Cook (1969), "The Validity of the Product Life Cycle," *Journal of Business,* 42 (October), 385–400.

Porter, Michael E. (1976), "Please Note Location of the Nearest Exit," *California Management Review,* XIX (Winter), 21–33.

———— (1979), "How Competitive Forces Shape Strategy," *Harvard Business Review,* 57 (March/April), 137–145.

Rink, David R. and John E. Swan (1979), "Product Life Cycle Research: A Literature Review," *Journal of Business Research,* 78 (September), 219–242.

Robinson, S. J. Q., R. E. Hichens, and D. P. Wade (1978), "The Directional Policy Matrix-Tool for Strategic Planning," *Long-Range Planning,* 11 (no. 3), 8–15.

Roll, Richard (1977), "A Critique of the Asset Pricing Theories Tests," *Journal of Financial Economics,* 4 (March), 129–176.

Rubinstein, M. (1973), "A Mean-Variance Synthesis of Corporate Finance Theory," *Journal of Finance,* 28 (March), 167–181.

Salop, Steven C. (1979), "Strategic Entry Deterrence," *American Economic Review,* 69 (May), 335–338.

Savich, R. S. and L. A. Thompson (1978), "Resource Allocation within the Product Life Cycle," *MSU Business Topics,* 26 (Autumn), 35–44.

Sharpe, W. F. (1964), "Capital Asset Prices: A Theory of Market Equilibrium Under Conditions of Risk," *Journal of Finance,* 19 (September), 425–442.

Shubik, M. (1959), *Strategy and Market Structure,* New York: Wiley.

———— (1975), *Games for Society, Business and War,* New York: Elsevier.

Simmonds, K. (1968), "Removing the Chains from Product Strategy," *Journal of Management Studies,* 5 (no. 1), 29–40.

Wensley, J. R. C. (1979a), "The Effective Strategic Analyst," *Journal of Management Studies,* 16 (October), 283–293.

———— (1979b), "Beyond the CAPM and the Boston Box: The Concept of Market Location," Bristol, England: Marketing Educators Group Conference.

———— (1981), "PIMS and BCG: New Horizons or False Dawn in Strategic Marketing," *Strategic Management Journal,* in press.

Weston, J. Fred (1973), "Investment Decisions Using the Capital Asset Pricing Model," *Financial Management,* 2 (Spring), 25–33.

Williamson, O. E. (1975), *Markets and Hierarchies: Analysis and Antitrust Implications,* New York: Free Press.

Wind, Yoram (1974), "Product Portfolio: A New Approach to the Product Mix Decision," *Proceedings of the 1974 AMA Conference,* 460–464.

————, and Vijay Mahajan (1980), "Design Considerations in Portfolio Analysis," working paper, Wharton School, University of Pennsylvania.

————, and T. Saaty (1980), "Marketing Applications of the Analytic Hierarchy Press," *Management Science,* 76 (July), 641–658.

Zakon, A. (1971), "Growth and Financial Strategies," working paper, Boston, MA: Boston Consulting Group.

Section
Five

The Planning Process
for Marketing Strategy

AN annual marketing plan typically contains sales and profit forecasts for each product category and brand over the coming year plus the level of expenditures budgeted to various marketing activities that will enable the firm to realize its forecasts. Most companies have well-defined procedures for producing the annual marketing plan and updating the plan at regular (quarterly) intervals. As we discussed in the introduction, the development of a marketing strategy involves more than simply producing a marketing forecast and budget. While the annual marketing plan translates a marketing strategy statement into operational terms, the development of the marketing strategy statement requires a distinct planning process.

In Table V.1, we have indicated four generic approaches for developing a strategic marketing plan. The appropriateness of these approaches depends upon the extent to which (1) the planning process is viewed as routine or unique and (2) the strategic issue or problem is focused (single-issue, such as an investment in a new-product development) or general (such as the positioning of an entire business unit).

In Sections II, III, and IV we describe a variety of analytical frameworks that can be used to develop the marketing strategy statement. These frameworks are typically used for examining unique but general strategic issues and focused strategic decisions. The articles in this section examine issues that

Table V.1   Generic Process Choices in the Management of Planning

	General	Focused
Routine	Marketing plan	Capital budgeting
Ad Hoc	External/internal consultants' report	Study group

arise when integrating the marketing strategy statement developed explicitly (by consultants, study groups, and planners) or implicitly (by capital budgeting committees) with the annual marketing plans developed at operating levels.

The development of a strategic marketing plan involves integrating the critical inputs discussed in Section II with the concepts and planning models presented in Sections III and IV. To examine how these factors are integrated, we need to consider the relationship between top-level managers, who are using the planning models to determine a strategic direction, and managers at the functional level—advertising and sales managers—who must use the allocated resources to implement the strategy. Inputs from both top-level and functional-level managers are required to develop an effective marketing strategy. The top-level managers possess a broad perspective on environmental trends and business capabilities, while the functional managers are in direct contact with the marketplace and have the best vantage point to determine what can be done. As we investigate the process of combining inputs from managers at various levels within the organization, we discover that the distinction between the strategic decisions of top-level managers and the tactical decisions of functional managers becomes blurred.

Marketing Strategy versus Marketing Tactics

In the introduction to the first section of this book, we attempted to make a clear division between a broad master strategy (focusing on the selection of both target product-markets and the nature of competitive advantage) and tactical decisions (such as the formulation of advertising themes or restocking policies for distributors).

George Steiner and John Miner have suggested the following set of dimensions with which to distinguish strategic from tactical decisions.[1]

1. *Importance.* Strategic decisions are significantly more important to the organization than tactical decisions. As Peter Drucker says, doing the right thing is more important than doing things right. If an organization directs its efforts toward the appropriate product-markets, it will be successful even if it makes mistakes in implementation. However, exceptionally good marketing tactics (advertising campaigns, sales contests, etc.), according to Drucker, will not overcome the selection of poor product-market targets.

2.   *Level at Which Conducted.* Due to their importance, strategic decisions are made by top-level marketing managers while tactical decisions are made at the level of product and functional managers.

3.   *Time Horizons.* Strategies last for long periods of time, while tactics have short durations. Strategic plans might have a ten year horizon, in contrast to annual marketing plans that deal primarily with tactical issues.

4.   *Regularity.* The formulation of strategy is continuous and irregular. The ongoing process of monitoring the environment might trigger an intense strategic planning activity when new opportunities or threats appear. Tactics are determined on a periodic basis with a fixed time schedule, typically designed to correspond to the annual budgeting cycle.

5.   *Nature of Problems.* Strategic problems are typically unstructured and unique. Hence, there is great uncertainty and risk associated with the formulation of strategies. Tactical problems, such as setting an advertising level or selecting salespeople, are more structured and repetitive in nature, so the risks associated with tactical decisions are easier to assess. In addition, strategy formulation involves the consideration of a wider range of alternatives than the formulation of tactics.

6.   *Information Needed.* Since strategies represent an organization's response to its environment, the formulation of strategies requires large amounts of information external to the organization. Much of the information is related to an assessment of the future and thus is quite subjective. Tactical decisions rely much more on internally generated accounting or market research information.

7.   *Detail.* Strategic plans are typically broad statements based on subjective judgments, while tactical plans are quite specific, supported by much more detailed information.

8.   *Ease of Evaluation.* Strategic decisions are much more difficult to evaluate than tactical decisions. The results of strategies might become evident only after many years. In addition, it is difficult to disentangle the quality of the decision from changes that might have occurred in the forecasted environment. In contrast, the results of tactical decisions are quickly evident and much more easily associated with the decision.

In this section, we will reexamine the proposal that a clear distinction can be drawn between strategy and tactics. We will consider the underlying logic, concepts of strategy, and actual managerial practice. As a first step in this reexamination, we look more closely at the assumptions underlying the sets of dimensions just listed.

Importance–Level–Time Horizon

The first three dimensions propose that, in general, strategic decisions are more important to the success of the business than tactical decisions, and thus strategic decisions are the responsibility of top-level management. As evidence of this proposition, we cited Peter Drucker's well-known aphorism, "It is more important to do the right thing than to do things right." Despite such powerful rhetoric, there is no evidence that strategy dominates tactics in terms of business unit performance. There may be a tendency to ascribe success to "good strategy" and failure to "poor strategy," but such an assessment is tautological.

There is a basic problem encountered in any attempt to determine whether performance is due to strategy or tactics. After the fact, many strategies can only be inferred, by outsiders, from a set of tactical actions taken. Some researchers have gone so far as to argue that this is true of insiders as well: the firm reveals its strategy to itself by its tactical actions.[2] There is little evidence that performance is improved when formal planning methods state the strategies explicitly before the tactical implementation programs are developed.[3]

In practice, both strategic and tactical decisions can have a substantial impact on business unit performance. Using football as an analogy, the success of the Dallas Cowboys under Tom Landry has been attributed to the brilliance of their strategic game plans, while the success of the late Vince Lombardi's Green Bay Packers has been ascribed to effective tactics—the fundamentals of blocking and tackling.[4]

Once we recognize that strategic and tactical decisions are so interwoven that it is difficult to determine which are more important, it becomes apparent that we can no longer assume that "important" decisions are made at higher levels in business. The blocking and tackling decisions of the Green Bay Packers are made by the linemen in the trenches, not by the coach or general manager. A final consideration is that strategic marketing plans, while written formally with a ten-year horizon, do not guarantee actual relevance over a time period longer than that of the tactical marketing plan. Indeed, much emphasis is placed on the need for periodic, often annual, reviews of the strategic plan.

The General Nature of Strategic Problems

The second group of dimensions, 4 through 6, focus on the nature of strategic versus tactical problems. These distinctions between strategic and tactical problems are quite similar to those developed by Robert Anthony to differentiate between the routine nature of capital budgeting and the regular and unstructured nature of strategic response.[5] Jospeh Bower subsequently found that such a distinction did not exist in large multidivisional corporations.[6] Although the distinction between routine and nonroutine problems can be rendered conceptually, there does not appear to be any justification for mapping this distinction onto the organizational decisions of capital budgeting and strategic reappraisal. Many strategic reappraisal decisions are imbedded in "routine" capital budgeting decisions. Thus, it seems more useful to identify the strategic and routine aspects of business decisions rather than to presort decisions into routine and strategic categories using a priori criteria.

Detail and Ease of Evaluation

There is less dispute concerning the last two dimensions as bases for discriminating between tactical and strategic decisions. Most people would agree that strategic statements are characterized by a lack of detail and thus are difficult to evaluate. Of course, one can adopt an alternative view that this difficulty in evaluating strategic decisions only reinforces the preceding argument—that a distinction is not possible. If strategic decisions are difficult to evaluate, then it must be an act of faith rather than empirical evidence that leads one to regard them as important. The issues raised in this reexamination show the need for better understanding of some of the underlying concepts about strategy itself, rather than resorting to unsubstantiated and rigid categorization of decisions.

Concepts of Strategy

The military perspective and an ecological viewpoint are two traditions that have influenced our thinking about the meaning of strategy in a business context. Although these analogies can provide some insight into the concept of strategy, we must recognize their limitations.

Military Analogy

Several recent articles have suggested that the military model can provide the missing links in our thoughts about marketing strategy.[7] Unfortunately, strategic military thinking is based on two assumptions that may not be appropriate bases for developing marketing strategies.

The first assumption is that certain resources are available only from directly controlled supplies. Clearly, there are critical resources in a business context analogous to the military resources of men, material, and supplies. Such resources in a strategic marketing context are cash, marketing and production capabilities, and managerial know-how. In a marketing context, these resources are generally available to the business from an external source. For example, a company can raise cash from outsiders if an attractive business opportunity arises. Contracts with advertising agencies can supply advertising creativity that may not be available within the firm. Independent manufacturer agents can be used to reach a new product-market.

In contrast, military strategy is based on the premise that resources may not be available from an external source when they are needed. Patton could not find an outsider to supply gasoline for his tanks.

The importance of resource control in military strategy provides an interesting focal point for marketing strategy. Perhaps marketing strategy should focus on resources that cannot be provided efficiently by external supply markets. In the previous section, we looked at strategic planning models that focused on cash, a resource that can be provided efficiently by capital markets. However, military strategy suggests we should base our analysis on marketing capabilities and know-how, resources that are not readily available from external sources.

The second assumption of traditional military strategy is that conflict must be viewed in terms of a direct readjustment of territorial boundaries at the expense of the enemy. This view that competition is a zero-sum game contrasts sharply with many marketing situations and is also at odds with the ecological model.[8]

Ecological Analogy

The ecological model concerns survival characteristics of the various species.[9] A basic premise of the ecological model is the so-called Principle of Competitive Exclusion which states that the environment cannot support two different species having identical needs. This premise suggests a more complex model of competitive behavior and survival than the "fight to the death" view propounded by military strategists and some strategic marketing analysts.

Another interesting premise of the ecological model is that we can distinguish between r-type species (those that survive on the basis of their rapid rate of reproduction) and k-type species (those that depend on their special abilities within an ecological niche). The product life cycle model discussed in Section III suggests that the effectiveness of these two types vary over the life cycle. In the early stages of the life cycle, r-types will be most effective because the primary concern is to expand a broad-based market. However, k-types will be more effective as the market matures because the emphasis then shifts to specialization and segmentation. William Hall has found that success in a business environment comes to companies that achieve either a low-cost position (r-type) or a highly differentiated position (k-type).[10]

One principal difference between the business and ecological perspectives is that while species are either one type or the other, no fundamental constraint prevents the metamorphosis of an r-type business to a k-type one at the appropriate stage in the market development. However, in practice, it seems that organizations undertake a change with difficulty. This is exemplified by the Ford Motor Company, which relentlessly and very effectively pursued efficiency in the Model T. This commitment was followed by the costly and difficult process of readapting to different market imperatives.[11] Another important difference lies in the substantial problems of classifying both individual firms and populations of firms (competitors) within an appropriate ecological framework.

In general, an ecological viewpoint implies a limited set of strategic alternatives for a firm. John Child, however, suggests that the body of strategic choices encompasses selection of the environment in which the organization wishes to exist (selection of product-markets) and includes the organization's attempts to manipulate its environment.[12] These proactive alternatives go beyond the "ecological" alternatives related to choice of organizational form and also raise important general issues about the ecological analogy. In particular, the widespread use of the term "market niche" in a marketing strategy context often fails to recognize the underlying issue of habitat (market) instability—changes in both customers and competitors.

In broad terms, the ecological analogy can suggest that one of the real issues in strategy formulation is the trade-off between specialization and adaptability. Unfortunately, it is much easier to recognize the criteria for a good specializer than for a good adapter. Thus, it is important to have a particular strategic focus at any one time and equally important to have a means of assessing the continuing relevance of such a focus, rather than to have the broad and nonoperational approach to strategy that relies on adaptive potential.

Nature of the Strategic Planning Process

The strategic concept adopted by an author has a strong influence on the nature of the planning process he or she advocates. However, all the articles in this section go beyond the simplistic idea that strategic planning is a one-way activity, from the top of an organization to the bottom. They share a concern for integrating top- and bottom-level perspectives, supporting the previous discussion that emphasized the intimate relationships between strategic and tactical decisions.

Balancing "Top-down" and Bottom-up" Processes

A commonly suggested method for integrating top-level and bottom-level perspectives is a process of successive approximations.[13] The planning process is divided into multiple stages in which corporate planners initially define objectives, constraints, plans, and goals. Business managers then take these inputs and develop a resource allocation plan while activity managers develop an action plan. Business managers evaluate the feasibility of the action plans and feed information about their likelihood of success back to corporate planners. Thus, the insights of activity managers are merged with the overviews of corporate planners through successive interactions across the three levels.

We should note, however, that the underlying assumptions of this process remain strongly hierarchical: the adjustment process accomplished lower down in the organization is generally conducted within the broader guidelines set at higher levels.

Article 18, "Strategic Market Analysis and Definition: An Integrated Approach," takes the move away from a purely top-down planning process significantly farther. George Day emphasizes not only that any broad definitions of strategic segments or market niches must be tested rigorously against detailed product-market data for evidence of discontinuities, but also that the more specific and detailed data may often be an undervalued asset in many planning processes. Such detailed data may in fact be a valuable source of ideas for effective market strategies. The article itself is not specific about the process implications of such a shift, but it assumes that the right balance can be achieved through dialogue and challenge between various managerial levels within the organization.

Strategic Incrementalism

At the opposite extreme from the dominant top-down view is the idea that the whole concept of grand strategy is fundamentally misleading. Proponents of this view argue that, in reality, strategy is the outcome of the whole series of minor tactical, and hence incremental, moves. Article 19, "Strategic Goals: Process and Politics," argues this position strongly. This view relates closely with the development of the concept of disjointed incrementalism in public policy analysis,[14] but it should be recognized that while this view has been accepted as having some validity in the public policy field, some have suggested that major systematic changes are also feasible in certain circumstances.[15] Others have argued that the analyst can use the process of analysis to facilitate change and development.[16] It is clearly true that in certain circumstances grand corporate strategy has been derived from a series of tactical decisions rather than providing a framework for tactical decisions. However, it is also true that some strategic decisions—the structure of the organization and its general direction and focus—exert significant impact on both the opportunities perceived within the organization and the ways in which these are assessed.

At least part of the reason for such differences in view can be explained by the distinction between an essentially normative rational analytic view at one extreme and a descriptive process view at the other. Two management researchers observing the same set of complex planning activities in any large diversified firm could come to very different conclusions as to what was actually going on. A simple way of drawing such a distinction is to consider the differences between the two underlying approaches that might be taken by such observers in practice,[17] as in Table V.2. We label such approaches "rational analytic" and "learning adaptive" to describe the overall perspective of the researchers. On this basis we can distinguish between what they will look for in terms of the role of senior executives, the forms their actions might take and the way of modeling the decision-making process itself in terms of both activities and outcomes.

Neither approach is "right" in an absolute sense but both, if applied properly, provide useful insights into the overall problem of development, including implementation, of marketing strategy.

Table V.2   The Impact of Different Research Approaches on What Is Seen

Overall Approach in Looking at:	Learning/Adaptive Researcher	Rational/Analytic Researcher
Role of Senior Executive	Context-Setting *Scene setting*	Prescriptive Action *Telling others what to do*
Strategy Variables	Organization Agendas Procedures *How the problem solution emerges.*	Analytical Frameworks *The forms of analysis that are used.*
Decision Model		
(a) Activities	Proposals Challenges Politicking *The taking of positions and the persuading of others.*	Parameter Estimation Outcome Calculation *Improving the inputs to the calculations and the evaluation of outcome.*
(b) Outcomes	A Strategy Choice Process *A more general way of describing the process that has taken place.*	A Form of Decision Analysis *An analytical method appropriate for the sort of decision made.*

Timing

Ever since the comment, "Nothing is more powerful than an idea whose time has come" was ascribed to Napolean, strategists have continued to emphasize the crucial role of timing in effective strategy development. The final article in this section, "Stragetic Windows," emphasizes the importance of timing in developing and implementing strategic marketing plans. This article illustrates, from a particular analytical perspective, that there is often a narrow time period during which the unique competitive advantages of a business match the opportunities arising in the changing environment.

However, again, life is rarely as clear-cut: some of the examples quoted in Article 20 remain less than obvious. Docutel went on to perform pretty well in the ATM business before being taken over much later by Olivetti, and Procter and Gamble, despite their significant entry, has more recently encountered problems in trying to shut-out new and existing competition in new markets. Like other key elements on the agenda for the development of a marketing strategy, the issue of correct timing cannot be evaluated by one particular approach.

Footnotes

1. George A. Steiner and John B. Miner, *Management Policy and Strategy* (New York: Macmillan, 1977), 22–24.

2. H. Mintzberg and J. Walters, "Of Strategies Deliberate and Emergent," *Strategic Management Journal* (July–September 1985):255–272.

3. Robert J. Kudla, "The Effects of Strategic Planning on Common Stock Returns," *Academy of Management Journal* 23 (1980):5–20.

4. While strategic parallels are often drawn between American football and business management, soccer is a more appropriate sport to use in deriving analogies. Business management, like soccer, is played continuously. Strategic decisions must be made while the game is being played. There are no opportunities to call time-outs in business for developing new plays. See B. S. Keristead, "Decision Making and the Theory of Games," in *Uncertainty and Expectations in Economics: Essay in Honour of G. L. S. Shakle,* ed. C. F. Carter and J. L. Ford (Oxford, England: Blackwell, 1972), 160–171.

5. Robert N. Anthony, *Planning and Control Systems: A Framework for Analysis* (Boston: Division of Research, Graduate School of Business Administration, Harvard University, 1965), in particular Appendix B: Robert H. Caplan, "Relationship between Principles of Military Strategy and Principles of Business Planning."

6. Joseph L. Bower, *Managing the Resource Allocation Process* (Boston: Division of Research, Graduate School of Business Administration, Harvard University, 1970).

7. H. Widmer, "Business Lessons from Military Strategy," *McKinsey Quarterly* (Spring 1980):59–67; and Philip Kotler and Pavi Singh, "Marketing Warfare in the 1980's," *Journal of Business Strategy* (Winter 1981):30–41.

8. Indeed, even in military terms there is a distinction between the direct territorial approach of a Klauswitz and the more subtle oriental views of a writer like SunTzu or Lidell Hart.

9. Howard E. Aldridge, *Organizations and Environments* (Englewood Cliffs, N.J.: Prentice-Hall, 1979); and Michael T. Hannan and John Freeman, "The Population Ecology of Organizations," *American Journal of Sociology* 82:929–965.

10. William K. Hall, "Survival Strategies in a Hostile Environment," *Harvard Business Review* (September–October 1974):75–85.

11.   W. J. Abernathy and K. Wayne, "Limits of the Learning Curve," *Harvard Business Review* (September–October 1974):109–119. (Article 9 of this book.)

12.   John Child, "Organizational Structure, Environment and Performance—The Role of Strategic Choice," *Sociology* 6 (January 1972):1–22.

13.   Peter Lorange and Richard F. Vancil, *Strategic Planning Systems* (Englewood Cliffs, N.J.: Prentice-Hall, 1977).

14.   Per Strangert, "Adaptative Planning and Uncertainty Resolution," *Futures* (February 1977):32–44.

15.   C. E. Lindbloom, "The Science of 'Muddling Through,'" *Public Administration Review* 19 (Spring 1959):79–88.

16.   K. Archibald, "Three Views on the Expert's Role in Policymaking: Systems Analysis, Incrementalism and the Clinical Approach," *Policy Science* 1 (1970):73–86.

17.   A wider range of perspectives on the nature of such phenomena are discussed and compared in much greater detail in Gareth Morgan, "Images of Organization," Beverly Hills, CA and London, England: Sage 1986.

Additional Readings for Section Five

Bracker, Jeffrey. "The Historical Development of the Strategic Planning Concept." *Academy of Management Review* 2 (1980):219–224.

Chakravarthy, B. S. "Adaptation: A Promising Metaphor for Strategic Management." *Academy of Management Review* 7 (1982):35–44.

Cosse, Thomas J. and John E. Swan. "Strategic Market Planning by Product Managers— Room for Improvement?" *Journal of Marketing* (Summer 1983):92–102.

Dyson, R. G. and M. J. Foster. "The Relationship of Participation and Effectiveness in Strategic Planning." *Strategic Management Journal* 3 (1982):77–88.

Emshoff, J. and I. Mitroff. "Improving the Effectiveness of Corporate Planning." *Business Horizons* (October 1978):49–60.

Fahey, L. "On Strategic Management Decision Processes." *Strategic Management Journal* 2 (1981):43–60.

Lindblom, C. E. *The Policy Making Process.* Englewood Cliffs, N.J.: Prentice-Hall, 1968.

Lindblom, C. E. "The Science of 'Muddling Through.'" *Public Administration Review* 19 (1959):79–88.

Mason, R. O. and I. I. Mittroff. *Challenging Strategic Planning Assumptions.* New York: Wiley, 1981.

Miller, D. and P. Friesen. "Momentum and Revolution in Organizational Adaptation." *Academy of Management Journal* 23 (1980):591–614.

Miller, D. and P. Friesen. "Structural Change and Performance: Quantum versus Piecemeal-Incremental Approaches." *Academy of Management Journal* 25 (1982):867–892.

Mintzberg, H. "What Is Planning Anyway?" *Strategic Management Journal* 2 (1981):319–324.

Mitroff, I. and J. Emshoff. "On Strategic Assumption-making: A Dialectical Approach to Policy and Planning." *Academy of Management Review* 4 (1979):1–12.

Quinn, J. B. *Strategies for Change: Logical Incrementalism.* Homewood, Ill.: Richard D. Irwin, 1980.

Rosenberg, Larry J. and Charles D. Schewe. "Strategic Planning: Fulfilling the Promise." *Business Horizons* (July–August 1985):54–62.

Stasch and Lanktree. "Can Your Marketing Planning Procedures Be Improved?" *Journal of Marketing* (Summer 1980):79–90.

Vancil, Richard and Peter Lorange. "Strategic Planning in Diversified Companies." *Harvard Business Review* (January–February 1975):77–84.

18

Strategic Market Analysis and Definition: An Integrated Approach

George S. Day

Effective strategy analysis hinges on the proper definition of the market. Yet, depending on the analyst's choice of served customer segments and the treatment of such issues as substitute technologies, geographic boundaries, and levels of production or distribution, the defined market may be very broad or comparatively narrow. At the same time, there may be no defensible basis for the choice of one definition over another, although the implications of a particular choice for strategy may be profound.

To further complicate the problem, the choice of market definition may also depend on the analysis approach that is employed. Two distinct approaches have evolved from different directions, each reflecting a different set of strategic concerns.

The first objective of this paper is to compare and contrast the two approaches. Generally we will find that *top-down* approaches reflect the need of corporate and business level management to understand the capacity of a business unit to compete and apply resources to secure a sustainable competitive advantage. *Bottom-up* approaches are usually employed by marketing planners and programme managers within the framework of a chosen product-market. The emphasis is on issues of product changes, advertising themes, promotional efforts, and price strategies, which imply a narrower tactical perspective.

With the increasing integration of corporate strategic planning and marketing planning (Hopkins, 1977) comes a need to reconcile the differences between mar-

This article first appeared in the *Strategic Management Journal*, vol. 2, pp. 281–299. © 1981 John Wiley & Sons Limited. Reproduced by permission of John Wiley & Sons Limited.

When this article was published the author was professor at the University of Toronto, Toronto, Canada.

ket analysis approaches that might materially influence strategic choices. Our second objective is to suggest a basis for better integration of top-down and bottom-up approaches. The issue is not which of the two perspectives is more valid, but how to harness them to achieve a balanced understanding. This can be achieved through the acceptance of multiple market definitions—each more or less appropriate depending on the strategic question—and the use of a mix of market analysis methods that can accommodate a variety of strategic questions. In particular, bottom-up methods have an untapped potential to broaden management's view of their market.

A prerequisite for effective integration of differing approaches to market analysis is a common model of the principal dimensions of a market. An emerging conceptual view of the multidimensional nature of markets promises to satisfy this requirement.

Multidimensional Market Definitions

A recent review of policy research has questioned the desirability of anchoring strategy in product-market space (Hatten, 1979), because of the restrictions imposed on thought by the common meanings of these words and concepts. Similarly, Abell (1980) has argued that it is dangerous for market definitions to be perceived as simply a choice of products, or business definitions as a choice of markets. Instead, he suggests the product be considered as a physical manifestation of the application of a particular *technology* to the provision of a particular *function* for a particular *customer group*.[1] A market is defined by the choices along these three dimensions. Also, Buzzell (1979a) has suggested that *level of distribution/production* be treated as a fourth dimension. These elaborations expand the conceptual power of the basic definition of a product-market as the set of substitutes which are perceived to satisfy the needs of a strategically distinct customer segment.

Customer Functions

Products or services can be thought of in terms of the functions they perform or the ways they are used. Thus, adjustable speed drives provide a speed control function, and pasta and macaroni may be used as nonvegetable meat supplements. It is the usage situation or application contemplated by the customer that dictates the benefits being sought. Then the manufacturer provides a package of functions, which may include auxiliary services and other enhancements, to deliver these benefits (Levitt, 1980).

It is useful to think of different levels of functions in a hierarchy beginning with a generic function. Thus, the speed control function can be subdivided by

---

[1]This section relies heavily on Abell's (1980) conceptual development. See also Abell and Hammond (1979) for application of this concept.

size of input power source, harshness of operating environment, sensitivity of control, and so forth. As the subfunctions become more narrowly defined, they will increasingly correspond to the specific benefits sought by the customer.

Technologies

The technologies are the alternative ways a particular function can be performed. Several different technologies may provide the same function or satisfy the same needs. For example, the generic medical diagnosis function can be served by X-ray, computerized tomography, and ultrasound technologies. Whether these technologies belong in the same market is a question that is usually resolved at the subfunction level. Often two technologies compete for some of the same functions, but in some specialized subfunctions only one can feasibly perform. This situation is often encountered with industrial materials such as engineered plastics.

Customer Segments

A segment is a group of customers with similar needs, sharing characteristics that are strategically relevant.

The choice of segments to include in the market definition is dictated by the significance of the differences between segments for the decisions to be made. For this reason, it is useful to think of hierarchies of segments, with diminishing differences between segments in the lower branches. At the top are "strategic" customer segments, which must be served by totally different marketing mixes; where virtually no element of the marketing programme for one segment is transferable to another strategic segment. This is the reason that tyre manufacturers approach OEM markets and replacement markets as entirely separate businesses, appliance manufacturers have different marketing strategies for retail buyers and contract buyers such as home builders, and food companies often have separate divisions for institutional markets. The need for different strategies leads to totally different cost and price structures.

Within each "strategic" customer segment, there will be further levels of groupings which are meaningful for strategy development—and hence lead to opportunities for differentiation from competitors. Much of the art and science of segmentation research (Frank, Massy, and Wind, 1972) has been directed at this type of segmentation. Geographic boundaries can define segments at virtually any level, depending on the extent to which travel time or transportation costs are a large element of total costs, or the market customs and competitive practices are significantly different.

Levels of Production–Distribution

In many markets, competitors have the choice of operating at only one level in the production–distribution process (either raw materials, intermediates, components, finished products, or distribution) or integrating forward or backward in the process (Rothschild, 1976). If different competitors operate on a number of different levels, then there is a question of whether the levels should be treated separately or combined.

Total and Served Market Definitions

The definition of the total market does not proceed one dimension at a time, but instead requires simultaneous consideration of customers, technologies, and functions. There are a myriad of possibilities, as the following illustrate:

(1) The Snap-on Tool Company defines its market as hand tools for the professional mechanic. This customer segment is reached solely with direct sales methods. No doubt Sears, Roebuck defines the market for the hand tools it sells to encompass many customer segments, beyond professional mechanics.

(2) A manufacturer of automated production equipment sells integrated systems that provide many distinct functions to one customer segment, the semiconductor industry. In contrast, a scientific instrumentation company defines its market as instruments for a single testing function sold to a distinct class of laboratories.

(3) At one time the market for liquid oxygen and other gases was supplied with bottled gas produced in central plants and trucked to customers. This market was redefined when small liquefaction plants could be built directly on customers' premises. The functions remained the same but the new technology created a distinct market of large customers with captive plants.

Each of these market definitions represents a choice of how far to proceed along each of the multiple dimensions of the market. Markets can be as narrowly defined as a single *market cell,* where each cell is described by a discrete category along each dimension, or be defined as a number of adjacent cells.[2] For planning purposes these combinations of cells are termed product-market units, or PMUs.

Within the total market, there is a further question of whether to serve the entire market or limit coverage to specific subsegments within market cells, such as retailers with central buying offices or utilities of a certain size. The choice of *served market* will be dictated by a variety of factors, including

(a) perceptions of which product function and technology groupings can best be protected and dominated,

(b) internal resource limitations which force a narrow focus,

(c) cumulative trial-and-error experience in reacting to threats and opportunities, and

(d) unusual competencies stemming from access to scarce resources or protected markets.

---

[2] This notion is developed further in Buzzell (1979a).

In practice, the task of grouping market cells to define a market is complicated. First, there is usually no one defensible criterion for grouping cells. There may be many ways to achieve the same function. Thus, boxed chocolates compete to some degree with flowers, records, and books as semicasual gifts (Cadbury, 1975). Do all of these products belong in the total market? To confound this problem, the available statistical and accounting data are often aggregated to a level where important distinctions between cells are completely obscured. Second, there are many products which evolve by adding new combinations of functions and technologies. Thus, radios are multifunctional products which include clocks, alarms, and appearance options. To what extent do these variants dictate new market cells? Third, different competitors may choose different combinations of market cells to serve or to include in their total market definitions. In these situations there will be few direct competitors—instead, businesses will encounter each other in different but overlapping markets, and, as a result, may employ different strategies.

Contrasting Top-down and Bottom-up Perspectives

There are pervasive differences between corporate-level planners and managers and business-level programme managers which stem from the breadth of the issues within their area of responsibility. In this and the following section we see how these differences may influence managers' views of the nature of markets and their preferences as to methods for defining markets.

The Top-down Perspective

A corporate-level planner or manager seeking to understand the strategic posture of a strategic business unit (SBU) or strategy centre[3] made up of one or more PMUs will want to know the following:

(1)   What is the *scope* of the business definition? A narrow definition will circumscribe the competitive arena. For example, the Letraset company could limit its scope to supplying dry transfer graphic designs to the commercial art market. A broader definition would recognize that Letraset is in the business of meeting the needs of commercial artists for convenient methods of creating graphic designs.

(2)   What is the basis for the choice of the currently *served* market? In particular, does the choice reflect the presence of significant discontinuities between the costs to serve different segments of the market?

---

[3]The terms business unit, strategic business unit (SBU) or strategy centre will be used interchangeably to refer to self-contained businesses with control over the key factors that determine their success in the market.

(3)   What is the current and forecast *performance* within the served market? What are the likely threats from present competitors finding better ways to satisfy market needs or achieve cost advantages, or from potential competitors entering from other geographic areas or offering substitute technologies?

(4)   What is the broad *strategic thrust* of the SBU, and what does it imply for resource requirements or contributions? This question will be assessed in the context of one or more portfolio representations which rely on forecasts of market share and growth, and stage of product life cycle analysis (Day, 1977; Hussey, 1978).

(5)   What are the *opportunities* for growth into new products or new markets that can best utilize the SBU experience base (Hanan, 1974)? That is, what is the most attractive growth sector for the SBU?

Underlying these questions is a view of markets as arenas of profitable competition where the corporate resources can be used to achieve a differential advantage. These resources are usually *supply factors:* such as raw materials, production processes, and technologies, plus the base of experience gained in serving the present market.

The Bottom-up Perspective

Within the SBU—and especially at the level of the product manager or market manager with responsibility for a PMU—there is a significant shift in orientation toward market analysis issues. The type and mix of markets are taken as given and the emphasis shifts to "how to be successful in the business." The salient questions thus relate in one way or another to short-run programmes for enhancing performance. They include such specific concerns as:

(1)   What is our present and forecast *performance* within our served market? Elements of this question deal with specific areas of vulnerability to competition, and ability to satisfy the evolving needs of customers within the served market.

(2)   How can we improve the *efficiency* of our programmes through better targeting of advertising promotions and purchase incentives, improving distribution coverage, and so forth?

(3)   What opportunities exist for improving *profitability* within the served market by price changes, repositioning, product enhancements and additions or deletions of items in the product line?

In terms of the multidimensional market definition, these questions deal with the fine-grained structure of the product alternatives and customer segments within the *market cells* (see Figure 1). A business may elect to serve a number of related market cells or parts of a few cells, but for each one it must tailor a marketing strategy. This is the locus of the short-run marketing plan.

The bottom-up market analysis issues can be grouped into two categories: *positioning* the company's offering and choosing *target customer segments* whose distinct patterns of needs dictate separate marketing programmes. The objectives

Figure 1 Multidimensional Market Analysis

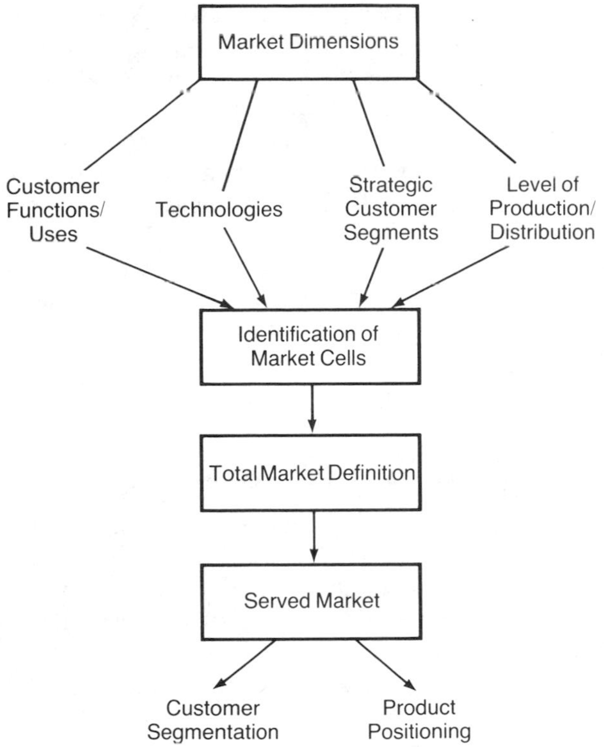

of both segmentation and positioning are the same: to seek competitive advantage through doing a better job of satisfying customer requirements.

Product positioning refers to the customer's perceptions of the place a product or brand occupies in a given market. In some markets a position is achieved by associating the benefits of the brand with the needs or life style of a customer group (as Brim decaffeinated coffee appeals to the concerned coffee drinker segment with the theme "you can drink as much as you used to"). More often, positioning involves the differentiation of the company's offering from the competition by making or implying a comparison in terms of specific attributes such as price or performance features. Thus, QYX line of computerized typewriters was introduced with a price range of $1,400 to $7,750, which corresponded to a gap in the IBM product line.

Customer segmentation is the process of subdividing the market into groups of customers whose members behave in the same way or have similar requirements. Actionable segments should be identifiable and accessible, represent enough volume potential to justify separate treatment (Kotler, 1977), and differ from other segments on dimensions that are meaningful for the design of strategy. This last condition means that distinctions between segments should relate to dimensions which influence the selection of one competitor over another.

The most widely used segmentation model (Wind, 1978) begins with the identification of a *basis for segmentation*—a product-specific factor which reflects differences in customer requirements and responsiveness to marketing variables. Possibilities include customers' product purchase patterns, product usage, benefits sought, price and technical service sensitivity, intentions-to-buy, and brand preference and loyalty. The choice will be largely dictated by the decision to be made.

Then, *segment descriptors* are chosen based on their ability to identify segments, account for variance in the segmentation basis, and invoke competitive strategy implications. These must be carefully tailored to the context. For example, a manufacturer of mining equipment has found that the value-in-use of his equipment (a function of initial and operating cost and productivity) relative to the competition depends less on the commodity being mined than on the specific physical profile of the mine (Johnson, 1978). Similarly, the geographic location of the mine affects its fixed cost structure and thus the comparative operating costs and productivity per unit of output for different types of equipment.

Implications of Differences in Perspective

Pervading the bottom-up perspective—and directing the search for protected market positions and target segments—is the customer's perspective. The product or market manager focuses on anticipating and reacting to shifts in the fine-grain structure of the market as a result of changes both in customers' requirements, needs, and capabilities and in the ability of competitors to satisfy these changes. This view of strategy as evolving from marketplace circumstances is very different from the top-down view which begins with supply factors. These differences are summarized and highlighted in Table 1. What should also be emphasized is that both perspectives are striving for the same end, which is the implementation of strategies which will yield a profitable competitive advantage.

Table 1   The View from the Top-down versus the Bottom-up

Issue	Top-down View	Bottom-up View
1. Definition of market	Markets are arenas of competition where corporate resources can be profitably employed	Markets are shifting patterns of customer requirements and needs which can be served in many ways
2. Orientation to market environment	Strengths and weaknesses relative to competition ▪ cost position ▪ ability to transfer experience ▪ market coverage	Customer perceptions of competitive alternatives ▪ match of product features and customer needs ▪ positioning
3. Identification of market segments	Looks for cost discontinuities	Emphasizes similarity of buyer responses to market efforts
4. Identification of market niches to serve	Exploits new technologies, cost advantages, and competitor's weaknesses	Finds unsatisfied needs, unresolved problems, or changes in customer requirements and capabilities
5. Time frame	2 to 5 years	1 to 3 years

Alternative Methods of Market Analysis and Definition

The characteristic differences between the top-down and bottom-up perspectives are reflected in their respective approaches to identifying competitive market cells.

Top-down Approaches to Market Analysis

The breadth of this perspective dictates consideration of a wide variety of present and prospective markets for resource allocation purposes. To implement this analysis, two requirements are paramount: (a) large amounts of data on market size, trends, plant capacities, and so forth must be in easily accessible form, and (b) the emphasis on resource allocation and competitive position puts a premium on the assessment of one's relative cost standing and the transferability of the experience base beyond presently served markets. These requirements dictate data of certain forms and types.

Supply-oriented Approaches

The first implementation requirement means a reliance on published data, which are almost invariably organized by industry group. The industry groups are defined according to supply criteria such as similarity of manufacturing processes, raw materials, physical appearance, technology, or method of operation. The virtue of such industry groups, which are the backbone, for example, of the Standard Industrial Classification system used in the United States, is their wide acceptance due to availability of data, ease of implementation, and seeming stability.

The problems are most apparent with the function and customer dimensions of markets. Two competitive products which may serve the same function but with different technologies are almost invariably in different SIC categories. For example, "polyvinyl" rain gutters and "sheet metal" gutters are in different 3-digit categories. These two technologies may not always compete directly, but when they do, they belong in the same market. This cannot be ascertained from data based on similarity of supply factors. Similarly, customer market segments defined by industries may be inappropriate either because they are too broad (and thus obscure important differences in needs and buying patterns) or too narrow (if the differences between segments are inconsequential for strategic purposes). In short, supply criteria seldom serve as a meaningful basis for grouping customers.

Identification of Cost/Investment Discontinuities

With this approach the analyst evaluates the market to see whether a significant discontinuity in the pattern of costs, capital requirements, and margins exists along one or more dimensions of the market. The resulting category boundaries represent barriers that insulate prices and profits from the activities of competitors outside the segment as well as discourage easy entry directly into the market by potential competitors. Thus, within the boundaries the relative profitability of competitors can be meaningfully compared.

The most important factors contributing to these discontinuities are:

(1)   economies of scale

(2)   transferability of experience

(3)   capital requirements.[4]

A boundary is encountered when participation in an adjacent category—whether a different technology, customer group, or function—is impeded by the need to enter with a large-scale operation to avoid a cost disadvantage, the need to invest substantial financial resources for fixed facilities, additional working capital, and start-up costs, or the need to employ a very different marketing mix. Conversely, barriers may not be severe if important elements of the company's experience base can be transferred. For example, a significant proportion of Texas Instrument's experience with semiconductor manufacturing is applicable to such related products as random-access memories and hand-held calculators. On the other hand, a producer of refractories for steel furnaces may find that most of its experience is limited to that specific setting.

Of course, experience is not restricted to production and technology factors but may reflect the accumulated output of all activities contributing to the value added of the product (Hedley, 1976). For example, the costs of marketing, distribution, and service often depend on experience and present a combination of scale and knowledge factors. Whether the company's experience and related resources can be employed more broadly depends on the similarity of requirements across customer segments, technologies, and functions. The identification of these similarities is analogous to the specification of the "common thread" (Ansoff, 1965).

Market boundaries identified in terms of cost discontinuities reveal opportunities for market niches which the firm can protect from competitive inroads and dominate for long-run profit.[5] Ideally there should be a minimum of direct competition within this market so the company can dominate the experience base necessary to serve that market. However, if the cost discontinuity is created by a cost element whose relative importance is declining, or the experience base is shared with outside suppliers of component parts or production technology who will sell to all prospective competitors, then the narrow market definition lacks enduring value.

When the market is defined very broadly in order to ensure competitive levels of experience and scale economies for a major cost element, it encompasses many related products whose principal common link is the shared experience base. For example, the cost position of many consumer packaged goods products is

---

[4]Porter (1979) discusses several other sources of discontinuities, including product differentiation (which limits the extent to which brand names can be utilized in adjacent markets) and lack of access to distribution channels.

[5]It may or may not be possible for a company to participate in the markets on both sides of a cost discontinuity. Sometimes this barrier is created by different customer segments, different patterns of needs, and responsiveness to marketing variables. For example, as some markets evolve toward maturity, the limited volume, high price, high cost-to-serve customer segment separates from the high volume, low cost-to-serve segment for the same function and technologies. Companies encounter serious problems in attempting to straddle two such disparate markets.

dictated by experience in sales and distribution through grocery outlets and advertising/promotion to mass markets, activities which are a significant proportion of total cost (Buzzell, 1979*b*). This broad perspective on market definition is very useful in the consideration of new ventures. It may be inappropriate for other purposes, such as evaluating performance in a served market, since it usually embraces a number of different competitive arenas. Similarly, a manufacturer of central air conditioners must adopt very different strategies for the modernization and new residential markets, yet product cost is dictated largely by the combined volume of sales in the two segments.

Bottom-up Approaches to Market Analysis

There is no lack of marketing research techniques that can be used for product positioning or identifying customer segments (Wind, 1978). Such methods as focus groups, problem detection studies, market mapping, conjoint analysis, trade-off analysis, and gain–loss brand switching analysis have proven their value in many applications. However, such studies are almost always undertaken from a bottom-up perspective. That is, the strategic market definition is taken as given and the focus is on the details of brand competition and customer differences within a market cell.

Yet, there is nothing inherent in many of these bottom-up techniques which mandates such a restricted role; it is a consequence of how and when they have been used. Consequently, their potential for clarifying strategic issues is largely untapped. The following discussion of one technique illustrates what can be done.

Substitution-in-Use Analysis

This category of techniques is based on the idea of strategically meaningful distinctions between functions and between technologies which represent the ways in which combinations of functions can be provided. But instead of starting with the function provided, situation-in-use analysis proceeds from the customer's perspective (Day, Shocker, and Srivastava, 1979).

Three premises underlie the concept of substitution-in-use:

1. People seek the benefits that products provide rather than the products *per se*.

2. The needs to be satisfied and the benefits which are sought are dictated by the usage situations or applications being contemplated.

3. Products/technologies are considered part of the set of substitutes if they are perceived to provide functions which satisfy the needs determined by intended usage.

Changing the perspective from function provided to benefits and needs which are contingent on the situation gives us another way of defining a market as the set of products viewed as substitutes within those usage situations in which similar patterns of benefits are sought. Customer segments are those groups for whom the usage situation is relevant.

This definition has several advantages over the technology/function approach, because the notions of benefits, usage situations, and consideration set are meaningful to customers and measurable. The introduction of intended usage into the definition also clarifies and enriches the complex nature of product "function."

Implications for Defining Markets for Strategic Planning Purposes

What is clearly needed is a dual approach to strategic market analysis, one which balances the production and cost-oriented top-down perspective with the customer's viewpoint. Otherwise, shifts in customer requirements and needs that may create new segments will be overlooked, and competitive threats from different technologies which can serve the same functions or satisfy similar needs will not be appreciated. By the same token, the customer perspective should not overwhelm the economic realities which dictate the ability to compete profitably.

This section explores various steps which can be taken to ensure that market definitions reflect a proper balance of cost and market factors and, thereby, yield meaningful strategic insights into the company's markets. The starting point is a recognition that different market definitions will be needed to satisfy different purposes, ranging from short-run performance evaluation to long-run analysis of threats and opportunities. This goal can be facilitated by ensuring that the strategic planning framework—which links business units or strategy centres and PMUs—is compatible with these different purposes. To test alternative planning frameworks for strategic relevance, explicit criteria are needed to analyse the interrelationships among PMUs. A key question is the relative importance of cost, demand, and other criteria for comparing PMUs. This question can be addressed by using the bottom-up market analysis techniques to understand the complexity of the market.

Multiple Market Definitions

There are many possible market definitions from which to choose. These alternatives are neither true nor false—only more or less useful for the purpose at hand.

Performance Evaluation and Short-Run Marketing Planning.   For these purposes emphasis should be on the presently served market, since this is the arena within which the organization is trying to satisfy customer needs. A single market share measure, however, does not provide much insight. Instead, shares should be determined for all relevant customer segments.

For short-run planning, the priority is to find subgroups of customers with distinctive patterns of needs and responsiveness to marketing variables in order to use these as a basis to gain and maintain a differential advantage within the served market. Such customer characteristics as industry type, volume requirements, reliance on technical service, and so forth provide useful bases for this kind of analysis. Competitors can build defensible positions based on vendor preferences and distribution/service coverage by tailoring their overall marketing strategy to the needs of these customer segments.

To evaluate the marketing plan, one should measure efficiency of performance within these defined target segments. This can provide diagnostic insights as a basis for continuing improvements. For the latter purpose, it is important to use all feasible units of measurements, such as share of revenue, unit volume, and number of transactions such as prescriptions (Majaro, 1977).

Strategic Planning.   For strategic planning, involving decisions about resource allocations within the business and product portfolio, and evaluation of financial and market performance objectives, broader market definitions may be required. The identification of strategically relevant boundaries will be guided by: (1) the extent to which relative scale economies and experience in key "cost sectors" are shared along the technology, function, and customer dimensions (Buzzell, 1979a); and (2) differentials in industry maturity or stage of life cycle as measured by current and prospective category growth, which in turn depends on untapped market potential and the presence of substitutes. Other indicators of appropriate boundaries include customer and technological stability, rate of competitive entry and exit, and the consequent distribution and stability of market shares. Patel and Younger (1978) note

> Such an examination may reveal considerable differences in industry maturity between car radios with built-in cassette players and traditional car radios. Differences in industry maturity and/or competitive position may also exist with regard to regional markets, consumer groups and distribution channels. For example, the market for cheap car radios sold by cash-and-carry discount houses to end-users doing their own installation may be growing much faster in some countries than the market served by specialty retail stores providing installation services.

This type of analysis requires the iterative use of top-down and bottom-up analysis, where the market definitions from one perspective are tested for strategic relevance and refined from other perspectives. Neither is adequate alone. We will return to this point in the discussion of the relationship of SBUs and PMUs.

Analysis of Threats and Opportunities.   Analysis of threats (competitive surveillance) and opportunities (new ventures) require the broadest definitions. As Simmonds (1968) noted, "the existence of an opportunity to make use of strengths is implicit in the definition of a strength—it implies a potentially profitable market given competitor's products, resources, and likely reactions." However, an adjacent market that represents a potential direction for future growth is also a possible source of new competition. Therefore, it is important to look at the market from the competitors' perspectives.

Various competitors may use quite different definitions for the same strategic purpose, and thus will arrive at different decisions. The concept of strategic groups (Porter, 1976) can be used to classify competitors according to the similarity or difference in their strategies, including degree of integration, extent of advertising and branding, use of captive or exclusive distributors, whether they are full-line or specialist sellers, and so forth. Each group reflects a choice which depends on its definition of the market and the resources it has available to compete.

The Strategic Planning Framework: Linking Business Units and Product-Market Units

For most multiple product firms, the SBU or strategy centre form of organization is regarded as a prerequisite to effective strategic management. A business unit is an independent component of the firm for which a discrete strategy can be developed. Ideally, it should have control over most of the factors that affect business-level strategy (Hall, 1978). This ideal is seldom achieved in practice, for most SBU definitions involve compromise and trade-offs. On the one hand, it is desirable that an SBU include as few product-market units (PMUs) as possible to encourage the development of focused product-market strategies (Hofer and Schendel, 1978). On the other hand, product-market units often cannot be treated as independent strategic entities either because they share resources with other PMUs, or there would be disjointed and ineffective strategies because of excessive fragmentation (Lorange, 1980).

A PMU is both the lowest level in the organization at which strategic planning takes place, and a building block which helps to make up an SBU. The choice of PMUs to group together within an SBU will depend on their similarity on strategically relevant factors. In effect, a clustering procedure is used in which each PMU is compared with every other PMU to determine their interrelationship along a variety of top-down (cost and technology-related) and bottom-up (market) criteria. This approach was used by a manufacturer of air conditioning equipment ranging from residential air conditioners to large commercial packages (self-contained units mounted in roof-tops or slabs) to custom engineered units for large-scale industrial cooling applications. The criteria used to compare the PMUs are similar to those suggested earlier in the discussion of strategically relevant boundaries. A simplified version of this manufacturer's work sheet is shown in Table 2 to illustrate how the criteria were employed. One major simplification is that the geographic dimension of the PMUs is not shown.[6] Also, for confidentiality reasons, the details of the technology criteria are not revealed.

Relative Importance of Cost and Demand Factors.　A quick scan of Table 2 reveals a common problem; there are no evident groupings for which there is not some overlap of PMUs. In part this problem is a consequence of assigning equal importance to each criterion, which will usually be inappropriate. However, the concepts developed earlier can be employed to identify circumstances where one set of factors should dominate the other, or facilitate subjective assessments of the relative importance of each criterion. Specifically, the relative importance of cost

---

[6] A good illustration of the definition of SBUs which balances global business considerations against local geographic market requirements can be found in the *Corning Glass Works: International (B)* case study (Intercollegiate Case Clearing House No. 9-379-052, 1978).

Table 2   Criteria for Comparing PMUs

	Product Market Units					
Criteria	Room Air Conditioners	Central Air Conditioners	Furnaces	Heat Pumps	Commercial Roof-top Units	Custom Engineered Units (E.M.)
Market Factors						
1. Shared competitors?		x		x	x	
2. Relative market share position?		x		x	x	
3. Industry maturity?	Mature	Growth (replacement cycle)	Mature	Embryonic	Growth	Mature
4. Shared customers?						
end users		x	x	x		?
contractor or dealer		x	x	x	x	
5. Substitutability in use?	x	x		x		?
Cost Factors						
1. Joint manufacturing cost?	x	x	x	x	x	?
2. Shared distribution?						
warehousing		x	x	x	x	?
transportation		x	x	x	x	
sales force	x	x	x	x	x	
Technology	x	x	x	x	x	x

x = PMUs are similar on this criterion.

or market factors will systematically vary with the degree of complexity of the market, as portrayed by the following dimensions:

1.   the number of distinctly different uses or applications for the products in the market;

2.   the number of usage situations encountered by each customer; and

3.   the size of the consideration set (the number of product types, product variants, brands and price feature combinations which the customer would consider during the choice process).

When there is only a single or very few uses, the product provides a single function, illustrated by farm equipment such as bean pickers or limited-function housewares such as crock-pots or hamburger cookers. These may be straightforward markets to understand, depending on the number of technologies and products considered feasible for providing the basic function, e.g. slow cooking at controlled temperature.

More complex environments are created when there are many possible ways to use the product but each user only considers it for one or two distinct uses. Most industrial materials and components fall into this category. For example, engineered plastics can be used for structural or decorative parts, containers, and so forth, and in each application there are many competitive materials, including metals and a whole spectrum of plastics entailing different cost–performance trade-offs.

The most complex markets are those where each customer has many uses for the product or service and many alternatives to consider.[7] Retail banking services are evolving toward this type of market as new competitors gain the franchise to collect deposits and give credits that was once restricted to commercial banks. Varying degrees of market complexity can be portrayed within the Product Usage Matrix of Figure 2.

More importantly, the matrix helps clarify the central issue in this paper— the relative balance of production and cost factors versus demand influences on the definition of the market. In general, with simpler environments the emphasis should be on cost and experience, but when there are complex usage patterns, and many alternative products/technologies which can satisfy customer needs, then the balance should shift toward a market perspective in the definition of both PMUs and SBUs. It was for this reason that General Foods redefined their product-oriented SBUs into menu categories, with SBUs like breakfast food, beverage, main meal, dessert, and pet food targeted toward specific usage situations, even though they often shared manufacturing and distribution resources (Hall, 1978).

---

[7]Within this market category are two subtypes which reflect differences in the *choice resolution process*. There is a variety switching or multiple product purchase subtype, in which the customer avoids compromises among benefits sought by choosing different convenience food outlets for different occasions or stocking many types of beverages to meet the needs of different circumstances. However, in the compromise subtype, the customer's product or service choice has to meet the needs of many conflicting situations. This is true of most big-ticket purchases, such as cooking appliances and automobiles (and perhaps vacations). For example, a family car may be used for family camping trips, shopping, daily commuting, and so forth. The ultimate choice is seldom best for each specific usage situation, but may be best for the expected combination of situations.

Figure 2   Product Usage Matrix

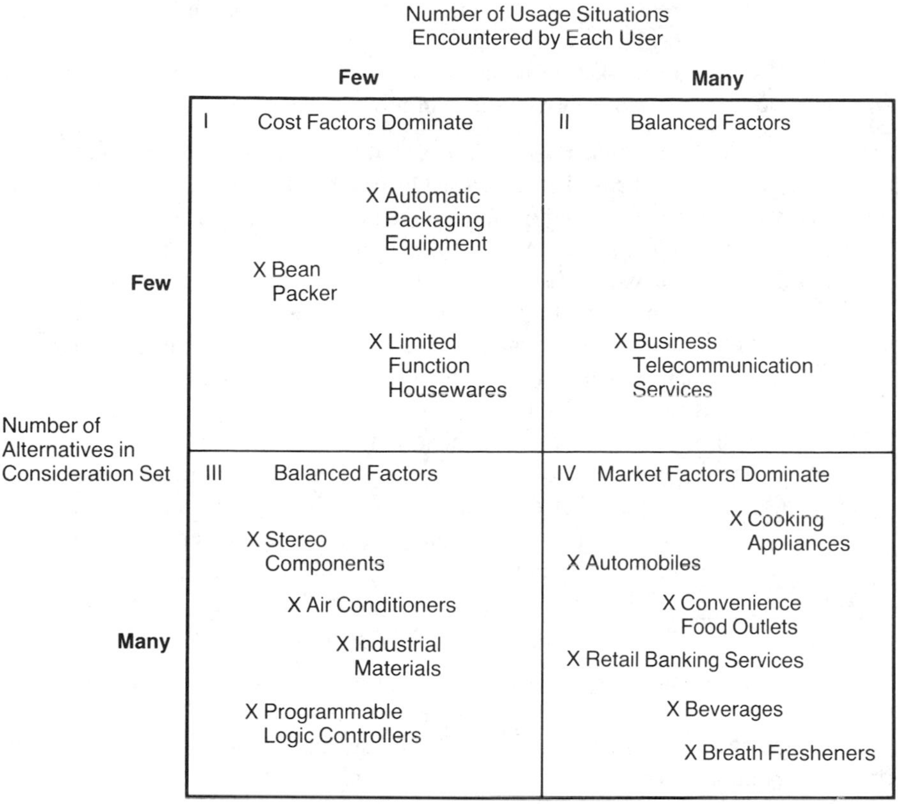

Number of Usage Situations
Encountered by Each User

	Few	Many

Few	I Cost Factors Dominate
	
	X Automatic
	   Packaging
	   Equipment
	X Bean
	   Packer
	
	X Limited
	   Function
	   Housewares
		II Balanced Factors
		
		X Business
		   Telecommunication
		   Services

Many	III Balanced Factors
	
	X Stereo
	   Components
	
	X Air Conditioners
	X Industrial
	   Materials
	
	X Programmable
	   Logic Controllers
		IV Market Factors Dominate
		
		X Cooking
		   Appliances
		X Automobiles
		X Convenience
		   Food Outlets
		X Retail Banking Services
		
		X Beverages
		X Breath Fresheners

Number of
Alternatives in
Consideration Set

Testing the Planning Framework.   The build-up approach to forming business units or strategy centres proceeds by grouping PMUs according to their similarity on appropriate cost, demand and technology factors. Alternatively, one can start with a corporation or a division and follow a *divide-up* approach, using those criteria for subdivision which yield the maximum strategic discrimination (as illustrated in the earlier example from Patel and Younger, 1978). Since only one or two criteria can be used at a time, the inevitable trade-offs which have to be made between cost and demand factors are not so evident.

Whether a build up or divide up approach is superior in any given situation can only be answered by testing the resulting planning framework for both strategic relevance and administrative feasibility.

(a)   *Strategic relevance tests.* The designation of a strategy centre or SBU is often a chicken-and-egg problem, in the guise of the continuing question of which comes first, strategy or structure? Different strategic thrusts may dictate the inclusion of different PMUs to form the business, yet strategic planning is conducted within the established structure of business units. Some useful questions to guide the necessary judgments are:

(i)   is the proposed planning structure capable of stimulating ideas for strategies which yield a future competitive advantage?

(ii)   is share of market an indication of relative cost or market power?

(iii)   can performance be measured in terms of profit or loss?

(b)   *Administrative feasibility tests.* One set of administrative issues deals with size and span of control trade-offs. On one hand, large business units are likely to encompass shared resource units such as pooled sales forces or joint production facilities, and they can help keep the span of control manageable. However, if too many dissimilar PMUs are lumped together, programme managers may be unable to perceive their contribution and important growth opportunities may be submerged within the bulk of the established business. But if the business units are narrowly focused on specific product-market opportunities the planning framework is likely to become fragmented into many small units. This places an unacceptable burden on the ability of corporate management to coordinate and control the individual units. This means, for example, that opportunities for collaboration between business units, such as adopting joint marketing programmes to reach international markets, may be overlooked since no single SBU has responsibility. Finally, if a business unit is too small it will not have the visibility or resources to warrant the development of separate strategic programmes.

The second administrative issue is the extent to which the planning framework of SBUs and PMUs should be forced into compatibility with the existing organization structure. If strategic realities dictate significant differences between the two structures, then, forcing them to be compatible for reasons of expediency may lead to excessive emphasis on short-run performance rather than a commitment to implementing a strategy to properly position the business in the long-run.

In the case of the air conditioner manufacturer described earlier, the strategic relevance test had primacy. The strategic planning framework which finally emerged in Figure 3 was adopted with the understanding that the existing organization would have to be quickly modified to ensure the desired strategic thrusts could be developed and executed.

Conclusion

Markets are complex, multidimensional arenas of competition composed of a myriad of niches and categories. The strategist seeking to understand a particular market is dealing with a moving target, for there is continuous change along each of the key market dimensions of function, technology, customer segmentation, and degree of integration. Barriers to competitive movement along these dimensions are constantly shifting, creating both threats and opportunities for protected market positions.

Both top-down and bottom-up analyses of strategic markets are necessary to avoid myopic market definitions, for there are inherent deficiencies to each approach which need to be balanced by the contrasting perspective. A top-down

Figure 3   Strategic Planning Framework

1. Corporate

2. Sector or Division

3. Strategy Centers
   Self Contained Businesses
   with Control over
   Key Factors That Determine
   Success in the Marketplace

4. PMUs
   Product-Market Units

5. Category and Segment
   Performance Units

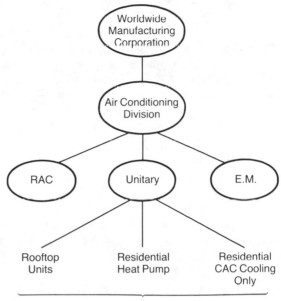

- Size and Type of Contractor
- Geographic Areas
- Size of Unit (Capacity)
- Replacement vs. New
  Installation

emphasis on markets specified in terms of company capabilities and resources can blind one to threats from competitors who are outside the presently served market, or can mean delayed response to shifts in customer requirements or usage patterns. Conversely, markets defined solely from the customer's perspective may ignore crucial economic factors which dictate relative cost position and may distort perceptions of opportunities where the competencies and experience base of the company can be effectively employed.

An integrated analysis of strategic markets begins with the acceptance of a need for multiple market definitions, each more or less suitable for particular strategic or tactical issues. Generally, broad definitions are necessary for the analysis of new ventures, or for competitive surveillance purposes, while narrower definitions are used for performance evaluation.

When the results of market analyses from the company and customer perspective are compared, it becomes evident that in many markets—especially those with complex patterns of product usage or product/service application—there is an untapped potential in methods which carefully distinguish between technologies and functions or uses. Finally, the planning process itself should have the capacity to seek out, understand, and exploit the differences in market definitions between top-down and bottom-up approaches. The pay-off will be clearer strategic thinking and faster response to emerging threats and opportunities.

References

Abell, Derek F. *Defining the Business: The Starting Point of Strategic Planning*. Prentice-Hall, Englewood Cliffs, N.J., 1980.

Abell, Derek F., and John S. Hammong, *Strategic Market Planning: Problems and Analytical Approaches*, Prentice-Hall, Englewood Cliffs, N.J., 1979.

Ansoff, H. Igor. *Corporate Strategy*, McGraw-Hill, New York, 1965.

Buzzell, Robert D. *Note on Market Definition and Segmentation*, Harvard Business School, Cambridge, Mass., 1979a.

Buzzell, Robert D. 'The dispute about high-share businesses', *PIMS/letter 19*. Strategic Planning Institute, 1976b.

Cadbury, N. D. 'When, where and how to test market', *Harvard Business Review*, May–June 1975, pp 96–105.

Day, George S. 'Diagnosing the product portfolio', *Journal of Marketing*, **41**, April 1977, pp. 29–38.

Day, George S., Allan D. Shocker, and Rajendra K. Srivastava. 'Customer-oriented approaches to identifying product-markets', *Journal of Marketing*, **43**, Fall 1979, pp. 8–19.

Frank, Ronald, William F. Massy, and Yoram Wind. *Market Segmentation*. Prentice-Hall, Englewood Cliffs, N.J., 1972.

Gluck, Frederick, Stephen P. Kaufman, and A. Steven Walleck. 'The evolution of strategic management', McKinsey Staff Paper, October 1978.

Hall, William K., 'SBUs: hot, new topic in the management of diversification', *Business Horizons*, February 1978, pp. 17–25.

Hanan, Mack. 'Reorganize your company around its markets', *Harvard Business Review*, November–December 1974, pp. 63–74.

Hatten, Kenneth J. 'Quantitative research methods in strategic management', in Dan Schendel and Charles W. Hofer (eds). *Strategic Management*, Little, Brown, Boston, 1979.

Hedley, Barry. 'A fundamental approach to strategy development', *Longe Range Planning,* December 1976, pp. 2–11.

Hofer, Charles W., and Dan Schendel. *Strategy Formulation: Analytical Concepts*, West Publishing, St. Paul, 1978.

Hopkins, David S. 'New emphases in product planning and strategy development', *Industrial Marketing Management*, **6**, 1977, pp. 410–419.

Hunt, Michael. 'Competition in the major home appliance industry: 1960-1970', *unpublished doctoral dissertation*, Harvard University, 1972.

Hussey, David E. 'Portfolio analysis: practical experience with the directional policy matrix', *Long Range Planning*, **11**, August 1978, pp. 2–8.

Johnson, William E. 'Trade-offs in pricing strategy', in *Pricing Practices and Strategies*, Conference Board, New York, 1978.

Kotler, Philip, *Marketing Management: Analysis, Planning, and Control*, Prentice-Hall, Englewood Cliffs, N.J., 1977.

Levitt, Theodore. 'Marketing success through differentiation—of anything'. *Harvard Business Review*, **58**. January–February 1980, pp. 83–91.

Lorange, Peter. *Corporate Planning: An Executive Viewpoint*, Prentice-Hall, Englewood Cliffs, N.J., 1980.

Majaro, Simon. 'Market share: deception or diagnosis?', *Marketing*, March 1977, pp. 43–47.

Patel, Peter, and Michael Younger. 'A frame of reference for strategy development', *Long Range Planning*, April 1978, pp. 6–12.

Porter, Michael E. *Interbrand Choice, Strategy and Bilateral Market Power*, Harvard University Press, Cambridge, Mass, 1976.

Porter, Michael. 'How competitive forces shape strategy', *Harvard Business Review*, March–April 1979, pp. 137–145.

Rothschild, William. *Getting It All Together*, AMACOM, New York, 1976.

Simmonds, Kenneth. 'Removing the chains from product strategy', *Journal of Management Studies*, February 1968, pp. 29–40.

Tilles, Seymour. 'Segmentation and strategy'. Perspectives Number 156. The Boston Consulting Group, Boston, Mass., 1974.

Wind, Yoram. 'Issues and advances in segmentation research', *Journal of Marketing Research*, **15**, August 1978, pp. 317–337.

19

Strategic Goals: Process and Politics

James Brian Quinn

Executives are constantly under pressure to:

- Define specific goals and objectives for their organizations.
- State these goals clearly, explicitly, and preferably quantitatively.
- Assign the goals to individuals or organizational units.
- Control the organization toward established measurable goals.

These have become almost biblical mandates for most managers. Yet at the strategic level in large companies one often finds that successful executives announce only a few goals. These are frequently broad and general. Only rarely are they quantitative or measurably precise. Further, managements tend to arrive at their strategic goals through highly incremental "muddling" processes rather than through the kinds of structured analytical processes so often prescribed in the literature and "required" according to management dogma.

This article documents why top managers act as they do. It also asserts that their practices are purposeful, politically astute, and effective. They do not represent breakdowns in management technique, sloppiness, or lack of top management sophistication—as critics of these practices so often suggest. Managers at all levels can be more effective if they understand the logic and process considerations behind such "broad goal setting" and "incremental" techniques.

The conclusions in this article come from systematic observation of some ten organizations over a period of several years. Examples are selected from these observations, from secondary sources, and from a current project on "Strategy Formulation in Major Organizations," in which the author has interviewed some 100 top managers in large U.S. and European companies.

This article first appeared in the *Sloan Management Review*. Reprinted from *Sloan Management Review* (Fall 1977): 21–37, by permission of the publisher. Copyright © 1977 by the Sloan Management Review Association. All rights reserved.

When this article was published the author was professor at Dartmouth College, Hanover, N.H.

Why Not Announce Goals?

Why don't top executives simply arrive at goals and announce them in the precise, integrated packages advocated by theoretical strategists and expected by their organizational constituents? In fact, they may establish a few broad goals by decree. But more often—and for good reason—they avoid such pronouncements. Why?

Undesired Centralization

Effective top managers understand that goal "announcements" centralize the organization. Such statements tell subordinates that certain issues are closed and that their thoughts about alternatives are irrelevant. Successful top executives know they cannot have as much detailed information about products, technologies, and customer needs as their line compatriots do. In formulating goals, they want both to benefit from this knowledge and to obtain the genuine participation and commitment of those who have it. For example:

- *Mr. James McFarland said that shortly after he became Chief Executive Officer, "I asked myself what was expected of me as CEO. I decided that my role was really to build General Mills from a good into a great company. But I realized this was not just up to me. I wanted a collective viewpoint as to what makes a company great. Consequently, we took some thirty-five top people away for three days to decide what it took to move the company from 'goodness' to 'greatness'. Working in groups of six to eight, we defined the characteristics of a great company from various points of view, what our shortcomings were, and how we might overcome these." Over time these broad goals were translated into charters for specific divisions or groups. They became the initial guidelines that stimulated the company's very successful development over the next decade.*
- *The president of another large consumer products company was trying to develop a posture to deal with ever increasing government regulations in his field. He said, "I have started conversations with anyone inside or outside the company who can help me. I don't know yet what we should do. And I don't want to take a stand we can't all live with. Before we make any irrevocable decisions, I'll want a lot of advice from those people in the company who understand the specific problems better than I do. And I'll want everyone pulling together when we do set our course."*

Far from stimulating desired participation, goal announcements can centralize the organization, rigidify positions too soon, eliminate creative options, and even cause active resistance to the goals themselves.

Focus for Opposition

Further, explicitly stated goals—especially on complex issues—can provide focal points against which an otherwise fragmented opposition will organize. Anyone with political sensibilities will understand this phenomenon. For example, President Carter's stated energy plan immediately drew the adverse comments of many parochial interests who only opposed a specific part of the plan. But soon these highly fragmented forces appeared unified in their opposition to the total plan, and each fragment gained added credibility from this apparent unity. In a like manner, a "land use plan" or a "zoning ordinance" quickly becomes a coalescing element for many disparate interests in a town. In industry, department or division heads, who compete fiercely on most issues, can become a formidable power bloc against some announced thrust which affects each only marginally. For example:

- *In a textile fibers company strong marketing, production, and R&D managers—who fought each other constantly—formed a potent coalition to resist a "product management" scheme to coordinate the very things that caused their friction. And in decentralized companies powerful product division heads have forced new CEOs to give up, get out, or revert to acquisitions—rather than accept new interdivisional goals pushed from the top.*

Because of such potential opposition, experienced executives are reluctant to put forward complete "goal packages" which could contain significant points of controversy. Instead they progress by building consensus around one—or a few—important new goal(s) at a time. This in part explains the "incrementalism" so often observed in organizations.

Rigidity

Once a top executive publicly announces a goal, it can become very difficult to change. Both the executive's ego and those of people in supporting programs become identified with the goal. Changing the goal broadcasts that the executive was in error and that all those pursuing the goal were on the wrong track. As a consequence, people doggedly prolong outmoded—but publicly committed—goals, rather than swallow losses and move on.

- *The government constantly continues obsolete military, energy, and social programs for just such reasons. Corporate bankruptcy lists are rampant with conglomerates, banks, transportation companies, and real estate ventures under duress because their officers tried frantically to fulfill announced—but unrealistic—growth goals.*
- *By contrast, the vice-chairman of a multibillion dollar consumer products company said, "We don't announce growth goals in new areas precisely because we don't want to be trapped into doing something stupid. We might be tempted to acquire a company when we shouldn't. Or we might hang on to an operation we really should sell off. Public statements can sometimes generate powerful expectations—internally and externally—that can pressure you to do the wrong thing."*

Top managers generally like to keep their options open as long as possible, consistent with the information they have. One way to accomplish this is to define only broad directions, then respond to specific, well-documented proposals. There is an additional advantage to this approach. The proposers are more likely to identify with their proposition and see it through. Again, this is part of the logic behind incrementalism.

▪ *As one vice-president in charge of diversification said, "Our management doesn't state a specific diversification goal requiring so many millions in profits and sales within five years. Instead we say 'we want to be a competitive factor in [a designated] industry in five years.' This keeps us free to approach each field flexibly as opportunities develop. And we don't get committed until we have concrete numbers and proposals to look at."*

Security

There are still other good reasons why effective top managers do not announce goals explicitly or widely. In any healthy organization good people constantly bubble out to head other enterprises. Thus top executives are justifiably reluctant to provide potential competitors with specific information about their future moves.

▪ *When talking to the investment community or his vice-presidents, Tex Thornton was never very specific about the sequence and timing of "his plan" during Litton's rapid growth phase. Advance knowledge of Litton's interest could have inflated an acquisition's stock price, activated other potential acquirers, or caused third parties to intervene. With large numbers of Litton executives being sought by other companies, it would have been folly to disclose acquisition goals in detail. In addition, more general goals allowed Litton needed flexibilities to consider new opportunities as they became available.*

Further, as one chief executive said, "the future can make fools of us all." There are many examples of former high executives ousted because unforeseen events made it impossible to fulfill ambitious announced goals.

▪ *In the late 1960s the president of a large consumer products company announced to all his goal of 10 percent profit growth per year. But many in the company regarded this as "his goal"—not theirs. Despite some impressive successes, the president was hung for a failure to meet this goal in two successive years while he was trying to develop some entirely new ventures within the company. When these were slow in materializing, his vice-presidents gleefully saw that the original goal was well-remembered at the board level. The embarrassed board, which had earlier approved the goal, terminated the president's career.*

There are many other situations—like divestitures, consolidations, or plant closures—where managers may not announce goals at all until after they are accomplished facts. These are just some of the reasons why top managers do not follow the conventional wisdom about announcing goals. The few goals top managers do announce tend: (1) to reflect or help build a developing consensus, (2) to be broad enough in concept to allow opportunism, and (3) to be sufficiently distant in time that a number of possible options could ensure their achievement.

When Should Goals Be General?

Conventional wisdom also requires that effective goals be specific, measurable, and preferably quantitative. Many managers actually express embarrassment or frustration when they cannot reach this "ideal." But more sophisticated executives find such highly precise goals useful only in selected circumstances. As an executive vice-president of a major automobile company said:

▪ *"The decisions where we can set specific numerical goals are the easy ones. Establishing the image of your car line, deciding what posture to take vis-á-vis developing legislation, determining what features the public will want in a car three years from now, setting goals for dealing with worker representation or host country demands abroad . . .those are the tough questions. And they don't have numerical answers."*

One can attempt to be verbally precise in such areas. Yet very often a broad goal statement is more effective than its narrower, more measurable counterpart might be. Why?

Cohesion

A certain generality in goals actually promotes cohesion. Many can support "continued growth," "greater freedom," "equal opportunity" "full disclosure," or "quality products" as organizational goals. But oddly enough, adding more specific dimensions to these broad concepts may quickly complicate communications, lose some individuals' support, and even create contention.

If a community tries to agree on its precise goals in building a new school, it may never reach a sufficient consensus for action. People can differ irreconcilably on whether a traditional, experimental, precollege, classical, or vocational approach should predominate. Yet they might easily agree on a goal "to build a new school." Once the broad program is approved, they can resolve some very fundamental value differences by compromising on the much less emotionally charged architectural details.

Similarly, top managers can often avoid serious rifts by focusing agreement on very broad objectives where substantial agreement exists, then treating more specific goal issues as decisions about concrete proposals or program details. Again, incrementalism is logical. For example:

▪ *The new principal stockholder in a mechanical equipment company wanted the company to grow relatively rapidly by selective acquisitions. One of the stockholder's board representatives prepared a detailed outline containing proposed areas for growth and diversification. Some other board members— based on limited experience—immediately took a rigid stance against one specific proposal, i.e. acquisitions in "service areas" supporting the company's line. Little progress could be made until the principal stockholder's representatives went back and sold the board on an idea they could all agree to, i.e., growth through acquisition. As the board becomes more comfortable with this broad concept, the principal stockholder's representatives still hope to bring in some "service company" candidates and allay their fellow directors' fears in terms of a specific example.*

Identity and Élan

Broad goals can create identity and élan. Effective organizational goals satisfy a basic human need. They enable people to develop an identity larger than themselves, to participate in greater challenges, to have influence or seek rewards they could not achieve alone. Interestingly enough, many employees can better identify with broad goals like being "the best" or "the first" in an area than they can with more specific numerical goals. As the chief executive of a major consumer products company said:

- *"We have slowly discovered that our most effective goal is to be best at certain things. We now try to get our people to help us work out what these should be, how to define best objectively, and how to become best in our selected spheres. You would be surprised how motivating that can be."*

Most companies devote great attention to measurable output goals—like size, productivity, profits, costs, or returns—that lack charisma and provide no special identity for their people. Yet they often fail to achieve these goals precisely because their people do not identify sufficiently with the company. To forge a common bond among individuals with widely diverse personal values, expectations, and capacities, such numerical goals must be teamed with goals that satisfy people's more basic psychological needs: to produce something worthwhile, to help others, to obtain recognition, to be free or innovative, to achieve security, to beat an opponent, or to earn community respect. While such organizational goals must be general enough to achieve widespread support, they must also clearly delineate what distinguishes "us" (the identity group) from "them" (all others).

To improve their competitive postures, executives often consciously define the "uniqueness" or "niche" of their company's products, processes, technologies, services, or markets. More thoughtful top managers also carefully analyze whether one strategic goal or another will better attract the skilled people and personal commitments they want. These people's talent and dedication then become the central strengths upon which the organization's success is built. An IBM salesman, a Bell Labs researcher, a *New York Times* stringer, or a Steuben glassblower all enjoy a special élan—as do millions of others whose organizations achieve a unique identity. This élan provides a special psychic compensation for the people involved, and symbiotically it becomes their organization's most priceless asset. More often than not such élan develops around broad conceptual goals, rather than precise mathematical targets.

When Should Goals Be Specific?

Contrary to conventional wisdom, relatively few strategic goals need to be mathematically precise. Properly derived, those few can provide essential focal points and stimuli for an organization. However, they should be generated with care and used with balance.

Precipitating Action

By making selected goals explicit at the proper moment, managers can create a challenge, precipitate desired discussions or analyses, or crystallize defined thrusts. For example:

■   *The president of a major packaging company wanted to move his organization in new directions. He first unleashed a series of management, staff, and consulting studies to help define the company's weaknesses and major opportunities for improvement. These were circulated as "white papers" for discussion by his top management team. After a while consensus began to emerge on critical issues and options. The president began to reinforce one: "the need to work existing assets much harder." In further discussions his organization crystallized this concept into a specific target return on net assets—vastly higher than the current return—as a principal goal for 1981. This goal triggered the shutdown of excess facilities, a new focus on profitability rather than volume, and a profit-centered decentralization of the whole organization.*

Under these circumstances, after building consensus around a broad goal, the top executive may merely approve its specific manifestation. Although the goal is a challenge, his own organization has recommended it. The executive knows that it is feasible, and key people understand and support the goal. The time horizon is sufficiently distant to allow for alternative approaches which will insure its achievement.

Major Transitions

Specific new goals can also help signal a major change from the past. Properly developed, they can challenge lower levels to propose specific solutions, yet not unduly constrain their approaches. To be effective they must build on some accepted values in the organization and leave time enough for proposed new programs to reach fruition. For example:

■   *After much discussion, an aerospace company's top management established the goal of moving 50 percent into nongovernment business within a decade. This started a furor of creative proposals. Research put forward new technical concepts. Each division proposed how it could best realign its own business. Corporate staff units investigated industries and specific companies for acquisitions. The administrative vice-president recommended a new control system to handle diversification. Revised banking relations were proposed. And so on. From all these thrusts top management slowly chose its desired pattern of internal vs. external growth, market sectors, organizational form, and financial structure. Throughout, lower levels felt their ideas were appreciated, and they identified with changes made.*

After a prolonged disaster or a major trauma, an organization often needs distinct and clear new goals. Typically, these must combine a broad definition of longer-term success and some specific, achievable, short-term goals to build confidence. Without visible intermediate goals, people can become frustrated and give up on the ultimate challenge.

Only a Few

At any given moment, an executive can push only a few specific new goals, giving them the attention and force they need to take hold. Fortunately, a top executive rarely needs to press more than a few significant changes simultaneously. In fact, the essence of strategy is to identify this small number of truly essential thrusts or concepts and to consciously marshall the organization's resources and capabilities toward them. Then—to capture the organization's attention—the executive must consistently reinforce these strategic goals through his statements, his decision patterns, and his personnel assignments. He must be willing to put his credibility on the line and use the power and sanctions of his office to achieve them. Still, the typical organization's ongoing momentum and resource commitments will allow it to absorb only a few major changes at once.

Two examples illustrate the complex interactions that lead to success or failure when setting specific goals at the top level:

- *In 1969, RCA's chairman, Robert Sarnoff, initiated several major new thrusts simultaneously. While repositioning RCA in its traditional electronics-communications markets, he actively diversified the company through acquisitions. At the same time he also strove: (1) to build RCA's computer activities into an effective direct competitor of IBM, (2) to move the company's technological efforts from research toward applications, and (3) to strengthen the company's lagging marketing capabilities. He implemented much of this through an enlarged central corporate staff. It was difficult for the organization to absorb so much top-level-initiated change at once. Various aspects of the program met intense resistance from existing divisions. The computer venture failed, and Mr. Sarnoff's credibility with the organization became strained to the breaking point.*

- *By contrast, shortly after Philip Hofmann became chairman of Johnson and Johnson, he announced a specific new goal of $1 billion in sales (with a 15 percent after tax return on investment) before his retirement some seven years later. Annual sales were then approximately $350 million. Though the challenge was startling in scale, it built upon an established growth ethic in the company, and it did not constrain potential solutions. Instead it stimulated each division to define how it could best respond, thus maintaining the company's intended decentralization. It also allowed sufficient time for managers to propose, initiate, and carry out their new programs. Performance ultimately surpassed the goal by a comfortable margin.*

At some point, of course, planning processes must refine goals into specific operational targets. As the examples of successful goal setting illustrate, this is best achieved through incremental, iterative processes which intimately involve those who have to implement the proposed strategic thrusts.

Are Effective Goals So Important?

All of the concepts above help insure that strategic goals are set: (1) at the right time, (2) with maximum input from those who have the most specific knowledge, and (3) with the genuine commitment of those who must achieve results. Why should managers take such care in developing and expressing organizational goals? Effective strategic goals do more than provide a basis for direction setting and performance measurement. They are essential to establishing and maintaining freedom, morale, and timely problem sensing in an enterprise. The benefits of effective goal setting are greatest when people throughout the organization genuinely internalize the goals and "make them their own."

Freedom with Control

If people share common purposes, they can self-direct their actions with minimum coordination from executive or staff groups. This is especially critical for creative groups like research, advertising, or strategic planning. Without such goal congruence, control of these activities is impossible. No amount of ex post facto performance measurement can insure that creative people imaginatively identify proper problems, generate imaginative alternatives, or invent new or responsive solutions. Such actions must be stimulated before the fact by ensuring that well-selected people understand and internalize goals.

Morale

Morale is a goal-oriented phenomenon. In a "high morale" organization people intensely share common performance goals. They ignore internal irritations and adapt rapidly to external stimuli which help or hinder goal accomplishment. Entrepreneurial organizations, project teams on urgent tasks, dedicated medical groups, or even whole societies (like Israel or Japan) exhibit these characteristics. A specific industrial example suggests how powerful the symbiotic effect of a stimulating goal and talented people can be:

- *From 1970–1976 tiny KMS Industries supported the world's most advanced laser fusion program for commercial energy production. As one executive said, "I don't know any of us who didn't agree that this was the most important task in the world. We thought we could lick the fight. If successful, we would have a new basis for creating energy, hydrogen, and hydrocarbons. It would make the U.S. and other nations independent of world energy markets. People on the fusion program had extremely high morale. They would work all night. They were thoroughly committed." On May 1, 1974— despite much larger AEC and Russian expenditures in the field—a KMS team achieved the world's first "unambiguous" release of neutrons from laser fusion.*

A contrasting example makes the opposite point:

- *The dominantly shared goal of many a government (or staff) department is the preservation of its members' positions and budgets. Lacking shared—or often even understood—performance goals, such organizations become "hotbeds of inertia." They focus extraordinary energies on minor internal irritants. When disturbed by external stimuli they operate with awesome tenacity to reestablish accepted interpersonal and political equilibria—even to the point of negating their own output and jeopardizing their continuation.*

Often managers spend enormous time trying to ease or resolve the interpersonal tensions in such organizations, but they accomplish little until they can get people to accept a new sense of common purpose.

Problem Sensing

Finally, goals help define problems. Organizations without a strong sense of broad purpose can precipitate their own demise by ignoring major problems or overlooking alternatives. Some companies define their services, concepts, and goals with such limited vision that they screen out major opportunities. Others have elaborately worked out goal statements covering broad issues, but their control and reward systems reinforce—and cause people to internalize—only a few. When people do not internalize an adequate range of goals, the consequences can be extremely costly.

- *In the late 1960s many conglomerates proudly concentrated on "managing business as a financial enterprise." Their control and reward systems focused so much attention on continuously improving short-term financial performance that their managers often screened out other important issues as "nonproblems." This led them to undercut research and technology, product and personnel development, plant investments, international relations, and perhaps even ethics to an extent that sometimes jeopardized their companies' very viability.*
- *Recently, the chairman of a multibillion dollar diversified company publicly decried the $35 million his divisions would expend on depolution measures. It was clear that he perceived "environmentalism" only as a threat. Yet one division of his company (auto exhaust systems) was likely to sell an additional $600+ million of its product annually—with corresponding profits— because of the same environmental standards he resisted as "a total loss to the company."*

Will Conventional Processes Work?

If goals are to stimulate freedom with control, high morale, and creative problem solving, people throughout the organization must understand and actively identify with them. Usually this requires the genuine participation of many individuals in setting and modifying the goals. Yet the manager must not lose control over this vital process. He must carefully blend consultation, participation, delegation, and guidance to achieve his purposes. How can he manage this complex art?

Bottom Up

The philosophers' ideal is to arrive at goal consensus through democratic discussion or through "bottom-up" proposals. These views often prevail within small-company, Japanese, or "Theory Y" managements, and they clearly have merit for some organizations.

However, such approaches are very time consuming and can prove to be frustrating, wasteful, or even divisive. Opaque committee discussions can go on endlessly and still leave individuals with different views of what goals were agreed on. People may expend extraordinary time and energy on proposals that management later rejects as "irrelevant." They feel angry or manipulated when "their" carefully prepared proposals or goals are overruled for other organizational purposes only fully appreciated from on high.

Unwitting Bureaucracy

Managers of larger enterprises rarely feel they can afford a purist approach to democratic goal setting. At the same time, they sense the shortcomings of goals announced from above. Consequently, a pragmatic compromise emerges. Top managers often provide a framework of broad goals for their subordinate units. They then encourage lower-level managers to make proposals which respond to these goals through planning, budgetary, and ad hoc processes. Before the proposals reach final approval stages, a series of staff interventions, personal discussions, and intermediate reviews tune them toward what various people think top management wants and will accept.

This process brings a kind of "collective wisdom" to bear. There is some personal involvement at all levels. But often a bland, committee-like consensus emerges. This process works moderately well for routine modifications of existing thrusts, but it discourages significant changes in organizational goals. Thus, unwittingly, most large enterprises become conservatively bureaucratized. They continue existing momenta and overlook major external changes or new opportunities.

How Do Managements Evolve Effective Strategic Goals?

Dramatic new strategic goal-sets rarely emerge full blown from individual "bottom-up proposals" or from comprehensive "corporate strategic planning." Instead a series of individual, logical, perhaps somewhat disruptive decisions interact to create a new structure and cohesion for the company. Top managers create a new consensus through a continuous, evolving, incremental, and often highly political process that has no precise beginning or end. A well-documented example—one with which many readers will be familiar—illustrates important dimensions of this "logical incremental" approach to strategic goal setting.

- *IBM's strategic goal of "introducing its 360 computers simultaneously as a single line with compatibility, standard interface, business and scientific capability, hybrid circuitry, and the capacity to open new markets" probably started in 1959 when T. Vincent Learson became head of the Data Systems and General Products divisions. The divisions' product lines had begun to overlap and proliferate, causing software, cost, and organizational problems. Top managers sensed this, but no clear solutions were at hand. In 1960-61 various specific decisions began to eliminate alternatives and define key elements of the new goal. Proposals for two new computers, "Scamp" and the 8000 series, were killed to avoid further proliferation. In mid-1961 Learson and a subordinate, Bob O. Evans, arrived at a broad concept "to blanket the market with a single product line," and they initiated exploratory studies on a new product line called simply "NPL." During 1961 a special Logic Committee recommended that IBM use "hybrid circuitry"— rather than integrated circuits—in any major new line. In late 1961 NPL was foundering. Learson and chairman Watson started a "series of dialogues on strategy" with division heads, but no clear concept emerged. Consequently, they formed the SPREAD committee of key executives to hammer out basic concepts for a new line. In January 1962, the committee reported and top management approved its recommended concepts for a new integrative product line, now worked out in some detail. Broad top management support and a genuine organization momentum were building behind the new concept.*

In 1962 development began in earnest, and IBM's board approved a $100-million manufacturing facility for hybrid circuits. Still, technical difficulties and differences in viewpoint persisted. In late 1962 a special programming meeting was held at Stowe to discuss software development, but major programming problems remained unresolved. In 1963 various groups openly resisted the new line. The opposition was broken up or removed. In December 1963, Honeywell precipitated action by announcing a strong competitor for IBM's successful 1401 computer. Shortly thereafter, in January 1964, Learson conducted a performance "shoot out" between the 360/30 and the 1401. The 360/30 was judged good enough to go ahead. Final pricing, marketing, and production studies were now made. In March 1964, top management approved the line in a "final risk assessment session" at Yorktown. And on April 7, 1964, Watson announced the 360 line. The decision now appeared irrevocable.

But in 1965 and later, new time-sharing features, smaller and larger computers, and peripheral equipment units were announced or "decommitted." IBM raised $361 million of new equity in 1965 to support the line— ultimately investing some $4.5 billion in the 360. Further changes occurred in the line and its supporting hardware and software. Finally, well into the 1970s, the 360 series provided IBM's essential strategic strength, its massive installed computer base. The decision and its impact extended over some fifteen years.

The pattern is common. At first there are simply too many unknowns to specify a cohesive set of new directions for the enterprise. More information is needed. Technical problems must be solved to determine feasibilities. Investments must be made in programs with long lead times. Trends in the market place must crystallize into sufficiently concrete demands or competitive responses to justify risk taking. Various resource bases must be acquired or developed. Different groups' psychological commitments must be diverted from ongoing thrusts toward a new consensus. Lead times for all these events are different. Yet logic dictates that final resource commitments he made as late as possible consistent with the information available—hence incrementalism.

To reshape an organization's accepted culture significantly, an executive must often overcome some potent psychological/political forces. His success will depend on the very group whose perceptions he may want to change. If he moves too precipitously, he can undermine essential strengths of his organization. All too easily he can alienate his people, lose personal credibility, and destroy the power base his future depends on. Unless a crisis intervenes, he cannot change the organization's ethos abruptly. Instead he usually must build commitment—and his own political support—incrementally around specific issues or proposals. The real art is to thoughtfully blend these thrusts together, as opportunities permit, into patterns which slowly create a new logical cohesion.

Changing strategic goals typically involves managing a complex chain of interacting events and forces over a period of years. How do successful managers approach this challenge?

Managing the Incremental Process

For the reasons cited above, a kind of "logical incrementalism" usually dominates strategic goal setting. This process is purposeful, politically astute, and effective. It starts with needs that may only be vaguely sensed at first and incrementally builds the organization's awareness, support, and eventual commitment around new goals. The stages in this process—though not always the same—commonly recur. These are set forth below. The management techniques used at each stage—also outlined below—are not quite the textbook variety. But seeing these in the context of the total process helps explain their wide use and notable effectiveness. It also explains some of the seeming anomalies and real frustrations of management in large organizations. Managers at all levels should understand how this process operates and how they can best fit into and manage their roles in it.

Sensing Needs.   Top executives very often sense needs for strategic change in quite vague or undefined terms, like IBM's "organizational overlap" or "too much proliferation." Early signals may come from almost anywhere, and they may initially be quite indistinct. Long lead times are often needed to make significant changes. Consequently, effective executives—like Mr. Learson—consciously seek multiple contact points with managers, workers, customers, suppliers, technologists, outside professional and government groups, and so on. They purposely short-circuit all the careful screens an organization builds to "tell the top only what it wants to hear" and thus delay important strategic signals. They constantly move around, show up at unexpected spots, probe, and listen.

Building Awareness.   The next step is very often to commission study groups, staff, or consultants to illuminate problems, options, contingencies, or opportunities posed by a sensed need. These studies sometimes lead to specific incremental decisions. More often they merely generate broadened or intensified perceptions of future potentials. At this stage managers may need to offset the frustration of study groups, who frequently feel they have "failed" because their studies do not precipitate direct action. But the organization is not yet ready for a decision. Key players are not yet comfortable enough with issues, variables, and options to take a risk. Building awareness, concern, and a "comfort factor" of knowledge about a situation is a vital early link in the practical politics of change.

Broadening Support.   This stage usually involves much unstructured discussion and probing of positions. Earlier studies may provide data or the excuse for these discussions—as in the case of the "strategic dialogues" at IBM. At this stage top executives may actively avoid decisions, other than agreeing to explore options. Instead, they may encourage other key players to see opportunities in a new light, define areas of indifference or concern, and identify potential opponents and points of contention. Whenever possible, the guiding executive lets others suggest new thrusts and maintains the originator's identity with the idea. He encourages concepts he favors, lets undesired or weakly supported options die, and establishes hurdles or tests for strongly supported ideas he may not agree with, but does not want to oppose openly. His main purpose is to begin constructive movement without threatening major power centers. Typically, goals remain broad and unrefined.

Creating Pockets of Commitment.   Exploratory projects—like NPL—may be needed to create necessary skills or technologies, test options, or build commitment deep within the organization. Initially, projects may be small and ad hoc, rarely forming a comprehensive program. The guiding executive may shun identity with specific projects to avoid escalating attention to one too quickly or losing credibility if it fails. To keep a low profile he may encourage, discourage, or kill thrusts through subordinates, rather than directly. He must now keep his options open, control premature momentum, and select the right moment to meld several successful thrusts into a broader program or concept. His timing is often highly opportunistic. A crisis, a rash of reassignments, a reorganization, or a key appointment may allow him to focus attention on particular goals, add momentum to some, or perhaps quietly phase out others.

Crystallizing a Developing Focus.   is another step. Ad hoc committees—like the SPREAD committee—are a favorite tool for this. By selecting the committee's membership, charter, and timing, the guiding executive can influence its direction. A committee can be balanced to educate, evaluate, or neutralize opponents. It can genuinely develop new options, or it can be focused narrowly to build momentum. Attention to the committee's dynamics is essential. It can broaden support and increase commitment significantly for new goals. Or it can generate organized opposition—and a real trauma—should top management later overrule its strong recommendations.

At crucial junctures the guiding executive may crystallize an emerging consensus by hammering out a few broad goals with his immediate colleagues and stating some as trial concepts for a wider group to discuss. He may even negotiate specific aspects with individual executives. Finally, when sufficient congruence exists or the timing is right, the goal begins to appear in his public statements, guidelines for divisions, and other appropriate places.

Obtaining Real Commitment.   If possible, the executive tries to make some individual(s) explicitly accountable for the goal. But he often wants more than mere accountability—he wants real commitment. A major thrust, concept, product, or problem solution frequently needs the nurturing hand of someone who genuinely identifies with it and whose future depends on its success. In such cases, the executive may wait for a "champion" to appear before he commits resources, but he may assign less dramatic goals as specific missions for ongoing groups. Budgets, programs, proposals, controls, and reward systems must now reflect the new goal, whether or not it is quantitatively measurable. The guiding executive sees to it that recruiting and staffing plans align with the new goal and, when the situation permits, reassigns its supporters and persistent opponents into appropriate spots.

Continuing Dynamics.   All of the above may take years to effect—as it did in IBM's case. Over this time horizon, the process is rarely completely orderly, rational, or consistent. Instead the executive responds opportunistically to new threats, crises, and proposals. The decision process constantly molds and modifies his own concerns and concepts. Old crusades become the new conventional wisdom; and over time, totally new issues emerge.

Once the organization arrives at its new consensus, the executive must move to ensure that this does not become inflexible. In trying to build commitment to a new concept, one often surrounds himself with people who see the world the same way. Such people can rapidly become systematic screens against other views. Hence, the effective executive now purposely continues the change process with new faces and stimuli at the top. He consciously begins to erode the very strategic goals he has just created—a very difficult psychological task.

Conclusion

Establishing strategic goals for complex organizations is a delicate art, requiring a subtle balance of vision, entrepreneurship, and politics. At the center of the art one finds consciously managed processes of "broad goal setting" and "logical incrementalism." Management styles vary, but effective top executives in larger enterprises typically state a few broad goals themselves, encourage their organizations to propose others, and allow still others to emerge from informal processes. They eschew the gimmickry of simplistic "formal planning" or "MBO" approaches for setting their major goals. Instead they tend to develop such goals through very complicated, largely political, consensus-building processes that are outside the structure of most formal management systems and frequently have no precise beginning or end.

Those who understand these processes can contribute more effectively, whatever their position in the organization. Those who wish to make major changes in organizations should certainly comprehend these processes, their rationale, and their implications. Those who ignore them may find the costs very high.

References

Bower, J. L. "Planning within the Firm." *American Economic Review,* May 1970.

Bowman, E. H. "Epistemology, Corporate Strategy, and Academe." *Sloan Management Review,* Winter 1974, pp. 35–50.

Cohen, K. J., and Cyert, R. M. "Strategy, Formulation, Implementation, and Monitoring." *Journal of Business,* July 1973.

Frank, A. G. "Goal Ambiguity and Conflicting Standards." *Human Organization,* Winter 1958.

Guth, W. D. "Formulating Organizational Objectives and Strategy: A Systematic Approach." *Journal of Business Policy,* Autumn 1971.

Hall, W. K. "Strategic Planning Models: Are Top Managers Really Finding Them Useful?" *Journal of Business Policy,* Winter 1972/1973, pp. 33–42.

Hunger, J., and Stern, C. "An Assessment of the Functionality of the Superordinate Goal in Reducing Conflict." *Academy of Management Journal,* December 1976.

Latham, G. P., and Yukl, G. A. "Review of Research on the Application of Goal Setting in Organizations." *Academy of Management Journal,* December 1975.

Lindblom, C. E. "The Science of 'Muddling Through.'" *Public Administration Review,* Spring 1959.

Mintzberg, H. "Strategy-Making in Three Modes." *California Management Review,* Winter 1973.

Pfiffner, J. M. "Administrative Rationality." *Public Administration Review,* 1960, pp. 125–132.

Simon, H. A. "On the Concept of Organization Goal." *Administrative Science Quarterly,* June 1964.

Soelberg, P. O. "Unprogrammed Decision Making." *Industrial Management Review,* Spring 1967, pp. 19–29.

Tosi, H. L.; Rizzo, J. R.; and Carroll, S. J. "Setting Goals in Management by Objectives." *California Management Review,* Summer 1970, pp. 70–78.

Vancil, R. F. "Strategy Formulation in Complex Organizations," *Sloan Management Review,* Winter 1976, pp. 1–18.

20

Strategic Windows

Derek F. Abell

Strategic market planning involves the management of any business unit in the dual tasks of *anticipating* and *responding* to changes which affect the marketplace for their products. This article discusses both of these tasks. Anticipation of change and its impact can be substantially improved if an organizing framework can be used to identify sources and directions of change in a systematic fashion. Appropriate responses to change require a clear understanding of the alternative strategic options available to management as a market evolves and change takes place.

Dynamic Analysis

When changes in the market are only incremental, firms may successfully adapt themselves to the new situation by modifying current marketing or other functional programs. Frequently, however, market changes are so far reaching that the competence of the firm to continue to compete effectively is called into question. And it is in such situations that the concept of "strategic windows" is applicable.

The term "strategic window" is used here to focus attention on the fact that there are only limited periods during which the "fit" between the key requirements of a market and the particular competencies of a firm competing in that market is at an optimum. Investment in a product line or market area should be timed to coincide with periods in which such a strategic window is open. Conversely, disinvestment should be contemplated if what was once a good fit has been eroded—i.e., if changes in market requirements outstrip the firm's capability to adapt itself to them.

This article first appeared in the *Journal of Marketing* (July 1978):21–26. Reprinted with permission from the *Journal of Marketing*, published by the American Marketing Association.

When this article was published the author was an Associate Professor of Business Administration at Harvard University, Graduate School of Business Administration, Cambridge, Mass.

Among the most frequent questions which management has to deal with in this respect are:

- Should funds be committed to a proposed new market entry? Now? Later? Or not at all? If a commitment is to be made, how large should it be?
- Should expenditure of funds of plant and equipment or marketing to support existing product lines be expanded, continued at historical levels, or diminished?
- When should a decision be made to quit and throw in the towel for an unprofitable product line or business area?

Resource allocation decisions of this nature all require a careful assessment of the future evolution of the market involved and an accurate appraisal of the firm's capability to successfully meet key market requirements. The strategic window concept encourages the analysis of these questions in a dynamic rather than a static framework, and forces marketing planners to be as specific as they can about these future patterns of market evolution and the firm's capability to adapt to them.

It is unfortunate that the heightened interest in product portfolio analysis evident in the last decade has failed to adequately encompass these issues. Many managers routinely classify their various activities as "cows," "dogs," "stars," or "question marks" based on a *static* analysis of the *current* position of the firm and its market environment.

Of key interest, however, is the question not only of where the firm is today, but of how well equipped it is to deal with *tomorrow*. Such a *dynamic* analysis may foretell nonincremental changes in the market which work to disqualify market leaders, provide opportunities for currently low share competitors, and sometimes even usher in a completely new cast of competitors into the marketplace. Familiar contemporary examples of this latter phenomenon include such products as digital watches, women's pantyhose, calculators, charter air travel, office copiers, and scientific instrumentation.

In all these cases existing competitors have been displaced by new contenders as these markets have evolved. In each case changing market requirements have resulted in a *closing* strategic window for incumbent competitors and an *opening* window for new entrants.

Market Evolution

The evolution of a market usually embodies more far reaching changes than the relatively systematic changes in customer behavior and marketing mix due to individual product life cycles. Four major categories of change stand out:

1. The development of new primary demand opportunities whose marketing requirements differ radically from those of existing market segments.

2. The advent of new competing technologies which cannibalize the existing ones.

3.   Market redefinition caused by changes in the definition of the product itself and/or changes in the product market strategies of competing firms.

4.   Channel changes.

There may be other categories of change or variants in particular industries. That doesn't matter; understanding of how such changes may qualify or disqualify different types of competitors can still be derived from a closer look at examples within each of the four categories above.

New Primary Demand

In a primary demand growth phase, decisions have to be reached by existing competitors about whether to spend the majority of the resources fighting to protect and fortify market positions that have already been established, or whether to seek new development opportunities.

In some cases, it is an original entrant who ploughs new territory—adjusting his approach to the emergent needs of the marketplace; in other cases it is a new entrant who, maybe basing his entry on expertise developed elsewhere, sees a "strategic window" and leapfrogs over the original market leader to take advantage of the new growth opportunity. Paradoxically, pioneering competitors who narrowly focus their activities in the early stages of growth may have the most difficulty in making the transition to new primary demand growth opportunities later. Emery Air Freight provides an example of a company that did face up to a challenge in such a situation.

Emery Air Freight.   This pioneer in the air freight forwarding business developed many of the early applications of air freight in the United States. In particular, Emery's efforts were focused on servicing the "emergency" segment of the market, which initially accounted for a substantial portion of all air freight business. Emery served this market via an extensive organization of regional and district offices. Among Emery's major assets in this market was a unique nationwide, and later worldwide, communications network; and the special competence of personnel located in the district offices in using scheduled carriers in the most efficient possible way to expedite deliveries.

As the market evolved, however, many new applications for air freight emerged. These included regular planned shipments of high value–low weight merchandise, shipments of perishables; "off-line" service to hard-to-reach locations, and what became known as the TCC (Total Cost Concept) market. Each of these new applications required a somewhat differenct approach than that demanded by the original emergency business.

TCC applications, for example, required detailed logistics planning to assess the savings and benefits to be obtained via lower inventories, quicker deliveries and fewer lost sales through the use of air freight. Customer decisions about whether or not to use air freight required substantially more analysis than had been the case for "emergency" use; furthermore, decisions which had originally been made by traffic managers now involved marketing personnel and often top management.

A decision to seek this kind of business thus implied a radical change in Emery's organization—the addition of capability to analyze complex logistics systems and to deal with upper echelons of management.

New Competing Technologies

When a fundamental change takes place in the basic technology of an industry, it again raises questions of the adaptability to new circumstances of existing firms using obsolete technology.

In many cases established competitors in an industry are challenged, not by another member of the same industry, but by a company which bases its approach on a technology developed outside that industry. Sometimes this results from forward integration of a firm that is eager to develop applications for a new component or raw material. Texas Instrument's entry into a wide variety of consumer electronic products from a base of semiconductor manufacture, is a case in point. Sometimes it results from the application by firms of a technology developed in one market to opportunities in another. Or sometimes a breakthrough in either product or process technology may remove traditional barriers to entry in an industry and attract a completely new set of competitors. Consider the following examples:

- *Watchmakers have recently found that a new class of competitor is challenging their industry leadership—namely electronic firms who are seeking end-market applications for their semiconductors, as well as a new breed of assemblers manufacturing digital watches.*
- *Manufacturers of mechanical adjustable speed drive equipment found their markets eroded by electrical speed drives in the early 1900s. Electrical drives were based on rotating motor-generator sets and electronic controls. In the late 1950s, the advent of solid state electronics, in turn, virtually obsoleted rotating equipment. New independent competitors, basing their approach on the assembly of electronic components, joined the large electrical equipment manufacturers in the speed drive market. Today, yet another change is taking place, namely the advent of large computer controlled drive systems. This is ushering yet another class of competitors into the market—namely, companies whose basic competence is in computers.*

In each of these cases, recurrent waves of new technology fundamentally changed the nature of the market and usually ushered in an entirely new class of competitors. Many firms in most markets have a limited capability to master all the technologies which might ultimately cannibalize their business. The nature of technological innovation and diffusion is such that most *major* innovations will originate outside a particular industry and not within it.

In many cases, the upheaval is not only technological; indeed the nature of competition may also change dramatically as technology changes. The advent of solid state electronics in the speed drive industry, for example, ushered in a number of small, low overhead, independent assemblers who based their approach primarily on low price. Prior to that, the market had been dominated by the large electrical equipment manufacturers basing their approach largely on applications engineering coupled with high prices and high margins.

The "strategic window" concept does not preclude adaption when it appears feasible, but rather suggests that certain firms may be better suited to compete in certain technological waves than in others. Often the cost and the difficulty of acquiring the new technology, as well as the sunk-cost commitment to the old, argue against adaption.

Market Redefinition

Frequently, as markets evolve, the fundamental definition of the market changes in ways which increasingly disqualify some competitors while providing opportunities for others. The trend towards marketing "systems" of products as opposed to individual pieces of equipment provides many examples of this phenomenon. The situation of Docutel illustrates this point.

Docutel.   This manufacturer of automatic teller machines (ATM's) supplied virtually all the ATMs in use up to late 1974. In early 1975, Docutel found itself losing market share to large computer companies such as Burroughs, Honeywell, and IBM as these manufacturers began to look at the banks' total EFTS (Electronic Funds Transfer System) needs. They offered the bank a package of equipment representing a complete system of which the ATM was only one component. In essence their success may be attributed to the fact that they redefined the market in a way which increasingly appeared to disqualify Docutel as a potential supplier.

Market redefinition is not limited to the banking industry; similar trends are underway in scientific instrumentation, process control equipment, the machine tool industry, office equipment, and electric control gear, to name but a few. In each case, manufacturers basing their approach on the marketing of individual hardware items are seeing their "strategic window" closing as computer systems producers move in to take advantage of emerging opportunites.

Channel Changes

Changes in the channels of distribution for both consumer and industrial goods can have far reaching consequences for existing competitors and would-be entrants.

Changes take place in part because of product life cycle phenomena—the shift as the market matures to more intensive distribution, increasing convenience, and often lower levels of channel service. Changes also frequently take place as a result of new institutional development in the channels themselves. Few sectors of American industry have changed as fast as retail and wholesale distribution, with the result that completely new types of outlets may be employed by suppliers seeking to develop competitive advantage.

Whatever the origin of the change, the effect may be to provide an opportunity for a new entrant and to raise questions about the viability of existing competitors. Gillette's contemplated entry into the blank cassette tape market is a case in point.

Gillette. As the market for cassettes evolved due to increased penetration and new uses of equipment for automotive, study, business, letter writing, and home entertainment, so did distribution channels broaden into an increasing number of drug chains, variety stores, and large discount stores.

Presumably it was recognition of a possible "strategic window" for Gillette that encouraged executives in the Safety Razor Division to look carefully at ways in which Gillette might exploit the cassette market at this particular stage in its evolution. The question was whether Gillette's skill in marketing low-priced, frequently purchased package goods, along with its distribution channel resources, could be applied to marketing blank cassettes. Was there a place for a competitor in this market to offer a quality, branded product, broadly distributed and supported by heavy media advertising in much the same way that Gillette marketed razor blades?

Actually, Gillette decided against entry, apparently not because a "strategic window" did not exist, but because profit prospects were not favorable. They did, however, enter the cigarette lighter business based on similar analysis and reportedly have had considerable success with their *Cricket* brand.

Problems and Opportunities

What do all these examples indicate? *First*, they suggest that the "resource requirements" for success in a business—whether these be financial requirements, marketing requirements, engineering requirements, or whatever—may change radically with market evolution. *Second*, they appear to suggest that, by contrast, the firm's resources and key competencies often cannot be so easily adjusted. The result is a *predictable* change in the fit of the firm to its market—leading to defined periods during which a "strategic window" exists and can be exploited.

The "strategic window" concept can be useful to incumbent competitors as well as to would-be entrants into a market. For the former, it provides a way of relating future strategic moves to market evolution and of assessing how resources should be allocated to existing activities. For the latter, it provides a framework for diversification and growth.

Existing Businesses

Confronted with changes in the marketplace which potentially disqualify the firm from continued successful participation, several strategic options are available:

1. An attempt can be made to assemble the resources needed to close the gap between the new critical marketing requirements and the firm's competences.

2. The firm may shift its efforts to selected segments, where the "fit" between requirements and resources is still acceptable.

3. The firm may shift to a "low profile" approach—cutting back severely on all further allocation of capital and deliberately "milking" the business for short-run profit.

4. A decision may be taken to exit from that particular market either through liquidation or through sale.

All too frequently, however, because the "strategic window" phenomenon is not clearly recognized, these strategic choices are not clearly articulated. Instead, "old" approaches are continued long after the market has changed with the result that market position is lost and financial losses pile up. Or, often only half-hearted attempts are made to assemble the new resources required to compete effectively; or management is simply deluded into believing that it can adapt itself to the new situation even where this is actually out of the question.

The four basic strategic choices outlined above may be viewed hierarchically in terms of *resource commitment*, with No. 1 representing the highest level of commitment. Only the company itself can decide which position on the hierarchy it should adopt in particular situations, but the following guideline questions may be helpful:

- To what extent do the changes call for skills and resources completely outside the traditional competence of the firm? A careful analysis has to be made of the gap which may emerge between the evolving requirements of the market and the firm's profile.
- To what extent can changes be anticipated? Often it is easier to adapt through a series of minor adjustments—a stepping stone approach to change—than it is to be confronted with a major and unexpected discontinuity in approach.
- How rapid are the changes which are taking place? Is there enough time to adjust without forfeiting a major share of the market which later may be difficult to regain?
- How long will realignment of the functional activities of the firm take? Is the need limited to only some functions, or are all the basic resources of the firm affected—e.g., technology, engineering, manufacturing, marketing, sales, and organization policies?
- What existing commitments—e.g., technical skills, distribution channels, manufacturing approaches, etc.—constrain adaption?
- Can the new resources and new approaches be developed internally or must they be acquired?
- Will the changes completely obsolete existing ways of doing business or will there be a chance for coexistence? In the case of new technologies intruding from outside industry, the decision often has to be made to "join-em rather than fight-em." Not to do so is to risk complete obsolescence. In other cases, coexistence may be possible.
- Are there segments of the market where the firm's existing resources can be effectively concentrated?

- How large is the firm's stake in the business? To the extent that the business represents a major source of revenues and profit, a greater commitment will probably need to be made to adapt to the changing circumstances.
- Will corporate management, in the event that this is a business unit within a multibusiness corporation, be willing to accept different goals for the business in the future than it has in the past? A decision not to adapt to changes may result in high short-run returns from that particular business. Looking at the problem from the position of corporate planners interested in the welfare of the total corporation, a periodic market-by-market analysis in the terms described above would appear to be imperative prior to setting goals, agreeing on strategies, and allocating resources.

New Entrants

The "strategic window" concept has been used implicitly by many new entrants to judge the direction, timing, and scale of new entry activities. Gillette's entry into cigarette lighters, major computer manufacturers entry into ATMs, and Proctor & Gamble's entry into many consumer markets *after* pioneers have laid the groundwork for a large-scale, mass-market approach to the specific product areas, all are familiar examples.

Such approaches to strategic market planning require two distinctly different types of analysis?

1. Careful assessment has to be made of the firm's strengths and weaknesses. This should include audits of all the key resources of the company as well as its various existing programs of activity.

2. Attention should be directed away from the narrow focus of familiar products and markets to a search for opportunities to put unique competencies to work. This requires a broader appreciation of overall environmental, technical and market forces and knowledge of many more markets, than is encountered in many firms today. It puts a particular burden on marketing managers, general managers, and business planners used to thinking in terms of existing activities.

Analysis of patterns of market evolution and diagnosis of critical market requirements in the future can also be of use to incumbent competitors as a forewarning of potential new entry. In such cases, adjustments in strategy can sometimes be made in advance, which will ultimately deter would-be new competitors. Even where this is not the case, resource commitments may be adjusted to reflect the future changes in structure of industrial supply.

Conclusion

The "strategic window" concept suggests that fundamental changes are needed in marketing management practice, and in particular in strategic market planning activities. At the heart of these changes is the need to base marketing planning around predictions of future patterns of market evolution and to make assessments of the firm's capabilities to deal with change. Such analyses require considerably greater strategic orientation than the sales forecasting activities which underpin much marketing planning today. Users of product portfolio chart analysis, in particular, should consider the dynamic as opposed to the static implications in designating a particular business.

Entry and exit from markets is likely to occur with greater rapidity than is often the case today, as firms search for opportunities where their resources can be deployed with maximum effectiveness. Short of entry and exit, the allocation of funds to markets should be timed to coincide with the period when the fit between the firm and the market is at its optimum. Entering a market in its early stages and evolving with it until maturity may, on closer analysis, turn out to be a serious management error.

It has been said that while the life of the product is limited, a market has greater longevity and as such can provide a business with a steady and growing stream of revenue and profit if managment can avoid being myopic about change. This article suggests that as far as any one firm is concerned, a market also is a temporary vehicle for growth, a vehicle which should be used and abandoned as circumstances dictate—the reason being that the firm is often slower to evolve and change than is the market in which it competes.

Bibliography

Ben M. Enis, Raymond LaGarce and Arthur E. Prell, "Extending the Product Life Cycle," *Business Horizons*, June 1977, pg. 46.

Nelson N. Foote, "Market Segmentation as a Competitive Strategy," presented at the Consumer Market Segmentation Conference, American Marketing Association, Chicago, February 24, 1967.

The Product Portfolio, Boston Consulting Group Perspective; see also, "A Note on the Boston Consulting Group Concept of Competitive Analysis and Corporate Strategy," Intercollegiate Case Clearing House No. 9-175-175; and George S. Day, "Diagnosing the Product Portfolio," *Journal of Marketing*, Vol. 41 No. 2 (April 1977), pg. 29.

See the following cases: Emery Air Freight Corporation (B); Gillette Safety Razor Division: The Blank Cassette Project; and Docutel Corporation; Intercollegiate Case Clearing House Nos. 9-511-044, 9-574-058 and 9-578-073 respectively.

A. C. Cooper, E. DeMuzzio, K. Hatten, E. J. Hicks, D. Tock, "Strategic Responses to Technological Threats," Proceedings of the Business Policy and Planning Division of the Academy of Management, Paper #2, Boston, Academy of Management, August 1974.

Derek F. Abell, "Competitive Market Strategies: Some Generalizations and Hypotheses," Marketing Science Institute, April 1975, Report No. 75-107.

Derek F. Abell, "Business Definition as an Element of the Strategic Decision," presented at the American Marketing Association/Marketing Science Institute Conference on Product and Market Planning, Pittsburgh, November 1977.

William E. Rothschild, *Putting It All Together: A Guide to Strategic Thinking* (New York: Amacom, 1976), pp. 103–121.

Theodore Levitt, "Marketing Myopia," *Harvard Business Review*, September-October 1975, pg. 26.

Section Six

Implementation of Marketing Strategies

IT is clear that a strategy becomes effective only when it influences action. However, this noncontroversial assertion masks an intractable dilemma in the application of strategic analysis.

Implementation is the process of translating strategic imperatives into various operating forms—including actions such as organizational designs for the control-and-reward system. No implementation decision excludes all others nor is it totally consistent within itself. At one end of the spectrum is an overemphasis on the definition of detailed tactical actions at a high level in the organization, suspiciously like the classic foolishness of "buying a dog and then barking oneself." At the other end, a reliance on a full feedback loop of monitoring, control, and adjustment can produce such delays that "the stable is locked after the horse has bolted." In this last section, we examine readings that cover, in more detail, the various options. Each article is characterized by an emphasis on the benefits of the particular form of implementation being considered.

Before we examine the various approaches, we will look at "implementation" in a complex diversified corporation. In Section V, we discussed some problems of understanding the impact of hierarchical decision making, particularly the role of senior divisional and corporate management in the development of the marketing strategy plan. These issues become even more critical during the process of implementation.

The two simplified models (Figure VI.1) of the process help in understanding some of the practical problems and provide a framework in which to compare the articles in this section.[1] The models are neither comprehensive nor exclusive but merely a starting point for a more comprehensive analysis. The first model, labelled "traditional," represents the basic thinking underlying the dilemma between setting broad objectives at one extreme and prescribing detailed implementation (tactical) actions at the other. In our simple distinction between corporate, business unit/division, and functional (marketing/sales) levels, we see the process as one in which the formulation of strategy at each higher level results in the transfer of objectives (and the presumed monitoring and control activity related to them) to each lower level with only the lowest (functional) level actually taking action. This view of the implementation process poses the uncomfortable choice between overly detailed but substantive instruction and broad objectives that are not specific enough.

An alternative view is labelled "interactive." In one sense, even the traditional model is interactive: feedback of information can improve the quality of the decisions on both objectives and actions. The alternative model, however, is truly interactive in that strategy at each level sets the context for strategy at other levels (either "up" or "down").

For example, marketing strategy at the functional level may attempt to redefine the bundle of product and service attributes offered to the consumer. This decision can influence the way in which the overall unit and its competitors are viewed at the business unit level, which in turn may influence the framework within which the corporate-level strategy is assessed. Such a process is common where a renewed focus on premium positioning and customer value requires the assessment of broad market options at the corporate level to be responsive to detailed and specific market evidence.

This interactive model for the process also reflects the "learning adaptive" model discussed previously. Strategy formulation is linked between different levels: what is transferred between levels includes form of organization, agendas, and procedures along with substantive detail.

The interactive model also recognizes two issues that were first raised in the introduction to this book: (1) there are both strategies and tactics at every level in the organization, and thus the use of the word "tactics" is possibly misleading, and (2) direct actions tend to be more appropriate in an "implementation" framework. Direct actions involve acquisition and divestment for corporate management, major capital investment in R&D, production or distribution for business unit management and detailed mix decisions (linked to market share and positioning strategies) for marketing/sales management.

Market Share Strategies

As we discussed in Section III, market share plays an important, possibly singular, role in the marketing strategy literature. The relationship between market share and ROI (see Figure III.1) suggests that businesses with high share make more money. Thus, implementation programs are typically developed with an

Figure VI.1   Two Models of Strategy and Implementation

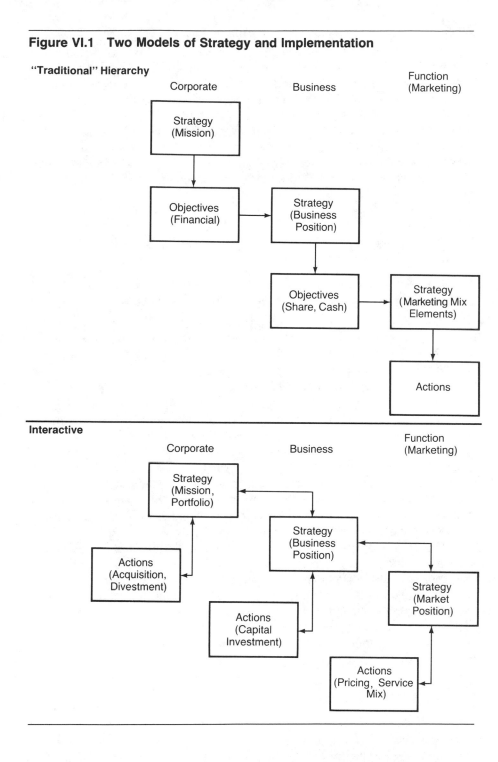

objective of increasing market share. However, the mere fact that share and ROI are correlated does not indicate conclusively that businesses should make investments simply to increase share. The benefit of achieving a high share may not justify the level of investment needed to achieve the position. For example, *Fortune* reports that DuPont cut prices for years to achieve a dominant position in the manufacturing of nylon, but was never able to make a significant profit.[2] Over the last 10 years research on the significance of this relationship between ROI and market share has been extensive but has not resulted in one widely accepted view. Three main issues arise in attempting to interpret the ROI and market share relationship for strategic prescriptions (market share strategies to improve profitability):

1. Market share explains only a small proportion of the variance in ROI.

2. Correlations between changes in market share and changes in ROI do not provide sufficient evidence to imply a causal relationship.

3. If market share is actually an intangible asset, it may be fairly priced; therefore, one cannot expect to make money soley by investing in it.

A number of important issues remain to be resolved, some of which are unresolvable within the context of the PIMS data base because of the limited types of models that can be specified and/or estimated. The first article in this section, "Is Market Share All That It's Cracked Up To Be?" examines this issue.

An important aspect of pursuing market share is, obviously, the sustainability of increases in market share gains. For example, a firm might achieve a significant gain in share by increasing advertising expenditures only to lose it when competitors respond by increasing their advertising expenditures. Several research studies have explored the effectiveness of various marketing mix variables in achieving a sustainable increase in share.[3] These studies suggest that investments in products and sales force are more effective at gaining share than investments in advertising and price decreases. These findings might be related to the notion that price and advertising changes are highly visible and can be responded to quickly.

Michael Porter, in his widely read books *Competitive Strategy* and *Competitive Advantage*, suggests two basic approaches for achieving a high ROI. One approach, cost leadership, proposes that a business focus on achieving a low-cost position relative to competition; the other approach, product differentiation, emphasizes offering a unique set of benefits and high product quality to customers. In Article 22, "Product Quality, Cost Position and Business Performance: A Test of Some Key Hypotheses," the effectiveness and potential interrelationships between these two approaches are examined empirically.

Customer Relationships

In Section One, we indicated that two important marketing-related sources of sustainable competitive advantage are customer loyalty and channel control. Article 23 discusses how customer loyalty can be achieved by positioning products to satisfy customer needs. Brand names are used to assure customers that a set of benefits will be provided consistently. Article 24 discusses the observation that brand names are a valuable asset to be exploited through brand extensions, but that such extensions must be undertaken with care. Finally, Article 25, "Making Sure Your Customers Keep Coming Back," describes how customer needs change over time and suggests that marketing strategies must adapt to these changes.

Channel Relationships

The potential for creating a sustainable competitive advantage through effective management of channel relationships is emphasized by Professor Raymond Corey:

> *A distribution system . . . is a key* external *resource. Normally, it takes years to build, and is not easily changed. It ranks in importance with key* internal *resources such as manufacturing, research, engineering, and field sales personnel and facilities. . . . It represents . . . a commitment to a set of policies and practices that constitute the basic fabric on which is woven an extensive set of long-term relationships.*[4]

Channel relationships play an important strategic role for two reasons. First, channel activities provide excellent opportunities for developing a superior offering from the customer's perspective, because distribution functions add significantly more value to a firm's offering than product development, manufacturing, or advertising activities. Second, enduring channel relationships are difficult to achieve and even more difficult to alter. Thus, advantages based on channel relationships are not easily attacked by competition.

There are four basic approaches or systems for coordinating and controlling the activities in a channel of distribution. In a *conventional channel,* the channel functions are provided by independent channel intermediaries. The agents, wholesalers, and retailers in conventional channels distribute the products offered by a number of producers. Each intermediary is primarily concerned with managing its immediate suppliers and customers to maximize its profits. Thus, a conventional channel involves a number of independent decision makers who focus on only one stage of the distribution process. Coordination of distribution functions is provided by market forces via the price mechanism. Producers compete against each other by offering products at attractive prices (margins) to secure the services of channel intermediaries. Conventional channels are characterized by a low level of coordination among channel members and limited control by the producers over activities performed by the channel members. However, market forces can induce very efficient performance of distribution functions. If a distributor fails to perform efficiently, producers and retailers will use other distributors who are available to provide services at lower costs.

In an *administered system,* a producer coordinates the distribution function by offering a program for a specific line of merchandise. The independent channel members can accept or reject the program. The typical program involves the producer offering guaranteed prices and delivery, customized sales aids (catalogs, point-of-purchase displays, demonstration equipment), advertising support, sales training, and assortment and floor plans. In exchange, the retailer agrees to display the producer's products in the suggested manner, maintain a specified level and assortment of inventory, and undertake appropriate advertising. Producers using an administered system to achieve control over the distribution function are exploiting their own expertise in merchandising their products. Furthermore, while the producer cannot force channel members to participate, the program is designed so that it is in the channel members' economic interest to adopt it.

In a *contractual system,* the activities to be performed by channel members and the producer are formalized in a contractual agreement. With this agreement, independent firms have a greater impact on the market than they could maintain through unilateral action. While there are many types of contractural systems, franchising is the most pervasive contractual system in the U.S. economy. More than 30 percent of all U.S. retail sales are made by franchise chains. The franchise contracts can coordinate activities between producers and retailers (General Motors and automobile dealerships), producers and wholesalers (Coca-Cola and soft-drink bottlers), wholesalers and retailers (Rexall drug stores), and developers of services and retailers (AAMCO, Midas, Holiday Inn, McDonald's, Kentucky Fried Chicken, and Kelly Services).

A *corporate channel* represents forward vertical integration by producers. All the channel functions are performed by organizational entities owned and operated by one firm. Singer (sewing machines); Sherwin-Williams (paints); and Hart, Schaffner, and Marx (men's clothing) are examples of corporations which have performed the production, wholesaling, and retailing functions for their products. By virtue of ownership, these firms maintained absolute control over the distribtuion activities for their products and had an opportunity to coordinate these activities to achieve a competitive advantage. However, significant administrative costs may be involved in effectively coordinating the distribution functions, and often becomes attractive to develop independent retail outlets at a later stage of market development.

Many marketers feel that greater control automatically leads to more efficiency in coordinating channel activities. However, the conventional systems employing the invisible hand of the marketplace can be more cost efficient than corporate systems. Article 26, "Make-or-Buy Decisions: A Framework for Analyzing Vertical Integration Issues in Marketing," discusses the conditions under which vertical integration (the corporate channel system) results in a more cost-effective channel than conventional systems.

Organization of Strategy Implementation

The organization of multiple-product, multimarket business must attempt to direct resources and programs to specific markets while exploiting the firm's capabilities across the entire range of product-markets in which it is participating. In general, effective action in a product-market is achieved through decentralization which places decision making in the hands of people who are in direct contact with the product-market environment. On the other hand, some centralization is needed to exploit synergies across product-markets. Article 27, "Managing Beyond Portfolio Analysis," explores this trade-off.

Some Cautions

The articles in this section examine how a chosen strategy might be implemented, but a few cautions are in order. Robert Hayes and William Abernathy have expressed concern than an overreliance on short-term performance measures (such as market share and profitability) can lead to a long-run decline in competitive position.[5] Such undesirable effects are, of course, increased when senior executives set hurdle rates for the returns on new investments, rates that exceed those derived from the financial markets, as discussed in Section III. Further problems are created when the crucial importance of timing is not recognized and too much emphasis is placed on certainty. If we wait too long to be certain that a marketing opportunity exists, then it will pass by if a competitor has responded more quickly.[6]

Article 12, "Strategic Responses to Technological Threats," provided an important, if restricted, test of the frequent underlying assumption that recognition of technological change in its markets provides the means for the dominant firm to react effectively by adapting. The actual evidence is distinctly pessimistic. Technological change often changes the nature of the market itself to the extent that previous competitive strengths count for little or, even worse, prove to be real handicaps. Others, have raised the concern that too much of strategic planning seems, in practice, to be directed toward broad and often trivial generalized strategies—such as cost leadership or market niches—rather than toward understanding the specifics and the opportunities of the product-market in question.[7]

A Partial Synthesis

As we suggested in Section I, our introduction to strategic marketing—and as many of the readings testify—the relationship between marketing strategy and action (implementation) poses a number of unresolved questions. The final conclusion about the current state of knowledge must be a personal one. While we hope we have made our own position clear, let us emphasize that it is very much our own position and that readers must make up their own minds on the basis of the conflicting arguments.

We choose to emphasize three particular apsects of strategic marketing. First, we believe that the process of thinking and acting strategically is a critical part of effective operations within an organization. Thinking strategically involves dialogue and debate. Assumptions must be made to surface and should be challenged. Any strategic action which seems initially to be obviously right must be severely tested. Second, it is not useful just to consider marketing strategy in broad terms of structure and organizational design at the corporate level and to leave more detailed market-based analysis solely to the operating level. A more interactive approach needs to be adopted between the various levels of analysis as well as between the various levels within the organization.[8] Third, to the extent that marketing strategy analysis embodies the evidence of empirical regularities in the competitive marketplace, a good understanding of the rules is a good basis on which to judge particular opportunities to beat the competition.

In summary, any student or practitioner of marketing strategy would be well advised to spend some time considering the following comment by Kiechel:

Strategic concepts may be a bit like the rules of the Assassins. That curious medieval sect of Muslim fanatics, we are told, had several orders or ranks, each with its own place in an ascending hierarchy. Upon being promoted into the next highest order, initiates would be given a new, and presumably loftier, set of rules to live by. After years during which these structures became second nature to them, the devout might even find a place in the ninth, or highest order. These few would wait with hushed reverence as the sect's leader welcomed them individually into the elect, whispering into the ear of each the final, ultimate wisdom. The message: "There are no rules."[8]

Footnotes

1. A more complex framework in which to assess the impact of organization, process, and substantive plans is provided by J. Galbraith and D. Nathanson, *Strategy Implementation: The Role of Structure and Process* (St. Paul, Minn.: West Publishing, 1978).

2. Walter Kiechel III, "The Decline of the Experience Curve," *Fortune,* October 5, 1984, 139.

3. Robert D. Buzzell and Fredrick D. Wiersema, "Modelling Changes in Market Share: A Cross-Sectional Analysis," *Strategic Management Journal* 2 (1981):27–42.

4. E. Raymond Corey, *Industrial Marketing: Cases and Concepts* (Englewood Cliffs, N.J.: Prentice-Hall, 1976), 263.

5. Robert M. Hayes and William J. Abernathy, "Managing Our Way to Economic Decline," *Harvard Business Review* (July–August 1980):67–77. This and related issues in the application of economic analysis to the identification of competitive opportunities are discussed in greater detail in Robin Wensley, "PIMS and BCG: New Horizon or False Dawn," *Strategic Management Journal* (April–June 1982):149–158.

6. J. Quincy Hunsicker, "The Malaise of Strategic Planning," *Management Review* (March 1980):8–14.

7. Michael Porter, in his book *Competitive Strategy: Techniques of Analyzing Business, Industry, and Competitors* (New York: The Free Press, 1981), uses the term generic rather than generalized to describe such strategies. Generic, however, implies that each is distinctly independent and the classification is not susceptible to further simplification. In fact, his three "generic" strategies (cost-leadership, differentiation, and focused) are all subsets of the basic strategy of maintaining competitiveness in a defensible market sector and it is not clear that the three are either the only or the most useful way of subdividing the basic strategy. In his more recent book, *Competitive Advantage: Creating and Sustaining Superior Performance* (New York: The Free Press, 1985), he apparently proposes a four-box classification based on breadth of competitive scope and degree of differentiation.

8.   This issue is discussed in more detail in P. J. Boxer and R. Wensley, "The Need for Middle-Out Development of Marketing Strategy," *Journal of Management Studies,* March 1986.

9.   Walter Kiechel III, "Playing the Rules of the Corporate Strategy Game," *Fortune,* September 24, 1979, 110–115.

Additional Readings for Section Six

Share Building Strategies

Allesco, J. "Market Share Madness." *Journal of Business Strategy* (Fall 1982):76–79.

Bloom, Paul E. and Philip Kotler. "Strategies for High Market Share Companies." *Harvard Business Review* (November–December 1975):63–72.

Burke, M. C. "Strategic Choice and Marketing Managers: An Examination of Business-Level Marketing Objectives." *Journal of Marketing Research* (November 1984):345–359.

Buzzell, Robert D. and Frederik K. Wiersema. "Modelling Changes in Market Share: A Cross-Sectional Analysis." *Strategic Management Journal* (1981):27–42.

Buzzell, Robert D. and F. Wiersema. "Successful Share-building Strategies." *Harvard Business Reviews* 59 (January–February 1981):135–144.

Buzzell, Robert D., Bradley T. Gale, and Ralph G. M. Sultan. "Market Share—A Key to Profitability." *Harvard Business Review* (January–February 1975):97–106.

Fogg, C. Davis. "Planning Gains in Market Share." *Journal of Marketing* (July 1974):30–38.

Gale and Branch. "The Dispute About High-Share Business." *Journal of Business Strategy* (Summer 1980):71–73.

Fruhan, William E. "Pyrrhic Victories in Fights for Market Share." *Harvard Business Review* (September–October 1972):100–107.

Hall, William K. "Survival Strategies in a Hostile Environment." *Harvard Business Review* (September–October 1980):75–85.

Hambrick, D. and S. Schecter. "Turnaround Strategies for Mature Industrial Product Business Units." *Academy of Management Journal* 26 (1983):231–248.

Hambrick, D. and S. Schecter. "High Profit Strategies in Mature Capital Goods Industries: A Contingency Approach." *Academy of Management Journal* 26 (1983):687–707.

Hamermesh, R. G., M. J. Anderson Jr., and J. E. Harris. "Strategies for Low Market Share Businesses." *Harvard Business Review* (May–June 1978):95–102.

Hamermesh, R. G. and Steven B. Silk. "How to Compete in Stagnant Industries." *Harvard Business Review* (September–October 1979):161–168.

Harrigan, K. "Strategies for Declining Industries." *Journal of Business Strategy* (Fall 1980):20–34.

Harrigan, K. and M. Porter. "End-Game Strategies for Declining Industries." *Harvard Business Review* (July–August 1983):111–120.

Hearne. "Fighting Industrial Senility: A System for Growth in Mature Industries." *Journal of Business Strategy* (Fall 1982):3–20.

Hofer, C. "Turnaround Strategies." *Journal of Business Strategy* (Summer 1980):19–31.

Kotler, Philip. "Harvesting Strategies for Weak Products." *Business Horizons* (August 1978):15–22.

Levitt, Theodore. "Marketing Success Through Differentiation—of Anything." *Harvard Business Review* (January–February 1980):83–91.

Wind, Yoram and Vijay Mahajan. "Market Share: Concepts, Findings and Directions for Future Research." In *Review of Marketing, 1981,* edited by Ben M. Enis and Kenneth J. Roering, 31–42. Chicago: American Marketing Association, 1981.

Woo, Carolyn Y. "Market Share Leadership—Not Always So Good." *Harvard Business Review* (January–February 1984):50–54.

Woo, Carolyn Y. "Evaluation of the Strategies and Performances of Low ROI Market Share Leaders." *Strategic Management Journal* (1983):123–135.

Woo, Carolyn Y. and Arnold C. Cooper. "The Surprising Case for Low Market Share." *Harvard Business Review* (November–December 1982):106–113.

Implementation Issues

Bonoma, T. "Making Your Marketing Strategy Work." *Harvard Business Review* (March–April 1984):69–76.

Bonoma, T. "Marketing Success Can Breed Marketing Inertia." *Harvard Business Review* (September–October 1981):115–121.

Bucklin, L. "A Theory of Channel Control." *Journal of Marketing* (January 1973):39–47.

Dearden, John. "The Case Against ROI Control." *Harvard Business Review* (May–June 1969):124–135.

Etgar, M. "Selection of an Effective Channel Control Mix." *Journal of Marketing* (July 1978):53–58.

Frohman, A. "Technology as a Competitive Weapon." *Harvard Business Review* (January–February 1982):97–104.

Galbraith J. and D. Nathanson. *Strategy Implementation: The Role of Structure and Process.* St. Paul, Minn.: West Publishing, 1978.

Guiltinan, J. "Planned and Evolutionary Changes in Distribution Channels." *Journal of Retailing* (Summer 1974):79–103.

Hanan, M. "Reorganize Your Company Around Its Markets." *Harvard Business Review* (November–December 1974):63–74.

Hauser, John and Steven M. Shugan. "Defensive Marketing Strategies." *Marketing Science* 2 (1983):319–360.

Hulbert, James M. and Norman E. Toy. "A Strategic Framework for Marketing Control." *Journal of Marketing* (April 1977):12–20.

Klein, B., R. Crawford, and A. Alchian. "Vertical Integration, Appropriable Rents, and the Competitive Contracting Process." *Journal of Law and Economics* 21 (1978):233–261.

Paul, Ronald M. and Neil Donovan. "The Reality Gap in Strategic Planning." *Harvard Business Review* (November–December 1976):66–72.

Resnik, A., P. B. Turney, and J. B. Mason. "Marketers Turn to Counter Segmentation." *Harvard Business Review* (September–October 1979):100–106.

El-Ansary, Adel and Robert Robicheaux. "A Theory of Channel Control: Revisited." *Journal of Marketing* (January 1974):2–7.

Robinson, William T. and Claes Fornell. "Sources of Market Pioneer Advantages in Consumer Goods Industries." *Journal of Marketing Research* (August 1985):305–317.

Schnaars, Steven P. "Timing Entry Into Growth Markets: A Comparison of Twelve Case Histories." *Business Horizons* (March–April 1986).

Weigand, R. C. "Buying Into Market Control." *Harvard Business Review* (November–December 1980):141–149.

Yip, George S. "Gateways to Entry." *Harvard Business Review* (September–October 1982):85–92.

21

Is Market Share All That It's Cracked Up to Be?

Robert Jacobson and David A. Aaker

A most influential development in strategic management has been the emergence of market share as a pivotal key to profitability.[1] One stimulus for this view was the empirical studies of the Boston Consulting Group and others that documented experience and economies of scale effects and the associated portfolio models that suggested, at least for some business types, that resources should be withdrawn unless the firm could obtain a relatively high market share position. Another impetus was the well-known research stream based upon the PIMS data base that empirically found a consistent association between market share and profitability.

The early highly visible PIMS based article of Buzzell, Gale, and Sultan (1975) reported that a 10 percent point difference in market share is accompanied by a 5 percent point difference in ROI. Based on a model that also controls for concentration, Gale and Branch (1982) came to the same conclusion. Further, the multivariable PIMS PAR ROI equation indicates that a 1 percent increase in market share leads to a .6 percent increase in ROI (Branch 1980; Gale, Heany, and Swire 1977).[2]

Two causal explanations are usually offered for the observed link between market share and profitability. First is the related effects of the experience curve and economies of scale. Through cumulative experience, tasks can be accomplished more efficiently by improving methods and procedures or by simple repetition. The desire to achieve cumulative experience effects can foster capital in-

---

[1]Profitability is used in the sense of economic profits/rents, i.e., a rate of return more than sufficient to maintain capital investment.

[2]Shepard (1972), making use of Fortune Directory data, reports two smaller estimates of the market share effect (.34 and .43).

This article first appeared in the *Journal of Marketing* 49 (Fall 1985):11–22. Reprinted with permission from *Journal of Marketing*, published by the American Marketing Association.

When this aticle was published the authors were Assistant Professor of Marketing, School of Business Administration, University of Washington; and J. Gary Shansby Professor of Marketing Strategy, School of Administration, University of California-Berkeley, respectively.

vestment in operations and product redesign efforts to reduce costs. Scale economies can be achieved by larger share businesses, as plant and equipment investment and expenses such as marketing and R&D can be spread over more units.

Although experience and scale effects have been observed literally thousands of times, they are neither universal nor automatic (Aaker 1984, Chapter 10). Experience effects tend to be found in industries with high levels of value added, continuous process manufacturing and high capital intensity. In other contexts, most notably service and extractive industries, experience effect strategies are rarely applied successfully. Further, experience effects are not automatic but require disciplined, effective programs in worker efficiency, product redesign, and capital utilization. In addition, economies of scale do not appear in all contexts, and, in fact, diseconomies of scale are very possible. Empirical evidence, e.g., Scherer (1980), suggests that minimum optimal scale can be achieved at output levels consistent with relatively small market shares.

A second causal explanation is that large market share can create market power over and above the cost advantage achieved by experience/scale effects. Large share firms may be able to extract favorable concessions from channel members because of their size and importance in the market. In addition, large market share may serve as an indicator of concentration, which may encourage collusive behavior and higher prices. However, this last argument is weakened by the results of Gale and Branch (1982) who find that when market share and concentration are both included in a model explaining profitability, the importance of concentration is insignificant.

There is, however, a third explanation for the observed association between market share and ROI. This explanation suggests the association is not causal but spurious, in that it is the result of both being jointly influenced by some third factor(s). One possible common causal factor is management quality. Good management may generate programs that make the marketing effort effective and the product line attractive and thereby achieve high market share. Good management may also initiate programs that encourage cost control, productivity gains, wise product line decisions, etc., and so achieve high ROI. Thus, the high ROI would not necessarily be caused by the high market share position; rather, both would be the joint outcome of the process of good management. To illustrate the implications, consider the futility of trying to enhance ROI through promotional efforts directed at increasing market share if the causal link from market share is much less than assumed.

Perhaps of equal or more importance is another possible common factor, luck. Based on pure chance, a business may be lucky enough to stumble onto one or more products or strategies that will prove to be successful. Mancke (1974) supports this argument with a simulation in which he demonstrates that an association between market share and profitability could be the result of lucky firms obtaining higher profits that could be reinvested so as to obtain more rapid growth than their less lucky rivals.

The existence of experience, scale, or market power effects based on market share provides the motivation, as posited by neoclassical economic/marketing theory, for a firm to follow a market share strategy as a means of achieving increased profitability. The implication is that market share has some intrinsic value by its direct impact on profitability. A gain in share will cause an increase in ROI. However, if the association between market share and ROI is largely based on a common association with a third factor and is therefore spurious, this type of strategy may be inappropriate. Gain in market share need not lead to increases in profitability and in fact could result in a decrease.

These explanations of the association between market share and ROI are not mutually exclusive. Theoretically, it is reasonable to expect that all three phenomena may be at work. The crucial question and the goal of this article is to determine to what extent is the association between market share and ROI causal and to what extent is the association spurious, i.e., reflecting common associations with third factors. At issue is determining the average increase in ROI if steps are taken to increase market share by 1 percent. The frame of reference is the various PIMS studies that have suggested that a 1 percent increase in market share would generate a .5 percent increase in ROI.

The PIMS data base, described in the next section, is also utilized in this study. However, unlike most previous studies, the analysis makes use of both cross-sectional and time series data. As a first step, the findings of Buzzell, Gale, and Sultan (1975) are replicated using regression analysis. Efforts are then made to separate the spurious from the direct influence of market share on ROI. First, lagged values of ROI are added to the ROI model as a means of capturing factors, such as luck and management quality, that may be a source of some spurious association. Second, to reduce potential contemporaneous spurious associations, market share is separated into two components: anticipated market share (the share explained by controllable or predetermined factors), and unanticipated market share (the share representing contemporaneous shocks). Third, additional explanatory factors, e.g., price, cost, promotion, are added to the ROI model so as to control for other influences. The result of these steps is an estimate of the market share effect with the bias caused by omitted variables substantially reduced. Our results are then contrasted with two previous studies with similar objectives. The possibility that market share might have a lagged effect or be enhanced under certain circumstances is then explored. Finally, some implications of the study are discussed.

The Data Base

The data used in this analysis are drawn from the PIMS (Profit Impact of Market Strategy) data base of the Strategic Planning Institute. PIMS data are based on reports of over 2,000 business units that are components of the over 200 corporations participating in the PIMS project. A business unit is defined as a division of the firm ''selling a distinct set of products to an identifiable set of customers in competition with a well-defined set of competitors.'' By use of a standardized form, information concerning the annual income statement, balance sheet, and other conditions such as market environment, is reported. Variables used in this study are defined in Table 1.

Because the data are kept confidential and participants are users of the data base, respondents are motivated to be accurate and conscientious when supplying

Table 1   Definition of Variables

Variable	Definition
Buyer Concentration	Number of immediate customers
Cap Util	Capacity utilization
Entry	Entry of competitors
Exit	Exit of competitors
Full PAR ROI	Estimate of ROI from PAR equation
Mrk Int	Marketing intensity[a]
MS	Market share
MS Rank	Market share rank
MSAN	Anticipated market share
MSLAG1	Market share in previous year
MSLAG2	Market share two years ago
MSUN	Unanticipated market share
Product Importance	Importance of product to immediate customers
Product Life Cycle	Life cycle stage of product category
Real Growth	Real long-term market growth
Rel Adver	Relative media advertising expenditures
Rel Cost	Relative direct costs
Rel Image	Relative product image/company reputation
Relative Market Share	Relative market share
Rel Price	Relative price
Rel New Prod	Relative new products[b]
Rel Promo	Relative promotion expenditures
Rel Qual	Relative product quality[c]
Rel SForce	Relative salesforce expenditures
ROI	Return on investment
ROILAG1	Return on investment in previous year
ROILAG2	Return on investment two years ago
Vert Int	Vertical integration[d]

[a]**marketing expenditures/revenue**
[b]**new products percent of sales (this business)—new products percent of sales (competition)**
[c]**percent of sales from superior products—percent of sales from inferior products**
[d]**value added/revenue**

data. In addition, the Strategic Planning Institute takes care to check any apparent inconsistencies in the data.

However, the data are not without limitations. The participating firms are not representative in that they tend to be large diversified corporations. There are very few small firms and new businesses in the project. Another limitation is that much of the data is subject to the assessment of the participant. The validity and/or consistency of subjective measures, such as relative product quality and defined market, might be subject to question. The ROI measure, based on accounting data that are often artifacts of the tax laws, e.g., depreciation, may also be a suspect indicator of the financial performance of a business (Fisher and McGowan 1983).

The PIMS project has two principal data bases. The most widely used is the SP14 data base which contains a cross-section of the four-year average of a business's report. The other is the SPIYR data base that contains combined cross-sectional time series data based on the cross-sectional data for the over 2,000 business units and the time series data for the number of years the business participated in the PIMS program. This study makes use of the SPIYR data base because, unlike the SP14 data base, it offers the possibility of capturing lagged effects and examining effects that might be averaged away in the SP14 data base.

The Market Share Effect

The ROI–Market Share Association

As evidenced by the regressions of equation 1 in Table 2, there is a significant association between market share and ROI.[3]

$$\text{ROI} = \beta_0 + \beta_1 \cdot MS + \epsilon \qquad (1)$$

The coefficient for the impact across all business units of market share on ROI of .5 is exactly in correspondence with empirical estimates reported in other studies. However, this regression does not indicate how much of the association is causal (whether it be through experience curve effects, economies of scale, or market power) and how much of it is spurious (the result of a common association with some third factor(s)). The estimate of the market share effect can be expected to be biased because there is a host of omitted factors that influence ROI and are correlated with market share.

Controlling for Lagged ROI

One way to capture some of the impact of these omitted factors is through the inclusion of previous years' ROI in the model. Previous years' ROI can act as a surrogate for firm specific factors occurring in previous periods that tend to be constant on a year-to-year basis, influence ROI, and may also influence market share. Past factors such as customer loyalty, distribution systems, advertising effectiveness, fortuitous circumstances, etc., have influenced ROI in previous periods and, if constant, may tend to influence current ROI in a similar manner. Lagged values of ROI can therefore serve to some extent as proxies for these factors.[4]

---

[3]The PIMS business units are identified as belonging to one of eight business types. For this study we have chosen not to analyze businesses classified as services or retail and wholesale distribution because of the relatively few number of businesses in these groups. Of the remaining businesses, analysis was done across all business types and by the groupings of (1) consumer products, (2) capital goods, and (3) materials, components, and supplies. The aggregation of the six business types into these three groupings was based on considerations of meaningful differences between regression coefficients of the various models explored. The difference between the consumer durables and consumer nondurable groupings was particularly small.

[4]The use of lagged values as surrogates for other factors is, in fact, the basis for the Box and Jenkins (1970) approach to time series analysis.

Table 2 ROI–Market Share Association

Coefficient Estimates	All Businesses	Consumer Goods Businesses	Capital Goods Businesses	Material, Components, and Supply Businesses
Intercept	10.16[a]	5.65[a]	4.14	13.84[a]
	(0.67)[b]	(0.94)	(2.62)	(0.69)
Market share	0.50[a]	0.74[a]	0.48[a]	0.42[a]
	(0.02)	(0.03)	(0.08)	(0.02)
R^2	0.05	0.16	0.02	0.07
Degrees of freedom	10213	2689	2011	5509

[a]significant at 99 percent level
[b]standard errors in parentheses

The inclusion of lagged dependent variables as explanatory factors, while rather common in time series studies, is often overlooked in cross-sectional studies. However, these terms may be able to capture some of the impact of past factors, even factors such as management quality and luck, which tend to be unobservable, on ROI and can help to reduce the potential for bias in estimates of the market share effect. In fact, ROI lagged one year is able to explain almost as much of the variation in ROI as the estimate of Full PAR ROI that is generated by the PIMS PAR ROI equation.[5]

A disadvantage of the inclusion of lagged ROI terms is the relative lack of dynamic variation, i.e., year-to-year movements in the data, which will not influence the consistency of coefficient estimates but may not allow adequate variation to isolate the impact of the various factors. However, this lack of variation is somewhat compensated by the large sample size available in the PIMS data base.

Table 3 reports the results of equation 2 that regresses ROI on market share and on ROI lagged one and two years, termed ROILAG1 and ROILAG2.[6]

$$ROI = \beta_0 + \beta_1 \cdot MS + \beta_2 \cdot ROILAG1 + \beta_3 \cdot ROILAG2 + \epsilon \quad (2)$$

Across all businesses lagged ROI was found to have a major impact and was able to substantially increase explanatory power. The relatively small standard errors for the coefficients indicate that the large sample size is able to overcome the relative lack of year-to-year variation so that the coefficients could be estimated with a relatively high level of precision. The impact of lagged ROI was very large for consumer goods and for materials, supplies, and components businesses and surprisingly small for capital goods businesses.

For each business grouping the coefficient for market share dropped from that of equation 1. For the aggregate grouping the market share effect reported in Table 3 is roughly half of that reported in Table 2, .22 versus .50. The implication is that a great deal of the association between market share and ROI is spurious and that the inclusion of lagged ROI is able to remove some of this spurious association by acting as a proxy for various third factors, such as management quality and luck.

However, there are differences between business types. The observed drop in the impact of market share was quite drastic for consumer product businesses (.74 to .17) and for materials, components, and supply businesses (.42 to .12). But the drop in capital goods businesses was relatively modest (.48 to .40). This modest drop suggests two possibilities that need to be explored further. First, the direct effect of market share may be more important in this business grouping. Second, for this grouping, lagged ROI may be an inadequate proxy for the third

---

[5]A regression of ROI on Full PAR ROI yielded an R-square of .32. The ROI on ROI lagged one year regression had an R-square of .28. Given that a regression of ROI on Full PAR ROI and ROI lagged one year yielded an R-square of .45 suggests that the explanatory power of the PAR ROI model can be improved by use of dynamic information.

[6]The sample size is reduced from that reported in Table 2 because observations that did not have data for the two preceding years were deleted.

Table 3 ROI–Market Share Association Controlling for Past ROI

Coefficient Estimates	All Businesses	Consumer Goods Businesses	Capital Goods Businesses	Materials, Components, and Supply Businesses
Intercept	5.20[a]	1.02	8.07[a]	4.91[a]
	(0.56)[b]	(0.71)	(1.93)	(0.59)
Market share	0.22[a]	0.17[a]	0.40[a]	0.12[a]
	(0.02)	(0.03)	(0.06)	(0.02)
ROI lagged 1 year	0.54[a]	0.71[a]	0.06[c]	0.67[a]
	(0.01)	(0.02)	(0.03)	(0.02)
ROI lagged 2 years	0.06[a]	0.11[a]	0.07[a]	0.06[a]
	(0.01)	(0.02)	(0.01)	(0.02)
R^2	0.39	0.70	0.07	0.58
Degrees of freedom	6350	1640	1267	3435

[a]significant at 99 percent level
[b]standard errors in parentheses
[c]significant at 95 percent level

factor(s) and so substantial bias may still remain in the estimate of the market share effect.[7]

What specifically the lagged ROI measures are reflecting is uncertain. We do not know to what extent they represent luck, elements of management quality (e.g., ability to generate effective advertising), or other factors such as brand loyalty or distribution strength. In fact, lagged ROI undoubtedly reflects different factors for different business units. A direction for future research might well be to determine the underlying structural phenomena that account for the usefulness of lagged ROI in explaining current ROI. However, we do know that lagged ROI is not representing market share as a market share term is explicitly modeled. Possible collinearity between lagged ROI and market share will not bias either the estimate of the market share effect or its standard error but will tend to increase the standard errors of the coefficients. However, even this influence of collinearity is not especially relevant in our analysis, since the large sample size allows for the construction of relatively small confidence intervals.

The Effect of Anticipated versus Unanticipated Market Share

By including the lagged ROI terms, third factors are controlled to the extent that they appeared in a previous period. However, it is reasonable to expect that situations exist where contemporaneous shocks will effect both ROI and market share during the current year. For example, a business might run into anticipated and perhaps uncontrollable production or marketing problems affecting both ROI and market share. Sales might be greater than anticipated because of unexpected market acceptance, exit of a major competitor, or distribution success. A new management team might institute a variety of changes/shocks that simultaneously affect both market share and ROI, but the change in ROI may not be directly influenced by the change in market share. Further, the reality is that some products do much better than others, even when they come from the same firm, have equal support, and an equal prior probability of success, just because of random shocks. By not incorporating the contemporaneous shock effect, a bias is still likely to exist in the market share coefficient reported in Table 3. What is needed is a means of isolating the intrinsic value of market share from that of shock that jointly influences both ROI and market share.

Towards this end, market share is separated into two components. The first component, which is termed *anticipated market share* (MSAN), is the market share that can be predicted based on controllable and/or predetermined factors. Anticipated market share is a variable that is purged of the effect of any contemporaneous shock and whose impact on ROI, as represented by β_1, equation 3, can be expected to better represent the intrinsic value of market share.

The second component, termed *unanticipated market share* (MSUN), is that market share that cannot be predicted based on the market share model. It is defined to be the difference between actual market share and anticipated market

---

[7]The relatively high year-to-year variation in ROI, and so the small impact of lagged ROI, might be explained by the fact that capital goods sales and ROI tend to be highly sensitive to fluctuations in the economy.

share, i.e., MS − MSAN. Unanticipated market share is to a large extent the market share that is the result of some unforeseen shock and whose impact on ROI, as represented by β_2 in equation 3, will include not only the impact of any shock but also the impact of any intrinsic value of market share.

$$ROI = \beta_0 + \beta_1 \cdot MSAN + \beta_2 \cdot MSUN$$
$$+ \beta_3 \cdot ROILAG1 + \beta_4 \cdot ROILAG2 + \epsilon \quad (3)$$

If neoclassical theory totally explains the association between market share and ROI, i.e., that the association is strictly causal, then one would expect, subject to the limitations of the PIMS data base, the impact on ROI of anticipated market share to be the same as that of unanticipated market share, i.e., $\beta_1 = \beta_2$. On the other hand, if the association of market share is solely the result of a joint dependency with some shock, then one would expect that anticipated market share would not have an impact on ROI but that unanticipated market share would have a positive impact on ROI, i.e., $\beta_1 = 0$ and $\beta_2 > 0$. If both theories are at work, then both anticipated and unanticipated market share will effect ROI. But since unanticipated market share may both reflect a common association and have a causal impact, its impact will differ from the impact of anticipated market share. The hypothesis that both views are at work but that the impact of anticipated market share is greater would imply that $\beta_1 > \beta_2 > 0$. However, the hypothesis that both views are at work but that the impact of unanticipated market share is greater would imply that $\beta_2 > \beta_1 > 0$.

The Market Share Model

In order to obtain measures of anticipated and unanticipated market share, the market share model depicted in equation 4 was developed and estimated. The model specification is very similar to that developed by Buzzell and Wiersema (1981). The most notable difference is that their analysis makes use of the average percentage change in market share over a four-year period, while we prefer to model the association of market share with previous years' market share with the use of lagged terms. Market share lagged one and two years is included in equation 4 following the similar logic that led to the inclusion of lagged ROI in the ROI model, i.e., to serve as surrogates for relevant factors not captured by other independent variables. MSAN is measured as the market share predicted by equation 4. The residual error from this equation, i.e., η, is the empirical estimate of MSUN. Table 4 reports the results. The R-square values in the range of .95 suggest that most of market share is anticipated, i.e., can be explained by controllable and/or predetermined variables. For each of the business groupings, the principal explanatory factor in the model is lagged market share.

$$MS = \delta_0 + \delta_1 \cdot MSLAG1 + \delta_2 \cdot MSLAG2$$
$$+ \delta_3 \cdot Entry + \delta_4 \cdot Exit$$
$$+ \delta_5 \cdot MSRank + \delta_6 \cdot MrkInt$$
$$+ \delta_7 \cdot RelPrice + \delta_8 \cdot RelQual$$
$$+ \delta_9 \cdot RelNewProd + \delta_{10} \cdot RelSForce$$
$$+ \delta_{11} \cdot RelAdver + \delta_{12} \cdot RelPromo$$
$$+ \delta_{13} \cdot RelImage + \eta \quad (4)$$

Other relevant factors in the model are competition entry and exit. As expected, competitor exit tends to increase share, while competitor entry does the reverse. The market share rank variable is significantly negative, perhaps because of ceiling effects; market share is more difficult to increase for larger share firms. Relative product quality and relative new product sales were both found to be positively related to market share. Of the relative marketing terms, only relative advertising was found to have a significant positive effect. A negative association was found to exist for market share with marketing intensity (except for consumer goods) and relative price.

There are two findings of Table 4 that warrant more detailed comment. First, the negative association found between market share and marketing intensity is consistent with an economies of scale argument discussed in Buzzell, Gale, and Sultan (1975). They suggest this is an indication that larger share firms are in fact able to obtain lower per unit marketing costs.

Second, Table 4 reports a negative association between relative price and market share. Certainly economic theory would expect nothing less. However, this finding is not completely consistent with other studies making use of PIMS data. Buzzell and Wiersema (1981) do not include a measure of relative price in their model based on a lack of predictive power. Phillips, Chang, and Buzzell (1983) found a positive association between market share and price. They suggest that this finding indicates that "no lawlike connection exists between price and share." Perhaps a more realistic explanation is that the measure of relative price available in the PIMS data base is a poor indicator of the competitiveness of the price charged by the firm. However, the coefficients reported in Table 4 indicating a negative although relatively small association between price and share suggest that the measure has some power of detecting the workings of the price mechanism.

Separating Anticipated from Unanticipated Market Share Effects

Table 5 shows the results of attempting to isolate the impact of the intrinsic value of market share by regressing ROI on anticipated market share (MSAN), i.e., the market share predicted by the market share model of equation 4, and unanticipated market (MSUN), i.e., the unexplained residual error from equation 4.[8]

The results suggest that both anticipated and unanticipated market share influence ROI. For each of the business groupings, it was found that the coefficient for unanticipated market share was far greater than that of anticipated market share. This would suggest that by not controlling for contemporaneous factors causing unexpected changes in market share, there is an upward bias in the estimate of the direct effect of market share. This bias is relatively small because unanticipated market share is a relatively minor component of market share. However, the market share impacts, as indicated by the unanticipated market share coefficients in Table 5, are all lower than the market share coefficients of Table 3

---

[8]The estimates of MSAN and MSUN appear insensitive to specification changes in equation 4, e.g., attempts to model interactive and nonlinear effects, apparently because of the crucial explanatory role played by lagged market share.

Table 4 Market Share Model

Coefficient Estimates	All Businesses	Consumer Goods Businesses	Capital Goods Businesses	Materials, Components, and Supply Businesses
Intercept	4.16[a]	2.71[a]	4.32[b]	4.22[a]
	(0.51)[c]	(0.60)	(1.65)	(0.74)
Market share lagged 1 year	0.89[a]	0.88[a]	0.79[a]	0.93[a]
	(0.01)	(0.02)	(0.03)	(0.02)
Market share lagged 2 years	0.04[a]	0.08[a]	0.10[a]	-0.004
	(0.01)	(0.02)	(0.03)	(0.02)
Entry	-0.50[a]	-0.44[a]	-0.71[b]	-0.38[b]
	(0.12)	(0.15)	(0.34)	(0.17)
Exit	0.32[b]	0.61[a]	0.48	0.19
	(0.13)	(0.16)	(0.37)	(0.19)
Market share rank	-0.89[a]	-0.57[a]	-1.50[a]	-0.77[a]
	(0.06)	(0.08)	(0.19)	(0.08)
Marketing intensity	-2.35[a]	1.19	-3.49	-5.74
	(0.72)	(0.81)	(0.19)	(1.35)

Rel price	-0.008^b	-0.009^b	0.02	-0.01^b
	(0.004)	(0.004)	(0.01)	(0.006)
Rel quality	0.01^a	0.004	0.03^a	0.008^b
	(0.002)	(0.003)	(0.006)	(0.003)
Rel new products	0.03^a	0.02^a	0.04^a	0.04^a
	(0.0005)	(0.006)	(0.009)	(0.007)
Rel salesforce	-0.07^b	-0.11	0.004	-0.08
	(0.004)	(0.07)	(0.16)	(0.08)
Rel advertising	0.15^b	0.15^b	0.18	0.21^b
	(0.06)	(0.07)	(0.17)	(0.09)
Rel promotion	0.006	-0.09	0.07	0.004
	(0.07)	(0.08)	(0.20)	(0.10)
Rel image	0.14^b	0.19^b	-0.32	0.23^b
	(0.07)	(0.09)	(0.21)	(0.09)
R^2	0.95	0.98	0.93	0.96
Degrees of freedom	6340	1630	1257	3425

[a]significant at 99 percent level
[b]significant at 95 percent level
[c]standard errors in parentheses

Table 5   ROI–Market Share Association Controlling for Past ROI and Unanticipated Market Share

Coefficient Estimates	All Businesses	Consumer Goods Businesses	Capital Goods Businesses	Materials, Components, and Supplies Businesses
Intercept	5.96[a]	1.53[b]	9.11[a]	5.52[a]
	(0.56)[c]	(0.70)	(1.91)	(0.59)
Anticipated market share	0.18[a]	0.15[a]	0.35[a]	0.09[a]
	(0.02)	(0.03)	(0.06)	(0.02)
Unanticipated market share	0.95[a]	1.17[a]	.94[a]	.74[a]
	(0.08)	(0.16)	(0.21)	(0.08)
ROI lagged 1 year	0.54[a]	0.71[a]	0.07[a]	0.68[a]
	(0.01)	(0.02)	(0.03)	(0.02)
ROI lagged 2 years	0.06[a]	0.11[a]	0.07[a]	0.06[a]
	(0.01)	(0.02)	(0.01)	(0.02)
R^2	0.39	0.70	0.07	0.59
Degrees of freedom	6349	1639	1266	3434

[a]significant at 99 percent level
[b]significant at 95 percent level
[c]standard errors in parentheses

(.18 vs .22; .15 vs .17; .35 vs .45; and .09 vs .12).

An alternate interpretation of the use of MSAN is that it is a means of removing simultaneous equation bias from the estimate of the market share effect that might result if a feedback from ROI to market share existed. Our procedure of obtaining an estimate of MSAN from equation 4 and then utilizing this estimate in equation 3 is analogous to two-stage least squares. Given that theory exists to support positive causal influences in both directions between market share and ROI, a positive bias in the least squares estimate might be hypothesized. The reduction in the magnitude of the estimates of the market share effect reported in Table 5 from that of Table 3 may be partially or even totally caused by the removal of simultaneous equation bias from the least squares estimates.

The Role of Other Factors

Although the lagged ROI terms are able to act as surrogates for influences on ROI that do not change substantially from year to year, they are obviously imperfect measures of key factors influencing profitability. To the extent that measures of potentially relevant explanatory factors of profitability are available, it is reasonable to employ them. Further, since an increase in market share is usually assumed to be caused by expenditures in marketing, quality, etc., which may tend to depress ROI in the short run, it becomes important to control for such variables to the extent possible. Equation 5 represents such an expanded regression model, the estimation of which is reported in Table 6.

$$
\begin{aligned}
\text{ROI} = \ & \beta_0 + \beta_1 \cdot \text{MSAN} + \beta_2 \cdot \text{MSUN} \\
& + \beta_3 \cdot \text{ROILAG1} + \beta_4 \cdot \text{ROILAG2} \\
& + \beta_5 \cdot \text{VertInt} + \beta_6 \cdot \text{MrkInt} \\
& + \beta_7 \cdot \text{CapUtil} + \beta_8 \cdot \text{RelPrice} \\
& + \beta_9 \cdot \text{RelCost} + \beta_{10} \cdot \text{RelQual} \\
& + \beta_{11} \cdot \text{RelNewProd} + \beta_{12} \cdot \text{RealGrowth} \\
& + \beta_{13} \cdot \text{RelSForce} + \beta_{14} \cdot \text{RelAdver} \\
& + \beta_{15} \cdot \text{RelPromo} + \beta_{16} \cdot \text{RelImage} + \epsilon
\end{aligned} \qquad (5)
$$

The estimate of the direct effect of market share as represented by the coefficient for anticipated market share has again rather dramatically fallen. The coefficient for the aggregated grouping is .09, less than one-fifth of the commonly cited estimate of .5. The smallest and the only statistically insignificant impact (.03) is reported for materials, components, and supplies businesses. The largest impact (.19) of market share was found for capital goods businesses. However, this is about one-half the size of the effect reported in Table 5 and is not statistically different from the impact (.13) found for consumer products businesses.

The impacts of the other variables in the model are consistent with the findings of other PIMS studies.[9] Value added, capacity utilization, relative quality, real market growth, and relative image were all positively related to ROI. Mar-

---

[9]Given that some of the same control variables appear in both equations 4 and 5, their impact in equation 5 indicates their direct influence on ROI, i.e., an effect net of any indirect impact they might have on ROI through an influence on market share.

Table 6 ROI Model

Coefficient Estimates	All Businesses	Consumer Goods Businesses	Capital Goods Businesses	Materials, Components, and Supplies Businesses
Intercept	-21.52[a]	-14.56[a]	-5.71	-22.35[a]
	(3.50)[b]	(4.36)	(14.46)	(3.66)
Anticipated market share	0.09[a]	0.13[a]	0.19[a]	0.03
	(0.02)	(0.03)	(0.06)	(0.02)
Unanticipated market share	0.89[a]	1.04[a]	0.77[a]	0.71[a]
	(0.08)	(0.16)	(0.20)	(0.08)
ROI lagged 1 year	0.50[a]	0.68[a]	-.02	.64[a]
	(0.01)	(0.02)	(0.03)	(0.02)
ROI lagged 2 years	0.07[a]	0.12[a]	0.06[a]	0.07[a]
	(0.01)	(0.02)	(0.01)	(0.02)
Vertical integration	29.16[a]	22.21[a]	51.96[a]	22.45[a]
	(2.16)	(3.05)	(8.12)	(2.19)
Marketing intensity	-36.90[a]	-18.88[a]	-116.24[a]	-18.98[c]
	(4.81)	(5.34)	(14.88)	(7.10)
Capacity utilization	0.17[a]	0.11[a]	0.34[a]	0.16[a]
	(0.02)	(0.02)	(0.05)	(0.02)
Rel price	0.08[c]	0.07	-0.02	0.06
	(0.03)	(0.04)	(0.12)	(0.04)

Rel cost	−0.07[c]	−0.05	−0.29[c]	−0.04
	(0.03)	(0.05)	(.12)	(0.04)
Rel quality	0.05[a]	−0.005	0.11[c]	0.04[a]
	(0.01)	(0.02)	(0.04)	(0.01)
Rel new products	0.03	−0.0001	−0.03	0.04
	(0.03)	(0.04)	(0.06)	(0.03)
Real market growth	0.14[a]	0.09[a]	0.11	0.12[a]
	(0.03)	(0.04)	(0.07)	(0.03)
Rel salesforce	−0.05	−0.46	0.10	0.39
	(0.35)	(0.46)	(1.12)	(0.38)
Rel advertising	−0.13	0.98[c]	−1.60	−0.07
	(0.37)	(0.42)	(1.22)	(0.43)
Rel promotion	−0.25	−0.21	1.32	−0.57
	(0.41)	(0.48)	(1.39)	(0.47)
Rel image	0.90[c]	0.44	1.83	0.79
	(0.43)	(0.58)	(1.49)	(0.44)
R^2	0.39	0.72	0.18	0.62
Degrees of freedom	6349	1627	1254	3422

[a]significant at 99 percent level
[b]standard errors in parentheses
[c]significant at 95 percent level

keting intensity had a negative relationship as did the three relative marketing variables, though not significantly. Relative cost had a negative effect, suggesting that lower costs were not entirely passed along to customers through lower prices. The positive impact of relative price perhaps indicates that businesses were, on the average, operating in an inelastic part of their demand curves. No consistent effect was found for relative new products.

Previous Studies Focusing on the Role of Third Factor Causation on the Market Share Effect

Two previous studies are particularly relevant to the findings discussed above. Gale and Branch (1982) conclude that the third factor effect exists but it is only a small part of the association between market share and ROI. In the other, Rumelt and Wensley (1980) suggest that the association between ROI and market share is solely the result of an association with a common factor. Problems relating to the experimental designs of these studies can perhaps explain the conflicting results.

Gale and Branch regress ROI on the level of market share and the change in market share, suggesting that the coefficient for the market share level represents the causal impact and the coefficient for the market share change reflects third factor effects. Both were found to be significant, but market share level had far greater explanatory power. Their finding that the third factor effect is only a small part of the explanation of the market share–ROI relationship may have been caused by a failure to adequately control for third factor effects. The inclusion of the change in market share to a large extent does control for the impact of contemporaneous shocks. However, results reported in this study make it clear that a number of other factors that are not controlled for by Gale and Branch, like management quality and luck, can also cause spurious association.

Rumelt and Wensley also explored the relative importance of the direct market share effect and stochastic (i.e., third factor) effects. They found no market share effect after market share is "cleansed" of its correlation with common third factors by use of an instrumental variable procedure. They attempted to cross-check their results by running a regression of the change in return on the growth in market share and a proxy (unanticipated growth in output) for the common third influence. They again find that the market share growth coefficient is insignificant and therefore conclude that the null hypothesis of no direct share effect on ROI cannot be rejected.[10]

This conclusion might not stem from a lack of relationship but perhaps from an inability of the approach to detect a relationship. First, as their authors note, since their instrumental variable estimate is a weak proxy for the change in market share, their tests to discern the direct market share effect will lack power, i.e., the tests will have a large Type II error in the detection of small market share effects. Second, the use of differenced data does not allow for the determination

---

[10]We tested the role of unanticipated output in equation 5 and found that it did not alter the impact of anticipated market share on ROI.

of what factors caused ROI to be at a specific level. One such factor might be market share. The change in market share, and, to a lesser extent, the change in ROI, involves an analysis of unexpected factors or shocks. The data used may well have differenced out a large amount of the underlying structural phenomenon, so that detecting possible impacts would be made more difficult. If differencing was indeed appropriate, the coefficient for ROI lagged one year should have been empirically observed to be approximately 1.00 instead of, for example, the estimate for all businesses of .50 reported in Table 6.

Conclusion

This investigation suggests that the direct impact of market share on ROI that was found using the PIMS data base is substantially lower than widely assumed. Instead of the commonly cited figure of a 1 percent change in market share being associated with a .5 percent change in ROI, we have found a 1 percent change in market share associated with a .1 percent change in ROI. The estimate of the market share effect reported in this study is 21 standard deviations less than the commonly cited estimate of .5. The discrepancy between the two estimates stems from the contention that a large amount of the correlation between ROI and market share is spurious, in the sense that they are both the joint outcome of some third factor(s).

Lagged Market Share Effects

Given the distinctly contrary nature of these findings, additional challenges would seem warranted. It could be possible that market share has delayed and/or carryover effects on ROI, in that the major impact of market share may not be contemporaneous but occur in some later periods. The activities required to generate the increase in market share could depress contemporaneous ROI but serve to increase ROI in subsequent years. The inclusion of variables such as marketing intensity and measures of the relative levels of price, quality, salesforce, advertising, and promotion in equation 5 reflect a concern to control for this possibility. However, it may be that such variables are not sufficiently sensitive to depict this effect. In addition, lagged ROI could be capturing the presence of a carryover effect via a Koyck (1954) distributed lag model.

To test the possibility that market share has a delayed/carryover effect on ROI, ROI was regressed on ROI lagged 1 and 2 years, the control variables in equation 5, current market share, and market share lagged 1, 2, 3, 4, and 5 years.[11] No such effect was detected. The sum of the coefficients involving market share was .09. The only significant impacts of market share were found contemporaneously and lagged 1 year. These impacts were exactly what would be ex-

---

[11]An equation involving higher order lagged terms of ROI was also tested. The estimate of the market share effect in a model involving ROI lagged 1, 2, 3, 4, and 5 years was virtually indistinguishable from that reported in Table 6.

pected, given the results of equation 5 and the high autocorrelation between market share and market share lagged 1 year.[12] The coefficients for the higher order lags were substantially smaller, insignificant, and added little explanatory power to the model. The hypothesis that the coefficients for these higher order lags were all equal to zero could not be rejected. This challenge failed to produce any evidence to indicate that market share has an impact different from that reported in Table 6.

Conditions under which Market Share Is More Important

Past studies, e.g., Buzzell, Gale, and Sultan (1975) and Woo and Cooper (1982), present evidence suggesting that the impact of market share differs under different circumstances. To test if our analysis averaged away a major market share effect, several variables that might be thought to interact with the market share impact were explored. ROI was regressed on market share, the control variables in Table 6, and dummy variables that allowed for differences in the intercept and the market share effect based on a determination of particular conditions being above or below the median. The regression coefficient for variables depicting interaction effects with market share thus provides estimates of how the market share effect differs under differing conditions.

This difference was small and insignificant for conditions relating to the product life cycle, product importance, vertical integration, and relative price. This indicates, for instance, that the market share effect was not significantly different for businesses with products early in the life cycle from businesses with products late in the life cycle. However, the market share effect did tend to be about 0.08 greater (with standard errors around .035) the more fragmented the buyer concentration, the less frequent the purchase, the higher the marketing intensity, or the higher the product quality.

The differences of impact of market share according to relative market share were large enough (.14), although insignificant (a standard error of .10), to warrant additional analysis. Following Hambrick and MacMillan (1982), who suggest that market share is more important for firms with very low or very high relative market share, the market share effect was separated by firms having a relative market share below .5, between .5 and 1.5, and above 1.5. While the difference

---

[12]The estimated coefficient values for current and lagged 1 year market share were .9 and $-.8$, respectively. To note the consistency with the estimates reported in Table 6, recall equation 5 models

$$ROI = \beta_1 * MSAN + \beta_2 * MSUN + \ldots$$

Since market share lagged 1 year, i.e., $MS(t-1)$, is found in Table 5 to provide the large percentage of explanatory power in predicting current market share, i.e., $MS(t)$ then $MSAN \cong MS(t-1)$ and so $MSUN \cong MS(t) - MS(t-1)$. Substituting these approximations in equation 5 yields:

$$ROI \cong \beta_1 * MS(t-1) + \beta_2 * (MS(t) - MS(t-1)) + \ldots$$

Upon rearranging:

$$ROI \cong (\beta_1 - \beta_2) * MS(t-1) + \beta_2 * MS(t) + \ldots$$

The estimated coefficient values reported in Table 6 would imply coefficient values of $-.8$ and .9 for $MS(t-1)$ and $MS(t)$, respectively. And, in fact, these were the values that were observed.

for high relative market share firms was both relatively small and insignificant, low relative market share firms had a market share effect .13 higher than that of firms with relative market share above .5. However, the standard error of this estimate (.10) was also large so that the null hypothesis of no difference in impact could not be rejected. Still, the size of the coefficient suggests that market share growth may be more important for small share firms, perhaps because of the greater importance of economies of scale to relatively low volume producers.

Suggestions for Future Research

Obviously there are unanswered questions about the impact of market share upon financial performance. It would be useful to:

- challenge our findings by making use of other data bases.
- learn more about the structure of the process generating ROI. Clearly there are factors and lagged effects in the causal structure that are difficult to effectively model but are important to strategic decision making. Clinical research of individual industries and firms might help to reveal the nature of the third factors giving rise to an association between market share and ROI.
- identify variables that could be employed to better identify those situations where experience, scale, or market power will be factors that will provide a substantial causal impact from market share to ROI.

Implications

The results of this study point to the conclusion that the direct impact of market share on ROI is substantially less than commonly assumed and, in fact, relatively minor. Market share would not appear to be, at least on the average, a key to profitability. Certainly this is not to suggest that market share is unimportant to the management of a business. High market share, together with high ROI, are indications that management has been following policies, whether by design or chance, that have proved to be successful. Market share can be used as an indicator of the effectiveness of current policies and suggestive of how these policies might be altered.

One implication of the conclusion that market share has been exaggerated as a causal determinant of ROI is that too much emphasis in planning and strategy development is focused on market share. Webster (1981) reports that top management view "marketing managers as unsophisticated in their understanding of the financial dimensions of marketing decisions" and tending to "focus more on sales volume and market share changes than on profit contribution and return on assets." Strategies placing strong emphasis on the attainment of high market share may be myopic and inconsistent with longer term horizons. Other fundamentals can be of equal or greater importance. More emphasis might be well-placed upon such key areas as product quality, customer satisfaction, productivity, corporate culture, product line appropriateness, and management effectiveness. In fact, situations could exist where a decline in market share may actually be an indication of good management. Efforts to keep or gain market share, for the sake of being number one or having a certain market share rank, may have a detrimental impact on ROI both in the short and long run. For example, the efforts of IBM in the 1970s to resist share erosion by aggressive price moves seem, at least in retrospect, to have been unwise.

There is no shortage of commentary in the management literature on how a smaller share competitor can achieve high returns without challenging on the basis of market share. One approach is to focus only upon part of the product line such as private labels, speciality, or high price/high quality products. Alternatively, the focus could be on a target segment, such as a regional market or those needing nonstandard products. There are numerous anecdotes about extremely successful businesses that have followed these kinds of niching strategies. Hamermesh, Anderson, and Harris (1978) studied three successful low share firms and concluded their success was due in part to good leadership, controlled growth, efficient use of R&D, and creative market segmentation.

The term *niche* has come to be associated with smallness and an inability to compete. Webster's dictionary defines niche more broadly as (i) a place, employment, or activity where an organism is best suited, or (ii) a habitat supplying the factors necessary for the existence of an organism. This view would seem to be a more insightful starting point for strategy development.

References

Aaker, David A. (1984), *Strategic Market Management*, New York: Wiley.

Box, G. E. P. and G. M. Jenkins (1970), *Time Series Analysis, Forecasting and Control*, San Francisco: Holden-Day.

Branch, Ben (1980), "The Laws of the Marketplace and ROI Dynamics," *Financial Management*, 9 (Summer), 58–65.

Buzzell, Robert D., Bradley T. Gale, and Ralph G. M. Sultan (1975), "Market Share—A Key to Profitability," *Harvard Business Review*, 53 (January-February), 97–106.

Buzzell, Robert D. and Frederick D. Wiersema (1981), "Modelling Changes in Market Share: A Cross-Sectional Analysis," *Strategic Management Journal*, 2 (January-March), 27–42.

Fisher, Franklin M. and John J. McGowan (1983), "On the Misuse of Accounting Rates of Return to Infer Monopoly Profits," *American Economic Review*, 73 (March), 82–97.

Gale, Bradley T. and Ben S. Branch (1982), "Concentration versus Market Share: Which Determines Performance and Why Does It Matter?," *The Antitrust Bulletin*, 27 (Spring), 83–103.

Gale, Bradley T., and Donald F. Heany, and Donald S. Swire (1977), "The PAR ROI Report: Explanation and Commentary on Report," Cambridge, MA: Strategic Planning Institute.

Hambrick, Donald C. and Ian C. MacMillan (1982), "The Product Portfolio and Man's Best Friend," *California Management Review*, 24 (Fall), 84–95.

Hamermesh, R. G., M. S. Anderson, and J. E. Harris (1978), "Strategies for Low Market Share Businesses," *Harvard Business Review*, 56 (May-June), 95–102.

Koyck, L. M. (1954), *Distributed Lags and Investment Analysis*, Amsterdam: North Holland.

Mancke, Richard B. (1974), "Causes of Interfirm Profitability Differences: A New Interpretation of the Evidence," *The Quarterly Journal of Economics,* 88 (May), 181–193.

Phillips, Lynn W., Dae R. Chang, and Robert D. Buzzell (1983), "Product Quality Cost Position and Business Performance: A Test of Some Key Hypotheses," *Journal of Marketing,* 47 (Spring), 26–43.

Rumelt, Richard P. and Robin Wensley (1980), "In Search of the Market Share Effect," working paper MGL-61, University of California at Los Angeles.

Scherer, F. M. (1980), *Industrial Market Structure and Economic Performance,* Chicago: Rand McNally.

Shepard, William G. (1972), "The Elements of Market Structure," *Review of Economics and Statistics,* 54 (February), 25–37.

Webster, Frederick E. (1981), "Top Management's Concerns about Marketing: Issues for the 1980s," *Journal of Marketing,* 45 (Summer), 9–16.

Woo, Carolyn Y. and Arnold C. Cooper (1982), "The Surprising Case for Low Market Share," *Harvard Business Review,* 60 (November-December), 106–113.

22

Product Quality, Cost Position, and Business Performance: A Test of Some Key Hypotheses

Lynn W. Phillips, Dae R. Chang, and Robert D. Buzzell

The Problem

Contemporary views of marketing strategy recognize two alternative approaches to achieving a differential advantage over competitors and earning supranormal rates of return (Hall 1980, Porter 1980). One approach, product differentiation, entails designing or marketing products so that they are perceived as unique by customers. Although many bases for differentiation exist, superior quality is the approach most often used to characterize this strategy (see Kiechel 1981). Differentiation by quality insulates a business from competitive rivalry by creating customer loyalty, lowering customer sensitivity to price, and protecting the business from other competitive forces that reduce price-cost margins (see Porter 1980, pp. 34–46).

An alternative strategy, overall cost leadership, involves generation of higher margins relative to competitors by achieving lower relative direct manufacturing and distribution costs. Higher margins are in turn reinvested in new manu-

This article first appeared in the *Journal of Marketing* 47 (Spring 1983):26–43. Reprinted with permission from *Journal of Marketing*, published by the American Marketing Association.

When this article was published the authors were Assistant Professor of Marketing at Stanford University, doctoral candidate at Harvard University in the Graduate School of Business Administration, and Sebastian S. Kresge, Professor of Business Administration, Harvard University, respectively.

facturing equipment and facilities to maintain cost leadership. Whereas high quality produces superior price-cost margins by operating on prices, cost leadership accomplishes the same by making costs the strategic target.

Literature pertaining to these two generic strategies emphasizes that they are basically incompatible. Indeed, conventional wisdom suggests that achieving higher relative quality or low relative costs are alternative goals that require different courses of action, resources and skills (Hall 1980, Kiechel 1981, Porter 1980). The rationale is that higher quality usually requires the use of more expensive components, less standardized production processes, and the adoption of other manufacturing and management techniques incompatible with achieving low costs. Furthermore, achieving a high quality position may require higher expenditures in other areas beyond the direct costs of manufacturing and distribution. Higher advertising and promotion expenditures may be necessary to convey a quality position to customers (Farris and Reibstein 1979); increased sales force spending may be needed to support the higher level of customer services that may accompany higher quality products; and a heightened emphasis on product innovation may be necessary to sustain a quality position. Finally, achieving such a position may require a perception of exclusivity, which is incompatible with the high relative market share needed for a volume-based cost leadership strategy (see Porter 1980, p. 38). Because of these and other strategic trade-offs between quality and cost, it is expected that higher quality will in most businesses be accompanied by higher costs. Although rare instances may exist where the cost and quality leader in a market are the same (see examples given by Hall 1980), these instances are usually treated as rare exceptions to a general strategic principle.

Despite persuasive arguments for viewing product quality and cost leadership as incompatible business strategies, recent evidence suggests that the incompatibility of quality and cost may be false and that, in fact, the two strategies may be much more conjunctive than conventional wisdom dictates. One line of evidence emerges from studies by manufacturing analysts who have observed that certain types of production processes, as well as certain approaches to managing manufacturing operations, may contribute simultaneously to creating high quality *and* low costs (see Fine 1983, Wheelwright 1981; cf Reddy 1980, Shapiro 1977, Smith 1980). Fine, for example, introduces the idea of a quality-based learning curve. According to his formulation, costs decline more rapidly with the experience of producing high-quality products than with the experience of producing low-quality products. This results because production workers must take more time and care with their work to produce high-quality items. Added care leads to the discovery and correction of defect-causing ''bugs'' in the production system that might otherwise be overlooked. Anecdotal evidence concerning Japanese and American manufacturing operations supports the idea that high quality and low costs are not incompatible (Fine 1983, Wheelwright 1981). In many industries, Japanese manufacturers are believed to be ahead of their U.S. counterparts on both quality and costs, and the observed cost advantages cannot be accounted for solely by differences in wage rates, capital investment, or factory automation (see Fine 1983, Chapter 1, for a review).

Recent studies reporting that product quality exerts a significant positive influence on market share (Buzzell and Wiersema 1981a, 1981b; Flaherty 1982) also support the view that achievement of a high quality position may actually exert a beneficial (i.e., lowering) effect on direct cost position in some markets. Specifically, these studies raise the possibility that product quality has an indirect lowering influence on direct costs via its effects on market position. According to this reasoning, higher quality results in higher market share, which in turn lowers direct costs due to absolute- and experience-based scale economies. Further, if product quality contributes to experience-based cost reductions via its influence on market share, and if experience economies apply not only to production costs but to all components of value added (Wensley 1981), this implies no necessary connection between higher relative quality and higher relative sales force, advertising or other marketing expenditures.

In sum, then, existing hypotheses disagree as to the compatibility of product quality and cost leadership as marketing strategies. One view predicts inherent trade-offs between quality and cost position; another suggests that no inherent trade-offs exist and that pursuit of a high quality strategy may actually have synergistic effects on cost position.

Complicating this picture is the fact that there is little convincing empirical evidence that quality and cost leadership are successful business strategies in the first place. To marshal support for this view, it is necessary to demonstrate that both lower direct cost position and higher product quality are associated with supranormal rates of return. There are almost no published studies showing a significant inverse relation between direct costs and return on investment across a broad sample of businesses, although specific industry case studies abound (see Henderson 1979).

The only evidence for a positive relation between product quality and ROI is that provided by the PIMS studies (Buzzell, Gale and Sultan, 1975; Schoeffler, Buzzell and Heany 1974), and there are methodological reasons to doubt these findings. In these studies, relative product quality is measured by an executive informant report on the percentage of the business unit's annual sales accounted for by products that, from the perspective of the customer, are assessed as superior, equivalent, and inferior to those available from the three leading competitors. PIMS uses estimates of these percentages to calculate a single measure of overall relative quality for each business, computed as percent superior minus percent inferior. As several analysts have noted (Phillips 1981, Rumelt and Wensley 1981, Scherer 1980), judgments of this type may be heavily influenced by informant biases, ignorance, the complexity of the judgment task and random factors, as well as the true state of affairs. If these sources of distortion are not accounted for, they can affect the precision of parameter estimates pertaining to the quality variable and introduce bias (Bagozzi 1980, Bagozzi and Phillips 1982, Phillips 1981). Yet in PIMS studies to date, no attempt has been made to model measurement error explicitly or to control for its potentially contaminating effects on substantive hypothesis testing. Until these measurement error issues are addressed, the integrity of any demonstrated relationships involving the product quality variable is still in doubt.

Beyond these methodological concerns surrounding the product quality–ROI relation, competing views exist as to how product quality actually influences ROI, if indeed it does. One view holds that product quality is a market niche strategy employed by smaller businesses against well-entrenched competitors. Higher quality enables the business to charge premium prices, which generate superior margins but also deter large-scale market penetration (Porter 1980). This scenario is inconsistent with the view that product quality increases ROI indirectly via its positive effects on market position. Whether the influence of product quality on ROI is direct, indirect or both has gone untested in previous studies, in large part because extant studies have relied on simple single equation models incapable of separating direct from indirect effects and controlling for the influence of intervening variables. Only by adopting simultaneous equation modelling procedures can more complex sequences of hypotheses be tested and conflicting hypotheses concerning the quality–ROI link be resolved.

The purpose of this study is to test competing hypotheses concerning the relationships among product quality, cost position and business performance. Specifically, a structural equation methodology is applied to data on businesses in the PIMS data bank to address the following issues:

- Does the achievement of a high relative quality or low relative cost position influence the extent to which a business earns supranormal returns on invested capital?
- If so, what are the mechanisms by which these effects occur? For example, does product quality exert a direct effect on return on investment as suggested in previous studies, or does it influence ROI only indirectly via its hypothesized effects on market position?
- Does the achievement of a high relative quality position necessarily entail trade-offs in terms of relative direct cost position and other cost components?
- To what extent are product quality and cost leadership complementary business strategies? In particular, to what extent does product quality exert an indirect, beneficial influence on relative direct cost position via its hypothesized effects on market share?
- To what extent are the relationships reported in previous PIMS studies involving the product quality variable and other competitive strategy variables spurious due to measurement error in key informant reports on these concepts?

To address these issues, a series of complex theoretical and methodological hypotheses is tested on data from over 600 businesses in the PIMS data base. In contrast to previous PIMS investigations, measurement error in key informant reports on relative product quality, relative direct costs and other key competitive strategy variables is explicitly represented and modelled within the context of a test-retest measurement framework. This approach affords an assessment of the reliability of measurements and control over the potential contaminating influence of measurement error on substantive hypothesis testing (Bagozzi and Phillips 1982). Further, as shown below, the structural equation methodology employed permits the modelling of complex sequences of causal relationships and the identification of direct versus indirect effects within a hypothesized causal system (Bagozzi 1980, 1981a, 1981b). By adopting econometric procedures that explicitly represent measurement fallibility and system complexity, we show how it is possible to distinguish among competing methodological and theoretical hypotheses that have gone untested in previous studies.

Research Methodology

Model

Figure 1 shows the causal model depicting the key relationships under investigation. Using the conventions of structural equation modelling common in the social sciences (e.g., Bagozzi 1980, Jöreskog and Sörbom 1979, 1982), circles represent latent variables and Greek letters depict parameters to be estimated.

In Figure 1, the key substantive hypotheses of the study are represented by the γ and β parameters. Each γ parameter represents a hypothesized causal path between the independent variable, product quality (ξ_1), and a latent dependent variable (η). Each β parameter represents a hypothesized causal path between two latent dependent variables, with the hypothesized directionality of causation shown by the direction of the arrow.

The measurements of the latent independent and dependent variables are shown as x's and y's, respectively. They are further denoted by the letters (t) or (t + 1) to convey that the measures are different informant reports taken at two points in time or, when denoted as (t, t + 1), averages of informant reports over two points in time.

The α's and λ's represent the factor loadings of the latent independent and dependent variables respectively. These values when squared represent the reliability of the measurements (Bagozzi 1980), which indicates the amount of variation in a measure due to the underlying concept. The δ's and ϵ's represent the random error components of the measures. ζ's reflect error in the dependent variables due to factors omitted from the model of Figure 1, and ψ indicates correlations among these error terms. A detailed presentation of the logic and assumptions of the methodology can be found in Bagozzi (1980), Bagozzi and Phillips (1982) and example applications can be found in Jöreskog and Sörbom (1979, 1982).

Below we describe the (1) key hypotheses associated with the model, (2) details of the measurement framework used to operationalize the model, (3) sample construction, and (4) model estimation.

Hypotheses

The Effects of Quality and Cost Position on ROI.   Two distinct views on the effects of product quality on ROI are represented by the parameters γ_1, γ_4 and β_{23}, on the one hand, and the parameters γ_3, β_{42}, β_{12} and β_{43}, on the other. The

Figure 1 Path Diagram Reflecting Key Relationships Being Tested[a]

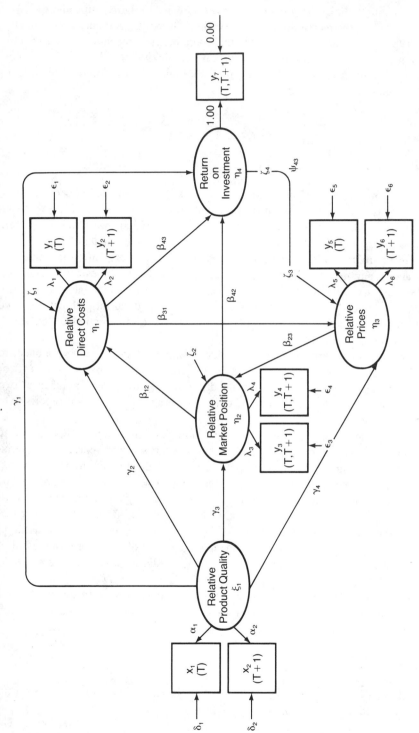

[a]Control variables omitted for simplicity; see Table 1. Equations for this model are presented in a technical appendix available from the authors (see Phillips, Chang and Buzzell 1982).

traditional PIMS–based view is that product quality has a positive direct influence on ROI (Buzzell 1978; Schoeffler, Buzzell and Heany 1974). That is,

H_1: The higher the quality of products in a business unit's portfolio relative to those of its leading competitors, the higher the business unit's return on investment.

Under this scenario, γ_1 is expected to be positive and statistically significant. The explanation usually advanced for the direct effects hypothesis, termed here the "niche theory," is that high-quality products allow the business to avoid profit-damaging competition on the basis of price (Gale and Swire 1977). Although the premium prices commanded by a high quality position may prevent the business from penetrating a large share of the market, this is not a deterrent to profitability. Successful differentiation through quality only requires that the business occupy a niche where it can command superior margins (Porter 1980). Thus, the mechanisms underlying the direct effects hypothesis may be summarized as follows:

H_{1a}: *The higher the quality of products in a business unit's portfolio relative to those of its leading competitors, the higher the level of prices charged relative to those of its leading competitors.*

H_{1b}: *Product quality has an indirect negative influence on market position via its positive effects on relative prices. Alternatively stated, higher relative prices derivable from higher relative quality undermine attainment of higher relative market share.*

Both H_{1a} and H_{1b} predict that γ_4 will be positive and statistically significant; H_{1b} further stipulates that β_{23} will be negative and statistically significant.

A competing view to the niche theory outlined above is that product quality influences ROI, but only indirectly through its effects on relative market position. According to this view, product quality is a major attribute driving customer preferences, and, therefore, relative market share (Buzzell and Wiersema 1981a, 1981b). Since market share presumably influences profitability via its effects on operating economies and other mechanisms (see Rumelt and Wensley 1981 for a review), it is possible that achieving a high quality position affects ROI only through its influence on market position. According to this formulation, market share is an intervening variable moderating the quality–ROI link. Therefore, we may hypothesize:

H_2: Return on investment is a positive function of relative market position and an indirect, positive function of relative product quality.

Support for this view is obtained only when γ_3 is positive and statistically significant and further, relative market position (η_2) is causally linked to return on investment (η_4). Evidence for the latter relationship may emerge in one of two ways. The traditional view is that higher market share causes lower direct costs, which in turn lead to supranormal returns on investment (see Henderson 1979, Porter 1980). This view predicts β_{12} and β_{43} will be negative and statistically significant. Alternatively, market position may influence ROI through mechanisms other than cost, such as market power and nonpecuniary economies of scale (see Scherer 1980 and Rumelt and Wensley 1981 for reviews). If this view is correct,

β_{42} should be positive and statistically significant, regardless of any effects observed for β_{12} and β_{43}. Overall, if any of the causal links between relative market position (η_2) and ROI (η_4) are statistically significant and are accompanied by a positive significant estimate for γ_3, it is appropriate to conclude that H_2 is supported by the data.[1]

The Effects of Product Quality on Relative Direct Cost Position.   The competing views regarding the relationship between product quality and relative direct cost position may be summarized as:

H_3: *The higher the quality of the products in a business unit's portfolio relative to those of its leading competitors, the higher the direct costs of the business's products relative to those of its leading competitors.*

H_4: *Product quality has an indirect beneficial (i.e., lowering) influence on relative direct cost position via its positive effects on relative market position.*

H_3 represents the view that inherent trade-offs exist between relative quality and direct cost position and predicts that γ_2 will be positive and statistically significant. Further, if the success of product quality strategy depends on commanding superior margins, the effect of quality on cost, represented by γ_2, should be less than or equal to the effect of quality on price, represented by γ_4.

Note that if quality exerts a beneficial effect on cost position via the quality–learning curve mechanism posited by Fine (1983), one would expect γ_2 to be negative and statistically significant, thus contradicting H_3. Even if quality fails to exert a direct beneficial effect on direct costs, the effect may be indirect via market share. This view is summarized in H_4 and predicts that γ_3 will be positive and statistically significant and that B_{12} will be negative and statistically significant.

Other Key Relationships.   To avoid misspecification of the model due to omitted causal paths, the effect of relative direct costs (η_1) on relative prices (η_3) is modelled by the parameter β_{31}, which we expected to be positive and statistically significant. As a final precaution to avoid model misspecification, it is necessary to control for the effects of other variables correlated with product quality that might also influence η_1, η_2, η_3 and η_4. Table 1 summarizes the variables used as controls and their hypothesized effects on the dependent variables. These variables were chosen because previous studies showed them to be important correlates of

---

[1]Since H_2 does not necessarily forbid H_1 or H_{1a} to occur, H_1 and H_2 are not entirely mutually exclusive hypotheses. Higher quality products may still command premium prices (H_{1a}), and a higher relative quality position may have direct effects on ROI above and beyond any indirect effects manifested via market share (H_1). However, simultaneous support for both H_{1a} and H_2 does contradict H_{1b}, in that it implies no inverse relation between prices and market share. Instead, H_{1a} and H_2 imply that prices and market position covary positively as a function of a common cause, namely product differentiation by quality.

quality and business performance outcomes (Gale and Swire 1977, Phillips and Buzzell 1982).[2]

Several of the control variables also bear on substantive hypotheses of the study. The view that relative product quality may involve systematic trade-offs in other cost areas, such as marketing expenditures, may be evaluated in our model by examining the magnitude and significance of the intercorrelations between the quality variable (ξ_1) and the control variables ξ_7, ξ_8 and ξ_9 in Table 1. To the extent that a higher relative quality position requires high relative levels of marketing expenditures with respect to innovative effort (ξ_7), sales force effort (ξ_8) and advertising/promotion (ξ_9), the correlations among ξ_1 and ξ_7, ξ_8 and ξ_9 should be positive and statistically significant. Failure to observe statistically significant correlations among these independent variables implies no significant trade-offs between quality and other value-added cost components.

Measurement Framework

Table 2 shows the measurements of the key variables represented in Figure 1. As shown in column 2 of Table 2, measures of ξ_1, η_1 and η_3 were obtained by asking executive informants in each business to respond to the standardized questions shown under column 3.

Ideally, one would like to model measurement error in informants' responses to these questions either by asking the same questions of different informants in the same and/or competitive businesses and comparing responses (see Phillips 1981, 1982), or by comparing informant reports on these variables versus organizational or institutional archives and records (see Pennings 1973). Unfortunately, when a business first enters the PIMS data base, no effort is made to obtain independent judgments from other informants or sources on product quality or other relative competitive strategy variables. While executives who supply this information are encouraged to consult records or other informants in answering certain questions, these controls are informal and fail to provide the multiple observations necessary to model measurement error explicitly.

To model the reliability of these measures, we used a test-retest measurement framework. When a company initially enters a business into the PIMS data

---

[2]Several aspects of our control variable strategy deserve mention. First, it was necessary to combine relative advertising and relative promotion expenditures into a single variable, since these measures are so highly correlated so to reflect almost the same concept (see Phillips and Buzzell 1982). Second, it should be noted that we originally included market concentration as a control variable in our model, but it was too collinear with the relative market position variable to allow its inclusion in the final model. More recent evidence on concentration effects shows, however, that its traditionally assigned importance as an ROI determinant by economists was overstated, since in industry-level studies it served largely as a proxy for aggregated market share (see Gale and Branch 1982, Ravenscraft 1981, Rumelt 1981a, Weiss and Pascoe 1981). Finally, it should also be noted that we attempted several other modifications to the model of Figure 1 to examine the sensitivity of our results to model changes. For example, we hypothesized a causal link between relative advertising/promotion and relative quality, rather than merely allowing them to be correlated. These and other changes failed to alter the substantive conclusions about the patterns of relationships shown in Figure 1.

Table 1   Other Variables Included as Controls in Model of Figure 1 and Their Hypothesized Effects on Dependent Variables

Independent Variables Other than Relative Product Quality (ξ_i) Used as Controls	Dependent Variables (Figure 1)[a]			
	(η_1) Relative Direct Costs	(η_2) Relative Market Position	(η_3) Relative Prices	(η_4) Return on Investment
ξ_2 Investment Intensity of Business	✓		✓	✓
ξ_3 Vertical Integration of Business	✓		✓	✓
ξ_4 Real Market Growth in Business's Product Market	✓		✓	✓
ξ_5 Percent Business's Employees Unionized	✓		✓	✓
ξ_6 Percent Business's Capacity Utilization	✓			✓
ξ_7 Percent of Business's Sales Derived from New Products		✓		✓
ξ_8 Sales Force Expenditures Relative to Competitors	✓	✓	✓	✓
ξ_9 Advertising/Promotion Expenditures Relative to Competitors		✓	✓	✓

[a]Checkmarks indicate hypothesized causal influences of control variables taken into account in the extended version of the model of Figure 1.

base, data are provided for the current year (time t) as well as for the previous four years (t − 1, . . . , t − 4). One year later at time (t + 1), remeasurement of a number of key variables is requested by PIMS researchers.

This annual update procedure is usually accomplished through personal interviews by PIMS service personnel. In these interviews there is limited reliance (if any) by informants on past records submitted to PIMS as a basis for providing new judgmental estimates. Due to promotions, resignations or reorganization, the informant interviewed in the annual update is often different from the one who provided the original information. Each of these factors contributes to the independence of the data collection efforts.

The year-to-year data points thus provided the multiple measurements necessary to model the reliability of PIMS measures of relative product quality, relative direct costs and relative prices. Test-retest reliability frameworks similar to the one employed in this study have been used in numerous investigations in other contexts, and the advantages and disadvantages of the approach are well known (Churchill 1979, pp. 260–261). Failure to observe high reliability of measures obtained at two or more points in time may be attributable to a change in the underlying latent variable rather than poor measurement. This would not appear to be a strong threat to valid inference in the present study, since the latent variables under investigation (e.g., product quality) are presumed to be stable characteristics of a business portfolio and are measured on a sample of businesses from mature, stable industries (Buzzell and Wiersema 1981b).

On the other hand, it is possible that high reliability values obtained for measures collected at two points in time may be attributable to methodological artifacts such as an informant's desire to maintain consistency in response, demand character in the items used, and so on. Threats due to these sources, while present in this research, are reduced by the use of a remeasurement approach that (1) occurs at a one-year interval (which reduces biases due to memory factors); (2) employs a personal interview (which reduces informant's reliance on past records); and (3) often entails interviews with a different informant (which attenuates informant-specific sources of distortion).

On balance, then, while the test-retest measurement framework employed in this study is not the strongest reliability assessment framework available, it is the only one applicable to the specifics of PIMS data collection procedures and, as will be shown below, it has sufficient probing value to provide insights as to the integrity of PIMS's measures, concepts and previously demonstrated relationships.

For purposes of this study, then, observations for ξ_1, η_1 and η_3 consisted of informant reports taken at two points in time: (time t) and a subsequent year (time t + 1) in which an annual update was completed. Observations for the relative market position variable consisted of the scores for y_3 and y_4 shown in Table 2, averaged over the periods t and t + 1. Observations for return on investment consisted of the single ROI measure, y_7, averaged over the periods t and t + 1. Because only a single average measure of ROI is used, it is necessary to assume that the return on investment variable is measured without error. This assumption is depicted in Figure 1 by the 1.00 and .00 values assigned to the factor loading and measurement error parameters, respectively, for y_7.

Table 2 Key Variables and Measurements Represented in Figure 1

Latent Variable	Type of Measure	Measure(s)		Corresponding Indicators in Model of Figure 1
Relative Product Quality (ξ_1)	Informant report based on response to standardized question	Estimate the percentage of this business's sales volume in this year accounted for by products and services that *from the perspective of the customer* are assessed as "Superior," "Equivalent," and "Inferior" to those available from the three leading competitors. (NOTE: The sum of these three percentages should be 100 percent.) In assessing quality, the customer's perception of both the intrinsic characteristics of the product or service and any associated services (delivery time, warranties, application assistance, etc.) should be taken into account where these are important in decisions to purchase. (Please see the *PIMS Data Manual* for a more detailed discussion of the procedure for estimating relative quality.)[a]	Superior [ ] % Equivalent [ ] % Inferior [ ] %	X_1 Informant report taken at time t X_2 Informant report taken at time $t + 1$
Relative Direct Costs (η_1)	Informant report based on response to standardized question	Estimate the average level of this business's direct costs per unit of products and services in this year, relative to the average level of the three largest competitors. Include costs of materials, production and distribution, but *exclude* marketing and administrative costs.[a]	[ ] %	Y_1 Informant report taken at time t Y_2 Informant report taken at time $t + 1$

Construct	Source	Definition	Indicator
Relative Market Position (η_2)	Informant report based upon consultation of organizational records	Market share of the business defined as the sales of the business as a percentage of the total dollar sales in the market served by the business. Served market definitions are determined by respondents in conjunction with SPI staff.	Y_3 Average computed over the time periods t and $t + 1$
		The percent market share of the business divided by the percent market share of the business's three largest competitors.	Y_4 Average computed over the time periods t and $t + 1$
Relative Prices (η_3)	Informant report based on response to standardized question	Estimate the average level of selling prices of this business's products and services in this year, relative to the average price of the three largest competitors. (Example: If this business's prices averaged 5 percent above those of leading competitors, report 105 percent).[a] ⬚ %	Y_5 Informant report taken at time t Y_6 Informant report taken at time $t + 1$
Return on Investment (η_4)	Informant report based on data from organizational records, computed according to standardized accounting practices	Net income as a percentage of invested capital. Net income is measured before taxes, interest and/or corporate finance charges and any unallocatable corporate overhead fees. Invested capital is the book value of fixed and working capital invested in the business and includes the capitalized value of major leases.	Y_7 Average computed over the time periods t and $t + 1$

[a]The standard of comparison in these questions is the *average* of the three largest competitors, weighted by their sales volumes if their market shares are not approximately equal. See *PIMS Data Manual* (Strategic Planning Institute 1978) for details on competitor definitions and further instructions.

Measurements for control variables ξ_8 and ξ_9 were constructed using the test-retest approach employed for ξ_1, η_1 and η_3. All other control variables were assumed to be measured without error by their respective indicators constructed from the PIMS survey by Strategic Planning Institute (SPI) staff. The *PIMS Data Manual* (SPI 1978) provides details on the measurements of these variables. For purposes of brevity control variables, their measurements, measurement properties and hypothesized causal effects are omitted from Figure 1 and from the presentation of statistical results.

Sample Construction

Although the PIMS research data base currently contains records on more than 2,000 businesses drawn from approximatley 600 corporations, the hypotheses were tested on a narrower sample of businesses. To estimate the model of Figure 1, it is necessary to restrict the analysis to businesses that provided data at two independent data collection efforts. Not all PIMS businesses satisfy this criterion since some businesses do not complete the annual update procedure, either because the business has been sold, management interest is in calibrating other businesses or for other reasons.

The analysis was also restricted to exclude any businesses identified as service or retail businesses since the theoretical issues under investigation pertain largely to manufacturing firms, and the problems of comparability of measures are severe between manufacturing concerns and retail or service businesses, especially with respect to relative direct costs and asset measurement (Rumelt and Wensley 1981).

Using the above screening criteria, observations were collected on 1,144 distinct two-year operating periods for 623 different businesses. The number of observations exceeded the number of businesses because some businesses, by having completed the update procedure several times, provided more than one set of two-year observations. We chose to retain multiple observations provided by a single business on two grounds. First, we expected the relationships under investigation to be generalizable over different operating periods, and selection of any two-year operating period from a set of multiple two-year periods provided by a business would have been arbitrary. Second, as we will show below, our parameter estimation procedures are maximum likelihood and depend upon relatively large samples for accurate estimates of causal paths and standard errors (Bagozzi 1980). We deemed these considerations more important than any unrepresentativeness in the sample that might arise from including multiple observations from the same business.

The two-year time periods covered by the observations ranged from the 1974–1975 to the 1980–1981 time period. Approximatley 80 percent of all observations were drawn from two-year time periods spanning the 1974–1977 era, and approximately 76 percent of the observations were drawn from industrial product as opposed to consumer product businesses. This skewness in observations with respect to time period and business type is consistent with the skewness in observations found in the entire PIMS sample (see SPI 1980).

To assess whether the businesses and time periods included in the study were unrepresentative of PIMS businesses and time periods in general, we compared mean differences between businesses included in our study versus those not included on the measures of the key variables shown in Figure 1 (see Phillips et al 1982 for details). The findings showed that businesses completing the update tended to be somewhat better performers than average PIMS businesses with respect to product quality, market share and ROI. Exactly how this self-selection bias might alter the internal consistency of the relationships under study cannot be ascertained with any certainty. For example, to the extent better performance is correlated with superior competitive intelligence, better record keeping and so on, it is possible that the quality of data is somewhat higher for businesses included here than for PIMS businesses in general. Consequently, any generalization of our findings to other PIMS businesses in particular, or to low-performing companies in general, must be viewed with caution. For further discussion of the representativeness of PIMS businesses overall, see Scherer (1980, p. 284) and Rumelt and Wensley (1981, p. 11).

Model Estimation and Evaluation

The model represented in Figure 1 may be estimated using the LISREL program (Jöreskog and Sörbom 1982) which provides an overall χ^2 goodness-of-fit test for the model being tested and maximum likelihood estimates for all parameters and standard errors. Satisfactory fits are based on the .05 level of significance. χ^2 values with an associated probability greater than .05 indicate that the hypothesized theoretical model provides a satisfactory fit to the data. Hypotheses as to the significance of specific causal paths and factor loadings are evaluated by examining their corresponding critical ratios (i.e., the estimate divided by its standard error). Critical ratios ≥ 1.96 are considered as evidence for the statistical significance of the parameter in question (see Bagozzi 1980, 1981a, 1981b).

Because of recent concerns raised about sole reliance on the χ^2 statistic as a measure of goodness-of-fit (Fornell and Larcker 1981), we also employed the Bentler and Bonett (1980) incremental fit index, Δ. This index provides an indication of the practical significance of a model in explaining data. Values of Δ of approximately .90 or greater indicate that the hypothesized model is capturing almost all of the information contained in the observations (relative to a baseline model, the "null model" of modified independence). Both the χ^2 and Δ measures of goodness-of-fit are reported for all models tested in this paper.[3]

[3]If the model of Figure 1 is rejected according to the goodness-of-fit measures, then the observed variance/covariance matrix of measurements cannot be accounted for by the hypothesized latent variables, error components and hypothesized causal paths. One aspect of the observed variance/covariance matrix that is not explicitly taken into account in Figure 1 is the potential influence of time-related factors on the measurements. To the extent that there is a common time component in informants' responses to measures collected at the same point in time, this will contribute to initial rejection of the model of Figure 1, since time factors are not explicitly represented. To model the effects of time-related factors, one may allow the error terms of the measures of Figure 1 to be correlated. By examination of the χ^2 and Δ goodness-of-fit measures for the models with and without correlated error terms, it is possible to ascertain the importance and significance of time-related factors in accounting for information contained in the measures and their contribution to model fit or lack thereof (see Results section below).

A final issue pertaining to model estimation concerns the homogeneity of the relationships under investigation across different types of businesses. Bass, Cattin and Wittink (1978) have shown how parameter estimates for causal paths may be seriously distored when one pools observations across heterogeneous industry groups. The rationale is that industry specific forces act as background factors influencing parameter estimates and that failure to take these factors into account by estimating separate models for different types of businesses results in a serious omitted variable problem.

To test the hypothesis of homogeneity or equivalence in parameter estimates across business groups, we first assigned all businesses and their corresponding observations to one of the six business categories used by PIMS researchers: consumer durables, consumer nondurables, capital goods, raw and semifinished materials, components and supplies businesses. We then employed the procedures for multiple group analyses recommended by Jöreskog and Sörbom (1982, pp. 78–87) to test hypotheses as to the homogeneity of the key causal paths (γ's, β's) and factor loadings (α's, λ's) shown in Figure 1. Homogeneity tests were conducted separately for causal paths and factor loadings and were done on a pairwise industry basis rather than comparing all six groups simultaneously.

The tests involved two steps: (1) estimating a model in which the parameters in question were constrained to be equal across the two groups being compared, and (2) comparing the fit of this model to one in which the parameters are unconstrained in each business group. Failure to observe a significant difference in the χ^2 test statistics for the two models implies that the null hypothesis of homogeneous parameters cannot be rejected. The χ^2 difference statistic (χ^2_d) used for evaluating this null hypothesis has degrees of freedom equal to the difference in degrees of freedom between the models being compared.

Table 3 shows the results for the tests for homogeneity. Note first that the χ^2 difference tests show that the null hypothesis of homogeneity in causal paths must be rejected in 13 of the 15 business group comparisons. Only in the comparison between consumer nondurables and capital goods businesses, on the one hand, and between consumer nondurables and supplies businesses, on the other, is the null hypothesis of homogeneous causal paths supported. Interestingly, however, the null hypothesis of equivalence in factor loadings cannot be rejected in all 15 of the pairwise comparisons. Thus, it may be concluded that the latent variables in the model of Figure 1 are measured with equal fidelity across the six business groups.

The findings for heterogeneity in causal paths indicate that data from the different types of businesses should not be pooled in estimating these parameters, thus supporting the arguments advanced by Bass, Cattin and Wittink (1978). Consequently, we estimated the model of Figure 1 separately for each of the six groups. While it would have been justified to pool the data for those sets of business groups with equivalent causal paths, we chose not to do so on other empirical grounds. When the tests for homogeneity of causal paths were expanded to include all control variable relationships as well as the key causal paths shown in Figure 1, the null hypothesis for homogeneity was rejected for both the consumer nondurables–capital goods business comparison ($\chi^2_{d(34)} = 81.6$, p $<$ .05)

Table 3 Results for Pairwise Tests for Homogeneity of Causal Paths and Measurement Relations, by Type of Business

χ^2_d Values for Homogeneity Tests: Key Causal Paths[a]

χ^2_d Values for Homogeneity Tests: Measurement Relations[b]

	Consumer Durables Businesses	Consumer Nondurables Businesses	Capital Goods Businesses	Raw and Semifinished Materials Businesses	Components Businesses	Supplies Businesses
Consumer durables businesses	—	17.9[c]	26.7[c]	25.3[c]	29.1[c]	21.5[c]
Consumer nondurables businesses	7.6	—	14.4	31.6[c]	36.8[c]	13.1
Capital goods businesses	11.2	5.2	—	30.5[c]	44.6[c]	33.8[c]
Raw and semifinished materials businesses	5.6	7.0	2.4	—	29.3[c]	48.1[c]
Components businesses	8.5	9.3	3.0	1.0	—	50.7[c]
Supplies businesses	5.6	7.2	10.5	5.7	8.9	—
Sample sizes[d]	132 (64)	134 (83)	238 (136)	129 (71)	299 (162)	212 (107)

[a]For $\chi^2_d(9) > 16.9$, p < .05
[b]For $\chi^2_d(6) > 12.6$, p < .05
[c]p < .05
[d]Number of unique businesses in parentheses

and the consumer nondurables–supplies business comparison ($\chi^2_{d(34)} = 89.3$, p < .05). These data further support the estimation of separate models for each business group.[4, 5]

Results

Measures of Model Fit

Table 4 reports the goodness-of-fit measures for the model of Figure 1 for the six types of businesses. As shown, the initial model (M_1) was rejected according to the χ^2 test in each sample. Note, however, that according to the Δ index, the hypothesized model fits the data quite well, capturing 89 to 96 percent of the information contained in the measures, depending on the sample.

A model hypothesizing correlated errors among indicators due to time-related factors (M_2) achieved a satisfactory fit according to both the χ^2 and Δ measures of it. Probability levels for the χ^2 statistic exceed .05 in all samples, and the Δ index shows that the hypothesized model captures at least 95 percent of the information contained in the measures in each sample. An indication of the amount of variation in measures due to time-related factors is given by comparison of the Δ values for M_1 and M_2 in Table 4. Depending on the sample, time-related factors add only 1 to 6 percent incremental information beyond that accounted for by the hypothesized latent variables, causal paths, random error and error-in-equa-

---

[4]Some analysts (e.g., Bass and Wittink 1975) have noted that pooling observations from various cross-sections of time may also distort parameter estimates unless the relationships are homogeneous over time. Ideally, then, one would also like to test for homogeneity of causal paths over time within each business group. Unfortunately, this could not be done since the procedures we used in testing for homogeneity are dependent on relatively large samples, a condition not satisfied in the present context. Within any business group the largest number of observations drawn from any one cross-section of time was 56, and it is recommended that one have a minimum of 50 observations plus an additional observation for each parameter to be estimated to use the maximum likelihood estimation procedures associated with multiple group analyses (Bagozzi 1980). Nevertheless, other studies that we conducted on PIMS data have shown strikingly similar parameter estimates over different time periods (Phillips and Buzzell 1982), suggesting that distortions in parameter estimates from pooling different cross-sections of time are likely to be minor.

[5]A final issue is whether parameter estimates for causal paths and factor loadings are heterogeneous within any of the six business groups. Hatten and Schendel (1977) have argued that relationships among strategic variables may vary dramatically depending on the position of a business within an industry—that is, whether it is a market share leader or follower, market pioneer or later entrant, and so on. If this is the case, pooling data from businesses in different strategic positions for purposes of parameter estimation may result in serious distortions. To address this issue, we divided each of the six business groups into market share leaders vs. followers and market pioneers vs. later entrants based on data supplied in the PIMS survey. Unfortunatley, only in the cases of capital goods, components and supplies businesses were there a sufficient number of observations in each category (leader/follower, etc.) to test hypotheses simultaneously across each group. Overall, the findings showed that the null hypothesis of homogeneous causal paths could not be rejected for either market leaders versus market followers or market pioneers versus later entrants for any of the business groups examined. This suggests that the internal consistency of the slope relationships under investigation is not significantly altered by background factors pertaining to a business's position within an industry. In turn, this supports the chosen strategy of model estimation on the basis of broad-based business categorizations, as opposed to model estimation based on within-industry categorizations. For similar results and conclusions pertaining to homogeneity of PIMS data, though in a different substantive context, see Rumelt and Wensley (1981).

Table 4 Goodness-of-Fit Measures for Model of Figure 1, by Type of Business

Models Tested	Consumer Durables Businesses	Consumer Nondurables Businesses	Capital Goods Businesses	Raw and Semifinished Materials Businesses	Components Businesses	Supplies Businesses
M_1: Causal Model with No Correlated Errors Among Measures	$\chi^2_{102} = 139.1,$ $p \approx .009$ $\Delta = .94$	$\chi^2_{102} = 242.8,$ $p \approx .000$ $\Delta = .89$	$\chi^2_{102} = 157.8,$ $p \approx .000$ $\Delta = .95$	$\chi^2_{102} = 148.8,$ $p \approx .002$ $\Delta = .94$	$\chi^2_{102} = 154.2,$ $p \approx .001$ $\Delta = .95$	$\chi^2_{102} = 156.1,$ $p \approx .001$ $\Delta = .96$
M_2: Causal Model with Correlated Errors Among Measures Due to Time-Related Factors	$\chi^2_{100} = 116.3,$ $p \approx .13$ $\Delta = .95$	$\chi^2_{86} = 101.2,$ $p \approx .13$ $\Delta = .95$	$\chi^2_{100} = 102.1,$ $p \approx .42$ $\Delta = .97$	$\chi^2_{97} = 112.3,$ $p \approx .14$ $\Delta = .95$	$\chi^2_{101} = 120.7,$ $p \approx .09$ $\Delta = .97$	$\chi^2_{95} = 107.2,$ $p \approx .19$ $\Delta = .97$

tion components. Variation in measures due to unmeasured time-related factors is therefore quite small. Overall then, the fit measures of Table 4 show that the hypothesized model of Figure 1 captures the data quite well across all six types of businesses.[6]

Reliability of Measures

Table 5 shows the standardized parameter estimates for the key measurement relations of Figure 1. Indicated are the reliabilities of each measure, which is equal to the squared value of the factor loading of the measure (α's and λ's in Figure 1). The amount of variation in a measure due to error factors, both random and time-related, is given by 1.00 minus the reliability coefficient. The reliability coefficients of Table 5 range from .77 to .99 across measures and samples, indicating that the latent variables are measured with a high degree of precision by the respective measures: Note also that the reliability values for the product quality measure (ξ_1) are remarkably high across all samples, being .86 or greater in each. Only in the case of the measures of relative direct costs for consumer durables businesses do reliability coefficients of both measures drop below .85. On balance, however, the high reliabilities and low measurement error components observed across measures and samples are consistent with the hypothesis that stable traits underlie the relative competitive strategy measures and that a high degree of correspondence exists between the measures and the concepts they represent.

Effects of Relative Product Quality and Direct Cost Position on ROI

Table 6 shows the standardized parameter estimates and critical ratios for the key causal paths depicted in Figure 1. Because they are standardized, these estimates reflect the relative influence of each variable within a particular business group; they are not, however, appropriate as a basis for comparisons across different types of businesses.

Looking first at the results for H_1, it may be seen that higher relative product quality has a direct positive influence on ROI in only three of the six types of businesses studied. Only in the cases of consumer nondurables, capital goods and components businesses are the coefficients for γ_1 positive and statistically significant. Thus, H_1 is rejected in half of the samples.

Looking next at the results for H_2, there is uniform support across all businesses for the view that product quality influences ROI indirectly via its effects on market position. Note first that relative product quality has a positive, statistically significant effect on relative market position across all businesses, as indi-

---

[6]The number of error terms correlated in order to achieve a satisfactory fit according to the χ^2 test statistic is given by the difference in degrees of freedom between M_1 and M_2 in Table 5. The models generally achieved a good fit according to the χ^2 test after correlating only a few error terms, but it was necessary to correlate others to avoid improper solutions in the standardized factor loading matrix (i.e., α's > 1.0). This latter condition probably arose because the factor loadings were forced to reproduce test-retest correlations that were quite high (i.e., .66 to .98).

Table 5 Standardized Parameter Estimates for Key Measurement Relation[a]

Concepts (ξ's, η's) and Measurements (X's, Y's)	Reliability Coefficients (α^2, λ'^2) by Type of Business					
	Consumer Durables Businesses	Consumer Nondurables Businesses	Capital Goods Businesses	Raw and Semifinished Materials Businesses	Components Businesses	Supplies Businesses
Relative Product Quality (ξ_1)						
$X_1(t)$	.88	.92	.95	.97	.86	.93
$X_2(t+1)$	.97	.99	.94	.96	.92	.99
Relative Prices (η_1)						
$Y_1(t)$	.98	.97	.93	.93	.96	.93
$Y_2(t+1)$	.82	.96	.88	.88	.89	.96
Relative Market Position (η_2)						
Y_3	.97	.97	.84	.86	.82	.94
Y_4	.86	.90	.99	.99	.99	.94
Relative Direct Costs (η_3)						
$Y_5(t)$	.83	.92	.92	.98	.96	.96
$Y_6(t+1)$	.77	.89	.94	.98	.92	.98

[a]All factor loadings had corresponding critical ratios greater than 1.96.

Table 6 Standardized Parameter Estimates for Causal Paths[a]

Causal Path	Parameter	Consumer Durables Businesses	Consumer Nondurables Businesses	Capital Goods Businesses	Raw and Semifinished Materials Businesses	Components Businesses	Supplies Businesses
		Parameter Estimates and Critical Ratios by Type of Business					
Influence of Relative Product Quality on:							
Return on Investment	γ_1	.02	.22	.19	-.09	.16	.03
		(.31)	(2.80)	(3.07)	(1.49)	(3.75)	(.57)
Relative Direct Costs	γ_2	-.08	.20	.40	.15	-.12	.06
		(.93)	(1.94)	(5.18)	(1.63)	(2.02)	(.76)
Relative Market Position	γ_3	.17	.38	.15	.30	.16	.38
		(2.24)	(4.39)	(1.96)	(3.22)	(2.51)	(5.50)
Relative Prices	γ_4	.19	.40	.27	.33	.41	.48
		(2.33)	(5.77)	(4.71)	(4.62)	(8.21)	(7.73)
Influence of Relative Market Position on:							
Relative Direct Costs	β_{12}	-.25	-.36	-.38	-.47	-.01	-.40
		(2.03)	(2.74)	(3.65)	(3.87)	(.14)	(3.83)
Return on Investment	β_{42}	.30	.15	.16	.03	.12	.40
		(2.93)	(1.50)	(2.62)	(.45)	(2.83)	(7.01)
Influence of Relative Direct Costs on:							
Relative Prices	β_{31}	.18	.24	.51	.60	.56	.48
		(1.83)	(3.09)	(8.16)	(7.57)	(11.40)	(6.71)
Return on Investment	β_{43}	.04	-.17	-.17	-.14	-.09	-.19
		(.46)	(2.38)	(3.00)	(2.21)	(2.05)	(4.13)
Influence of Relative Prices on:							
Relative Market Position	β_{23}	.18	.17	.30	.07	-.06	.24
		(2.13)	(1.82)	(2.99)	(.49)	(.81)	(2.82)

[a]Critical ratios in parentheses.

cated by the γ_3 estimates and critical ratios. Further, the estimates for β_{12}, β_{42} and β_{43} show that relative market position has a positive, significant influence on ROI, though the mechanisms by which this occurs vary by type of business.

In the case of consumer nondurables and materials businesses, relative market position influences ROI only by its effects on cost position. This is reflected by the significant negative estimates for β_{12} and β_{43} and the insignificant estimate for β_{42}, which reflects the influence of market position on ROI via mechanisms other than cost economics. In the case of consumer durables and components businesses, an opposite conclusion emerges. Market position influences ROI only via mechanisms other than cost, as reflected in the significant positive estimates for β_{42} and the insignificant estimates for β_{43} (in the case of consumer durables) and β_{12} (in the case of components). Finally, in the case of capital goods and supplies businesses, relative market position influences ROI indirectly by its beneficial effects on relative direct cost position and directly via mechanisms other than cost. The estimates for β_{12}, β_{42} and β_{43} are all statistically significant and have the signs predicted by theory.

In sum, the data are consistent in supporting, on the one hand, a causal link between relative product quality and relative market position, and relative market position and ROI, on the other. H_2 is thus supported across all business groups. Further, the data support the view that achieving a low relative cost position is one way to earn supranormal returns, since cost position is a significant determinant of ROI in all businesses except consumer durables (see estimates of β_{43}).

Support for H_2 across all samples casts doubt on hypotheses emerging from the market niche theory of how quality influences performance. While there is evidence that higher quality does lead to higher prices ($H_{1(a)}$), as shown by the positive and significant coefficients for γ_4 in all six business groups, no evidence exists that these higher prices deter market penetration ($H_{1(b)}$). In no case is the estimate for β_{23} negative and statistically significant. Rather, the consistent results for H_2 across samples show that higher quality contributes to—rather than undermines—market position and is, therefore, much more than a niche strategy option—at least in the businesses under investigation.[7]

Effects of Relative Product Quality on Relative Direct Cost Position

The results for H_3, as given by the estimates for γ_2, show that H_3 must be rejected in all but one of the samples. Only in the case of capital goods businesses is there evidence for the hypothesis that higher relative quality results in higher relative direct costs per unit. In consumer durables, nondurables, materials and supplies businesses, the estimates for γ_2 are statistically insignificant. In components businesses, higher relative product quality results in lower direct costs per unit, as

---

[7]In another set of analyses we tried to marshall support for the niche theory by hypothesizing a direct link between relative prices and ROI (i.e., β_{43}). However, only in two of the six samples was this parameter positive and statistically significant. In all other samples β_{43} was negative. Thus, there is little evidence for a direct quality-price-ROI sequence.

indicated by the negative and statistically significant estimate for γ_2. This finding is consistent with the quality–learning curve model posited by Fine (1983). Overall, there is limited support for the view that achieving a high relative quality position comes only by making systematic trade-offs versus relative direct cost position.

Five of the six types of businesses studied support the view that product quality has indirect beneficial effects on relative direct cost position (via its influence on relative market position). For all businesses except components, the estimates for β_{12} are negative and statistically significant and are accompanied by a positive and significant estimate for γ_3. Note, however, that even in components, product quality exerts a beneficial influence on relative direct cost position, although the effect is direct (via γ_2) rather than indirect via market position. Thus, the conclusion that relative product quality actually has a beneficial influence on relative direct cost position is supported across all six types of businesses under investigation.

Table 7 shows the correlations between the relative product quality variable and relative sales force expenditures, advertising and promotion expenditures, and percentage of sales derived from new products. The data show that in consumer nondurables, materials and component businesses, achieving a high relative quality position does not generally entail higher relative marketing expenditures or a higher relative level of innovative effort. Only in consumer durables is there consistent evidence that higher product quality may be accompanied by increased marketing expenditures. In the other three types of businesses, only three of the nine relevant intercorrelations are positive and statistically significant, and these are quite small. On balance, little evidence exists to support the view that achieving higher relative product quality requires systematic trade-offs in other cost areas such as marketing.

Error in Equation Estimates

Table 8 reports the error in equation parameters for the model of Figure 1 and Table 6. Looking first at the estimates of the error variances of the ζ's in Figure 1, shown as ψ_{11}, ψ_{22}, ψ_{33}, ψ_{44} in Table 8, one may ascertain the proportion of variation explained in each of the four dependent variables (η's) by the independent variables (ξ's). Variance explained, given by $1.00 - \psi$, ranges from 7 to 31 percent for relative direct costs, 9 to 39 percent for relative market position, 35 to 54 percent for relative prices and 39 to 66 percent for ROI. Given that these estimates reflect only moderate levels of variance explained and that relative product quality is only one of many causes of these phenomena, the ultimate effect of product quality on business performance outcomes, while significant, is relatively small. This conclusion is further supported by the moderate size of the estimated coefficients linking product quality to ROI, product quality to market position and market position to ROI (Table 6).

Looking next at the estimates for covariance among error in equation parameters, we can see that four of the six estimates for ψ_{43} are statistically significant. This indicates that there are common causes of both ROI (η_4) and relative prices (η_4) omitted from the model of Figure 1 and Table 1 in all but the consumer

Table 7   Correlations Between Relative Product Quality and Other Relative Marketing Mix Variables

Correlation of Relative Product Quality with:	Consumer Durables Businesses	Consumer Nondurables Businesses	Capital Goods Businesses	Raw and Semifinished Materials Businesses	Components Businesses	Supplies Businesse
			Type of Business			
Relative sales force expenditures	.25[a]	−.03	.10	.05	.10	.12
Relative advertising/promotion expenditures	.39[a]	−.09	.19[a]	.08	.08	.18[a]
Relative percentage of sales from new products	.37[a]	−.16	.06	.01	.00	.19[a]

[a]Parameter estimate is at least 1.96 times its standard error.

Table 8 Standardized Parameter Estimates for Variances and Covariances of Error in Equation Terms[a]

Parameter Estimates and Critical Ratios by Type of Business

Parameter	Consumer Durables Businesses	Consumer Nondurables Businesses	Capital Goods Businesses	Raw and Semifinished Materials Businesses	Components Businesses	Supplies Businesses
ψ_{11}	.69	.90	.89	.72	.93	.84
	(5.48)	(6.79)	(9.02)	(7.70)	(12.11)	(9.39)
ψ_{22}	.61	.67	.75	.82	.91	.66
	(7.26)	(7.21)	(8.73)	(6.06)	(8.61)	(8.84)
ψ_{33}	.65	.59	.50	.46	.57	.64
	(8.12)	(7.32)	(9.19)	(6.63)	(10.47)	(9.25)
ψ_{44}	.61	.56	.59	.35	.48	.34
	(8.05)	(7.99)	(10.76)	(7.99)	(12.11)	(10.08)
ψ_{43}	−.14	−.01	−.11	.07	.13	−.01
	(2.35)	(.14)	(2.80)	(1.97)	(4.03)	(.13)

[a]ψ is the variance of the error term ζ in Figure 1. Critical ratios in parentheses.

nondurables and supplies businesses samples. However, given that the significant covariance estimates are quite low (.13 to − .14), if variables are omitted from the model, their effects are quite small in magnitude.

Discussion

To the best of our knowledge, this is the first study to examine competing methodological and theoretical hypotheses in the PIMS data base using a causal modelling methodology. Unlike the methods used herein, earlier PIMS studies estimated simple single equation models and assumed that all variables were measured perfectly and without error. Complex sequences of relationships went untested, and reliability and validity issues were not explicitly treated. This approach stands in stark contrast to the fact that, as strategy researchers, we are investigating a very complex system via indirect observation through potentially highly fallible measurements. By adopting econometric procedures that explicitly represent system complexity and measurement fallibility, our study has produced tentative answers to important methodological and theoretical questions omitted in previous studies.

Methodological Findings

From a methodological perspective, our study allays at least some key concerns regarding measurement error in PIMS' measures of certain competitive strategy variables. The high reliabilities observed for the measures of product quality and other relative competitive strategy variables across samples (Table 5) suggest that stable traits underlie the measures and that variation due to time related and random error factors is small. Moreover, as shown in Table 3, the concepts are measured with equal fidelity across diverse types of businesses. On balance, this suggests a very high quality data collection process by PIMS researchers. Apparently the distortions that one would normally expect in self-reported measures comparing a business to its leading competitors are offset by such factors as effective safeguards against the release of information in individual businesses, voluntary contribution of data by PIMS participants, and skilled staff work with respect to data collection, preparation and screening. Indeed, the data appear relatively free of the clerical errors and inconsistencies in response that are likely to corrupt much of the data traditionally employed by economists and strategy researchers.

The results for the measurement parameters (Table 5) also reduce the skepticism surrounding the findings of numerous other PIMS studies that made no efforts to control for the contaminating effects of measurement error in informant reports on causal analysis. Had the results of Table 5 shown poor reliability of measurements, the findings of previous studies relying on these measures would be called into question. Instead our findings suggest that previous studies that naively assumed no measurement error likely suffered little attenuation in observed relations due to time and random error components.

Our findings do not, or course, allay certain concerns over measurement error in PIMS' participants' self-reports. Because our reliability estimates were obtained from an application of a monomethod measurement framework (i.e., the same question asked in many cases to the same informant at one-year intervals), it is not possible to rule out completely methods factors such as demand character in the items, informant biases, or other external confounds as spurious sources of covariation in the year-to-year measurements. Studies in other contexts that have explicitly modelled these sources of variation in informant reports have found them to be significant and have reported measurement error components substantially higher than those found in the present study (see Phillips 1981). At present, all that can be concluded is that (1) the PIMS measures of product quality and other relative competitive strategy variables were exposed to a series of logical, internally consistent validation tests that offered numerous opportunities for the measurements to fail; (2) these tests were the only ones possible within the confines of PIMS data collection procedures; and (3) the measures repeatedly survived these efforts at disproof as demonstrated on six different samples representing a diversity of businesses.[8]

Theoretical Findings

From a theoretical perspective, our findings in part converge with and in part diverge from received views on product quality and cost leadership as generic marketing strategies (see Hall 1980, Porter 1980). Relative direct cost position was a significant determinant of business performance in all but one of the six types of businesses studied (consumer durables, Table 6). Product differentiation by high relative quality, in contrast, was a significant determinant of ROI in all six types of businesses, though the manner in which this effect was manifested varied across businesses (Table 6). Considered together, these findings support Porter's and Hall's arguments that differentiation and cost-based strategies are both viable routes for competitive success.

Our findings diverge from previous literature in explaining the mechanisms by which quality-based strategies influence ROI, and how quality- and cost-based strategies interact. In contrast to previous studies, our findings indicate that product quality does not have a consistently direct effect on business unit ROI. This effect was observed in only half of the businesses studied (consumer nondurables, capital goods and components, Table 6). However, across all businesses quality was shown to influence ROI indirectly via its positive effects on market position. Overall, this implies that, at least in some businesses, product quality is not intrinsically valuable and plans or strategies aimed solely at the attainment of a high quality position may be ill-conceived. By contrast plans that view investments in product quality as a determinant of future market position and, in turn, subsequent ROI are entirely appropriate. This latter perspective contradicts prevailing views (e.g., Porter 1980, pp. 34–46), suggesting that pursuit of a high quality strategy often requires the perception of exclusivity, which is incompatible with high relative market share. Indeed, our results suggest that, at least for the businesses

---

[8]For further tests on the reliability of PIMS data, see Phillips and Buzzell (1982).

studied herein, quality is consistently an important factor determining market position and is not merely a strategy to be used only by small companies facing
well-entrenched competitors.

Our results also question existing views that attainment of a high quality
position is likely to come only at a cost premium (e.g., Hall 1980, Porter 1980).
For the six types of businesses studied, only one (capital goods) showed a positive
systematic relationship between relative product quality and relative direct costs
(Table 6), and only one (consumer durables) showed a positive systematic relationship between relative quality and relative marketing expenditures (Table 7).
Of the 24 parameter estimates in Tables 6 and 7 that could have reflected a quality–cost trade-off, only seven did, and these tended to be small. In contrast, the
view that relative product quality exerted a beneficial effect on relative direct cost
position via market share was supported across all types of businesses studied.
Thus, our findings clearly indicate that attainment of a high quality position and
pursuit of a low direct cost position are not necessarily incompatible business
strategies, as both the academic and popular literature on the subject would lead
us to believe (see e.g., Kiechel 1981, Porter 1980; for an exception, see Wheelwright 1981). Some areas of complementarity actually exist.

The finding that both higher relative quality and costs lead to increased
prices (Table 6), combined with the finding that quality does not significantly
influence direct costs across most businesses, suggests that pursuit of a quality
strategy enables the company to command profit margins superior to lower quality
competitors. This conclusion is consistent with those of previous PIMS studies
(e.g., Buzzell, Gale and Sultan 1975, Farris and Reibstein 1979, Gale and Branch
1982). However, the higher prices that emerge from a high quality strategy apparently do not deter market penetration, as demonstrated by the coefficients for
β_{23} across samples (Table 6). These findings refute the inverse price–share relationship predicted by economic models and market niche theories of product quality. We must conclude that no lawlike connection exists between price and share
in mature markets and that, instead, these two variables covary positively as a
function of some common cause such as product differentiation.

To this point discussion has focused on those findings that are more or less
generalizable across the types of businesses under study. In many respects, this
masks much of the great diversity that our findings display across different types
of businesses. To illustrate this point, consider the different marketing strategy
scenarios that emerge from Table 6 for components, capital goods and supplies
businesses. Looking first at the results for components businesses (Table 6), we
see that product quality has a direct, positive effect on ROI and an indirect positive effect on ROI via market position. Moreover, it has a direct and beneficial
(i.e., lowering) effect on direct costs which in turn significantly affects ROI. Further, achieving a high quality position does not entail cost trade-offs in other
value-added expenditure areas (Table 7). Clearly, in components businesses, relative quality and cost position are not alternative strategic objectives requiring
different courses of action. Higher relative quality requires no significant trade-
offs in terms of cost position and, in fact, facilitates achievement of a low cost
position. Quality is not one of several ways to win in components; it is the only
way. Whether this is due to the adoption of manufacturing and/or marketing op-

erations that simultaneously produce high quality and low cost goes unanswered in our study.

These results for components businesses may be contrasted to the scenario emerging from capital goods businesses. As in components, relative product quality exerts both a direct influence on ROI and an indirect influence via relative market position. However, higher product quality does require a trade-off in direct cost position (Table 6) and advertising/promotion expenditures (Table 7). The increase in direct costs attributable to quality is in part compensated for by the ability of the business to command higher prices, though the effect of quality on prices is less than its effect on costs (Table 6), a finding unique to capital goods. Cost increases are also made up for by the indirect beneficial influence that quality exerts on cost position via market position and the fact that higher relative costs get reflected in higher relative prices (Table 6). Thus, while higher relative quality is a profitable strategy for capital goods businesses, it does entail some of the cost trade-offs suggested by conventional wisdom.

Still another pattern of findings is given by the scenario for supplies businesses. In contrast to components and capital goods, relative product quality influences ROI only indirectly via market position. It involves no significant trade-offs with relative direct costs (Table 6) and only minor trade-offs with respect to relative marketing costs (Table 7). Unlike components businesses, relative direct cost position is determined in part by relative market position, and both of these variables directly influence ROI (Table 6).

These contrasting findings across different types of businesses underline the point that marketing strategy analysis must be situational (Rumelt 1981b). While our analysis has produced generalizable results showing that certain types of generic strategies do lead to success, the exact manner in which these strategies are translated into success in specific industries varies dramatically by type of business. As Rumelt has argued, there appears to be no generalizable algorithm for creating wealth. Rather, strategic prescriptions that apply to broad classes of businesses can only aid managers in avoiding mistakes, not in designing specific routes to competitive advantage. The task of creating sound marketing strategies, while significantly aided by theoretical generalizations, remains a situation specific exercise.

Summary and Conclusions

Product quality is often cited as a panacea for the problems currently afflicting American business. In view of the potential importance of product quality, it is surprising so little attention has been paid to it by marketing scholars. Marketing management texts generally ignore the topic, and only a handful of empirical studies exist.

The present study provides strong evidence for the influence of product quality on business performance, albeit a different and relatively smaller role than that suggested in previous studies. Moreover, the high reliability values observed for PIMS measures of relative product quality show that the concept is subject to meaningful operationalization and testing. Finally, for the samples studied, attainment of a high quality position was not generally found to involve many of the strategic trade-offs such as higher relative direct costs or marketing expenditures, often attributed to quality strategies by business analysts. Considered together, these findings indicate that strategic options involving the product quality variable are worthy of more attention from marketing researchers and practitioners alike.

References

Bagozzi, Richard P. (1980), *Causal Models in Marketing*, New York: John Wiley and Sons, Inc.

_____ (1981a), "An Examination of the Validity of Two Models of Attitude," *Multivariate Behavioral Research*, 16 (July), 323–59.

_____ (1981b), "Attitudes, Intentions, and Behavior: A Test of Some Key Hypotheses," *Journal of Personality and Social Psychology*, 41 (October), 607–26.

_____ and Lynn W. Phillips (1982), "Representing and Testing Organizational Theories: A Holistic Construal," *Administrative Science Quarterly*, 27 (September), 459–489.

Bass, Frank M. and Dick R. Wittink (1975), "Pooling Issues and Methods in Regression Analysis with Examples in Marketing Research," *Journal of Marketing Research*, 12 (November), 414–25.

_____, Philippe Cattin and Dick R. Wittink (1978), "Firm Effects and Industry Effects in the Analysis of Market Structure and Profitability," *Journal of Marketing Research*, 15 (February), 3–10.

Bentler, Peter M. and Douglas G. Bonett (1980), "Significance Tests and Goodness-of-Fit in the Analysis of Covariance Structures," *Psychological Bulletin*, 88 (no. 3), 588–606.

Buzzell, Robert D. (1978), "Product Quality," *PIMSLETTER No. 4*, Strategic Planning Institute.

_____, Bradley Gale and Robert Sultan (1975), "Market Share—A Key to Profitability," *Harvard Business Review*, 53 (January–February), 97–106.

_____ and Frederik D. Wiersema (1981a), "Successful Share Building Strategies," *Harvard Business Review*, 59 (January–February), 135–144.

_____ and _____ (1981b), "Modelling Changes in Market Share: A Cross-Sectional Analysis," *Strategic Management Journal*, 2 (January–March), 27–42.

Churchill, Gilbert (1979), *Marketing Research: Methodological Foundations*, New York: Dryden.

Farris, Paul and Davis Reibstein (1979), "How Prices, Ad Expenditures and Profits are Linked," *Harvard Business Review*, 57 (November–December), 173–184.

Fine, Charles H. (1983), "Quality Control and Learning in Productive Systems," Ph.D. dissertation, Stanford University, Graduate School of Business.

Flaherty, M. Therese (1982), "Market Share, Technology Leadership and Competition in International Semiconductor Markets," working paper, Harvard University, Graduate School of Business Administration.

Fornell, Claes and David F. Larcker (1981), "Evaluating Structural Equation Models with Unobservable Variables and Measurement Error," *Journal of Marketing Research*, 18 (February), 39–50.

Gale, Bradley T. and Ben S. Branch (1982), "Concentration versus Market Share: Which Determines Performance and Why Does It Matter?," *The Antitrust Bulletin*, 27 (Spring), 83–105.

—— and Donald J. Swire (1977), *The Limited Information Report: A Strategic Planning Tool for Business Decision Making When Information is Difficult to Obtain,* Cambridge, MA: Strategic Planning Institute.

Hall, William K. (1980), "Survival Strategies in a Hostile Environment," *Harvard Business Review,* 58 (September–October), 75–85.

Hatten, Kenneth and Dan Schendel (1977), "Heterogeneity Within an Industry: Firm Conduct in the U.S. Brewing Industry," *The Journal of Industrial Economics,* 26 (December), 97–112.

Henderson, Bruce D. (1979), *Henderson on Corporate Strategy,* Cambridge, MA: Abt Books.

Jöreskog, Karl and Dag Sörbom (1979), *Advances in Factor Analysis and Structural Equation Models,* Cambridge, MA: Abt Books.

—— and —— (1982), *LISREL: Analysis of Linear Structural Relationships by Method of Maximum Likelihood,* Chicago, IL: National Educational Resources.

Kiechel, Walter (1981), "Three (or Four, or More) Ways to Win," *Fortune,* 104 (October 19), 181, 184, 188.

Pennings, Johannes (1973), "Measures of Organizational Structure: A Methodological Note," *American Journal of Sociology,* 69, 41–52.

Phillips, Lynn W. (1981), "Assessing Measurement Error in Key Informant Reports: A Methodological Note on Organizational Analysis in Marketing," *Journal of Marketing Research,* 18 (November), 395–415.

—— (1982), "Explaining Control Losses in Corporate Marketing Channels: An Organizational Analysis," *Journal of Marketing Research,* 19 (November), 525–549.

—— and Robert D. Buzzell (1982), "An Examination of the Reliability of PIMS Relative Competitive Strategy Measures," paper presented at American Institute for Decision Sciences Conference, San Francisco, November.

——, Dae Chang and Robert D. Buzzell (1982), "Product Quality, Cost Position and Business Performance: A Test of Some Key Hypotheses," working paper, Graduate School of Business, Stanford University.

Porter, Michael E. (1980), *Competitive Strategy,* New York: The Free Press.

Ravenscraft, David J. (1981), "Structure-Profit Relationships at the Line of Business and Industry Level," working paper, Bureau of Economics, Federal Trade Commission.

Reddy, Jack (1980), "Incorporating Quality in Competitive Strategies," *Sloan Management Review,* 21 (Spring), 53–60.

Rumelt, Richard P. (1981a), "How Important is Industry in Explaining Firm Profitability," working paper, Graduate School of Management, University of California, Los Angeles.

—— (1981b), "Toward a Strategic Theory of the Firm," paper presented at a conference on "Non-Traditional Approaches to Policy Research," University of Southern California, November 12–13.

—— and J. Robin C. Wensley (1981), "Market Share and the Rate of Return: Testing the Stochastic Hypothesis," working paper, Graduate School of Management, University of California, Los Angeles.

Scherer, F.M. (1980), *Industrial Market Structure and Economic Performance,* Chicago, IL: Rand McNally Publishing Company.

Schoeffler, Sidney, Robert D. Buzzell and Donald F. Heany (1974), "Impact of Strategic Planning on Profit Performance," *Harvard Business Review,* 52 (March–April), 137–45.

Shapiro, Benson P. (1977), "Can Marketing and Manufacturing Coexist?," *Harvard Business Review,* 56 (September–October), 104–114.

Smith, Ward C. (1980), "Finding New Opportunities for Profitability in Manufacturing Cost," *Management Review,* 69 (March), 60–62.

Strategic Planning Institute (1978), *The PIMS Data Manual,* Cambridge, MA: SPI.

———— (1980), *The SPI Research Data Bases,* Cambridge, MA: SPI.

Weiss, Leonard and George Pascoe (1981), "Some Early Results on the Concentration-Profits Relationship from the FTC's Line of Business Data," working paper, Federal Trade Commission.

Wensley, J. Robin C. (1981), "Strategic Marketing: Betas, Boxes, or Basics?," *Journal of Marketing,* 45 (Summer), 173–82.

Wheelwright, Steven C. (1981), "Japan—Where Operations Really are Strategic," *Harvard Business Review,* 59 (July–August), 67–74.

23

Positioning Your Product

David A. Aaker and J. Gary Shansby

How should a new brand be positioned? Can a problem brand be revived by a repositioning strategy? Most marketing managers have addressed these and other positioning questions; however, "positioning" means different things to different people. To some, it means the segmentation decision. To others it is an image question. To still others it means selecting which product features to emphasize. Few managers consider all of these alternatives. Further, the positioning decision is often made ad hoc, and is based upon flashes of insight, even though systematic, research-based approaches to the positioning decision are now available. An understanding of these approaches should lead to more sophisticated analysis in which positioning alternatives are more fully identified and evaluated.

A product or organization has many associations which combine to form a total impression. The positioning decision often means selecting those associations which are to be built upon and emphasized and those associations which are to removed or de-emphasized. The term "position" differs from the older term "image" in that it implies a frame of reference, the reference point usually being the competition. Thus, when the Bank of California positions itself as being small and friendly, it is explicitly, or perhaps implicitly, positioning itself with respect to Bank of America.

The positioning decision is often the crucial strategic decision for a company or brand because the position can be central to customers' perception and choice decisions. Futher, since all elements of the marketing program can potentially affect the position, it is usually necessary to use a positioning strategy as a focus for the development of the marketing program. A clear positioning strategy can insure that the elements of the marketing program are consistent and supportive.

What alternative positioning strategies are available? How can positioning strategies be identified and selected? Each of these questions will be addressed in turn.

This article first appeared in the *Business Horizons* (May-June 1982):56–62. Copyright, 1982, by the Foundation for the School of Business at Indiana University. Reprinted by permission.

When this article was published the authors were Professor of Marketing and Professor of Marketing Strategy, respectively, at the University of California at Berkeley.

Positioning Strategies

A first step in understanding the scope of positioning alternatives is to consider some of the ways that a positioning strategy can be conceived and implemented. In the following, six approaches to positioning strategy will be illustrated and discussed: positioning by (1) attribute, (2) price–quality, (3) use or applications, (4) product user, (5) the product class, and (6) the competitor.

Positioning by Attribute

Probably the most frequently used positioning strategy is associating a product with an attribute, a product feature, or customer benefit. Consider imported automobiles. Datsun and Toyota have emphasized economy and reliability. Volkswagen has used a "value for the money" association. Volvo has stressed durability, showing commercials of "crash tests" and citing statistics on the long average life of their cars. Fiat, in contrast, has made a distinct effort to position itself as a European car with "European craftsmanship." BMW has emphasized handling and engineering efficiency, using the tag line, "the ultimate driving machine" and showing BMWs demonstrating their performance capabilities at a race track.

A new product can upon occasion be positioned with respect to an attribute that competitors have ignored. Paper towels had emphasized absorbency until Viva stressed durability, using demonstrations supporting the claim that Viva "keeps on working."

Sometimes a product will attempt to position itself along two or more attributes simultaneously. In the toothpaste market, Crest became a dominant brand by positioning itself as a cavity fighter, a position supported by a medical group endorsement. However, Aim achieved a 10 percent market share by positioning along two attributes, good taste and cavity prevention. More recently, Aqua-fresh has been introduced by Beecham as a gel paste that offers both cavity-fighting and breath-freshening benefits.

It is always tempting to try to position along several attributes. However, positioning strategies that involve too many attributes can be most difficult to implement. The result can often be a fuzzy, confused image.

Positioning by Price/Quality

The price/quality attribute dimension is so useful and pervasive that it is appropriate to consider it separately. In many product categories, some brands offer more in terms of service, features, or performance and a higher price serves to signal this higher quality to the customer. Conversely, other brands emphasize price and value.

In general merchandise stores, for example, the department stores are at the top end of the price/quality scale. Neiman Marcus, Bloomingdale's, and Saks Fifth Avenue are near the top, followed by Macy's, Robinson's, Bullock's, Rich's, Filene's, Dayton's, Hudson's, and so on. Stores such as Sears, Montgomery Ward, and J.C. Penny are positioned below the department stores but above the discount stores like K-mart. Sears efforts to create a more upbeat fashion image was thought to have hurt their "value" position and caused some share declines.[1] Sears' recent five-year plan details a firm return to a positioning as a family, middle-class store offering top value. Sears is just one company that has faced the very tricky positioning task of retaining the image of low price and upgrading their quality image. There is always the risk that the quality message will blunt the basic "low-price," "value" position.

Positioning with Respect to Use or Application

Another positioning strategy is associating the product with a use or application. Campbell's soup for many years was positioned for use at lunch time and advertised extensively over noontime radio. The telephone company more recently has associated long-distance calling with communicating with loved ones in their "reach out and touch someone" campaign. Industrial products often rely upon application associations.

Products can, of course, have multiple positioning strategies, although increasing the number involves obvious difficulties and risks. Often a positioning-by-use strategy represents a second or third position designed to expand the market. Thus, Gatorade, introduced as a summer beverage for athletes who need to replace body fluids, has attempted to develop a winter positioning strategy as the beverage to drink when the doctor recommends drinking plenty of fluids. Similarly, Quaker Oats has attempted to position a breakfast food product as a natural whole-grain ingredient for recipes. Arm & Hammer baking soda has successfully positioned their product as an odor-destroying agent in refrigerators.

Positioning by the Product User

Another positioning approach is associating a product with a user or a class of users. Thus, many cosmetic companies have used a model or personality, such as Brut's Joe Namath, to position their product. Revlon's Charlie cosmetic line has been positioned by associating it with a specific life-style profile. Johnson & Johnson saw market share move from 3 percent to 14 percent when they repositioned their shampoo from a product used for babies to one used by people who wash their hair frequently and therefore need a mild shampoo.

In 1970, Miller High Life was the "champagne of bottled beers," was purchased by the upper class, and had an image of being a woman's beer. Phillip Morris repositioned it as a beer for the heavy beer-drinking, blue-collar working man. Miller's Lite beer, introduced in 1975, used convincing beer-drinking personalities to position itself as a beer for the heavy beer drinker who dislikes that filled-up feeling. In contrast, earlier efforts to introduce low-calorie beers positioned with respect to the low-calorie attribute were dismal failures. One even

---

[1]"Sears' New 5-year Plan: To Serve Middle America," *Advertising Age*, December 4, 1978.

claimed its beer had fewer calories than skim milk, and another featured a trim personality. Miller's positioning strategies are in part why its market share has grown from 3.4 percent in 1970 to 24.5 percent in 1979.[2]

Positioning with Respect to a Product Class

Some critical positioning decisions involve product-class associations. For example, Maxim freeze-dried coffee needed to position itself with respect to regular and instant coffee. Some margarines position themselves with respect to butter. Dried milk makers came out with instant breakfast positioned as a breakfast substitute and a virtually identical product positioned as a dietary meal substitute. The hand soap "Caress" by Lever Brothers positioned itself as a bath-oil product rather than a soap.

The soft drink 7-Up was for a long time positioned as a beverage with a "fresh clean taste" that was "thirst-quenching." However, research discovered that most people regarded 7-Up as a mix rather than a soft drink. The successful "un-cola" campaign was then developed to position 7-Up as a soft drink, with a better taste than the "colas."

Positioning with Respect to a Competitor

In most positioning strategies, an explicit or implicit frame of reference is the competition. There are two reasons for making the reference competitor(s) the dominant aspect of the positioning strategy. First, a well-established competitor's image can be exploited to help communicate another image referenced to it. In giving directions to an address, for example, it's easier to say it is next to the Bank of America building than it is to detail streets, distances, and turns. Second, sometimes it's not important how good customers think you are; it is just important that they believe you are better (or as good as) a given competitor.

Perhaps the most famous positioning strategy of this type was the Avis "we're number two, so we try harder" campaign. The strategy was to position Avis with Hertz as a major car rental agency and away from National, which at the time was a close third to Avis.

Positioning explicitly with respect to a competitor can be an excellent way to create a position with respect to an attribute, especially the price/quality attribute pair. Thus, products difficult to evaluate, like liquor products, will often be compared with an established competitor to help the positioning task. For example, Sabroso, a coffee liqueur, positioned itself with the established brand, Kahlua, with respect to quality and also with respect to the type of liqueur.

Positioning with respect to a competitor can be aided by comparative advertising, advertising in which a competitor is explicitly named and compared on one or more attributes. Pontiac has used this approach to position some of their cars as being comparable in gas mileage and price to leading import cars. By compar-

[2]"A-B, Miller Brews Continue to Barrel Ahead," *Advertising Age,* August 4, 1980:4.

ing Pontiac to a competitor that has a well-defined economy image, like a Volkswagen Rabbit, and using factual information such as EPA gas ratings, the communication task becomes easier.

On Determining the Positioning Strategy

What should be our positioning strategy? The identification and selection of a positioning strategy can draw upon a set of concepts and procedures that have been developed and refined over the last few years. The process of developing a positioning strategy involves six steps:

1.   Identify the competitors.

2.   Determine how the competitors are perceived and evaluated.

3.   Determine the competitors' positions.

4.   Analyze the customers.

5.   Select the position.

6.   Monitor the position.

In each of these steps one can employ marketing research techniques to provide needed information. Sometimes the marketing research approach provides a conceptualization that can be helpful even if the research is not conducted. Each of these steps will be discussed in turn.

Identify the Competitors

This first step is not as simple as it might seem. Tab might define its competitors in a number of ways, including:

a.   other diet cola drinks;

b.   all cola drinks;

c.   all soft drinks;

d.   nonalcoholic beverages;

e.   all beverages.

A Triumph convertible might define its market in several ways:

a.   two-passenger, low-priced, imported, sports car convertibles;

b.   two-passenger, low-priced, imported sports cars;

c.   two-passenger, low- or medium-priced, imported sports cars;

d.   low- or medium-priced sports cars;

e.   low- or medium-priced imported cars.

In most cases, there will be a primary group of competitors and one or more secondary competitors. Thus, Tab will compete primarily with other diet colas, but other colas and all soft drinks could be important as secondary competitors.

A knowledge of various ways to identify such groupings will be of conceptual as well as practical value. One approach is to determine from product buyers which brands they considered. For example, a sample of Triumph convertible buyers could be asked what other cars they considered and perhaps what other showrooms they actually visited. A Tab buyer could be asked what brand would have been purchased had Tab been out of stock. The resulting analysis will identify the primary and secondary groups of competitive products. Instead of customers, retailers or others knowledgeable about customers could provide the information.

Another approach is the development of associations of products with use situations.[3] Twenty or so respondents might be asked to recall the use contexts for Tab. For each use context, such as an afternoon snack, respondents are then asked to identify all appropriate beverages. For each beverage so identified respondents are then asked to identify appropriate use contexts. This process would continue until a large list of use contexts and beverages resulted. Another respondent group would then be asked to make judgments as to how appropriate each beverage would be for each use situation. Groups of beverages could then be clustered based upon their similarity of appropriate use situations. If Tab was regarded as appropriate with snacks, then it would compete primarily with other beverages regarded as appropriate for snack occasions. The same approach would work with an industrial product such as computers, which might be used in several rather distinct applications.

The concepts of alternatives from which customers choose and appropriateness to a use context can provide a basis for identifying competitors even when market research is not employed. A management team or a group of experts, such as retailers, could employ one or both of these conceptual bases to identify competitive groupings.

Determine How the Competitors are Perceived and Evaluated

The challenge is to identify those product associations used by buyers as they perceive and evaluate competitors. The product associations will include product attributes, product user groups, and use contexts. Even simple objects such as beer can evoke a host of physical attributes like container, aftertaste, and price, and relevant associations like "appropriate for use while dining at a good restaurant" or "used by working men." The task is to identify a list of product associations, to remove redundancies from the list, and then to select those that are most useful and relevant in describing brand images.

One research-based approach to product association list generation is to ask respondents to identify the two most similar brands from a set of three competing brands and to describe why those two brands are similar and different from the

[3]George S. Day, Alan D. Shocker, and Rajendra K. Srivasta, "Customer-Oriented Approaches to Identify Product Markets," *Journal of Marketing*, Fall 1979:8–19.

third. As a variant, respondents could be asked which of two brands is preferred and why. The result will be a rather long list of product associations, perhaps over a hundred. The next step is to remove redundancy from the list using logic and judgment or factor analysis. The final step is to identify the most relevant product associations by determining which is correlated highest with overall brand attitudes or by asking respondents to indicate which are the most important to them.

Determine the Competitors' Positions

The next step is to determine how competitors (including our own entry) are positioned with respect to the relevant product associations and with respect to each other. Although such judgments can be made subjectively, research-based approaches are available. Such research is termed multidimensional scaling because its goal is to scale objects on several dimensions (or product associations). Multidimensional scaling can be based upon either product associations data or similarities data.

Product Association–based Multidimensional Scaling. The most direct approach is simply to ask a sample of the target segment to scale the various objects on the product association dimensions. For example, the respondent could be asked to express his or her agreement or disagreement on a seven-point scale with statements regarding the Chevette:
"With respect to its class I would consider the Chevette to be:

- sporty
- roomy
- economical
- good handling.''

Alternatively, perceptions of a brand's users or use contexts could be obtained:
"I would expect the typical Chevette owner to be:

- older
- wealthy
- independent
- intelligent.''

"The Chevette is most appropriate for:

- short neighborhood trips
- commuting
- cross-country sightseeing.''

In generating such measures there are several potential problems and considerations (in addition to generating a relevant product association list) of which one should be aware:

1. The validity of the task. Can a respondent actually position cars on a "sporty" dimension? There could be several problems. One, a possible unfamiliarity with one or more of the brands, can be handled by asking the

respondent to evaluate only familiar brands. Another is the respondent's ability to understand operationally what "sporty" means or how to evaluate a brand on this dimension.

2.   Differences among respondents. Subgroups within the population could hold very different perceptions with respect to one or more of the objects. Such diffused images can have important strategic implications. The task of sharpening a diffused image is much different from the task of changing a very tight, established one.

3.   Are the differences between objects significant and meaningful? If the differences are not statistically significant, then the sample size may be too small to make any managerial judgments. At the same time, a small difference of no practical consequence may be statistically significant if the sample size is large enough.

4.   Which product associations are not only important but also serve to distinguish objects? Thus, airline safety may be an important attribute, but all airlines may be perceived to be equally safe.

Similarities-based Multidimensional Scaling.   Product-association approaches have several conceptual disadvantages. A complete, valid, and relevant product association list is not easy to generate. Further, an object may be perceived or evaluated as a whole that is not really decomposable in terms of product associations. These disadvantages lead us to the use of non-attribute data—namely, similarity data.

Similarity measures simply reflect the perceived similarity of two objects. For example, respondents may be asked to rate the degree of similarity of assorted object pairs without a product association list which implicitly suggests criteria to be included or excluded. The result, when averaged over all respondents, is a similarity rating for each object pair. A multidimensional scaling program then attempts to locate objects in a two-, three- (or more if necessary) dimensional space termed a perceptual map. The program attempts to construct the perceptual map such that the two objects with the highest similarity are separated by the shortest distance, the object pair with the second highest similarity are separated by the second-shortest distance, and so on. A disadvantage of the similarity-based approach is that the interpretation of the dimensions does not have the product associations as a guide.

Analyzing the Customers

A basic understanding of the customer and how the market is segmented will help in selecting a positioning strategy. How is the market segmented? What role does the product class play in the customer's lifestyle? What really motivates the customer? What habits and behavior patterns are relevant?

The segmentation question is, of course, critical. One of the most useful segmentation approaches is benefit segmentation which focuses upon the benefits or, more generally, the product associations that a segment believes to be important. The identity of important product associations can be done directly by asking customers to rate product associations as to their importance or by asking them to make trade-off judgments between product associations[4] or by asking them to conceptualize and profile "ideal brands." An ideal brand would be a combination of all the customer's preferred product associations. Customers are then grouped into segments defined by product associations considered important by customers. Thus, for toothpaste there could be a decay preventative segment, a fresh-breath segment, a price segment, and so on. The segment's relative size and commitment to the product association will be of interest.

It is often useful to go beyond product association lists to get a deeper understanding of consumer perceptions. A good illustration is the development of positioning objectives for Betty Crocker by the Needham, Harper & Steers advertising agency.[5] They conducted research involving more than 3,000 women, and found that Betty Crocker was viewed as a company that is:

- honest and dependable
- friendly and concerned about consumers
- a specialist in baked goods but
- out of date, old, and traditional
- a manufacturer of "old stand-by" products
- not particularly contemporary or innovative.

The conclusion was that the Betty Crocker image needed to be strengthened and to become more modern and innovative and less old and stodgy.

To improve the Betty Crocker image, it was felt that an understanding was needed of the needs and lifestyle of today's women and how these relate to desserts. Thus, the research study was directed to basic questions about desserts. Why are they served? Who serves them? The answers were illuminating. Dessert users tend to be busy, active mothers who are devoted to their families. The primary reasons for serving dessert tend to be psychological and revolve around the family.

- Dessert is a way to show others you care.
- Dessert preparation is viewed as an important duty of a good wife and mother.
- Desserts are associated with and help to create happy family moments.

Clearly, family bonds, love, and good times are associated with desserts. As a result, the Betty Crocker positioning objective was to associate Betty Crocker uniquely with the positive aspects of today's families and their feelings about dessert. Contemporary, emotionally involving advertising was used to associate Betty Crocker with desserts that contribute to happy family moments.

---

[4]Paul E. Green and Yoram Wind, "New Ways to Measure Consumers' Judgments," *Harvard Business Review*, July-August 1975:107–115.

[5]Keth Reinhard, "How We Make Advertising" (presented to the Federal Trade Commission, May 11, 1979):22–25.

Making the Positioning Decision

The four steps or exercises just described should be conducted prior to making the actual positioning decision. The exercises can be done subjectively by the involved managers if necessary, although marketing research, if feasible and justifiable, will be more definitive. However, even with that background, it is still not possible to generate a cookbook solution to the positioning questions. However, some guidelines or check-points can be offered.

1. Positioning usually implies a segmentation commitment.   Positioning usually means that an overt decision is being made to concentrate only on certain segments. Such an approach requires commitment and discipline because it's not easy to turn your back on potential buyers. Yet, the effect of generating a distinct, meaningful position is to focus on the target segments and not be constrained by the reaction of other segments.

Sometimes the creation of a "diffuse image," an image that will mean different things to different people, is a way to attract a variety of diverse segments. Such an approach is risky and difficult to implement and usually would be used only by a large brand. The implementation could involve projecting a range of advantages while avoiding being identified with any one. Alternatively, there could be a conscious effort to avoid associations which create positions. Pictures of bottles of Coca-Cola with the words "It's the real thing" superimposed on them, or Budweiser's claim that "Bud is the king of beers," illustrate such a strategy.

2. An economic analysis should guide the decision.   The success of any positioning strategy basically depends upon two factors: the potential market size × the penetration probability. Unless both of these factors are favorable, success will be unlikely. One implication of this simple structure is that a positioning strategy should attract a sizeable segment. If customers are to be attracted from other brands, those brands should have a worthwhile market share to begin with. If new buyers are to be attracted to the product class, a reasonable assessment should be made of the potential size of that growth area. The penetration probability indicates that there needs to be a competitive weakness to attack or a competitive advantage to exploit to generate a reasonable market penetration probability. Further, the highest payoff will often come from retaining existing customers, so this alternative should also be considered.

3. If the advertising is working, stick with it.   An advertiser will often get tired of a positioning strategy and the advertising used to implement it and will consider making a change. However, the personality or image of a brand, like that of a person, evolves over many years, and the value of consistency through time cannot be overestimated. Some of the very successful, big-budget campaigns have run for ten, twenty, or even thirty years.

4. Don't try to be something you are not.   It is tempting but naive—and usually fatal—to decide on a positioning strategy that exploits a market need of opportunity but assumes that your product is something it is not. Before positioning a product, it is important to conduct blind taste tests or in-home or in-office use tests to make sure that the product can deliver what if promises and that is compatible with a proposed image.

Consider Hamburger Helper, successfully introduced in 1970 as an add-to-meat product that would generate a good-tasting, economical, skillet dinner.[6] In the mid-1970s, sales suffered when homemakers switched to more exotic, expensive foods. An effort to react by repositioning Hamburger Helper as a base for casseroles failed because the product, at least in the consumers' mind, could not deliver. Consumers perceived it as an economical, reliable, convenience food and further felt that they did not need help in making casseroles. In a personality test, where women were asked to describe the product as if it was a person, the most prevalent characteristic ascribed to the product was "helpful." The result was a revised campaign to position the product as being "helpful."

Monitoring the Position

A positioning objective, like any marketing objective, should be measurable. To evaluate the positioning and to generate diagnostic information about future positioning strategies, it is necessary to monitor the position over time. A variety of techniques can be employed to make this measurement. Hamburger Helper used a "personality test," for example. However, usually one of the more structured techniques of multidimensional scaling is applied.

A variety of positioning strategies is available to the advertiser. An object can be positioned:

1. by attributes—e.g., Crest is a cavity fighter.

2. by price/quality—e.g., Sears is a "value" store.

3. by competitor—e.g., Avis positions itself with Hertz.

4. by application—e.g., Gatorade is for flu attacks.

5. by product user—e.g., Miller is for the blue-collar, heavy beer drinker.

6. by product class—e.g., Carnation Instant Breakfast is a breakfast food.

The selection of a positioning strategy involves identifying competitors, relevant attributes, competitor positions, and market segments. Research-based approaches can help in each of these steps by providing conceptualization even if the subjective judgments of managers are used to provide the actual input information to the positioning decision.

[6]Reinhard: 29.

24

Brand Franchise Extension: New Product Benefits from Existing Brand Names

Edward M. Tauber

Some of the most successful companies in the United States have begun to offer new products which capitalize on the firm's most valuable assets: well-known trademarks on brand names. Items such as General Foods' Jello pudding pops, Chesebrough Ponds' Vaseline Intensive Care bath beads, Bic disposable lighters, Woolite rug cleaner, Sunkist orange soda, and Clairol hair blow dryers are extensions of a previously known brand name employed by the parent company to enter a new category.

This "new type" of business opportunity is being pursued by an increasing number of firms, though the franchise extension approach to new-product development is still in its infancy. As a result, very little has been written about its merits and pitfalls or how to pursue it in a systematic fashion.

The purpose of this article is to distinguish how brand franchise extensions differ from other opportunities, outline their benefits and drawbacks, specify some conditions under which they are and are not appropriate, and overview a procedure for identifying and evaluating alternative extensions for a given brand. An important by-product of this effort offers management a strategic look at alternative ways of defining what business they are in.

This article first appeared in *Business Horizons*, 47 (March–April 1981):36–41. Copyright, 1981, by the Foundation for the School of Business at Indiana University. Reprinted with permission.

When this article was published the author was Professor and Chairman of Marketing at the University of Southern California.

Franchise Extensions

Differentiation of franchise extension from other new-product forms is best understood by viewing opportunities from the standpoint of the parent firm. In Figure 1, four types of opportunities are characterized according to whether they are in a product category new to the company (brand) and whether the brand name used is new or already familiar to the consumer.

When a new entry employs a new brand name and the product or service is in a category new to the company, this is a traditional *new product*. If the item employs a new brand but is introduced into a category where the firm already has a market position, it is called a *flanker brand*. Ralston Purina's entry of Butchers Blend Dry Dog Food is a flanker to their Dog Chow line. *Line extensions* represent new sizes, flavors, and the like where items use an existing brand name in a firm's present category. Ragu's Italian Cooking Sauce is an extension of their line of other bottled spaghetti sauces.

In contrast to these three, *franchise extensions* take a brand name familiar to the consumer and apply it to products that are in a category new to the parent firm. In effect, franchise extension is one method for a company to enter a new business through the leverage of its most valuable asset—the consumer awareness, good will, and impressions conveyed by its brand name.

Figure 1   New Opportunities from the Company's Viewpoint

	Product Category		
	New	Existing	
	New Product	Flanker Brand	New
			Brand Name
	Franchise Extension	Line Extension	Existing

Opportunities for Growth

Probably the most difficult challenge facing the large corporation today is how to achieve significant sales and earnings growth at acceptable risk within the no/slow growth environment of the American economy. As a result of a variety of factors, new-product development is undergoing a dynamic transition, especially among heavy new-product marketers such as package goods firms. This transition is reflected in a number of trends that have significantly affected new-product development during the seventies and will continue to affect opportunities in the eighties.

The number of new items introduced has dramatically declined. The number introduced in the supermarket in 1979 was half the level monitored in 1972, according to the A. C. Nielsen Company.[1] Further confirmation of this trend is the year-to-year decline in new products in 1978 and 1979, according to the *New Product News*.[2]

A comparative study of the success rate of package goods introduced in 1971 versus 1977 uncovered a sizeable decrease. A. C. Nielsen found 47 percent of new products introduced in 1971 were successful while only 36 percent of those introduced in 1977 met the same criteria.[3]

Compounding the problem for the future is the lower commitment to new-product R&D. McGraw Hill's annual survey of planned R&D expenditures revealed an average 2 percent of sales in 1979, one third lower than the mid-sixties peak. Companies are expected to allocate only 35 percent of these monies to new-product development.[4]

Some of the contributing factors that have led to the deceleration of new-product activity and the increased risk include increasing cost (technology, production, media, promotion), stable volume for supermarket and other consumer items, declining to stable GNP (and therefore disposable real income), inflation pressures due to energy and other resources, and increasing competition both here and abroad from foreign products.

With continuing supply pressures and demand stagnation, I see four major opportunities for the individual firm:

- Market expansion through new distribution channels or untapped areas, especially abroad.
- Acquisition and merger—a continuing trend.
- Line extensions and flanker brands—a defensive tactic to tie up shelf space and "share of mind," and
- Franchise extensions—leveraging existing brands into new categories.

[1] "New Product Success Ratios," *Nielsen Researcher*, A. C. Nielsen Company, Chicago, Illinois, 1979.

[2] *New Product News*, Dancer Fitzgerald Sample, Inc., New York, December 1979.

[3] *Nielsen Researcher*, 1979.

[4] "R&D Planned Expenditures," McGraw Hill Publishing Company, New York, 1979.

Defining the Business

The process of exploring franchise extensions represents a reasoned approach for selecting what new categories a company might enter. Inherent in this process is the identification of alternative definitions of what business we are in.

Theodore Levitt highlighted this basic strategic question in his now classic paper, "Marketing Myopia," written almost twenty years ago. He challenged management to think broadly about what was or could be their domain, pointing out that the failure of the railroads was due to not recognizing they were in the transportation business. The result was missed opportunities and stiffer competition from other transportation carriers. What Levitt did not do was to provide guidelines or research techniques to aid management in determining how to define their business and what product or service categories to include.

Levitt's example suggests that railroads should have defined their business in terms of all competition that would supply similar transportation service. This is only one way of redefinition. For example, Figure 2 reveals some alternative business extensions. BIC has defined its business, not by competition in pens, but instead by a product attribute—disposability. Clairol defined its business by items that offer a head-care benefit. Sunkist has limited its extensions to products which have an orange flavor association. Thus, there are many creative ways for any firm to define its territory. A systematic approach to aid management in this task will be presented later. It is important to note here that investigating franchise extensions will likely result in offering new ways of looking at one's business.

It is particularly interesting to note that BIC's decision to define their business as inexpensive consumer disposables led them to razors and lighters. Their initial success with disposable pens could have led them into stationery supplies or office equipment, natural additions given their channel of distribution. Leveraging their production capability of plastic disposables rather than their distribution channel was a critical strategic decision.

Benefits of Franchise Extensions

Extending a franchise offers a number of benefits which traditional new-product development does not. The major one is that extension capitalizes on the company's most valuable assets—its brand names. Thus, the company moves into a new category from a position of strength—the immediate consumer awareness and impressions communicated by the brand.

Figure 2   What Business Are We In?

Railroads	OR	Transportation
Jello pudding	OR	Snacks and desserts
Clairol shampoo	OR	Head care
Bic pens	OR	Disposables
Sunkist oranges	OR	Orange-flavored foods and beverages

A further benefit is that investment outlays typically necessary to establish a new brand—a significant expense—are minimized. An important related payoff is that introduction of a franchise extension can increase sales for the parent brand. The advertising and heightened awareness of the new entry can have a synergistic effect on the original product. This corporate or umbrella effect can create important advertising efficiencies.

Finally, there *may* be reduced risk of failure of the new item when the brand name already strongly conveys benefits desired in the new category.

Appropriateness

Each contemplated case of extending a franchise is unique and requires custom analysis. Nevertheless, there are certain conditions which I believe are necessary for a franchise extension to be successful. The parent brand should provide leverage in the new category. There must be a rub-off of perceived superior know-how, effectiveness, or appropriate imagery. Most highly advertised brands are known. They provide significant leverage in a new category. Thus, there should be a benefit of the parent brand that is the same benefit offered and desired in the new franchise extension. For example, Sunkist orange soda "promises" the same orange taste as obtained from Sunkist oranges.

Consumers should perceive the new item to be consistent with the parent brand name. Most consumers would probably accept Planters peanut butter candy as a logical extension of the franchise.

Finally, it is critical that the company enter the new category with comparable or superior production/distribution/merchandising and advertising capability. A number of successful franchise extensions have occurred without any technological breakthroughs or product improvements. However, competitive parity is necessary. One case in point is Coleman's successful extension from the camp stove and lantern business to the camping equipment business, offering tents, sleeping bags, and so on.

Franchise extension is not without risk. In fact, its major strength—capitalizing on a previously established brand name—also reflects its number one risk: potential dilution of the brand franchise in the long run.

There are a number of conditions that can contribute to franchise deterioration. What might appear to be a "natural" extension short term should be pursued with caution as most deleterious effects to a franchise occur gradually over time. Brands like General Electric, Betty Crocker, Quaker, and Gillette have been extended profusely. While they have not stopped being household words, the strong associations they once had with specific products (television, cake mix, oatmeal, and razors) and their related qualities have been diluted.

For this reason franchise extension always carries greater risk when a brand name is used almost synonymously with a specific product. The great lengths to which manufacturers go to protect their trademarks from being judged legally generic testifies to the market value such brands possess. The only thing worse than competitors breaking this brand-product link in the consumer's mind is companies doing it to themselves. A Tab is a sugar-free cola. Now, the Coca-

Cola Company offers Tab in a variety of flavors. Other examples of brands that are not legally generic but are often used synonymously with the category are: Kleenex = facial tissues; Perrier = naturally carbonated bottled water; Coke = cola; Scotch Tape = transparent tape; Tampax = feminine hygiene tampon; Band-Aid = adhesive bandages.

Another risky condition when extending a franchise occurs when the new item could create confusion or a negative image for the parent brand.

Finally, sometimes the new item's failure could seriously affect the parent brand. Some years ago, Carnation Company announced its intent to introduce a contraceptive dog food, Lady Friskie, knowing that if this medicated product generated any adverse publicity, even in an isolated test market, sales of the parent brand (Friskies) could be impaired. Later, they tried naming the test product Extra Care. It was never introduced to the market.

Search and Evaluation

Implicit in Levitt's concept of how to define one's business is the notion that it should go beyond product description (such as railroads) to benefits, attributes, meanings, and associations. Franchise extension search is based on the question, "What's in a name?"

The franchise extension search is a two-stage consumer research method employing bright, articulate people who have the ability to think abstractly. No attempt is made to locate an average or a "representative" group. During the first half of the ideation session, consumers generate meanings and associations surrounding the brand name. In stage two, the consumers are asked to identify product or service categories that are related to each association.

Figure 3 is a condensed version of the output from a franchise extension search for Vaseline Intensive Care. The brand leads to alternative definitions of the business (moisturizer, medicinal, body care, etc.) and each definition has a list of related product categories. Each chain represents a potential franchise extension. For example, one option is to define the business as offering lotions and introduce products such as Vaseline Intensive Care sunburn cream or Vaseline Intensive Care baby lotion.

Deciding on the appropriateness of a franchise extension entails using these three criteria which are related to consumer perception.

- The consumer perceives the new item to be consistent with the parent brand.
- The parent brand provides leverage in the new category which the existing competitors do not have.
- A benefit associated with the parent brand is the same one offered and desired from the new franchise extension.

These criteria—perceptual fit, competitive leverage, and benefit transfer—are used when quantitative study is conducted where respondents are asked how likely they would be to expect alternative products such as soap or baby oil from a brand name such as Vaseline Intensive Care (perceptual fit). For each product

Figure 3   Franchise Extension Search

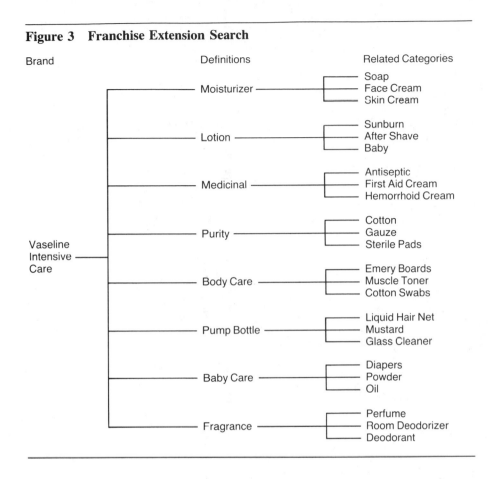

which is likely, they are asked to list any brands they believe the new item would compete with. Then, they report in what ways, if any, the new product might be better than the competitors and in what ways it might not be as good (competitive leverage). In the final step, each participant thinks of any benefit or advantage the parent product has (Vaseline Intensive Care lotion) that could be associated with each new item (benefit transfer). See Figure 4.

Too often, new-product programs are undertaken without sufficient guidance from top management. A key source of direction is a tightly written definition of what business the firm wishes to pursue. This initial step is easy to ignore or assume since the products or services the companies offer tend to become the definition of the business—pens, shampoo, jeans, etc. The strategic task of defining a business by product attributes, consumer benefits, or other more abstract associations broadens horizons while at the same time delineates the areas the firm will pursue.

A second key to successful new-product activity is management's recognition of what assets it has which are leverageable, such as resource purchasing

Figure 4   Franchise Extension Search

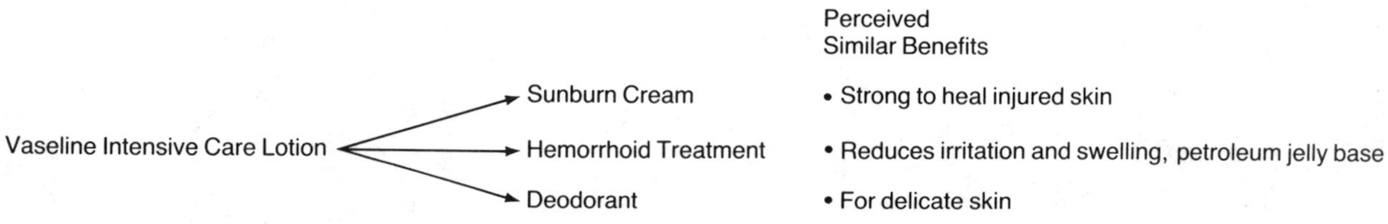

Vaseline Intensive Care Lotion

→ Sunburn Cream

→ Hemorrhoid Treatment

→ Deodorant

Perceived
Similar Benefits

• Strong to heal injured skin

• Reduces irritation and swelling, petroleum jelly base

• For delicate skin

power, technology, processing capability, and distribution channels. Well-known brand names are for many firms among the most leveragable assets they own.

The process proposed here begins with the brand name, generates alternative definitions of the business through meanings and associations to the brand, and seeks related product categories. These categories become candidates for consideration of a franchise extension. Business judgment and economic factors must be applied to eliminate categories that are of no interest to the firm. Consumer research can be used to evaluate the fit of the brand name to the category, and any competitive leverage that would exist.

25

Make Sure Your Customers Keep Coming Back

F. Stewart DeBruicker and Gregory L. Summe

Jerry Evans, a sales applications engineer for Polyplastics, a plastic resin manufacturer, expected a rewarding day. For the better part of two years he had been calling on Universal Electric's new product design group. In the last year his efforts had paid off in hefty orders, as the group included several of his modified-nylon resins in their specifications for a promising new line of home appliances.

True, he now seemed to be spending increasing amounts of time with the procurement manager rather than with his original benefactor, the design group's leader. But the project leader had specifically asked to meet with him today. Jerry welcomed the chance to talk over some of the new applications he had in mind.

Jerry's optimism was short-lived. The design group leader greeted him with the announcement that the team was winding up its current assignment and members were being reassigned to various new projects in the company. In the future, he said, reorders of the modified nylon Jerry sold would be handled exclusively by the procurement manager.

Later, meeting alone with the procurement manager, Jerry tried to establish rapport and stimulate interest in his product. He mentioned how much he had enjoyed working with the design group and began to describe ideas for other product applications. "We appreciate that, Jerry—we do," the procurement manager interrupted, "but I'll have to be honest with you. I'm looking for three things: price, price, and price. What can you do for us?"

This article first appeared in the *Harvard Business Review*. Reprinted by permission of the *Harvard Business Review* (January–February 1985):92–98. Copyright © 1985 by the President and Fellows of Harvard College; all rights reserved.

When this article was published the authors were Adjunct Associate Professor of Marketing at the Warton School of the University of Pennsylvania and an associate in the Atlanta office of McKinsey Company who specializes in business strategy marketing for technology-based companies, respectively.

Surprised at the manager's bluntness, Jerry floundered, joking lamely, "Well, as you know, we're not exactly the Chevrolet of the industry." Even as the words were coming out, he could see his customer's interest slipping. Later, when walking to his car, Jerry had the uneasy feeling that he was losing the account—worth more than half a million dollars in annual orders. It had all happened so suddenly.

Jerry Evans is a hypothetical salesman, but his problem is real and increasingly common. He has confronted the industrial marketing phenomenon of evolving customer experience. That is, his customer has evolved from an inexperienced buyer that leaned heavily on the support and services Jerry's company offered to an experienced buyer more interested in other benefits—in this case, price.

Jerry walked away with an empty order sheet because his marketing department had not prepared him for this predictable change in customer behavior. Had he been alert to the change, he would have noticed some telling signals: the increasing participation of a purchasing agent in the buying decision and the dwindling interest of the team in his application suggestions.

Jerry's problem illustrates a marketing strategy issue that affects all manufacturers of products sold to other businesses. Whether the product is a standard industrial product like sheet steel or a high-tech item like telecommunications equipment, the company will confront customer changes that result from this customer experience effect. Understood in its relation to the product life cycle, this effect provides insight into the customer's needs and serves as a guide for planning marketing strategies.

The Customer Experience Effect

As customers gain familiarity with a product, they find a manufacturer's support programs to be of declining value. Their buying decisions become increasingly price-sensitive. They unbundle into components the products they once purchased as systems and open their doors to suppliers who sell on price and offer little in the way of product support. Even the most remote observer, once instructed, can spot this pattern.

The Inexperienced Generalist

Naturally, when a product family is at the beginning of its life cycle, most customers are inexperienced. Even as the product matures, it will continue to attract inexperienced customers. Novice customers are distinguished by two characteristics: they are generalists, and they place a premium on technical and applications support in making purchases.

They are generalists because companies dealing with a new product usually assign responsibility to people who are competent in traditional skills and trustworthy in dealing with uncertainties. In some cases, these people will be, by default, members of general management. There may be no other member of the organization who will take on the political risk of being associated with a bad decision.

Other inexperienced customers will be design engineers, systems analysts, and other "professional" generalists who are rewarded for introducing major new products and processes and for moving their companies into new businesses.

Inexperienced customers place strong emphasis on product support. They are attracted by a bundle of vendor-supplied benefits and proven technology. Their decision processes are slow and they rely on vendors for guidance throughout.

In such a market situation, vendors with strong marketing and account management resources compete most effectively. Companies that are unwilling or unable to manage prolonged decision processes and to provide turnkey solutions to problems will fail with this type of customer.

A look at the history of the mainframe computer industry's environment tells us much about inexperienced customers and the strategies that serve them. This industry got off the ground in the 1960s, when a few large corporations decided to remain a jump ahead of competitors (and get a better handle on working capital) by computerizing the enormous task of record keeping.

Since the purchase decision involved changes in internal information flows and procedures and large financial commitments, it was usually made by a committee of senior managers—each with a functional ax to grind. Decision making took 18 to 24 months.

IBM dominated this market from the outset because it had tailored its marketing strategy to the inexperienced buyer. Its marketing program included complete systems of reliable (rather than technologically advanced) hardware and software; a wide product line permitting future upgrading; extensive human resources for installation, education, service, and account management; rental options with liberal system-upgrading privileges and fees quoted on a whole-system basis; and a pricing strategy that yielded margins much higher than systems offered by smaller competitors.

IBM's was a formidable strategy, not so much because of the enormous resources behind it but because it was tailored to a market of inexperienced generalists.

Similarly, the robotics industry today confronts a market in which most customers are inexperienced and risk-averse. Buyers are less interested in the performance-price ratios of component robots than in proven, comprehensive, packaged solutions. Only companies that offer complete systems and products with unassailable reputations for reliability will succeed in this environment. Strong marketing resources are much more important than low price.

In short, inexperienced generalists buy systems, and they take a long time to reach a decision. Any strategy that offers them less than a complete, systematic solution is unlikely to succeed.

The Experienced Specialist

The initially successful vendor will falter, however, if it fails to respond to the growing sophistication and self-confidence of its customer base.

As companies become more familiar with a product and more confident of their ability to make judgments about it, they shift the purchasing responsibility from general management or support professionals to either functional specialists with detailed knowledge of the product or purchasing agents, who base the buying decision on standard specifications. In robotics purchasing, for example, the corporate-level committee at Fisher Body has in recent years been replaced by a smaller group of manufacturing and production specialists. They are more knowledgeable about component performance and system applications and rely much less on the guidance of manufacturers' account management teams.

Product experience emboldens customers to assume certain risks they once deferred to the vendor. No longer do they look for a comprehensive bundle of benefits. The bundle's components can be seen, sorted, and valued. Some of those components may be purchased from the original systems vendor, others are likely to be made by the customers themselves, and still others bought from specialist suppliers. When this unbundling takes place, customers tend to base buying decisions not on strong support from the account manager or on turnkey systems but on price-performance trade-offs. Decision making is less time-consuming. (The few exceptions are products with complex component interfaces, such as integrated office systems and flexible manufacturing systems.)

Customers in the telecommunications industry have already embarked on the transition. Prodded by AT&T's divestiture and industry deregulation to make their own choices of equipment and long-distance service vendors, businesses are beginning to develop in-house staffs to manage their telecommunications needs. As these staffs become more experienced, they will increasingly unbundle telecommunications products. They will buy some components of equipment from one vendor and some from another, and select more carefully between service vendors. They will *build* their systems using the products and services offering the best price-performance benefits.

The point of transition from inexperienced generalist to experienced specialist is, of course, rarely as clear-cut as in the hypothetical situation described at the outset of this article. But certainly inexperienced and experienced customers base their buying decisions on quite different factors.

Customer Sophistication and Product Maturity

How does the customer's evolution relate to the product life cycle? The two can evolve in parallel, as in the telecommunications industry today, but the transition from inexperienced to experienced customer often takes place independent of product maturation. Product market evolution, in other words, is driven by customer forces as well as by product forces. The engineering plastics story with which we started illustrates the point: as the customers mature, purchase decisions are made first by applications engineers, later by purchasing agents, and then, in some cases, by the many thousands of operators of molding companies that process resins into finished plastic parts. Other factors, such as the length of time required to make the purchase decision and the benefits sought, also change as the customer gains experience (see Exhibit I). No wise marketer makes the mistake of assuming that customer evolution parallels a company's product life cycle.

The patterns of product benefits customers desire are definable and predictable. As Exhibit II shows, a product's market will be a mosaic of four customer

Exhibit I   Effects of Customer Experience in the Engineering Plastics Industry

| | Customer Groups | |
	Inexperienced Customers	Experienced Customers
Decision-making Unit	Applications engineers	Purchasing agents
Decision-making Process	New tasks, two years	Routine repurchases, four to five per year
Marketing Policy Areas:		
Dominant Product Benefits	Technical assistance, applications support	Performance, availability, price
Price/Value Considerations	Enhanced competitive position	Low cost
Sales Program	Account management via industry specialists	Field sales on a geographic basis
Key Success Factors	Account management and technology	Low cost of goods sold, low or parity prices

profiles. These four possible stages (no customer goes through all four) can provide the basis for targeted marketing programs:

1. Early in the development of an industry, customers can be expected to reward vendors who provide not only reliable new technology but also high levels of technical and applications support. These first-purchase decisions, while potentially rewarding, are risky, and customers proceed cautiously for fear of failure. Customers may be attracted to promising new products, but the so-called FUD factor—fear, uncertainty, and doubt—will predispose them to pay a premium price for a product of known reliability coupled with effective support. Products whose markets currently fit this profile include aseptic packaging (which is familiar to consumers as the latest packaging for beverages), fiber optics, and powdered metals.

2. As customers gain knowledge, they purchase the product primarily for its performance characteristics. However, the vendor can still deliver value by helping develop new applications. For example, polycarbonates now face a market composed largely of experienced buyers, as do industrial robots (while many buyers of robots are inexperienced, most of the volume in that market is presently controlled by experienced buyers).

3. Customers entering the market late will be influenced by the availability of substitute products. Since competing vendors may have lower product development costs (by virtue of their later entry) and lower application costs (because they can imitate the innovating company), they are likely to offer lower prices. Customers in this environment, while seeking technical sup-

Exhibit II   Product Benefit Profiles

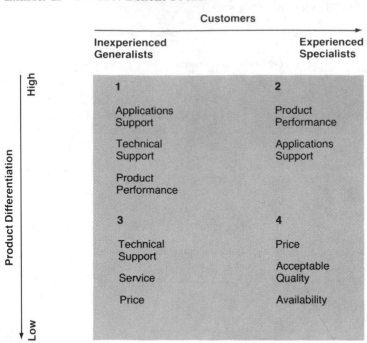

port and responsive service, will also tend to be price sensitive. Portions of the electric switch-gear and long-distance telephone service markets fall into this category.

4.   Under the pressure of customer and competitive forces, most of the market will eventually assume the profile of the experienced customer buying an undifferentiated product. At this stage, customers will unbundle the original product-benefit package and strip away the benefits not directly related to their dominant buying needs. They will seek adequate rather than superlative quality, assured availability to ensure stable production planning and efficient use of related resources, and the lowest possible price. Polyvinylchloride, sheet steel and glass containers are among the commodity products that fit this profile.

Marketing Strategy Implications

Once a good customer relationship has been established, the seller tends to cherish and sustain the status quo. But as customer needs change over time, sellers can be left holding an empty bag. Conversely, a competitive advantage exists for the vendor who understands and anticipates the customer experience effect and who designs strategies based on the benefits a given group of customers desires.

These benefits can be provided in many ways to the advantage of both buyer and seller. Four primary approaches, outlined in Exhibit III are as follows.

Account Management Strategies

As long as most competitors fail to duplicate a product's core technology, the principal evolution in the product-market environment takes place on the customer side. In industries with a brisk rate of new-product development, the vendor can slow this evolution by emphasizing account management—strengthening the account management representation and perhaps even adding top management to the team. This strategy is designed to keep purchasing decisions under the regular review of general managers in senior positions, thereby limiting the impact of experienced specialists on important decisions. Its purpose is to sustain the vendor's influence and block competitive inroads into the account.

IBM used this strategy to great advantage in the computer industry. The company inhibited customers' transitions from inexperienced to experienced buyers by using a multilevel team account management approach. Including both high-level managers and data processing specialists in the decision-making unit ensured the continued involvement of inexperienced generalists in the decision-making process. These moves enabled IBM to retain most of its customer base

Exhibit III   Marketing Strategies that Recognize Customer Experience*

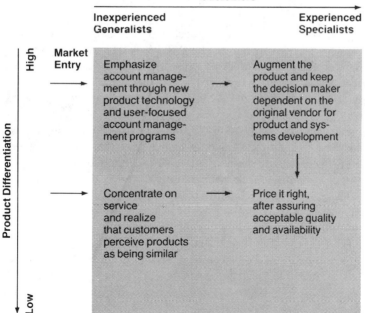

*Customers begin as inexperienced generalists and through product usage become experienced. As products mature, customers purchase less differentiated products.

over the long term. Not until recently was IBM forced to address the price-sensitive needs of experienced customers.

In high-tech industries, the fast pace of product and systems development makes account management a feasible strategy, even when customers have achieved some sophistication. Making the strategy work, however, requires an enormous commitment to support skilled marketing resources. And to succeed, the strategy must add real value; in other words, the involvement of higher level managers must result in superior responsiveness based on a genuine commitment to meet the customer's needs efficiently and economically.

Product Augmentation Strategies

Advanced products eventually spawn imitations, and inexperienced customers become experienced specialists. Theodore Levitt has suggested that at this point ''it makes sense to embark on a systematic program of customer-benefiting, and therefore customer-keeping, product augmentation.''[1] In other words, sellers should emphasize a particular benefit—say, new applications support—that they know the customer is seeking. The thrust of this strategy is to keep differentiating the product in the customer's eyes, thereby drawing attention away from the price appeal of competing products. To do so, the vendor identifies the customer's product needs and adapts offerings to serve them. A supplier who can identify an associated product need and fill it through a unique service of continuing value to the customer will not be forced to compete on the basis of price.

In the industrial market for converted paper products, for example, one U.S. producer is differentiating its product on the basis of reliability and specialization. Its paper products, which are considered a mature line, account for a very small percentage of the cost of the customer's final product. But when they fail, the end product usually suffers costly damage. Having tested all the competitive offerings, this producer took steps to lower its failure rate through design and manufacturing changes. Next the company began working with its major customers to design products with superior loading characteristics for their particular applications. It is now changing its sales emphasis from customer relationships to applications expertise.

With its new augmentation strategy, this company expects to provide a product that commands both a significant premium and a large share of the market. The supplier benefits by slowing the movement of its product into the commodity category, where purchase decisions are based mainly on price. The customer receives real value through increased reliability of its end product.

Customer Service Strategies

Sellers seeking to attract inexperienced customers who enter the market late in the product life cycle may find a service strategy to be appropriate. The presence of substitute products in the market will make even first-time decision makers aware

---

[1]Theodore Levitt, ''Marketing Success Through Differentiation—Of Anything,'' HBR January–February 1980, p. 83.

of how few differences exist between the offerings of competing suppliers, rendering product performance characteristics less important than they would be early in the cycle. Customer interest will likely focus not on product but on service—the distribution, customer education, and aftermarket support elements of the marketing mix.

Consider the situation in the microcomputer industry. Dozens of competitors have entered the market, with most products based on the same Intel 8088 chip. Their products are virtually identical in performance capabilities. This proliferation of vendors with similar products has affected end-user decisions by shifting the purchase decision away from issues of technical product capability. Some vendors—notably Apple Computer—have followed a product augmentation strategy for experienced users by developing extensive software for particular customer applications. Apple, along with others, targeting the inexperienced customer, have emphasized service areas: training, product maintenance, and related support. Still others, unprepared for this shift in customer needs, have fallen victim to the current industry shakeout.

The telecommunications industry provides another example. A current AT&T ad has this lead: "Our products come with the following standard equipment: technical consultant, account executive, systems technician." In other words, the strategy is service, and it is targeted toward the great mass of companies, inexperienced with large telecommunications systems, that can now select among competitive products.

Pricing Strategies

Eventually, customer and competitive forces combine to drive a marketplace into a highly price-sensitive mode. If the vendor is to protect its market position, strategies that emphasize account management, product augmentation, and customer service must give way to a strategy based at least partly on price.

A Supplier's Strategic Evolution

Companies can use an aggressive market-development strategy to respond to the mosaic of customer profiles that prevail at any given time. The experience of one company—a major producer of engineering plastics in Europe—illustrates how to do so successfully.

Historically, this company used strongly differentiated products and extensive customer-support programs to attract customers who were insensitive to price. The company simply avoided markets that had become price-sensitive as products aged and users became sophisticated.

Through the late 1970s, the company's sales growth and profit margins outpaced the industry's. But by 1982, as one of the company's products, a branded resin, was maturing, several other companies had entered the market. These competitors sold standard grades of the resin at prices 10 percent to 20 percent less than the European company's. None of the newcomers offered comparable customer-support programs, but by concentrating on price-sensitive customers they succeeded in establishing positions in the industry.

Using customer-experience and product-differentiation analyses as guide-lines (segmenting customers according to knowledge of the product and products according to intensity of the competition), the company discovered that its strategy of avoiding experienced, price-sensitive users no longer made sound strategic sense. It learned via interviews with former customers that while its applications development efforts were still expanding the market, the company was losing many customers who were switching to less differentiated, standard grades. Fur-ther, it was giving aid and comfort to price-cutting competitors by avoiding price-sensitive business. Management finally concluded that the price-sensitive segment was the largest and fastest-growing segment in a slow-growing market and that its market leadership would be jeopardized if the company let its customers slip away by failing to recognize both their experience and the commodity nature of the product.

Based on its customer-experience analysis, the company revised its strategy in three ways. First, it decided to continue the traditional strategy of developing new products for designated industries. It expected this portion of the overall strategy to be a vigorous generator of net income in the near term but to diminish in the longer term due to technical limits.

Second, the company elected to reduce prices on products for which the total contribution from price-sensitive customers (experienced specialists) was greater than performance-sensitive customers (inexperienced generalists). To pre-serve margins, it also cut back on the support resources allocated to these products internally.

Third, the company took steps to slow the passage of the remaining custom-ers who were experienced but still performance-sensitive to the price-sensitive category. These actions included active pursuit of legal protection of patent and licensing rights, development of new product grades, and the further augmentation of the product by offering associated services, such as computer-aided design.

This story stands in sharp contrast to our opening anecdote. Two things, however, are clear from both: the effect of customer experience is a potent factor in the marketplace and does not exist in isolation from the product life cycle. The two forces are interactive elements in the evolution of a market. Companies have often ignored the customer-experience factor because it is not readily measured—it is a concept that pertains to the forest, not to the trees. But successful companies choose and manage their customers with the same care they put into choosing and managing their products. Anticipating the patterns of evolution in customer deci-sion making is as vital to success as is the most technically sophisticated product development program. In their final product-market choices, customers are as im-portant as products.

26

Make-or-Buy Decisions

Erin Anderson and Barton A. Weitz

Improving marketing productivity is a major corporate concern, especially in view of the rapid escalation of media costs and direct sales costs.[1] Although productivity gains can be made in many areas, the Conference Board reports that reallocating field salesforces and revamping distribution systems are the most frequent actions taken.[2] These salesforce and distribution decisions often prompt examination of the following make-or-buy question: should a marketing activity be performed within the organization by company employees or should the organization contract with an external agent to perform the activity? In other words, to what extent should the firm vertically integrate the performance of marketing activities?

Vertical integration is defined as the combination of technologically distinct economic processes within the confines of a single firm.[3] Thus, the firm is pondering a vertical integration question when a direct salesperson is considered as an alternative to a manufacturer's representative, when an in-house advertising agency is weighed against a traditional full-service agency, and when decisions are made concerning the organization of the distribution channel. The question also arises in international marketing when a firm chooses among the options of entering a market directly, establishing an independent subsidiary, or using local representatives. Furthermore, strategy development, market research, and new-product development may be delegated to outside agents. The resolution of these questions defines the boundary of the firm[4] by determining the degree to which a firm internalizes marketing functions.

This article first appeared in the *Sloan Management Review*. Reprinted from *Sloan Management Review* (Spring 1986) by permission of the publisher. Copyright © 1986 by the Sloan Management Review Association. All rights reserved.

When the article was published the authors were Assistant Professor in the Marketing Department at The Wharton School of the University of Pennsylvania; and Professor of Marketing and the J.C. Penny Eminent Scholar Chair in Retail Management at the Graduate School of Business Administration of the University of Florida, respectively.

Objective

Even though make-or-buy decisions arise frequently and have important productivity implications, there is little theory or research to guide managers in analyzing these issues. The objective of this article is to provide a framework for analyzing make-or-buy decisions and to stimulate empirical research in this area by describing a set of variables and proposed relationships. Rather than identifying all of the variables that might affect vertical integration decisions, the framework focuses on a key set of variables associated with the efficiency with which the marketing activity is performed.

The marketing literature suggests a wide variety of alternative criteria for evaluating the performance of a marketing activity, such as the cost associated with undertaking the activity; the sales generated or market share realized; the degree of communication and coordination between people performing and activity; the level of risk; innovativeness and adaptability; and the degree to which entry barriers are established. These alternative criteria can be all related to the criterion of long-term efficiency, examined herein.

Scope

This article focuses primarily on two vertical integration alternatives: the firm either performs the activity internally using company employees (a "make" decision) or contracts with an external agent to perform the activity (a "buy" decision). For many marketing activities, a wider set of alternatives exists. For example, there are four basic organizational patterns for distribution channels: conventional or traditional, administered, contractual, and corporate.[5] The conventional channel represents a "buy" decision, since distribution activities are performed by independent companies, while the corporate channel constitutes a "make" decision, since distribution activities are performed by units owned and operated by the firm. The remaining two organizational forms, administered and contractual, are aspects of vertical integration not considered directly here. These forms represent intermediate levels of vertical integration in which the company exerts more control than it can in a conventional channel but less than in a corporate channel. Similarly, salespeople compensated by straight commission can be viewed as an intermediate level of integration between the company employee compensated by straight salary and the independent agent compensated by commission on sales. In presenting the framework, only the black and white extremes on the vertical integration spectrum are discussed; however, extensions to the gray area are considered in the final section.

Organization

Following a brief review of the traditional viewpoint on vertical integration decisions in marketing and economics, a framework for analyzing vertical integration issues is presented. The key variables in the framework are defined, logical arguments are presented to justify the proposed relationships, and these relationships

are summarized as a proposition. The variables in the framework are operational-
ized in the form of questions to be answered when analyzing a vertical integration
problem. The article concludes with suggestions concerning future investigations.

Marketing Perspectives on Vertical Integration
Variations without a Theme

The wide variations in the degrees of vertical integration observed indicate the
complexity of the vertical integration issue in marketing. This variability occurs
across both different activities and industries. In 1977, both advertising and distribution functions were performed largely by external agents: 90 percent of national advertising was placed by full-service agencies and 75 percent of all distribution activities was performed by merchant wholesalers. In contrast, the personal
selling function tends to be performed internally: only 10 percent of sales activities
was performed by manufacturers' representatives. These patterns have been relatively stable in recent years. From 1972 to 1977, there was a slight decrease in
the level of vertical integration in sales and wholesaling, while the level of integration in advertising changed little.[6]

These aggregate figures, however, obscure considerable differences across
industries. In selling, for example, the percentage of sales made through manufacturers' representatives is 43 percent for electrical goods, 32 percent for furniture
and home furnishings, 19 percent for apparel, 12 percent for machinery, 4 percent
for groceries, and only 2 percent for alcoholic beverages.[7] Advertising activities,
while typically performed by independent agencies, are frequently internalized for
industrial products,[8] services,[9] retailing,[10] and new-product introductions.[11]

Scale Economies versus Control

The marketing literature on vertical integration of advertising, sales, and distribution has focused upon the trade-off between scale economies achieved through
the use of external agents and the benefits of increased control and coordination
achieved through vertical integration. The following is a brief review of the marketing literature on several functions.

The Sales Function.   For selling activities, most textbooks and practitioners indicate that a direct salesforce is preferable to independent agents because of the
difficulty of controlling reps.[12] These control problems arise because it is assumed
that agents are too short-term oriented and will not engage in activities with a
long-term payoff, such as filling out reports, promoting new products, collecting
market research, cultivating new accounts or small customers with growth potential, and performing service and support functions. In contrast, direct salespeople
are thought to enjoy more job security, to be more susceptible to influence by
superiors, and to be less subject to short-term pressures, especially if paid on a
salary.

The use of independent sales agents is usually recommended only for small companies, for territories with low sales potential, or for entering a new market. In these situations, the benefits from scale economies outweigh the control problems. Since reps are more difficult to control than company employees, it is considered preferable to switch to direct salespeople as soon as a company or territory can support their higher fixed costs.

The Channel Function.   Similarly, most marketers contend that vertical integration improves channel performance by providing better control over channel activities. In addition, independent wholesalers are characterized as small businesses with limited marketing and managerial capabilities. Thus, firms should use corporate, vertically integrated channels when they can achieve the necessary scale economies. When scale economies do not justify vertical integration, companies should achieve coordination through the use of power.[13]

The Advertising Function.   The principal reasons for using external advertising agencies are related to lowering costs and improving advertising effectiveness.[14] Costs are lowered through the economies of scale achieved by contracting advertising functions to external organizations, since the costs associated with supporting a highly creative and highly paid staff are shared by a number of clients. However, there are many companies that continue to use external agencies even though their advertising expenditures are sufficient to achieve the necessary scale economies.[15]

Administrative Costs

The writing on vertical integration in marketing has largely ignored the administrative costs associated with vertical integration. There is an implicit assumption that the control benefits offered by vertical integration are achieved at minimal costs.

Some marketers have explicitly recognized the administrative costs incurred through vertical integration.[16] In sales force management, Shapiro has suggested that these administrative costs are leading to a new perspective concerning the advantages of independent agents.[17] Shapiro contends that due to the highly competitive nature of the marketplace in which reps engage, reps tend to be well organized, cost conscious, highly motivated, and excellent salespeople. Thus reps can offer an efficient alternative to large, unresponsive, bureaucratic direct sales forces. Therefore, Shapiro suggests the sales function should be performed internally only by companies large enough to support the overhead, yet small enough to manage it well.

In sum, even though two considerations affecting make-or-buy decisions (scale vs. control) have been identified in the marketing literature, there is little discussion of how these factors should be weighed against each other when making a vertical integration decision.

Economic Perspectives on Vertical Integration

From the perspective of economics, there are two motives for vertical integration: (1) cost reduction and (2) environmental control.[18] The cost-reduction motive arises when the efficient performance of a function requires close coordination of several processes. The manufacturing of steel provides a classic example of vertical integration to achieve cost reductions. By integrating blast furnaces, converters, and primary reduction mills, the cost of handling the metal is reduced by eliminating reheating between stages.

Firms also vertically integrate to gain greater control over their economic environment. Backward integration can be used to ensure the supply of scarce raw materials, while forward integration ensures market access through limited distribution channels. By assuming greater control over suppliers or market access, the firm reduces the probability of suppliers or other channel members exerting monopolistic power and charging excessive prices for their products or services. Thus vertical integration can reduce both risk and cost when channel members or suppliers can become powerful.

The control gained through vertical integration can also be used to achieve a strategic advantage over competition.[19] By controlling the supply of key raw materials or a distribution channel to a market, a firm creates a strategic advantage over competition. This advantage enables the firm to either differentiate its offerings or charge lower prices than the competition and thus achieve superior performance.

Both the cost-reduction and environmental control motives suggest that the primary reason for vertical integration is the *absence of competitive markets for products and services needed by the firm.* Clearly, the need for environmental control arises when firms anticipate that competitive markets for channel functions will be supplanted by powerful monopolists who will charge excessive prices for their products and services.

The need for cost reduction in performing technologically related activities can also be traced to anticipated failure of competitive markets. Even though the activities in the steel process are technologically related, these activities could be performed by independent firms. A firm with excess processing capacity could contract with an independent firm to build blast furnaces adjacent to the processing plant. There would be a competitive market for molten steel composed of several firms interested in building adjacent blast furnaces. However, once a contract is drawn and the blast furnaces are built, the processing firm no longer faces a competitive market for molten steel. The firm initially selected to build the blast furnaces and supply molten steel has a strong competitive advantage over all other potential suppliers because it now has operating blast furnaces adjacent to the processing plant. Due to this unique asset, the site, the blast furnace company has achieved a monopolistic position and can charge excessive prices for molten steel provided to the processing plant. To prevent this situation from occurring, firms vertically integrate technologically related activities (or enter into extremely complex contingent claim contracts with independent suppliers). By vertically integrating, firms prevent a competitive market, *ex ante* to the initial contract, from degenerating into a noncompetitive *ex post* market.

Thus, the economic perspective on vertical integration focuses on anticipated market imperfections. If markets for selling, advertising, or distribution services were perfectly competitive, outsiders would be pressured to keep costs and prices down. Hence, there would be no need to vertically integrate to assure low-cost supply. However, the traditional industrial organization literature does not delineate the specific conditions under which markets become noncompetitive, necessitating vertical integration to contain costs.

The framework presented in this article explicitly addresses factors that characterize nonperfectly competitive markets. In addition, issues concerning scale economies, control, and administrative costs that arise in the marketing literature are also considered. The proposed interrelationships between these variables is based on an approach for analyzing the cost of transactions, developed principally by Oliver Williamson.[20] Williamson's transaction cost analysis blends institutional economics, organizational theory, and contract law to examine the following question: under what conditions are transactions performed more efficiently within an organization under hierarchical control (achieved through vertical integration), as opposed to between independent entities under market control (achieved through contracting in the marketplace)? Here, the transactions considered are the payment of compensation to develop an advertising campaign, sell a product, or perform distribution functions.

If one can assume opportunism does not exist, firms would simply extract promises from independent agents that they will behave in good faith. Accordingly, contracting in the marketplace to perform a marketing function would always be efficient. But the difficulty of discerning when independent agents will be opportunistic is the principal cause of market failures.

A Framework for Analyzing Vertical Integration Issues

Overview

The proposed framework, shown in Figure 1, enumerates the factors affecting the efficiency with which marketing activities are performed and indicates the conditions under which efficiency can be improved through the use of vertical integration (hierarchical control). The efficiency [1][21] of a marketing activity is affected by the net contribution or effectiveness [2] resulting from the marketing activities and the administrative overhead cost [3] associated with monitoring and controlling the activity. Net contribution is the revenues produced by the marketing effort minus the direct costs of engaging in the activity, while the overhead cost associated with the activity constitutes the fixed cost of running an administrative mechanism. Efficiency is the ratio of these components. Thus, net effectiveness has a positive impact on efficiency while administrative overhead has a negative impact on efficiency. This rather arbitrary division of efficiency into two components is useful for discussing the impact of integration on efficiency.

Within this framework, net effectiveness is negatively affected by [1] the lack of competition in the supplier market [2A]; [2] the uncertainty of the environment within which the marketing activity is performed [2B]; [3] the difficulty

Figure 1   Framework Factors Affecting Efficiency

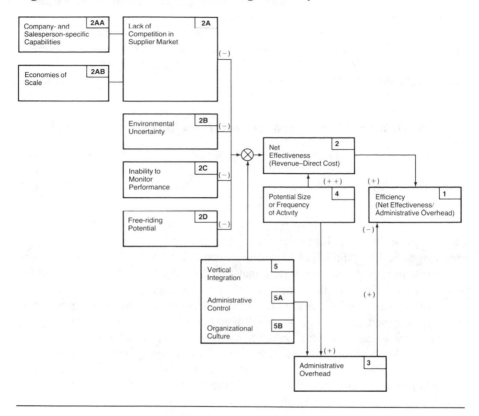

of accurately assessing (monitoring) the performance of the marketing activity [2C]; [4] the potential for "free riding" on the efforts of other parties [2D].

If scale economies arise in the performance of a marketing activity, increasing the level of the marketing activity or the frequency with which the activity is performed [4] will raise net effectiveness [1] by raising total revenue and [2] by enabling a firm to move down the experience curve, thereby decreasing direct cost per unit. Of course, total direct cost will rise, but not as steeply as revenue will rise. The impact, then, is a sharp increase in net effectiveness, indicated by (+ +). A partially offsetting factor is a steep increase in administrative overhead [3] that occurs periodically as the scale of the marketing activity increases. This is indicated by (+). Ultimatley, increasing the level or frequency of a marketing activity can increase efficiency, as long as the increase in overhead is more than offset by the increase in net effectiveness.

The net effectiveness achieved by external agents is usually maximized by the control arising from the invisible hand of a highly competitive market. However, when the market becomes less competitive [2A] or when it is difficult to enforce contracts because of environmental uncertainty [2B], performance assessment problems [2C], or free-riding potential [2D], the resulting reduction in effectiveness can be controlled by vertically integrating [5]. Through vertical integration, administrative controls [5A] and organizational culture [5B] can be used to minimize potential losses arising from opportunism.

In the following section, the factors that reduce net effectiveness are discussed in detail and the methods by which these factors can be controlled through vertical integration are presented. Finally, the costs of imposing these administrative controls are addressed.

Factors Reducing Net Effectiveness—Lack of Competition [2]

The framework presented in Figure 1 delineates four factors that have a negative impact on net effectiveness. The first factor, lack of competition in the supplier market [2A], plays a central role. This factor is discussed in detail in the following section.

Company-specific Capabilities [2AA].   The existence of company- and sales-person-specific capabilities [2AA] and significant scale economies [2AB] creates an opportunity for people performing marketing activities to engage in opportunistic behavior because of the reduced level of competition in the supplier market. Company-specific capabilities are the specialized knowledge and skills required to perform a marketing activity for a particular firm. These capabilities may be thought of as assets, since they generate value added by enhancing performance. Typically, these capabilities arise from specialized training and experience with the company.

Company-specific capabilities include the knowledge required to perform the activity, the knowledge of how the firm operates (its people, methods and procedures, and its unique language and terms), and the set of relationships that develop between the people performing the activity and the people using the end result. For example, company-specific capabilities arise when a unique set of capabilities is required to develop an advertising campaign for a brand or to distribute the brand. Developing the campaign may require intimate knowledge of the advertiser's market research and close, well-coordinated teamwork with the brand manager's office. Distributing the brand may demand knowledge of the brand's particular storage requirements and a good relationship with factory personnel.

Note that ''company-specific'' capabilities are not the same as ''rare'' or ''unusual'' capabilities. For example, the technical knowledge possessed by a computer salesperson is rare, but is company-specific only if the knowledge is germane to the computers manufactured by just one company. One indicator of the degree to which company-specific capabilities are required to perform a function is the time and difficulty of replacing experienced external agents or company employees with someone already familiar with the industry but not the company.

When company-specific capabilities are required to perform a marketing activity, the people who are performing the activity have acquired these idiosyncratic assets and they are able to engage in opportunistic behavior. Opportunism means that agents and managers are inclined to be self-interest seeking *in a deceitful manner*. Opportunism can take many forms: withholding or distorting relevant information, favorably reinterpreting explicit or implicit contract provisions, shirking, and so forth. Such opportunistic behavior may be practiced by either party, the principal or the agent, or by both.

Some idiosyncratic assets are transferable. For example, a salesperson's close relationship with a key customer is a considerable asset to a company—and might be used to the benefit of a competitor if the salesperson switches employers. When idiosyncratic assets are transferable, they become salesperson-specific, not company-specific, and different implications arise.

Consider the following situation: a salesperson threatens to leave the firm unless his or her pay is increased. If the assets possessed by the salesperson are company-specific and not transferable (such as technical knowledge applicable to only one brand), the threat may be empty. If the company refuses to meet the salesperson's demands, the salesperson may not be able to secure greater rewards from a competitor because the idiosyncratic assets are associated with the salesperson's present employer, not the salesperson. When the salesperson's threat is costly, the company may be willing to undertake the expenses associated with hiring and training a new salesperson.

However, if the assets are salesperson-specific and transferable (such as friendships with purchasing agents), the threat will be more believable. The salesperson has actually acquired assets for which another employer would be willing to pay. Thus, the threat of opportunistic behavior is greatest when assets are salesperson-specific rather than company-specific.

When employees or agents possess company- and salesperson-specific assets, the firm is willing to tolerate opportunistic behavior because of the high cost of locating and training new personnel.[22] Furthermore, the firm may tolerate inflexibility (noncooperation, unwillingness to adapt) because the people presently performing the activity are shielded from the threat of easy replacement. A latitude of acceptance is created, and, within this zone, the people presently performing the activity know that opportunism and inflexibility will be tolerated. They can, for example, attempt to skim a sales territory, demand higher sales commissions, or demand more margin to perform distribution functions. In short, company- and salesperson-specific capabilities are the mechanisms by which a highly competitive market for performing a marketing activity breaks down, creating a situation in which poor performers are tolerated, not replaced.

Scale Economies [2AB]. Free entry is critical to the operation of a competitive marketplace. Entry barriers take many forms; however, the principal form for our purposes is the presence of economies of scale in the performance of a marketing function, e.g., distribution.

Although company-specific capabilities and scale economies have the same impact (reducing competition), they have very different implications. Both the potential for *ex post* scale economies and the potential for *ex post* company-specific capabilities can be evident before the signing of a contract with an agent. In the case of scale economies, both the company and the agent realize that the agent can collect higher profits than in fully competitive markets, due to the limited number of suppliers in the market. In the case of company-specific capabilities, such as the steel processing example used earlier, both parties could realize the specific capabilities being created by locating the processing capacity near the blast furnace. However, the difference between these two problems lies in the ability of vertical integration to solve them. Vertical integration will, at least in part, solve the opportunistic behavior problem, but it cannot of itself create scale economies for the firm. Thus, in the case of very strong scale economies, the contracting firm may be willing to tolerate more opportunistic behavior with an independent agent than in the case of creation of company-specific assets.

Other Factors Reducing Net Effectiveness

Company-specific capabilities and scale economies, considered in the previous section, reduce net effectiveness by decreasing the level of competition in the supplier market. The three factors discussed in this section—environmental uncertainty [2B], inability to accurately measure performance [2C], and free-riding potential [2D]—reduce net effectiveness by making it difficult to enforce contracts with external agents. These difficulties arise because the "arms-length" relationship with external agents impedes a free flow of information.

Environmental Uncertainty [2B].   A high level of complexity and turbulence in a firm's environment results in a high level of environmental uncertainty. The effect of uncertainty is to render prediction difficult, which makes it hard to specify the tasks that must be performed, in what manner, and at what level. In uncertain environments, firms frequently find their definition of the marketing tasks out of step with unanticipated changes. This forces frequent reassessments and redefinition of the marketing tasks.

Environmental uncertainty has a negative impact on net effectiveness in both "make" and "buy" situations. Clearly, writing and enforcing contracts with external agents is quite difficult in uncertain environments. However, vertically integrated organizations also have difficulties in dealing with environmental uncertainty. In fact, many scholars argue that uncertainty poses more difficulties for a centralized system than for a decentralized one.[23] Should a shift in strategy be needed, it may be easier to negotiate with or change independent agents than to pressure an entrenched division to change its ways.

Thus, vertically integrating to exert more control over employees may be useful to reduce the opportunism that arises in an uncertain environment. However, this reduction in opportunism may be achieved by sacrificing the flexibility needed to cope with uncertainty, suggesting that firms may be better off buying rather than making under uncertainty.

However, the use of external agents to provide flexibility is only effective when the supplier market is competitive. When company-specific capabilities are required, agents are not easily replaceable, so flexibility is already lost. In sum, uncertainty alone does not favor integration but uncertainty combined with company-specific capabilities makes integration the efficient solution.

Difficulty of Assessing Performance [2C].   A second form of uncertainty is the firm's ability to assess performance using output measures, such as sales. When it is difficult to assess performance using output measures, the effectiveness of independent agents falls because it is difficult to determine how well activities were performed. These assessment problems can be minimized under vertical integration, since the employment contract legitimizes the employers' authority to examine inputs, such as number of sales calls made or amount of time spent working on an advertising campaign.

Difficulties in assessing performance also arise when responsibilities are shared, which is frequently accompanied by high coordination needs. For instance, when team selling is used, it is difficult to ascertain the contribution of each individual to the final sale (or lost opportunity).

In addition, when many factors can affect sales, it is difficult to assess the contribution of a single factor. For example, the impact of trade selling on sales of consumer packaged goods is difficult to measure in the presence of substantial advertising and promotion efforts. Shared responsibilities and multiple factors affecting sales cause problems for controlling *both* independent agents and company employees. Vertical integration (using employees) is a partial solution because it enables a firm to monitor the salesperson's inputs.

Free-riding Potential [2D].   When people performing a marketing function can "free ride" on the efforts of others, effectiveness declines. The classic example is a highway restaurant franchise of a well-known firm. The efforts of the firm and its franchisees *as a whole* create a good reputation for the name. The highway franchisee may "ride" on this reputation (enjoy its benefits), yet cut costs by not performing up to standard. Customers leave with a lower opinion of the chain; the specific franchisee suffers little because the customer base is transient. Other franchises may do the same, perhaps because customers have few alternatives or because owners believe their slippage won't be detected. In general, the potential for free riding is high when the activities of individual agents affect each other but agents do not absorb all the costs (or benefits) of their actions. (Economists call this problem one of "externalities.") This frequently occurs in distribution, where one retailer's poor after-sales service or repair, for example, may affect the brand's reputation and reduce sales for other retailers. The growth of chain-style franchises, in which considerable supervision and seemingly harsh noncompliance penalties are common, may be due to the considerable free-riding potential in many retail operations.

Controlling Reductions in Net Effectiveness because of Excessive Opportunism

The previous section outlined four factors—lack of competition; uncertainty; inability to measure performance; and free riding—that encourage opportunistic behavior and reduce net effectiveness. These factors make it difficult to write, monitor, and enforce contracts and to replace parties who prove to be opportunistic or inflexible. In this section, two methods for controlling losses due to opportunism—administrative control and organizational culture—are discussed.

Administrative Control [5A].   The classic method for controlling opportunistic behavior and reducing subsequent losses in net effectiveness is to vertically integrate and perform the activity within a bureaucratic structure. Bureaucracies control opportunism by (1) reducing the potential gains that can be realized by opportunistic behavior; (2) using authority to direct behavior; (3) improving access to information and thus auditing performance better; and (4) offering a broader, more subtle range of incentives to the people performing the activity.

An organization can reduce the gains to be had from cheating and inflexibility because employees, unlike independent agents, do not have preemptive title to the profits resulting from their activities. Employees receive payment determined by management, and usually cannot benefit directly from profits realized through opportunism.

The firm's ability to direct behavior comes from its legitimate authority, granted by employees. Thus, the firm can resolve disputes by fiat, can demand different behavior in response to circumstances, and can dictate the activities of employees by rules and directives. While a firm's authority is limited, authority is greater with an employee than with an independent agent.

Organizations can also curb opportunism with their greater capacity for accessing information and auditing the activities, inputs, and performance (outputs) of their employees. The firm is not constrained to simply reviewing written documents on clearly relevant issues; it can delve into side issues and review informal evidence. Furthermore, employees may cooperate with an insider, yielding more and better information.

The organization has far more flexibility for curbing opportunism. It can offer a broader, more subtle range of incentives than can the market. These incentives can serve to make employees identify to some extent with the company's goals and feel that they have a stake in the company. This range of incentives includes job security, status in the hierarchy, etc.

Organizational Culture [5B].   Ouchi has suggested an alternative method for controlling lost effectiveness due to opportunism.[24] He proposes that employee commitment can be increased using "organizational culture." Through socialization, individual goals are merged with the company's goals so that individuals are motivated to serve the organization. Employees will suspend a calculative orientation and accept short-run inequities. They do this because they have good reason to expect equity in the long run. Thus, culture can be used to decrease monitoring costs and increase compliance. When successfully implemented, the organization becomes a "clan" in which an informal social system, based on worker commitment and organizational trust, reduces the needs for bureaucratic surveillance and explicit evaluation. Thus, clans can provide high net effectiveness and avoid the disadvantage of large bureaucracies. While Japanese firms are popular examples of clans, Ouchi describes clan-type control used by U.S. firms.

Costs of Vertical Integration

Administrative control and organizational culture implemented through vertical integration are effective means of dealing with opportunism. However, there are administrative costs [4] associated with the solution of making rather than buying. One element is administrative overhead: the setup and maintenance of a company involves overhead, which decreases efficiency. For marketing activities which occur infrequently or have low level of expenses, it is unlikely that this overhead can be justified, since efficiency losses for a small operation will be small relative to allocated overhead. However, even when transactions are large, administrative costs can be substantial—in fact, much greater than the losses due to opportunism. Unless the losses due to uncompetitive markets, free riding, and assessment problems are substantial, the use of external agents controlled by the market mechanism offers significant cost savings.

Advantage of Using External Agents

Competitive forces in the marketplace, business norms that encourage good working relationships between independent organizations, and some inherent inefficiencies in bureaucratic organizations create a situation in which contracting with independent agents will typically result in high net effectiveness and low administrative costs. The administrative costs associated with external agents are quite low and they are simply the cost of preparing and administrating a contract. The "invisible hand" of the market places substantial pressures on independent agents to provide a marketing activity efficiently. In short, replaceability creates superior performance.

In addition, market relationships are not always cold, calculative, arm's-length arrangements in which parties are looking for chances to engage in opportunistic behavior. Efficient relationships develop between independent parties in this manner because (1) business people have a reputation to protect; (2) the norm of reciprocity prevails; and (3) people involved in transactions insist on introducing satisfying, trust-based elements to their dealing.

Finally, the inefficiencies of large, bureaucratic organizations are well documented.[25] Company employees may not maintain efficiency because they are sheltered from the competitive forces of the marketplace, managers are reluctant to terminate inefficient internal programs or personnel, large organizations breed alienation, and the goals of individual managers may not be related to the performance of the organization.

Because of these inefficiencies in bureaucratic organizations and the efficiency inherent in the marketplace, the transaction cost approach proposes that, in general, greater efficiency is achieved when marketing activities are performed by independent agents rather than by vertically integrated firms. Figure 1, then, presents deviations from this premise, that is, the conditions under which the market mechanism fails and it is most efficient to vertically integrate the activity.

Operationalizing the Framework

In summary, the relative efficiency of performing a marketing activity through vertical integration as opposed to independent agents increases as:

1.   The degree of competition in the supplier market decreases;

2.   The degree to which the performance of the activity can be assessed using output measures decreases;

3.   The potential for free riding increases;

4.   The uncertainty of the environment in which the activity is performed increases, given a high level of company-specific capabilities; and

5.   The scale on which the activity is performed increases.

In Table 1 a series of proposed questions for assessing the factors are presented. If the responses for a given situation are in the right-hand column, the framework suggests that the marketing activity should be vertically integrated. If the responses are in the left-hand column, the framework indicates the marketing activity will be more efficiently performed by external agents.

Implications

A Need for Hybrid Systems

This article has focused on the make or buy issue rather than the broader issue of marketing control. However, the application of this framework (the answering of the questions in Table 1) demonstrates that most situations do not possess *all* the characteristics for a ''make'' decision or *all* the characteristics for a ''buy'' decision. Many situations fall in the gray area between these two extremes on a control dimension, where neither make nor buy is clearly superior. These situations call for the use of ''obligational contracting,'' i.e., a hybrid system.

Marketers have recognized this need for hybrid systems, particularly in the channels area. Perhaps the most common example is franchising, which has some of the authority and supervision of the make option but the separate ownership of the buy option. The difficulty of managing such a system is so great that one may wonder why firms do not simply integrate. The explanation provided by this framework, based on transaction cost analysis, is that company-specific capabilities and the reduction in marketplace competition are not enough of an issue to justify abandoning the market's advantages. Yet the opportunities to free ride are great enough and specificity and uncertainty high enough that some degree of control is justified, creating a hybrid with harsh penalties for noncompliance.

Another response to the need for hybrid systems in channels has been the use of vertical market restraints. Many people have focused on the negative social welfare implications of vertical market restraints; however, the use of these restraints as a managerial response to a difficult control problem has received little attention. For example, the assignment of exclusive territories enables a manufacturer to protect distributor margins and encourage distributors to provide additional services such as training and educating potential customers and providing demonstration facilities.

In selling, the growth of hybrid systems has been limited to investigations of different compensation schemes. Commission compensation is usually accompanied by low control, while salary compensation is associated with high control. Thus the use of commission is akin to the use of market control, while salary is akin to vertical integration (administrative control). This framework would suggest that the commission (market control) is more efficient when selling products re-

Table 1   Summary and Measures of Key Variables in Framework

Key Variables	Buy	Make
Competition in Supplier Market [2A]	low	high
—Are there many agents available that can perform the marketer's activity satisfactorily?	yes	no
—How costly would it be to switch from your present agent to a new agent?	not very costly	very costly
Company- and Salesperson-specific Capabilities [2AA]	low	high
—How long does it take a new agent with industry experience to achieve the performance level of the previous agent?	short time	long time
—Does your company use terms or have procedures not used by other companies in your industry?	no	yes
—How much training is required to bring a new agent with industry experience up to speed?	little	a lot
—Is your marketing offering:	standard	differentiated
—Is the buying decision for your offering:	simple	involved
—Is close coordination between your company and the agent needed to perform the marketing activity well?	no	yes
—Are there many products or services similar to yours on the market?	no	yes
—Are customers' loyalties directed primarily toward:	company	salesperson
Economies of Scale [2AB]	low	high
—Are large providers of marketing services significantly more efficient than small ones because of:		
more intense utilization of personnel and facilities?	no	yes
a better ability to attract and hold quality personnel?	no	yes
an ability to obtain quantity discounts, e.g., favorable advertising rates?	no	yes
an ability to gain entry and develop relationships, e.g., with prospective customers?	no	yes
Environmental Uncertainty [2B] If Significant Company-specific Capabilities*	low	high
—How accurate are your sales forecasts?	accurate	inaccurate
—Is your business environment (technological, competitive, social) changing rapidly?	no	yes
—How great is the variance in sales from year to year?	low	high
—How frequently are competitive new products introduced into your market?	low	high
Inability to Monitor Performance [2C]	low	high
—Is a team effort required to accomplish the marketing activity?	no	yes
—Can you accurately evaluate the performance of the marketing activity using output measures?	yes	no
—Is there a wide variety of factors affecting your output measures?	no	yes
—Do you keep accurate records related to the performance of the marketing activity?	yes	no

continued

Table 1   *Continuing*

Key Variables	Buy	Make
—Can you tell from output measures what each individual's contribution is?	yes	no
Free-riding Potential [2D]	low	high
—Do customers purchase from the same person who makes the presentation? (sales)	yes	no
—Are all channel members of the same level required to provide the same level of service and support? (distribution)	yes	no
—Is the reputation of the channel member more important than the reputation of the brand?	yes	no
Potential Size of Transaction [4]	low	high
—What are the sales per square mile in the typical territory? (sales)	low	high
—How many new advertising campaigns are developed each year? (advertising)	few	many
—What is the size of your advertising budget? (advertising)	small	large
—What is the average order size? (distribution)	small	large
—Do your customers order many products from you to be delivered at once? (distribution)	no	yes

*If such capabilities are insignificant, neither system is preferable.

quiring low company-specific capabilities (standardized products needing little co-ordination with the factory), when performance is easily measured, when there is little free-riding potential, when there is low environmental uncertainty, and when transaction size is small (low sales potential).

Another example of hybrid systems involves advertising. The limited use of in-house ad agencies is often attributed to size: few firms advertise enough to achieve economies of scale in an in-house operation. However, a recent study suggests that "economies of scale" do not seem sufficient to explain the low incidence of "in-house" advertising agencies.[26] One marketing scholar, Leonard Lodish, argues that full-service outside agencies are popular because they relieve management from carrying out a murky, hard-to-control function.[27] Lodish suggests that a better strategy than bringing advertising in-house is to break advertising into its three components—copy development, media scheduling, and media buying—and consider setting up a mixed (hybrid) structure. Integrating copy development makes sense for very specialized or technical products because the creative person must spend months learning about the business in order to be able to write copy. Media scheduling should often be integrated as well because good judgments depend on intimate knowledge of the product, the market, the competition, and the customer. Such knowledge of the business is a valuable company-specific capability. This should make firms consider employing the copy writer or media scheduler themselves, rather than becoming wedded to the agency that employs these people.

On the other hand, Lodish argues that media buying is best left to outsiders. By placing many ads, the buyer can develop critical experience about media buying in general; seldom does the buyer need to know information germane to just one advertiser. Hence, a reasonable scenario for many firms would be a hybrid structure consisting of in-house copy development and/or media scheduling complemented by media buying, through a media-buying service.

Product Life Cycle and Vertical Integration

The transaction cost analysis framework suggests that the efficiency of the make and buy governance modes will change over the product life cycle. During the introductory phase of the product life cycle, significant company-specific capabilities are required to market new products. Unique knowledge and perhaps equipment are required to advertise, sell, and distribute the products. Few, if any, independent agents will possess these capabilities, and thus competition in the supplier market will be minimal after a selected agent is trained.

In addition, the uncertain nature of demand during the introductory phase suggests that it will be difficult to monitor the performance of marketing activities using output measures. For example, it is difficult to determine whether the failure of a new product was due to a deficiency in the product, a poorly executed advertising program, or weak distribution.

In sum, during the introductory phase of the product life cycle, company-specific capabilities are high, uncertainty is high, and the ability to monitor performance is low. Under these conditions, the transaction cost analysis framework says that marketing activities are performed more efficiently by internal agents compared to external agents.

However, as the product matures, the nature of the transaction (the payment for performance of marketing activities) changes. During maturity, several imitators will join the initial product in the marketplace. Therefore, the company-specific skills required to market the product are reduced. There is often a very competitive market of external agents interested in and capable of performing marketing activities for the products. With a longer history, sales are more predictable and it is easier to detect the impact of specific marketing activities.

Thus, the later stages of the product life cycle are characterized by lower company-specific capabilities, greater ability to monitor performance, and lower uncertainty. These changes in the nature of the transaction suggest that the efficiency of external agents will increase relative to internal agents as the product matures. Vertical integration will be most appropriate during the introductory phase and least appropriate during the mature phase.

Product Differentiation and Vertical Integration

Highly company-specific capabilities are a natural consequence of product differentiation. The more unique a market offering is, the more specialized are the capabilities required to market the product. The reverse can also be true. In fact, there are many examples of product differentiation that have been created through specialized marketing activities, such as the specialized salesforce used by Cole

National to train and service key-making machines in retail outlets or the displays for L'Eggs hosiery in grocery stores.

When a company elects to pursue a differentiation strategy, company-specific capabilities will be high and the competition among external agents to provide marketing services will be low. Thus, vertical integration will be the most efficient way to perform marketing activities more often for differentiated products than for nondifferentiated products. Since differentiated products typically service a narrow market, scale economies may be economically infeasible for such products. If the only alternative is to use external agents to market a differentiated product, the company must be prepared to incur the higher costs that result from inefficient performance of marketing activities.

Conclusions

The implications of a framework based on transaction cost analysis for examining make-or-buy decisions are considerable.

This framework begins with a bias toward the market mode. It assumes that control is *undesirable* in competitive markets, since dysfunctional outcomes may result. More faith is placed in the workings of the invisible hand than in the judgment of a "channel captain," manufacturer, or other contractor. The ruthlessness of market workings is thought to be highly beneficial in that competitive outcomes often prevent errors. Errors that are made are penalized, which pressures managers to learn and to correct their mistakes. Transaction cost analysis values the benefits of control *only* when the competitive marketplace breaks down, i.e., when bargaining over just a small number of suppliers is inevitable. Thus, the framework points toward a make decision in situations where specialization in performing a marketing activity occurs.

The transaction cost approach offers a way to unify seemingly isolated variables and arguments, many of which are aspects of specialization, uncertainty, and the conflict between the ruthless wisdom of market outcomes and the benefits of control. For example, the marketing literature comparing manufacturers' representatives with direct salesforces veers back and forth between the benefits of each option, with no conclusion emerging. Some writers emphasize the advantages of control, while others expound on the virtues of independence. The framework in this article delineates the conditions under which each perspective is appropriate. It provides a good organizing device and "first-cut" analysis. Other variables not included in the framework may add insight (or even dominate the analysis) in a specific setting; however, a number of examples considered in the article indicates that the framework has a wide range of useful applications.

Notes

1.   E. Webster Jr., "Top Management Views of the Marketing Function," Working Paper No. 80–108 (Cambridge, MA: Marketing Science Institute, 1980).

2.   M. S. Miller, "Increasing Marketing Productivity," Information Bulletin No. 86 (New York: The Conference Board, 1980).

3.   M. Porter, *Competitive Strategy: Techniques for Analyzing Industries and Competition* (New York: The Free Press, 1980; p. 300.

4.   W. G. Ouchi, "A Conceptual Framework for the Design of Organization Control Mechanisms," *Management Science* 25 (1979):833–848.

5.   L. W. Stern and A. I. El-Ansary, *Marketing Channels,* Second Edition (Englewood Cliffs, NJ: Prentice-Hall, 1982).

6.   R. E. Pulver, "Advertising Services: Full Service Agency, A La Carte, or In-House?" (New York: Association of National Advertisers, 1979); T. C. Taylor "A Raging 'Rep'idemic," *Sales and Marketing Management,* 8 June 1981, pp. 33–35; U.S. Bureau of Census, *1977 Census of Wholesale Trade,* Geographic Area Services, Report #WC77-A-52, 1980.

7.   Taylor (1981).

8.   Pulver (1979).

9.   W. R. George and H. C. Barksdale, "Marketing Activities in the Service Industries," *Journal of Marketing,* 30 October 1974, pp. 65–69.

10.   W. M. Weilbacher, *Advertising* (New York: MacMillan Publishing Co, 1979).

11.   T. J. Gage, "Quaker Shows Commitment to Ad Division," *Advertising Age,* 5 February 1980, p. 12.

12.   R. W. Haas, *Industrial Marketing Management* (New York: Petrocelli/Charter, 1976); G. Risley, *Modern Industrial Marketing* (New York: McGraw-Hill, 1972).

13.   Stern and El-Ansary (1982).

14.   O. Kleppner, *Advertising Procedure,* Seventh Edition (Englewood Cliffs, NJ: Prentice-Hall, 1979).

15.   E. C. Bursk and B. S. Sethi, "The In-House Advertising Agency," *Journal of Advertising* 10 (1976):24–27.

16.   R. D. Buzzell, "Is Vertical Integration Profitable?" *Harvard Business Review,* January-February 1983, pp. 92–102.

17.   B. Shapiro, *Sales Program Formulation* (New York: McGraw Hill, 1977).

18.   F. M. Scherer, *Industrial Market Structure and Economic Performance,* Second Edition (Chicago: Rand NcNally, 1980), p. 78.

19.   K. Harrigan, "A Framework for Looking at Vertical Integration," *The Journal of Business Strategy,* February 1983, pp. 30–37.

20.   O. Williamson, *Markets and Hierarchies: Analysis and Antitrust Implications* (New York: The Free Press, 1975); "Transaction-Cost Economics: The Governance of Contractual Relations," *Journal of Law and Economics,* October 1979, pp. 233–62; "The Economics of Organization: The Transaction-Cost Approach," *American Journal of Sociology* 87 (1981):547–77.

21.   The designation in brackets refers to the designation in the upper right-hand corner of the related box in Figure 26.1.

22.   R. E. Weigand, "Buying In to Market Control," *Harvard Business Review,* November–December 1980, pp. 141–149 offers some interesting examples of how vendors can take advantage of situations in which specific capabilities and assets exist. For example, government contractors frequently submit bids below cost on an initial order for equipment. While they lose money on the initial order, they develop unique know-how and production equipment (transaction-specific assets) that "lock" them into follow-on orders. They "get well" during this following period by charging high prices (engaging in opportunistic behavior).

23.   K. J. Arrow, *Limits of Organization* (New York: N. W. Norton and Company, Inc., 1974). R. H. Miles, *Macro Organizational Behavior* (Santa Monica: Goodyear Publishing Company, 1980).

24.   W. G. Ouchi, *Theory Z* (Reading, MA: Addison-Wesley Publishing Company, 1900).

25.   A. Downes, *Inside Bureaucracies* (Cambridge, MA: Little, Brown, 1966).

26.   R. Schmalensee, A. J. Silk, and R. Bojanek, "The Impact of Scale and Media Mix on Advertising Agency Costs," *Journal of Business* 56 (1900):453–475.

27.   L. M. Lodish, "Advertising: Make, Lease, or Buy?" *The Wharton Annual* 8 (1983):105–110.

Manage beyond Portfolio Analysis

Richard G. Hamermesh and Roderick E. White

Several years ago, a company lay at the door of bankruptcy. Following the best available advice, management had targeted a few of its divisions for rapid sales growth. To encourage growth and entrepreneurial behavior, corporate management granted these divisions considerable latitude to conduct their business and rewarded their executives for growth. Meanwhile, the company used the remaining divisions to produce the cash to fuel the growth of their sister units. It tightly controlled these cash-generating divisions and tied their managers' small bonus incentives to stringent cost-reduction goals.

During the first few years this approach seemed to work splendidly. Sales and earnings rose dramatically while the growing divisions introduced new products at a rapid rate. Then problems began to emerge.

First, key personnel in the cash-producing divisions began to resign with greater and greater frequency. During their exit interviews the executives revealed that they felt no confidence in corporate management's commitment to these divisions.

Second, the growing divisions evinced disturbing signs of loss of control: high inventory levels, high warranty costs, and frequent complaints about new products began to depress sales and particularly earnings. Compounding this problem, some key managers in the growth divisions, many of whom had been richly rewarded for their prior accomplishments, resigned when headquarters started to ask probing questions about their activities.

This article first appeared in the *Harvard Business Review*. Reprinted by permission of the *Harvard Business Review* (January–February 1984):103–109. Copyright © 1984 by the President and Fellows of Harvard College; all rights reserved.

When this article was first published the authors were Associate Professor of General Management at the Harvard Business School and Assistant Professor at the School of Business Administration, University of Western Ontario, respectively.

Eventually, the company's profits turned to losses, and, in an attempt to rectify the situation, the board of directors brought in new management.

This case is neither extreme nor uncommon. It illustrates that the way corporate management interacts with its operating divisions can have a major impact on those divisions' performance. Despite awareness of this, many top managers have difficulty knowing what stance to take with their divisions, and many times they set up inappropriate relationships.

Two main causes lie behind these misguided actions. First, many managers have been seduced by corporate portfolio strategies that focus their attentions on market share and cash flow objectives.[1] In many instances, top managers have accepted this orientation without considering their divisions' competitive strategies or seeing whether market share and cash flow objectives provide a meaningful basis for building the relationship between headquarters and the business units.

Second, when corporate managers do turn to the question of how to structure relationships with their operating divisions, they find few existing guidelines. The advice they uncover tends to be very general, such as "closely control mature divisions," "create an entrepreneurial atmosphere in growth divisions," or (even more glib) "match a manager's personal orientation or style with operating strategy."

But this advice doesn't tell a manager how much autonomy to give different divisions, how large a bonus payment is appropriate, or how reporting relationships between key functions and shared departments should be structured. In looking at how the corporate management of 12 multibusiness companies structure these relationships with 69 of their business units, we tried to answer these questions. (See the accompanying insert for a description of our methodology.) In the following pages we present the results of our research.

What's behind Business Unit Performance

Profitability is of course the end result of a complex set of market, competitive, and organizational interrelationships. An important but difficult task for practitioners, consultants, and business researchers is to distinguish the effects of these different relationships.

Earlier explanations of performance have focused on only one or two of these factors. We think that the situation is more complicated than that, and in our research we considered the effects all of them have on business unit performance. While an industry's environment and a business's competitive position within the industry as well as the competitive strategy the business employs to take advantage of the aforementioned factors together determine a business's performance potential, our notion is that the business will realize that potential *only*

---

[1]In a recent *HBR* article entitled, "Portfolio Planning: Uses and Limits," January–February 1982, p. 58, Philippe Haspeslagh estimated that as of 1979, 45 percent of the *Fortune* "500" industrial companies had introduced portfolio planning to at least some extent.

if it is appropriately organized to exploit its strategic position and to deal with its competitive environment.[2]

Although common measures for important industry characteristics, competitive position, and strategy are available, there is less understanding of those aspects of corporate–business unit relationships that influence performance, namely the organizational and administrative arrangements between the corporate office and the business unit. We refer to these as the unit's organizational context.

We studied the following three aspects of business unit organizational context:

Study Methodology

This study is made up of a subset of the PIMS (profit impact of market strategies) research base. Twelve PIMS member companies agreed to supply us with organizational information about 69 of their business units. No more than 8 businesses came from any one company. To the existing PIMS data base, which primarily included each unit's industry, market characteristics, competitive position and measures of performance we added organizational information.

We collected the organizational data in late 1979. Performance, market, and competitive data were four-year averages. Although we present the data in cross-tabular form with cell averages in this article, we conducted the analysis using multiple regression, with performance (either ROI or sales growth) as the dependent variable and the aspects of organizational context as independent variables. In order to control for their effects, we included measures of market factors and competitive position in the right-hand side of the equation. A comparable type of control was used for the data reported in this article. Unless otherwise noted, the performance results reported have been adjusted to remove the linear effects of real market growth and relative market share. Using multiple regression, we found that the relationships reported in this article had a confidence level greater than or equal to 95 percent.

1. **Autonomy,** or the degree to which business unit managers can make decisions independent of other parts of the company, especially the corporate head office.

[2]See our article, "Toward a Model of Business Unit Performance: An Integrative Approach," *Academy of Management Review,* 1981, vol. 6, p. 213.

2. **Line responsibility,** or the degree to which business unit managers have direct and complete responsibility for key functions (sales, marketing, manufacturing, engineering, and so forth) or share responsibility for some of these with other unit managers.

3. **Incentive compensation,** or the percentage of the business unit general manager's total cash compensation attributable to the unit's performance.

What Makes a Successful Relationship

Although we did not uncover any easy or precise ways of structuring corporate–business unit relationships, we did isolate those situations where organizational context has the greatest effect on performance and those factors that are the most important in structuring these relationships. Specifically, we found that organizational context does affect performance and that the business unit feels these effects the most when it competes in a dynamic, changing industry. The organizational context has less effect on (and is frequently mismanaged in) business units competing in stable, slowly changing industries.

Previous research on business unit performance that considered only the industry environment and competitive position variables has explained a large part of the variance in return on investment (ROI) among business units.[3] Our research, which used fewer industry and competitive position variables but which included measures of organizational context, explains a comparable amount.[4] (Even though we did not consider such important administrative variables as the person who manages the business unit or the subtle import of day-to-day communications between corporate and business unit managers, the organizational context is still of great significance.)

In fact, we found that corporate managers can have as much impact on a business unit's performance by attending to its administrative ties to headquarters as they can by managing according to detailed strategic portfolio analyses. Moreover, executives can affect the organizational context more easily than they can the competitive and environmental conditions confronting that unit.

Despite the close relationship that organizational context has with performance, however, it is important to recognize that no simple, dominating association between any of the elements of organizational context and performance holds for all business units. Any executive who looks for one best level of autonomy, incentive compensation, or line responsibility will be disappointed. If, however, the executive takes the environment in which the business unit operates and its competitive strategy into account as well, then he or she will find that different relationships between headquarters and business units do have significant connections with business unit performance.

[3]Sidney Schoeffler, Robert D. Buzzell, and Donald F. Heany, "Impact of Strategic Planning on Profit Performance," *HBR* March-April 1974, p. 137.

[4]Roderick E. White, "Structural Context, Strategy and Performance," unpublished doctoral dissertation, Harvard Business School, 1981.

To determine the effect of these relationships on performance, we split the business units in our study into two groups—those in dynamic environments with frequent product introductions, sweeping technological changes, and fluctuating market shares between competitors; and those in stable environments, which have the opposite characteristics.

In Dynamic Environments

For those business units that compete in dynamic environments, we found that the kind of relationship the unit has with headquarters has a significant impact on performance Exhibits I and II show, for example, that in stable environments a business unit's level of autonomy has little impact on either sales growth or ROI. But for business units in dynamic environments, high autonomy is associated with rapid sales growth, while low autonomy is associated with much higher ROI.

Judging from our experience, we think these findings make sense for two reasons. First, managers of units competing in dynamic environments have so many options to choose from that when corporate managers get involved they will inevitably influence the units' strategies and, ultimately, performance. Second, business unit managers given much autonomy tend to pursue sales opportunities rather than profitability. To ensure that sales growth is balanced with profitability, corporate management may have to step in and tighten the reins a bit.

The amount of line responsibility unit managers have also carries a strong correlation with the business unit's performance. As Exhibits III and IV show, in dynamic markets business units that share responsibility for key functions have sales growth roughly equivalent to, but profitability higher than, that of business units having direct line responsibility for sales, marketing, manufacturing, and engineering. In dynamic environments shared responsibility for functions pays off. For business units in stable environments, the opposite relationship exists. Higher sales growth and profitability result when reporting relationships are self-contained within the unit.

Again sifting through our experience, we think that one reason this situation occurs may be that in a changing market units share functional responsibilities so that the competencies of the entire company can be applied flexibly to meet the numerous opportunities a dynamic environment presents, even though it takes extra time and effort for business units to coordinate functions. The sharing process may lead to a cross-fertilization of ideas and allow each unit to have access to

Exhibit I   Sales Growth According to Degree of Autonomy and the Volatility of the Business Environment

	Autonomy		
	Low	High	Number of Observations
Total sample	4.9%	9.0%	69
Business units in dynamic environments	5.9%	12.0%	35
Business units in stable environments	3.7%	6.8%	34

Exhibit II ROI According to Degree of Autonomy and the Volatility of the Business Environment

| | Autonomy | | |
	Low	High	Number of Observations
Total sample	23.0%	18.2%	69
Business units in dynamic environments	23.3%	14.3%	35
Business units in stable environments	22.7%	20.9%	34

costly functions, such as engineering and sales, that otherwise may not be justified for units facing a shifting market.

Because organizational context can have such an impact on the performance of business units competing in dynamic markets, the implications for corporate managers are great. Rather than taking a hands-off stance toward growth businesses, as management in our opening example did, corporate managers need to carefully consider the influences that the organization itself has on business units facing dynamic environments. Precisely because some environments change so rapidly and the range of outcomes that business units can achieve in these environments is very wide, the organizational context surrounding these business units can have a strong influence on the results they achieve and on whether the business units achieve fast growth or high ROI. At General Electric, for example, corporate managers actually oversee growth businesses and spotlight the performance of venture managers.

In Stable Environments

Corporate managers in both dynamic and stable environments need to pay attention to the organizational arrangements between business units and headquarters. But whereas our data suggest that direct involvement in business decisions has a significant positive impact on the profitability of businesses in dynamic environments, whatever effect it has on the results of business units in stable environments may be negative (see Exhibits I and II). In our view, stable environments

Exhibit III Real Sales Growth According to the Structure of Reporting Relationship and the Business Environment

| | Reporting Relationship for Key Functions | | |
	Shared	Self-contained	Number of Observations
Total sample	5.9%	7.2%	69
Business units in dynamic environments	8.7%	6.1%	37
Business units in stable environments	3.2%	8.1%	32

Exhibit IV   ROI According to the Structure of Reporting Relationship and the Business Environment

	Reporting Relationship for Key Functions		
	Shared	Self-contained	Number of Observations
Total sample	20.3%	21.5%	69
Business units in dynamic environments	22.2%	18.4%	37
Business units in stable environments	18.5%	25.8%	32

provide clear signals to the managers of business units. Because the range of feasible competitive strategies and performance outcomes for these businesses is narrow and changes little, too much corporate attention is unnecessary and can prove counterproductive.

Our opening example illustrates that when top management involves itself too much with business units in stable environments, it can cause problems. In this case, management tightly controlled these businesses and targeted them to produce high cash flows. Eventually the businesses lost their competitive edges in their markets. In discussing these issues with managers, we found that such situations are not unusual. In what we have labeled "self-fulfilling prophecy of portfolio management," the decision to harvest a business for cash leads to tighter controls and less autonomy, which leads to lower morale in the business unit, which leads to worse performance and the resignations of key managers, and possibly the eventual disposition of the business unit. But this pattern can be broken. To get the results they desire, corporate managers don't have to restrict the autonomy of businesses in stable environments.

Top managers also have difficulty establishing the appropriate incentive compensation for managers of business units competing in stable environments. Even though the managers in our sample indicated that their incentive compensation was based on measures such as profits, residual income, and return on investment, Exhibit V shows that for businesses in both stable and dynamic environments, higher levels of incentive compensation are related to lower average return on investment.

This unexpected relationship is particularly strong for business units in stable environments. As Exhibit V illustrates, the managers of these businesses who received high bonuses had an average ROI of only 17.4 percent, eight percentage points less than their counterparts who got lower bonuses. While it is possible that higher levels of base compensation may offset lower levels of incentive compensation, our findings suggest that although many top managers talk about rewarding the managers of mature, cash-cow businesses with high incentives based on cash flow and return on investment, they do not translate these ideas into meaningful action.

None of the exhibits, of course, shows what is cause and what is effect. But as Exhibit VI illustrates for this sample, high sales growth and high ROI are,

Exhibit V   ROI in Relation to Incentive Compensation and the Business Environment

| | Return on Investment | | |
| | Business-based Incentive as a Percentage of Total Compensation | | |
	Low	High	Number of Observations
Total sample	23.5%	18.5%	65
Business units in dynamic environments	21.9%	20.0%	32
Business units in stable environments	25.7%	17.4%	33

understandably, both necessary for large bonus payments. Executives of business units with low growth in sales but *high* ROI, however, received the lowest level of incentive compensation: on average, only 8.6 percent. On average, managers of units with high sales growth were rewarded well regardless of the return generated. Clearly, the connection between incentive compensation and business unit performance is not easily explained and we suspect often mismanaged, especially for units facing stable environments.

Unit Strategy and Organizational Context

In considering how managers relate their business units' strategies to the organizational contexts they establish, we find that market share and cash flow objectives based on build, hold, or harvest portfolio strategies do not provide a useful guide to how corporate managers ought to structure their relationships with their units. On the other hand, an understanding of the business unit's *competitive* strategy can provide corporate managers with guidelines.

Of course, all business units end up generating or consuming cash and gaining, holding, or losing market share. But it is important not to regard these vari-

Exhibit VI   Cash Bonus in Relation to Sales Growth and Profitability*

| | | Real Sales Growth | |
		Low	High
ROI	*Low*	12.3%	15.5%
	High	8.6%	22.7%

*Cell averages are cash bonuses as a percentage of total compensation.

ables as if they comprise a strategy but rather to see them as the result of strategic actions. A group vice-president of a large industrial company illustrated the difference when he said:

Two of the divisions that report to me are in very sluggish industries. In one case, we have been able to develop more original strategies, we have the employees all fired up, and we're making a good return. But I have had to fight to keep the corporate planners from giving their view of the situation. In the other division, the view from the top that has permeated the unit is that it is a cash-generating division and should be squeezed. I feel we could do some original things there to improve our competitive position, but it's impossible to get anyone in the division very excited to try something new. Eventually, we'll probably sell or liquidate the division.

In his book *Competitive Strategy*, Michael Porter argues that the essence of strategy is the creation of sustainable competitive advantage.[5] Managers can achieve this advantage in one of two basic ways: by establishing an overall low-cost position or by effectively differentiating the product and charging a premium price for it. As Exhibit VII demonstrates, these approaches can result in several possible generic strategies. With a pure cost strategy, the business has a low-cost position and low price. Its key competitive advantage is its cost position. On the other hand, managers of businesses with a pure differentiation strategy are able to command a premium price but also incur higher costs. Naturally, the most desirable, but hardest to achieve, position is to have both cost and differentiation advantages. For example, Caterpillar Tractor has a low-cost position but also has differentiated its product on the basis of reliability and after-sales service and parts-supply operations.

Our research suggests that corporate administrators can enhance performance by tailoring the organizational context to the business units' competitive strategy. Exhibit VIII illustrates that for businesses with pure cost strategies, low autonomy is related to much higher ROI.

For a pure cost strategy to be successful managers typically must pay attention to operational details, relentlessly pursue productivity improvements and reduction of defects, centralize purchasing, and standardize components. To carry

Exhibit VII   Generic Business Strategies

		Relative Price Position	
		Low	**High**
Relative cost position	*Low*	Pure cost	Cost and differentiation
	High	No competitive advantage	Pure differentiation

[5]Michael E. Porter, *Competitive Strategy: Techniques for Analyzing Industries and Competitors* (New York: Free Press, 1980).

Exhibit VIII   Impact of Organizational Context and Generic Business Strategy on ROI*

Strategy	Autonomy		Responsibility for Key Functions	
	Low	High	Shared	Self-contained
Pure cost	37.9%	17.9%	40.7%	20.5%
Pure differentiation	20.9%	23.0%	12.3%	25.3%
Cost and differentiation	31.6%	29.5%	29.1%	32.0%
No competitive advantage	9.7%	−1.6%	1.7%	7.8%

***This exhibit uses unadjusted ROI data.**

out these kinds of activities, managers have to direct their attention to the internal aspects of their units, primarily to the production and engineering functions. When the division has low autonomy and top management is in strong control and involved, its managers have the support and impetus they need to keep them focused on the necessary tasks.

In contrast, with an externally oriented differentiation strategy, because business unit management is closer than top management to the customer and the market, corporate involvement can contribute little to a unit's success. (See Exhibit VIII.)

The strategy of the division also determines how line responsibilities should be structured. As Exhibit VIII shows, business units that have pure cost strategies and also share line responsibilities with others have much higher ROIs than units that have self-contained functions. As we have discussed, sharing costly functions helps minimize overall costs.

The Gap in Portfolio Analysis

In sum, a strong relationship exists between the organizational and administrative structures surrounding a business unit and its performance. In recent years, planners have zealously applied sophisticated strategic planning techniques to the problems of managing multibusiness companies. These techniques focus exclusively on industry and competitive conditions as the determinants of business unit performance and on market share and cash flow objectives. While we do not dispute the importance of factors such as competitive dynamics, market share, and cash flow, some corporate executives have watched these variables exclusively and ignored the important relationship between organizational context and business unit performance. Also, executives can affect the context far more easily than they can competitive and environmental factors.

Our research suggests that rather than focusing exclusively on portfolio management variables, one of corporate management's principal roles is establishing an appropriate organizational context for each of its business units, and that the character of each business's environment and strategy must condition the design of its organizational context.

Given the limited size of our sample and the complexity of the phenomenon, managers need to apply our specific findings with caution. But to our minds, what is more important than any of the individual relationships we uncovered is the overall finding that the appropriate design of organizational contexts requires that top managers be sufficiently aware of the affairs of their business units to appreciate and understand the market conditions they face and the competitive strategies they are trying to implement.

When managers design organizational contexts in light of these considerations, they can anticipate the impact of the contexts on business unit performance. Even the most sophisticated of strategies can fail if corporate managers pay insufficient attention to the organizational and administrative variables in the performance equation. And questionable strategies can produce acceptable results when corporate executives organize and implement them appropriately.

Index

A.C. Nielson, 481
A M International, 250
Administrative control, 509–510
Advertising, 502
Advertising and product life cycle, 214–215
Agents, external, 511
Allis Chalmers, 170–171
American Locomotive Co., 230
American Motors, 171–175
American Safety Razor Corp., 230
Amoco, 404
Ansoff matrix, 252–253
Apple Computer, 250, 497
Appliance industry, 61
Armour Leather Co., 232
Armstrong, 238
Aston-Tate, 152
AT&T, 59, 492, 497
Atari, 57
Automatic teller machine, 349, 393, 396
Automobile industry, 171–175
Auto producers, 94
Avis, 470, 477

Babcock and Wilcox Co., 230
Baldwin Locomotive Works, 230, 234–235
Bank of America, 467, 470
Bank of California, 467
BCG product portfolio, 248–251, 295–306
    assumptions, 329–331
Beechem, 468
Beer industry, 89
Beta, 328
Bic, 238, 479, 482
Black and Decker, 96
Bloomingdale's, 468
BMW, 468
Booz-Allen-Hamilton, 118
Boston Consulting Group, 2, 13, 38, 153, 162,
    178–179, 194, 217, 249, 258–260, 269–271,
    302
Bowmar, 168
Brand franchise, 479–487
Brands and product life cycle, 206–210
Brand switching, 71, 73
Brewing industry, 190
British motor industry, 172
Bullock's, 468
Burroughs, 393
Business mission, 8–10
Business unit, 520–529
    dynamic environment, 523–524
    organization, 521–522, 526–529
    performance, 520–521
    stable environment, 524–526
    strategy, 526–527
Buyers, power of, 93–94

Campbell, 469
Capabilities, 62–63. See also Competitive
    advantage
Capital Asset Pricing Model, 151–152, 161–176,
    327–328
Capital budgeting, 150–153
    drawbacks, 152–153
Capital requirements, 89–91
Carnation, 484
Carnation Instant Breakfast, 467
Cash balance, 251, 329–330
Cash cow, 249–251, 258, 271, 297–298
Cash flow, 250, 297
    market growth, 296–297
    market share, 250
Caterpillar Tractor, 527
Channel of distribution, 502
Chemical industry, 310–313
Chesebrough Ponds, 479
Chrysler Corporation, 49, 171–173, 299
Coca-Cola, 60, 97–98, 209, 404, 476, 483–484
Coleman, 483
Colgate-Palmolive, 209, 222
Columbia Broadcasting System (CBS), 230
Combustion Engineering Inc., 230
Commodore, 57
Compaq, 3, 59
Competition, 87–99
Competitive advantage, 5–6, 252–253, 312–313,
    334–338
    channel control, 403–404
    customer loyalty, 402–403
Competitors, 62–63
Computer industry, 89
Computerland, 57
Control, 381, 403–404
Cost advantages, 90–91. See also Experience
    curve
Cost reduction, 164
    via vertical integration, 499–516
Costs
    administrative, 502
    allocation, 105
    controllable versus uncontrollable, 103–104
    cost comparison curves, 183–184
    cost compression curves, 183
    cost differentials, 184–185, 194
    experience curve, 153–155, 183–197
    fixed, 102
    labor, 103
    market definition, 359–361
    reduction strategy, 195–196
    relation with product quality, 435–462
    relation with ROI, 435–462
    variable, 102
Cross elasticity of demand, 71–72
Crown Cork & Seal, 95
Curtiss-Wright, 230, 239

Customer, 60–62, 489–498
  decision process, 75–76
  experience effect, 490–492
  sophistication & product maturity, 492–494
  strategic alternatives, 60–62, 352–353
  usage behavior, 72–73
  versus competitor orientation, 23
Customer judgments analyses, 75–82

Decision sequence analysis, 75–76
Design and manufacturers, 61
Direct grouping, 79
Directional policy matrix, 307–323, 331–332
Discounted cash flow, 326–327
Distribution channel, 92
  market definition, 353–354
Distribution channels
  cost allocation, 105–116
  market definition, 393–394
Docutel, 393
Dogs, 249, 258, 271, 298
Dollar metric approach, 79
Du Pont, 157, 208, 238, 402

Ecological analogy, 346
Economies of scale, 89, 501–505, 507
EFTS (electronic funds transfer system), 393
Electric generator industry, 168–171
Electronic calculator industry, 155, 165–168
Electronic funds transfer system (EFTS), 393
Emerson Electric, 95
Emery Air Freight, 391–392
Entry barriers, 96, 335–336
Entry, threat of, 89–92
Environmental uncertainty, 508
Environment audit, 123–124
Esterbrook Pen Co., 230
Eversharp, Inc., 230
Exit barriers, 96, 335
Experience curve, 90–91, 153–155, 162–168,
    177–197. See also Costs
  concept, 177–182
  extensions, 335–337
  limitations, 154–155
  low growth, 168
  market definition, 359–361
  profitability, 168–171
  sources, 180–181
  strategic implications, 164–175
  types, 182–189

Fairchild Semiconductor, 238
Fiat, 468
Filene's, 468
Financial analysis
  evaluation of alternatives, 149–153, 161–176,
    326–328
  segments, 101–116
Fisher Body, 492
Fisher-Pry model, 231–233
Fixed cost allocation, 105
Ford, 171–173, 195, 225, 336, 346
Fortune, 402
Fortune-1000, 249
Free response approach, 78–79
Free riding potential, 509
French perfumes, 204
FTC, 152

General Electric (GE), 68, 69, 122, 170–171, 217,
    223, 225, 258, 281, 483
General Foods, 68, 152, 366, 479
General Mills, 74, 152, 374
General Motors (GM), 51, 129, 171–174, 191, 233,
    299, 404
Geritol, 209
Gillette, 69, 230, 252–253, 394, 483
GNP, 192
Goals. See also Objectives
  effective, 381–385
  general versus specific, 377–380
Goodrich, 238, 334
Goodyear, 334
Green Bay Packers, 344
Grinding wheel industry, 194
Group Lotus, 174
Growth, 481
Growth vector matrix, 252–253

Harvest, 249
Hendry model, 73–75
Hertz, 470, 477
Holiday Inn, 404
Honeywell, 393
Hudson's, 468

IBM, 20, 59, 61, 250, 299, 357, 380, 383–386,
    393, 430, 491, 495–496
Implementation, 11, 399–406
Incrementalism, 347–348, 373–388
Industry structure, 87–99
Innovation, 243
Intel Corp., 20, 497
International Telephone & Telegraph, 122
Investment intensity, 242, 288

J.C. Penney, 468
Johnson & Johnson, 255, 380, 469

Kelloggs, 74, 152
Kelly Services, 404
Kentucky Fried Chicken, 404
Kleenex, 209, 484
K Mart, 469
KMS Industries, 381
Kodak, 92
Kophers Corp., 230

Learning curve, 434. See also Experience curve
Lever Brothers, 470
Leyland, 172–174
Litton, 145, 376
Lotus development, 152

Macy's, 468
Make or buy decision, 499–516. See also Vertical
    integration
Marlboro, 209
Market analysis, 361–362
Market behavior, 28
Market definition, 352–355, 359–361
  experience curve, 153–155
  redefinition, 393
Market evolution, 30–31, 390–393. See also
    Product life cycle

Market growth, 243, 296–297
  BCG product portfolio, 330–331
  directional policy matrix, 310–311
  portfolio strategy, 299–300
Marketing audit, 117–134
  benefits, 126–127
  data collections, 127
  inside audit, 119, 122–123
  pitfalls of, 127–128
Marketing myopia, 482
Marketing productivity audit, 125–126
  problem, 127–128
Marketing Science Institute, 205
Marketing strategy
  audit of, 124
  definition, 2
  customer implications, 494–497
  the planning process, 6–11, 341–349
  versus corporate strategy, 4
  versus tactics, 3–4, 342–345
Marketing systems audit, 124–125
Marketing theory, 17–28, 30–33
Market models. See Theories of the firm
Market share, 153–155
  anticipated versus unanticipated, 417–423
  cash flow, 250
  effect of, 413–417, 426–428
  experience curve, 168–171
  gaining share, 250
  implications, 429–430
  model, 418–421
  PIMS, 409–423
  ROI, 249, 409–430
  strategies, 400–402
MBO (management by objectives), 387
McCullough, 96
McDonald's, 404
McGraw-Hill, 481
Measurement sensitivity, 196
Microcomputer industry, 57–59
Microsoft, 152
Midas, 404
Military analogy, 2, 59, 345
Milk, 249
Miller Beer, 89, 469–470, 477
Mobility barriers, 335, 337
Model specification, 197
Montgomery Ward, 468
Morale, 381–382
Multidimensional scaling, 473–474

National, 470
National Can, 95
Needham, Harper & Steers, 475
Neiman Marcus, 468
Net present value, 150–153
New product benefits, 479–487
Niches, 135–147, 346, 430
Nonprofit organizations, 127
North American Rockwell, 145

Objectives, 10–11, 119–120, 150–151
  goals, 374–376
OPEC, 48
Opportunism, 509–510
Organization
  audit of, 124
  planning, 404–405

Organizational boundaries, 29
Organizational culture, 510
OSHA, 48

Papermate, 238
Paradigm
  dyadic exchange, 22
  integrative, 24–25
  Kuhnian, 38
  shift, 21
Parker Pen, 230, 235, 238
PAR ROI, 244–248, 409, 415
  model, 244–248, 282, 326–328
Pepsi-Cola, 60, 97–98, 209
Perceptual mapping, 76–77
Performance assessment, 508–509
Perrier, 484
Phillip Morris, 89, 469
Phillip N.V., 334
PIMS, 38, 168, 184, 195, 242–248, 281–291, 402,
    409–423, 435–462, 521
  limitations, 244, 248, 282–291
Planning
  adaptive, 348
  marketing audit, 117–134
  prescriptive versus actual, 12–13, 373–388
  process overview, 6–11, 341–349, 351–369
  product life cycle, 208–210
  strategic, 32–33, 37, 50–52
  top-down versus bottom-up, 32, 355–358, 383
Planters Peanuts, 209
Polaroid, 92, 225
Portfolio analysis, 248–252, 519–529. See also
    Product portfolio model
  approaches, 258–261
  corporate, 4
  market growth/market share, 249–251
Portfolio management, 302–305
Pricing
  experience curve, 167
Problem child, 249, 258, 271
Procter and Gamble, 192, 349, 396
Product benefits, 494, 496
Product definition, 220–221, 225, 482–487
Product demand, 68–69
  product life cycle, 156–157
Product differentiation, 243
  vertical integration, 515–516
Product Life Cycle, 155–158, 201–213, 217–226
  application, 222–223
  biological analogy, 202, 226
  customer and the PLC, 489–498
  exceptions, 204–206
  general model, 201, 218–220
  market evolution, 390–393
  product definition, 220–221, 225
  product portfolios, 331
  relationship with experience curve, 186–189,
    196–197
  vertical integration, 515
Product Life Cycle and Process Life Cycle,
    223–224
Product line, 108
Product markets, 67. See also Strategic
    alternatives
  boundaries, 57–61, 193–194, 68–82, 155,
    352–355, 360
  evaluation of, 149–158
  measurement, 71–82

Product portfolio model, 248–252
market attractiveness/competitive capabilities,
251–252, 307–323
market share/market growth, 249–251, 295–306,
329–332
Product positioning, 357, 467–477. *See also*
Niches; Product market boundaries
definition, 467
strategies, 468–475
Product quality, 243, 434–445, 452–462
relation with cost, 435–462
relation with ROI, 435–462
Product substitution, 95
market definition, 361–362
technological change, 231–233
Product-by-uses analyses, 79–80
Productivity, 243

Quaker Oats, 469, 483
Question marks, 258, 298–299

Radio Shack, 57
Ralston Purina, 480
Raytheon, 230, 235, 238, 239
RCA, 230, 235, 239, 299, 380
Reliance Electric, 145
Resource allocation, 10–11, 29–30, 59, 241–253
Revlon, 469
Rexall Drug Store, 404
Rheem, 235
Rich's, 468
Rivalry, 96
ROI, 281–289, 435–462, 521–528. *See also*
Market share
effect of market share, 409–430
par model, 244–249
PAR ROI, 409, 415
PIMS, 242–248
Rolls Royce, 174, 223

S.C. Johnson & Sons, 222
Saks Fifth Avenue, 468
Salesforce, 501–502, 507
Schick, 238
Sears, 129, 354, 468, 477
Segmentation, 116
Segments, strategic, 20–28, 71, 136–137,
357–358
experience curve, 172–173
financial analysis, 102–116
Segments, types of
common buying factor, 141–144
customer-size, 144–145
end use, 138
geographic, 138–139
product, 139–141
Seton Leather Co., 231
Seven-Up (7 Up), 97, 209, 470
Shared costs, 155
Sheaffer Pen Co., 230
Shell, 310
Sherwin-Williams, 404
Singer, 404
Situation analysis, 9, 101–116. *See also* Marketing
audit
Snap-on Tool, 354
Soft drink industry, 60, 97–98
Standard Industrial Classification, 70
Star, 249, 258, 271, 297–298

Steam turbine generators, 181
Stockholders' wealth, 150–151
Strategic alternatives
definition, 10
identification, 10–12
Strategic Business Unit (SBU), 4, 282–283, 332,
335–356, 363–368
Strategic management, 19–20, 25, 94–95, 97
Strategic marketing, 25–26. *See also* Marketing
strategy
illustration, 11–12
Strategic Planning Institute, 242, 244, 281–283,
288, 411–412, 446
Strategic planning
product life cycle, 217–226
STRATPORT, 257–277
Strategic window, 349, 389–397
dynamic analysis, 389–390
Strategy
business units, 526–527
definition, 2
ecological analogy, 346
management, 19
market entry, 222–223
military analogy, 2, 345
orientation, 17
for product positioning, 468–475
technological change, 229–240
versus tactic, 3–4, 342–345
STRATPORT model, 241–242, 257–277
functions, 267–270
limitations, 276–277
optimization module, 270
overview, 261–264
structure, 264–266
use, 271–274
Substitution-in-use analysis, 80–81
Supplier's strategic evolution, 497–498
Suppliers, power of, 93–94
SWOT, 63
Sylvania, 230, 234
Synergy
growth vector model, 252–253
PIMS, 283

Tactics
implementation, 399–400
product life cycle, 201–204
versus strategy, 3–4
Target group index, 208
TCC (total cost concept), 391
Technology
market definition, 353
strategic response, 229–240
technology substitution analysis, 71, 78,
392–393
Texas Instruments, 11–12, 61, 168, 223–224, 360,
392
Theories of the firm, 39–50
agency costs model, 41–42
behavioral model, 42–43
market value model, 40–41
neoclassical model, 39
resource dependence model, 43–44
Theory development, 196
Theory 'Y' management, 383
3M Company, 122
Timex, 92
Toyota, 468

Transparent Paper, 171
Triumph, 472

UAW, 50
United Aircraft, 230, 238
Universal Electric, 489
University of California, 12
U.S. brewing industry, 190

Vaseline Intensive Care, 479, 484
Vauxhall, 172
Vertical integration, 243, 499–516
   costs of, 502–511
   efficiency of, 504–511
   hybrid systems, 512–515
   marketing perspectives, 501

   objective, 500
   product differentiation, 515–516
   product life cycle, 515
Victor Comptometer, 222
Volkswagen, 468, 471
Volvo, 468

WACC, 327
Walt Disney Productions, 11
Waterman, 230, 238
Westinghouse, 170
Wine industry, 92

Xerox, 89, 299

Zero-based budgeting, 125–126